Physical Constants

Name	Symbol	Value	Units
Speed of light in vacuum	c	3.00×10^8	m/s
Boltzman's constant	k_B	1.38×10^{-23}	J/K
Charge on electron	q	1.60×10^{-19}	C
Thermal voltage (@ 300 K)	$\phi_T = k_B T/q$	25.9	mV
Permittivity of vacuum	ε_0	8.85×10^{-12}	F/m
Permeability of vacuum	μ_0	$4\pi \times 10^{-7}$	H/m

Silicon Constants

Name	Symbol or Formula	Value	Units	Alternate Units
Permittivity of Silicon	$\varepsilon_{Si} = \varepsilon_{rSi} \bullet \varepsilon_0$	1.04×10^{-10}	F/m	104 aF/μm
Permittivity of SiO_2	$\varepsilon_{Si} = \varepsilon_{rSiO2} \bullet \varepsilon_0$	3.45×10^{-11}	F/m	34.5 aF/μm
Breakdown Voltage, SiO_2		7×10^8	V/m	0.7 V/nm
Bulk Mobility, Electrons	μ_n	0.135	m^2/V$\bullet$s	
Bulk Mobility, Holes	μ_p	0.048	m^2/V$\bullet$s	
Intrinsic Carrier Concentration in Silicon	n_i	1.45×10^{16}	$1/m^3$	

Bulk Resistivity of Various Pure Metals (ρ in $\Omega \bullet$m)

Material	Value
Silver (Ag)	1.6×10^{-8}
Copper (Cu)	1.7×10^{-8}
Gold (Au)	2.2×10^{-8}
Aluminum (Al)	2.8×10^{-8}
Tungsten (W)	5.3×10^{-8}

Relative Permittivity (Dielectric Constant, ε_r) of Various Materials

Material	Value
Silicon Dioxide (SiO_2)	3.9
Silicon Nitride (Si_3N_4)	7.5
Beryllia (BeO)	7.3
Alumina (Al_2O_3)	9.5
Epoxy Glass (FR-4)	4.5–5.0
Polyimide	3.5–4.5
Teflon	2.2–2.8

MOSFET Equations

Drain Current

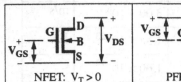 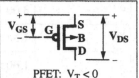

NFET: $V_T > 0$ PFET: $V_T < 0$

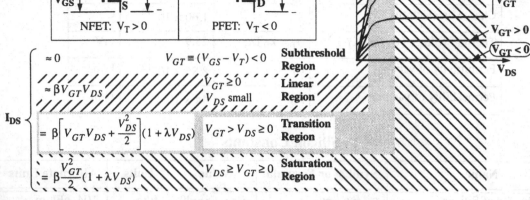

$$I_{DS} \begin{cases} \approx 0 & V_{GT} \equiv (V_{GS} - V_T) < 0 \quad \text{Subthreshold Region} \\[2mm] \approx \beta V_{GT} V_{DS} & V_{GT} \geq 0, \; V_{DS} \text{ small} \quad \text{Linear Region} \\[2mm] = \beta\left[V_{GT}V_{DS} + \dfrac{V_{DS}^2}{2}\right](1 + \lambda V_{DS}) & V_{GT} > V_{DS} \geq 0 \quad \text{Transition Region} \\[2mm] = \beta \dfrac{V_{GT}^2}{2}(1 + \lambda V_{DS}) & V_{DS} \geq V_{GT} \geq 0 \quad \text{Saturation Region} \end{cases}$$

increasing V_{GT}

$V_{GT} > 0$

$V_{GT} < 0$

Device Transconductance $\quad \beta = k\dfrac{W}{L} \quad$ W, L = width, length of device

Process Transconductance $\quad k = \dfrac{\mu \varepsilon_{SiO2}}{T_{OX}} \quad$ $\mu = \mu_n$, electron mobility (NFETs) $= \mu_p$, hole mobility (PFETs)

Subthreshold Conduction

$I_{DS} \neq 0 \quad$ when $\quad V_{GT} < 0$

Subthreshold Drain Current $\quad I_{DS} = I_{ST}\exp\left[\dfrac{V_{GS} + \sigma V_{DS} - V_T}{n\phi_T}\right] \quad$ I_{ST}, σ, and n are process dependent

Body Effect

Body-Effect Threshold Voltage $\quad V'_T = V_T\big|_{V_{SB} > 0} = V_{TO} + \gamma[(2|\phi_F| + V_{SB})^{1/2} - (2|\phi_F|)^{1/2}]$

$V_{TO} = V_T\big|_{V_{SB} = 0} \quad$ and $\quad |\phi_F| = \dfrac{kT}{q}\ln\dfrac{N}{n_i} \quad$ N is the dopant atom concentration

Typical Parameters for 0.35μm Process

Parameter	Description	NFET	PFET
V_T	Threshold voltage	+0.5 V	−0.5 V
k	Process transconductance	200 μA/V^2	50 μA/V^2
T_{OX}	Gate oxide thickness	7 nm	
λ	Channel length modulation	0.1 V^{-1}	
γ	Body effect parameter	0.3 V$^{1/2}$	

Inverters

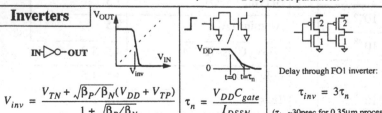

IN ▷○ OUT

Delay through FO1 inverter:

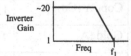

Gain-bandwidth product of inverter:

$$V_{inv} = \dfrac{V_{TN} + \sqrt{\beta_P/\beta_N}(V_{DD} + V_{TP})}{1 + \sqrt{\beta_P/\beta_N}}$$

$$\tau_n = \dfrac{V_{DD}C_{gate}}{I_{DSSN}}$$

$$\tau_{inv} = 3\tau_n$$
($\tau_{inv} \sim$30psec for 0.35μm process)

$$\omega_1 = \dfrac{g_m}{C} = \dfrac{I_{DSS}}{V_{DD}C} = \dfrac{1}{\tau_{inv}}$$

Power and Noise

Bypassing

Resonant Frequency of LC Circuit

$$\omega_C = \frac{1}{\sqrt{LC}}$$

Bypass Capacitor Sizing

$$C_B > \frac{I_{avg}}{\Delta V}\left(k_i t_{ck} + \frac{L I_{avg}}{\Delta V}\right)$$

t_{ck} is the clock period, I_{avg} is the time-averaged current consumption, and ΔV is the maximum allowed ripple voltage.

$$k_i = \frac{max\left|\int_0 (I - I_{avg}) dt\right|}{I_{avg} t_{ck}}$$

Typical values for k_i are 0.25–0.5

Noise

Noise in a Signaling System

$$V_{Noise} = K_N V_{Signal} + V_{NFixed}$$

For **homogeneous** coupled lines, $k_C = k_L$, and:

Crosstalk coefficients between coupled transmission lines

$$k_{NearEnd} = \frac{k_C + k_L}{4}$$

$$k_{FarEnd} = \frac{(k_C - k_L)}{2}$$

where k_C and k_L are the capacitive and inductive coupling constants between the two lines.

$$k_{NearEnd} = \frac{1}{4}\left(\frac{C_M}{C} + \frac{L_M}{L}\right) = \frac{C_M}{2C}$$

$$k_{FarEnd} = \frac{1}{2}\left(\frac{C_M}{C} - \frac{L_M}{L}\right) = 0$$

Johnson (Thermal) Noise in Resistors

$$V_{jR} = (4k_B TRB)^{1/2}$$

where T is temperature in K, R is the resistance in Ω, and B is the bandwidth in Hz; V_{jR} is in volts.

Shot Noise

$$I_{sR} = (2qIB)^{1/2}$$

where q is the electron charge, I is the current in the circuit, and B is the bandwidth in Hz; I_{sR} is in amperes.

Bit Error Rate (BER)

$$P(error) = \exp\left(\frac{VSNR^2}{2}\right)$$

P is the probability of an error in a signaling system with VSNR voltage signal-to-noise ratio. In typical signaling systems P is sampled once per bit, and $P = BER$.

Thermal Conductivity of Various Materials (κ in W/m•K)

Material	Value
Silicon (Si)	150
Silicon Dioxide (SiO_2)	1.5
Copper (Cu)	420
Aluminum (Al)	240
Berylia (BeO)	220
Alumina (Al_2O_3)	35
Epoxy Glass (FR-4)	0.2
Polyimide/Glass	0.3
Teflon/Glass	0.3

Transmission-Line Equations

Slightly Lossy Line

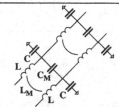

Characteristic Impedance
$$Z_0 = \sqrt{\left(\frac{R+Ls}{G+Cs}\right)} = \sqrt{\frac{L}{C}}\Bigg|_{R,\,G\approx0}$$

Propagation Velocity
$$v = \frac{1}{\sqrt{LC}}\Bigg|_{R,\,G\approx0}$$

Coupled Lines

 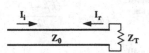

Even-Mode Impedance
$$Z_{Evn} = \sqrt{\frac{L+L_M}{C-C_M}}$$

Odd-Mode Impedance
$$Z_{Odd} = \sqrt{\frac{L-L_M}{C+C_M}}$$

Telegrapher's Equation

Reflection Coefficient
$$k_r = \frac{V_r}{V_i} = \frac{I_r}{I_i} = \frac{Z_T - Z_0}{Z_T + Z_0}$$

Skin Effect

Skin Depth
$$\delta = \frac{1}{\sqrt{\pi f \mu \sigma}}$$

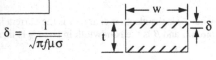

Skin Depth Frequency
$$f_s = \frac{\rho}{\pi\mu(t/2)^2} \qquad f_s = \frac{\rho}{\pi\mu r^2}$$

Skin Depth Resistance
$$R(f) = \frac{\sqrt{\pi f\mu\rho}}{2w} = R_{DC}\left(\frac{f}{f_s}\right)^{1/2} \qquad R(f) = \frac{\sqrt{f\mu\rho/\pi}}{2r} = \frac{R_{DC}}{2}\left(\frac{f}{f_s}\right)^{1/2}$$

Attenuation in Lossy Line

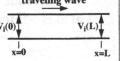

traveling wave

Attenuation
$$\frac{V_i(L)}{V_i(0)} = \exp[-(\alpha_R + \alpha_D)L] = \exp\left[-\left(\frac{R}{2Z_0} + \frac{GZ_0}{2}\right)L\right]$$

Conductor Loss
$$\alpha_R(f) = \frac{R_{DC}}{4Z_0}\left(\frac{f}{f_s}\right)^{1/2} \textbf{(Round)} \qquad \alpha_R(f) = \frac{R_{DC}}{2Z_0}\left(\frac{f}{f_s}\right)^{1/2}\textbf{(Strip)}$$

Dielectric Loss (Homogeneous)
$$\alpha_D(f) = \frac{\pi\sqrt{\varepsilon_r}\tan\delta}{c}f$$

Dielectric Loss Tangent
$$\tan\delta = \frac{G}{\omega C} = \frac{\sigma_{Diel}}{\omega\varepsilon_r}$$

R, C, Z_0 for Various Geometries (Homogeneous Dielectric, L = εμ/C)

$$R_{DC} = 2\frac{\rho}{wh}$$
$$C = \frac{\varepsilon w}{s}$$
$$Z_0 = \sqrt{\frac{\mu}{\varepsilon}}\frac{s}{W}$$

$$R_{DC} = \frac{\rho}{\pi r_1^2} + \frac{\rho}{\pi(r_3^2 - r_2^2)}$$
$$C = \frac{2\pi\varepsilon}{\log(r_2/r_1)}$$
$$Z_0 = \sqrt{\frac{\mu}{\varepsilon}}\frac{\log(r_2/r_1)}{2\pi}$$

$$R_{DC} = \frac{2\rho}{\pi r^2}$$
$$C = \frac{\pi\varepsilon}{\log(s/r)}$$
$$Z_0 = \sqrt{\frac{\mu}{\varepsilon}}\frac{\log(s/r)}{\pi}$$

$$R_{DC} = \frac{\rho}{\pi r^2}$$
$$C = \frac{\pi\varepsilon}{\log(2s/r)}$$
$$Z_0 = \sqrt{\frac{\mu}{\varepsilon}}\frac{\log(2s/r)}{\pi}$$

$$R_{DC} = \frac{\rho}{wh}$$
$$C \approx \frac{\varepsilon w}{s} + \frac{2\pi\varepsilon}{\log(s/w)}$$
$$Z_0 = \frac{\sqrt{\varepsilon\mu}}{C}$$

DIGITAL SYSTEMS ENGINEERING

What makes some computers fast and others slow? What makes some digital systems operate reliably for years while others fail mysteriously every few hours? Why do some systems dissipate kilowatts whereas others operate from batteries? The answers to these questions of speed, reliability, and power are all determined by the system-level electrical design of a digital system: issues of power distribution, noise management, signaling, timing, and synchronization.

Digital Systems Engineering presents a comprehensive treatment of these topics. It combines a rigorous development of the fundamental principles in each area with down-to-earth examples of circuits and methods that work in practice. The book not only can serve as an undergraduate textbook, filling the gap between circuit and logic design, but also can help practicing digital designers keep up with the speed and power of modern integrated circuits. The techniques described in this book, which were once used only in supercomputers, are now essential to the correct and efficient operation of any type of digital system.

Overall, the book describes the fundamental engineering problems of digital systems: power, noise, signaling, and timing. The best known techniques are presented for dealing with these problems, and working circuits that implement these techniques are discussed. At all levels the material is developed rigorously, and equations are derived from first principles. The book avoids the handbook approach of describing how things are done and focuses on why things are done, pointing out the limitations of current approaches. Emerging techniques are introduced that are likely to be how things will be done in the future. The book has been used in an undergraduate Digital Systems Engineering course at MIT. Materials from this course, including lecture notes, simulations, and laboratory assignments, will be available via the Web.

William J. Dally is Professor of Electrical Engineering and Computer Science at Stanford University. He has held positions at Bell Telephone Laboratories, the California Institute of Technology, and the Massachusetts Institute of Technology. He regularly consults for companies in the area of high-speed digital design. His clients include SGI/Cray Research, Digital Equipment Corp., and Intel Corp. His research interests include computer architecture, parallel computing, computer graphics, computer-aided design, and VLSI design.

John W. Poulton has been a faculty member in the Computer Science Department at the University of North Carolina at Chapel Hill since 1981 and currently holds the position of Research Professor. He was the co-inventor (with Henry Fuchs) and lead engineer on the development of several generations of Pixel-Planes graphics engines. These machines were among the first graphics systems to use custom logic-enhanced memory chips for pixel processing, which today are widely employed in graphics hardware architectures. His research interests include parallel computing, computer graphics, and circuit design of memory and communications systems in VLSI.

DIGITAL
SYSTEMS
ENGINEERING

WILLIAM J. DALLY   JOHN W. POULTON

CAMBRIDGE
UNIVERSITY PRESS

CAMBRIDGE UNIVERSITY PRESS
Cambridge, New York, Melbourne, Madrid, Cape Town, Singapore, São Paulo

Cambridge University Press
The Edinburgh Building, Cambridge CB2 8RU, UK

Published in the United States of America by Cambridge University Press, New York

www.cambridge.org
Information on this title: www.cambridge.org/9780521592925

First published 1998
Reprinted 1999, 2000, 2001
This digitally printed version (with corrections) 2008

A catalogue record for this publication is available from the British Library

Library of Congress Cataloguing in Publication data
Dally, William J.
Digital systems engineering / William J. Dally, John W. Poulton.
p.   cm.
Includes bibliographical references
ISBN 0-521-59292-5 (hb)
1. Electronic digital computers – Design and construction.   2. Digital Integrated circuits.
I. Poulton, John W.   II. Title.
TK7888.3.D2934   1998
621.39 – dc21   97–43730
                                                                              CIP

ISBN 978-0-521-59292-5 hardback
ISBN 978-0-521-06175-9 paperback

Cambridge University Press has no responsibility for the persistence or
accuracy of URLs for external or third-party Internet websites referred to in
this publication, and does not guarantee that any content on such websites is,
or will remain, accurate or appropriate.

About the cover: The photo on the cover shows three of the authors' projects. In the foreground is
an oscilloscope trace showing an eye diagram of an equalized 4Gb/s signaling system jointly
developed by the authors. Behind this trace is a 512-processor J-Machine, an experimental parallel
computer developed by Dally and his group at MIT. In the background is a plot of the layout of a
PixelFlow EMC chip, the heart of a high-performance graphics system developed by Poulton and
his colleagues at UNC.

CONTENTS

PREFACE

Today we are on the brink of a major change in the way digital systems are designed. In the past, many digital designers successfully ignored electrical issues, designing their systems in terms of discrete logic. Only the designers of supercomputers and high-speed communication systems needed to look past the digital abstraction. This is no longer the case. As technology has advanced, the systems-level engineering problems of digital systems have become critical to the success of all digital systems.

As technology continues to advance, issues of signaling, timing, power, and noise become increasingly important. At high signaling frequencies, wires can no longer be considered equipotential regions and must be modeled as transmission lines. The number and speed of gates on a chip have increased faster than the number and speed of pins, making inter-chip communication a system bottleneck and placing a premium on efficient signaling and timing conventions. With reduced supply voltages and higher currents, power distribution becomes a more challenging engineering problem. At high frequencies, timing conventions must be carefully designed to prevent skew and jitter of clock signals from degrading system performance. Because of these trends, the techniques described in this book, once used only in supercomputers, are now essential to the correct and efficient operation of any type of digital system.

We were motivated to write this book for two reasons. First, in our research building high-speed digital systems (parallel computers, network switches, and high-performance graphics systems) we developed a number of signaling, timing, and power distribution techniques that overcame the limitations of conventional methods. We were eager to share these methods and the engineering science behind them with other practicing engineers. Our second motivation was to avoid repetitions of many disasters we encountered in our interactions with industry. Over a year was spent at one company chasing noise problems before a system would operate reliably. Another system went through several iterations of ASICs due to timing problems. A third system failed periodically due to on-chip power supply fluctuations. A fourth system product was delayed by six months because of a subtle failure in the flip-flops used throughout a custom chip design. These problems delayed system delivery by months to years and in some cases directly contributed to the failure of companies. Band-aid fixes rarely exist for these types of problems; however, they could have been easily avoided by proper design if the engineers involved had been knowledgeable about noise, signaling, timing, and power. By writing this book, we hope to help eradicate the widespread ignorance, and often misinformation, in these areas and in doing so, help avoid disasters of this kind in the future.

Organization

The book begins by describing the major engineering problems of digital systems: power, noise, signaling, and timing. It presents the best known techniques for dealing with these problems and describes working circuits that implement these techniques. At all levels material is developed rigorously, deriving equations from first principles. The book avoids the handbook approach of describing how things are usually done. While it gives a good description of current industrial practice, it emphasizes why things are done, points out the limitations of current approaches, and describes emerging techniques, such as low-voltage signaling and closed-loop timing, that are likely to be how things are done in the future.

The book introduces the topic of digital systems engineering by describing the major engineering problems associated with digital systems and the technology trends affecting them. The book then devotes three chapters laying the groundwork for the treatment of these problems by describing computer elements: wires and circuits. These chapters examine the components and interconnections used to build modern digital systems and develop engineering models of these components to facilitate the study of systems engineering problems in later chapters.

After this preamble, the book deals with the problem of power distribution in Chapter 5. Digital logic requires a stable, quiet, DC supply voltage while drawing a large AC current with frequency components comparable to signal rise times. This chapter develops circuit models for both on-chip and off-chip power distribution networks and loads. Off-chip distribution methods including bypass capacitors, local regulation, shunt regulators, and clamps are discussed, as are on-chip distribution methods including power grid layout, on-chip regulation, and symbiotic bypass capacitors. The chapter closes with the presentation of an example distribution system. Since power supply noise is one of the largest noise sources in digital systems, this chapter lays the groundwork for the treatment of noise in Chapter 6, which in turn lays the groundwork for the discussion of signaling conventions in Chapter 7.

Noise, the topic of Chapter 6, is one of the most important factors in the engineering of digital systems, yet it is also one of the least understood. Most noise in digital systems is created by the system itself, and hence is truly interference and not noise. This chapter gives an in-depth treatment of major noise sources including power supply noise, signal return coupling, crosstalk, inter-symbol interference, and parameter offsets. Lower-level noise sources including alpha particles, thermal noise, shot noise, and flicker noise are briefly treated. The engineering models of these noise sources are then used to introduce the use of noise budgets, the concept of noise immunity, and the calculation of error rate based on statistical noise models. This treatment of noise prepares the reader to understand the major problem in the design of signaling systems presented in Chapters 7 and 8.

Signaling, the method used to transmit a bit of information from one location to another, is central to the design of digital systems. A signaling convention involves encoding information into a physical quantity (typically current or voltage), providing a reference against which this quantity is measured, the design of transmitters to couple signal energy into the transmission medium and terminators to absorb energy and prevent unwanted reflections, and a method for controlling signal transitions to limit the spectrum of transmitted energy. The signaling convention determines to a large extent the reliability, speed, and power consumption of a system. A good signaling convention isolates a signal from noise, providing noise immunity, rather than attempting to overpower the noise with noise margin. Most signaling conventions in common use are quite poor, based on standards that are accidents of history rather than on careful design to isolate noise sources. For this reason, many modern systems define their own signaling conventions rather than employ these standards.

Chapter 7 deals with the basics of signaling over LC transmission lines and lumped LRC interconnect. This chapter introduces the concepts of voltage-mode and current-mode transmission, unipolar and bipolar signaling, series and parallel termination, references, and differential signaling. Undertermination, rise-time control, pulsed signaling, and multi-level signaling are also described. We develop methods for calculating the signal magnitude required to transmit a signal reliably in the presence of noise and show that, with adequate noise isolation, very low voltage signal swings (100 mV) are sufficient. Chapter 8 describes more advanced concepts including techniques for dealing with lossy RC and LRC transmission lines, simultaneous bidirectional signaling, and AC signaling.

A digital system uses a timing convention, along with a signaling convention to govern when to place a new symbol on a signal line and when to sample the line to detect the symbol. A good timing convention is one that maximizes performance by reducing and compensating for sources of timing noise, skew and jitter. It is the uncertainty in the timing of a signal, not the delay, that limits the rate at which a system can operate. Chapter 9 discusses the fundamentals of timing conventions. The methods used to encode timing on signals are described and the concepts of timing noise and timing budgets are introduced. The chapter goes on to develop methods for minimizing skew and jitter using both open-loop and closed-loop timing. A discussion of clock distribution techniques closes the chapter.

Closely related to timing is the problem of synchronization, determining the relative order of two events, which is discussed in Chapter 10. Synchronization is required when sampling asynchronous inputs into a synchronous system, or when a signal traverses the boundary between two clock domains. When a signal is synchronized there is some probability that the synchronizer will be driven into a metastable state, unable to resolve which event came first, and stay in that state long enough to cause a synchronization failure. This chapter introduces the problem of synchronization, describes metastability, synchronization failure, and gives methods to calculate the probability of synchronization failure. A section on synchronizer design recognizes several special cases of synchronization and describes how to build fast synchronizers that exploit these special cases to avoid the normal synchronizer delays. Finally, the chapter describes methods for asynchronous design that avoid the problem of synchronization.

Circuits for signaling and timing are described in Chapters 11 and 12 respectively. Chapter 11 presents working circuits for the transmitters, receivers, and terminations needed to build the signaling systems described in Chapters 7 and 8. Particular attention is paid to techniques for managing noise and compensating for process, voltage, and temperature variations. Timing circuits are described in Chapter 12 including flip-flops, delay lines, VCOs, phase comparators, and clock drivers. The emphasis here is on minimizing skew and jitter. Each of these chapters closes by describing an example system that ties together the concepts of Chapters 7 through 10 with the circuit details of Chapters 11 and 12.

Teaching Digital Systems Engineering

The best way to empower engineers with mastery of digital systems engineering is to teach this material as part of the undergraduate curriculum in electrical engineering and computer engineering. There is currently a gap in the curriculum between circuit design, which covers the electrical design of individual logic and memory elements, and logic design and architecture, which deal with the logical organization of digital systems. System-level electrical issues, while critically important, are absent from the curriculum.

This book is intended to fill this gap in the electrical engineering and computer engineering curriculum. It is written as a textbook with the material presented in an order suitable for teaching and with exercises at the end of each chapter. The material is at a level appropriate for seniors or first-year graduate students in electrical engineering. Drafts of the book have been used to teach digital systems engineering courses at MIT (by Dally) and Washington University (by our colleague Fred Rosenberger). Starting with Autumn Quarter 1998, a course on digital systems engineering based on this book, EE273, will be offered at Stanford University.

Supplementary teaching materials, including course schedules, lecture slides, simulation models, problem sets and solutions, will be available via the world-wide web at http://www.cambridge.org/9780521592925

We learned a great deal and had a great deal of fun in the process of creating this book. We hope that you get at least a bit of the insight and enjoyment out of reading it that we got out of writing it.

William J. Dally, *Stanford, California*
John W. Poulton, *Chapel Hill, North Carolina*

ACKNOWLEDGMENTS

We would like to thank all of the people who have contributed to the creation of this book. Fred Rosenberger at Washington University carefully reviewed the draft manuscript and was the first brave soul (other than the authors) to teach a course from this book. His insightful comments greatly improved the quality of the resulting book.

Many people reviewed one or more draft chapters. Of these people, Tom Knight (MIT), Gill Pratt (MIT), and Rich Lethin (Equator Technologies) deserve special thanks for suggesting significant improvements.

The students who took 6.891 at MIT during Fall Semester 1996 helped greatly to debug the material and an early draft of the text.

Steve Tell and Robert Palmer at UNC performed many of the measurements that are presented in Chapter 3.

Our view of this material, as presented here, has been greatly influenced by interactions with our colleagues including (in no particular order) Mark Horowitz (Stanford), Kunle Olukotun (Stanford), Tom Lee (Stanford), Ken Yang (Stanford), Vernon Chi (UNC), John Eyles (UNC), Rich Brown (Michigan), Tom Knight (MIT), Gill Pratt (MIT), Steve Ward (MIT), Anant Agarwal (MIT), Chuck Seitz (Myricom), Al Barber (HP), Dan Dobberpuhl (Digital), Steve Oberlin (Cray), Mark Birrittella (Cray), Dan Mansour (Cray), Doug Kervin (Cray), Dave Dunning (Intel), Craig Peterson (Intel), Randy Mooney (Intel), Greg Fyler (Intel), Greg Papadopoulos (Sun), Lance Glasser (KLA), Phil Carvey (Avici), Steve Molnar (IDT, Inc.), Trey Greer (PixelFusion, Ltd), and Fred Heaton (Secant Network Technologies).

We learned much from the students and staff that worked with us on research projects related to this work including Larry Dennison, Whay Lee, Duke Xanthopoulos, Mike Noakes, Jeff Bowers, Steve Keckler, Andrew Chang, Ed Lee, and Richard An.

Alan Harvey at Cambridge University Press helped us throughout the project. Our project manager Andrew Wilson and our copy editor John Joswick took a very rough manuscript and turned it into a polished book.

Gill Weigand, Bob Parker, and Bob Lucas at DARPA had the foresight to fund research in these areas before it became a pressing problem.

Finally, our families, Sharon, Jenny, Katie, and Liza Dally and Susan, Sarah, and Winona Poulton made significant sacrifices so that we could have the time to devote to writing.

INTRODUCTION TO DIGITAL SYSTEMS ENGINEERING

1

Digital systems are pervasive in modern society. We use computers for bookkeeping, engineering, publishing, and entertainment. Digital communications systems handle our telephone calls and enable our Web browsing sessions. Other uses of digital systems are less visible. Most consumer electronics products are largely digital and becoming more so. Music today is distributed digitally on compact optical disks, and video production is rapidly becoming a digital process. A typical appliance is controlled digitally by a microcomputer. As many as ten microcomputers can be found in the average car for controlling functions ranging from the sound system to the antilock brakes.

A *digital* system represents information with discrete symbols (of which digits are a special case) rather than with a continuously varying quantity, as in an *analog* system. Most systems use just two symbols, often denoted by the binary digits (or *bits*) 0 and 1, to represent all information. Simple truth propositions are represented directly with a single bit, whereas strings of bits are used to represent more complex data.

In a digital system, noise below a given level can be completely rejected. Symbols are encoded into ranges of voltage or current level. If we add a small amount of voltage, V_N, to the nominal voltage for the 0 symbol, V_0, the resulting voltage, $V_0 + V_N$, will still be in the range for a 0 symbol and, more importantly, can be restored to the nominal level, V_0. This property allows us to process information through many noisy stages of logic with no accumulation of noise. In an analog system, in contrast, disturbing an information voltage, V_x, with noise gives a voltage, $V_y = V_x + V_N$, that represents a different piece of information. The analog signal cannot be restored and will be severely degraded after many stages of noisy processing.

All digital systems, whether used explicitly for computation or as part of an entertainment system, are constructed from three basic components: logic, memory, and communication channels. Logic operates on symbols, for example adding two numbers together or comparing two characters. Memory stores symbols, moving them in time so that information computed at one point in time can be recalled later. Communication channels, usually wires, move information in space so that values generated by logic in one location can be stored in memory, used by logic in a different location, or both.

The development of a digital system involves circuit and logic design, architecture, and systems engineering. Individual components such as logic gates and memory arrays are designed at the circuit level. At the logic level we compose these individual components into subsystems such as adders and finite-state machines. At a higher level the instruction-set and register-level organization of the system is governed by the principles of computer architecture.

This book addresses digital systems engineering. The systems-level engineering issues in a digital system include power distribution, noise management, signaling, timing, and synchronization. Power distribution deals with how to distribute a controlled DC voltage level throughout a system that draws considerable amounts of AC current. Transmitting digital symbols over wires at maximum speed and with minimum power is the challenge of signaling. Timing deals with how computations and communications are sequenced within and between modules. The design of signaling and timing conventions is dominated by considerations of noise or uncertainty; thus, the successful digital designer must understand noise sources and formulate methods for managing noise. Synchronization is required to coordinate the operation of two systems operating from separate time bases or to sample an input that may change asynchronously.

We address these issues from systems and circuits perspectives. For each topic, we start by giving the big picture with circuit details abstracted and then return to the topic and present detailed circuits.

1.1 WHY STUDY DIGITAL SYSTEMS ENGINEERING?

As technology has advanced, the systems-level engineering problems of digital systems have become more critical. At high signaling frequencies wires can no longer be considered equipotential regions and must be modeled as transmission lines. On-chip wires are becoming more resistive, presenting a significant signaling challenge. The number and speed of gates on a chip have increased faster than the number and speed of pins, making interchip communication a system bottleneck and placing a premium on efficient signaling and timing conventions. With reduced supply voltages, higher currents, and thinner metal layers, power distribution is an increasingly challenging engineering problem. At high frequencies timing conventions must be carefully designed to prevent skew and jitter of clock signals from degrading system performance.

Careful attention to digital systems engineering issues makes an enormous difference in the performance, reliability, and power dissipation of a system. Too often, lack of attention to these issues results in a system that is unreliable or simply does not work. Recently, a major computer manufacturer delayed the release of a new system because several custom chips failed to operate at any speed owing to excessive clock skew. Another manufacturer had to revise several chips in a new system because noise problems led to unacceptable error rates on interchip signals.

Digital systems engineering has largely been ignored by the academic community. Most curricula include courses on circuit design of logic elements, logic design, register-transfer-level design, and high-level architecture. However, the engineering problems of composing circuits into systems are only briefly touched upon. A frequent misconception at the system level is that one must abstract away the electrical properties of the system and deal with discrete symbols at the logic or architectural level. To the contrary, careful management of electrical issues at the system level is critical to the success of any modern system.

In fact, to do a credible job of computer architecture one must have an intimate understanding of system-level engineering issues. Architecture deals with organizing a system and defining interfaces (e.g., instruction sets and channel protocols) to achieve cost and performance goals. System-level engineering constrains what the architect can do and is a major determinant of the cost and performance of the resulting system. It is far too easy for one to abstract these issues and architect a system that, owing to bandwidth limitations, is unrealizable or suboptimal.

Many in industry have taken ad hoc appoaches to systems engineering problems. Clocks are distributed by open-loop trees that are tuned until the circuit works. Power is distributed on wide metal lines. Full-swing signals are used for signaling on and between chips. Typically, a company addresses a systems engineering problem using the same approach taken with its last system. This often leads to a false sense of security. As technology advances, ad hoc approaches that worked in the past become suboptimal and often fail. Many companies have been caught unawares by excessive power supply noise, unreliable signaling, and badly skewed clocks. In one classic example, manufacturers designed standard logic components using the high-inductance corner pins of their packages for power and ground. This was originally done to simplify routing of printed circuit (PC) boards without power planes. Over the years, standard logic parts increased in speed until their switching current induced so much noise across the supply inductors that the output could not reliably be detected. Only after many parts failed in systems did the manufacturers relocate the pins to the center of the package.

In this book we will take an engineering science approach to systems engineering problems; that is, we will study the underlying physical and electrical mechanisms that relate to power distribution and signaling and timing conventions. We will develop models for these mechanisms and use these models to analyze the performance of potential solutions. We will present specific solutions to these problems that work under today's constraints, and, more importantly, we will give you the tools to understand why these solutions work and to evaluate whether they will continue to work under future constraints.

Standards, both published and de facto, have historically played a large role in digital engineering. The use of full-swing underterminated voltage-mode signaling and edge-triggered synchronous timing is almost universal even though, as we will see, there are far better signaling and timing alternatives. The popularity of the prevailing approaches derives from the many catalog parts available using these conventions and to a lesser extent to the lack of understanding about alternatives and the criteria for evaluating them.

The trend toward building digital systems from custom or semicustom very large scale integrated (VLSI) components such as application specific integrated circuits (ASICs) has lessened the importance of catalog parts, except for memories, and hence enables the system designer to control signaling and timing conventions. Because these ASICs largely communicate with one another, the system designer is free to choose any convention she wishes for communication between these components. The designer is also free to choose the conventions employed by and between the components on a single chip. Thus, at the same time that continued advances in VLSI fabrication technology drive many of the challenging systems problems, VLSI also offers an opportunity to solve these problems by adding degrees of freedom in the choice of signaling and timing conventions.

1.2 AN ENGINEERING VIEW OF A DIGITAL SYSTEM

An engineer views a digital system in terms of information flow, power flow, and timing. For example, Figure 1-1 is an engineering view of a node of a modern multicomputer. The arrows in the figure illustrate the information flow and are annotated with the signaling convention employed, and the individual components are annotated with their power and timing information. As we shall see, these are not independent variables. The choice of a signaling convention, for example, can determine both the available bandwidth from a component and the power it requires.

The heart of the system is a central processing unit (CPU) operating at 500 MHz and dissipating 80 W of power from a 2.5-V supply. The CPU is connected to a set of cache chips via data and address lines and to a controller chip via two unidirectional channels. The controller in turn connects via channels to a router,

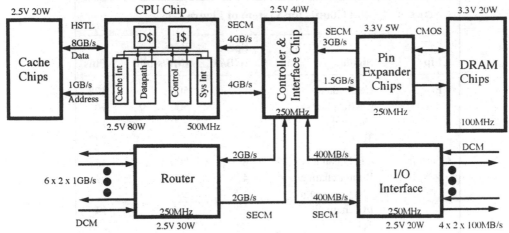

FIGURE 1-1   A Systems View of a Multicomputer Node

an I/O interface, and, via some pin expanders[1] to a set of dynamic random access memory (DRAM) chips. The router has six bidirectional channels that connect to the routers on other nodes, and the I/O interface has four channels that connect to peripherals.

1.2.1 Feeds and Speeds

Much of the art of digital systems design is managing the movement of information. A good design balances demands for bandwidth against the constraints of limited numbers of chip and module pins and limited amounts of wiring area on chips and boards. The designer controls the partitioning of the system and the topology of connections to strike the appropriate balance. This is a critical task. The efficient use of available bandwidth is probably the single most important determinant of overall system performance.

A key tool in the process of balancing a system is a diagram, like Figure 1-1, that shows the *feeds*, where information flows, and the *speeds*, how fast (in bits/s) the information flows along each path. This information is used in two ways. First, together with the signaling rate, the combined speeds into and out of each component or module indicate how many pins are required. Second, system performance can be predicted from the bandwidths at various points in the system in conjunction with an architectural model (usually a simulator).

For example, suppose our architectural model indicates that the bandwidth from the CPU to the second-level cache should equal the bandwidth from the CPU to the rest of the system. Our packaging allows at most 300 signal pins on

---

[1] A pin-expander chip takes a few pins that use a high-speed signaling convention, like single-ended current mode (SECM) at 500 Mb/s, and converts them to a larger number of pins in a slower signaling convention such as full-swing complementary metal-oxide semiconductor (CMOS) at 100 Mb/s.

TABLE 1-1   **Pin Counts for System of Figure 1-1**

Chip	Signal	Speed (GB/s)	Rate (Mb/s-pin)	Pins
CPU	Cache data	8	500	128
	Cache address	1	500	16
	Channels	8	500	128
	Total			272
Controller	CPU channels	8	500	128
	Router channels	4	500	64
	Memory channels	4.5	500	72
	I/O channels	0.8	500	14
	Total			278
Router	Controller channels	4	500	64
	Router channels	12	250	384
	Total			448

a component. Our signaling convention dictates that all signals must be point-to-point. Signals on the board operate single-ended at 500 Mb/s-pin, and signals that go off the board (router and I/O outputs) operate at differentially 500 Mb/s over a pair of pins for 250 Mb/s-pin. Using these numbers, Table 1-1 shows the number of pins required by the three major chips in the system.

The table shows that the CPU and controller chip are within the pin budget, and a few pins are left over. The router, however, is way over the pin budget, and thus the system as currently sketched cannot be implemented with the planned packaging. At this point the designer needs to repartition the system (see Exercise 1.1) to eliminate this bottleneck, reduce the router bandwidth, with possible performance penalties, or attempt to remove the constraint by getting a package with more pins or using a faster signaling convention.

1.2.2   Signaling Conventions

A signaling convention is the method used to encode symbols (usually 1 and 0) into physical quantities (e.g., voltage and current). An efficient signaling convention is one that maximizes the bandwidth per pin, minimizes power dissipation, and provides good noise immunity. Such a signaling convention can dramatically increase available bandwidth and hence system performance. Suppose, for example, the entire system in Figure 1-1 were implemented using a full-swing CMOS signaling convention that was limited to 100 Mb/s-pin. The CPU and controller chips would require about 1,400 signal pins! With CMOS signaling, a system of this level of performance simply could not be implemented.

Most of the channels between chips on the same PC board in Figure 1-1 use single-ended current-mode (SECM) signaling. This convention encodes the symbol 1 as a +2.5-mA current and a 0 as a −2.5-mA current. The wire over which a signal travels is designed to be a 50-Ω transmission line and is parallel-terminated with a 50-Ω resistor on the receiving chip into a midrail (1.25-V) supply. This gives a voltage swing of 250 mV, from 1.125 to 1.375 V. The receivers detect the arriving signal by measuring the voltage across the termination resistor with a sensitive amplifier.

In contrast, most systems today use a form of full-swing signaling. For example, the CMOS signaling convention, as employed by the DRAMs in Figure 1-1, encodes 1 as the positive supply voltage (3.3 V) and 0 as the negative supply voltage (0 V). The impedance of the wires is uncontrolled, and the lines are unterminated. A CMOS inverter is used to detect the received voltage in the reference frame of the receiver power supplies.

Why is current-mode signaling preferable to CMOS signaling? Current-mode signaling offers lower power, faster operation, and better noise immunity. The only advantage of CMOS signaling is that it is used by the vast majority of standard parts. To interface to such parts (e.g., the DRAMs in Figure 1-1) one must use this signaling convention.

1.2.2.1 Signaling Speed

Current-mode signaling offers faster operation because it employs incident wave signaling for minimum delay and uses a terminated transmission line to minimize intersymbol interference. Suppose the average on-board wire is 30 cm long. The current-mode signaling system injects a 250-mV signal at one end of this line, and 2 ns later the wave carrying this signal arrives at the termination and is absorbed into the terminator. No residual energy is left on the line to corrupt subsequent bits. Thus, the line can immediately be used to send a second bit. In fact, several bits can be pipelined on a long wire. By getting the symbol on and off the line quickly, current-mode signaling enables fast signaling rates.

In contrast, the average CMOS driver, with an output impedance of 200 Ω cannot drive the 50-Ω line through 3.3 V in a single step. To do so would require a very low output impedance and enormous current (66 mA). Instead this driver injects a 660-mV (13-mA) signal into the line. After 2 ns, this wave reflects off the receiving end of the line, giving 1.3 V. Only after the wave reflects off the source and then the receiver for a second time is the line voltage sufficiently high to be detected as a logic 1. Even after 10 ns (2.5 round trips) the line is still over a half volt short of 3.3 V. This residual state leads to intersymbol interference. Because CMOS signaling takes a long time to get a symbol on the line, it is limited to signaling periods that are many times the delay of the line.

1.2.2.2 Signaling Power

By operating with a small signal swing, current-mode signaling dissipates much less power. The current-mode signaling convention draws 2.5 mA from a 2.5-V supply for a power dissipation of 6.2 mW. The actual signal power is ten times less, 620 μW (2.5 mA times the 250-mV signal swing). Operating at 500 Mb/s, the signal energy per bit is 1.25 pJ (2 ns times 620 μW), and the power supply energy per bit is 12.5 pJ.

In contrast, the CMOS system operates with a peak current of 13 mA and an average current of 9.4 mA (assuming the line toggles each cycle) from a 3.3-V supply for a power dissipation of 31 mW. Operating at 100 Mb/s, for the reasons described above, the signal energy per bit is 310 pJ or about 250 times that of the current-mode system![2] The power supply energy is the same here as the signal energy (about 25 times that of the current-mode system).

1.2.2.3 Signal Integrity

At this point you might think that with such a large signal swing the CMOS system must be much more reliable in the presence of noise. In fact the opposite is true. As we shall see in Chapter 7, the current-mode system has better noise immunity because it isolates the signal from external noise sources, such as power supply noise, and reduces internal noise sources, such as receiver sensitivity and intersymbol interference.

1.2.2.4 Other Signaling Conventions

The same arguments apply to signaling conventions on-chip. For example, using full-swing signaling to communicate between the instruction cache, I$, and control unit in Figure 1-1, would waste power. However, the constraints for on-chip signaling are different, and hence different solutions are appropriate.

Two other off-chip signaling conventions appear in the channel labels of Figure 1-1. A differential current-mode signaling convention (DCM) is used for all signals that leave the PC board to avoid the problems of signal-return cross talk that would otherwise occur owing to the large return impedance of typical off-board cables and connectors. The cache static random access memory (SRAM) chips are shown using HSTL,[3] an underterminated signaling convention (Section 7.3.4) that is just beginning to be offered in standard parts such as SRAMs.

1.2.3 Timing and Synchronization

A timing convention governs the sequencing of data through logic and across channels. The convention governs when signals can change and when they are sampled.

1.2.3.1 Synchronous Timing

Within a *clock domain*, an area where all signals have their timing referenced to a single clock signal, the convention may be built around edge-triggered flip-flops or level-sensitive latches. Some conventions, such as using multiple nonoverlapping clock phases, are very tolerant of clock skew, whereas others require very careful clock distribution to minimize skew.

---

[2] The fact that the CMOS system does not reach 3.3 V after 10 ns works in its favor here. The energy to charge a 30-cm, 50-pF line to 3.3 V is 545 pJ ($3.3^2 \times 50$ pF).

[3] HSTL is an acronym for high-speed transceiver logic.

For example, the system of Figure 1-1 employs a separate clock domain for the core logic of each chip. Most of the chips operate at 250 MHz, whereas the CPU operates at 500 MHz. The internal logic in each clock domain uses level-sensitive latches and a single-phase clock. Minimum delay constraints are used to relax clock skew tolerances.

1.2.3.2 Pipelined Timing

With all signals referenced to a single clock, the maximum operating frequency depends on the propagation delay through the logic or across the channel. In situations where data flow primarily in one direction and delays are predictable (e.g., most channels), substantially higher throughput can be realized by using *pipelined timing*. With pipelined timing, each pipeline stage operates in its own clock domain, and the phase of the clock is delayed to match the delay of the data. Therefore, the maximum throughput is independent of propagation delay and is limited only by the uncertainty in the delay: skew and jitter. In Figure 1-1, the channels between the controller and the other components all operate using pipelined timing, allowing operation with clock periods much shorter than the delay of the wires. Pipeline timing is also occasionally used to advantage in the design of pipelined arithmetic units. In this context, it is sometimes referred to as *wave-pipelining*.

1.2.3.3 Closed-Loop Timing

The static portion of delay uncertainty, skew, can be eliminated by using a control loop that measures the relative delay or phase of two signals and adjusts a variable delay or frequency element to match delays. This form of closed-loop timing allows operation at very high frequencies without requiring very tight tolerances or matching of wire and logic delays. The dynamic portion of uncertainty, jitter, can be reduced by using a phase-lock loop that tracks the low-frequency variations in an incoming signal while rejecting high-frequency jitter.

1.2.3.4 Clock Distribution

Distributing a clock over a large clock domain with low skew and controlled duty factor is a challenging engineering problem. Off-chip, clock trees with matched transmission lines and buffers are typically used. On-chip, the problem is more difficult, for the lossy nature of on-chip wires leads to large diffusive delays, and power supply variations modulate the delay of clock buffers. The CPU chip in Figure 1-1, for example, uses a six-level clock tree with the leaves shorted in a low-resistance, two-dimensional grid to control clock skew across the chip to within 300 ps. This skew is large compared with the typical gate delay (100 ps). However, by using a timing convention that employs a two-phase nonoverlapping clock driving transparent latches and that constrains the minimum delay between latches, the design easily tolerates the 300-ps skew without increasing the cycle time and without any danger of hold-time violations. In designing the timing of a system, an engineer chooses between methods to control skew and methods that tolerate skew. A well-designed system usually balances the two approaches.

1.2.3.5   Synchronization

Before signals from different clock domains can be combined, they must be *synchronized* to a common clock. For example, the receiving side of each channel in the controller chip of Figure 1-1 operates in its own clock domain as a result of the pipelined timing employed. Before these signals can be combined in the core of the controller, they must be synchronized to the core clock. In general, synchronizing a signal to a clock requires a delay as the synchronizer waits for metastable states to decay. However, the synchronization being performed in Figure 1-1, and in most digital systems, is a special case in that the events being synchronized are periodic. Thus, future transitions can be predicted in advance and the signals synchronized without delay.

1.2.4   Power Distribution

A digital system requires a stable DC supply voltage, to within a few hundred millivolts, to ensure proper operation of logic and communication circuits. The power distribution system must provide this steady voltage in the presence of very large AC current demands. The resistive nature of on-chip wires and the inductance inherent in most packaging elements make this a difficult problem.

A modern CMOS circuit can vary its current draw from 0 to a maximum value in a fraction of a clock cycle. In the system of Figure 1-1, for example, the CPU dissipates 80 W at 2.5 V for an average current of 32 A. The peak current is easily twice this amount, 64 A, and current demand can readily change from zero to this maximum value in half a clock cycle, 1 ns, for a peak derivative of $di/dt = 64$ GA/s. Even with hundreds of supply pins (of a few nH each), this current transient induces an unacceptable voltage transient across the parasitic inductance of the package. On-chip bypass capacitors and perhaps regulators are required to manage this transient.

A typical power distribution system is a hierarchy. Small local elements, like on-chip bypass capacitors and regulators, provide small amounts of energy to local regions and handle the high-frequency components of transients. Larger elements supply larger regions and handle lower-frequency components of the transients. Because of their physical distance from the point of use, and the inductance that implies, they are not able to manage the high-frequency transients. At higher levels of the hierarchy, the supply voltage is usually raised to allow distribution to be performed with lower currents and hence smaller and less expensive bus-bars and cables.

1.2.5   Noise

Noise is a major concern in the engineering of digital systems. It corrupts signals on channels between modules, disturbs the state of logic networks and memory cells, and adds jitter and skew to the timing of signals. Signaling and timing conventions are designed around the constraints of system noise. For example, both the amplitude of signal swing and the clock cycle of a pipelined timing system are determined primarily by noise constraints.

TABLE 1-2   **An Example Noise Budget**

Noise Source	Type	Amount (%)	Amplitude (mV)
Gross margin			125
Receiver offset	Fixed		±10
Receiver sensitivity	Fixed		±10
Unrejected power supply noise	Fixed		±5
Transmitter offset	Proportional	5	±13
Cross talk	Proportional	10	±25
Intersymbol interference	Proportional	10	±25
Total noise			±88
Net margin			37

Operating digitally, of course, we can recover the correct symbol and timing in the presence of noise as long as the noise does not exceed a fixed threshold, often called the *noise margin*. Careful design is required, however, to make the probability of exceeding this margin appropriately small.

Most noise in digital systems is created by the system itself and thus should properly be called *interference*.[4] The most significant noise sources are power supply noise, cross talk, and intersymbol interference. Power supply noise, voltage fluctuations of the power supply caused by the AC current demand, couples into signals and modulates the delay of timing elements. Cross talk occurs when a symbol on one signal line interferes with the symbol carried on another signal line and is caused by capacitive and inductive coupling between signal lines and their returns. Intersymbol interference occurs when symbols placed on a signal line interfere with later symbols on the same line because of parasitic tank circuits, slow circuit nodes, and reflections from imperfect terminations.

As engineers, we manage noise by using a *budget* that allocates our gross noise margin to expected sources of noise. For example, Table 1-2 shows the noise budget for the ±2.5-mA current-mode channels of Figure 1-1. These signals have a 250-mV swing and hence a 125-mV *gross noise margin*. This is the amount of noise that can be tolerated before a symbol will be incorrectly detected. We perform a worst-case analysis to see if this margin is adequate to account for expected noise sources. The table shows that if the six noise sources have maximum amplitude and sum in the same direction, the worst possible case, the maximum noise is 88 mV. This leaves a *net noise margin* of 37 mV to provide safety and allow for unexpected noise sources.

In designing a system to deal with noise, it is useful to separate noise sources into those that are *fixed*, independent of signal magnitude, and those that are *proportional* and scale with signal magnitude. Three of the noise sources in

---

[4] In this text we reserve the term *interference* to refer to interference between digital signals (e.g., crosstalk and intersymbol interference). We refer to interference from other sources simply as *noise*.

Table 1-2 are fixed, whereas the remaining three are proportional, totaling to 25% of the signal swing (which is 50% of the gross margin). The fixed sources can be dealt with by increasing signal swing. This would have no effect, however, on the proportional sources, for they would increase at the same rate. They must be reduced or rejected. They cannot be overpowered.

An efficient system design cancels noise where possible. For example, the third noise source in Table 1-2 is *unrejected* power supply noise. The system has ±150 mV of supply noise. All but 3% of this noise is rejected as common-mode between the signal and the return. It would be far more expensive to attempt to overpower this supply noise.

1.2.6 A Systems View of Circuits

When designing signaling and timing conventions and budgeting for noise, the digital systems engineer is constrained by what can be practically built. Any real receiver will have a finite offset and sensitivity, any real flip-flop will have finite setup and hold times, and any real delay line will introduce some amount of jitter. These circuit constraints play a major role in the design of a system such as that of Figure 1-1. It is important to appreciate how these implementation constraints arise and to determine which are controllable and which are not. For this reason, we will take an in-depth look at circuits in this book from a systems perspective. Rather than study amplifiers or flip-flops in isolation, we will look at how their design affects system properties, such as required signal amplitude and cycle time.

1.3 TECHNOLOGY TRENDS AND DIGITAL SYSTEMS ENGINEERING

The phenomenal growth in the performance and range of applications of digital systems is fueled by an exponential rate of improvement in the underlying semiconductor technology. Every three years, the number of devices that can be fabricated on a chip, and more importantly the number of wiring *grids* on a chip, quadruples.

As chip density improves, however, the problems of digital systems engineering get harder. For example, smaller devices operate at lower voltages to maintain constant fields, and at the same time the increased number of devices draws larger AC currents, making the power distribution problem doubly hard. Similarly, timing and signaling are also becoming more difficult as technology advances.

1.3.1 Moore's Law

Gordon Moore [Moore79] observed that the number of devices that could be economically fabricated on a single chip was increasing exponentially at a rate of about 50% per year and hence quadrupling every 3.5 years. At the same time,

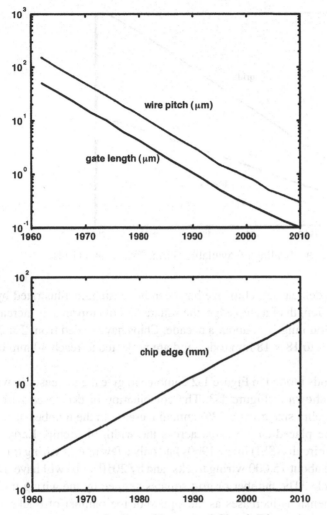

FIGURE 1-2 Scaling of Integrated Circuit Dimensions

the delay of a simple gate has been decreasing by 13% per year, halving every 5 years. The semiconductor industry has maintained this breakneck trend for the past 27 years, and there is every reason to expect that it will continue for at least the next decade.

Figure 1-2 is a plot of the exponential scaling of integrated circuit feature size and linear dimension as a function of time.[5] The upper graph shows how gate length and wire pitch decrease at a rate of 13% per year, halving every 5 years. Gate lengths have scaled from 50 μm in the 1960s to 0.35 μm today and are projected to reach 0.1 μm by 2010. At the same time that the sizes of features

---

[5] The scaling figures in this section make use of data from several sources. Historical data are based on surveys, including that by Hennessy and Jouppi [HennJoup91]. Future trends are based largely on projections by the Semiconductor Industry Association [SIA94], and some adjustments are based on the authors' expectations.

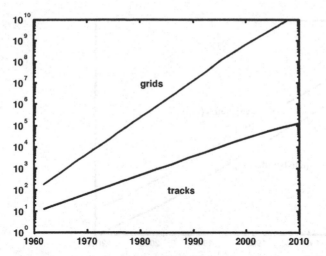

FIGURE 1-3   Scaling of Available Wiring Tracks and Grids

have been decreasing, chip size has been increasing, as illustrated by the lower panel. The length of a chip edge, the square root of chip area, is increasing by 6% per year, doubling after about a decade. Chips have scaled from 2×2 mm in the early 1960s to 18×18 mm today and are projected to reach 40 mm on a side by 2010.

The trends plotted in Figure 1-2 combine to give the increases in wiring tracks and grids shown in Figure 1-3. The combination of decreased wire pitch with increasing chip size gives a 22% annual increase in the number of wiring tracks that can be placed side-by-side across the width of a chip. Early small-scale integrated circuits (SSI) in the 1960s had only a few tens of wiring tracks. Today's chips have about 15,000 wiring tracks, and by 2010 chips will have over 100,000 wiring tracks. The number of grid squares defined by the wiring tracks in the x and y dimensions increases as the square of the number of tracks, or 50% per year, quadrupling every 3.5 years and increasing by an order of magnitude every 6 years.

The number of *grids* on the chip is a good measure of the amount of functionality that can be implemented on the chip. A bit of a given type of memory or a certain arithmetic function requires a number of grids of a chip area that remains roughly constant over time.[6] Early chips in the 1960s had only a few hundred grids. Modern chips have 10^8 grids, and by 2010 chips will have 10^{10} grids. This increase of six orders of magnitude over the last 35 years in the functionality that can be placed on a chip has led to major challenges and opportunities in deciding how to organize a system efficiently to use all this area.

The speed of on-chip functions is also increasing exponentially with time. To first order, the delay of a simple gate decreases linearly with gate length. As

---

[6] Of course major advances in memory or arithmetic circuits, such as the development of the one-transistor DRAM in the middle 1970s or recoded multipliers in the 1950s, can greatly reduce the number of grids required for a particular function. However, advances of this magnitude are relatively rare today.

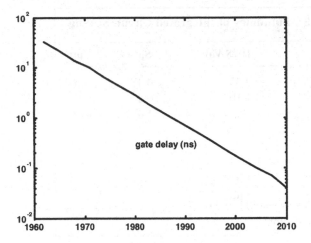

FIGURE 1-4   Scaling of Gate Delay

illustrated in Figure 1-4, gate delay decreases by 13% per year, halving every 5 years. The delay of a simple 2-input NAND gate with a fan-out of four has gone from tens of nanoseconds in the 1960s to a few tenths of a nanosecond today and is projected to be a few tens of picoseconds by 2010. Unfortunately, as described in the following paragraphs, the blinding speed of these gates is likely to be masked by wire delays that increase over time.

The overall capability of a chip depends on the number of functions it contains and the speed of these functions. Combining this 13% per year increase in speed with the 50% per year increase in grids gives an overall increase in capability of 70% per year. This measure of capability increases by an order of magnitude roughly every 4 years. Figure 1-5 plots capability, measured as grids divided by gate delay, as a function of time. This measure of capability has gone from 5 in the early 1960s to about a billion today and is projected to reach nearly a trillion by 2010.

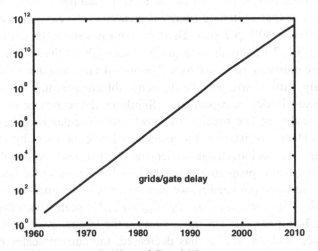

FIGURE 1-5   Scaling of Capability

TABLE 1-3 Summary of Integrated Circuit Scaling			
Parameter	1998 Value	S_P[a]	Units
Gate length, L_d	0.35	0.87	μm
Wire pitch, χ	1.10	0.87	μm
Chip edge	19	1.06	mm
Tracks	1.8×10^4	1.22	χ
Grids	3.2×10^8	1.49	χ^2
Gate delay	0.23	0.87	ns
Capability	1.4×10^9	1.71	χ^2/ns
Pins	549	1.11	

[a] Annual scale factor.

Such a rapid increase in capability makes time a key variable in measuring performance. For example, if a new technology offers a factor of two increase in capability but is delayed for 2 years, the advantage is more than negated. A quantitative increase in capability of this magnitude also implies a qualitative difference in machine organization. The organization that worked best at one level of capability is unlikely to be optimum for a machine built from chips that are 100 times more capable.

Table 1-3 summarizes the scaling of the parameters described in this section. For each parameter, P, the table gives its 1998 value, $P(1998)$, and its annual scale factor, S_P. The value of the parameter for a given year, x, can be estimated by

$$(1\text{-}1) \qquad P(x) = P(1998)S_P^{(x-1998)}$$

1.3.2 Scaling of Chip Parameters

As linear dimensions scale by a factor, x, chip parameters scale, as illustrated in Table 1-4, so that switching energy decreases as the cube of x while current draw increases at 30% per year. The first five rows show the scaling described in Section 1.3.1. To maintain constant field strength, as linear dimensions scale by x, voltage must also be scaled by x. The area of a minimum-sized device scales quadratically with x, whereas the dielectric thickness scales linearly, giving a linear decrease in device capacitance. Similarly, the resistance of a minimum-sized wire scales as $1/x$ because the cross section scales as x^2 and the length scales as x. Hence, resistance of a device-sized wire increases by 15% per year. As to first approximation, charge carriers travel at constant speed under a constant field, device speed is proportional to gate length and thus scales linearly with x.

From these basic parameters, we can derive how the energetics of the technology scale. The switching energy, $E_{sw} = C_{dev}V^2$ scales with the cube of x, decreasing 34% per year! However, because the frequency of switching events has increased and the voltage has decreased, the current scales only linearly with x. More importantly, the current per unit area scales as $1/x$, increasing by

TABLE 1-4   **Scaling of Chip Parameters**

Parameter	Symbol	Scaling		Per Year
Wire pitch	x			0.87
Chip edge	y			1.06
Area	A		y^2	1.13
Tracks/chip	T		y/x	1.22
Grids/chip	G	T^2	$(y/x)^2$	1.49
Voltage	V		x	0.87
Wire capacitance	C_{dev}		x	0.87
Wire resistance	R_{dev}		$1/x$	1.15
Switching time	τ		x	0.87
Switching energy	E_{sw}	$C_{dev}V^2$	x^3	0.66
Current	I_{dev}	$C_{dev}V/\tau$	x	0.87
	I_{area}	I_{dev}/x^2	$1/x$	1.15
	I_{chip}	AI_{area}	y^2/x	1.30

15% per year and, because area increases as well, the current per chip is increasing even faster at 30% per year. Although the energy of each switching event is decreasing at a phenomenal rate, the current draw per chip is increasing nearly as fast.

1.3.3   Scaling of Wires

As technology scales, wires become increasingly important compared with devices in terms of power, delay, and density. The reasons for this are illustrated in Table 1-5, which shows how wire properties scale as linear dimensions decrease and chip area increases. The table contains three pairs of columns. They show the scaling formula and the change per year for a device-sized wire, a 1-μm wire, and a wire that crosses the entire chip. The first two rows show how the capacitance and resistance of these wires scale over time. Although the capacitance of a device-length wire decreases over time, the capacitance for a fixed-length wire

TABLE 1-5   **Scaling of Wire Properties**

Parameter	Device		1-μm		Chip	
C	x	0.87	1	1.00	y	1.06
R	$1/x$	1.15	$1/x^2$	1.32	y/x^2	1.40
I	x	0.87	1	1.00	y	1.06
IR	1	1.00	$1/x^2$	1.32	$(y/x)^2$	1.49
IR/V	$1/x$	1.15	$1/x^3$	1.51	y^2/x^3	1.71
RC	1	1.00	$1/x^2$	1.32	$(y/x)^2$	1.49
RC/τ	$1/x$	1.15	$1/x^3$	1.51	y^2/x^3	1.71

remains constant, and the capacitance for a *global* wire that crosses the width of the chip increases. The resistance of all three wires increases but at a significantly more rapid rate for the longer wires.

1.3.3.1   Scaling of Power Distribution

Rows three through five of Table 1-5 show how distributing power becomes increasingly difficult as technology scales. These three rows consider the current supplied by a single supply wire. The current draw of a device-wide region is a constant times the length of the region, decreasing for a device-long region and increasing with chip length for a chip-long region. This increasing current must be carried over wires with resistance that is increasing rapidly over time. Row four shows that the *IR* drop of a constant-length wire is increasing at 32% per year, and the drop across a chip-long wire is increasing at 49% per year. Worse yet, as voltages decrease, the tolerable *IR* drop decreases proportionally. Thus, the relevant parameter is the *IR* drop as a fraction of voltage, IR/V. This scales as $1/x$, even for a device-sized wire, and as y^2/x^3 for a chip-sized wire, increasing at a whopping 71% per year! In short, if a power distribution strategy is left unchanged while all the linear dimensions and voltages decrease by 13%, the *IR* power supply noise, as a fraction of voltage, nearly doubles.

Careful engineering is required to combat this increase in supply noise. Brute-force solutions like more and thicker metal layers for power distribution or area bonding play an important role. These methods are costly, however, and economical chips complement them with better power distribution techniques involving on-chip regulation and bypass capacitors as well as low-power design methods. These issues are discussed in depth in Chapter 5.

1.3.3.2   Scaling of On-Chip Communication

The increasing difficulty of on-chip communication is shown in rows six and seven of Table 1-5. The RC delay of a constant-length wire increases by 32% per year, and the delay of a cross-chip wire increases by 49% per year. The relevant quantity, however, is how the delay of the wire compares with the decreasing device delay. This parameter, RC/τ is increasing by 51% and 71% for the constant length and cross-chip wire, respectively. To complicate matters, this delay is diffusive, and thus the rise-time, and hence the uncertainty of the delay, increase at the same rate.

In the near future this scaling will cause wire delay to dominate gate delay entirely in most systems. In 1998, the delay of a loaded gate, 200 ps, is about the same as the delay of a 5-mm on-chip wire. In 2008, the gate delay decreases to 50 ps, whereas the wire delay increases to 12 ns. The 1:1 ratio becomes 250:1. In the future, systems must be organized to keep wires short, and signaling methods that make the most of lossy RC wires must be employed to reap the advantages of faster gates.

This dramatic increase in the delay of a global wire relative to gate delay, almost doubling every year, affects the signaling, timing, and architecture of digital systems. Signaling conventions tailored to RC lines involving repeaters and pulsed low-voltage swing drivers are needed to get the maximum performance

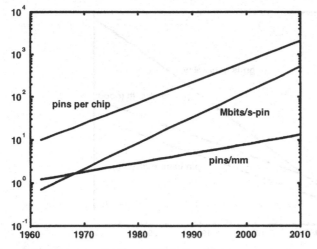

FIGURE 1-6   Scaling of Pins per Chip

from these lossy wires. The lossy nature of the wires makes it extremely difficult to distribute a global clock with low skew. A brute-force solution to this problem involves devoting a large quantity of metal to building a low-impedance clock grid. More clever solutions relax the need for global synchrony by dividing the chip into separate clock domains or employing asynchronous design techniques. Finally, architectures that exploit locality, thus reducing the need for communication over global wires, will perform much better than those that incur the long latencies inherent in global communication over lossy wires.

1.3.3.3   Scaling of Off-Chip Communications

The number of pins that can be economically fabricated on a chip increases as the perimeter of the chip times the linear density of pins. This is true even for area bonding because the pins must still be routed out from under the perimeter of the chip in the next-level package. As illustrated in Figure 1-6, pin count increases by 12% per year. Early chips had only about ten pins, contemporary chips have hundreds of pins, and chips with several thousand pins should be economical by 2010. The growth in pin count is due to the 6% annual increase in chip perimeter combined with a 6% annual increase in pin density. Pin density depends on the track spacing of the second-level packaging technology, which typically scales at about half the rate as on-chip wire spacing.

To complicate matters, off-chip signaling rates have historically trailed on-chip clock rates. The bandwidth per pin for an average chip is also shown in Figure 1-6. Signaling rates of about 1 Mb/s-pin were typical in the 1960s, whereas modern chips approaching 100 Mb/s-pin and rates of 500 Mb/s-pin should be widespread by 2010. A chip using aggressive signaling technology can do about an order of magnitude better than this curve.

The number of available pins is being rapidly outpaced by the amount of on-chip functionality. The bandwidth demand of a partition of an architecture is often captured in a rule-of-thumb known as *Rent's rule*. This rule states that the

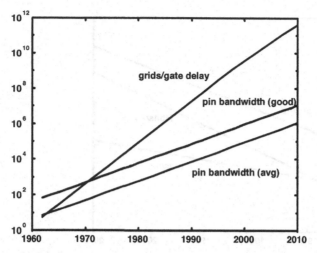

FIGURE 1-7   Scaling of the Gap Between Pin Bandwidth and Capability

bandwidth,[7] $B(b/s)$, from a module with capability C (gates × Hz) grows as C^α

$$(1\text{-}2) \qquad\qquad B = K_R C^\alpha$$

For machines designed without much concern for locality, the exponent α is typically in the range 0.5 to 0.75, with 0.7 being typical.

It was possible to build machines with Rent exponents of 0.7 in the 1960s when this rule was coined; however, the relative scaling of capability to off-chip bandwidth will not sustain such a large exponent. As illustrated in Figure 1-7, capability increases annually by 71%, whereas the available pin bandwidth increases annually by only 28%. The largest exponent that can be sustained under this scaling is 0.46 (log 1.28/ log 1.71). The gap between the required bandwidth (with $\alpha = 0.7$) and the available bandwidth (with $\alpha = 0.46$) is large and growing.

The widening gap between available bandwidth and demand poses many challenges for the digital systems designer. For many systems, off-chip bandwidth is the single largest performance bottleneck. As with on-chip communication, this problem must be addressed through better signaling and better architecture. With good signaling techniques (Chapter 7), off-chip signaling can operate at speeds higher, rather than lower, than the on-chip clock and increase at the same rate.

A switch to faster signaling gives a one-time increase in off-chip bandwidth that, however large, is rapidly canceled by the 33% annual growth in the capability-to-bandwidth ratio. For example, the order of magnitude increase between the average and good bandwidth curves in Figure 1-7 only postpones a bandwidth problem for 8 years. In the long run, better architecture is needed to keep most communication on-chip, thus reducing demand.

---

[7] The original Rent's Rule [LandRuss71] relates the number of pins on a module to the number of gates. When the clock cycle and the signaling rate are identical, this rule is the same as ours. We prefer to relate bandwidth to capacity, however, because it covers the more general (and quite common) case in which the signaling rate and clock cycle differ.

1.3.4   High Levels of Integration Permit New Approaches

The rapid improvement of VLSI technology gives us the tools to tackle many of the technical challenges that the evolving technology has created. Modern VLSI chips have several hundred million grids of chip area containing millions of transistors. Using a small fraction of this area, we can build circuits that solve many of the system-level electrical problems. By applying logic, we can solve these problems without the need for brute-force application of power, large pin-counts, or expensive package design. Some examples include the following:

1. Using custom VLSI chips at both ends of a signal allows us to tailor a signaling convention that isolates noise sources to enable signaling at rates significantly higher than in systems employing conventional signaling.
2. By encoding a stream of symbols before transmission, we can solve a multitude of problems. Band-limited coding reduces the problems of frequency-dependent attenuation and aids clock recovery. DC-balanced coding greatly reduces signal-return cross talk (sometimes called ground bounce).
3. Using pipelined timing conventions can increase both throughput and reliablity over that achieved with conventional synchronous timing.
4. Rather than carefully matching the delay of signal paths and still having a considerable amount of residual skew, using closed-loop per-line clock recovery can completely eliminate skew between a clock and a data signal.
5. Regulating the power at the point-of-use to address the problems of on-chip power distribution locally.

This book explores these examples, and others, in detail.

1.3.5   Digital Systems Problems and Solutions Continue to Change

The rapid advance of VLSI technology and the pace of change in applications make digital systems engineering a very dynamic field. Solutions that work today may neither be appropriate nor adequate in the future. Each generation of technology and each new application area demand new solutions.

Often, compatibility with existing parts, processes, and infrastructure along with a reluctance to try new techniques acts as a retardant, slowing the rate of change. Many engineers prefer tuning to innovation and operate by making a few small changes to an existing solution. Time is usually a factor as well. With today's short development cycles there is little time for experimentation or risk taking. In the end, the marketplace sorts out the prudent from the reactionary and generally rewards those who take calculated risks.

Decoupling technology development from product development reduces the risks associated with new techniques. Developing a new signaling, timing, or power distribution technology independent of, and in advance of, a product development limits the impact of technology failures on product development and creates an atmosphere that is more conducive to innovation. Unfortunately, few companies today have the foresight to invest in such advanced development.

1.4   ORGANIZATION OF THIS BOOK

This book is organized into three main sections. In Chapters 2 to 4, we discuss the elements of digital systems design: wires, transistors, and simple circuits. These chapters lay the groundwork for the remainder of the book by developing engineering models of the important digital systems building blocks. Chapter 2 begins by discussing how digital systems are packaged into chips, modules, circuit boards, and chassis and how these modules are interconnected with various forms of wires. In Chapter 3, we look at the electrical properties of these packaging technologies and develop a set of engineering models for wires that are used throughout the rest of the book. Finally, in Chapter 4 we investigate the properties of the metal-oxide semiconductor (MOS) transistor and the composition of transistors into simple digital circuits.

The next part of the book, Chapters 5 to 10, investigates the key issues of digital systems engineering at the system level. We begin with the problem of power distribution in Chapter 5. Noise is discussed in Chapter 6. Signaling methods are covered in Chapters 7 and 8. Timing conventions are discussed in Chapter 9, and synchronization issues are explored in Chapter 10.

The final part of the book, Chapters 11 and 12 describe circuits for signaling and timing, respectively. The discussion of signaling circuits in Chapter 11 complements the system-level treatment of signaling in Chapters 7 and 8. Similarly, the treatment of timing circuits in Chapter 12 complements the system-level discussion of timing in Chapters 9 and 10.

1.5   BIBLIOGRAPHIC NOTES

Two excellent texts on topics relating to Digital Systems Engineering are Bakoglu [Bakoglu90] and Johnson and Graham [JohnGrah93]. Bakoglu gives a strong theoretical treatment of VLSI circuits and interconnects. Johnson and Graham give a more practical treatment of topics relating to system-level interconnects and timing. The example discussed in Section 1.2 is based loosely on modern multicomputers such as the Cray T3E [Scott96] and the SGI Origin 2000 [LaudLeno97]. The scaling of integrated circuit technology is described in [Moore79], [HennJoup91], and [SIA94]. Rent's rule, relating module pinout-to-gate complexity is discussed in [LandRuss71].

1.6   EXERCISES

1-1   **Pin Budgets:** The router chip in Figure 1-1 is over the pin budget, as indicated in Table 1-1. The following suggestions have been proposed to repartition the system to bring the individual chips within pin budget:

   1. Make the router channel pins single-ended on the router chip and use single-ended-to-differential converter chips to generate differential versions of these signals.

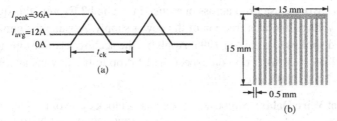

FIGURE 1-8 Current Waveform and On-Chip Power Distribution

2. Partition the router across two chips with each handling three of the incoming channels. The controller bandwidth is split evenly across these two subrouters, and a 2-GB/s channel is used for communication between the two half routers.

Evaluate these suggestions in terms of total numbers of chips and pins required. Which would you pick?

1-2   **Signaling:** The system shown in Figure 1-1 uses four types of signaling: SECM (single-ended current mode), DCM (differential current mode), CMOS (full-swing), and HSTL. Compare the first three of these in terms of power per bit. Assume that all signal lines are 50-Ω and parallel-terminated.

1-3   **Off-Chip Power Distribution:** Suppose the router chip from Figure 1-1 draws an average current of 12 A from the 2.5-V supply over an inductance of 20 nH. The supply network must be designed so that when the router idles and draws zero current, the supply voltage of the router must remain below 2.75 V. Draw a simple circuit that illustrates this situation. How large a capacitor must be connected across the router to meet this requirement? How low must the lead inductance of this capacitor be?

1-4   **Noise Budgets:** If the signal swing of the SECM channels of Figure 1-1 is doubled from 250 to 500 mV, what happens to the noise budget of Table 1-2? What is the new net noise margin? What is the ratio of gross noise margin to noise before and after this change?

1-5   **Arithmetic Scaling:** A 32-bit integer multiplier uses a 32×16 array of full adders.[8] Each full adder, along with its associated multiplexer, is 16χ on a side. How many chips, or what fraction of a chip, does it take to make a 32×32 integer multiplier in 1965, 1985, and 2005? Each full adder has a delay of one *gate delay* (as shown in Figure 1-4), and the worst-case path through the multiplier goes through nine full adders. How many multiplications per second can be realized per chip in 1965, 1985, and 2005? At what rate does this quantity scale?

1-6   **Scaling of On-Chip Power Distribution:** The router chip of Figure 1-1 draws 12 A *average* current with the waveform shown in Figure 1-8(a). The peak instantaneous current here is 36 A. This power is distributed over a comb of thin-film aluminum conductors, as shown in Figure 1-8(b). If these conductors have a resistivity of 0.04 Ω/square, and the current draw is distributed uniformly across the chip,

---

[8] Booth recoding allows the multiplication to be performed with a 32×16 array rather than a 32×32 array.

what is the worst-case drop across one *tine* of the comb? Express this quantity as an absolute voltage and as a fraction of the power supply. Assume the number you just calculated applies to a chip in 1995. Applying the scaling relationships for I, R, and V from Table 1-5, what do you expect the IR drop to be (in volts and % supply) in the years 2000, 2005, and 2010?

1-7 **Scaling of Wire Delay:** Suppose a system has a clock cycle of ten gate delays. What clock frequency does this imply in the years 1990, 2000, and 2010? In these same years, how many clocks, or what fraction of a clock, does it take to drive a wire from one corner of the chip to the opposite corner? Assume this wire runs only horizontally and vertically so that its length is twice the linear dimension of the chip. For now, assume that the delay of a wire is its RC time constant. We will see how to do better in Chapter 8.

1-8 **Chip Architecture:** As described above in Exercise 1-5, a full-adder takes an area of $256\chi^2$ (16χ on a side). Thus, a 32-bit adder is $8K\chi^2$, and a 32-bit recoded multiplier is $128K\chi^2$. How many multiplications and additions per second can be performed on a chip in 2005 and 2010? Discuss some possible uses for chips with this level of performance.

1-9 **Component Specification:** One task of a digital systems engineer is keeping up-to-date on the specifications of available *standard* components – memory components in particular. Using a Web browser (the new way) or a databook library (the old way), look up the specifications of two competing contemporary memory chips. For example you could investigate high-bandwidth DRAM components (RAMBUS versus synchronous DRAM) or static memory components (HSTL versus TTL SRAMs). Describe the two components you have chosen and evaluate their advantages and disadvantages. Which would you choose? For which application?

1-10 **Literature Search:** It is also important for a digital systems engineer to keep up-to-date with the latest custom chips and the techniques employed in their design. These chips are reported in conferences such as the International Solid-State Circuits Conference (ISSCC), the Microprocessor Forum, and Hot Chips. Industry newsletters such as *Microprocessor Report* are also a good source of information on this topic. Look up a contemporary microprocessor chip in a recent copy (within the last year) of one of these conference proceedings or newsletters. Discuss the digital-systems techniques employed. How is clock distribution performed? How are on-chip power supplies handled? What types of signaling conventions are used?

2 PACKAGING OF DIGITAL SYSTEMS

Digital systems are packaged in a hierarchy of chips, carriers, circuit boards, chassis, and cabinets. Signals are transported on batch-fabricated thin-film and thick-film wires on chips, carriers, and boards, and over cables between boards and chassis. The physical characteristics of the wires at each level determine their electrical properties, their cost, and the maximum signal density that can be supported.

At the lowest level, electronic components (mostly field-effect transistors) are fabricated on the surface of silicon integrated circuit *chips* and interconnected by layers of thin-film metal wiring. One or more of these chips are mounted in a *package* that connects their pads to package pins. Packages are mounted on a circuit board that provides low-impedance power and signal return planes and interconnects the package pins with thick-film metal layers. Circuit boards in turn may be connected to one another by other circuit boards (backplanes or mother boards) or by cables. To share mechanical support, several circuit boards are usually packaged together in a chassis, and several chassis may be housed in a cabinet or rack.

At each level of the hierarchy, from chips to cables, a set of design rules governs the physical size and spacing of wires and connections. The geometry that arises from these design rules constrains available wire density and determines the electrical properties of the resulting wires. In this chapter we discuss available packaging technology at each level of the hierarchy and survey current design rules. In Chapter 3, we study the electrical properties and cost models of the wires at each level of the hierarchy.

Wires are not the only means available for moving digital symbols from one place to another in a system. For completeness, we will briefly review the two principal *wireless* signaling technologies: optical and radio. Although a complete discussion of these technologies is beyond the scope of this book, we present sufficient information for the digital systems engineer to understand the capabilities and limitations of these techniques and where they can be best applied.

The remainder of this section discusses in more detail each level of the packaging hierarchy. We begin in Section 2.1 by examining a complete digital system to see how the different packaging levels fit together. We then work from the bottom up, examining each packaging level, from chips to cables, in detail in Sections 2.2

through 2.8. Finally, we give a brief overview of optical signaling in Section 2.9 and radio communications in Section 2.10.

2.1   A TYPICAL DIGITAL SYSTEM

Figure 2-1 is a photograph of a typical digital system, a high-end personal computer. The system's main components, including its processor and memory interfaces, are mounted on a larger mother board. Specialized I/O hardware plugs into an I/O bus card, which itself plugs into the mother board. Memory is mounted on SIMs (single in-line modules). Power is distributed from a central power supply in the lower part of the cabinet to the boards, discs, and other components over wiring harnesses made up of individual conductors. Data are distributed from boards to discs (e.g., over ribbon cables). Like all but the highest performance computers, this machine is air-cooled; a single fan pulls air in through the bottom of the enclosure past the power supply, discs, and circuit cards. The entire system is housed in a metal enclosure welded from individual pieces of stamped steel and covered with plastic panels that provide noise reduction and improved appearance.

Table 2-1 summarizes the properties of the packaging levels in a digital system built using 1997 technology. For each level the table shows the size of the level, the number of wiring layers typically used (for both signals and power), various wire properties, and the number of pins to the next level. The wire properties include pitch (the spacing between two adjacent wires on the same layer), wire cross section, resistance per unit length, and the type of transmission line used to

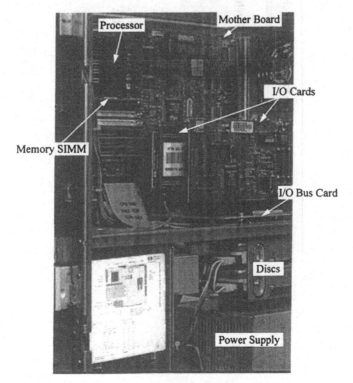

FIGURE 2-1   Packaging of a Typical Digital System

TABLE 2-1 Properties of Packaging Levels

Level	Size	Layers	Pitch (μm)	Tracks/Layer	Wire Cross Section (μm)	Resistance (Ω/mm)	Wire Model	C (pF/mm)	Pins
Chip	15 × 15 mm	4	1.2	12,500	0.6 × 0.6	150	C/RC	0.2	500
Package	5 × 5 cm	4	150	333	75 × 20	1 Ω (total)	LC	1 pF (total)	500
Circuit board	40 × 30 cm	8	625	2000	125 × 20	0.05	LC/LRC	0.1	2,000
Backplane	40 × 30 cm	8	625	2000	125 × 20	0.05	LC/LRC	0.1	1,000
Chassis	40 × 40 × 40 cm	N/A	N/A	N/A	N/A	N/A	LRC		1,000
Cabinet	1.5 × .6 × .6 m	N/A	N/A	N/A	N/A	N/A	LRC		3,000

model the wire. Perhaps the single most relevant number is the number of tracks per layer (the linear dimension divided by the wire pitch) because this is a good measure of the wiring capacity of a given level.

The numbers in this table are for a typical system. Examples exist of systems with larger chips and boards, finer wiring pitches, more layers, and more pins between levels. However, exceeding these typical numbers usually carries a heavy price premium.

As technology advances, the numbers in this table will improve. However, they do not all improve at the same rate. Integrated circuit wire density is advancing at a rate of 22% per year, doubling about every 3 years. The number of tracks per layer on a circuit board, on the other hand, increases by only about 7% per year, doubling only after 10 years. This nonuniform scaling changes the nature of the digital system design problem over time, making solutions that were optimal 10 years ago inappropriate today.

2.2   DIGITAL INTEGRATED CIRCUITS – ON-CHIP WIRING

Integrated circuits are at the core of a modern digital system. In fact, today there are many systems that fit entirely on a single integrated circuit. A single 15-mm square chip today (1997) can hold up to 64 Mbits of memory, several million gates, or some combination of the two. A simple 32-bit CPU (without memory) can be realized in an area just 1 mm on a side. Over 200 of these simple CPUs would fit on a 15-mm square chip!

A typical 0.35-μm CMOS chip has four wiring layers on which 0.6-μm square aluminum wires are routed.[1] Aluminum wires (resistivity, $\rho = 2.65 \times 10^{-8}$ Ω-m) of this size have a resistance of 0.04 Ω/square, which implies 74 Ω/mm for a minimum-width wire at 25°C. The top layer may be made thicker, with coarser design rules, to facilitate power distribution at the expense of signal density.

The signal layers on such a chip are spaced by 0.6-μm dielectric layers of SiO$_2$ (dielectric constant, $\varepsilon_r = 3.9$) that are sometimes doped with other materials. Silicon nitride (Si$_3$N$_4$, $\varepsilon_r = 7.5$) is used for the top-most dielectric layer. A wire in a dense region of a chip is surrounded by minimum-pitch parallel wires on its layer and minimum-pitch perpendicular wires on adjacent layers. Such a wire has a significant capacitance, not to ground or the substrate, but to these other wires. Only the bottom wiring layer has a significant capacitance to the substrate. The total capacitance for a wire in a dense region is 160 fF/mm. As described in Section 6.3.1, the presence of this capacitance between signal wires leads to capacitive crosstalk between signals.

Because of their high resistivity, short length, and tight pitch, on-chip wires almost always have an inductance low enough to be safely ignored. Thus, in our analysis we will model short on-chip wires as lumped capacitive loads and longer on-chip wires as lossy RC transmission lines. Any wire whose resistance is small compared with the circuit driving it will be considered short. Typically, wires

---

[1] Some chips use refractory metals such as tungsten (W) for on-chip wiring to allow high-temperature processing after the wiring layer is deposited.

under 1 mm are short, but resistance must be considered for all longer wires. Because of their resistivity, driving long on-chip wires at high speed is among the most difficult signaling challenges we will encounter.

Wire density is a limiting factor in most integrated circuits. Except for very regular arrays (such as memories), on-chip function units tend to be *wire-limited*. That is, their area is determined not by the number of gates or transistors but rather by the wiring required to connect them.

Perhaps the biggest limitation of a modern digital integrated circuit is the large reduction in signal count between on-chip wires and package pins. With over 10^4 wiring tracks in each dimension on each of four layers, it is not unusual to have several million on-chip signals. However, packaging constraints require that only 500 or fewer signals can leave the chip. For inexpensive plastic packages, fewer than 200 signals can leave the chip. Because of this limitation, chips are often *pad-limited*, and the area of the chip is determined by the number of pads required to bring signals off-chip and not by the density of on-chip circuits. This is particularly common with peripheral-bonded chips for which the required chip area increases as the square of the number of pads.

2.3   INTEGRATED CIRCUIT PACKAGES

Most integrated circuits are bonded to small ceramic or plastic packages. Although it is possible to attach chips directly to boards, a method used extensively in low-cost consumer electronics, placing the chips in packages enables independent testing of packaged parts, simplifies reworking of boards, and eases the requirements on board line pitch by spreading out the pins. In some cases, several chips are packaged together on a ceramic or laminated module. Such *multichip modules* allow high-density interconnection between the chips packaged together.

Electrically, the signal leads of first-level packages have significant mutual and self-inductance. If the leads are fabricated in pairs or at uniform height over a return plane, the lead is best modeled as a transmission line. With proper control of conductor size and spacing, the impedance of this line can be matched to other transmission media (e.g., a 50-Ω stripguide on a PC board). If spacing to a return is large or irregular, the lead is modeled as a lumped inductor. Depending on how the chip is bonded and packaged, it is not unusual for the conductor from the chip pad to the PC board to have as much as 10 nH of self-inductance and 5 nH of mutual inductance to adjacent conductors.

2.3.1   Wire Bonds and Solder Balls

Figure 2-2 illustrates the most common technique for electrically attaching chips to packages. Wire bonds are formed by compression welding one end of a thin (1-mil-diameter) gold wire to a bond pad (typically 100 μm on a side on 125 μm centers) on the chip and the other end to a pad on the package. Wire bonds are inexpensive and compliant, allowing unequal thermal expansion of the chip and package. However, they have significant inductance, about 1 nH/mm, and only allow one or two rows of pads around the periphery of the chip.

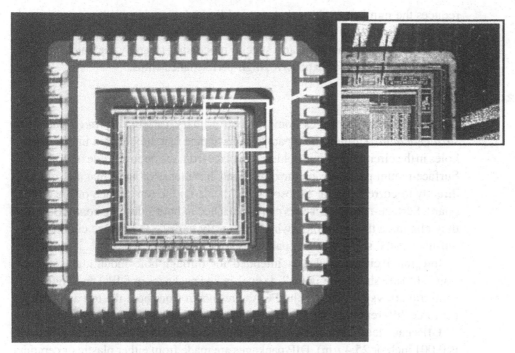

FIGURE 2-2   Wire-Bonding a Chip to a Package

An area array of solder balls can also be used to attach a chip to a package, as in Figure 2-3. In this case, a chip's aluminum bond pads are processed with additional metal layers to allow adhesion of solder balls to pads. This style of die-to-package connection is often called "C4" or "flip-chip" after pioneering packaging processes developed at IBM. Connections to a PC board or package are made by depositing a solder paste on an array of contacts (on either side of the board), placing the chip in rough alignment, and then heating the assembly to reflow the solder. The surface tension of the solder pulls the chip into precise alignment. Solder ball contacts are typically placed on 250-μm centers, and the balls themselves are 100 μm or less in diameter.

Solder balls have the advantages of very low inductance (a few tenths of a nanohenry per contact) and the ability to form contacts with pads located over the entire area of the chip, not just the periphery. Area bonding is particularly advantageous for power distribution because it allows the global power distribution to be done in thick-film (20 μm typical) power planes in the package rather than in thin-film (1 μm typical) wires on the chip. Area bonding also significantly

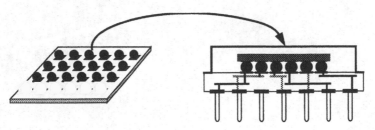

FIGURE 2-3   Flip-Chip Bonding

reduces the number of chips that are pad-limited, since a very large number of pads can be placed in a small area. However, because area bonding requires expensive multilayer packages and special processing to apply the solder, its use tends to be reserved for expensive, high-performance chips.

2.3.2 Package Types

Integrated circuit packages come in two primary varieties: *through-hole* and *surface-mount*. Through-hole packages have pins that are inserted into through-holes in the circuit board and soldered in place from the opposite side of the board. Surface-mount packages, on the other hand, have leads or lands that are soldered directly to corresponding exposed metal lands on the top surface of the circuit board. Surface-mount packages can be attached to both sides of a board. Because they eliminate through-holes, which are costly to drill, and reduce circuit-board wiring density, surface-mount packages are generally preferred.

Integrated circuit packages intended for through-hole mounting (see Section 2.4.6) are shown in Figure 2-4 (dual-in line packages or DIPs) and Figure 2-5 (pin-grid arrays or PGAs). The PGAs are shown from both the top and bottom for three different pin counts.

DIPs have lead counts between 8 and 64, with leads on 100-mil centers (a *mil* is 0.001 inch or 25.4 μm). DIP packages are made from either plastic or ceramic materials, as discussed in the next section. They have the unpleasant characteristic that their corner leads are much longer than their center leads, and thus there is a wide range of parasitic lead inductance and capacitance. DIPs are large by today's standards, generally have poor high-frequency performance, and are nearly obsolete.

Pin-grid arrays are usually made of ceramic materials, but relatively inexpensive plastic versions are also available. They have lead counts that range from 64 up to 500 or so. The smaller pin-count packages have pins on 100-mil centers in several rows around the outside of the package; larger PGAs, such as the one shown on the right of Figure 2-5, have pins on 50-mil centers in staggered rows. This example package also has provisions for mounting discrete power supply bypass capacitors.

Most modern IC packages are intended for surface attachment to a PC board. Examples of the most common types are shown in Figure 2-6. Leaded chip carriers

FIGURE 2-4   Examples of Dual-In Line (DIP) Packages

FIGURE 2-5   Examples of Pin-Grid Array (PGA) Packages

(LCCs) are shown at the center of the figure. They have leads emerging from all four sides of the package, and the external part of each lead is bent into a J form that tucks up underneath the package. This arrangement allows some flexibility in the lead so that, as the board and package heat up at different rates, differential expansion between the two can be accommodated. LCCs are made using plastic, ceramic, or metal manufacturing processes. Their leads are on 50-mil (1.27-mm) centers, and the packages are available in lead-counts from 20 to 84.

Small-outline (SO) packages, shown at the right of Figure 2-6, were intended to replace DIPs. They are found with gull-wing leads, like those shown in the figure, and less often with J leads; both lead types provide thermal expansion compliance. These packages are generally made of plastic. Lead pitch is 50 mils for all but the TSOP (tiny small-outline package) style, which has smaller, typically 25-mil, pitch.

At the left side of the figure are quad flat pack (QFP) packages. Available in plastic, metal, and ceramic variations, these packages have gull-wing style leads and pin counts ranging from 44 to 352. QFPs are available in "families," which share a fixed body size but have varying lead counts. Lead pitch varies from 1.00 mm down to 0.40 mm.

FIGURE 2-6   Examples of Surface-Mount Packages

FIGURE 2-7   Ball-Grid Array (BGA) Packages

Figure 2-7 shows a typical ball-grid array (BGA) package. These packages are made using either ceramic or PC-board-like laminates. Package "leads" consist of a solder ball attached to a package pad, and these balls are arranged in a grid on the bottom of the package.

There are two types of BGAs. Type-I or *cavity-up* BGAs have a die-attach cavity and wire bond pad area on the top of the package. These are wired through internal wiring layers in the package to the bottom pads and balls, and the array of ball connections generally covers the entire bottom of the package. Type-II or *cavity-down* BGAs have their die-attach area on the bottom of the package, with several rows of balls surrounding the die cavity, like the package shown in Figure 2-7. The advantage of this arrangement is that the top of the package can be made into a thick metal heat slug to which the die is attached on the bottom side. This heat slug can easily be augmented with an external heat sink. Thus, where Type-I's are usually limited to dissipation less than a watt or so, Type-II BGAs can handle chips that have power dissipation up to tens of watts. BGAs are still fairly new (1997), and standards for size, shape, and lead count have not been fully settled. Currently, off-the-shelf packages are available with lead counts up to 400 or so and with balls on a 50-mil (or greater) grid. Some custom BGA packages have been built with lead counts up to 1,000.

Most of the package types we have discussed are available in two different forms, cavity-up and cavity-down, a designation that describes which side of the package has the die-attach cavity. As with Type-II BGAs, cavity-down packages mount the IC die into the bottom of the package and allow heat to be drawn out of the top of the package, often with an attached heat sink. Cavity-down packages can therefore handle much higher power dissipation than cavity-up packages, which shed heat mainly through their leads into the PC board.

Lastly, each of the package types we have discussed is generally available in a range of die cavity sizes. This avoids the necessity of placing a small die in a large cavity, a situation which would result in very long bond wires. Designers usually want to keep bond wires as short as possible to reduce their electrical parasitics and improve their mechanical robustness.

2.3.3 Package Manufacturing Processes

Integrated circuit packages are made from plastic, ceramic, PC-board-like laminates, and metal. Often, IC manufacturers will encode the material type in the package abbreviation, and thus a "PQFP" is a plastic quad flat pack, a "CERDIP" is a ceramic DIP, and so forth.

Plastic packages are formed by die-bonding and wire-bonding the chip to a metal (usually copper) lead frame and then encapsulating the assembly in injection-molded plastic. Plastic packages are inexpensive, but, because they lack ground planes, leads do not have controlled impedances and generally have high inductance. Plastic packages usually have high thermal resistance, making it difficult to cool a chip that dissipates a great deal of power. An array of thermal vias or a metal *slug* is often used to improve the heat conduction of a plastic package.

Metal package analogs exist for the plastic LCC and QFP packages. In these packages, the integrated circuit die is mounted and wire-bonded to a metal lead frame that is then captured between two thin metal shells. An epoxy resin is injected between the shells to seal the assembly, to insulate the lead frame from the case, and to cement the assembly together. The lead frame is in thermal contact with the metal shell, thereby greatly improving the thermal performance of the package relative to the plastic version. The leads of the package emerge through thin slits in the metal case, and the proximity of the (electrically floating) metal case reduces the lead mutual and self-inductances. Metal QFPs generally have exactly the same outside dimensions as their plastic cousins and so can be used interchangeably in a given PC-board design.

A ceramic package consists of several layers of conductors, usually about $100\ \mu$m wide on 200-μm centers separated by layers of insulating ceramic, usually alumina (Al_2O_3). The chip is placed in a cavity in the package and bonded (wire or solder ball) to the conductors. A metal lid is then soldered on the package to seal the cavity against the environment. Because multiple layers are used, power supply and signal return planes can be included in the package, reducing supply inductance and providing controlled-impedance signal paths. One disadvantage is that the high permittivity of alumina ($\varepsilon_r = 10$) results in a low propagation velocity in the package but is advantageous for power–ground connection layers because additional capacitance is a significant benefit for supply bypassing. It is also possible to include discrete bypass capacitors within a ceramic package.

Laminated packages are similar to ceramic ones but are built using the same materials and processes used for PC boards. Like the ceramic package, a chip is placed in a cavity in the laminated package and bonded to the conductors. The multiple layers of conductors permit the use of supply and return planes and controlled impedance lines. Compared with ceramic packages, laminated packages enjoy the advantage of a relatively low permittivity ($\varepsilon_r = 4$). They have the disadvantage that they are not as well sealed, particularly against water vapor, as a ceramic package, making them unsuitable for use in a hostile environment.

2.3.4 Multichip Modules

With multiple wiring layers and supply planes, ceramic and laminated packages can hold and interconnect several integrated circuits. By making interchip connections locally, these *multichip* modules or MCMs reduce the pin count of the package and the capacitance of the interchip wires. However, MCMs are usually more expensive than single-chip packages and increase the size (and cost) of the smallest unit that can be independently tested and replaced.

2.3.5 A Typical Package Model

In this section we will develop a simple electrical model for a typical package, a type-II BGA. We will assume that the 30-mm square package houses a 15-mm square chip and provides about 300 signal pins between chip and board.

2.3.5.1 Physical Construction

The construction of a typical type-II BGA is shown in Figure 2-8. It is built using PC board fabrication techniques. The interconnect for the package is of multilayer laminated construction and is bonded to a metal substrate that serves as the heat sink for the package. The interconnect portion of the package has a large central hole that allows a die to be bonded onto the metal heat slug. Solder balls (shown at the top of the figure) make connections to a PC board, and thus the package is referred to as a cavity-down design because the die is toward the bottom of the package.

Copper conductors in the laminate are 20 μm thick, and signal leads are drawn about 75 μm wide. Planes are provided for power supply and ground connections. A dozen or so solder balls are used to connect each of these planes to the printed circuit on which the package is mounted. Plane conductors are wrapped around the edges of their dielectrics to form continuous annular metal lands around the die area. Power and ground bond wires can be connected anywhere along these lands. Signal and plane layers are separated from neighboring planes by 150 μm. Some of the details of BGA construction can be seen in Figure 2-8.

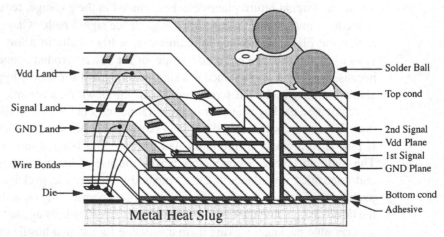

FIGURE 2-8   Typical Type-II BGA Construction

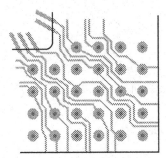

FIGURE 2-9   Typical Signal Wiring Pattern

The chip's I/O pads are connected to package lands with 50-μm-diameter bond wires. There are two tiers of signal lands on the package to which bond wires are attached. The longest bond wires, connected to the upper tier at the package corners, are about 6 mm long; the shortest, connected to the lower tier at the center of each side, are about 3 mm long.

A typical wiring pattern for a signal layer in a lamintated BGA is shown in Figure 2-9. The following features are worth noting:

1. A typical wiring trace may run at minimum distance from other traces for a substantial fraction of its total length, and thus neighboring traces are strongly coupled.
2. Wiring traces are often run from the wire-bond land to a via (that connects to a solder-ball land on the surface) and then onward to the edge of the package. Package laminates are made up on large panels that hold many packages, and, before these are cut into individual parts, wiring traces are connected to a common terminal that allows gold to be electroplated onto the wire-bond lands. Unfortunately, the vestigial traces out to the package edge form unterminated stubs that tend to degrade signal quality. Not all package manufacturing processes require these extra traces, and they should be avoided if possible.
3. Signal wiring traces are 10–15 mm in length. Signals propagate along them at about half the free-space speed of light, about 150 mm/ns, and thus package traces represent a delay of about 100 ps. This time is short compared with most signal rise and fall times; therefore, we can treat package leads as lumped circuit elements with reasonable accuracy.

2.3.5.2   Package Electrical Model

The package electrical model has four parts, as shown in Figure 2-10: the bond wire between chip and package, the package land to which the bond wire is attached, the signal trace between land and via, and the via and solder ball (perhaps including the PC board land to which the ball is attached). In principle, an electrical model of this package would have to take into account all of the currents and charges on a complex three-dimensional arrangement of conductors and dielectrics. In practice, we can use fairly simple tools to build a lumped-circuit-element equivalent model that will serve well for most high-performance signaling designs.

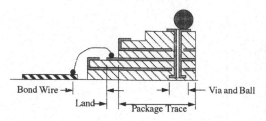

Bond Wire → | → | ← Via and Ball
Land → | ← Package Trace →

FIGURE 2-10   Package Electrical Model

For the bond wire, we can develop a crude model by assuming that the wire is a uniform round conductor over a conducting plane. In Chapter 3 we will develop some simple formulas for capacitance and inductance per unit length for this situation (Eqs. 3-6 and 3-9, respectively); applying these formulas and assuming a 50-μm-diameter ($2r$) wire 0.5 mm away from a plane

$$(2\text{-}1) \qquad C = \frac{2\pi\epsilon_0}{\ln\left(2\frac{s}{r}\right)} = 15 \text{ fF/mm}$$

$$L = \frac{\mu_0 \ln\left(2\frac{s}{r}\right)}{2\pi} = 0.75 \text{ nH/mm}$$

The capacitance of a bond wire is almost always negligible compared with the capacitance at its two ends (the chip I/O pad and the wire-bond land), and thus a single lumped inductor is a reasonably accurate model. A value of 1 nH per millimeter of length is a good rule of thumb for the inductance of bond wires.

The signals on neighboring bond wires interact via coupling capacitance and mutual inductance. We can estimate these effects either by using exact or empirical formulas (outlined in Chapter 3 and in several of the references) or by using a two-dimensional field solver such as LINPAR [DjorHarr89]. Bond wires typically run parallel for their entire length, spaced apart by about 200 μm or so. Mutual capacitance is about 20 fF/mm between neighboring bond wires. Next nearest neighbors are reasonably well shielded for mutual capacitance; therefore, this coupling can usually be ignored. However, mutual inductances may need to be considered for wires that are some distance apart. Mutual inductance coupling coefficients are about 0.4, 0.3, and 0.2 for the geometry we have assumed for wires that are 1, 2, and 3 spacings apart, respectively.

A 2D solver is also useful for estimating the effects of the land and package trace in our model. The actual impedances of traces and coupling between neighboring traces are quite complex, but a useful model can be constructed assuming uniform traces spaced an "average" distance apart. If we assume an average 100-μm spacing for lands and traces and a dielectric constant of 4.7 (for the glass-epoxy material typical of laminated packages), then the lands can be modeled as small lumped capacitors of about 0.15 pF and coupling capacitors between lands of about 0.08 pF. The package traces have capacitance to the neighboring planes of about 90 fF/mm; coupling capacitance to the neighboring lines of about 40 fF/mm; series inductance of about 0.7 nH/mm; and first, second, and third mutual inductive coupling coefficients of about 0.5, 0.3, and 0.2, respectively.

The via, solder ball, and PC board trace have very low inductance compared with the signal traces on the package and board; a reasonably accurate model is

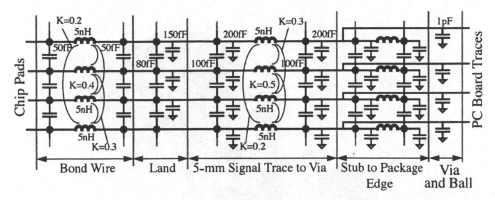

FIGURE 2-11   Package Lumped-Element Model

a single lumped capacitance for this part of the model of about 1 pF. This part of the model is difficult to determine from a simple analytical model but can be measured using techniques we will outline in Section 3.7.

The series resistances of bond wires, package signal traces and planes, and other package elements could also be included in a lumped-element model, but these are often small enough to ignore for many applications.

A simplified lumped-element package model is shown in Figure 2-11. Note that the ground symbol in the figure is assumed to be the package ground-plane node.

A more complete model would split this capacitance between ground and power planes. Chip power and ground are connected typically through several parallel bond wires (inductors) to these planes, and it may be necessary to model the (small) additional inductance of the vias and balls that connect package power planes to board power planes.

This example should be considered only the outline of a starting point for developing a detailed package model. In critical applications, many more details may be required to capture the behavior of the package.

2.4   PRINTED CIRCUIT BOARDS

Packaged chips are usually interconnected using PC boards. Like laminated packages, PC boards consist of layers of conductors separated by insulating layers. The conductors are typically copper, and the insulator is usually some form of fiberglass composited with epoxy resin. The minimum wire dimensions for a board today (1996) are 100-μm-wide lines on 200-μm centers. However, vias between layers are much larger, as we will discuss below. When wires are routed through areas with many vias, typical wire pitch (χ) is about 625 μm.

Figure 2-12 shows a typical PC board (a graphics accelerator for a personal computer) that typifies several techniques used in modern board construction. The board itself does not have sufficient area to mount all the components; therefore, some parts are mounted on an additional *mezzanine* card (parallel to the main card at the upper right). Memory chips are mounted on a SIMM plugged into a socket that holds it at a 45° angle to the main board (to reduce overall height). A variety of surface mount packages are used on this board; the larger chips are all mounted in

FIGURE 2-12 A Printed Circuit Board (courtesy AccelGraphics, Inc.)

QFPs, memories in small outline packages, and a few smaller chips in leaded chip carriers. Much of the circuitry for this board is contained in a single large custom integrated circuit near the center of the board. This circuit dissipates so much heat that it has its own cooling fan attached directly to the package. The board also contains several tiny leadless discrete components (resistors, capacitors, crystal resonators, and so forth).

2.4.1 PC Board Construction

Typical PC boards for high-performance digital systems have four to eight layers of wiring and an equal number of power and ground return planes, though it is feasible to fabricate boards with twenty or more wiring–plane layers. High-quality controlled-impedance transmission lines can be constructed by spacing the signal wiring layers an appropriate distance above and below a pair of planes.

The PC board industry had its beginnings in the United States before metric dimensional units were universally adopted for manufacture, and PC board fabrication vendors continue to use apparently whimsical dimensioning based on the English system of units. Board dimensions are often specified in *inches* (1 inch = 25.4 mm), and dielectric thickness and conductor widths are usually measured in *mils* (1 mil = 0.001 inch = 25.4 μm). The thickness of the copper wiring layers is expressed in ounces (oz), the weight of copper metal in a square foot of material. Typical copper thicknesses are 0.5, 1.0, and 2.0 oz, corresponding to 0.7 mil (17.5 μm), 1.4 mil (35 μm), and 2.8 mil (70 μm), respectively. Advanced processes, particularly those used for laminated IC packages, sometimes use 0.25-oz copper.

Printed circuit boards are constructed from alternating layers of *core* and *B-stage* or *prepreg*. A core is a thin piece of dielectric with copper foil bonded

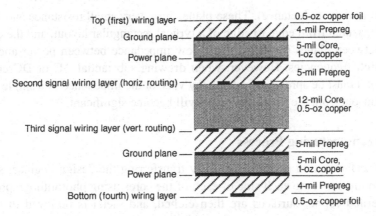

Top (first) wiring layer — 0.5-oz copper foil
4-mil Prepreg
Ground plane —
5-mil Core,
1-oz copper
Power plane —
5-mil Prepreg
Second signal wiring layer (horiz. routing) —
12-mil Core,
0.5-oz copper
Third signal wiring layer (vert. routing) —
5-mil Prepreg
Ground plane —
5-mil Core,
1-oz copper
Power plane —
4-mil Prepreg
Bottom (fourth) wiring layer —
0.5-oz copper foil

FIGURE 2-13   Typical Printed Circuit Board Stackup

to both sides; prepreg is a dielectric material mixed with expoxy resin which, when heated and pressed together in a stack of cores and prepreg layers, forms a strong bond with neighboring cores. Once cured, prepreg becomes identical to the dielectric material inside a core. By far the most common dielectric is fiberglass–epoxy, though other dielectrics such as Teflon and polyimide are used for some special applications.

The arrangement of cores and prepreg layers that make up a PC board is called a *stackup*. Figure 2-13 shows one of several possible stackups for an eight-layer board suitable for a high-performance digital system. Stackups for modern multilayer boards are usually arranged so that the outermost layers are prepregs with copper foil bonded to the outside for the outermost (top and bottom) wiring layers. In the interior of the board, pairs of signal layers are placed between pairs of planes to form stripline transmission lines. Wires on one signal layer are routed mostly orthogonally to the wires on the adjacent signal layer to avoid crosstalk. The stackup is symmetric about the center of the board in the vertical axis; this arrangement is usually recommended by fabricators to avoid mechanical stress in the board under thermal cycling.

2.4.2   Electrical Properties

For the stackup shown in Figure 2-13, internal 0.5-oz traces drawn 6 mils wide (152×17.5 μm) will have a DC resistance of about 5 Ω/m, inductance of about 350 nH/m (8.8 nH/inch), capacitance of about 122 pF/m (3.1 pF/inch), and a characteristic impedance of about 53 Ω. Microstriplines on the surface of this board stackup can be adjusted to about 50-Ω impedance by drawing them 8 mils (200 μm) wide, with $R = 4.5$ Ω/m, $L = 280$ nH/m, and $C = 106$ pF/m.

Power planes are often built on the thinnest core available from a fabrication vendor (to maximize the capacitance between the planes) and often use thicker copper layers than on signal layers to reduce resistance. The solid 1-oz (35-μm)-thick power and ground planes in Figure 2-13 have a resistance of 490 $\mu\Omega$/square. The parallel plate capacitance between the two planes, separated by 5 mils (130 μm,) is about 270 nF/m^2, and the inductance is about 0.165 nH/square (planes pairs are two-dimensional transmission lines; equation 3-8 can be used to find the inductance). These planes have very small resistance and inductance, measured from edge to edge of a typical rectangular layout, and the capacitance between planes provides a very low impedance between power and ground at high frequencies. However, when drawing substantial AC or DC currents, the load must be spread out over many vias, or the impedance of a single via and the fan-out from the via to the plane will become significant.

2.4.3   Manufacturing Process

The fabrication process begins by transferring the design engineer's pattern of conductors onto each side of each of the cores using photolithography. The patterned copper surfaces are then etched, and metal is removed in the process everywhere but on the conductor patterns. Next the cores, prepreg, and surface foils are stacked, carefully aligned, and heated under pressure to bond the assembly together. The surface copper layers are patterned and etched to form the surface conductors. Holes, both for mechanical assembly and for interlayer vias, are drilled through the entire thickness of the board. The surface layers are then photolithographically repatterned, exposing only the copper conductors and holes that are to become vias, and copper is plated onto the exposed areas and into the exposed holes. A solder mask, a thin (typically 2-mil) layer of polymeric material, is often bonded to the top and bottom surface. The solder mask protects the copper conductors on the surfaces, exposing only those locations where components are to be soldered to the board. These areas, *solder pads*, are usually coated with solder as part of the board fabrication process to avoid copper corrosion during handling before assembly. Finally, milling operations can be used to add slots, cutouts, and other nonround shapes.

Most PC board processes support gold flashing, which permits selected surface conductors to be electroplated with a thin layer of gold, either to allow direct wire bonding of integrated circuits or a conductor pattern to be used as a connector.

Some vendors offer flexible PC board processes that are useful for applications in which the board must conform to an unusual mechanical shape. An example is shown in Figure 2-14. The board shown on the right of the figure has rigid sections for mounting components and flexible sections that allow the overall assembly to be folded into a compact package (the system shown contains six special cameras for real-time tracking in a virtual-reality application). Components are soldered onto the rigid sections by reflow; then the assembly is cut free of the larger board and assembled into the package.

2.4.4   Vias

Vias are much larger than conductors, and thus via diameter, not conductor spacing, usually limits the wiring density that can be achieved in a board design. Fabricators use the *aspect ratio* of a via, the ratio of board thickness to via diameter, to judge its manufacturability. The larger the aspect ratio, the more difficult it is to plate the inside surface of the hole reliably. As a rule of thumb, most vendors charge a premium for holes with aspect ratios much over about 8:1 or so. For a typical board thickness of 62 mils (1.6 mm), a 10-mil drill hole is usually the

FIGURE 2-14   Example of Flexible PC Board Fabrication and Assembly

smallest practical size. Holes are plated to a thickness of about 1–3 mils, and the *finish hole size*, usually specified by the designer, is therefore 2–6 mils smaller than the drill hole.

Vias in a multilayer board are fairly complex structures, as shown in Figure 2-15. Vias require *pads* on each layer to which they connect, and consequently there will be an annulus of copper around the plated hole. Because the holes are not guaranteed to be perfectly aligned with the copper traces, these annuli are needed to ensure that the copper is not broken by the drilling operation. Inner pads are often larger than outer pads to allow for even greater dimensional tolerances on inner layers. Where a via passes through a plane, a clearance hole is required large enough to guarantee that no accidental connection will be made. Where a via is supposed to connect to a plane, as in a power or ground via, a *thermal relief* structure (usually four small metal bridges between via and plane) is often required to isolate the via thermally from the plane to facilitate soldering operations.

Because vias are so much larger than signal wires and occupy all layers of the PC board, it is very expensive for a signal to change layers. Some PC

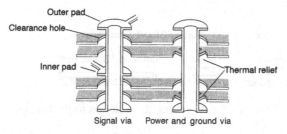

FIGURE 2-15   Cutaway of Vias in a Multilayer PC Board

manufacturing processes support very small *blind vias* that connect only two (typically inner) layers of the board. Though they save considerable space, blind vias are usually quite expensive.

2.4.5 Dimensional Constraints

Boards are fabricated from *panels*, large sheets of core and prepreg material, typically 18×24 in. (460×610 mm). Small board designs are replicated and tiled onto a panel so that they fill up as much of the panel as possible. However, if the outline size of the board is, for example, slightly larger than half the size of a panel, only one instance of the design will fit on the panel, and much of the material will be wasted. Such considerations can substantially affect the overall cost of a board.

In any case, overall board dimensions are usually kept much smaller than a full panel; some automated assembly equipment cannot handle boards larger than 400 mm or so.

Most manufacturers control their inventory of material by offering a limited selection of core and prepreg thicknesses. Achieving a particular desired characteristic impedance for a board trace requires setting the ratio of conductor width to dielectric thickness; consequently, the menu of dielectric thicknesses becomes an important constraint for signaling.

Vias are drilled using a series of standard-sized drills, and thus the designer is also limited to a small selection of possible via sizes. Fabricators charge a premium for retooling a drilling station, and designers therefore usually avoid specifying more than a few different hole sizes in a design.

2.4.6 Mounting Components: Surface-Mount and Through-Hole

Packaged integrated circuits, as well as discrete components (resistors, capacitors, etc.), are attached to the board either by bonding to surface pads (surface-mount) or by inserting pins into a via (through-hole). Figure 2-16 illustrates the common lead types for through-hole and surface-mount attachment of integrated circuits.

Surface-mount packaging is by far the preferred method, for it obviates the need to drill large-diameter holes through the board, reduces the inductance of the connection, and allows components to be mounted on both sides of the board. Figure 2-12 shows a typical PC board manufactured with (mostly) surface-mount techniques. The tiny two-terminal devices scattered around the board are discrete resistors and capacitors. Most passive components are available in these tiny

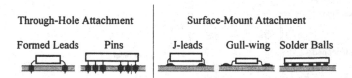

FIGURE 2-16   Methods for Attaching IC Packages to PC Boards

packages, which are usually designated by their size in mils (e.g., an "0402" package is 40×20 mils, or about 1.0×0.5 mm). The figure presents a variety of the IC package types discussed in Section 2.3.2.

Surface-mount assembly techniques have reached the point at which it is difficult or impossible to place and solder components onto boards by hand. Leaded integrated-circuit packages may have hundreds of delicate leads, typically on 0.5-mm centers, easily damaged by handling. Ball-grid array packages, now fairly common, are much more robust to handling but require solder joints that are hidden from normal visual inspection once a part is mounted to a board. Discrete components, such as resistors, capacitors, and inductors, are packaged in surface-mount packages as small as 0.5×1.0 mm. For these reasons, automated component placement and soldering processes are the rule for modern PC board assembly.

Typical assembly processes begin by silk-screening solder paste, a mixture of granulated solder alloy and cleaning flux, onto a board. The silk screen template is aligned with the solder mask to apply solder paste only to pads. Next, a robot, programmed with component placement and orientation data, picks up parts from feeders and component handlers, aligns them with their associated solder pads, and places them on the board. For larger components, the damp solder paste holds the component in place until the soldering operation is complete; smaller components, such as resistors and capacitors, are often cemented onto the board with epoxy-based glue also screened onto the board. Soldering is usually performed as a batch operation in a special oven that gradually heats the board to the solder melt temperature and then gradually cools the board, for too-rapid heating and cooling may introduce mechanical stress in the board.

Most surface-mount boards require at least a few through-hole components and thus are actually examples of *mixed* assembly, whose process flow concludes with mounting the through-hole parts and wave-soldering them.

In any soldering operation, there is some probability that a given joint will be faulty, either an open circuit or a short to a neighboring joint. Failure rates are radically different for different package types. For example, fine-lead-pitch leaded chip carriers (0.5-mm pitch or finer) experience failure rates per pin as high as 50 parts per million, whereas BGA packages have failure rates about an order of magnitude lower. Complex boards may have several thousand solder joints, and the probability of a bad joint on a board, the failure rate times the number of joints, can be quite high. Inspection and identification of failed joints is therefore an absolute requirement. Typically the defects are correlated within a board so that a single observed defect can hint at the existence of other defects on the board or portend future intermittent failures.

Most processes still depend on human visual inspection to identify bad solder joints and other defects, though mass-production processes increasingly use robotic vision systems. Some solder joints, such as those underneath BGA packages, cannot be visually inspected, and X-ray inspection is increasingly common. Electronic inspection using special "boundary scan" circuitry that links all of the I/O pads on all of the chips on a board into a bit-serial data chain is sometimes

FIGURE 2-17   Some Example Sockets for DIPs and Leadless Chip Carriers

used to check for correct board assembly and soldering. Poor soldering can also produce intermittent heat-related failures. Boundary-scan circuitry is particularly helpful in isolating these postassembly failures.

2.4.7   Sockets

To allow for replacement or rework, packaged integrated circuits and multichip modules are sometimes attached to a board using *sockets* that permit the chips to be "easily" removed and replaced without the need to reflow solder. All sockets, however good, degrade the electrical quality of the signal path by adding parasitic circuit elements, predominantly inductance, between the package and the board.

Some typical sockets are shown in Figure 2-17; sockets for DIPs are shown on the left and for LCCs on the right. Traditionally sockets have involved wiping pin-in-socket connections. Such sockets usually have an insertion and removal force of several ounces per pin. Inserting and removing chips with 500+ pins into these sockets requires considerable force and care. Cam-actuated zero-insertion-force or ZIF sockets simplify the insertion and removal process but at considerable cost.

A typical ZIF socket for a leaded chip carrier is shown (on its side) in Figure 2-18. In use, a packaged chip is placed in the bottom (left) part of the socket against a series of spring-loaded fingers that contact the package pins. The lid then hinges down and locks to hold the pins firmly agains the contact fingers.

Some land-grid-array packages are attached to circuit boards by compressing a conductive *interposer* between the package and a land pattern on the board. This gives a high-quality, low-profile connection that is relatively easy to assemble and disassemble.

FIGURE 2-18   A Zero-Insertion-Force (ZIF) Socket for LCCs

2.5   CHASSIS AND CABINETS

One or more PC boards are usually assembled together in a box that is called a card cage or chassis. Power supplies, cooling fans, and other support equipment are also often included in a chassis. The chassis provides mechanical support for the circuit cards as well as the backplanes or cabling, or both, that electrically connect them. The chassis also includes mechanical structures for guiding cooling fluids (liquid or air) and serves as a shield to prevent unwanted electromagnetic radiation from entering or leaving the system's circuits and wiring.

Several chassis are often combined in a single enclosure called a cabinet or rack (after the old telephone relay racks). The cabinet serves to stack several chassis in a small amount of floor space and provides room for cabling the chassis together. Cabinets often include cabling *bulkheads* where cables that connect chassis in the cabinet to other cabinets are terminated. Cabinets are cabled together with cables running through the walls to adjacent cabinets, passing under the floor between cabinets, or traversing overhead trays.

One of the most popular types of enclosures is the rack-mountable card cage. Many card cages conform to a set of standards that allow off-the-shelf mechanical components to be combined in a large variety of ways to build a semicustom enclosure for a system. The basic component of these enclosures is a mechanical support for PC card assemblies that bolts into a standard 19-inch "relay" rack. This assembly includes card guides to help align card connectors with backplane connectors and provisions for attaching a backplane PC board. The standards are intended to be compatible with a variety of backplane and daughter card pin-in-socket connector systems. Also available are standard front panel blanks in various width and heights, fan assemblies, shelves, drawers, and all types of related hardware. Dimensioning for standard card cages is rather strange: the height of card cage assemblies is measured in units of "U" (1 U = 1.75 in or 44.45 mm); 3, 6, 9, and 12 U are common standard heights. Width of front panels (and therefore card spacing) is measured in units of "HP" (1 HP = 0.2 in or 5.08 mm). Most card cages have a total width of 84 HP.

2.6   BACKPLANES AND MOTHER BOARDS

2.6.1   Daughter Cards

For purposes of modularity, small circuit boards, often called *daughter cards*, can be attached to a larger circuit board, the *mother board*, to assemble a system. Perhaps the most familiar type of daughter card is the *SIMM* (single in-line memory module); several SIMMs are usually mounted parallel to one another and perpendicular, or at an angle, to the mother board, as shown in Figure 2-19. Linear or area connectors may be used to attach a daughter card, whose plane is parallel to the mother board. This arrangement, called a *mezzanine*, allows just enough spacing for component height and cooling air. In effect, the mezzanine card is a large multichip module that plugs into a rather unusual socket on the mother board. Mother boards usually include other active components besides the daughter cards. Examples of both construction techniques are shown in Figure 2-19, a photograph of a UNIX workstation mother board. A mezzanine board is mounted to the mother board at the right of the figure; a mezzanine arrangement is also used for I/O boards at the left of the figure. A row of SIMM sockets is provided for memory expansion at the upper right, and two SIMMs are shown installed.

2.6.2   Backplanes

A classic physical arrangement for digital systems is a set of parallel circuit cards interconnected over one or two edges by a *backplane*. Figure 2-20 shows a typical backplane and daughter card arrangement. Connectors along the daughter

FIGURE 2-19   Daughter Card and Mother Board Packaging

FIGURE 2-20 Backplane and Circuit Card Packaging

card edge contact connectors on the backplane. The backplane is a PC board that often contains nothing but wiring traces and connectors; it is essentially a special-purpose rigid cable. Although most backplanes contain only passive circuitry, this is not a restriction, and in some cases connector pin count can be reduced by placing some active components on the backplane.

2.7 WIRE AND CABLE

2.7.1 Wires

Cabling is used to distribute power and signals within and between system modules. Low-current power supply distribution and non-speed-critical signaling are often routed within an enclosure in cable harnesses and multiconductor cables built from groups of individual insulated wires. Resistance, physical size, and maximum current-carrying capacity of wires are the primary concerns for designing wiring harnesses. The resistance of a wire is determined by its cross-sectional area, often specified using wire *gauge*.

Table 2-2 shows some common sizes of wires in units of American Wire Gauge (AWG) along with their properties. As shown in the table, the AWG is a logarithmic scale, like dB, with the cross-sectional area of a wire decreasing

TABLE 2-2   **American Wire Gauges and Their Properties**

Gauge (AWG)	Wire Diameter (mils)	Wire Diameter (mm)	DC Resistance $(\times 10^{-3}\ \Omega/\text{m})^a$	Maximum Current (A)	f_1^b (kHz)	Attenuation at 1 GHz (dB/m)
000	409.6	10.404	0.203	175	0.16	0.02
0	324.9	8.252	0.322	125	0.26	0.03
4	204.3	5.189	0.815	70	0.65	0.04
6	162.0	4.115	1.297	50	1.03	0.06
8	128.5	3.264	2.061	35	1.64	0.07
10	101.9	2.588	3.277	25	2.61	0.09
12	80.81	2.053	5.210	20	4.15	0.11
14	64.08	1.628	8.268	15	6.59	0.14
18	40.30	1.024	20.95	5	16.7	0.22
20	31.96	0.8118	33.31	3	26.5	0.28
22	25.35	0.6439	52.95		42.1	0.35
24	20.10	0.5105	84.22		67.0	0.45
28	12.64	0.3211	213.0		169	0.71
30	10.03	0.2548	338.2		269	0.90
32	7.950	0.2019	538.4		428	1.13
34	6.310	0.1602	854.6		680	1.42

^{a}For annealed copper at 20°C.
^{b}Skin-effect frequency.

by an order of magnitude, and hence the resistance increasing by an order of magnitude, each 10 gauges. The gauge of a wire with cross-sectional area A in m^2 is approximately given by

$$(2\text{-}2) \qquad\qquad AWG = -10 \ln\left(\frac{A}{A_0}\right)$$

where A_0 is the area of a zero-gauge wire ($5.07 \times 10^{-5}\ m^2$).

The current-carrying capacity of a wire is determined not only by its size but also by the permissible temperature rise due to resistive heating in the wire, the type of insulation surrounding the conductor, how the wire is packed with other wires, and various safety and regulatory factors. The column of the table labeled maximum current gives the numbers recommended by the American Insurance Association. Slightly higher numbers (e.g., 20A for 14 AWG) are used in the National Electrical Code.

Wire is available either as a single strand of metal (solid wire) or as a bundle of smaller wires twisted together to form a larger wire (stranded wire). An AWG 22 stranded wire, for example, might contain seven strands of AWG 30 wire, a bundle that has about the same cross-sectional area as a single AWG 22 conductor. Stranded wire is usually used in cable assemblies and harnesses because it is more flexible than solid wire.

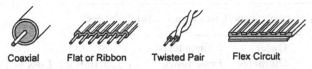

Coaxial   Flat or Ribbon   Twisted Pair   Flex Circuit

FIGURE 2-21   Types of Signaling Cables

The high-frequency performance of a wire is indicated by the last two columns of Table 2-2. The column labeled f_1 gives the skin-effect frequency of the wire. This is the frequency at which the skin depth of the signal equals the radius of the wire. Below this frequency the entire conductor carries current, and the AC resistance is equal to the DC resistance. Above this frequency, only the outer *skin* of the conductor carries current, and the resistance of the wire increases with the square root of the frequency, as discussed in Section 3.3.4.4. This frequency-dependent resistance increases attenuation as frequency increases. The attenuation per meter in deci-Bells or dB for each wire gauge at 1 GHz is given in the final column of the table.

2.7.2   Signaling Cables

Cabling for high-speed and high-frequency signaling in digital systems requires a well-controlled characteristic impedance and a well-defined signal current return path physically close to the signal conductor. To satisfy these two requirements, signaling cables are usually arranged in one of the basic forms shown in Figure 2-21. We will see in Chapter 3 how the geometry of these cables affects signaling properties such as impedance, cross talk, and attenuation.

2.7.2.1   Coaxial Cable

Coaxial cable (often called "coax") has the advantage that, when signal and return currents are equal, both the magnetic and electrical fields associated with the signal are entirely contained within the cable, thus reducing interactions with neighboring signals to a large extent. To improve propagation speed and reduce losses, these cables are often built so that the space between inner and outer conductors is only partially filled with dielectric material (thin spirals of dielectric are common, for example, in closed circuit TV cables). The outer conductor is often made of braided small copper wires to give the cable improved flexibility. Characteristic impedances of coaxial cables are typically 50–100 Ω. Signal attenuation is frequency dependent, as we will see in Section 3.3.4, and cables differ widely in the amount of loss per unit length.

Table 2-3 shows the characteristics of several popular coaxial cable types. Capacitance per unit length is often useful when the coaxial cable's length is short compared with the shortest wavelength of interest in the signal (the lumped approximation; see Section 3.3.1). Losses are measured in dB (ten times the base 10 log of the ratio of power levels at two points 100 m apart on the cable). Note that losses are higher for smaller cables, in general, and also depend on the dielectric material. The velocity factor, v/c, is the ratio of speed of signal propagation on

TABLE 2-3   **Characteristics of Some Common Coaxial Cables**

Cable Designation	Dielectric	Outer Diameter (in)	Characteristic Impedance (Ω)	Capacitance (pF/m)	Loss @ 1 GHz (db/100 m)	v/c^a
RG-11A/U	Polyethylene	0.405	75	67.3	7.1	0.66
RG-8A/U	Polyethylene	0.405	52	96.8	8.0	0.66
RG-59/U	Polyethylene foam	0.242	75	56.7	10.9	0.78
RG-58A/U	Polyethylene foam	0.198	50	85.3	14.5	0.78
RG-62A/U	Polyethylene/ air	0.238	93	44.3	8.7	0.84
RG-174/U	Polyethylene	0.101	50	101.0	34.0	0.66
RG-178B/U	Teflon	0.071	50	95.1	46.0	0.70
RG-179/U	Teflon	0.096	75	64.0	24.0	0.70
M17/133	Teflon	0.086	50	105.0	22.0	0.70

^{a} Velocity factor.

the cable to the speed of light in vacuum, which is mainly a function of ϵ_r of the cable dielectric. Although the types listed above have a single inner (signal) conductor and an outer (return) conductor, there also exist cables with two signal conductors and an outer shield called "twinax." Twinax is sometimes used for differential signaling systems.

2.7.2.2   Ribbon Cable

Ribbon cable has many small, usually stranded, wires embedded in a flat strip of dielectric. Typical ribbon cables have conductors spaced on a 50-mil (1.27-mm) pitch and are available in several standard widths, typically from 9 to 64 conductors. A signal and its return are usually run on neighboring wires to minimize interactions with other signals. In single-ended signaling systems (systems in which the signal return is shared across many signals), the single return is repeated on every other conductor so that each signal wire lies between a pair of return wires. When used in this way, the characteristic impedance of each signal wire is 110–130 Ω in typical cables.

Ribbon cables are available in many varieties. To reduce cross talk, some ribbon cables offer twisted pairs of conductors. The twisted sections alternate with short sections of untwisted wire to allow easy connectorization (see Section 2.8). Another strategy for improving signal integrity is to embed a ground plane in the cable. Signal return currents flow in this ground plane much as in a PC board microstrip. One wire of the ribbon is bonded to the ground plane so that the plane can be connected to circuitry at each end. Note that in this style of cable, all of the signal return currents flow through this single pin; consequently, this type of cable may not be the best choice for high-performance signaling systems with many parallel wires. Ribbon cables are also available with shields, usually made from thin metal foil, that completely surround the signal and return conductors. Shields of this sort are usually used to reduce capacitive coupling and not as signal returns. Yet another variation on this theme is to package several coaxial cables in a ribbon. These cables, available in 50-, 75-, and 93-Ω characteristic impedances, have individual coaxials on 100-mil (2.54-mm) centers.

2.7.2.3 Twisted Pair

Cross talk between neighboring wires (Section 6.3) can be reduced dramatically by twisting together the wires carrying a signal and its return. A neighboring signal wire finds itself alternately close to the signal and then close to the return along the length of the twisted pair. The currents and voltages on the signal and return wires are opposite, and thus the effects of the electric and magnetic fields on nearby wires are nearly canceled by each successive half twist. Twisted-pair cables have impedances in the range of 100–150 Ω. Groups of twisted pairs are often bundled into a single jacket, sometimes with an outer electrostatic shield. With their well-controlled impedance, surprisingly low loss at high frequencies, and low cost, twisted pair cables are widely used in voice and data networks and can support signaling rates up to 100 Mbits/s and higher. The Cray supercomputers from the Cray-1 through the Cray C-90 also use twisted-pair cabling for carrying high-speed signals between modules at data rates up to 250 MHz.

2.7.2.4 Flex-Circuit Cable

A variation on ribbon cable, flex-circuit cable, consists of a series of flat conductors embedded in a dielectric. Flex cables are made by rolling round copper conductors flat and embedding them in an insulator or by etching flexible PC board material. Flex-circuit cables for very high-performance signaling systems may include one (microstrip) or two (stripline) signal return planes.

2.7.3 Bus Bars

Large digital systems typically require power supplies of a few volts (3.3 and 5.0 V are common standards) and may dissipate hundreds of watts per board. Current flow in power supply conductors can reach hundreds of amperes, and this current must be delivered to loads with small voltage drops. A few feet of even the largest diameter wire (see Table 2-2) can introduce a few tens of millivolts of loss in a few feet of cable at these current levels. Worse, connectors attached to the ends of power supply wiring tend to introduce additional resistance, and heating at these points can lead to reliability problems.

For high-current supply wiring applications, *bus bars*, solid bars of a conductive metal, are used to carry supply currents from power supply to boards and backplanes. Bus bars are often bolted to backplanes to augment or replace PC board conductors for supply current delivery. Bus bars are often made from copper plated with solder or tin to avoid corrosion. Brass and aluminum are also commonly used bus bar materials. Figure 2-22 shows an example of bus bar

FIGURE 2-22   An Application of Bus Bars for Supply Current Delivery

construction. Large rigid copper straps connect a group of four switching power supplies to a backplane. Current distribution over the backplane is augmented with additional plated bus bars bolted onto the backplane in contact with large surface traces on the backplane PC board.

2.8   CONNECTORS

Most digital systems are *modular*, that is, they are built up of testable, repairable, and maintainable subunits and are *externally connected* to power sources, networks, and devices that support human–machine interaction (keyboards, displays, printers, etc.). These characteristics require that connections within a system and connections between a system and its environment be capable of being broken and reestablished repeatedly and reliably. Connectors are the components that support this vital function.

Connectors link the electrical and mechanical parts of a design problem. Finding elegant solutions in both domains is among the most challenging parts of digital systems engineering. To get a feel for the level of difficulty, the reader should examine the catalogs and Web pages of electronic parts vendors that deal in a wide variety of components. Invariably, the connector sections of these catalogs are the largest sections. The enormous variety of connectors is a reflection of the design difficulties associated with them. Connector costs, in monetary terms, the space they take up in a system, and the engineering effort associated with them are often a significant part of the overall cost of a system.

Connector reliability often determines the overall reliability of the system. Where other interfaces between the wires in a system are typically made by *alloying* two metals (e.g., wire bonds, solder joints, etc.), connectors cause current to flow from one piece of metal to another simply by being in physical contact. All connectors include some type of mechanical spring to provide connection force when the connector is mated and a set of conductors to carry current.

The metal surfaces of connector conductors are inevitably exposed to air, which can convert a high-conductivity metal surface into an insulating metal oxide. Moisture and corrosive contaminants dissolved in air can greatly accelerate this process. Connector manufacturers usually try to find a way to make the area of contact in a connector *gas-tight* to avoid this problem. Vibration and other mechanical forces that may act on the connector during its operational lifetime serve initially to undo gas-tight connections and can lead to early failure. It is easier to make a small gas-tight joint than a larger one, and thus this characteristic is at odds with overall current-carrying capacity.

Most premium connectors are plated with noble metals, mainly gold, that resist corrosion and promote long-life, low-resistance connections. Gold-plated connectors are almost universally used in high-performance signaling systems. Gold plating is expensive, however, and therefore much less expensive connectors are available that are coated with cheaper metals, such as tin. The cost of the engineering effort required to analyze the reliability and acceptability of a "cheap" connector and the possibility of a very expensive field replacement, however, may easily outweigh the savings in component costs. Inexpensive connectors should only be used in noncritical applications and where volume production can recover costs.

Connectors constrain the design of a signaling system. Connector-pin density places limits on how a system can be decomposed into PC boards and modules and on how many signal wires can be brought into a system from the environment. Connectors introduce impedance discontinuities into a signaling system, and, as we will see in Chapters 3 and 6, these discontinuities establish limits on signaling rates and are signficant sources of noise. Impedance discontinuity at a connector interface, particularly the physical separation of a signal current from its return current, is often the main culprit in unwanted radiation (*EMI*, or electromagnetic interference) into and out of a system.

A full discussion of the engineering issues of interconnection is beyond the scope of this text. We will briefly introduce the most important applications and types of connectors and refer the reader to the list of references for a study of this issue.

2.8.1   PC Board Connectors

Many types of connectors are used to attach circuit boards to mother boards and backplanes. Historically, the most common type of connector has been the *edge connector*, a set of gold-plated fingers along one edge of the card. Because the male side of the connector is fabricated as part of the board, these connectors are relatively low cost. Because the PC-board half of the connector is rigid, the connector mating force is provided by fingers of springy material in the female connector. Connection density for card-edge connectors is fairly low relative to pin-and-socket types (typically 20 connections per inch or less). This is particularly true when a signal return plane is required; all of the connector fingers on one side of the board will be taken up for this purpose. Because of their low density relative to the alternatives, edge connectors today are only found in high-volume, low-performance applications where cost is more important than signal density. They are used, for example, to attach PCI-bus peripheral cards to PC backplanes and in the ubiquitous SIMMs that house memory ICs in computers.

Pin-in-socket connectors are the most commonly used board-to-board connections today. They can be purchased in up to six-row configurations with connection densities up to 80 conductors per inch. Some families of connectors have integral ground planes that provide a controlled impedance on the signal lines. The connector mating force is provided by spring fingers inside the female (socket) half of the connector.

Dense, controlled-impedance connectors can be made out of flexible circuit board material. A flex circuit, with exposed plated terminals along one surface and often a signal return plane in an inner layer, is wrapped around a form. The assembly accepts a high-density set of mating terminals along a board edge (daughter card) and surface mounts to a mother board or backplane. Flex connectors are usually built with mechanical actuators that pull the edges of the connector apart for removal and insertion of the mating connector and force them together for a secure connection once the connector is mated.

Connectors are attached to PC boards in a variety of ways. The oldest method of attachment is by through-hole soldering; the connector terminates on the board side in a series of wire tails that are inserted in plated-through holes on the board and soldered in place. In recent years, this process has been largely replaced with a press-fit technique in which the connector tails have been modified with a springy section, which, when pressed into a plated through-hole, makes a secure, gas-tight connection. Some modern, high-density connectors, and nearly all flex-circuit connectors, are mounted to the board using surface-mount techniques similar to those used for IC packages. Because all but zero-insertion-force types of connectors require some amount of force per pin during mating operations, mating forces for large pin-count connectors can be quite large. Mounting brackets and headers are often used to take up these forces to avoid flexing connector-to-board connections.

2.8.2   Interposers

Pairs of planar structures are sometimes connected over an area array of connection points using an *interposer*. Interposers are used, for example, to connect a mezzanine board to a mother board, to connect a stack of peer PC boards into a three-dimensional package, to attach a land-grid array to a PC board, and to make temporary connections between test, measurement, and programming equipment and boards or chips under test.

Interposers can be constructed from arrays of spring-loaded pins (sometimes called "pogo pins") or using *fuzz buttons*, small balls of wadded-up gold wire that are both conductor and spring. More recently, low-cost interposers have become available consisting of individual S-shaped gold springs embedded in an elastomeric material. Pogo pins and fuzz buttons require an insulating mechanical part to hold them vertically in place and to ensure alignment with the mating boards or packages. Interposers, particularly those made with fuzz buttons, offer fairly large numbers of low-inductance connections in a given volume and allow mating and demating for test and repair. However, mating an interposer assembly is usually not a routine service operation, for the process may require considerable care to avoid damage to the connecting parts, particularly fuzz buttons, and to achieve proper alignment. Fuzz-button interposers offer very high reliability (much higher than sliding contact connectors, such as pin-in-socket types).

2.8.3   Elastomeric Connectors

Elastomeric connectors combine the conductor and spring into a single entity. There are two types: *layered elastomeric* and *metal-on-elastomer* connectors. Layered elastomeric connectors consist of alternating stripes (in the strip version of the connector) or filaments (in the area version) of conducting and insulating silicone rubber. The basic silicone rubber material, which is an insulator, is made conductive by including carbon or silver in the rubber composition. Metal-on-elastomer connectors have metal foil, typically gold-plated copper, bonded to a slab of silicone rubber. Area elastomers are often fabricated by embedding short pieces of wire, bent into springs, in a compliant rubber material. A typical application, in which two identical area arrays of conducting pads are interconnected by an area elastomer, is shown in Figure 2-23.

Elastomeric connectors make connections by *redundancy*. That is, the pitch of the stripes or filaments of conducting material is usually much finer than the area pads that mate with the connector, and thus generally a few or many stripes carry the current for each signal. Because the connector is mechanically much like a strip or slab of rubber, it must be held in place by a rigid holder. In the case of

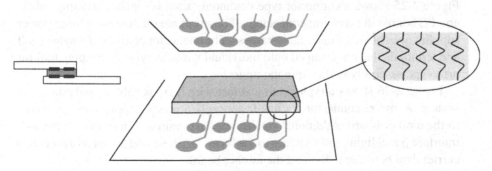

FIGURE 2-23   Area Elastomeric Connector

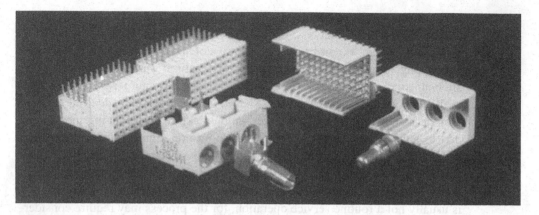

FIGURE 2-24   Power Connectors Compatible with Backplane Connectors

a strip connector, the holder not only positions the connector but also guarantees that it is compressed by just the right amount during assembly.

2.8.4   Power Connectors

In low-end digital systems it is not unusual to see power brought onto cards over connector pins that would otherwise be used for signals. In high-performance digital systems, however, this is almost never done. Pins designed to handle 10-mA signals are not appropriate for 300-A power feeds. Special power connectors that bring wide areas of copper together with high force are usually used to bring power onto high-performance boards. A power connector intended for use with a compatible type of backplane–daughter card connector is shown in Figure 2-24. The standard multipin connector modules intended for signals are shown in the background. In the foreground are special high-current pin connectors and their plastic headers, which are mechanically compatible with the signal connectors.

2.8.5   Wire and Cable Connectors

2.8.5.1   Wire Harness Connectors

Figure 2-25 shows a connector type commonly used for interconnecting cables and PC boards in a system; connectors of this type are often used to bring power supplies onto boards from a cable harness. The connector consists of a nylon shell and terminals that are crimped onto individual wires. A typical crimping tool for prototype assembly is shown in the figure.

Figure 2-26 shows a typical intracabinet wire harness cabling and connector system. A nylon connector (in hand) connects a power supply wiring harness to the mother board. Additional smaller cables terminated in plastic connectors interface panel lights and switches to the board. A ribbon-cable assembly (center) carries data between a disc and the mother board.

Figure 2-27 shows the back of a typical workstation cabinet and the variety of connectors and cables used to connect the workstation to networks, keyboards,

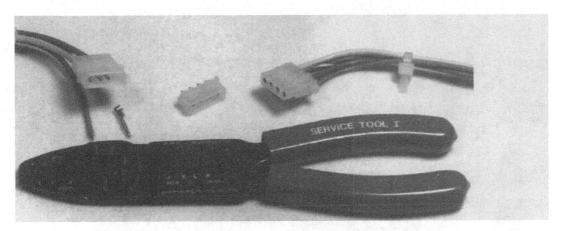

FIGURE 2-25 Typical Nylon-Shell Connectors with Terminals and Crimper

displays, and other external equipment. At the left is a small "phone" plug, ubiquitous in audio systems, used here to connect a microphone for speech input to the workstation. Several D-type connectors are pictured, including the second from the left, which is used to deliver video signals to a display, and next to it a somewhat larger, 25-pin D that is one of the standard connectors for RS-232 serial port connections. D-type connectors are available in standard sizes from 9 to 56 pins. The small, round DIN (Deutsche Industrie Norm) connector near the center of the photo is used here for the keyboard connection but is sometimes used for other serial interfaces because it has the advantage of taking up very little rear-panel space. The connecter at the center is a special 50-pin high-density

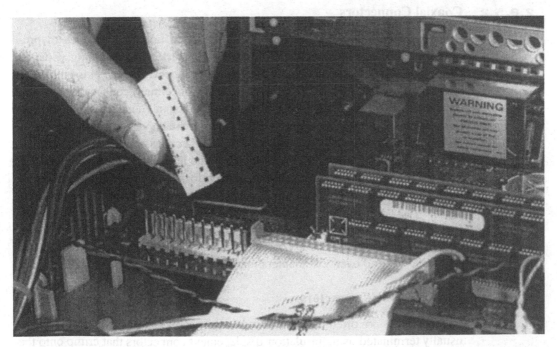

FIGURE 2-26 A Typical Intracabinet Wiring Application

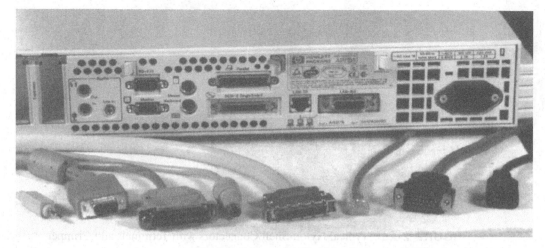

FIGURE 2-27 Typical Connectors Used for Between-Cabinet Interconnect

version of the D-connector that supports the Small Computer Systems Interface (SCSI) and is used here to connect the workstation to an external disc. To its right is an RJ-45 connector for attaching a thin-wire Ethernet; the RJ series of connectors is available in a variety of forms, the most common of which, by far, is the RJ-11 used on virtually all telephones in the United States. Another type of network connection available on this workstation is the Ethernet transceiver cable terminated in the D-type 15-pin connector second from the right. Finally, at the right side of the photo is a modular 3-pin power connector used almost universally on computer and instrumentation equipment powered from the 120-V AC mains.

2.8.5.2 Coaxial Connectors

Sensitive, high-frequency signals are often carried on coaxial cables to provide a controlled-impedance environment and interference shielding. Coaxial connectors, illustrated in Figure 2-28, are used to connect these cables to bulkheads and circuit cards. The BNC (for bayonet Neill Concelman) connector, shown in the center of the figure, is the most widely used coaxial connector today. It has the advantage of being inexpensive and is easy to attach with a bayonette action. However, it is limited to frequencies of 500 MHz or less. The SMA (subminiature microwave type-A) connectors shown at the left of the figure are expensive but smaller and have good high-frequency performance up to 10 GHz. Type-N connectors (right-hand side of the figure) are often used at frequencies of 1 GHz and above, particularly for microwave instruments that require very high-quality, low-loss connections. A remarkable variety of coaxial connectors are available; one vendor that specializes in coaxial connectors lists some 550 different types of connectors and over 350 adapters that mate one type to another.

2.8.5.3 Ribbon-Cable Connectors

Ribbon cables are often used to connect circuit cards within a chassis. They are usually terminated using insulation-displacement connectors that crimp onto the

FIGURE 2-28 Some Examples of Coaxial Connectors

cable to provide two rows of pins on 100-mil centers. Ribbon-cable connectors are very inexpensive; however, their application is usually limited to within-chassis use because they lack the mechanical integrity of the connectors shown in Figure 2-27.

Figure 2-29 shows a typical ribbon-cable insulation displacement connector before (left) and after (upper right) attachment to a ribbon cable. The mating connector, in this case intended for through-hole solder attachment to a PC board, is shown at the lower right.

2.8.5.4 Methods of Attachment

Connectors are attached to wires in a variety of ways. Perhaps the oldest method, which goes back to the invention of electrical technology for lighting, is to capture the wire between two pieces of metal that are part of the connector using a threaded

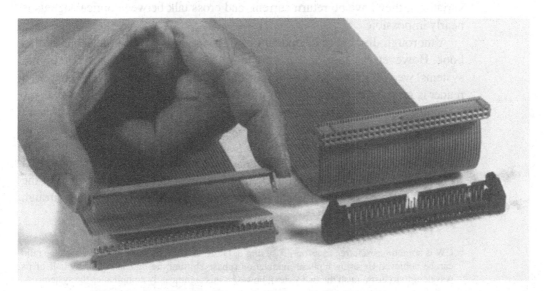

FIGURE 2-29 An Example Ribbon-Cable Connector

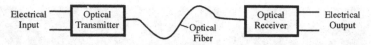

FIGURE 2-30   An Optical Communications Channel

fastener to provide the necessary force. Audio and power connectors, for example, use this method to this day. Soldering, used widely in cable connectors in the early development of electronic technology, is less common today. Crimping, in which a portion of the connector is mashed together with the wire, is a very common technique in modern wire and coaxial connectors. Most crimp-style cable–connector families require a special hand or power tool called a *crimper* to effect the connection. Some crimpers (e.g., those for coaxial cable connectors) perform a gang-crimp, making several connections in one operation. Finally, as described in Section 2.8.5.3, insulation displacement is widely used to attach connectors to multiconductor cables.

2.9   OPTICAL COMMUNICATION

Transmitting signals optically as modulated light has several advantages beyond isolation. Most importantly, light can be sent long distances (over 100 km) through high-quality fiber with little dispersion or attenuation. This property makes optical communication the method of choice for distances over 100 m. Second, the bandwidth of an optical channel is extremely high. The 1.5-μm wavelength that is commonly used in communications systems corresponds to a frequency of 2×10^{14} Hz. A bandwidth of even 0.1% of this carrier, 100 GHz, is wider than any encountered in electrical systems. Finally, optical signals are inherently isolated from most sources of interference. They are not affected by power supply variations, they have no return current, and cross talk between optical signals is nearly impossible.

A thorough discussion of optical communication is beyond the scope of this book. However, because of the importance of optical signaling in large digital systems, we will give a quick overview of the field in this section. The interested reader is referred to [Wilson97] for more detail.

Figure 2-30 shows a basic optical communications system. An electrical input signal modulates a light source, a light-emitting diode (LED) or laser diode, in the optical transmitter. The modulation is usually CW, that is, in one input state the transmitter is on and in the other the transmitter is off.[2] The optical signal from the transmitter is coupled into an optical fiber that guides the light to the receiver. In some cases the fiber may be omitted and the signal propagated through

---

[2] CW is sometimes referred to as on-off keying or OOK. A small increase in signal-to-noise ratio can be achieved by using biphase modulation (phase shifting the optical signal by half of its wavelength to distinguish the two states); however, this significantly complicates the system.

free space between the transmitter and receiver. The receiver detects the arriving optical energy and demodulates it to generate an electrical output signal.

2.9.1 Optical Transmitters

2.9.1.1 LEDs

Inexpensive low-speed optical communications systems use light-emitting diodes (LEDs) for the transmitter. An electrical current in the LED stimulates emission of photons of a particular energy (wavelength) that depends on the material from which the LED is constructed. The major advantage of LEDs is their low cost (a few tens of cents each). However, they have poor conversion efficiency (a few percent), limited bandwidth, and low optical power output. Thus, LED transmitters are only used in optical links that operate at modest bit rates (< 100 Mbits/s) over short distances (up to a few kilometers).

2.9.1.2 Laser Diodes

Higher bandwidth and better efficiency can be achieved by using a laser diode to convert electrical signals to optical signals. Although considerably more expensive (up to several hundred dollars each for high-power units), laser diodes have much better conversion efficiency (typically 25–30%) and produce much higher output power (up to 1 W or so). The optical output of a laser diode is coherent, which is a requirement for long-haul optical links.

Many optical communications systems modulate the light from the laser or LED by simply turning the power to the emitter on and off, as illustrated in Figure 2-31(a). However, the bandwidth of the circuit that switches the power and the ability of the emitter itself to respond to power switching can limit the maximum speed of the system. For this reason, very-high-bandwidth systems using laser diodes usually leave the diode on continuously and modulate the output beam of the laser using an electro-optic modulator. Several types of modulators are available. Many act to vary the length of the optical path, and hence the phase of the optical signal (indicated by the gray paths in Figure 2-31), in response to the voltage on an electrical signal. A phase-shifting modulator can be used directly, as illustrated in Figure 2-31(b), to implement a phase-shift keying system. As shown in Figure 2-31(c), a phase-shifting modulator can also be used to realize on-off keying by splitting the output power of the laser into two signals, phase

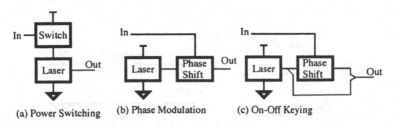

(a) Power Switching   (b) Phase Modulation   (c) On-Off Keying

FIGURE 2-31   Modulating the Transmitter

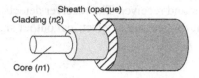

FIGURE 2-32   Cutaway View of an Optical Fiber

shifting one of the two signals, and recombining the result. If the relative phase shift of the two combined signals is zero, they will constructively interfere, and the full laser power will appear on the output. If the relative phase shift is 180°, on the other hand, the two signals destructively interfere, and there is very little power on the output.

2.9.2   Optical Fiber

The construction of a typical optical fiber is shown in Figure 2-32. The core and cladding are made of plastic or glass silica and doped so that the index of refraction of the core, $n1$, is greater than the index of refraction of the cladding, $n2$. The sheath is an oqaque protective jacket. The core and cladding work together to form a dielectric waveguide for light. This type of fiber is called a *step-index fiber* because the index of refraction as a function of radius is a step function at the boundary between core and cladding.

In the left half of Figure 2-33, when light passes across a boundary between a region of higher refractive index into a region of lower refractive index, part of the light is reflected from the boundary and part is transmitted across the boundary. If the incoming light ray is incident on the boundary with angle Θ_i, then the transmitted light makes an angle Θ_t with the normal to the surface, where the relationship of the angles is given by Snell's law as follows:

$$(2\text{-}3) \qquad \sin \Theta_t = \frac{n1}{n2} \sin \Theta_i$$

If $n1$ is greater than $n2$, as Θ_i increases, Θ_t also increases, always remaining larger than Θ_i and reaching 90° when the incident angle reaches the critical angle Θ_c given by

$$(2\text{-}4) \qquad \sin \Theta_c = \frac{n2}{n1}$$

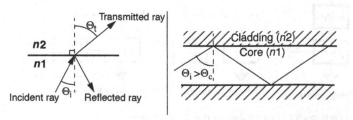

FIGURE 2-33   Light Transmission at a Boundary and in an Optical Fiber

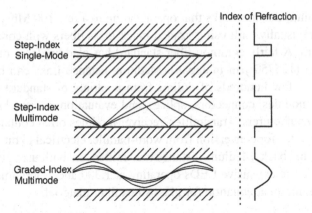

FIGURE 2-34   Propagation in Various Types of Fibers

When the incident angle is greater than Θ_c, light undergoes total internal reflection at the boundary. Optical fiber is constructed so that light that enters the fiber with the incident angle between $\pi/2$ and Θ_c undergoes total internal reflection at the boundary between the core and the cladding, and, when it is repeatedly reflected from one boundary to the opposite one, makes its way down the fiber with little attenuation. Each incident angle defines a *mode* for the fiber, and because of the small dimensions of most optical fibers, the wave properties of the light in the fiber cause these modes to be discretized. The number of such modes is proportional to the ratio of the fiber diameter d to the wavelength of light λ as follows:

$$(2\text{-}5) \qquad\qquad n \propto d/\lambda$$

In a step-index multimode fiber, different modes experience different path lengths and therefore different delays, leading to *intermodal dispersion*. This dispersion (in addition to material dispersion and absorption) degrades the signal impressed on the light as it travels down the fiber.

Intermodal dispersion can be avoided in one of two ways. As indicated by Eq. (2-5), the number of modes can be reduced by decreasing the fiber diameter. If the fiber is sufficiently small, only one mode is supported. This type of fiber, a *single-mode step-index* fiber, is often used for long-distance communications. The performance of multimode fibers can be greatly improved by building the core with an index of refraction that varies with radius. Such a *graded-index* fiber can be designed so that all rays experience the same path delay independent of incident angle. Light propagation in each of the fiber types is shown in cartoon form in Figure 2-34.

2.9.2.1   Multimode Fiber

Multimode fibers are used for short- and medium-length interconnects. Very inexpensive step-index plastic fibers are available with core diameters of 1–2 mm, suitable for links that operate at a few megabits per second over a few meters. Short-haul, megabit-per-second links can be built for a few dollars using plastic fibers and LED transmitters that operate at wavelengths between 650 and

950 nm. Medium-distance links that operate at up to a few 100 Mb/s over a few kilometers are usually built using graded-index glass fibers with core diameters of 50–200 μm. A fairly common fiber standard has cladding/core diameters of 125/62.5 μm (125/50 μm in Japan). Medium-distance links can be built for a few tens to a few hundreds of dollars from a variety of standard transmitter and receiver modules, connectors, splices, and evaluation kits available from a number of manufacturers. Transmitter–receiver modules often contain all of the necessary circuitry for conversion from word-parallel electrical to bit-serial optical signaling and back. Medium-distance transmitters are built using laser diodes or somewhat more expensive LEDs operating at 1,300 and 1,500 nm, the wavelengths of minimum attenuation for glass silica fiber material.

2.9.2.2   Single-Mode Fiber

Single-mode step-index fibers are used for long-haul links. These fibers have small cores, typically 8–10 μm, and must be fabricated with better dimensional tolerances; thus, they are more expensive than multimode fibers. They must be driven with coherent light from laser-diode transmitters and require more precise alignment of optical components. Single-mode fiber systems, although more expensive than multimode systems, can support data rates of several gigabits per second over distances up to 100 km or more on a single link.

2.9.2.3   Optical Connectors

To enhance the versatility and ease of use of optical interconnects, manufacturers have developed connector systems that make optical fibers nearly as easy to mate and demate as electrical cables. Multimode fibers have relatively noncritical optical alignment, and connectors have been developed for these fibers that resemble their SMA and BNC electrical cousins. Snap-together connectors and multiple-fiber connector assemblies, analogous to mass-termination electrical connectors, are available. Figure 2-35 outlines the design of a typical multimode fiber connector.

The male part of the connector is often integrated with a photoemitter or photodetector package and contains a built-in lens and a threaded receptacle for the fiber. The female connector crimps onto the outer sheath of the fiber, which has been stripped to expose a few millimeters of the fiber. The fiber is contained within a ferrule that fits snugly inside the male connector and is held securely near the window by a ring and coupling nut. Inexpensive kits are available from connector manufacturers that allow the fiber to be stripped, polished, and crimped onto the female connector in the field.

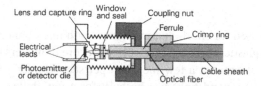

FIGURE 2-35   A Typical Optical Connector for Multimode Fiber

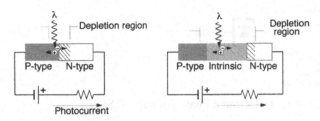

Conventional Junction Photodiode **PIN Photodiode**

FIGURE 2-36 Junction Photodiode (left) and PIN Diode (right)

Interconnection of single-mode fibers is somewhat more difficult because of the more demanding requirements on optical alignment and flatness at the end of the fiber. Mating a single-mode fiber to a transmitter or detector is particularly difficult because it is essential that the optical interface be of the highest quality to ensure maximum power transfer in or out of the cable. Some laser diodes and detectors are available with optical "pigtails," short sections of fiber that are permanently attached and optically coupled to the semiconductor package. These flexible pigtails can be brought out to connectors or splices to permit the optoelectronic device to be connected to a long-haul cable. Standard splices and connectors are manufactured for single-mode fiber; they can be attached in the field using a suitcase-sized kit of parts and tools.

2.9.3 Optical Receivers

The most common optical receivers use a PIN (P-intrinsic-N) photodiode to convert light intensity to current, though conventional silicon junction photodiodes and phototransistors can be used for optical links with low data rates. Conventional photodiodes operate as shown on the left of Figure 2-36. A reverse-biased P/N junction creates a depletion region in and around the junction. If a photon of sufficient energy arrives in this region, it liberates an electron-hole pair, which is separated by the field in the depletion region, leading to a photocurrent in the external circuit that sets up the reverse bias. The width of the depletion region determines how much collection area there is for photons. The depletion region can be made larger by increasing the bias or increasing the area of the junction; both of these approaches make the diode's response time longer, however, and in practice junction photodiodes are too slow for data rates above a few megabits per second.

In the PIN diode this problem is overcome by the insertion of an undoped (intrinsic) silicon region between the P- and N-doped regions. The depletion region set up by the reverse bias extends through the entire intrinsic region, greatly increasing the photon collection volume, and the junction capacitance is reduced by the larger separation. PIN photodiodes are much more sensitive than conventional diodes and can switch at gigahertz rates.

Avalanche photo diodes (APD) are often used in very-high-performance optical receivers. APDs *multiply* the single electron-hole pair generated by an arriving photon through a chain reaction so that a single arriving photon results in a large

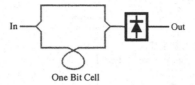

FIGURE 2-37   Detecting a Phase-Modulated Signal

number of charge carriers and hence generates a more substantial current. In effect, an APD receiver combines the detector and preamplifier in a single device.

Photodector diodes of all three types are often combined with a transimpedance amplifier on the same die to amplify the weak current-mode signal from the diode into a voltage-mode logic signal to drive external circuitry.

All three types of photodiodes detect the intensity of the received optical signal. Thus, they can directly detect a bit stream that is modulated using on-off keying. To detect a bit stream that is encoded using phase-shift keying (PSK), however, requires that the optical phase first be converted to intensity before imaging the beam on the photodiode. Figure 2-37 illustrates one method for detecting a PSK optical signal. The input power from the fiber is split into two optical paths. The lower path in the figure is configured to be exactly one bit cell longer than the upper path to within a small fraction of a wavelength. After this differential delay, the optical signals are recombined and the combined light is imaged on the photodiode. If the current bit and the last bit have the same phase, the two signals constructively interfere, and a large intensity is detected by the photodiode. If the phase of the two bits is different, however, the two signals destructively interfere, and a very low intensity is detected by the photodiode.

The sensitivity of optical receivers is limited by the shot noise of the receiving photodiode. The very best optical receivers are able to detect a bit of information reliably from the arrival of a few tens of photons.

2.9.4   Multiplexing

In long-haul communication systems much of the cost of the system is in the fiber. By one estimate, it costs about $30,000 per mile to install a cable with about 200 single-mode fibers. Because of the high cost of the fiber, there is economic advantage to squeezing as much information into a single fiber as possible. Because the bandwidth of a single optical channel is limited, the capacity of a fiber can be increased by multiplexing several optical channels together onto a single fiber. This multiplexing can be performed either in the frequency or the time domains.

2.9.4.1   Wavelength-Division Multiplexing

Wavelength-division multiplexing (WDM) involves combining optical channels operating at different frequencies (colors) into a single fiber. As illustrated in Figure 2-38, the outputs of N lasers (and modulators), each operating at a slightly

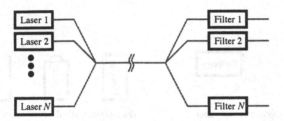

FIGURE 2-38 Wavelength-Division Multiplexing

different frequency, are combined into a single fiber. This combining can be performed using either fiber combiners or free-space optics to image all of the beams on the core of the transmission fiber. At the receiver, a beam splitter divides the received power from the transmission fiber across N receive fibers. The optical signal in each receive fiber is then passed through an optical filter to select the wavelength of just one laser and drop the others. The N receive signals are then independently demodulated and detected (not shown).

Although simple, this arrangement is rather inefficient because the filters discard $N - 1/N$ of the received power. In power-limited systems, an N-fold improvement in power margins can be achieved by replacing the beam splitter and filters with a diffraction grating. The grating separates the received signal energy by color so that all of the power from each transmit laser is directed into the corresponding receive fiber.

In a recent demonstration of WDM, researchers at Fujitsu demonstrated 1.1 Tb/s transmission over a 150-km fiber by multiplexing together 55 sources, each generating a 20-Gb/s optical signal. The individual channels had wavelengths centered on 1.55 μm separated by 0.6 nm. This corresponds to a center frequency of 194 THz with a 75-GHz channel spacing.

2.9.4.2 Time-Division Multiplexing

An optical time-division multiplexing system is illustrated in Figure 2-39. An optical pulse source generates a periodic train of very narrow, subpicosecond pulses. This pulse train is fed to an array of fixed delays (lengths of optical fiber) to generate a staggered array of pulses. For example, suppose the source generates 1-ps

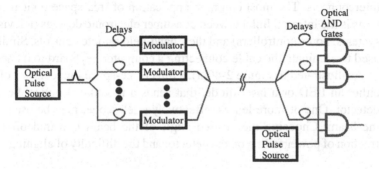

FIGURE 2-39 Optical Time-Division Multiplexing

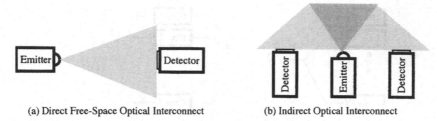

(a) Direct Free-Space Optical Interconnect   (b) Indirect Optical Interconnect

FIGURE 2-40   Free-Space Optical Interconnect

pulses with a repetition frequency of 10 GHz (100-ps pulse spacing). Ten delays with 10-ps spacing generate ten staggered channels with 1-ps pulses separated by 10 ps each. The delayed pulses are then modulated by electrical signals, using either OOK or PSK, and the modulated pulses are recombined for transmission. The dispersive nature of a long optical transmission line acts to spread out the pulses in time just as it spreads out the frequency lines of the optical carrier.

At the far end of the line, the received signal is split, and a complementary set of delays is used to align all of the channels in time. A set of optical AND gates, a nonlinear optical element, combines the delayed signal from the line with an optical pulse source to separate the individual channels.

2.9.5   Optical Amplifiers

In many optical communication systems it is desirable to amplify the power level of an optical signal without the cost of optical-electrical and electrical-optical conversion associated with a conventional repeater. Optical amplifiers fill this need. They accept an optical input and produce an optical output, which is the input with the power level boosted by some amount. Both semiconductor optical amplifiers and erbium-doped optical fiber amplifiers are used in this capacity. Typical amplifiers have bandwidth wide enough to support WDM signals.

2.9.6   Free-Space Optical Interconnect

It is, of course, possible to transmit signals on light beams that are not confined to a fiber waveguide. Such communications systems are called *free-space* optical interconnects. The most common application of free-space optical communications is the infrared link between consumer electronic devices (televisions, audio systems, home controllers) and their hand-held remote controls. Similar links are used to eliminate the cable connecting a computer keyboard to its host.

As illustrated in Figure 2-40(a), a direct free-space link consists of an emitter, either an LED or a laser diode, that sends a modulated optical beam toward a detector. One or more lenses, effectively a telescope, may be used to collimate the beam. Choosing the desired angle of the beam is a tradeoff between the fraction of power falling on the detector and the difficulty of aligning[3] the detector

---

[3] And maintaining alignment in the presence of vibration.

and the emitter. Such direct links are limited to applications where there is a clear optical line-of-sight between the emitter and detector. In applications where the emitter and detector cannot *see* each other but can see a common reflecting surface, an *indirect* free-space link, illustrated in Figure 2-40(b), may be used. The emitter illuminates a reflective surface, either specular or diffuse, which reflects the modulated light to several detectors. This arrangment is useful, for example, in networking computers in a large room by bouncing light off the ceiling. Wired repeaters between rooms can extend the network further.

By varying power level and angle of beam, free-space optical systems can be configured to operate over a wide range of distances and bit rates. At the low end, systems using LEDs with wide beams over room-sized distances can be operated at about 1 Mb/s. At the opposite extreme, systems employing lasers with optical amplifiers and large (10-cm) telescopes to generate a very narrow beam have been proposed for communication between spacecraft[4] over distances of 100,000 km at bit rates of 1 Gb/s. There are many possibilities between these two extremes.

Currently, considerable research is aimed at developing free-space optical communications at the discrete IC level. The idea behind this research is to combine optical emitters and detectors (gallium–arsenide semiconductors), silicon-based logic and memory ICs, and glass or plastic holographic lenses and light guides to build large systems in which optical pathways take the place of wires, thus providing higher bandwidth, shorter delays, and lower noise.

2.10   RADIO COMMUNICATION

Sending digital signals over radio links is another alternative to wires. Radio transmission is to wired digital communication as free-space optics are to guided optics. Compared with optical communication, radio transmission has the advantage that it can, to some extent, penetrate obstacles that are opaque to an optical signal such as walls, trees, and fog. Its primary disadvantage is its longer wavelength that both limits its bandwidth and requires much larger apertures to achieve a narrow beam.

As with optical communication, a detailed discussion of radio frequency (RF) communication would fill several volumes and is beyond the scope of this book. Here we attempt to give a brief overview of what the capable digital designer should know about radio communication.

2.10.1   A Typical Digital Radio

A typical digital radio link is illustrated in Figure 2-41. The digital signal modulates the output of an *intermediate frequency* (IF) oscillator. The modulated IF signal is then *mixed* (multiplied) by the output of the RF oscillator. The mixer

---

[4] These systems are limited to much shorter distances in terrestrial applications because of the attenuation of the atmosphere and the distortion caused by atmospheric turbulence.

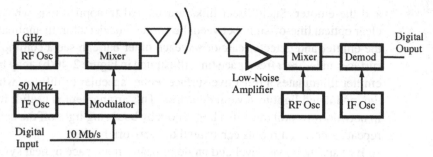

FIGURE 2-41   A Digital Radio Link

exploits the trigonometric identity

(2-6) $\cos(\omega_{IF}t)\cos(\omega_{RF}t) = 0.5\cos[(\omega_{RF} - \omega_{IF})t] + 0.5\cos[(\omega_{RF} + \omega_{IF})t]$

to generate a pair of modulated RF signals at the sum and difference frequencies of the two oscillators.[5] The output of the mixer is then amplified (not shown) and driven into a matched antenna. The transmitted signal propagates through the ether in a beam pattern determined by the transmit antenna.

The receive antenna intercepts a small fraction of the transmitted signal power and inputs this low-level signal to a low-noise RF amplifier. The signal-to-noise ratio, and hence the bit rate, of the link is largely determined by the ratio of the signal power detected by the antenna to the noise figure of this amplifier. The amplified RF signal is then downconverted to IF by mixing with an RF oscillator, demodulated, and detected (not shown) to yield a digital output.

There is a trend toward implementing the entire IF section, the IF oscillator and modulator–demodulator, of many radios entirely digitally. In these *digital radios* the RF section is still implemented using an analog oscillator and mixer because extremely high sample rates would be required for a digital implementation.

2.10.2   The Power Equation

The achievable data rate and bit-error rate of a radio link is largely determined by the ratio of signal power to noise power at the input of the low-noise amplifier. If the *noise-effective temperature* of the receive amplifier is T_R, typically 290 K, and the bandwidth is B, the input referenced noise in the receiver is given by

(2-7) $$P_N(B) = Bk_B T_R$$

where k_B is Boltzmann's constant (1.38×10^{-23} J/K). If our example radio of Figure 2-41 has a bandwidth of 10 MHz (for the 10-Mb/s signal), the noise[6] at the input of the low-noise amplifier (LNA) is $(10^7)(1.38 \times 10^{-23})(290) = 4 \times 10^{-14}$ W or -104 dBm.

---

[5] By mixing with a complex signal, both sine and cosine waves, one of these two *sidebands* can be eliminated, resulting in more efficient use of the RF spectrum.

[6] It is often convenient to express power in decibels of milliwatts or dBm. If P is the power in watts, then $10\log_{10}(P \times 10^3)$ is the power in dBm.

The signal power starts with the transmitter output power, P_T, and is reduced for losses along the link. The largest loss is usually the $1/r^2$ dropoff in power width distance between the transmitter and receiver. Suppose we have an omni-directional transmitter antenna, and the receiver antenna has an effective area[7] of $A_R = 0.01$ m². At a distance r from the transmitter, the spherical wavefront of the signal has an area of $4\pi r^2$. Thus, the fraction of transmitted power absorbed by the receiver antenna is

$$(2\text{-}8) \qquad k_r = A_R/(4\pi r^2)$$

For example, with $A_R = 0.01$ m², at a distance of $r = 10^3$ m, $k_r = 8 \times 10^{-7}$ or -61 dB.

If we lump the additional losses due to multipath fading, scattering off obstacles, and propagation through lossy material into a factor, k_L, we can calculate the received signal power, P_S, and the signal-to-noise ratio, P_S/P_N as

$$(2\text{-}9) \qquad P_S = P_T k_r k_L$$

$$(2\text{-}10) \qquad \frac{P_S}{P_N} = \frac{P_T k_r k_L}{B k_B T} = \frac{P_T A_R k_L}{4\pi r^2 B k_B T}$$

For our example system, suppose our transmitter power, P_T, is 0.5 mW or -3 dBm, and our additional link losses, k_L, sum to 20 dB. Then from Eq. (2-9) we have a signal-to-noise ratio (SNR) of $P_S/P_N = 100$ or 20 dB. As we shall see in Chapter 6, this corresponds to a bit-error rate[8] (BER) of about $\exp(-P_S/2P_N)$, which is about 10^{-22}.

The power margins of a radio link can be improved by increasing the effective area, and hence narrowing the beam pattern, of either the transmit or receive antenna. The improvement in power due to a larger antenna is often referred to as *antenna gain*. This is a bit of a misnomer, for the antenna is a passive element that does not add any power to the signal; it simply directs the power into a narrower beam. The gain, G, of an antenna is related to its effective area, A, and is given by

$$(2\text{-}11) \qquad G = \frac{4\pi A}{\lambda^2}$$

Rewriting Eq. (2-10) to account for the area of both the transmitting and receiving antennae gives

$$(2\text{-}12) \qquad \frac{P_S}{P_N} = \frac{P_T A_R G_T k_L}{4\pi r^2 B k_B T} = \frac{P_T A_R A_T k_L}{\lambda^2 r^2 B k_B T}$$

Equation (2-12) shows how one can trade off transmitter power, antenna area, distance, and bandwidth to achieve the desired signal-to-noise ratio.

---

[7] The effective area of a half-wave dipole is $1.6\lambda^2/4\pi$ or about 0.01 m² for a 1-GHz frequency, $\lambda = 0.3$ m.

[8] To a good first approximation, BER is given by $10^{-0.2\text{SNR}}$, where SNR is the ratio of signal power to noise power.

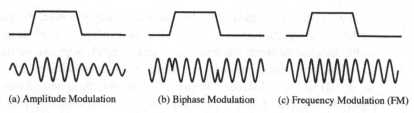

(a) Amplitude Modulation   (b) Biphase Modulation   (c) Frequency Modulation (FM)

FIGURE 2-42   Amplitude, Biphase, and Frequency Modulation

2.10.3   Modulation

A digital signal requires bandwidth from DC to half the bit rate. Most radio links, on the other hand, rely on resonant circuits and antennae that can handle only a small fractional bandwidth. To reduce the fractional bandwidth (the bandwidth divided by the center frequency) of a digital signal, it is used to modulate a high-frequency *carrier*, almost always a sine wave. The effect is to encode the 1 and 0 symbols into a waveform with a narrow fractional bandwidth. As illustrated in Figure 2-42, the modulation can be performed by varying one or more of the following parameters: amplitude, phase, or frequency of the carrier waveform.

2.10.3.1   Amplitude Modulation

Amplitude modulation (AM) is illustrated in Figure 2-42(a). The simplest form of AM is on-off keying in which the full carrier is transmitted for a 1 and no carrier is transmitted for a 0. This is rarely used, because the receiver may lose lock with the carrier during a long string of zeros. A more robust system sends a 1 as one amplitude and a 0 as a different, but nonzero, amplitude, as illustrated in the figure. If the channel has a high SNR, several bits may be transmitted in a single *baud* by using several different amplitudes (e.g., two bits can be encoded into four amplitude levels).

Amplitude-modulated transmission suffers from two problems. First, many factors, such as scattering and fading, can cause the amplitude of the signal to vary. These problems are most acute in mobile systems but also occur with fixed stations owing to moving reflectors in the environment. Such environmentally induced variations in amplitude may be difficult to discriminate from signal changes. The second problem with AM is that it does not make the best use of the transmitter's power. The average transmitter power is much less than the peak.

2.10.3.2   Phase Modulation (PM)

The problems of amplitude modulation can be overcome by varying the phase rather than the amplitude of the carrier. Biphase, the simplest form of phase modulation, varies the phase by $180°$, encoding a 1 as $\sin(\omega t)$ and a 0 as $-\sin(\omega t)$. Several bits can be encoded at a time into a larger number of phases (e.g., 2 bits can be encoded into four phases separated by $90°$).

In band-limited channels with good signal-to-noise ratios, large numbers of bits can be encoded into a single symbol by varying both the phase and amplitude of the signal. As illustrated in Figure 2-43(a), an arbitrary combination of phase and amplitude can be realized by summing a weighted combination of sine and

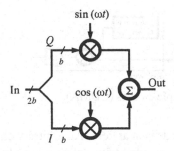

(a) Quadrature Amplitude Modulation

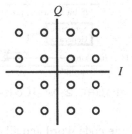

(b) Typical "Constellation"

FIGURE 2-43   Quadrature Amplitude Modulation (QAM): Combining Phase and Amplitude Modulation

cosine waveforms, a method known as *quadrature amplitude modulation* or *QAM*. Each $2b$-bit input symbol is divided into a b-bit inphase component, I, and a b-bit quadrature component, Q. The I component is multiplied by the cosine wave, whereas the Q component is multiplied by the sine wave, and the two outputs are summed.

The resulting set of symbols can be plotted on a set of I and Q axes, as shown in Figure 2-43(b). The I axis corresponds to the relative amplitude of the inphase component, while the Q axis corresponds to the relative amplitude of the quadrature component. For example, the case shown corresponds to four bits per symbol, two bits of I and two bits of Q, centered around the axis. With QAM we are able to pack four bits per symbol while resolving only four voltage levels. With straight AM, packing four bits per symbol would require resolving sixteen voltage levels.

2.10.3.3   Frequency Modulation

As shown in Figure 2-42(c), frequency modulation (FM) involves varying the frequency of the carrier wave to encode information. As with the other modulation schemes, we can encode one bit per symbol by switching between a pair of frequencies, or we can pack b bits per symbol if we are able to discriminate between 2^b frequencies. Frequency modulation shares PM's insensitivity to the amplitude of the signal.

2.10.3.4   Code-Division Multiple Access (CDMA)

Several data signals can be sent simultaneously in the same frequency band if their information is spread out by multiplying each data stream by an orthogonal code word. A simplified CDMA system is illustrated in Figure 2-44. The transmitter performs an exclusive-OR (XOR) between the data signal and a repeating code word, a 128-bit sequence that repeats once each microsecond. If the data word and code word are both thought of as sequences over $\{-1, +1\}$,[9] this XOR corresponds to a multiplication. The code word set is selected so that the correlation between

---

[9] Here a 1 bit corresponds to $+1$ and a 0 bit to -1.

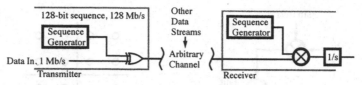

FIGURE 2-44   Code-Division Multiple Access (CDMA)

one code word and all other code words is near zero. An arbitrary channel sums the encoded data stream with streams encoded with orthogonal code words.

At the receiver, the summed data streams are multiplied by the original sequence.[10] The data stream encoded with the same sequence is perfectly correlated and thus sums coherently in the integrator. All other data streams are completely uncorrelated and therefore contribute only a small amount to the integrated value. The result is that the transmitted data are separated from the summed data streams.

Code-division multiple access has two primary advantages over the more conventional forms of modulation described above. First, it avoids the frequency allocation problem. All channels share a common frequency. As more channels are combined on the frequency, the interference beween channels increases, forcing each channel to drop its data rate to maintain an acceptable bit error rate. Thus, the data rate can be adapted, depending on traffic rather than on a fixed frequency allocation.

The second major advantage of CDMA is that it spreads the data signal out over a much wider RF bandwidth than in a conventional system. For example, our CDMA system spreads a 1-Mb/s data signal over a 128-MHz bandwidth. Although this wide bandwidth puts considerable demands on the RF design, it provides considerable resistance to fading caused by multipath problems, as described in Section 2.10.4.

2.10.4   Multipath

A typical environment has many reflectors of radio signals; almost any piece of metal qualifies. As a result, radio signals bounce and scatter and may reach the receiver over several different paths, as illustrated in Figure 2-45. This phenomenon, called multipath, accounts for the ghost images often seen on television sets. When the two paths differ by π (mod 2π) radians and are of similar amplitude, they destructively interfere, and the signal level may fade or drop below

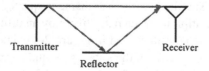

FIGURE 2-45   Multipath Radio Transmission

---

[10] Synchronizing the sequence generators at the transmitter and receiver is a nontrivial task that we will not address here.

detection. In a mobile system, the difference in path length is usually changing constantly with the signal fading in and out. Even without fading, multipath results in intersymbol interference because the difference in path lengths may be several baud times in a high-speed system.

The solution to multipath is diversity – either frequency diversity, spatial diversity, or both. With spatial diversity several receive antennae are employed positioned in such a way that it is unlikely that all antennae will be in a fade simultaneously. Frequency diversity, on the other hand, is acheived by spreading the transmitted signal across a large enough bandwidth that the entire signal cannot be lost in single frequency fade. This can be accomplished by sending the data on two frequency channels or by a method like CDMA that spreads the data out across a single wide-frequency channel.

2.11   BIBLIOGRAPHIC NOTES

Two excellent textbooks have been written about packaging and related issues in digital systems: [JohnGrah93] and [Bakoglu90]. [HoroHill86] is a broad compendium on electronic design with excellent chapters on packaging, powering, cooling, and connectors. The Institute for Interconnecting and Packaging Electronic Circuits has published a series of handbooks on standards and design practice for the design and analysis of printed circuit boards; these include [IPCD95], [IPCD91], and [IPCSM96]. For information on components, cables, materials, and much else, refer to [RefDat93], a publication that should be included on every practicing engineer's bookshelf. [Tewksbur94] contains a collection of papers on theory and modeling of digital systems interconnects. [LeeMess94] is an excellent textbook on digital communications, including chapters on modulation schemes and signal analysis. [KrauBost80] is an old but still very useful introduction to the design of radio transmitters and receivers.

2.12   EXERCISES

2-1   **Backplane and Daughter-Card Wiring Density:** Obtain a catalog of connectors for attaching daughter cards to a backplane and find the highest-density connectors available that also provide reasonable signal integrity (controlled impedance and cross talk). Calculate the maximum number of signals that can reasonably be passed between neighboring daughter cards, assuming a maximum board dimension of 15 in. Describe your assumptions.

2-2   **Printed Circuit Boards Stackup:** In a PC board technology with 6 mil line and space rules, find a stackup that will support six internal signal layers (three pairs of layers like the inner layers of Figure 2-13), each with 50-Ω impedance. A spreadsheet is a very convenient way to do this; use the empirical formulas in [JohnGrah93], the plots in [RefDat93], or some other reference for calculating the impedance. What is the smallest practical via possible with your stackup?

2-3 **Power Supply Wiring:** A power supply must deliver 300 A to a pair of backplane connections 25 cm distant. Ignoring losses in the end connections, what wire size would be required to deliver the current with no more than a 0.1-V drop? If a bus-bar were used instead, what would its cross-sectional area have to be? How much power is dissipated in the interconnect?

2-4 **Optical Communication:** Describe situations in which you would prefer using a fiber-optic data link to using an electronic link over a cable. Under which situations would you prefer to use a cable? List as many situations as possible of both types.

2-5 **Digital Radio:** Consider a digital radio link between a laptop computer and a network basestation in the same building. The maximum distance is 100 m, and the link losses are no more than 20 dB. The link must carry a 10-Mb/s (ethernet rate) signal with a BER of 10^{-22} or better. The antennae are both nondirectional (unity gain). How much transmitter output power is required for the link?

3 MODELING AND ANALYSIS OF WIRES

Wires are used in a digital system to communicate signals from one place to another and to distribute power and clock. In these capacities wires dominate a modern digital system in terms of speed, power, and cost. The time required to drive wires and for signals to propagate over wires is often the largest factor in determining cycle time. The bulk of the power in many systems is dissipated driving wires, on-chip and off. The amount of wiring, not the number of transistors or gates, usually determines the amount of area required by a function on a chip. The number of terminals required is a major factor in the area and cost of chips, packages, and circuit boards. Economically achievable wire density is a major influence on the architecture of a system. One can envision many organizations that simply cannot be wired economically.

Despite the importance of wires in a digital system, they are usually all but ignored in most courses on digital electronics. Too often such courses, and real designers, treat wires as ideal equipotential regions that present no load to the driver and change value instantaneously at all points along their length. Real wires are not ideal but rather have parasitic capacitance, resistance, and inductance. If not handled properly, these parasitic circuit elements will add delay, degrade signal quality, and even cause oscillations. With proper engineering techniques, however, they are easily tamed.

Most off-chip wires are LC *transmission lines* along which waves can propagate. These wires look like a resistive load to the driver and a Thévenin-equivalent source to the receiver. When terminated into a matched impedance, a transmission line is an ideal signaling medium: the driver places a signal on the line and it propagates at near the speed of light to the receiver, where it is detected and then absorbed into the termination. The signal arrives with this *incident wave*, and there are no reflections to interfere with subsequent signals on the line. However, with a mismatched termination at the ends of the line, or no termination at all, the traveling wave from the driver will reflect back and forth across the line, causing interference.

On-chip wires are lossy RC transmission lines that diffuse sharp signal edges into slow rise times. Long off-chip wires also have a resistive component that leads to attenuation. Because of the *skin effect* the resistance of a line increases with frequency. This frequency-dependent attenuation can lead to signal distortion as the unattenuated low-frequency components of a signal are summed with the attenuated high-frequency components at the receiver.

Many designers also have a tendency to ignore the cost of wires and use gate count or transistor count to estimate the cost of a function. This can be an expensive mistake, as many have discovered, for many functions with low gate count (e.g., a crossbar switch) are extremely costly in terms of wires. Often much less expensive alternatives exist and are easily discovered if the right cost models are used.

The remainder of this chapter discusses wires from the perspective of a digital systems designer. We begin in Section 3.1 by discussing how to calculate the resistance, capacitance, and inductance of a wire given its geometry and material properties. In Sections 3.2 and 3.3, we introduce the electrical models we use in practice to analyze wires. Depending on the circumstances, we model wires as lumped resistance, capacitance, or inductance, or as distributed RC, LC, or LRC transmission lines. The special properties of multidrop buses, differential balanced lines, and electrically isolated lines are discussed in Section 3.4. Section 3.5 treats the topic of wire cost models. The chapter closes in Section 3.6 with a discussion of tools for modeling wires and laboratory instruments and techniques for measuring their properties.

3.1   GEOMETRY AND ELECTRICAL PROPERTIES

We often think of wires as being ideal by having zero resistance, capacitance, and inductance. However, real wires have nonzero values of all three of these values. A real wire is not an ideal conductor but rather an unintended or *parasitic* circuit element. A good designer develops an intuition about how the geometry of the wire, its shape and spacing to other conductors, affects its electrical properties. Before diving into detailed electrical models of wires, we will take a moment to present some simple formulas for deriving the electrical properties: resistance, capacitance, and inductance given the rough geometry of a set of conductors and their separating insulators. These formulas will be useful in computing the properties of the wires and pins in the different packaging levels and in developing electrical models for these components. Although computer analysis is usually required to solve for these values exactly, we hope that by working a few simple geometries by hand you will begin to develop an intuition about the relationship between geometry and electrical properties.

3.1.1   Resistance

The resistance of a conductor is proportional to its length divided by its area. When dealing with rectangular or circular conductors with dimensions as illustrated in Figure 3-1, the resistance is given by Eq. (3-1) below. For more complex geometries, (e.g, curves, corners, and changes in diameter) numerical methods are usually used to calculate resistance.

$$(3\text{-}1) \qquad R = \frac{\rho l}{A} = \begin{cases} \rho l/(wh) & \text{rectangular} \\ \rho l/(\pi r^2) & \text{circular} \end{cases}$$

where the constant ρ is the resistivity of the material (in Ω-m).

For rectangular conductors we often express the resistance in units of Ω/square, for the resistance of a square ($w = l$) conductor of thickness h is independent of

FIGURE 3-1   Resistance of a Conductor

TABLE 3-1   **Resistivity of Common Conductive Materials**

Material	Symbol	$\rho(\Omega\text{-m})$
Silver	Ag	1.6×10^{-8}
Copper	Cu	1.7×10^{-8}
Gold	Au	2.2×10^{-8}
Aluminum	Al	2.7×10^{-8}
Tungsten	W	5.5×10^{-8}

its absolute size (w and l). The resistance per square, R_{sq}, is given by

$$(3\text{-}2) \qquad\qquad R_{sq} = \rho/h$$

Table 3-1 lists the resistivity of conductive materials commonly found in electronic packaging. The numbers are for a temperature of 20°C. The resistance increases with temperature by about 4,000 ppm/°C.

Although silver has the lowest resistivity, it is seldom used in electronic packaging because of its high cost. Copper, the second most conductive element, is the most commonly used material for electrical conductors. It is used for cabling, ground planes, and stripguides in circuit boards and bus bars. Aluminum, although less conductive than copper, offers a higher conductivity per dollar and is more compatible with integrated circuit fabrication. It is widely used for wiring on integrated circuits, low-cost power cables, and bus bars. Tungsten and other refractory metals are used in applications where high-temperature processing follows the deposition of the metal.

3.1.2   Capacitance

The capacitance between two conductors depends on their global environment, because intervening or nearby conductors can screen or divert field lines. Because of the global nature of capacitance, numerical methods are almost always needed to calculate accurate capacitance numbers for complex geometries. However, back-of-the envelope calculations using simplified geometries are useful for estimating rough capacitance values.

Figure 3-2 illustrates four common wire cross sections. We can calculate the capacitance per unit length from these cross sections by assuming that there is a charge per unit length, Q, of 1 on one of the conductors, solving for the field, E, using Gauss's law, and then integrating the field along a path from one conductor to the other to determine the voltage. The simplest situation is the parallel plate capacitor. When the width, w, is large compared with the spacing, we can assume that the field is entirely contained within the two plates, giving a uniform E field of $Q/(w\varepsilon)$ and thus a capacitance per unit length of

$$(3\text{-}3) \qquad\qquad C_a = \frac{w\varepsilon}{s}$$

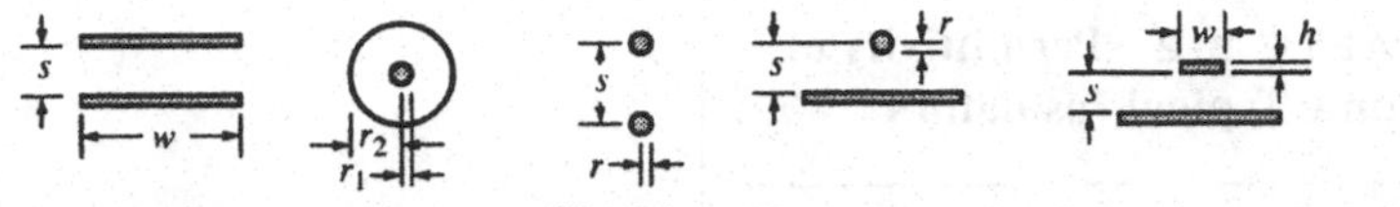

Parallel Plate   Coaxial   Wire Pair   Wire over ground   Rectangle over ground
(a)   (b)   (c)   (d)   (e)

FIGURE 3-2   Common Wire Cross Sections

For the coaxial conductor the field is also completely contained between the two conductors. However, in this case the field is nonuniform. At a distance, $r_1 < r < r_2$, from the center of the conductor, $E = Q/2\pi r$. Integrating E from r_1 to r_2 gives

$$(3\text{-}4) \qquad\qquad C_b = \frac{2\pi\varepsilon}{\log(r_2/r_1)}$$

For a parallel pair of wires, we determine the field by superposition, considering just one wire at a time. Each wire gives $E = Q/2\pi x$. We then integrate this field from $x = r$ to $x = s$ and combine the two voltages, giving

$$(3\text{-}5) \qquad\qquad C_c = \frac{\pi\varepsilon}{\log(s/r)}.$$

For single wire over a ground-plane, we apply the principle of charge image, which states that a charge a distance, s, above the plane induces a charge pattern in the plane equivalent to a negative charge an equal distance below the plane. Thus, the capacitance here is equal to twice that of a pair of wires spaced by $2s$.

$$(3\text{-}6) \qquad\qquad C_d = \frac{2\pi\varepsilon}{\log(2s/r)}$$

Our final geometry, a rectangular conductor over a ground plane, is usually called a *microstripline*. Because its width is comparable to its height, we cannot approximate it by a parallel plane, and because it lacks circular symmetry we cannot easily calculate its E field. To handle this difficult geometry we will approximate it by a parallel plate capacitor of width, w, to account for the field under the conductor, in parallel with a wire over a ground plane, to account for the fringing field from the two edges. This approximation is not exact, but it works well in practice.

$$(3\text{-}7) \qquad\qquad C_e = \frac{we}{s} + \frac{2\pi\varepsilon}{\log(4s/h)}$$

All of these expressions for capacitance depend on the permittivity of the material, ε. We usually consider ε to be the product of two components, $\varepsilon = \varepsilon_0\varepsilon_r$. Here $\varepsilon_0 = 8.854 \times 10^{-12}$ F/m is the permittivity of free space, and ε_r is the relative permittivity of the material. Table 3-2 gives the relative permittivity of several insulating materials typically used in electronic packaging. In general, it is advantageous to use a material with the lowest possible permittivity, for it gives not only lower capacitance but also a higher propagation velocity.

TABLE 3-2   **Permittivity of Some Typical Insulators**

Material	ε_r
Air	1
Teflon	2
Polyimide	3
Silicon dioxide	3.9
Glass-epoxy (PC board)	4
Alumina	10
Silicon	11.7

3.1.3   Inductance

Although we could calculate the inductance of our typical wire cross sections directly, it is simpler to take advantage of the fact that, whenever the conductors of a transmission line are completely surrounded by a uniform dielectric, the capacitance and inductance are related by

(3-8) $$CL = \varepsilon\mu$$

Thus, for example, the inductance of a round conductor over a ground plane completely surrounded by a homogeneous medium is

(3-9) $$L_d = \frac{\mu \log(2s/r)}{2\pi}$$

For most situations we will encounter, the permeability, μ, is the permeability of free space, $\mu_0 = 4\pi \times 10^{-7}$ H/m.

In situations where there is a dielectric boundary near the transmission line conductors, such as a microstripline on the surface of a PC board with dielectric below and air above the line, Eq. (3-8) does not hold. However, it is usually possible to develop approximate formulas for capacitance that define an "average" dielectric constant for these situations, and the inductance can be calculated approximately as shown above.

3.2   ELECTRICAL MODELS OF WIRES

3.2.1   The Ideal Wire

When we draw a line connecting two components in a circuit diagram, we tend to think of this line representing an *ideal wire*. Such a wire has no resistance, no inductance, and no capacitance to any other circuit element. Moreover, it has no delay. A voltage change at one end of the ideal wire is immediately visible at the other end, even if it is some distance away; the whole wire is an *equipotential region*. Clearly such an ideal wire is not physically realizable. Although superconductors can reduce the resistivity to zero (at considerable expense), the inductance and capacitance cannot be eliminated, and the delay of the wire is bounded by its length divided by the speed of light.

The ideal wire is a useful approximation in many situations because it lets us ignore the parasitic circuit elements contributed by the wire and concentrate on the circuit properties of the components being connected. In many cases, where the effect of the parasitic elements is small, this approximation is appropriate, and we need look no further at wires. However, in most digital systems this is not the case. In digital systems, wire delay is a substantial fraction of overall delay, and the parasitic resistance, inductance, and capacitance of wires have appreciable effects.

3.2.2 The Transmission Line

In Section 3.1, we saw that real wires are not ideal but rather have series resistance and inductance and parallel capacitance and conductance. Considering these parasitic circuit elements gives an electrical model for an infinitesimal section of line (of length dx) as shown in Figure 3-3(a). The values R, L, and C here are per unit length (ohms/meter, henrys/meter, and farads/meter, respectively).

3.2.2.1 Partial Differential Equation

It is important to note that the circuit elements of a wire are *distributed* along its length and not *lumped* in a single position. The behavior of this distributed system cannot be described by an ordinary differential equation but rather requires a partial differential equation. Considering voltage, V, to be a function of position, x, and time, t, we can derive an equation describing V from examination of Figure 3-3(a). First observe that the gradient of V is the drop across the series elements and the gradient of I is the current through the parallel elements

$$\frac{\partial V}{\partial x} = -RI - L\frac{\partial I}{\partial t}$$

(3-10)

$$\frac{\partial I}{\partial x} = -GV - C\frac{\partial V}{\partial t}$$

Then, differentiating the first equation with respect to x and substituting the second equation into the result gives

(3-11)
$$\frac{\partial^2 V}{\partial x^2} = RGV + (RC + LG)\frac{\partial V}{\partial t} + LC\frac{\partial^2 V}{\partial t^2}$$

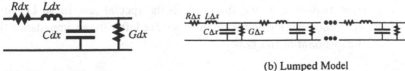

(a) Infinitesimal Model

(b) Lumped Model

FIGURE 3-3   Infinitesimal and Lumped Models of a Transmission Line

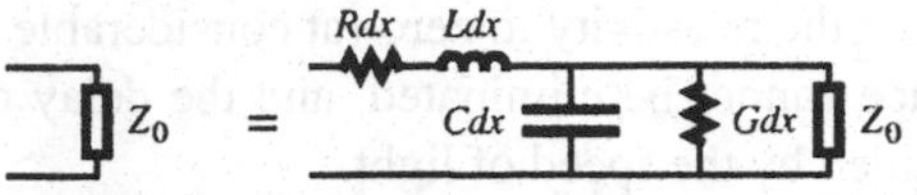

FIGURE 3-4   Derivation of Line Impedance

or, if we ignore conductance and set $G = 0$,

$$(3\text{-}12) \qquad \frac{\partial^2 V}{\partial x^2} = RC\frac{\partial V}{\partial t} + LC\frac{\partial^2 V}{\partial t^2}$$

We will spend much of the remainder of this section discussing solutions to special cases of this equation, which governs the propagation of waves in transmission lines. We will see that for largely resistive lines, such as long on-chip wires, where the inductance is negligible, this equation becomes the diffusion equation, and signals diffuse down the line. For lines that are primarily inductive with negligible resistance, on the other hand, such as PC board strip guides and board-to-board cables, this equation becomes the wave equation, and signals propagate down the line as traveling waves.

3.2.2.2   Impedance of an Infinite Line

Figure 3-4 illustrates how we calculate the impedance of an infinite length of line. If we assume that the line presents some impedance, Z_0, as shown on the left side of the figure, then that value must be equal to a short section of line concatenated with an impedance of Z_0, as illustrated on the right side of the figure.

Equating the impedance of the two networks gives[1]

$$(3\text{-}13) \qquad Z_0 = Rdx + Lsdx + \frac{1}{Csdx + Gdx + 1/Z_0}$$

Simplifying gives

$$(3\text{-}14) \qquad (Z_0 - Rdx - Lsdx)(Csdx + Gdx + 1/Z_0) = 1$$

$$Z_0^2(Cs + G) - Z_0(R + Ls)(Cs + G)dx - (R + Ls) = 0$$

Because dx is infinitesimal, the Z_0 term in the middle term vanishes, and we have

$$(3\text{-}15) \qquad Z_0 = \left(\frac{R + Ls}{G + Cs}\right)^{1/2}$$

In the general case this impedance is complex valued and frequency dependent. However, as we shall see, in the special case of an LC line, $R = G = 0$, the frequency terms cancel, and we are left with an impedance that is real and independent of frequency.

---

[1] Where $s = j\omega = 2\pi jf$.

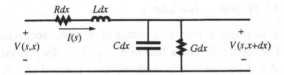

FIGURE 3-5 Derivation of Frequency-Domain Solution for a Transmission Line

3.2.2.3 Frequency-Domain Solution

We can solve for voltage, $V(s)$, as a function of position, x, from examination of Figure 3-5. Observing that the drop across the incremental resistor and inductor is $\partial V(s)/\partial x$ and that $V(s) = I(s)Z_0$, we get

(3-16)
$$\frac{\partial V(s)}{\partial x} = -(R + Ls)I(s) = -\frac{(R + Ls)V(s)}{Z_0}$$

and substituting Z_0 from Eq. (3-15) gives

(3-17)
$$\frac{\partial V(s)}{\partial x} = -[(G + Cs)(R + Ls)]^{1/2}V(s)$$

Which has the solution

$$V(s, x) = V(s, 0)\exp\{-[(G + Cs)(R + Ls)]^{1/2}x\}$$

(3-18)

$$V(s, x) = V(s, 0)\exp(-Ax)$$

where

(3-19)
$$A = [(G + Cs)(R + Ls)]^{1/2}$$

is the *propagation constant*. For a given frequency, the magnitude of A determines the amount by which a signal of that frequency is attenuated per unit distance, and the phase of A determines the amount of phase shift per unit distance.

3.2.2.4 Signal Returns

As illustrated in Figure 3-3, a transmission line is a four-port network. The upper conductive path in both parts of Figure 3-3 represents the signal path, whereas the lower path represents the *signal return*. Kirchoff's current law tells us that the net current out of a subnetwork is always zero. Thus if a transmitter injects a current, i, into the signal conductor, a corresponding current, $-i$, must flow in the return. The characteristics of the transmission line depend strongly on the signal return and its relationship to the signal conductor. The capacitive element in the line is largely capacitance between the signal and the return, and the inductive element is largely the self-inductance of the loop formed by the signal and its return. Although the returns in Figure 3-3 are shown with zero impedance, real returns have some finite impedance. With symmetric transmission lines such as twisted-pair cable, the return impedance equals the signal impedance. Very often we will ignore the return, for example by drawing only the signal conductor in a circuit schematic. However, as we will see later in this book, a host of problems can result from poorly designed signal returns.

3.2.2.5   Lumped Models of Transmission Lines

One can model a transmission line as a series of lumped sections, as shown in Figure 3-3(b). The figure shows a line that has been discretized into short sections of length Δx. Each section is modeled by a lumped circuit consisting of two resistors, one inductor, and one capacitor for each section. This lumped model is often used to simulate a transmission model using a circuit simulator, like SPICE,[2] that solves ordinary differential equations.

Accurately modeling a transmission line with a lumped circuit requires discretizing both space and time into sections that are small compared with the shortest wavelengths of interest. As a rule of thumb, the resonant frequency of the LC circuit in each section should be at least an order of magnitude higher than the highest frequency of interest in the simulation. The timestep Δt used to integrate the equations numerically to simulate the lumped model in turn needs to be made short compared with the period of the LC circuit in each section.

(3-20)
$$\Delta t \ll 2\pi \Delta x \sqrt{LC} \ll 2t_r$$

where t_r is the shortest rise time expected in the system.

3.3   SIMPLE TRANSMISSION LINES

3.3.1   Lumped Wires

Although all wires have some amount of resistance, capacitance, and inductance, in many cases we can accurately model the wire as consisting of a single lumped component. Most short signal lines, and short sections of low-impedance transmission line, appear to signals as lumped capacitors. On-chip power supply wires are usually modeled as lumped resistors. Off-chip power supply conductors and short high-impedance sections of transmission lines are modeled as lumped inductors.

In general, a short wire can be modeled as a lumped capacitor (inductor) if the source and load impedances are both significantly higher (lower) than the impedance of the line, Z_0.

3.3.1.1   Lumped Capacitive Loads

If the time required to traverse a wire is short compared with the rise time of the fastest signal that will travel over the wire, and if there is no DC current draw over the wire, then both the inductive and resistive elements of the transmission line can safely be ignored and we can accurately model the wire as a lumped capacitor. Such a model is typically used for short ($<1000\chi$) on-chip wires that drive static gates (no DC load) and short ($x < t_r v/5$, where t_r is the rise time and v

---

[2] SPICE is a circuit simulator originally developed at the Univ. of California at Berkeley in the 1960s and now widely available in commercial versions.

the propagation velocity) off-chip wires.[3] As will be discussed in Section 7.4.2.1, the rise time of off-chip signals is often purposely slowed, thus increasing the size of a wire that can be considered a lumped capacitor. For 1997 technology, $\chi = 1.2\,\mu m$, and on-chip lines shorter than 1 mm can be considered lumped. With rise-time control, $t_r = 2$ ns, and $\varepsilon_r = 4$, and off-chip lines shorter than 6 cm can be considered lumped. Without rise-time control, $t_r = 0.5$ ns, and lines longer than 1.5 cm must be considered as transmission lines.

For short off-chip wires, the capacitance of a short line is almost entirely to a plane in the PC board, either a dedicated signal return plane or a shared return–power plane. Only a small portion of the capacitance, typically less than 5%, is to other conductors. Thus, for these short lines, cross talk is relatively small, and the primary effect of the capacitance is to slow the signal swing. For long off-chip wires, however, cross talk can be a factor, as discussed in Section 6.3.2.

On-chip wires run in multiple layers with no return planes. Thus, almost all of the capacitance of an on-chip wire is to *other wires*. As discussed in detail in Section 6.3.1, the capacitance to other lines introduces significant cross talk. This cross talk acts both to degrade noise margins and to increase delay. The delay increases because twice as much charge must be transferred to the capacitor if the line that forms the other plate switches in the opposite direction, a phenomenon called the Miller effect. As we shall see, cross talk is particularly damaging in cases where a line carrying a signal with a large swing is coupled to a line that has a small signal swing.

For a typical on-chip wire, that is $0.6\text{-}\mu m$ square spaced 0.6 μm from parallel wires on either side and runs 0.6 μm above and below layers of perpendicular wires with a dielectric of SiO_2, the capacitance is usually about 0.16 fF/μm or 160 pF/m (see Section 6.3.1.3). A typical PC-board trace, 8 mils (200 μm) wide and 6 mils (150 μm) above and below a return plane with $\varepsilon_r = 4$, has a capacitance of about 150 pF/m (see Section 6.3.2.4). It is no surprise that the capacitance per unit length is relatively constant across these packaging layers because the conductor spacing scales by approximately the same factor as the conductor width.

As discussed in Section 7.4.1, signaling strategies for capacitive lines focus on diminishing the signal swing to reduce the amount of delay and energy involved in switching the line (charging the capacitor).

3.3.1.2 Lumped Resistive Lines

A line used to distribute substantial amounts of DC current (e.g., for power distribution) can usually be modeled as a lumped resistor. Although such a line does have appreciable capacitance, it can safely be ignored because the line holds a relatively steady DC voltage and thus does not charge or discharge the capacitor.

---

[3] This *critical length*, x, corresponds to about $1/10$ of the wavelength ($\lambda \sim 2 t_r v$) of the fundamental frequency associated with a rising or falling edge. As a rule of thumb, wires longer than $0.1\,\lambda$ should be treated as transmission lines.

For such lines, the major concern is the IR drop over the wire. For example, a 0.6-μm square wire (0.07 Ω/square) that is 5-mm long has a resistance of 583 Ω. If such a line supplies a current of 0.5 mA, the IR drop is almost 300 mV. As we will see in Section 5.3, these IR drops are the major problem in on-chip power distribution.

3.3.1.3   Lumped Inductive Lines

A short wire that carries substantial amounts of AC current[4] (e.g., for power distribution) is often modeled as a lumped inductor. As with the resistive line, such a line does have appreciable capacitance; however, for power distribution, the inductance is the dominant effect. For example, a typical 8-mil transmission line spaced 6 mils above and below return planes has an inductance of about 300 nH/m or 3 nH/cm.

3.3.1.4   Lumped Models of Impedance Discontinuities

As we will see in Section 3.3.3.2, an LC transmission line has a characteristic impedance that is given by $Z_0 = \sqrt{L/C}$. If a section of line has an impedance $Z_1 > Z_0$, and the length of this line is short compared with the rise time of the signal, then the line can accurately be modeled by a line of impedance Z_0 in series with an inductor with value

$$(3\text{-}21) \qquad L_1 = l\left(Z_1^2 C - L\right) = lC\left(Z_1^2 - Z_0^2\right)$$

where l is the length of the discontinuity. Similarly, a short section of line with an impedance lower than normal, $Z_2 < Z_0$, can be modeled as a lumped capacitor in parallel with a line with impedance Z_0 with the capacitance given by

$$(3\text{-}22) \qquad C_2 = l\left(\frac{L}{Z_2^2} - C\right) = lL\left(\frac{1}{Z_2^2} - \frac{1}{Z_0^2}\right)$$

For example, the bond-wire that connects a chip to its package usually has considerably higher impedance than the transmission lines it connects to and thus is often modeled as a lumped inductor (usually about 1 nH/mm). Connectors between PC boards and cables, unless carefully designed, also have short high-impedance sections that are usually modeled as lumped inductors.

3.3.2   RC Transmission Lines

For long on-chip lines that carry signals, both the resistance and the capacitance of the line are significant, but the inductance is negligible; therefore, the line must be modeled as an RC transmission line. Signal propagation on an RC line is

---

[4] Although off-chip wires and on-chip wires carry AC and DC currents, we tend to approximate the on-chip wires as lumped resistors and the off-chip wires as lumped inductors based on the relative values of their inductance and resistance.

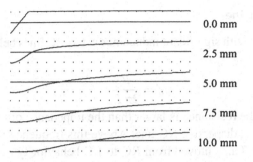

0.0 mm

2.5 mm

5.0 mm

7.5 mm

10.0 mm

FIGURE 3-6   Response of a Lossy RC Line

governed by Eq. (3-12) with the inductive term dropped. The result is the familiar heat (or diffusion) equation

$$(3\text{-}23) \qquad \frac{\partial^2 V}{\partial x^2} = RC \frac{\partial V}{\partial t}$$

Thus, the signal *diffuses* down the line, and edges are widely dispersed with distance. Because both the resistance and capacitance increase with the length of the line, the delay of a signal on an RC line is *quadratic* with line length.

3.3.2.1   Step Response of an RC Line

A typical 0.6-μm square wire on an integrated circuit, $R = 0.12$ Ω/μm and $C = 0.16$ fF/μm, has a time constant of $RC = 2 \times 10^{-17}$ s/μm^2. Although this seems like a small number, the quadratic delay adds up quickly. A 10-mm wire, for example, has a delay (to first order) of 2 ns.

In many cases the degradation of rise time caused by the diffusive nature of RC lines is as much of a problem as the delay. Figure 3-6, for example, shows waveforms for a 10-mm lossy RC line driven by a signal with a 200-ps rise time. Waveforms are plotted each 2.5 mm along the line. The tick marks are placed every 100 ps, and the full-scale x axis corresponds to 2 ns. The figure shows that the line delays the signal by about 0.8 ns and increases its rise time by almost 2 ns. Such a slow rise time converts even a small amount of voltage noise into large amounts of jitter, causing serious problems when distributing timing signals.

As a rule of thumb, the delay, t_d, and rise time, t_r, of the step response of an RC line of length d are given by

$$t_d = 0.4 d^2 RC$$

$$(3\text{-}24)$$

$$t_r = d^2 RC$$

where R and C are resistance and capacitance per unit length, respectively.

Driving lossy on-chip RC lines is perhaps the hardest signaling problem encountered in modern digital systems design. As illustrated in Figure 3-6, driving these lines is like wiggling a wet noodle. A fast sharp edge injected at one end degrades into a slow, poorly defined edge along the line. We will examine a number of techniques for dealing with these lines in Section 8.1.

3.3.2.2   Low-Frequency RC Lines

Even transmission lines with significant inductance act as RC lines below a cutoff frequency,

$$(3\text{-}25) \qquad f_0 = \frac{R}{2\pi L}$$

Below this frequency, the resistance is larger than the impedance of the inductor, and the line behaves as a dispersive RC line. Above this frequency the line acts as an LC or LRC line. This cutover from RC to LC behavior typically occurs between 10 kHz and 1 MHz, depending on line configuration.

Perhaps the best example of a low-frequency RC line is a telephone subscriber loop. The loop is up to several kilometers of AWG24 twisted pair with $R = 0.08\ \Omega/\text{m}$, $C = 40$ pF/m, and $L = 400$ nH/m. The cutoff frequency, f_0, of the loop is about 33 kHz. Above this frequency, the line has a real characteristic impedance of 100 Ω. Below this frequency the impedance is a function of frequency given by Eq. (3-15). Over the telephone band, from 300 Hz to 3 kHz, the impedance ranges from 1,500 to 500 Ω with a phase angle that is nearly constant near $-45°$. Telephone circuits operate with 600-Ω impedance, which reflects the impedance of the line near the middle of the band.

For digital systems, low-frequency RC behavior will be a factor any time long LRC lines are used. The dispersive behavior at low frequencies will cause intersymbol interference. This problem is usually dealt with by band-limiting the signal to eliminate components below f_0.

3.3.3   Lossless LC Transmission Lines

Most off-chip lines, both PC-board traces and cables, fall into a category in which they are too long to be modeled as lumped capacitors but short enough that we can safely ignore their resistance. Dropping the resistive term from Eq. (3-12) gives the familiar wave equation that governs the propagation of signals on LC lines.

$$(3\text{-}26) \qquad \frac{\partial^2 V}{\partial x^2} = LC \frac{\partial^2 V}{\partial t^2}$$

3.3.3.1   Traveling Waves

One set of solutions to Eq. (3-26) are of the form

$$(3\text{-}27) \qquad V_f(x, t) = V\left(0, t - \frac{x}{v}\right)$$

$$V_r(x, t) = V\left(x_{\max}, t - \frac{x_{\max} - x}{v}\right)$$

where the propagation velocity, v, is given by

$$(3\text{-}28) \qquad v = (LC)^{-1/2}$$

The two parts of Eq. (3-27), V_f and V_r, correspond to forward and reverse traveling waves, respectively. That is, they are waveforms that propagate down the line with velocity, v, without any distortion of their waveform.

A traveling wave of arbitrary shape is a solution to the wave equation because propagation at a constant velocity turns a temporal derivative into a spatial derivative and vice versa. If a signal is traveling with velocity, v, then its first spatial derivative (gradient) is

$$(3\text{-}29) \qquad \frac{\partial V(x,t)}{\partial x} = \frac{\partial V\left(0, t - \frac{x}{v}\right)}{\partial x} = -\frac{1}{v}\frac{\partial V(x,t)}{\partial t}$$

Repeating the process gives the second spatial derivative (the divergence)

$$(3\text{-}30) \qquad \frac{\partial^2 V}{\partial x^2} = \frac{1}{v^2}\frac{\partial^2 V}{\partial t^2}$$

The expression for the second derivative is the wave equation. Thus, a traveling wave is a solution. Because the velocity term is squared, the polarity of the velocity does not matter, and both forward and reverse traveling waves satisfy the equation.

3.3.3.2 Impedance

To a driving circuit, an LC transmission line presents the same impedance as a resistor with value

$$(3\text{-}31) \qquad Z_0 = \left(\frac{L}{C}\right)^{1/2}$$

This impedance, from Eq. (3-15), is independent of both the length of the line and the frequency of the applied signal. That a line of arbitrary length has a constant real impedance greatly simplifies the design of signaling conventions and circuits to drive the line. One simply designs driver circuits to drive a resistor. Except for reflections off the far end of the line, the reactive nature of the line is not visible to the driver. The real impedance also gives a simple V–I relationship for the line. At any point along the line, the currents associated with the forward and reverse traveling waves are

$$(3\text{-}32) \qquad \begin{aligned} I_f(x,t) &= \frac{V_f(x,t)}{Z_0} \\[2mm] I_r(x,t) &= -\frac{V_r(x,t)}{Z_0} \end{aligned}$$

The current is negative for the reverse traveling wave because, by convention, current flowing in the positive x direction is positive and in the negative x direction is negative.

The impedance of transmission lines encountered in electronic systems ranges from 20 to 300 Ω, and 50 Ω is typical for both strip guides on boards and coaxial cables. Twisted-pair cables typically have an impedance of about 100 Ω.

3.3.3.3 Driving LC Transmission Lines

The traveling wave solution to the wave equation dictates that a waveform imposed at a point on the line will propagate with velocity, v, in both directions. Most often we inject a waveform by forcing either a voltage or a current into one end of the

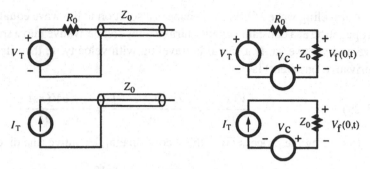

FIGURE 3-7   Driving an LC Line

line, as illustrated in Figure 3-7. The top left quarter of the figure shows a line being driven by a voltage source with an output impedance R_0. We illustrate an LC transmission line schematically as a cartoon of a coaxial cable regardless of whether the line is coaxial or not. For the time being we will assume that the line is of infinite length. This allows us to defer discussion of reflected waves and how the other end of the line is terminated.

As shown in the equivalent circuit in the top right quarter of Figure 3-7, to solve for the incident voltage in the line we model the line as a resistor with value Z_0 and a voltage source with value V_C to represent the initial voltage to which the capacitance of the line is charged. If we assume the initial voltage, V_C, is zero, the line forms a voltage divider with the output impedance of the source giving a foward-traveling *first incident* wave with amplitude

$$(3\text{-}33) \qquad V_i(x, t) = \left(\frac{Z_0}{Z_0 + R_0} \right) V_T \left(t - \frac{x}{v} \right)$$

The bottom left quarter of Figure 3-7 shows a current source driving the line. Injecting current into the line generates a forward traveling wave that adds to this original voltage.

$$(3\text{-}34) \qquad V_i(x, t) = Z_0 I_T \left(t - \frac{x}{v} \right)$$

The transmission line is a linear element, and thus we can apply the principle of *superposition* to solve for the voltage on the line as the sum of contributing voltages. For example, suppose that the line driven by a voltage source in the top half of Figure 3-7 is initially charged to 2 V and the voltage source drives a unit step, $V_T = U(t)$, into the line. We can solve for the waveform on the line by combining the result of driving an uncharged line (a + 1-V step) with the result of connecting a line charged to 2 V to a zero source (a − 2-V step) to get the result of the source driving the charged line (a − 1-V step).

The rest of our treatment of transmission lines will assume that the line is initially uncharged and will replace the V_C sources in Figure 3-7 with shorts. This simplifies the solution for the incident wave, and superposition can be used to include the effect of any initial charge on the line. As we will see shortly, super-position also plays a critical role in handling reflections. Although superposition

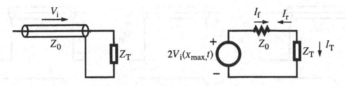

FIGURE 3-8   Terminating a Transmission Line

allows us to deal with one traveling wave at a time propagating down an uncharged line, it is important to remember that the voltage of a traveling wave is
incremental and thus is added to the other traveling waves and the initial state of
the line to give an absolute voltage.

The topic of driving transmission lines with current and voltage sources is
treated in more detail in Section 7.3.

3.3.3.4   Reflections and the Telegrapher's Equation

With a finite length transmission line, we must consider what happens when a
traveling wave reaches the end of the line. The left side of Figure 3-8 illustrates the
situation where an incident wave, V_i, reaches the end of a transmission line with
impedance, Z_0, terminated in an impedance of Z_T. The right side of the figure
gives a Thévenin-equivalent model of the line. The impedance is Z_0, and the open
circuit voltage is *twice* the amplitude of the incident wave. To see why the voltage
is double V_i, consider replacing Z_T with another section of transmission line with
impedance Z_0. The output impedance and the line would form a divide-by-two
voltage divider. Thus, to get a voltage of V_i on the line, the open-circuit voltage
must be $2V_i$.

With this model, the total current through the terminator, I_T, is

(3-35)
$$I_T = \frac{2V_i}{Z_0 + Z_T}$$

This terminator current is the superposition of the current due to the forward traveling wave, I_f, and the current due to the reflection, I_r. We know that the forward
current is given by Eq. (3-32), and thus we can solve for the reverse current.

$$I_r = I_f - I_T$$

(3-36)
$$I_r = \frac{V_i}{Z_0} - \frac{2V_i}{Z_T + Z_0}$$

$$I_r = \frac{V_i}{Z_0}\left(\frac{Z_T - Z_0}{Z_T + Z_0}\right)$$

Slightly rewritten, this is the famous *Telegrapher's equation* that relates the magnitude and phase[5] of the incident wave to those of the reflected wave.

(3-37)
$$k_r = \frac{I_r}{I_i} = \frac{V_r}{V_i} = \frac{Z_T - Z_0}{Z_T + Z_0}$$

---

[5] Note that for complex termination impendances, Z_T, the reflection coefficient, k_r, may be complex,
and the reflected wave may be phase shifted from the incident wave. For real-valued Z_T, the
reflection coefficient is real, and the phase is either 0 (k_r positive) or π (k_r negative).

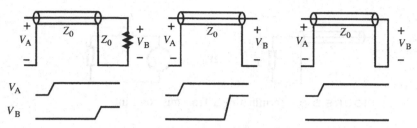

FIGURE 3-9   Matched, Open-Circuit, and Short-Circuit Terminations

3.3.3.5   Some Common Terminations

Figure 3-9 illustrates three special cases of line termination. From left to right the figure shows, matched, open-circuit, and short-circuit terminations along with sketches of the waveforms at the two ends of the line. The sketches consider only the first incident and first reflected wave. As discussed below, the behavior in the latter two cases also depends on subsequent reflections.

The matched termination, Figure 3-9 left, is the simplest and most common method of terminating a line. When $Z_T = Z_0$, the Telegrapher's equation tells us that $V_r = 0$. The forward traveling wave is absorbed entirely in the termination and no reverse traveling wave is reflected. In this case, V_B is just a delayed version of V_A. The matched termination simulates an infinite transmission line. As far as the traveling wave is concerned, a transmission line of impedance Z_0 is indistinguishable from a resistor with value Z_0, and thus the wave continues on into the terminator as if it were just more line.

Matched terminations are widely used in signaling systems because they reduce intersymbol interference. The termination absorbs all of the energy in the incident wave corresponding to one symbol; therefore, it cannot interfere with the waves corresponding to subsequent symbols. Stated differently, a line with a matched termination arrives at a steady-state response to an excitation in the minimum amount of time.

Figure 3-9 (center) illustrates the case when the far end of the line is left unconnected, an *open-circuit termination*. With an infinite termination impedance, $Z_T = \infty$, Eq. (3-37) tells us that $V_r = V_i$. Without any termination, the forward-traveling wave is completely reflected. The voltage at the open end of the line, V_B, is the sum of V_r and V_i and thus is twice the magnitude of the incident wave injected at V_A.

Open-circuit terminations (unterminated lines) are often used in systems where the driver has too high an output impedance to switch the line with the first incident wave. In such systems multiple reflections are required to *ring-up* the line to the switching point. Open terminations are also sometimes used in conjunction with a matched source termination to reduce power dissipation and to take advantage of the voltage doubling effect. However, as we will see in Section 7.3.3, such systems are usually more susceptible to noise as the voltage at the receiver is referenced to the transmitter.

The final case shown in Figure 3-9 (right) is a short-circuit termination. With a termination impedance, $Z_T = 0$, $V_r = -V_i$; the reflected wave is equal and opposite to the incident wave and thus $V_B = V_r + V_i = 0$ (no surprise because it is shorted).

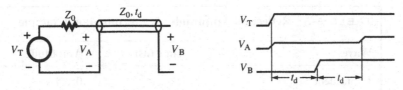

FIGURE 3-10   A Source-Terminated Line

Short-circuit terminations are occasionally used to generate short pulses from sharp voltage steps. However, they are more commonly encountered when modeling reflections off of low-impedance sources.

3.3.3.6   Source Termination and Multiple Reflections

If there is any mismatch in the termination, $Z_T \neq Z_0$, a reflected wave with nonzero magnitude, V_r, will arrive back at the source. This wave itself will reflect off the source with an amplitude V_{r2} given by Eq. (3-37). This second reflection travels down the line, and the reflections continue.

To avoid these multiple reflections it is often useful to match the source impedance to the line impedance. This has the added benefit of absorbing any spurious reverse traveling waves (e.g., due to cross talk) at the source. Figure 3-10 illustrates such a *source-terminated* line with an open circuit at the far end. The right side of the figure shows the response of this configuration to a step on the source V_T. The source impedance and line impedance divide this voltage, giving a half-amplitude step at the source end of the line, V_A. At time t_d later, this half-amplitude step reflects off the open end of the line. The superposition of the half-amplitude forward and reverse traveling waves results in a full-amplitude step at the far end of the line, V_B. After another line delay, t_d, this wave returns to the source, where it brings V_A up to full amplitude. It is then absorbed into the source impedance, and there are no further reflections.

Source termination is by no means limited to use with an open-circuit termination at the far end of the line. Many systems provide matched terminations for both ends of the line.

3.3.3.7   Arbitrary Termination

In the general case illustrated in Figure 3-11, neither end of the line has a matched termination, and thus waves reflect off of both ends. In this case the first step in computing the response of the line to a source transition is calculating the

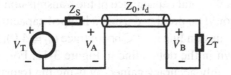

FIGURE 3-11   Arbitrary Termination

TABLE 3-3   Reflection Amplitudes for Termination Example

Wave	Time (ns)	Amplitude	Total
1st incident	0	0.111	0.111
1st reflection from term	4	0.101	0.212
1st reflection from source	8	0.078	0.290
2nd reflection from term	12	0.071	0.361
2nd reflection from source	16	0.055	0.416
3rd reflection from term	20	0.050	0.465
3rd reflection from source	24	0.039	0.504
4th reflection from term	28	0.035	0.539
4th reflection from source	32	0.027	0.566
5th reflection from term	36	0.026	0.591

reflection coefficients for the termination (K_{rT}) and source (K_{rS}).

$$K_{rT} = \frac{Z_T - Z_0}{Z_T + Z_0}$$

(3-38)

$$K_{rS} = \frac{Z_S - Z_0}{Z_S + Z_0}$$

For example, suppose $Z_0 = 50\,\Omega$, $Z_T = 1\,\text{k}\Omega$, and $Z_S = 400\,\Omega$ (typical values for an 8-mA CMOS driver with a 1 kΩ pullup); then we have $K_{rT} = 0.90$ and $K_{rS} = 0.78$.

Using these reflection coefficients, we compute the magnitude of each reflected waveform until the magnitude of the reflections drops below some threshold. The reflection magnitudes for our example, assuming V_T is a unit step and the line is 4 ns long, are listed in the Table 3-3. Even after nine traversals of the wire, the signal is still 123 mV (17%) short of its final value of 0.714 V. For space we have terminated the signal at this point. In practice we would continue computing reflections until the total amplitude was within 5% of the steady-state value. In this case, the signal reaches this amplitude after 16 traversals of the wire or 64 ns.

If the next signal transition occurs before the current transition has settled at its steady-state value, we apply superposition by computing the response to the two transitions separately and then summing them in the area that they overlap. This overlap corresponds to intersymbol interference, a source of noise that we will discuss further in Section 6.4.

If one smooths the response of this example system (with mismatched terminations at both ends of the line) the result is an exponential with a time constant, $\tau = (R_S \| R_T)C_1$, where C_1 is the total capacitance of the transmission line. This is exactly the response that would be predicted using a lumped capacitive model of the line, assuming the transmission line is a PC board trace ($\varepsilon_r = 4.0$), $C_1 = 80\,\text{pF}$, and the response is as shown in the dotted line in Figure 3-12. For systems that slowly ring up the line, the only accuracy gained by using the transmission-line model is the discrimination of the discrete steps as the line rings up.

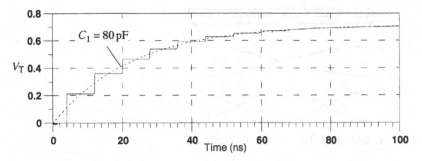

FIGURE 3-12 Waveforms for Termination Example

This example highlights the fact that a line that is not terminated at least at one end with a matched impedance introduces either significant delay or intersymbol interference, or both, because of the time required for reflections to *ring out*.

3.3.3.8 Standing Waves

When an unterminated, or underterminated, transmission line is driven by any periodic waveform, then the forward- and reverse-traveling waves combine to form a *standing wave* that appears to be stationary. For example, consider the case of a sine wave with a period that evenly divides twice the line length

$$(3\text{-}39) \qquad V_i(t) = \sin\left[\frac{\pi n}{d}(vt)\right]$$

The forward- and reverse-traveling waves sum to give the standing wave

$$
\begin{aligned}
V_s(x,t) &= V_f(x,t) + V_r(x,t) \\
&= \sin\left[\frac{\pi n}{d}(vt - x)\right] + \sin\left[\frac{\pi n}{d}(vt - 2d + x)\right] \\
&= \sin\left[\frac{\pi n}{d}(vt - x)\right] + \sin\left[\frac{\pi n}{d}(vt + x)\right] \\
&= 2\sin\left(\frac{\pi n v}{d}t\right)\cos\left(\frac{\pi n}{d}x\right)
\end{aligned}
$$

(3-40)

As shown in Eq. (3-40) and illustrated in Figure 3-13 the standing wave has a cosine envelope that has *nulls* where $nx/d = 1/2 + m$ for integer m. The figure shows the envelope for $n = 1$ and $n = 2$. For $n = 1$ there is a single null at the midpoint of the line, while for $n = 2$ there are two nulls at the $1/4$ and $3/4$ points. Modulo the sign of the envelope, the oscillations over the entire line are in phase.

Standing waves do have a few useful applications in digital systems, such as distributing a clock with zero skew (Section 9.7.1.3). However, for most signal lines, they represent noise that interferes with detection of the signal. They are most often a problem when an open or underterminated line is driven by a high-impedance driver with a clock period that evenly divides twice the line length.

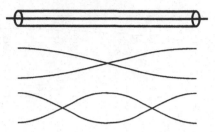

FIGURE 3-13   Standing Waves

3.3.3.9   Summary

To sum up, although an RC line is like a wet noodle, an LC transmission line is a taut guitar string. It will cleanly propagate arbitrary waveforms over substantial distances. However, just like the guitar string, it will oscillate or ring if not terminated.

3.3.4   Lossy LRC Transmission Lines

Losses in long LC transmission lines are too large to be neglected. The resistance in conductors and the conduction in dielectrics attenuate the traveling wave and give a response that is a hybrid of the traveling wave of the LC line with the diffusive response of an RC line. The *skin effect* causes the series resistance of the line to vary with frequency, and *dielectric absorption* causes the conductance of the line to vary with frequency; both effects result in increased attenuation at higher frequencies.[6]

3.3.4.1   Wave Attenuation

For the time being ignore the skin effect and frequency-dependent dielectric absorption and consider a transmission line with a fixed resistance, R, and a fixed conductance, G, per unit length. A lumped electrical model for a short section of line is shown in Figure 3-14 (repeated from Figure 3-3). From Eqs. (3-18) and (3-19) the magnitude of a traveling wave, $V_i(x)$, at any point along the line is related to the magnitude, $V_i(0)$, at a given frequency by

(3-41)
$$\frac{V_i(x)}{V_i(0)} = \exp(-Ax)$$

$$A = [(G + j\omega C)(R + j\omega L)]^{1/2}$$

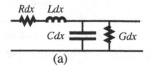

(a)

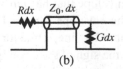

(b)

FIGURE 3-14   Model of a Lossy LRC Transmission Line

---

[6] Radiation of electromagnetic waves from the line is an additional component of loss. For most lines, however, this component is small compared with line resistance and dielectric absorption.

If the losses G and R are small, then at high frequencies A can be rewritten as

$$A \approx (j\omega RC + j\omega GL - \omega^2 LC)^{1/2}$$

(3-42)
$$= j\omega\sqrt{LC}\left(1 - j\frac{RC + GL}{\omega LC}\right)^{1/2}$$

Because the losses G, R are small, we can replace the square root with a Taylor expansion, keeping only the first term to give

$$A \approx j\omega\sqrt{LC}\left(1 - j\frac{RC + GL}{2\omega LC}\right)$$

(3-43)
$$= j\omega\sqrt{LC} + \frac{R}{2Z_0} + \frac{GZ_0}{2}$$

The first term describes how the phase of the traveling wave varies along the line, and the second two terms describe the loss in amplitude of the wave along the line. The amplitude of the traveling wave at any point along the line is given by

$$\frac{|V_i(x)|}{|V_i(0)|} = \exp\left[-(\alpha_R + \alpha_D)x\right]$$

(3-44)
$$\alpha_R = R/(2Z_0)$$

$$\alpha_D = GZ_0/2$$

Thus, the amplitude of a traveling wave is reduced exponentially with distance along the line with attenuation factors α_R and α_D due to conductor resistance and dielectric loss, respectively. The terms R, G, α_R, and α_D are all per unit length.

3.3.4.2 DC Attenuation

In most real transmission lines, the DC conductance of the dielectric is zero. For a line with a matched termination, the steady-state response is attenuated by an amount proportional to the inverse of the length of the line. To see this, consider a DC model of a line of length d and the matched termination as illustrated in Figure 3-15. The output voltage across Z_0 is

(3-45)
$$\frac{V_{DC}(d)}{V_T} = \frac{Z_0}{Rd + Z_0} = \frac{1}{2\alpha_R d + 1}$$

where $\alpha_R = R/2Z_0$ is the same attenuation factor as for Eq. (3-44).

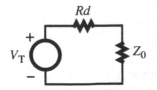

FIGURE 3-15 DC Model of Lossy Line and Matched Termination

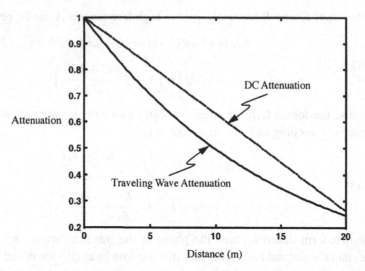

FIGURE 3-16   Traveling Wave and DC Attenuation Versus Distance

In the steady state, the voltage has a constant gradient; thus

$$(3\text{-}46) \qquad \frac{V_{DC}(x)}{V_T} = 1 - \frac{2\alpha_R x}{2\alpha_R d + 1}$$

Figure 3-16 plots the two attenuation formulas of Eqs. (3-44) (with α_R only) and (3-46) at bottom and top, respectively, as a function of distance (in meters) for a 20-m, 5-mil stripguide with a fixed resistance of 7 Ω/m.

3.3.4.3   Combined Traveling Wave and Diffusive Response

Figure 3-17 shows how the response of a lossy LRC line to a unit step combines a traveling wave component with a diffusive component. The figure shows the waveform at 4-m intervals along a 20-m line with a fixed resistance of 7 Ω/m. At

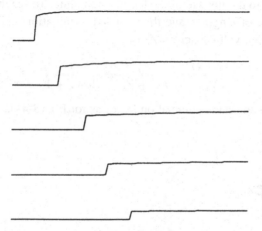

FIGURE 3-17   Response of a Lossy LRC Line As a Function of Distance

each point, x, along the line the response is a step to an amplitude of exp $(-\alpha_R x)$, the amplitude of the traveling wave at point x, followed by a diffusive relaxation to the steady-state value at point x. The diffusive relaxation has a time constant that is proportional to the square of the position along the line.

This response is *dispersive* in that it spreads out a pulse in time. The dispersion here is due to the frequency-dependent nature of the response of the line at low frequencies. Above a cutoff frequency, f_0, given by Eq. (3-25), our approximation that led to Eq. (3-43) holds, and the line looks like an LC line with a fixed resistive attenuation per unit length, independent of frequency. Below this frequency, the line looks like an RC line with a low-pass frequency response that rolls off linearly with frequency. For a 5-mil stripguide with $R = 7\ \Omega/\text{m}$ and $L = 300\ \text{nH/m}$, $f_0 = 3.7\ \text{MHz}$.

The difference between the AC (traveling wave) attenuation and the DC attenuation along with the long tails of the response due to the diffusive relaxation results in significant intersymbol interference. The situation is made worse by the frequency-dependent nature of wire resistance and dielectric absorption.

3.3.4.4 The Skin Effect

High-frequency current flows primarily on the surface of a conductor with current density falling off exponentially with depth into the conductor

$$(3-47) \qquad J = \exp\left(-\frac{d}{\delta}\right)$$

The skin depth, δ, the depth where the current has fallen off to exp (-1) of its normal value is given by

$$(3-48) \qquad \delta = (\pi f \mu \sigma)^{-1/2}$$

where $\sigma = 1/\rho$ is the conductivity of the material, and f is the frequency of the signal.

Although the current falls off exponentially with depth, we approximate this effect by assuming that the current flows uniformly in an outer shell of the conductor with thickness δ. Figure 3-18 illustrates this effect for a round conductor and a stripguide. Because the stripguide width is much greater than its height, we ignore the contributions from the sides of the stripguide. The cross-sectional area

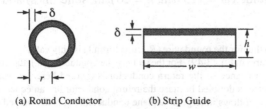

(a) Round Conductor   (b) Strip Guide

FIGURE 3-18 Skin-Effect Resistance for Round Wire and Stripguides

that is carrying current is

$$A_a = 2\pi r\delta - \pi\delta^2 \approx 2\pi r\delta = 2\pi r(\pi f\mu\sigma)^{-1/2}$$

(3-49)

$$A_b = 2w\delta = 2w(\pi f\mu\sigma)^{-1/2}$$

At very high frequencies the skin depth is small compared with the diameter; therefore, we ignore the quadratic term in the expression for A_a, giving for both geometries an expression that is the approximate surface area times the skin depth. Substituting Eq. (3-49) in Eq. (3-1) gives a resistance per unit length[7] of

$$R_a(f) = \frac{1}{2r}\left(\frac{f\mu\rho}{\pi}\right)^{1/2}$$

(3-50)

$$R_b(f) = \frac{1}{2w}(\pi f\mu\rho)^{1/2}$$

The skin effect does not affect a conductor unless the frequency is above a frequency, f_s, where the skin depth is equal to the radius of the conductor (or half the height for a rectangular conductor).

(3-51)

$$f_s = \frac{\rho}{\pi\mu r^2}$$

Below this frequency, all of the area of the conductor is carrying current, and the wire has a constant DC resistance, R_{DC}. Above this frequency, the resistance increases with the square root of frequency. Thus, an alternate and often more convenient form of Eq. (3-50) is

$$R_a(f) = \frac{R_{DC}}{2}\left(\frac{f}{f_s}\right)^{1/2}$$

(3-52)

$$R_b(f) = R_{DC}\left(\frac{f}{f_s}\right)^{1/2}$$

and the attenuation factors in Eq. (3-44) for the two types of line are

$$\alpha_{aS}(f) = \frac{R_{DC}}{4Z_0}\left(\frac{f}{f_s}\right)^{1/2}$$

(3-53)

$$\alpha_{bS}(f) \approx \frac{R_{DC}}{2Z_0}\left(\frac{f}{f_s}\right)^{1/2}$$

Figure 3-19 shows resistance and attenuation as a function of frequency for a 5-mil copper stripguide ($w = 125\ \mu m$, $h = 20\ \mu m$, solid lines) and a 24 AWG

---

[7] It should be emphasized that for the round wire (R_a), this formula is only valid for $f \gg f_s$ because it ignores the quadratic term in Eq. (3-49). For the rectangular conductor (R_b), this formula is valid for $f \geq f_s$. Also, the resistance of the return conductor is ignored here. For symmetric lines the effective line resistance is doubled because the return conductor has an equal resistance. For striplines, the return current flows in large-area plane conductors but is distributed over a narrow band under the signal trace at high frequencies. The return current distribution can be crudely approximated by assuming that it flows uniformly in a band in each return plane that is the width of the signal conductor.

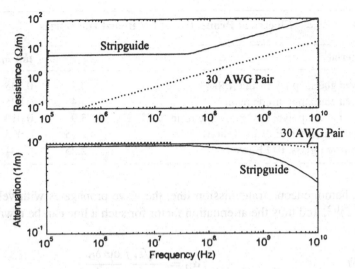

FIGURE 3-19 Resistance and Attenuation of 5-mil Stripguide and 30 AWG Pair

($r = 250\,\mu$m, dotted lines) twisted pair. The stripguide has a DC resistance of R_{DC} of 7 Ω/m and skin-depth frequency, $f_s = 43$ MHz. At $f = 1$ GHz its effective resistance is 33 Ω/m, and signals are attenuated by 0.72 (2.9 dB) per meter. For comparison, the 24 AWG pair has $R_{DC} = 0.08\,\Omega$/m, $f_s = 67$ kHz, and at 1 GHz, $R = 6.6\,\Omega$/m, attenuating signals by 0.94 (0.57 dB) per meter.

Figure 3-19 does not quite tell the whole story because it neglects the fact that below f_0, 3.6 MHz for the stripguide, the line behaves like an RC transmission line with a low-pass frequency response. However, for short lines, where the total attenuation in this region below f_0 is small, we can safely ignore this effect.

The frequency-dependent attenuation due to skin effect low-passes the traveling wave, giving a step response with an increased rise time and a tail that extends to $1/f_1$. This dispersion of the waveform leads to intersymbol interference as the tails of the responses to past symbols on the line interfere with new symbols placed on the line.

3.3.5 Dielectric Absorption

Dielectric loss for printed circuit materials is usually expressed in terms of the *loss tangent* defined as

$$(3\text{-}54) \qquad \tan\delta_{\mathrm{D}} = \frac{G}{\omega C}$$

This quantity is approximately constant with frequency. The attenuation factor is, then,

$$\alpha_{\mathrm{D}} = \frac{GZ_0}{2} = \frac{2\pi fC \tan\delta_{\mathrm{D}}\sqrt{L/C}}{2}$$

$$(3\text{-}55)$$

$$= \pi f \tan\delta_{\mathrm{D}}\sqrt{LC}$$

TABLE 3-4   **Electrical Properties of PC Board Dielectrics**

Material	ε_r	tan δ_D
Woven glass, epoxy resin ("FR-4")	4.7	0.035
Woven glass, polyimide resin	4.4	0.025
Woven glass, polyphenylene oxide resin (GETEK)	3.9	0.010
Woven glass, PTFE resin (Teflon)	2.55	0.005
Nonwoven glass, PTFE resin	2.25	0.001

For a homogeneous transmission line, the wave propagates with velocity, $v = 1/(LC)^{1/2}$, and thus the attenuation factor for such a line can be rewritten in the form

$$(3\text{-}56) \qquad \alpha_D = \frac{\pi \sqrt{\varepsilon_k} f \tan \delta_D}{c}$$

where c is the speed of light in vacuum, and ε_r is the relative permittivity of the material. Properties of some commonly used PC board dielectrics are shown in Table 3-4.

It should be noted that both ε_r and tan δ_D vary with frequency, substantially for some materials (those in the table were measured at 1 MHz) [IPCD95]. In some PC-board dielectric materials, these parameters also vary with thickness. Generally, materials with lower ε_r and tan δ_D are more expensive than materials with higher values; for example, Teflon board materials are roughly ten to twenty times as expensive as standard glass/epoxy materials. Printed circuit fabricators should be consulted about the relative costs and electrical and mechanical properties of their materials before committing to a board design for high-performance signaling.

3.4   SPECIAL TRANSMISSION LINES

3.4.1   Multidrop Buses

For many years, a popular method of connecting digital systems was the multidrop bus illustrated in Figure 3-20. Several modules, usually PC boards, connect to the bus via transceivers and wiring stubs. At any given point in time, one module is authorized to transmit and the other modules listen. From an abstract point of view, the bus is very convenient, for it permits, albeit in a serialized manner, any

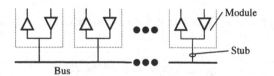

FIGURE 3-20   A Multidrop Bus

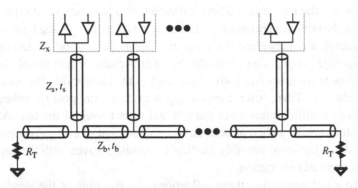

FIGURE 3-21   Electrical Model of a Bus

module to communicate with any other module. However, buses are rarely used today in high-performance digital systems because electrically the stubs severely limit the bandwidth at which the bus can operate.

Figure 3-21 shows an electrical model of a bus. The bus itself consists of several sections of transmission line with impedance Z_b and delay t_b between modules. Each module connected to the bus is modeled as a stub of transmission line with impedance Z_s and delay t_s along with a lumped load Z_x representing the transceiver. As shown, buses typically are parallel-terminated at both ends into a matched terminator R_T.

The distributed load of stubs and transceivers greatly lowers the effective impedance and propagation velocity of the bus. Consider a bus where $Z_b = Z_s = 50\,\Omega$; the lines have $C = 150$ pF/m and $L = 375$ nH/m; the stubs are 10 cm (≈ 700 ps) long; the spacing between modules is 3 cm; there are 10 slots; and Z_x is 15 pF of capacitance. Because the stubs themselves have a capacitance of 15 pF the combination stub and transceiver adds 30 pF of load every 3 cm or 1 nF/m. The bus–stub combination has a capacitance of 1.15 nF/m. This high capacitance reduces the impedance (Eq. (3-31)) to 18 Ω and the velocity (Eq. (3-28)) to 4.8×10^7 m/s (about $1/3$ normal speed). To cancel reflections, the terminations at the ends of the bus should both be 18 Ω. A driver sees a line with this impedance in either direction and thus must drive half of this impedance or 9 Ω.

The low impedance by itself would not be a problem were the bus driven with a low voltage swing and terminated in a matched load. Most buses, however, are driven by high-impedance, high-swing drivers that take several round trips to ring up the bus to a detectable voltage level. With the low velocity, this adds considerable delay. For our 30-cm, 10-slot bus, each traversal takes 6 ns, and four or more traversals may be required to get the bus to an appropriate level.

To further complicate the impedance problem, many systems allow users to *partially populate* buses, which leads to impedance discontinuities. Consider, for example, the bus model shown in Figure 3-21, where several of the modules in the center of the bus and their stubs are not present. This unloaded section of bus is a 50-Ω line surrounded by 18-Ω lines on either side. Significant reflections will occur at either end of the unloaded section because of this impedance mismatch.

Even if the transmission line is driven with a low swing and is properly terminated, the nonuniform nature of the stubs and interstub spacing limit the maximum
frequency and hence the rise time of a signal that can be carried by the bus. A
sharp edge propagating down the bus will partially reflect off of each stub. The
incident wave gives a negative reflection as the current divides between the stub
and the bus. Then, after a round-trip stub delay, the positive reflection off the
end of the stub divides over the left and right halves of the bus. Also, because
the stub is mismatched at both ends, a fair amount of energy remains ringing up
and down the stub, possibly leading to standing waves with the appropriate (or
inappropriate) excitation.

To avoid generating these reflections, the rise time of the signals on the bus
must be significantly longer than the round-trip delay of the stub so that the stub
acts as a lumped capacitance. A stub has a round-trip delay of 1.4 ns, so using our
rule of thumb that $t_r > 5\, t_d$, rise times must be limited to be no faster than 7 ns. The
rise time is also limited by the nonuniformity of the capacitance represented by
the stubs. To approximate lumped capacitors spaced every 3 cm as a uniform capacitor, the rise time must be large compared with the 700-ps delay between slots.
For this example this is a less restrictive constraint than the stub length. However,
on a bus with short stubs, the interstub spacing may be the limiting factor.

Buses can be made to go very fast by keeping the stub lengths and spacings
very small. RAMBUS,[8] for example operates a bus at 500 Mb/s per wire by
connecting specially designed chip packages directly to the bus with close spacing.
For distances associated with PC board modules, 2–3-cm spacing and 5–20 cm
stubs; however, even with good drivers and terminators buses are limited to no
more than 100 Mb/s.

Because of these geometry-related limitations, point-to-point links that can
signal at 5–10 times these rates are rapidly replacing buses in high-end systems.[9]

3.4.2   Balanced Transmission Lines

Up to this section, we have assumed that the return path in a transmission line has
zero inductance, as illustrated in the line section of Figure 3-22(a). However, in
reality all lines have some nonzero return inductance, as shown in Figure 3-22(b).
In this model of a line section we have divided the inductance per unit length, L,
into signal and return portions, $L = L_s + L_r$. For some lines, such as coaxial
cables and stripguides between return planes, L_r is much less than L_s and is often
safely approximated by zero inductance.

A *balanced* or *symmetric* transmission line is one for which $L_s = L_r$. Twisted-
pair cables where the signal and return are carried on identical conductors, for
example, are symmetric transmission lines. Voltage drops across the return inductance of any line, in particular symmetric lines, can be a significant factor in
a signaling system.

---

[8] RAMBUS is a standard for memory system interconnect, introduced by RAMBUS, Inc. and widely
adopted by DRAM vendors.
[9] See Exercise 3-7, however, for a method of building buses without the effect of stubs.

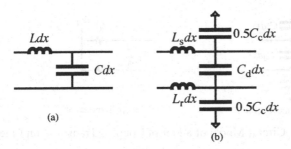

(a)

(b)

FIGURE 3-22 Return Inductance in an LC Transmission Line

A symmetric transmission line has both a differential mode impedance, Z_0, and a common-mode impedance, Z_1. A signal applied differentially across the line sees the sum of L_s and L_r and the sum of C_d and $0.25C_c$. If both conductors of the line are tied together and driven with the same signal, the resulting common-mode signal sees the parallel combination of L_s and L_r and only C_c. Thus, to first approximation,[10] Z_0 and Z_1 are given by

(3-57)

$$Z_0 = \left(\frac{L_s + L_r}{C_d + 0.25C_c} \right)^{1/2}$$

$$Z_1 = \left[\frac{L_s L_r}{(L_s + L_r)C_c} \right]^{1/2}$$

Figure 3-23 shows the step response of a symmetric line. When the voltage source produces a unit step, equal amounts of voltage are dropped across the equal signal and return inductances of the line. Thus, relative to a ground at the far end of the line, the voltage on the signal conductor at the near end, V_s, rises by a half volt, and the voltage on the return conductor, V_r, falls by a half volt. The wave propagates in this *balanced* manner with $I_s = -I_r$ until it reaches the termination. Here, the full signal appears across the matched termination as V_3.

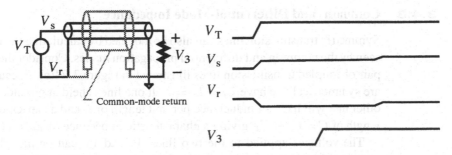

FIGURE 3-23 Step-Response of Symmetric Transmission Line

---

[10] The situation is a bit more complicated because of mutual inductance between the two conductors, but we will ignore that effect for the moment. We will revisit this simplification in Section 3.4.3 below.

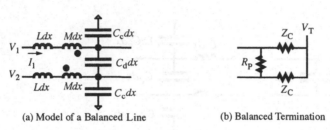

(a) Model of a Balanced Line   (b) Balanced Termination

FIGURE 3-24   Circuit Model of a Pair of Coupled Transmission Lines

If there is no other connection between the two sides of the transmission line, the system will be stable at this point, with V_r again equal to the "ground" at the termination.

If, however, there is a separate ground connection[11] between the source and termination, denoted by the shaded line in Figure 3-23, the situation may not be stable. The half-volt drop around this *ground loop* causes a *common-mode* current of $0.5/Z_1$ to flow back across the line toward the source. After a line delay, this common-mode wave reaches the source and causes a bump in V_s and V_r. This common-mode wave will reflect off the source with some attenuation, depending on the common-mode impedance of the source and ring up and down the line. Most often the common-mode line is underterminated, causing the ringing to settle with an exponential envelope.

Each time the common-mode wave reaches the unbalanced terminator at the end of the line, energy will be exchanged between the differential-mode wave and the common-mode wave. This *mode coupling* between the common-mode wave and the differential-mode wave leads to intersymbol interference.

To avoid problems with common-mode waves and mode-coupling between differential mode and common-mode transmission lines, care should be taken to terminate both the differential and common modes properly at the receiver. In general, transmission lines with significant return inductance should not be used to carry single-ended signals. They should only be used with differential signals and balanced terminations.

3.4.3   Common- and Differential-Mode Impedance

Symmetric transmission lines can also be modeled by calculating the impedances seen by the common and differential propagation modes. Consider the model of a pair of coupled transmission lines illustrated in Figure 3-24(a). Because the lines are symmetrical, we have $L_s = L_r = L$. If one line is held at ground, $V_2 = 0$, the other line will have an inductance per unit length of L and a capacitance per unit length of $C = C_c + C_d$, giving a characteristic impedance of $Z_0 = (L/C)^{1/2}$.

The voltages applied to the two lines, V_1 and V_2, can be thought of as the superposition of a common-mode voltage, V_C, and a differential-mode voltage,

---

[11]   Our model in Figure 3-22 is approximate in that it does not include the inductance per unit length of this common-mode return.

ΔV, where

$$V_C = \frac{V_1 + V_2}{2}$$

(3-58)

$$V_D = \frac{V_1 - V_2}{2}$$

When a differential-mode signal is applied, equal and opposite currents flow in the two lines, and the voltage drop across the mutual inductance is in the direction opposite that of the self-inductance. With this situation, the mutual inductance, M, acts to reduce the inductance seen by the differential mode signal to $L - M$. With the two signal lines moving in opposite directions, however, the effect of the mutual capacitance, C_d, is doubled, increasing the capacitance seen by the differential signal to $C + C_d$. Thus, the differential-mode impedance, Z_D, is given by

(3-59)
$$Z_D = \frac{V_D}{I_1} = \left(\frac{L - M}{C + C_d}\right)^{1/2}$$

When a common-mode signal drives the lines, equal currents flow in the two signal lines in the same direction. This causes the voltage drop across the mutual inductance to be in the same direction as that of the self-inductance. Thus, the inductance seen by the common-mode signal is increased to $L + M$. With this signal, there is no voltage change across the coupling capacitor, C_d. Thus, the common-mode signal sees only the capacitance of C_c, or $C - C_d$. Consequently, the common-mode impedance is given by

(3-60)
$$Z_C = \frac{V_C}{I_1} = \left(\frac{L + M}{C - C_d}\right)^{1/2}$$

Increasing the coupling capacitance gives a better differential transmission line because the differential-mode impedance is reduced and the common-mode impedance is increased. An asymptote is eventually reached, however, for the common-mode impedance cannot exceed the impedance of free-space (about 377 Ω).

A balanced termination, shown in Figure 3-24(b), can be used to match the differential and common-mode impedances of a line simultaneously. The circuit in the figure terminates common-mode signals with an impedance of Z_C and differential signals with an impedance of $Z_C \parallel R_P$, which is equal to Z_D if R_P is chosen as

(3-61)
$$R_P = 2\left(\frac{Z_D Z_C}{Z_C - Z_D}\right)$$

When both propagation modes are properly terminated in this manner, there are no reflections of either the differential or the common-mode components of the signal and hence no mode coupling.

3.4.4 Isolated Lines

Cabinets that have separate AC power feeds often have grounds that differ by several or even a few tens of volts. This is due to unbalanced AC power current

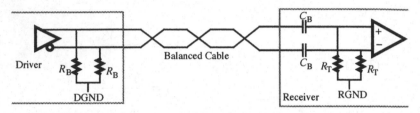

FIGURE 3-25   An AC-Coupled Transmission Line

flowing in the neutral lead of the distribution network. This potential ground shift makes it undesirable to couple transmission lines directly between cabinets that do not share a common ground point. Such direct coupling may result in signals being outside the dynamic range of the receivers, permanent damage to driver and receiver circuits, and large currents flowing in the signal returns.

3.4.4.1   AC Coupling

The simplest method of isolating DC signal levels is to AC-couple signals using blocking capacitors, as shown in Figure 3-25. The driver generates signals referenced to its local ground, DGND. If the driver operates in the current mode, bias resistors, R_B, are used as shown to reference the voltage on the cable to the driver. Because they are for DC bias only, these bias resistors can be quite large. They are not needed at all if a voltage-mode driver is used. A pair of blocking capacitors, C_B, at the receiver,[12] along with the termination resistors, R_T, level shift this voltage to be referenced to the receiver ground, RGND.

An AC-coupled signal must be DC-balanced (equal numbers of 1's and 0's) with no frequency components below the cutoff frequency of the high-pass filter formed by C_B and R_T. For example, if R_T is 50 Ω and C_B is 0.1 μF,[13] the cutoff frequency is $f_c = 200$ kHz. If a 100-Mb/s bit stream is coded so that DC balance is achieved at least every 20 bits, then the lowest frequency component is 5 MHz, which is well above the cutoff frequency. Methods for coding signals for balance are discussed in Section 8.4.

Capacitor coupling is inexpensive and can be used for very-high-bit rate signaling because the capacitors pass the high-frequency components of the signal without loss or distortion. The only disadvantages of capacitor isolation are that the signal needs to be DC-balanced, the isolation range is limited by the breakdown voltage of the capacitors, and only the low-frequency (below f_c) components of the ground shift are isolated.

Transformers can also be used to AC-couple signals, as illustrated in Figure 3-26. The figure shows transformers at both ends of the line. In practice, isolation can be achieved using a transformer at only one end of the line. Air-core

---

[12] The blocking capacitors could also be palced at the transmitter or at any point along the cable. There is no particular advantage to placing them at the receiver.

[13] Small ceramic capacitors are typically used for blocking capacitors because they are inexpensive, available in small surface-mount packages with low inductance, and have breakdown voltages of 100 V or more.

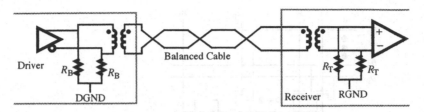

FIGURE 3-26 Transformer Coupling

transformers are used to couple high-frequency signals to prevent frequency-dependent core losses from distorting the signal. In addition to isolating signals, transformers can also be used to convert impedances. For example, a transformer with a 1.4:1 turns ratio will convert a 100-Ω input impedance to a 50-Ω output impedance. In this capacity they are often used to couple high-swing, high-impedance drivers and receivers to low-impedance transmission lines.

Compared with capacitive coupling, transformer coupling is expensive, consumes a great deal of board area, and is prone to cross talk due to coupling of flux between transformers. For this reason, it is only used where impedance conversion is required in addition to isolation.

3.4.4.2 Optical Isolation

A signal can be isolated from wide-spectrum ground shift without the need for DC balance by converting it from electrical to optical and back, as illustrated in Figure 3-27. The current, i_{in}, causes an LED to emit light, which in turn induces an output current, i_{out}, to flow in an appropriately biased phototransistor. Thus, current-encoded digital signals on the input are reproduced, modulo the bandwidth limitations of the LED and phototransistor, as a current-encoded digital signal on the output. The input need not be DC-balanced, and the output is isolated from high-frequency ground shift as well as low frequency. The isolation voltage is limited only by the breakdown of the insulator used for the optical path (1 kV is typical for single-chip optocouplers), and much higher isolation voltages can be achieved by using free-space or optical fiber for isolation.

3.5 WIRE COST MODELS

Wires account for much of the cost of a digital system. Although the final cost of the system is determined by tabulating the bill of materials, at early design stages we use simpler *wire cost models* to estimate the wiring feasibility and cost of design alternatives. At each level of the packaging hierarchy the design is limited

FIGURE 3-27 Optical Isolation

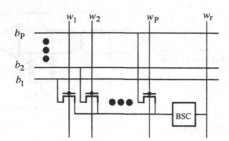

FIGURE 3-28   A Register-File Cell Is Wire-Limited

either by the number of available wiring tracks (or grids) or by the number of pins to the next level of the hierarchy. In analyzing high-level alternatives, we abstract details such as wire routing, cable selection, and connector selection and use wire cost models that assign rough costs (dollars) to wiring tracks and pins at each level of the hierarchy.

3.5.1   Wire Area Costs

More often than not, the chip area of a function unit is determined by the wiring required to connect the function unit rather than by the number of transistors or gates that are being connected. For such *wire-limited* function units, the cost of the unit is determined by counting the wiring tracks required for connection.

As an example of a wire-limited function, consider a register file with P read-write ports, W words, and B bits. A schematic for one of the WB cells in such a register file is shown in Figure 3-28. In a typical design the base storage cell (BSC), with zero ports, requires six transistors. Thus, the number of transistors required by the cell is $6 + P$. The area required by these transistors is swamped by the required wiring area. Neglecting the tracks required to implement BSC, to supply power, and to connect to the switching device, the cell requires an area of $P^2 + P$ tracks-squared (χ^2), P horizontal wiring tracks by $P + 1$ vertical tracks. Its area grows quadratically with the number of ports.[14] When weighing the possibility of adding a port to a register file, one needs to consider not the linear increase in transistors but the quadratic increase in wiring area.

A typical 1996 15-mm square chip with a wire pitch, χ, of 1.2 μm has 12,500 tracks in each dimension or 1.6×10^8 tracks squared (χ^2) of area and costs[15] about \$50 to fabricate,[16] test, and package. Thus, the cost per unit area is 3.1×10^{-7}

---

[14] Strictly speaking, a register file with R read ports and W write ports can be implemented in area proportional to $(R + W)W$. The read ports can be added with a linear increase in area by simply replicating the entire register file. Adding a write port, however, has quadratic cost because it requires adding a word line and a bit line to each cell of each replicated register file.

[15] The *cost* of an article is the amount of money a manufacturer spends making it. The *price*, the amount the buyer pays for it, may be much higher. It is not unusual for a chip with a per-unit cost of \$50 to have a price of \$500 or more. Intel's high-end microprocessors are good examples.

[16] The cost of integrated circuit fabrication is largely due to depreciation of capital equipment. For example, our example 15- $\times$ 15-mm 0.35-μm chips are fabricated on 8-inch-(200-mm) diameter

TABLE 3-5 **Wire Costs**

Level	Size	Cost	χ/Layer	Signal Layer	$/\chi^2$	$/mm
Chip	15 mm	50	1.2×10^4	4	3.1×10^{-7}	2.7×10^{-4}
MCM	50 mm	50	333	4	4.5×10^{-4}	1.5×10^{-3}
4-layer PCB	30 cm	50	1,200	2	3.4×10^{-5}	1.4×10^{-4}
16-layer PCB	30 cm	500	1,200	8	3.4×10^{-4}	3.5×10^{-4}

dollars/χ^2. With these numbers, a 64-bit by 64-word 5-port register file costs $WB(P^2 + P) = 1.2 \times 10^5 \chi^2$, or about 4 cents. A 10-port register file, in contrast, costs $4.5 \times 10^5 \chi^2$ or about 14 cents.

To first order, the cost of most function units can be estimated by counting the number of wiring tracks required in each direction. This usually gives an underestimate, for additional tracks are required for power, ground, and local signals. Estimating area and cost from gate or transistor counts (as is still practiced by many engineers) tends to give completely erroneous measures. This is particularly apparent when considering function units that require *only* wire. For example, a 32×32 port crossbar switch with 64 bits per port requires $64K\chi^2$ of area but zero gates. This is much more than would be estimated by an average area of about $10\chi^2$ per gate. Other wire-only functions include permutations and bit-selections, for example as encountered in common cryptography algorithms such as data encryption standard.

Global wiring is considerably more expensive than local wiring because it runs a longer distance. Consider, for example, a group of 64 signals that run the length of a 12-mm datapath. Each wire runs a length of 10^4 tracks, giving a cost of $6.4 \times 10^5 \chi^2$ or about 20 cents for the entire bus, which is more than was required for ten times as many wires in the register file example above.

Printed circuit boards can also be wire-limited when there is little locality of connection. For example, if every pin on twenty 500-pin 30-mm square packages must cross the center of a 200-mm board, the required wire density is 50 wires/mm or 20 μm/wire. With a typical pitch of 250 μm, a minimum of thirteen signal layers in just this one direction would be required to carry the wires, not counting area required by vias. Adding in power, ground, and return planes as well as signal layers in the perpendicular directions, the number of layers would be prohibitively expensive.

Table 3-5 gives a rough tabulation of wire costs at different levels of a system in terms of both dollars per χ^2 and dollars per millimeter of wire. The χ^2 numbers

wafers that yield about 100 good chips each. The incremental cost of fabricating a wafer, labor and materials, is about $200 ($2 per chip). Silicon foundries, however, may charge as much as $3,000 per wafer ($30 per chip) to cover the depreciation on their very expensive fabrication equipment. After several years, when a process is mature and the equipment is *paid for*, fabrication costs approach the incremental costs. For this reason, high-volume, price-sensitive chips are often made in an older technology (e.g., 0.5 μm) where the wafer fabrication costs are much lower.

assume a single signal layer in each direction (as is usually the case when wiring a function unit), whereas the millimeter numbers assume that half of the signal layers are running in either direction. The table illustrates several interesting points. First, the cost per χ^2 of wire is two orders of magnitude cheaper on-chip than for the cheapest off-chip interconnect. This is one major reason why integration pays off. It is cheaper to integrate many functions on one large chip (until yield starts to fall off) than it is to connect several smaller chips using a higher level of packaging. Second, the cost per millimeter of wire remains roughly constant across the batch-fabricated portion of the packaging hierarchy (chips, MCMs, and boards). However, one can do a lot more with a millimeter of wire on a chip than at a higher level. In 1 mm, an on-chip wire can connect to several function units; an off-chip wire, on the other hand, must typically run 10 mm or more just to connect two chips. Finally, one pays a premium for dense off-chip interconnection as reflected in the price of the MCM and the 16-layer PC board.

3.5.2 Terminal Costs

If a chip or a board is *pin-limited*, the dominant cost becomes the cost of a terminal or pin. The cost of a pin-limited chip is the area required to support a given number of pins. For a peripheral-bonded chip, with a pad pitch of x (typically 125 μm), the area required for P pads is $(Px)^2/16$ (typically $9.8 \times 10^{-4} P^2 \text{mm}^2$). For example, a 500-pad chip (say 400 signal pads with 100 power pads) requires an area of at least 2.5×10^2 mm^2 (e.g., a square chip 15.6 mm on a side). If the logic on the chip is simple, most of this area will be unused and will serve only to provide room for the pads.

For area-bonded chips, the area required for a given number of pads increases linearly with the number of pads. For example, if the pads are on $x = 250$-μm centers, then the area for P pads is Px^2 (0.062 Pmm^2). In this case our 500-pad chip requires only 31 mm^2 (e.g., 5.6 mm on a side).

The cost of pin-limited chips increases linearly with area over a much larger range than for logic-limited chips because defects in the unused portions of the chip have little effect. For a 1996 chip with a cost per unit area of about 0.22 \$/mm^2, the cost per pin on a pin-limited chip is 11 cents for peripheral bonding and 1.4 cents for area bonding.

Packages affect the cost of terminals in a very nonlinear manner. Plastic packages, up to 352-pin plastic QFPs, are very inexpensive (about \$0.01 per pin) but often have poor electrical properties and can handle limited amounts of power. At the other extreme, large ceramic PGAs or BGAs with power planes, multiple signal layers, and heat *slugs* to aid thermal conduction can be very expensive (about \$0.10 per pin).

Circuit boards can be pin-limited in the same manner as chips. However with boards the cost is less severe because the unused area on the board is not populated with chips. Thus, with boards, the cost per pin is primarily the cost of the connector and its mate. For high-quality connectors, the cost is about 10 cents per pin.

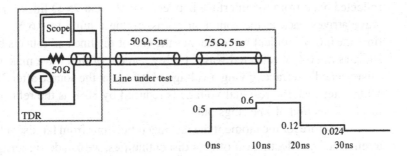

FIGURE 3-29   The Time-Domain Reflectometer

3.6   MEASUREMENT TECHNIQUES

Real transmission lines are complicated enough that the closed-form equations for electrical properties in Section 3.1 are not adequate to model a line accurately. In practice, engineers construct detailed electrical models of lines by first constructing detailed physical models of the line components (stripguide, cable, connectors, packages, etc.) and then using CAD software that numerically solves Maxwell's equations to extract the electrical parameters from the physical model.

Once the components for a line have been fabricated, the electrical model is validated in the laboratory. This validation can be performed either in the time domain using a time domain reflectometer or in the frequency domain using a network analyzer.

3.6.1   Time-Domain Measurements

3.6.1.1   The Time-Domain Reflectometer

A time-domain reflectometer (TDR) consists of a step generator and an oscilloscope configured as shown in Figure 3-29 to measure the step response of the source end of the line. The TDR is the most popular measuring instrument for characterizing interconnect because it requires access to only one end of the line (an important consideration in situations where it is hard to get at the other end of the line, let alone connect an instrument to both ends at the same time) and because it gives a measurement from which the line impedance as a function of length can be calculated. Thus, the TDR can be used to identify the location and nature of any discontinuities, including the end of the line, if it is unmatched.

As an example of TDR operation, the response to the two-segment line shown in Figure 3-29 is given in the figure. The unit step generator is matched to the line,[17] giving an initial voltage of 0.5 V. After 5 ns, 20% of the incident wave is

---

[17] If the line is other than 50 Ω, it is customary to add series or parallel resistance as required to match the source to the line. Although not strictly required, a matched source eliminates the problem of reflections off the source interfering with reflections from discontinuities.

reflected back from the interface between the 50- and 75-Ω lines. This reflected wave arrives back at the source at 10 ns, giving a jump to 0.6 V. At the same time the 0.6-V incident wave reaches the end of the line and reflects back off the short as a -0.6-V reflected wave. Eighty percent of this wave makes it past the mismatched interface, giving a voltage of 0.12 V at the source after 20 ns. Every 10 ns after that, the residual voltage is reduced by 80% as the reflected wave in the 75-Ω section of line rings out.

If we ignore for the moment the fact that reflections from far discontinuities are attenuated by reflecting off of near discontinuities, we can derive an approximate equation that relates impedance as a function of position to our observations of source voltage; beginning with Eq. (3-37), we get

$$(3\text{-}62) \qquad Z(x) = Z_0 \left[\frac{V(2x/v)}{1 - V(2x/v)} \right]$$

For a clean line, where all discontinuities are small, this equation works well because reflected signals arrive back at the source essentially unscathed. However, in extreme situations, such as the 50% mismatch illustrated in Figure 3-29, the effect of upstream discontinuities on reflected signals cannot be ignored.

A more accurate approximation considers the second reflection of the incident wave, ignoring the third and subsequent reflections. To derive the impedance equation for this approximation, assume that we have segmented the line into sections of roughly uniform impedance and that the voltage observed at the source from the reflection off the interface of sections i and $i - 1$ is V_i. Let the actual voltage induced at this interface by the incident wave be U_i. Then from Eqs. (3-62) and (3-37) the reflection coefficient and transmission coefficient at the interface between sections i and $i - 1$ are given by

$$(3\text{-}63) \qquad k_{ri} = \frac{U_i - U_{i-1}}{U_i + U_{i-1} - 2U_iU_{i-1}}$$

$$k_{ti} = 1 - |k_{ri}|$$

To calculate the observed voltage we must consider the change in the voltage at the interface, $\Delta U_i = U_i - U_{i-1}$. At each interface, a portion of this change is reflected, and a portion is transmitted with the relative amounts given by Eq. (3-63). Thus, the change in observed voltage $\Delta V_i = V_i - V_{i-1}$ is given by

$$(3\text{-}64) \qquad \Delta V_i = \Delta U_i \prod_{j=1}^{i-1} k_{tj}$$

This equation can be rewritten to give an iterative expression for actual voltage in terms of observed voltage.

$$(3\text{-}65) \qquad U_i = U_{i-1} + \frac{\Delta V_i}{\prod_{j=1}^{i-1} k_{tj}}$$

Because the k_{tj} terms in Eq. (3-65) only depend on prior values of U, we can solve for the actual voltages along the line by starting at the source and working to the right.

TABLE 3-6 **Example Calculation of Impedance from Observed Voltage**

i	V_i (V)	ΔV_i (V)	k_{ri}	k_{ti}	U_i (V)	Z_i
0	0.5				0.5	50
1	0.5	0	0	1	0.5	50
2	0.6	0.1	0.2	0.8	0.6	75
3	0.12	−0.48			0	0

Table 3-6 illustrates this calculation for the example transmission line and reflectometer waveform shown in Figure 3-29. The first row of the table, $i = 0$, corresponds to the section of line in the instrument and is used to initialize the calculation with $V_0 = U_0 = 0.5$. Each of the next three rows corresponds to an interface: $i = 1$ is the matched interface between the 50-Ω line and the interface, $i = 2$ is where the line jumps to 75 Ω, and $i = 3$ is the short at the end of the line. The second column lists the observed voltage from each of these interfaces taken directly from the waveform in Figure 3-29. The next column gives the differential version of the observed voltage, ΔV_i. The next two columns give the reflection and transmission coefficients for the interface calculated from Eq. (3-63) using the values of U_i from lines above. The next column gives the actual voltage at the interface, U_i, from Eq. (3-65) using the values of transmission coefficients from the lines above. The final column gives the impedance, Z_i, calculated from Eq. (3-62). In this case the impedance is exact because the observed waveforms do not yet include any contributions from tertiary or greater reflections. This will not always be the case. However, the effect from later reflections is usually small, for these reflections are attenuated by the cube of the reflection coefficient or more.

3.6.1.2 Rise Time and Resolution

The spatial resolution of a TDR is set by the rise time of the step.[18] A step with rise time t_r is able to resolve a discontinuity with length

$$(3\text{-}66) \qquad \Delta x > t_r v$$

Because of frequency-dependent attenuation, the rise time is sharper and the resolution finer at the source end of the line, but both degrade as the step propagates down the line. This degradation is caused by two phenomena. First, the skin-effect resistance of the line disperses the pulse, as discussed in Section 3.3.4.4. Second, an isolated lumped element or a section of mismatched line has a low-pass effect that further increases the rise time. Thus, the resolution of a TDR is limited both by the rise time of the source and by the frequency response of the line. The saving grace here is that if the line low-passes the TDR step so that it cannot measure a small discontinuity, then the line will also low-pass signals so they are not affected by the discontinuity.

---

[18] Of course the resolution can be no better than the frequency response of the scope. However, usually the rise time is the limiting factor, not the scope bandwidth.

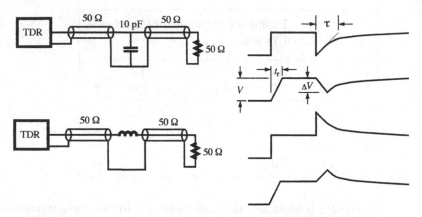

FIGURE 3-30 TDR Response from Lumped Discontinuities

3.6.1.3 Lumped Discontinuities

The TDR is also quite effective at measuring the position and value of a lumped load on a line. Figure 3-30 illustrates the TDR response from a parallel capacitor (top) and a series inductor (bottom). For each case, two traces are shown. The top trace of each set shows the response for an ideal step with zero rise time. The bottom trace shows the response where the step has a rise time t_r. Because a capacitor is an AC short, its TDR response with an ideal step goes momentarily to zero and then returns to 0.5 V with a time constant, τ_C. Inasmuch as the capacitor sees the parallel combination of the line impedance in each direction, this time constant is

$$(3\text{-}67) \qquad \tau_C = Z_0 C / 2$$

Similarly, because an inductor is an AC open, its response momentarily doubles to 1 V and then decays back to 0.5 V with a time constant, τ_L. Here the inductor is in series with the two line sections; consequently, the time constant is

$$(3\text{-}68) \qquad \tau_L = L/(2Z_0)$$

When the lumped circuit element is hit with a step with a nonzero rise time, t_r, the response does not go all the way to zero. Because the portion of the response from the early part of the step has decayed before the latter parts of the step arrive, the peak magnitude of the discontinuity is

$$(3\text{-}69) \qquad \frac{\Delta V}{V} = \left(\frac{\tau}{t_r}\right)\left[1 - \exp\left(-\frac{t_r}{\tau}\right)\right]$$

Thus, three quantities can be measured from the shape of the response. The position of the lumped discontinuity is given by the onset of the response. The time constant of the tail of the response gives the magnitude of the discontinuity, and the rise time can be calculated from the peak magnitude of the response.

Unfortunately, lumped discontinuities low-pass the incident wave from the TDR with cutoff frequency of $f_c = 1/\tau$, resulting in degraded spatial resolution.

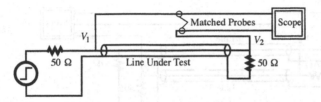

FIGURE 3-31   Transmission Measurement of a Line

In practice this is one of the most difficult measurement problems because even the best connectors used to attach the TDR to the line under test, such as edge-launch SMAs, will have enough lumped inductance and capacitance to low-pass the 20-ps edge of a good TDR head, such as a Tektronix 11801B with an SD-32 sampling head.

3.6.1.4 Transmission Measurements

If an additional scope channel of the TDR is connected to the far end of the line under test, as illustrated in Figure 3-31, transmission measurements can be performed to measure dispersion. The attenuation and delay of the line as a function of frequency can be determined from the Fourier transforms of the transmitted and received waveform. For accuracy, transmission measurements are performed differentially by comparing the waveform at the beginning of the line to the waveform at the end of the line using matched probes. This eliminates errors due to the nonzero rise time of the step and frequency-dependent attenuation of the step between the generator and the line under test.

The transmission measurement in effect measures the transfer function, $H(j\omega)$, for the line. If the measured source voltage is V_1, and the measured receive voltage is V_2, as illustrated in Figure 3-31, then the transfer function is calculated by numerically computing the Fourier transforms of the two voltages, $V_1(j\omega)$ and $V_2(j\omega)$, and dividing as follows:

$$(3\text{-}70) \qquad\qquad H(j\omega) = V_2(j\omega)/V_1(j\omega)$$

Using this measured transfer function, the response of the line to any input, V_x, can be calculated by transforming the input to the frequency domain, computing $V_y(j\omega) = V_x(j\omega)H(j\omega)$, and transforming the result back to the time domain. As described in Section 3.6.2, a network analyzer measures this frequency response in a more direct manner.

Transmission measurements are very poor at locating or isolating discontinuities because the effect of all the discontinuities along the line is superimposed on a single arriving edge at the far end. Reflection measurements are better for these purposes because the effect of the discontinuities are spread out in time.

3.6.1.5 Cross Talk Measurements

By taking measurements from two lines as illustrated in Figure 3-32, a TDR can make direct measurements of forward and reverse cross talk. As with the transmission measurement on a single line, the cross talk transfer functions, H_f

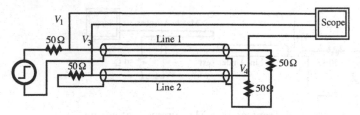

FIGURE 3-32 Setup for Cross talk Measurement

and H_r, are calculated by numerically transforming the measurements to the frequency domain and dividing.

3.6.2 Network Analysis

The internal components of a typical network analyzer are shown in Figure 3-33. The *source* is a sinusoidal generator whose output frequency can be swept over the frequency bands of interest. The *receiver–detector* can perform phase-sensitive measurements on any of several input channels, usually two or more. Phase measurements are made relative to the source oscillator. Phase and amplitude from each of the receiver input channels are passed to the *computation and display* unit, which computes any of a large number of possible measurements (transmission, reflection, scattering matrices, equivalent impedances, etc.) and displays the results, usually on a raster display that presents numerical and graphical information simultaneously. Graphical information is usually in the form of a plot of electrical parameters versus frequency. The *test set* is an interconnection box that is configured differently for each kind of measurement to be performed; the interconnections to and from the test set are transmission lines. In general, the test set contains circuitry to measure the incident and reflected energy at each port of the network under test.

Test sets in network analyzers for higher frequencies (1 GHz and higher) make use of *directional couplers*. A directional coupler is shown in cartoon form on the left side of Figure 3-34. It consists of two transmission lines that are coupled over a short distance. If the short line is terminated at Z_A in its characteristic impedance and the coupling parameters between the lines are set appropriately, the voltage across Z_A is proportional *only* to the amplitude of the forward-traveling wave from the source to Z_1, independent of the value of Z_1. A coupler of this sort is symmetric, and thus a signal reflected from the load back to the source produces a voltage on Z_B that depends only on the amplitude of the reflection, provided

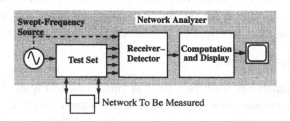

FIGURE 3-33 Network Analyzer Block Diagram

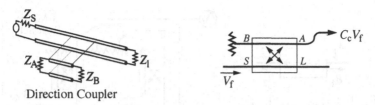

Direction Coupler

FIGURE 3-34 Directional Coupler

Z_B is set at the characteristic impedance of the short line. The behavior of a directional coupler can be understood qualitatively based on the derivation of cross talk in coupled transmission lines (Section 6.3). The interested reader is referred to [Mat69] for a derivation of the remarkable properties of directional couplers.

Figure 3-35 shows simple test sets configured to measure the transmission coefficient on a two-port network (left). A directional coupler samples the forward-traveling wave input to the network into one receiver channel, and the network's output is sampled by a second receiver channel. Such a setup could be used to find the transfer function for a piece of lossy transmission line, as shown in Eq. (3-70), for example. Network analyzers are handy for measuring impedances of components (single-port networks); a test set for impedance measurements is shown on the right side of Figure 3-35 that samples the forward and reflected signals on the line between the source and the impedance under test.

Scattering matrices or *S-matrices* provide a concise way of specifying all of the properties of a network, and many network analyzers are configured for S-matrix measurements. As shown in Figure 3-36, the S-matrix relates the (complex) amplitudes of the signals leaving a network (B_i) to the amplitudes of the signals incident on the network (A_i). A test set that simultaneously measures the four S-parameters of a two-port network is shown on the right side of the figure.

The design and assembly of *fixturing* suitable for accurate high-frequency measurements are complex. At the least, test fixtures that connect the analyzer to the device under test consist of short lengths of transmission line. These lines present an impedance between the instrument and the device to be tested, thereby altering any measurements that are made. Modern analyzers include a set of standard terminating devices (shorts, opens, and resistive terminations); by making measurements on these standard terminators attached successively at the DUT connections of the fixture, the effects of the fixture can be subtracted from later

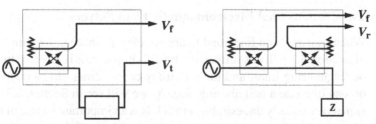

Test Set for Transfer Function   Test Set for Impedance Measurements

FIGURE 3-35 Test Sets for Transfer Function and Impedance

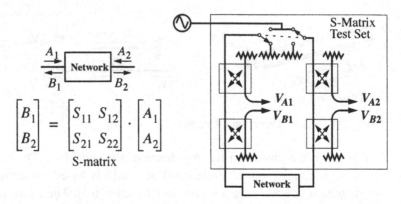

FIGURE 3-36   S-matrix Measurements with a Network Analyzer

measurements. Fixtures and standard terminations are precision-machined items and require careful handling in order to make accurate, repeatable measurements.

3.6.3   CAD Tools for Characterizing Wires

A vital part of a practicing engineer's working knowledge is facility with tools to *design and specify* the wires that carry the signals in a system and to *analyze* wires that are generated by board and chip design systems. We briefly outline some of the commonly used tools for this purpose.

3.6.3.1   Spreadsheets

In Section 3.1 we developed simple formulas for capacitance, inductance, resistance, and characteristic impedance for some simple arrangements of transmission line conductors. These formulas, and others that have been published for more complex situations, can readily be entered into a general-purpose computer spreadsheet such as Microsoft EXCEL or into math-oriented packages such as MATLAB. With modest effort, a spreadsheet can be constructed that will simultaneously compute the characteristic impedances of all signal layers in a PC board stackup, allowing the designer to balance wire impedance and signal integrity issues against mechanical constraints such as available material and overall thicknesses. The reader is referred to [Matick95] and [JohnGrah93] for a variety of formulas suitable for this kind of calculation; the authors of the latter reference offer their formulas on computer-readable media for use with MATHCAD.

3.6.3.2   Two-Dimensional Electromagnetic Field Solvers

When transmission line conductors are closely spaced, the simple formulations of Section 3.1 will not suffice. Each line's impedance is affected by the proximity of neighboring lines, and the proximity causes *cross talk*, a coupling of signals on one line into a neighboring line. As we will see in Section 6.3, these coupled signals are usually undesirable; cross talk is an important source of noise in digital systems. As a first step in both design and analysis of closely spaced signal wires, we can make the approximation that wires are infinitely long. This approximation reduces a three-dimensional problem to a two-dimensional problem that can be solved numerically with relatively modest computational requirements. A two-dimensional analysis will yield inductance, capacitance, and resistance per unit length for each line, and capacitance and inductance matrices that describe the coupling between each pair of lines. These can be plugged into a lumped-element circuit model for AC and transient analyses in a circuit simulator. A popular program for personal computers that supports this type of analysis is LINPAR [DjorHarr89]; a user inputs the dimensions and geometry of one of a variety of common multiconductor transmission line arrangements, and the program calculates characteristic impedances, line losses due to DC resistance and skin effect, and capacitance and inductance matrices. Some circuit simulators, such as HSPICE, support 2D multiconductor transmission line models as parameterized circuit elements where the parameters include the geometry and dimensions of the wires and dielectrics.

3.6.3.3 Signal Integrity Software Packages

Figure 3-37 shows an X-ray view of a small area and a few layers of a modern PC board. The figure shows a small region of the layout, displaying only three of twelve signal layers. Visible on the left are the lands for a ball-grid array. Near the center are the rectangular pads for a quad flat-pack. The figure is about 3 times actual size.

In a complex board, each of several thousand signal traces can potentially interact with any of the other traces on the board. Because of this combinational explosion, it is practically impossible to analyze by hand the impedance of each single trace and its coupling to neighboring traces. To meet this formidable challenge, commercial CAD vendors have introduced tools that perform a cross talk triage on all of the traces on a board extracted automatically from the board layout. Problem traces, identified on the basis of signal integrity rules, can then

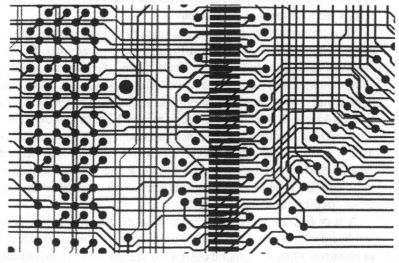

FIGURE 3-37 PC Board Routing Example (courtesy Steve Tell)

be analyzed in detail by employing field solvers. Tools of this kind, for example Quad Design's tool package, work with the layout design tools from other vendors; they tend to be quite expensive but may pay for themselves by identifying problems in aggressive designs in advance of fabrication and prototyping.

3.6.3.4   3D Electromagnetic Field Solvers

Many of the interconnect structures that support signaling in digital systems cannot be characterized using the 2D, long-conductor approximation. Examples include vias in multilayer PC boards, MCMs, and connector and socket pins. For signaling rates of tens or even hundreds of megabits per second, edge rates are sufficiently slow that these 3D structures can be approximated as small lumped elements. As signaling speeds increase, however, new tools will be needed that can analyze the effects of 3D structures on wave propagation. 3D field solvers have been topics of research for some years. Some experimental software packages have been developed and tested, and a few have begun to make their way into more general use. The LC package [Thomas97], developed at Cray/Silicon Graphics and based on results of several university research projects, is an example of a 3D field solver package that is approaching general usability. A full solution to a complex 3D conductor geometry is very demanding computationally; hours of computation on a parallel supercomputer may be required to analyze a single small structure. Computing cycles are getting cheaper all the time, however, and we expect to see 3D field solvers in general use in the not-too-distant future.

3.7   SOME EXPERIMENTAL MEASUREMENTS

In this section we present some typical measurements one might want to perform in support of the design and analysis of a signaling system. In each case we will compare the experimental results with the predictions of the simple theoretical results we have derived in this chapter.

Measurements of impedance, attenuation, and interaction between individual transmission lines are extremely difficult to perform on "real" PC boards – boards designed to support and interconnect the components of an actual system. First, instruments such as TDRs and network analyzers require cabling from their front-panel connectors to the circuit under test. It is almost impossible to attach a cable to board solder pads or lands intended to receive IC packages or connectors without introducing a significant impedance discontinuity. This large discontinuity will usually mask various subtle effects one might wish to measure accurately. Second, "real" boards may have thousands of interacting traces, and thus it is generally quite difficult to separate the various interactions that affect the impedance of a given circuit trace along its length.

A very fruitful approach to measuring PC board behavior is to construct a test board whose only purpose is to provide sites for measuring transmission-line phenomena. Once the general design parameters for an interconnect system have been selected, a test board can be constructed that has the same layer stackup,

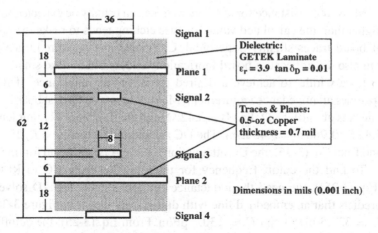

FIGURE 3-38 Test Board Dimensions and Parameters

geometric design rules, and materials as the final system board. The cabling problem is solved by providing *edge launchers* at each end of each test structure on the test board. These are special connectors, usually of the SMA variety, designed to provide a constant impedance transition from cable to board trace. The complexity problem is addressed by placing only the simplest structures on the test board; each test structure should be designed so as to vary only one parameter of interest, while others are held constant. Simple "straight-through" board traces with edge launchers should be included to assess the quality of the cable-to-board connections. Test boards of this sort are used in the measurements outlined in the following sections.

3.7.1 Frequency-Dependent Attenuation in a PC Board Trace

In Section 3.3 we developed simple models for frequency-dependent attenuation due to conductor skin effect and dielectric absorption. In this section we will show how closely these simple models approximate the behavior of an embedded strip-line in a test PC board.

The test board's stackup is intended to model that of a typical six-layer board of 0.062-in. thickness. The board stackup dimensions and material parameters are summarized in Figure 3-38. The dimensions shown are intended to yield 50-Ω microstrips on the board surface and 50-Ω embedded striplines between the planes. The measurements in this section are on two test structures. The first (line A) is approximately 0.2 m long; the second (line B) is about 1 m long.

3.7.1.1 DC Resistance and Attenuation Calculations

The exact lengths of the two test lines are best found from the PC board design system; line A is 0.988 m long, and line B is 0.206 m long. The cross section of the two lines is 8×0.7 mils or 203×17.8 μm. The DC resistance is found from $R = \rho L/A$, where $\rho = 1.7 \times 10^{-8}$ $\Omega \cdot$m is the resistivity of copper. Line A's resistance should be 0.97 Ω, line B's resistance is 4.65 Ω.

Measured resistance for a PC board trace can usually be expected to be slightly higher than the calculated value because etching tends to make the cross section of board traces slightly trapesoidal. Calculated and measured trace resistances can also differ because board fabrication vendors often make small adjustments to trace widths to achieve a desired characteristic impedance, if the designer specifies an impedance requirement. Measurements on the test board indicate that line A is about 1.13 Ω, line B is 5.42 Ω, and the resistance per unit length is $R = 5.42\,\Omega/0.988\,\text{m} = 5.48\,\Omega/\text{m}$. The DC attenuation factor, $\alpha_R = R/2Z_0$, is 0.0548, and from Eq. (3-46), the DC attenuation for line A is 0.978 and for line B is 0.907.

To find the cutoff frequency for the transition from RC to RLC behavior (Eq. (3-25)), we need the inductance per unit length. The 2D solver LINPAR predicts that an embedded line with dimensions shown in Figure 3-38 will have $L = 327.5$ nH/m and $C = 130.7$ pF/m. From Eq. (3-25), the cutoff frequency for RC behavior is $f_0 = R/(2\pi L) = 2.66$ MHz. The time constant (RC) for this line is $5.48\,\Omega \cdot 130.7\,\text{pF} = 716$ ps.

For the (shorter) line A terminated at 50 Ω, we would expect to see a steady-state attenuation of 0.98, from Eq. (3-25), and an exponential tail with time constant $(0.206\,\text{m})^2 \cdot 716\,\text{ps} = 30$ ps given by the second of Eqs. (3-24). For the (longer) line B, the steady-state attenuation is 0.91, and the RC time constant is $(0.988\,\text{m})^2 \cdot 716\,\text{ps} = 699$ ps. The response of each line to a fast pulse is shown in Figure 3-39. The figure shows screen dumps from a Tektronix 11801A sampling scope. A TDR head was used to produce the fast ($\sim$20 ps) input pulse to the line, and a sampler was used to record the output shown in the figure.

The response of a physical lossy line does not look exactly like the waveforms in Figure 3-17, because, in addition to the DC losses, the real lines exhibit frequency-dependent losses due to skin effect and dielectric absorption. These effects slow and round off the initial part of the output edge. However, the tail of the response conforms well to our simple development for RC behavior in Section 3.3.2.

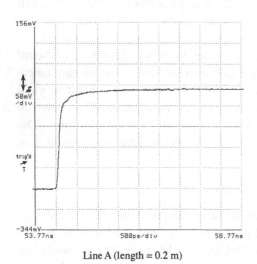

Line A (length = 0.2 m)

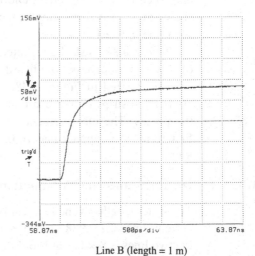

Line B (length = 1 m)

FIGURE 3-39 Response of Embedded Striplines to Fast Edge

TABLE 3-7   Calculated and Measured DC Loss Terms in Striplines

	Calculated DC Attenuation	Measured DC Attenuation	Calculated $\tau = RC$(ps)	Measured $\tau = RC$(ps)
Line A	0.98	0.97	30	29
Line B	0.91	0.90	699	700

Table 3-7 summarizes the calculated and measured response in the long tails. Measurements were made on a numerical dump of the screen data shown in Figure 3-39 (often the most convenient form), and they are in good agreement with calculation.

3.7.1.2   High-Frequency Attenuation Factors

The skin-effect frequency is found from Eq. (3-51) (with $\mu = \mu_0 = 4\pi \times 10^{-7}$ H/m, and $r = t/2 = 8.9\,\mu$m); $f_s = 54.4$ MHz. To compute the attenuation factor for the embedded line, we must take into account the losses in the return planes because these are significant at high frequencies. As a crude estimate, we will assume that the current flows in a region whose width is the same as the stripline conductor and whose thickness is one skin depth. This estimate just doubles the skin-depth resistance of the line. From Eq. (3-53), the attenuation factor is, then, $\alpha_S = 0.470\,f^{1/2}$ per meter, where f is in gigahertz.

From Eq. (3-56) we can calculate the attenuation factor for dielectric absorption in the GETEK board material used for the test board. Permittivity ε_r, is 3.9, and $\tan \delta_D$ is about 0.01, from which $\alpha_D = 0.207 \cdot f$ (1/m, f in gigahertz).

A network analyzer is an ideal instrument to examine these effects. Figure 3-40 is a photograph of the setup used for measuring the frequency-dependent attenuation in our test board, which is connected to a Hewlett–Packard 8753D Network Analyzer.

The network analyzer is configured to measure S_{21}, the ratio of power out of the output port to power into the input port of a 2-port network. Figure 3-41 shows the results for the 1-m line (line B). The power ratio (in decibels) has been converted to an amplitude ratio and plotted against the log of the frequency. For comparison, we have included a simple calculated model for the attenuation. Below the skin-depth frequency ($f_s = 54.4$ MHz), we assume that the losses are entirely due to line resistance, which varies linearly with frequency between $R = R_{DC} = 5.48\ \Omega$/m at low frequencies to $2R$ at the skin-depth frequency.

$$(3-71) \qquad \frac{|V_X|}{|V_0|} = \exp\left[-\frac{R_{DC}(1 + f/f_s)}{2Z_0}x \right]$$

This crudely accounts for the variation in resistance in the signal return planes with frequency. Above the skin-depth frequency, we compute the attenuation using the previously calculated attenuation factors for skin effect and dielectric

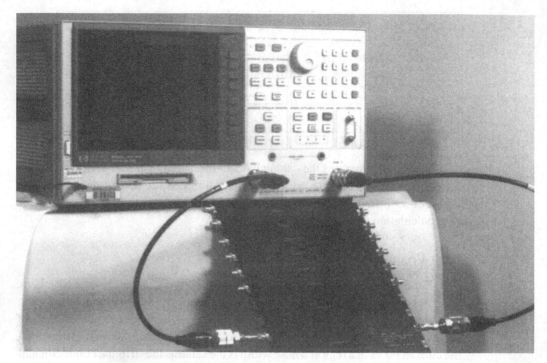

FIGURE 3-40 Test Setup for Measuring Frequency-Dependent Attenuation

loss as follows:

$$(3\text{-}72) \quad \frac{|V_X|}{|V_0|} = \exp(-\alpha_D x) \cdot \exp(-\alpha_S x)$$

$$= [\exp(-0.207 f \cdot 0.988) \cdot \exp(-0.470 f^{1/2} \cdot 0.988)]$$

The data shown in Figure 3-41 indicate that this simple model accounts reasonably well for the observed losses in a PC board transmission line.

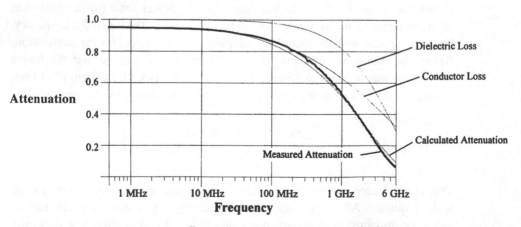

FIGURE 3-41 Comparison of Measured and Calculated Loss in Line B

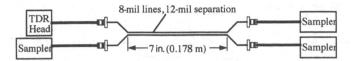

FIGURE 3-42   Cross-Talk Test Structure for Embedded Striplines

3.7.2   Cross Talk in Coupled Lines

When two transmission lines run parallel for some distance, a forward-traveling wave on one line will induce, in general, both forward and reverse traveling waves on the second, close-by line. As we discussed in Section 3.6.2, useful devices such as directional couplers can be constructed from coupled transmission lines. In a signaling system, however, coupling between adjacent signal lines is usually an unwanted source of noise called cross talk. In this section, we will outline the measurement of cross talk between pairs of lines on a test board.

3.7.2.1   Coupled Embedded Striplines

This test structure, included on the same test board as the attenuation test site, is sketched in Figure 3-42.

In this test setup, a TDR is used to drive one of the lines with a fast-rise-time pulse. Samplers are connected to the far end of the driven line and to both ends of the quiet line. All of the connections between the TDR/samplers and the board are made using low-loss, semirigid coaxial cables, which are all cut to exactly the same length (to simplify timing measurements). The test setup, using a Tektronix 11801A sampling oscilloscope with an SD-24 TDR/sampling head and SD-26

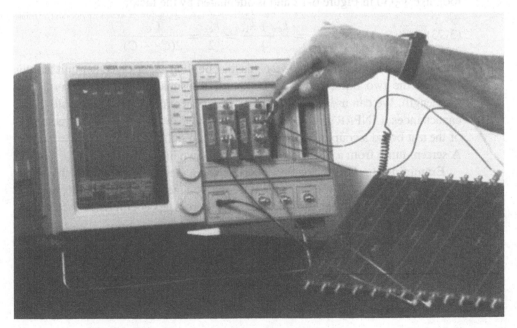

FIGURE 3-43   Photograph of Cross-Talk Measurement Setup

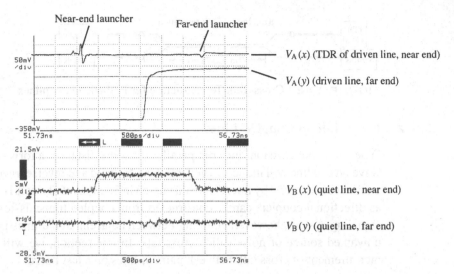

FIGURE 3-44   Cross-Talk Measurement in Coupled Embedded Striplines

dual sampler, is shown in Figure 3-43. Note that four equal-length semirigid coaxial lines connect the instrument to the test board. An operator is tightening an SMA connector with a special torque wrench.

As discussed in Section 6.3.2.3 and Section 6.3.2.4, under the special conditions that two coupled lines are homogeneous transmission lines terminated in their characteristic impedance, we expect to see no forward cross talk. The coupling terms due to mutual capacitance and to mutual inductance are identical in a homogeneous line and cancel in Eq. (6-19) for forward cross talk. For reverse cross talk, given by Eq. (6-16), the signal at the near end of the quiet line should look like $V_B(x)$ in Figure 6-12 and is attenuated by the factor

$$(3\text{-}73) \qquad k_{rx} = \frac{k_{cx} + k_{lx}}{4} = \frac{k_{cx}}{2} = \frac{C_C}{2(C_C + C)}$$

where the last step uses Eq. (6-8), C_C is the coupling capacitance per unit length between the two lines, and C is the single transmission line capacitance per unit length. We can use a field solver or empirical expressions to estimate these capacitances; LINPAR gives $C_C = 8.26$ pF/m and $C = 120$ pF/m for the geometry of the test board's coupled embedded striplines. From these values, $k_{rx} = 0.032$. A screen dump from a Tektronix 11801A is shown in Figure 3-44.

Examining the figure, we find that the voltage at the near end of the quiet line rises to about 7.5 mV (note the different voltage scales used for V_A and V_B measurements); therefore, the observed reverse cross talk coefficient is $7.5/250 = 0.03$, in agreement with the calculated value.

Note that the near-end signal persists for about 2.4 ns; this should correspond to twice the time required for a signal to traverse the coupled portion of the line (see Figure 6-12 and the accompanying discussion). The speed of light in the dielectric of the test board is $c(\varepsilon_r)^{-1/2} = 1.519 \times 10^8$ m/s or about 6 in./ns. The 7-in. of coupled trace should produce a near-end signal that persists for about

TABLE 3-8 Capacitance, Inductance, and Mutuals for Microstrip	
C	97 pF/m
C_S	10.2 pF/m
L	294 nH/m
M	58 nH/m

$2 \cdot 1.17$ ns $= 2.3$ ns, which is in reasonable agreement with the time measurement from the waveform $V_B(x)$.

The far-end cross talk is not zero but is very small ($k_{fx} < 0.1k_{rx}$), as we would expect for a homogeneous line. Note that the test structure is a directional coupler.

3.7.2.2 Coupled Inhomogeneous Lines

The test board also includes a site for cross-talk measurement between a coupled pair of *in*homogeneous transmission lines. For this measurement, we will use a pair of microstrips (striplines on the surface of the board, referenced to an internal plane). The setup is similar to that of Figure 3-42, except that the lines are drawn 36 mils wide separated by 16 mils.

The waveforms in Figure 3-45 show that there is significant far-end cross talk. Microstrips are explicitly inhomogeneous because there is a physical discontinuity in dielectric constant at the surface of the board with PC-board dielectric below and air above. On the basis of the discussion in Section 6.3.2, we would expect the forward cross talk coefficient to be nonzero because the inductive and capacitive coupling constants are not equal. The LINPAR results give, from Eqs. (6-8)

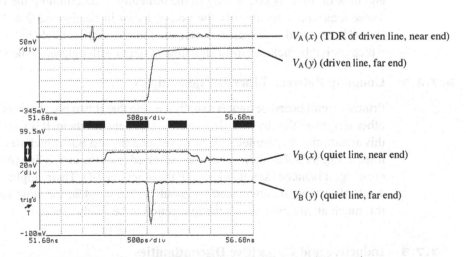

FIGURE 3-45 Cross-Talk Measurement in Coupled Microstrips

and (6-11),

$$k_{cx} = \frac{C_S}{C_S + C} = \frac{10.2}{10.2 + 97} = 0.095$$

(3-74)

$$k_{lx} = \frac{M}{L} = \frac{58}{294} = 0.196$$

and from Eqs. (6-16) and (6-19),

$$k_{rx} = \frac{k_{cx} + k_{lx}}{4} = 0.073$$

(3-75)

$$k_{fx} = \frac{k_{cx} - k_{lx}}{2(4)} = -0.051$$

The amplitude of the reverse cross-talk signal is about 17 mV, and thus the measured reverse cross-talk coefficient is 17 mV/250 mV = 0.068, in reasonable agreement with calculation.

The forward cross-talk amplitude depends not only on the forward cross-talk coefficient but also on the length of coupled section and the rise time of the edge that is generating the cross talk. The LINPAR solver predicts that the propagation speed in this microstrip is about 7 in./ns; therefore, the propagation time for the coupling is about 1.0 ns. Estimating the edge rise time is difficult because the rise time degrades as the edge propagates along the line. From the scope data, the rise time at the far end of the driven trace is about 125 ps; consequently, we might estimate the "average" edge rate along the coupled section at about 100 ps. From Eq. (6-18), we can calculate an expected amplitude of

(3-76) $$\frac{V_B(y)}{V_A(x)} = \frac{k_{fx} t_x}{t_r} = \frac{-0.051 \cdot 1.0}{0.1} = 0.5$$

The observed amplitude is 80/250 = 0.32, and the difference between calculation and measurement is due mainly to the difficulty of determining the rise time t_r. These measurements amplify the points drawn in Section 6.3.2.4. Microstrips should be avoided in situations where far-end cross talk is likely to be a problem, which probably includes most signaling systems with tight noise budgets.

3.7.2.3   Coupling Between Lines at Right Angles

Printed circuit board designers usually assume that if two board traces cross each other at right angles, there will be no cross talk between them. It is worth verifying this assumption experimentally, however, and the test board includes a site, outlined in Figure 3-46, for this purpose. As the edge on the driven line (A) passes the crossing, it launches small pulses into the quiet line (B). Their amplitude is about 1 mV; thus they are attenuated by about 1/250 = 0.4%; for most applications, this much attenuation allows the interaction to be safely ignored.

3.7.3   Inductive and Capacitive Discontinuities

In Section 3.3.1.4 we developed a simple model for the effect of point discontinuities, both capacitive and inductive, in transmission lines. Figure 3-47 shows

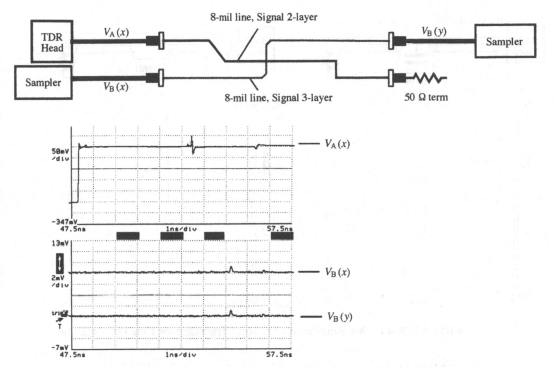

FIGURE 3-46 Test Structure and Measurements for Crossing Striplines

TDR screen dumps for two fairly extreme examples by way of illustrating the elements of the model.

These scope traces should be compared with the drawings in Figure 3-30. The measured decay times for the capacitive and inductive discontinuities are compared with calculations from Eqs. (3-67) and (3-68) in Table 3-9.

The rise time of the TDR step is much smaller than the decay time of either of these large discontinuities; consequently, the amplitude of the reflection at the discontinuity from Eq. (3-69) is approximately

$$\frac{\Delta V}{V} = 1 - \frac{1}{2}\frac{t_r}{\tau}$$

(3-77)

Note that the reflection at the capacitive discontinuity has a short positive spike ahead of the negative reflection from the capacitor; this is due to a small series–inductive discontinuity introduced in the process of attaching the capacitor to the cable. Working backwards from Eq. (3-77), we calculate the rise time for the edge as

$$t_r = 2\tau\left(1 - \frac{\Delta V}{V}\right) = 420\,\text{ps}$$

(3-78)

This calculation should be taken with considerable skepticism, for real inductors such as the 220-nH one we used for this experiment are far from ideal components. Most exhibit significant series resistance and capacitance in parallel with the inductance.

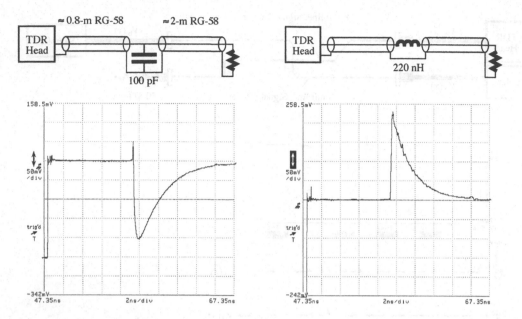

FIGURE 3-47   Measurements of (Large) Transmission Line Discontinuties

Many of the discontinuities of interest in real signaling systems have time constants that are comparable to or smaller than the rise time of the signal. We often want to know what effect these discontinuities will have on signal integrity, and part of a typical design process is constructing a circuit model that accurately represents the effects of such discontinuities. We conclude this section by investigating two physical structures often found in signaling systems, the *via* (a metal-plated hole that connects vertically between two wiring layers on a board), and the *slot* (a hole in the reference plane for a stripline).

A simple model for estimating the size of *small* lumped discontinuities assumes that $\tau \ll t_r$, and from Eq. (3-69)

$$(3\text{-}79) \qquad \tau = t_r \frac{\Delta V}{V}$$

Further, we will estimate t_r by measuring the leading edge of the reflection at the discontinuity.

Figure 3-48 outlines the results from the test board for TDR measurements on vias of two different sizes. From the TDR plots, vias appear to be almost

TABLE 3-9   **Measured Versus Calculated Decay Times for Point Discontinuties**

	τ_C	τ_L
Measured	2.6	2.1
Calculated	2.5	2.2

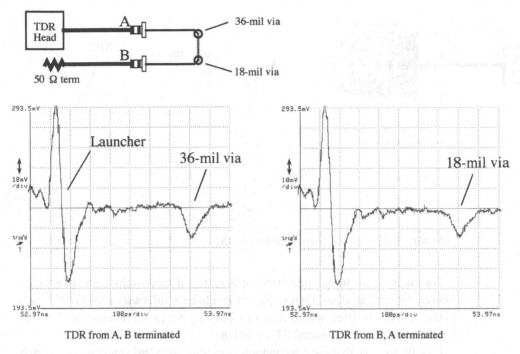

TDR from A, B terminated   TDR from B, A terminated

FIGURE 3-48   TDR Measurements on Vias

entirely capacitive discontinuities, and larger via diameters lead to larger capacitance, not surprisingly. Using the simple model of Eq. (3-79), for the large via we estimate t_r at about 50 ps, and $\Delta V/V = 15\,\text{mV}/250\,\text{mV} = 0.06$, and thus $\tau = 3$ ps, and $C_{\text{via}} = 0.12$ pF. A similar reading of the TDR for the small via gives $C_{\text{via}} = 0.096$ pF.

These measurements confirm the conventional wisdom that vias can safely be ignored in most signaling systems (see, for example, the discussion in Chapter 7 of [JohnGrah93]). However, your results may vary; in some special circumstances, (e.g., very small clearance holes, many planes), via capacitance could become significant. Measurements on a physical model are often inexpensive insurance against signaling problems.

As a second example, we examine a test structure for a slot in the return planes of a stripguide. Slots are often generated inadvertently in signal return planes in areas of a PC board that contain many closely spaced signal vias. Clearance holes are required around a signal via in each plane layer to prevent the signal from shorting to the plane. When many vias are clustered together, the clearance holes in the planes coalesce, removing a large continuous area of metal on the plane layer and thereby creating a slot.

A test structure and its TDR are shown in Figure 3-49. The slot is inductive; this is physically reasonable, for the return currents in the plane, which normally flow in a narrow band below the stripguide, must take a long diversion around the slot. Examining the TDR, t_r is about 50 ps, as in the via measurements, and $\Delta V/V = 75\,\text{mV}/250\,\text{mV} = 0.3$, from which we calculate an inductance of 3.5 nH.

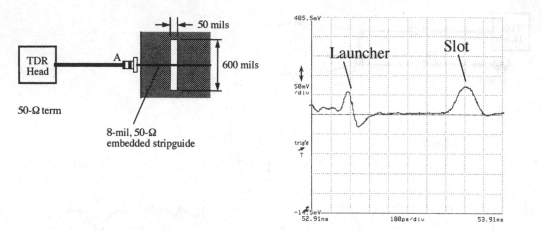

FIGURE 3-49   TDR Measurements on a Slot

For many applications, this large an inductive discontinuity cannot be safely ignored. In general, slots in return planes should be assiduously avoided. Not only do they adversely affect signal integrity, but they are excellent antennas that can generate significant unwanted RF radiation.

Finally, we note that the edge launchers on the test board are themselves fairly large impedance discontinuities (unfortunately!). The portion of the launcher that connects to the board appears to represent an inductance followed by a capacitance. The inductance arises from our failure to bring the board's reference planes all the way to the edge of the board; the capacitive discontinuity is associated with the connection of the lead to the board through a via.

For careful measurements, a better launcher would be desirable. Both edge launchers and right-angle launchers can provide good impedance matches to PC boards. The quality of the launch depends critically on the details of the board layout for the launcher attachment. Recommendations for using a right-angle launcher are outlined in Figure 3-50. The board has a higher dielectric constant than the dielectric in the connector (usually Teflon), and thus this layout attempts to minimize the capacitance between the plated-through hole that accepts the center pin of the launcher and the surrounding clearance holes in the board planes. It turns out that, even with as large a clearance hole as practicable, the capacitance is still too large; therefore, the connector is mounted a small distance off the board to introduce a tiny compensating inductance in the center lead.

A TDR comparison of a high-quality right-angle launcher installation with our somewhat poorer edge launchers is shown at the bottom of the figure.

3.7.4   Measurement of IC Package Parasitics

In Section 2.3.5 we outlined some ideas for developing an electrical model for a package, if none is available. Such a model should, if possible, be confirmed by measurement, and a high-speed TDR with special fixturing is the appropriate

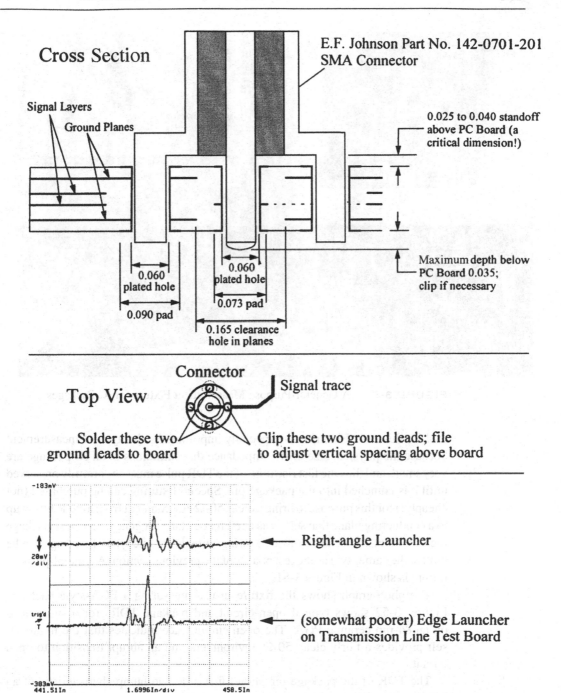

Cross Section

E.F. Johnson Part No. 142-0701-201
SMA Connector

Signal Layers

Ground Planes

0.025 to 0.040 standoff
above PC Board (a
critical dimension!)

0.060
plated hole

0.060
plated hole

0.090 pad

0.073 pad

0.165 clearance
hole in planes

Maximum depth below
PC Board 0.035;
clip if necessary

Top View

Connector

Signal trace

Solder these two
ground leads to board

Clip these two ground leads; file
to adjust vertical spacing above board

Right-angle Launcher

(somewhat poorer) Edge Launcher
on Transmission Line Test Board

FIGURE 3-50   PC Board Layout for a Right-Angle SMA Launcher (courtesy Al
Barber, Hewlett–Packard Laboratories)

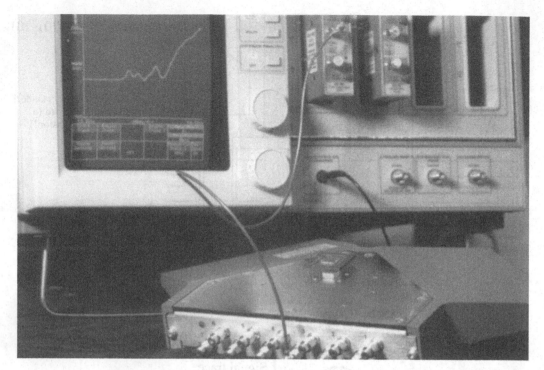

FIGURE 3-51   A General-Purpose Measurement Fixture for IC Packages

tool for this task. Fixturing is especially important for this type of measurement because the physical size of the impedance discontinuities in an IC package are very small, and thus the fast rise time of the TDR pulse must be carefully preserved until it is launched into the package pin. Special fixturing can be purchased (not cheaply!) for this purpose to bring a clean 50-Ω environment from a cable fitting up to a conducting plane that serves as a reference plane for general-purpose package measurements. Special-purpose fixturing suitable for one type of package can be built in the same style as the test boards of the previous section. A general-purpose fixture is shown in Figure 3-51.

The photograph shows the fixture in use measuring a PGA-style package. Figure 3-52 shows typical open-circuit and package TDRs for a signal lead on an 84-pin ceramic PGA. The open circuit trace indicates that the fixture it-self provides a fairly clean 50-Ω environment and an abrupt transition to open circuit.

The TDR of the package pin shows first a double-hump characteristic of an L-C-L lumped discontinuity corresponding to the package's external pin. Next, a short, reasonably flat portion of trace corresponds to the package's printed trace between the external pin and the bond wire land. Finally, the trace shows a large inductive discontinuity followed by a capacitive one arising from the bond wire and chip bond pad.

We could estimate the values of the equivalent lumped components in this trace using the informal methods discussed in Section 3.7.3, but more precise

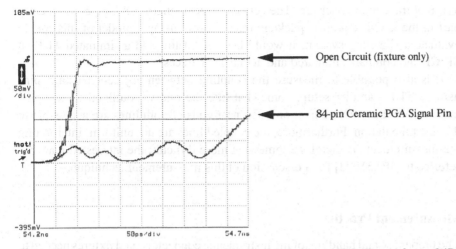

FIGURE 3-52 Open-Circuit and Package TDR Traces for an 84PGA

estimation of these parameters is possible taking into account the discussion in Section 3.6.1.1. There we noted that reflection from a downstream impedance discontinuity is affected by all of the discontinuities upstream of that point. These effects can be deconvolved numerically in a method called *Z-profiling*.

The Tektronix 11801A TDR/sampler we have been using for the measurements of this chapter can be equipped with a package that performs Z-profiles. Further, this software package can build approximate lumped-constant circuits for each user-identified portion of the TDR trace. Figure 3-53 shows the TDR of Figure 3-52 after Z-profile processing. With the leading double-hump approximated by an L-C-L circuit, the central flat portion by an ideal transmission line, and the last feature before the open-circuit by an L-C, the software produces the circuit shown at the right of the figure.

For this particular chip, the bond pad capacitance is 950 fF (from circuit extraction). The bond wire is 4.5 mm long; therefore, our rule of thumb (1 nH/mm) predicts 4.5 nH. Both are in good agreement with the extracted circuit. The speed of light in the aluminum oxide ceramic material of the package ($\varepsilon_r \approx 8.8$) is about 0.1 mm/ps, and thus the transmission line portion of the trace corresponds to about

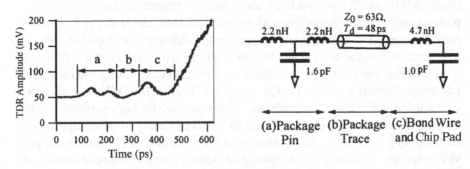

FIGURE 3-53 Z-Profile Data and Lumped Circuit Model for 84PGA

5 mm of trace in the package. The actual physical length is 8 mm; consequently part of the L-C-L circuit is package trace. Before using a model of this sort to evaluate a signaling system, it would be prudent to build a simulated TDR in SPICE and compare simulated and actual TDR traces.

It is also possible to measure the coupling between adjacent package pins using a TDR–sampler setup, somewhat like the one we outlined for coupled transmission lines. Of course, only the near ends of both lines are accessible to the instrumentation. Furthermore, the coupled lines are not uniform. Interpreting the measurements is therefore somewhat more difficult; the interested reader is referred to [IPA31093] for a discussion of this measurement technique.

3.7.5 Measurement Practice

The proper use and handling of the instruments, connectors, and fixtures needed to make high-frequency measurements is a fairly extensive subject in itself. High-frequency and microwave analysis equipment (e.g., TDR and sampling heads for high-frequency oscilloscopes) have voltage-sensitive input stages; great care should be taken to avoid applying voltages outside their allowed range, either from powered circuits or from accumulated static electrical charge. High-frequency connectors should be handled in such a way as to avoid introducing dirt and corrosion to their mating surfaces. Most high-performance connectors that use threaded fasteners have a specific torque to which they should be tightened for best impedance match; there are special torque wrenches for SMAs, for example, that simplify proper tightening. Before setting out to do measurements of the sort outlined in this section, it is advisable to consult instrument manuals, which often have useful outlines of proper measurement technique.

3.8 BIBLIOGRAPHIC NOTES

The classic text on transmission line is [Matick95]; it was so well-written (in 1969) that IEEE press reprinted the original text of the book in 1995. [Dworsky88] is another excellent text about transmission lines. Another excellent textbook is [Bakoglu90], which covers a large set of related subjects, including packaging, power, cooling, and signaling circuit design. Both [Matick95] and [JohnGrah93] provide empirical expressions for computing the characteristic impedance of various forms of transmission lines; the latter text has expressions suitable for use in a spreadsheet. The publications of the Institute for Interconnecting and Packaging Electronic Circuits were cited in Chapter 2; publication [IPCD95] contains much useful information about materials and design practice for high-performance PC boards. Information about cables (and an amazing variety of other topics) is to be found in [RefDat93]. The publications [SakuTama83] and [YuanTric82] provide empirical equations for computing capacitive coupling between conductors in a multiconductor interconnect. [JohnGrah93] provides considerable practical advice on the construction of effective signaling systems.

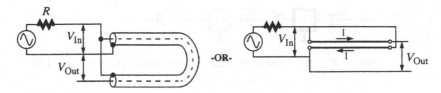

FIGURE 3-54   Transmission-Line Transformer

3.9   EXERCISES

3-1   **Example Transmission Lines:** Calculate the electrical properties (R_{DC}, C, L, and Z_0) of the following common transmission media: (a) a twisted pair made of "wire-wrap" wire; (b) RG-58 coaxial cable (compare your results with the published values); (c) a wire-wrap wire glued to the surface of a PC board, $\varepsilon_r = 4.5$ and 6 mil dielectric thickness to first plane layer (for this one, you can either ignore that the line is inhomogeneous or find the appropriate empirical formulas in one of the references). For this exercise, go to the manufacturer's data on common wire and cable to find the various physical and electrical parameters.

3-2   **Mismatched Terminations:** Section 3.3.3.7 works out the waveforms for an under-terminated transmission line. Find the reflection coefficients for an *over*terminated line, $Z_0 = 50\,\Omega$, $Z_T = 5\,\Omega$, $Z_S = 1\,k\Omega$. Assuming a traversal time of 2 ns, construct the equivalents of Table 3-3 and Figure 3-12. Build a SPICE deck that models this circuit. Perform a transient simulation and compare the results with your hand-constructed solution.

3-3   **Standing Waves:** Section 3.3.3.8 describes standing waves on a line terminated in an open circuit. Does a line driven sinusoidally at one end and terminated in a short circuit at the other exhibit standing waves? If so, write an expression for the location of the nodes on such a line.

3-4   **Transmission-Line Transformer:** Consider the circuit in Figure 3-54. Assume the frequency of the generator is high enough that the transmission line's outer conductor represents a large reactive impedance. What is the relationship between the output voltage and input voltage? What is the relationship between the impedance at the V_{Out} terminals and the input impedance, R? (Hint: The signal and return currents in an ideal transmission line are equal and opposite. In a real transmission line, this will be true if the inductive coupling between the two conductors is large.)

What are the voltage and impedance relationships in the circuit of Figure 3-55? If you have the means to do so, construct these circuits and verify your results with measurements. What happens at low frequencies? If a toroidal core of high-permeability

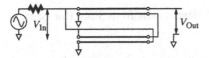

FIGURE 3-55   Mystery Transformer

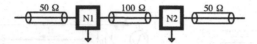

FIGURE 3-56   Resistive Matching Networks (for Exercise 3-6)

material is available, try wrapping your transmission line around this core. How does this affect the low-frequency behavior?

3-5 **Impedance Transformation:** If a lossless transmission line of characteristic impedance, Z_0, and length, l, driven sinusoidally, is terminated in an arbitrary impedance, Z_l, show that the impedance at the drive end is

(3-80)
$$Z_{\text{ln}} = Z_0 \left[\frac{Z_l + jZ_0 \tan \beta l}{Z_0 + jZ_l \tan \beta l} \right]$$

$$\beta = \omega\sqrt{LC}$$

The term β determines the rate at which the phase changes along the line and is equal to $2\pi/\lambda$, where λ is the wavelength of the excitation frequency. If the length of the line is $\lambda/4$, what is the input impedance as a function of load impedance? What is the input impedance when the line is shorted? Open?

3-6 **Resistive Matching Networks:** One can propagate a signal between transmission lines of differing impedance without reflections by inserting a matching network between the two lines. Consider the situation in Figure 3-56 where a signal is transmitted first over a 50-Ω line, then a 100-Ω line, then back to a 50-Ω line. Using only resistors, design the networks, N1 and N2, so that there are no reflections from a wave traveling from left to right. (Hint: This can be done with a single resistor for each network.) Now modify your design so that it works for a wave traveling in either direction. How much signal level is lost passing through the two networks? How much signal energy?

3-7 **Buses Without Stubs:** One can build a bus (multidrop transmission line) in which there are no reflections off the stubs by placing matching networks at each drop across the line, as shown in Figure 3-57.[19] Design the resistive matching network, N, shown in the figure so that a signal transmitted to the network from any of its three terminals is propagated out the other two terminals (possibly attenuated) with no reflections.

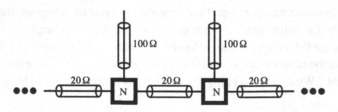

FIGURE 3-57   A Bus with No Reflections from Stubs (for Exercise 3-7)

---

[19] To avoid reflections off the end of the stubs, each stub is terminated into its characteristic impedance (100 Ω). This termination is not shown in the figure.

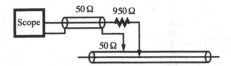

FIGURE 3-58   A Passive Attenuating Probe (for Exercise 3-8)

With the impedance values shown in the figure, 20-Ω bus and 100-Ω stubs, how much energy is lost from the signal traveling down the bus at each stub? How much energy would be lost if both the stubs and the bus were 50-Ω lines?

3-8   Bus with Attenuating Probes: In measuring signals on high-speed lines, it is common practice to use an *attenuating probe*, as illustrated in Figure 3-58. A 50-Ω transmission line with a 950-Ω series resistor taps the signal with a 20:1 attenuation while providing a negligible (1 kΩ) load to the line. Show how such a probe can be used to design a bus that has no reflections from the stubs (as in Exercise 3-7). (Hint: Because the end of the stub toward the bus is clearly mismatched, it must be driven with a source-terminated driver.) Give a formula that relates how the attenuation of the *probe* stubs can be traded off against the attenuation of a signal traveling along the bus.

3-9   Nonsinusoidal *Standing* Waves: Consider the circuit of Figure 3-59(a) below. The voltage source generates a periodic trapezoidal signal with the waveform shown in Figure 3-59(b). This signal is coupled to one end of a 5-ns-long 50-Ω line through a 100-kΩ resistor. The other end of the line is left open. Sketch the steady-state voltage at the open end of the line.

3-10   Nonlinear Termination: Consider the circuit of Figure 3-60. A voltage source with a 10-Ω output impedance drives a transmission line terminated into a pair of diodes (assume these are ideal diodes with no voltage drop) that restrict the range of the signal between 0 and 1 V. Sketch the waveforms that result at both ends of the line in response to a unit step on the voltage source.

3-11   Frequency-Dependent Termination: Often a termination includes a reactive element (intentionally or otherwise) that gives it a frequency-dependent impedance. Four frequency-dependent terminations are illustrated in Figure 3-61. In (a) a capacitor has been intentionally added to reduce the DC power dissipation of the termination. A series inductor in (b) models the bond-lead inductance seen by a signal before it arrives

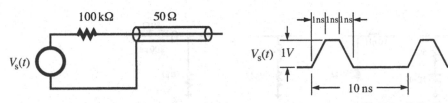

(a) Periodic Voltage Source Driving a Line   (b) Waveform from Voltage Source

FIGURE 3-59   Periodic Excitation of an Open Line (for Exercise 3-9)

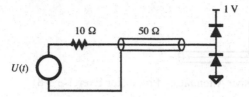

FIGURE 3-60   Nonlinear Termination (for Exercise 3-10)

at an on-chip termination resistor. The inductance on the side-path in (c) models the lead inductance of an off-chip terminator in a high-inductance (radial-lead, SIP, or DIP) package. The transmission-line stub in (d) models the case in which the termination is placed a small distance from the actual end of the line. For each of these four cases (1) plot the impedance seen by the signal as a function of frequency, and (2) sketch the waveform received (at the right side of the circuit) and reflected (from the left side of the circuit). Assume the termination is at the end of a 50-Ω transmission line. Consider signal rise times of 100 ps and 1 ns.

3-12   **Losses in Coaxial Cables:** Show that the high-frequency resistance of a coaxial cable is

(3-81)
$$R = \frac{1}{2}\sqrt{\frac{\rho\mu f}{\pi}}\left(\frac{1}{r_1} + \frac{1}{r_2}\right)$$

where r_1 and r_2 are the radii of the inner and outer conductors, respectively. Further, show that the losses due to the skin effect are minimized for a particular value of the ratio r_1/r_2.

An RG-58/U cable (a common 50-Ω coaxial) has an inner conductor of 0.032-in.-diameter copper wire, a solid polyethylene dielectric whose outer diameter is 0.116 in., and a braided copper outer shield. [Harper92] lists the electrical properties of (low-density) solid polyethylene as $\varepsilon_r = 2.28$, tan $\delta_D = 0.002$. Approximating the outer conductor as a solid copper cylinder, calculate and plot the loss per meter as a function of frequency up to 10 GHz. Find a reference that describes the losses in this cable and compare your results with the published data (usually reported in units of db/foot).

3-13   **Return Impedance and Coupled Lines:** Expand Eq. (3-57) to include the effects of mutual inductance.

3-14   **TDR Plots:** (a) Draw an idealized TDR trace for the circuit of Figure 3-29 but with an open circuit at the end instead of a short. (b) Assuming an idealized TDR with a

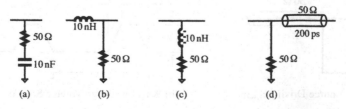

FIGURE 3-61   Frequency-Dependent Terminations (for Exercise 3-11)

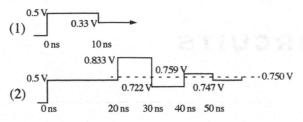

FIGURE 3-62   TDR Traces for Problem 3-14

50-ohm source step generator like the one in Section 3.6.1.1 (0.5-V step into 50 Ω), draw a schematic of the transmission line circuit that would produce each of the idealized TDR traces in Figure 3-62. (c) Draw idealized waveforms for the signal at the far end of the transmission line in (a) and both cases for (b).

3-15   **Lumped Discontinuities:** Idealized TDR traces for lumped parallel capacitive and series inductive discontinuities are shown in Figure 3-30; draw the waveforms you would expect to see at the far end of such a line, assuming that the line is terminated resistively in its characteristic impedance. What would the idealized TDR and far-end signals look like for a *series* capacitive and *parallel* inductive discontinuity?

3-16   **Extracting Parasitics:** Figure 3-63 shows a TDR trace from an unknown circuit. Develop a model circuit composed of ideal transmission lines, inductors, and capacitors that gives the same response. You may find it useful to simulate your model circuit with HSPICE to verify correspondence.

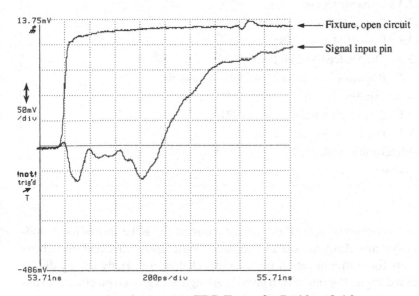

FIGURE 3-63   TDR Traces for Problem 3-16

4 CIRCUITS

Metal-oxide-semiconductor (MOS) transistor circuits lie at the core of most modern digital systems. They are used to construct logic, memories, and the drivers and receivers for communication lines. In this chapter we briefly survey digital MOS circuit design. The intent is to provide enough background on circuits to understand the circuit constraints on the system-level electrical problems discussed in later chapters.

We begin by describing the structure and operation of the metal-oxide-semiconductor field-effect transistor or MOSFET. The I–V characteristics of the MOSFET are described. We also address lumped circuit models of device parasitics and introduce a number of simpler models that are useful for approximate hand analysis of circuits.

After presenting the basic circuit elements, we move on to describe common circuit building blocks or idioms such as switches, gates, source followers, current mirrors, and source-coupled pairs. These idioms form the basic building blocks or subcircuits from which larger circuits are built. The first step in analyzing or designing a circuit is always to partition the circuit into a number of these idioms. The overall function of the circuit is then easily discerned, and its parameters follow from the parameters of its constituent subcircuits.

Our exploration of circuits starts in Section 4.3.1 with an examination of switch circuits. Many MOS circuits, including pass-transistor networks, Manchester carry chains, and multiplexers can be accurately modeled by considering each MOSFET to be a switch with a series resistance. The switch model also gives a rough approximation of the behavior of other circuits, including complementary MOS or CMOS gates.

The ubiquitous CMOS gate is the next step on our tour. This gate forms the core of most modern digital systems. In Section 4.3.2 we explore the properties of static CMOS gates by computing their DC transfer function, their AC step response, and their propagation delay. The discussion addresses device sizing and performance tuning. In Section 4.3.3 we see how the performance of a CMOS gate can be improved further by making it dynamic and discuss the properties of precharged CMOS gates and domino logic.

The high-performance digital signaling and timing systems we will encounter in Chapters 7 through 12 require fast and accurate amplifiers, comparators, and delay elements. Such circuit elements are normally used in *analog* circuits. When we apply these elements to digital systems we optimize their design for speed and large-signal performance. We are less concerned with analog issues of linearity and small-signal performance. We discuss basic amplifier forms and related circuits in Sections 4.3.4 through 4.3.7. Particular attention is paid to differential circuits and regenerative amplifiers because these are the basic building blocks of signaling and timing systems.

4.1 MOS TRANSISTORS

The active components on most modern integrated circuits, and hence in most modern digital systems, are metal-oxide-semiconductor (MOS) field-effect transistors (FETs). The FET is a four-terminal device. Voltage applied to the *gate* terminal controls the flow of current between the *source* and *drain* terminals. The *body* terminal forms the second terminal of many parasitic circuit elements. Voltage on the body terminal modulates the characteristics of the device.

In the simplest analysis, a MOSFET is a switch in which the connection between the source and drain terminals is controlled by the voltage applied to the gate terminal. Schematic symbols and *switch-level* models for two types of MOS transistors are shown in Figure 4-1. In an n-type MOSFET or NFET, a positive voltage on the gate, relative to the source, turns the device on. In a PFET, on

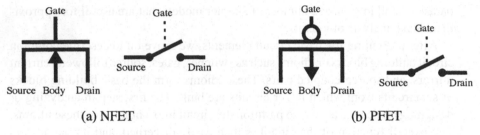

(a) NFET   (b) PFET

FIGURE 4-1   MOS Transistors

the other hand, a negative voltage applied between the gate and source turns the device on. In most MOSFETs, the source and drain are physically identical[1] and their identity is determined by the applied voltage. In an NFET, the more negative of the two terminals is the source, and the other is the drain. In a PFET, the source is the more positive terminal.

4.1.1   MOS Device Structure

Figure 4-2 shows the structure of an n-channel MOSFET or NFET from two views along with the schematic symbol for the device. The upper drawing is a top view, looking down on the chip. The lower drawing is a side view showing a cross section of the chip. The source and drain terminals are regions of n-type silicon[2] surrounded by the p-type silicon body region, usually the substrate of

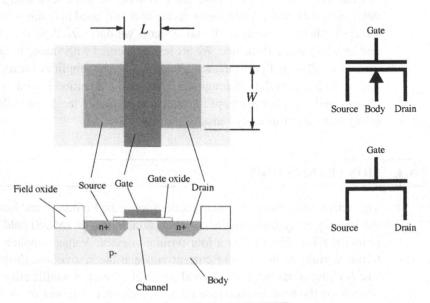

FIGURE 4-2   Structure of a n-Channel MOSFET

---

[1] This is true for all MOSFETs used in digital circuits but is not true for some power MOSFETs where very different doping densities are used in the source and drain.

[2] n-type silicon is implanted with group V *donor* ions, whereas p-type silicon is implanted with group III *acceptor* ions.

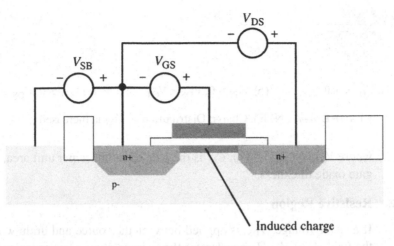

Induced charge

FIGURE 4-3 An NFET with Positive Gate Bias

the chip. The p–n junctions between the source and drain terminals and the body form diodes. In normal operation the voltages on the source and drain are positive relative to the body, and thus these junctions are reverse biased. They act as capacitors with small leakage currents. The portion of p-type silicon between the source and drain is the *channel* where most of the action in the device occurs. The gate terminal is formed by polycrystalline silicon (poly)[3] insulated from the channel, the region of the body below the gate, by a thin layer of oxide.

The length, L, and width, W, of the channel are under control of the mask designer. As described in Sections 4.1.2 and 4.2, these dimensions control the transconductance of the device as well as its parasitic capacitances.

4.1.2 Current–Voltage Characteristics

4.1.2.1 Threshold Voltage

As a positive voltage is increasingly applied to the gate terminal, the holes in the p-type channel are increasingly repelled. When the voltage reaches a *threshold voltage*, V_T, that depends on the equilibrium potential of the material and the potential due to surface ions, enough holes have been driven away so that electrons become the majority carriers and the material at the surface of the channel has effectively become n-type and forms a conductive region between the source and drain. At this point we say that the channel surface is *inverted* from p-type to n-type. As the gate voltage is increased above the threshold voltage, a charge Q_{ch} is induced in the channel, as illustrated in Figure 4-3. The amount of charge induced is given by

$$(4\text{-}1) \qquad Q_{ch} = V_{GT}LWC_{ox} = \frac{V_{GT}LW\varepsilon_{ox}}{t_{ox}}$$

---

[3] In early MOSFETs the gates were made from aluminum; hence, the name metal-oxide-semiconductor (MOS) transistors. Today the gates are no longer metal, but the name has stuck.

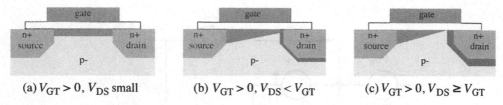

(a) $V_{GT} > 0$, V_{DS} small   (b) $V_{GT} > 0$, $V_{DS} < V_{GT}$ (c) $V_{GT} > 0$, $V_{DS} \geq V_{GT}$

FIGURE 4-4 NFET Charge Distribution as V_{DS} is Increased

where $V_{GT} = (V_{GS} - V_T)$, C_{ox} is the gate capacitance per unit area, and t_{ox} is the gate oxide thickness.

4.1.2.2 Resistive Region

If a small voltage, V_{DS}, is applied between the source and drain while $V_{GT} > 0$, the field, $E = V_{DS}/L$, accelerates the induced charge to a velocity of $v = E\mu_n$, where μ_n is the *mobility* of the charge carriers (electrons for the NFET). Each carrier has to travel the length of the device. The time for one carrier to traverse the channel is $v/L = E\mu_n/L$, and the current is given by

$$(4\text{-}2) \qquad I_{DS} = \frac{E\mu_n Q_{ch}}{L} = \mu_n C_{ox}\left(\frac{W}{L}\right)V_{GT}V_{DS} \qquad \text{(for } V_{DS} \ll V_{GT})$$

Thus, for small V_{DS}, the FET is essentially a linear resistor with resistance controlled by the gate voltage.

As V_{DS} is increased, the charge distribution across the channel becomes nonuniform, as illustrated in Figure 4-4(b). Near the source, where the full V_{GS} falls across the gate oxide, a large amount of charge is induced. Closer to the drain, where the smaller V_{GD} falls across the channel, less charge is induced. To keep the current constant across the channel, the field varies inversely with charge, giving a nonlinear variation in voltage with distance. The result is that current increases less than linearly with V_{DS}, as expressed by

$$I_{DS} = k_n\left(\frac{W}{L}\right)\left(V_{GT}V_{DS} - \frac{V_{DS}^2}{2}\right)$$

$$\text{(for } V_{DS} < V_{GT})$$

$$(4\text{-}3) \qquad = \beta_n\left(V_{GT}V_{DS} - \frac{V_{DS}^2}{2}\right)$$

where $k_n = \mu_n C_{ox}$ (with units of A/V^2) is the process transconductance parameter and $\beta_n = k_n(W/L)$ is the device transconductance parameter.

The nonlinear region of operation, where V_{DS} is less than V_{GT} but large enough that the quadratic term of Eq. (4-3) is significant, is often called the *transition region* because it represents a transition between the linear resistive region described by Eq. (4-2) and the linear saturation region described in Section 4.1.2.3.

4.1.2.3 Saturation Region

When V_{DS} is equal to V_{GT}, the voltage across the gate oxide at the drain end of the channel is just V_T, and thus the channel charge near the drain drops near zero.

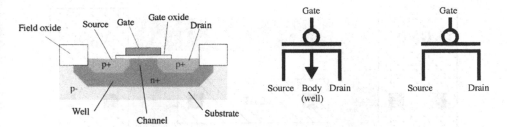

FIGURE 4-5 Structure and Symbol for a P-channel MOSFET (PFET)

At this point the channel is *pinched off*, as illustrated in Figure 4-4(c), and further increases in V_{DS} have little effect, to first order, on current flow. In this *saturation* or *current-source* region of operation, the FET acts as a current source with the current set by V_{GT}

$$I_{DS} = \frac{k_n}{2}\left(\frac{W}{L}\right)V_{GT}^2$$

(4-4)   (for $V_{DS} \geq V_{GT}$)

$$= \frac{\beta_n V_{GT}^2}{2}$$

4.1.2.4 p-Channel FETs

A p-channel MOSFET or PFET is constructed as illustrated in Figure 4-5. An n-doped well region in the substrate forms the body terminal of the device,[4] and p-doped regions within this well form the source and drain terminals. A PFET operates in the same way as an NFET except that all of the polarities are reversed. The source is typically the most positive of the three main terminals with V_{GS}, V_{Tp}, k_p, and V_{DS} all negative. When dealing with both types of devices, we denote the transconductance and threshold voltage of NFETs and PFETs as k_n, k_p, V_{Tn}, and V_{Tp}, respectively. The magnitude of the threshold voltages is usually comparable. However, because the mobility of holes is significantly lower than the mobility of electrons, the magnitude of k_p is usually 1/2 to 1/3 that of k_n. Because of this low transconductance, CMOS circuit design favors NFETs in applications where performance is critical.

The schematic symbols for PFETs are illustrated at the right side of Figure 4-5. An *inversion bubble* is added to the gate terminal to remind us that a negative gate voltage turns the device on. In the four-terminal symbol the diode connection to the well is reversed to indicate the correct polarity.

The astute reader will have noticed that a PFET built in an N-well forms a three-layer PNP structure that resembles a bipolar transistor. The source (or drain) forms the emitter of the transistor, the well forms the base, and the substrate forms the

---

[4] These figures assume a p-type substrate where the NFETs are formed in the substrate and the PFETs are formed in n-wells. With an n-type substrate the PFETs are formed in the substrate, and the NFETs are formed in p-wells.

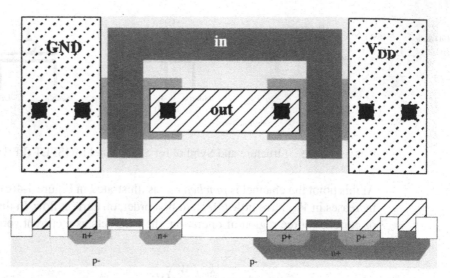

FIGURE 4-6   Complementary MOS (CMOS) Devices

collector. This parasitic PNP transistor is of limited utility, for it has a very thick base region and its collector is shorted to the substrate.

Figure 4-6 illustrates the structure of a CMOS circuit that incorporates both a PFET and an NFET. The figure shows a CMOS *inverter* incorporating a single PFET and a single NFET. In addition to combining the devices from Figures 4-2 and 4-5, this figure also shows metal wiring, the cross-hatched regions that are used to connect the source and body terminals of the devices to GND and V_{DD} and the drains of the two devices together. Although the figure shows nice square edges between the regions, in real chips the geometry is rougher and more irregular.

If one were to draw a line from the source or drain of the PFET through the well, through the substrate, to the source or drain of the NFET, the line would pass through a PNPN stack of layers. These four layers form a parasitic silicon-controlled rectifier (SCR) structure that, if triggered, can *latch up*, leading to catastrophic failure. Layout guidelines for connecting power supplies to well and substrate spoil the gain of this parasitic device to prevent it from becoming a problem.

4.1.2.5   Channel-Length Modulation

A MOSFET in the saturation region is not a perfect current source. As illustrated in Figure 4-7, as V_{DS} is increased, the depletion region at the drain junction grows, reducing the effective channel length. This *channel-length modulation* results in a finite output impedance to the current-source; that is, I_{DS} increases with V_{DS}. The effect, as you would expect, is most pronounced on short-channel devices where the depletion region becomes a significant fraction of the zero-bias channel length. Thus, where high-impedance current sources are needed, devices with nonminimum length are often used.

FIGURE 4-7   Channel-Length Modulation

We empirically model channel length modulation by adding a term to the I–V equations for the device

$$(4\text{-}5) \qquad I_{DS} = \begin{cases} 0 & \text{if } V_{GT} < 0 \\[2mm] \beta_n\left(V_{GT}V_{DS} - \frac{V_{DS}^2}{2}\right)(1 + \lambda V_{DS}) & \text{if } V_{GT} > V_{DS} \geq 0 \\[2mm] \frac{\beta_n}{2}V_{GT}^2(1 + \lambda V_{DS}) & \text{if } V_{DS} \geq V_{GT} \end{cases}$$

Here $\beta_n \lambda / 2$ represents the incremental conductance of the device in the saturation region. We add the $(1 + \lambda V_{DS})$ term to the resistive region equation as well to ensure continuity of I_{DS} when we switch between the two equations at $V_{DS} = V_{GT}$.

4.1.2.6 Body Effect

The threshold voltage of a device is increased as the bias between the source and body terminals, V_{SB}, is increased.[5] This bias increases the depletion layer charge that must be displaced by the threshold voltage to drive the channel into inversion. The resulting modulation of threshold voltage is given by

$$(4\text{-}6) \qquad V_T(V_{SB}) = V_{T0} + \gamma[(2|\phi_F| + V_{SB})^{1/2} - (2|\phi_F|)^{1/2}]$$

where ϕ_F is the *bulk Fermi potential* of the material

$$(4\text{-}7) \qquad |\phi_F| = \left(\frac{k_B T}{q}\right)\ln\left(\frac{N_a}{n_i}\right)$$

The first term here is the thermal voltage $k_B T/q$, which is about 25 mV at room temperature, and the second term is the log of the ratio of acceptor ion concentration, N_a, to intrinsic carrier concentration, n_i. For typical values, the potential is about 300 mV.

The *body-bias coefficient*, γ, is given by

$$(4\text{-}8) \qquad \gamma = \frac{(2q\varepsilon N_a)^{1/2}}{C_{ox}}$$

and is typically about 0.3 $V^{1/2}$.

---

[5] Note that V_{SB} must always be greater than −0.6 in an NFET. Otherwise, the source-body diode would be forward biased.

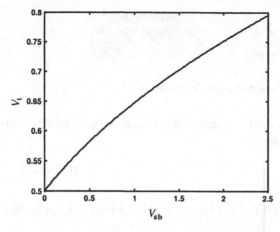

FIGURE 4-8   Body-Effect on Threshold Voltage

Figure 4-8 illustrates the body effect on threshold voltage for typical parameters of $|\phi_F| = 300$ mV and $\gamma = 0.3$ V$^{1/2}$. As the source becomes more positive with respect to the substrate, the threshold voltage increases gradually from 500 to 800 mV.

4.1.2.7   Velocity Saturation

At very high fields, the charge carriers fail to follow the linear velocity and field relationship from which Eqs. (4-2) through (4-5) are derived. The carrier velocity becomes *saturated* at $v_{sat} \approx 1.7 \times 10^5$ m/s and does not increase further with increased field. In terms of device equations, this implies that above a certain V_{GS} the device enters saturation before V_{DS} reaches V_{GT} at

$$(4\text{-}9) \qquad\qquad V_{sat} = \frac{v_{sat} L}{\mu}$$

and the device equations are modified by substituting V_{DE} for V_{DS} in Eq. (4-5), where V_{DE} is given by[6]

$$(4\text{-}10) \qquad\qquad V_{DE} = \min(V_{DS}, V_{sat})$$

4.1.2.8   Subthreshold Conduction

When $V_{GS} < V_T$, I_{DS} is small but not zero. In this *subthreshold* region of operation the mobile charge in the channel, and hence the current, depends exponentially on V_{GS}. To first approximation the subthreshold current is given by

$$(4\text{-}11) \qquad\qquad I_{DS} = I_{st} \exp\left(\frac{V_{GS} + \sigma V_{DS} - V_T}{nkT/q}\right)$$

The coefficient I_{st} and the parameters σ and n are determined empirically.

---

[6] This simplified equation does not match empirical data well in the transtition region. A smoother and more accurate curve in this region is given by

$$V_{DE} = V_{DS} + V_{sat} - \left(V_{DS}^2 + V_{sat}^2\right)^{1/2}$$

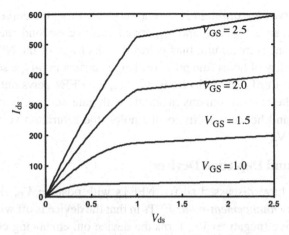

FIGURE 4-9 I–V Curves for a Typical 0.35-μm NFET

Subthreshold conduction is important in dynamic circuits because it is the primary mechanism by which stored charge leaks from capacitive storage nodes.

4.1.2.9 Typical I–V Curves

Figures 4-9 and 4-10 show the I–V curves for a typical $W = 1.0\,\mu$m, $L = 0.35\,\mu$m NFET and PFET, respectively, calculated from Eqs. (4-5) and (4-10). The vertical axis of each curve shows the drain-source current, I_{DS}, in microamperes as a function of the drain-source voltage, V_{DS}. The multiple curves reflect different gate-source voltages, V_{GS}.

The NFET curves clearly show the effects of velocity saturation. Once V_{GT} is increased above the saturation voltage, $V_{sat} = 1$ V, the current becomes linear rather than quadratic with increasing gate voltage. The nonzero slope of the curves in the saturation region reflects a λ of 0.1. The sharp corner on the transition from the transition to the saturation region is an artifact of the simple model and does not occur in empirical measurements.

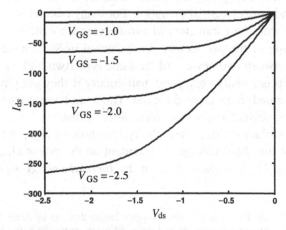

FIGURE 4-10 I–V Curves for a Typical 0.35-μm PFET

The PFET curves are different is several respects. First, the curves are in the third quadrant because V_{DS}, I_{DS}, and V_{GT} are all negative. Second, the magnitude of the drain current at maximum bias is less than half that of the NFET. This is because the mobility of holes (the positive charge carriers in p-type semiconductors) is about one third that of electrons. Finally, the PFET stays out of velocity saturation, and the current remains quadratic with gate voltage. Because of the lower mobility, and hence velocity, of the holes, the saturation voltage for the PFET is about 3 V.

4.1.2.10   Enhancement and Depletion Devices

The devices we have discussed so far, NFETs with positive V_{Tn} (PFETs with negative V_{Tp}) are *enhancement-mode* FETs in that the device is off with $V_{GS} = 0$; applying a positive (negative) V_{GS} turns the device on, enhancing conductivity. By implanting a surface charge below the gate it is also possible to build NFETs with a negative V_{Tn} (PFETs with positive V_{Tp}). Such *depletion-mode* FETs are on with $V_{GS} = 0$; applying a negative (positive) voltage turns the device off, depleting conductivity. Depletion-mode NFETs were widely used in the late 1970s and early 1980s as loads in NMOS circuits. They are rarely used, however, in CMOS circuits.

4.1.3   Parameters for a Typical 0.35-μm CMOS Process

Table 4-1 shows typical device parameters for a typical 0.35-μm (drawn gate length) CMOS process. These numbers do not reflect any single real process but rather were compiled from several open sources, such as IEDM and ISSCC proceedings. The performance of the devices is largely determined by the effective gate length,[7] 0.25 μm, and the gate oxide thickness, 70 Å. Along with the mobility, these determine C_{ox} and the process transconductance. The table includes values for parasitic capacitances and resistances that are discussed in the next section.

The parameters shown in Table 4-1 are *nominal* parameters that reflect the average value for a typical device operating at a temperature of 25°C. The parameters of a given device may vary from these nominal values because of variations in processing and temperature of operation. For many circuits we are concerned more with how well the parameters of two devices are matched and less with the absolute value of the parameters. As discussed in Section 6.5.3, matching of parameters between two devices of the same type (two NFETs for example) on the same chip is usually very good, particularly if they are physically close together and oriented in the same direction. There are larger variations between different types of devices and devices on different chips.

Temperature variations affect the mobility, threshold voltage, and subthreshold conduction. The threshold voltage is dependent on the potential, ϕ_F, which, as described by Eq. (4-7), is dependent on the *thermal voltage* $k_B T/q$. The net

---

[7] The *drawn* gate lenth, L_{drawn}, is the minimum gate length that can be defined on a mask. As a result of lithography and the source and drain diffusion under the gate, the *effective* gate length, L_{eff}, is often significantly shorter. It is L_{eff} that determines the electrical properties of the transistor.

TABLE 4-1   **Parameters for a Typical 0.35-μm Process**

Symbol	Description	Value	Units
L_{drawn}	Device length (drawn)	0.35	μm
L_{eff}	Device length (effective)	0.25	μm
t_{ox}	Gate oxide thickness	70	Å
N_a	Density of acceptor ions in NFET channel	1.0×10^{17}	cm^{-3}
N_d	Density of donor ions in PFET channel	2.5×10^{17}	cm^{-3}
V_{Tn}	NFET threshold voltage	0.5	V
V_{Tp}	PFET threshold voltage	-0.5	V
λ	Channel modulation parameter	0.1	V^{-1}
γ	Body-effect parameter	0.3	V$^{1/2}$
v_{sat}	Saturation velocity	1.7×10^5	m/s
μ_n	Electron mobility	400	cm^2/Vs
μ_p	Hole mobility	100	cm^2/Vs
k_n	NFET process transconductance	200	μA/V^2
k_p	PFET process transconductance	50	μA/V^2
C_{ox}	Gate oxide capacitance per unit area	5	fF/μm^2
C_{GSO}, C_{GDO}	Gate source and drain overlap capacitance	0.1	fF/μm
C_J	Junction capacitance	0.5	fF/μm^2
C_{JSW}	Junction sidewall capacitance	0.2	fF/μm
R_{poly}	Gate sheet resistance	4	Ω/square
R_{diff}	Source and drain sheet resistance	4	Ω/square

result is that threshold voltage *decreases* by about 1.5 mV/°C as temperature *increases*. A major effect of this decrease in threshold voltage is an increase in subthreshold conduction, which roughly doubles for every 10°C increase in temperature. As a result, charge leaks off of dynamic nodes significantly faster at high temperatures. Thus, the maximum operating temperature often governs the constraint on minimum clock period or minimum refresh time.

The largest effect of temperature on performance is due to mobility, which decreases with increasing temperature according to the empirical relation

$$(4\text{-}12) \qquad \mu(T) = \mu(300\,\text{K})(T/300)^{-a}$$

where T is the temperature in Kelvin, and a is an empirical parameter that is typically about 1.5. Designers have exploited this relation to build very fast MOS circuits by cooling the transistors with liquid nitrogen to 77 K. At this temperature, mobility is increased by a factor of 7.7! Of course, the designers of chilled MOS circuits must still deal with the problem of velocity saturation.

4.2   PARASITIC CIRCUIT ELEMENTS

An MOSFET includes many parasitic circuit elements, both resistors and capacitors, as illustrated in Figure 4-11. In the figure, the NFET symbol represents an

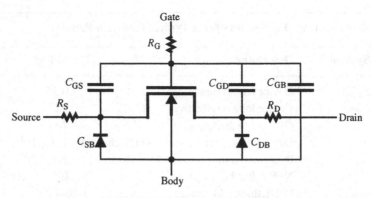

FIGURE 4-11 MOSFET Parasitic Circuit Elements

ideal MOSFET described by the I–V in Eqs. (4-5) through (4-11) without any parasitic elements. Any real MOSFET includes the other elements shown in the figure: capacitance from the gate to the three other terminals; source and drain diodes to the body terminal; and source, drain, and gate series resistance. In addition to the device parasitics shown in this figure, circuits are also affected by wiring parasitics, as described in Chapter 3.

4.2.1 Parasitic Capacitors

Device capacitance is of first-order importance in digital MOS circuit design because the performance of most circuits is determined by the ratio of device transconductance to the capacitance being driven.

4.2.1.1 Gate Capacitance

Perhaps the most significant parasitic circuit element is the gate capacitance, C_G, which determines the amount of charge required to switch the gate. As illustrated in Figure 4-12, C_G includes two fixed components, C_{GSO} and C_{GDO}, due to overlap of the gate with the source and drain regions, and a variable component, C_{GC}, due to the gate to channel capacitance. The gate to channel capacitance, C_{GC}, varies in both magnitude and in its division among the three terminals (B, S, and D), depending on V_{GS}, and V_{DS}. As shown in Figure 4-12(a), when $V_{GS} < V_T$, the channel is not inverted, and C_{GC} is entirely between the gate and body. When $V_{GS} > V_T$, the inverted channel shields the body from the gate, and C_{ox} is entirely between the gate and the channel. We model this distributed capacitance as two

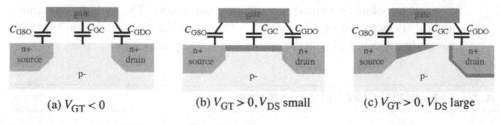

(a) $V_{GT} < 0$ (b) $V_{GT} > 0$, V_{DS} small   (c) $V_{GT} > 0$, V_{DS} large

FIGURE 4-12 Gate Capacitance

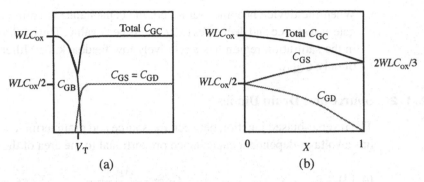

FIGURE 4-13   Gate Capacitance as a Function of V_{GS} and V_{DS}

lumped capacitors, one between the gate and the source and the other between the gate and the drain. When V_{DS} is small, the capacitance is divided evenly between the source and drain (Figure 4-12(b)). When V_{DS} is large, the device is in saturation with the drain end of the channel pinched off, and C_{GC} is entirely between the gate and the source.

Figure 4-13(a) shows the dependence on V_{GS} when $V_{DS} = 0$. When $V_{GS} = 0$, the inverted channel has not been formed; thus C_{GC} is entirely to the body terminal. The capacitance at this point is $C_{GB} = WLC_{ox}$. As V_{GS} is increased, a depletion layer is formed, effectively moving the back plate of the capacitor away from the gate and decreasing the capacitance. When $V_{GS} = V_T$, a conducting channel is formed that shields the body from the gate. From this point forward, C_{GB}, is essentially zero, and the gate capacitance is entirely to the source and drain. With a small V_{DS}, $C_{GS} = C_{GD} = WLC_{ox}/2$.

When the device is on, $V_{GS} > V_T$, the division of capacitance between the source and drain depends on the degree of saturation, $X = V_{DS}/V_{GT}$, as illustrated in Figure 4-13(b). As the device becomes saturated, C_{GD} drops to zero, and C_{GS} increases to 2/3 of WLC_{ox}. The capacitance in this region is calculated by taking the partial derivative of channel charge with respect to terminal voltages. This derivation gives

$$C_{GS} = C_{GSO} + \frac{2}{3}WLC_{ox}\left[1 - \left(\frac{1-X}{2-X}\right)^2\right]$$

(4-13)

$$C_{GD} = C_{GDO} + \frac{2}{3}WLC_{ox}\left[1 - \left(\frac{1}{2-X}\right)^2\right]$$

These detailed capacitance equations are typically used only for numerical analysis. For purposes of design and hand analysis, it suffices to remember the following two key points about gate capacitance:

1. There is a large discontinuity in the capacitance as the device turns on. The capacitance shifts from the body to the source or drain terminals, and the magnitude fluctuates around $V_{GT} = 0$. When using a MOS capacitor to store a voltage, for example in a PLL charge pump, avoid operation in this region.

2. When the device becomes saturated, the capacitance is entirely between the gate and source and decreases to 2/3 of its peak value. Thus, a device operating in the saturation region has a relatively low feedback, or Miller capacitance, of only C_{GDO}.

4.2.1.2   Source and Drain Diodes

The reverse-biased junction between the source and drain terminals and the body has a voltage-dependent capacitance proportional to the area of the junction.

$$(4\text{-}14) \qquad C_J = \frac{A_J C_{J0}}{\left(1 + \frac{V_J}{\phi}\right)^{1/2}}$$

where A_J is the area of the junction, C_{J0} is the zero-bias capacitance per unit area, and ϕ is the built-in potential of the junction. The junction area includes both the bottom surface of the junction as well as the sidewall.

For most digital circuits, we can safely ignore the voltage dependence of the diode capacitors and model them as fixed capacitors with components due to the area and perimeter of the source or drain as follows:

$$(4\text{-}15) \qquad \begin{aligned} C_{SB} &= C_J A_S + C_{JSW} P_S \\ C_{DB} &= C_J A_D + C_{JSW} P_D \end{aligned}$$

where A_X and P_X are the area and perimeter of terminal X (the source or drain).

Depending on process parameters, the source and drain capacitance of a device are each typically between 1/4 and 1/2 the gate capacitance. This capacitance can be significantly reduced by *folding* the device, as illustrated in Figure 4-14. This geometry significantly reduces the perimeter of the source and drain and hence the sidewall capacitance, a large component of the total source and drain capacitance. Processes with shallow junctions or with oxide isolation of the source and drain have markedly reduced sidewall capacitance, whereas processes with heavy field doping have narrow depletion regions and hence higher area and sidewall capacitance.

4.2.2   Parasitic Resistance

The doped silicon used to form the terminals of a MOSFET is much less conductive than the metal wires used to interconnect the devices. The thin layers of silicon have a sheet resistance of 20 to 100 Ω/square by themselves. Most modern processes form a thin layer of a more conductive silicide on the surface

(a) Straight, single contacts

(b) Folded and ample contacts

FIGURE 4-14   Transistor Geometry

of the silicon, reducing this sheet resistance to 1 to 4 Ω/square.[8] Many modern devices also have a lightly doped drain (and source) region that covers the area within 0.1 to 0.5 μm of the gate and has a very high resistance of 1 to 2 kΩ/square.

With a process that includes a silicide layer and proper attention to layout, parasitic resistance is not significant. However, careless layout can result in resistances that severely degrade device performance. Figure 4-14 illustrates the wrong (a) and right (b) way to lay out a transistor. The straight transistor in Figure 4-14(a) has only a single contact to each terminal. Suppose the device had a W/L of 400, a drawn width of 140 μm (rather than the W/L of 16 and width of 5.6 μm, shown). The gate would have a resistance of 1,600 Ω and a capacitance of about 240 fF, resulting in a time constant of 380 ps, which is significantly longer than the rise time of most signals in a modern process. In the resistive region of operation, the device itself would have an on resistance of about 4 Ω, which is swamped by the 400-Ω resistance of the silicon between the source and drain contacts. Devices with a single contact on a terminal also reduce yield because failure of any one contact will render the device inoperative.

By folding a transistor into a number of parallel sections or *fingers* and making dense contacts to the source and drain region, as illustrated in Figure 4-14(b), the parasitic resistances can be reduced to negligible levels. Assume that our device with a W/L of 400 is divided into eight fingers each with a W/L of 50. The gate on each finger now has a time constant of 200 $\Omega \times$ 30 fF = 6 ps. With 200 contacts on each source and drain, the silicon resistance becomes about 0.02 Ω, which is small enough to be ignored.

4.2.3 A Typical Device

To get a feel for the rough proportions of parasitic circuit elements, consider the $W/L = 16$ NFET folded into four fingers, as shown in Figure 4-14(b). The parameters for this device are given in Table 4-2.

The source, drain, and gate resistances are small enough to be safely ignored.

4.2.4 SPICE Models

Table 4-3 below shows the HSPICE Level 3 NFET model[9] that is used in simulations in this book. Table 4-4 shows the PFET model. Only parameters that are different from the NFET model are shown.

Figures 4-15 and 4-16 show the simulated I–V characteristics for the NFET and PFET, respectively. These curves agree reasonably well with our calculated I–V curves in Figures 4-9 and 4-10.

---

[8] For comparison recall that the aluminum wiring connecting these devices has a sheet resistance of about 0.05 Ω/square.

[9] In general, one would not use Level 3 models for short-channel devices such as these. For accurate modeling of real short-channel devices, the BSIM2 and BSIM3 models are preferred. For the purposes of this book we provide Level 3 models because they are supported by almost all circuit simulators.

TABLE 4-2   **Parameters for** $W/L = 16$ **NFET**

Symbol	Description	Value	Units
β	Device transconductance	1.7	mA/V^2
R_{on} ($V_{GS} = 2.5$ V, $V_{DS} = 0$)	On resistance ($1/\beta\,V_{GT}$)	150	Ω
I_{DSS} ($V_{GS} = V_{DS} = 2.5$ V)	Saturation current	3.3	mA
C_G	Gate capacitance	10	fF
A_S	Source area	3	μm^2
P_S	Source perimeter	13	μm
C_{SB}	Source junction capacitance	4	fF
A_D	Drain area	2	μm^2
P_D	Drain perimeter	8.4	μm
C_{DB}	Drain junction capacitance	2.7	fF

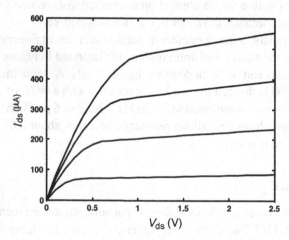

FIGURE 4-15   Simulated NFET I–V Characteristics

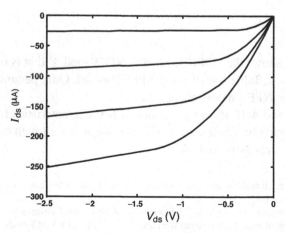

FIGURE 4-16   Simulated PFET I–V Characteristics

TABLE 4-3　**HSPICE Level 3 NFET Model**

Name	Description	Value	Units
LEVEL	Model identifier	3	
TOX	Gate oxide thickness	70×10^{-10}	m
UO	Mobility	600	cm^2/Vs
VTO	Threshold voltage	0.5	V
LD	Lateral diffusion of source and drain	5×10^{-8}	m
VMAX	Saturation velocity	1.5×10^5	m/s
KAPPA	Saturation field factor	0.3	V^{-1}
THETA	Mobility degradation factor	0.2	V^{-1}
NSUB	Bulk surface doping	1×10^{17}	cm^{-3}
ACM	Area calculation method (for source and drain diodes)	2	
CGDO	Gate-drain overlap capacitance	1×10^{-10}	F/m
CGSO	Gate-source overlap capacitance	1×10^{-10}	F/m
CJ	Bulk junction capacitance	5×10^{-4}	F/m^2
CJSW	Bulk sidewall junction capacitance	2×10^{-10}	F/m
LDIF	Length of lightly doped source and drain region adjacent to gate	1×10^{-7}	m
HDIF	Length of heavily doped source and drain region from contact to lightly doped region	3×10^{-7}	m
RS	Lightly doped source sheet resistance	2,000	Ω/square
RD	Lightly doped drain sheet resistance	2,000	Ω/square
RSH	Heavily doped source and drain sheet resistance	4	Ω/square

4.3　BASIC CIRCUIT FORMS

Circuits are composed from a relatively small set of basic circuit building blocks. Blocks such as switch networks, gates, source followers, current sources, and source-coupled pairs act as circuit idioms. In analyzing a circuit, a block, once recognized, is replaced with a functional model, and analysis of the circuit is greatly simplified. In designing circuits, one thinks about which idioms to select and how to combine them. One rarely thinks of individual transistors in all their generality. In this section we examine the most common idioms in use in MOS digital circuits.

TABLE 4-4　**HSPICE Level 3 PFET Model (Differences from NFET)**

Name	Description	Value	Units
UO	Mobility	150	cm^2/Vs
VTO	Threshold voltage	−0.5	V
LD	Lateral diffusion of source and drain	4×10^{-8}	m
KAPPA	Saturation field factor	1.8	V^{-1}
NSUB	Bulk surface doping	2.5×10^{17}	cm^{-3}

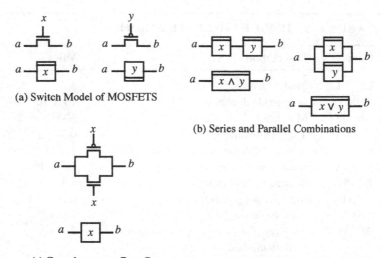

(a) Switch Model of MOSFETS

(b) Series and Parallel Combinations

(c) Complementary Pass Gate

FIGURE 4-17   Switch Networks of MOSFETs

4.3.1   Switch Networks

Modeling a MOSFET as a switch, as illustrated in Figure 4-1, is adequate for many purposes. It is adequate, for example, when the MOSFET is being used as a current switch in a differential circuit, as a multiplexer, or in performing logical analysis of gate circuits. In general we can use a switch to model a MOSFET if its gate terminal is driven by a full-swing logic signal (one of the supply voltages) and its application is not sensitive to the details of its I–V characteristics.

4.3.1.1   Pass Gates

As shown in Figure 4-17(a), we model an NFET by a switch that is *on* when its gate terminal is high. We represent the switch by a box labeled with the gate signal, x. We draw a bar across the top of the box, as shown, to indicate that the NFET does not pass high signals. If signal x is at V_H, and signals a and b rise above $V_H - V_T$, $V_{GS} < V_T$, and the NFET turns off. In a similar manner, we represent a PFET as a switch that is on when the gate signal is low. We draw the PFET with a bar across the bottom of the box to denote that it does not pass low signals. For the purposes of analyzing switch networks, we have abstracted all of the details of the MOSFET I–V characteristics. When the switch is on, current flows between the switch terminals; when the switch is off, no current flows. In some cases we will find it useful to augment this simple model by adding a resistance parameter to describe the I–V characteristics when the switch is on.

A switch that passes both high and low signals can be constructed by connecting an NFET switch that passes low signals in parallel with a PFET switch that passes high signals, as shown in Figure 4-17(c). The gates of the two devices are controlled by complementary signals so that they are on at the same time. We denote this complementary pass gate as a box labeled by the logical condition under which it is true.

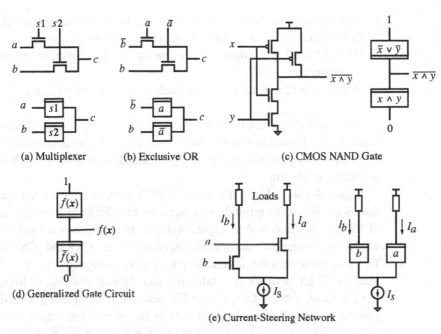

(a) Multiplexer   (b) Exclusive OR   (c) CMOS NAND Gate

(d) Generalized Gate Circuit

(e) Current-Steering Network

FIGURE 4-18 Switch Circuits

4.3.1.2 Logic with Switches

As shown in Figure 4-17(b), a series network of switches is equivalent to a switch that is on only when *all* of the switches are on. Only when x and y are both true does current flow between a and b. We represent this as the logical AND, $x \wedge y$, of logical variables x and y. Similarly, wiring switches in parallel is equivalent to a switch that is on when *any* of the inputs are true. The composite switch is on when the logical OR, $x \vee y$, of inputs x and y is true. More complex logic equations can be realized by series and parallel connections of these composite switches. Switching functions can also be realized by networks that are not series–parallel connections.

4.3.1.3 Circuits Using Switches

Figure 4-18 illustrates several MOSFET circuits that can be analyzed using the switch model of the MOSFET. A two-input multiplexer is shown in Figure 4-18(a). When $s1$ is true, signal a is connected to the output c, and when $s2$ is true, signal $s2$ is connected to the output c. This circuit differs in four important respects from the multiplexer one would construct from AND and OR gates. All of these differences are captured by the switch model.

1. The NFET-only circuit attenuates high levels by a threshold drop. For example, if $s1 = 2.5$ V and $a = 2.5$ V, c would be driven no higher than about 1.7 V. The NFET switch model qualitatively captures this behavior. A complementary multiplexer is required to get full levels on the output.

2. The circuit works in both directions. It acts as a demultiplexer if c is driven, distributing c to a or b, depending on the value of $s1$ and $s0$.
3. When $s1 = s2 = 0$, output c is left floating; it is not driven to zero as in a logical multiplexer.
4. When $s1 = s2 = 1$, all three terminals are connected together.

This multiplexer circuit can be configured to act as an exclusive-OR gate, realizing the logical function $c = (a \wedge \bar{b}) \vee (\bar{a} \wedge b)$, by appropriate connections to its inputs, as shown in Figure 4-18(b). This pass-transistor XOR is often used in multiplier circuits.

Figure 4-18(c) shows a CMOS NAND gate. A *gate* circuit has an output that is connected to ground via a network of NFETs and to V_{dd} via a network of PFETs, as illustrated in Figure 4-18(d). In a well-formed gate, the two networks have complementary functions denoted as $f(\mathbf{x})$ and $\bar{f}(\mathbf{x})$ in the figure. The gate computes the logical function $f(\mathbf{x})$ of input vector $\mathbf{x}$. When $f(\mathbf{x})$ is true, the PFET network is conducting and the output is V_{dd} or logical 1. When $f(\mathbf{x})$ is false, $\bar{f}(\mathbf{x})$ is true, the NFET network is conducting, and the output is ground or logic 0. The simplest gate is an inverter for which $f(x) = \bar{x}$. The NAND gate in Figure 4-18(c) computes the function $\overline{x \wedge y}$. To see that the two networks compute complementary functions, we apply DeMorgan's law, giving $f(x, y) = \bar{x} \vee \bar{y} = \overline{x \wedge y}$. We will examine the properties of gate circuits in more detail in Section 4.3.2.

The final example is a current steering network, as shown in Figure 4-18(e). The source current I_S is *steered* into one of the two loads, depending on the state of the inputs. When a is true, the current is directed into the right load, and when b is true the current is directed into the left load. To first order the voltage developed across the load is determined by I_S and the load resistance, independent of the properties of the switch. We will see this current-steering idiom in many current-mode MOS circuits.

Modeling transistors as switches is accurate only for some operating points and circuit topologies. If inputs a and b to the circuit of Figure 4-18(e) differ by only a small voltage, ΔV, the switch model is not useful, and we must model the input transistors as a source-coupled pair (Section 4.3.6). When the inputs swing to the supply rails, we model the transistors they control as switches.

4.3.1.4   Transient Analysis of Switch Networks

When the devices in switch networks are operated in the resistive region, we can compute the transient response and delay of the network by modeling it as an RC network. For example, consider the incrementer carry chain shown in Figure 4-19. This circuit uses switch logic to compute the carries in an incrementer. If the propagate signal, P_i, is true, the circuit propagates carry C_i to C_{i+1}. Otherwise the circuit *kills* the carry, setting C_{i+1} to zero. The recursive logic equation for this circuit is thus

$$(4\text{-}16) \qquad\qquad C_{i+1} = P_i \wedge C_i$$

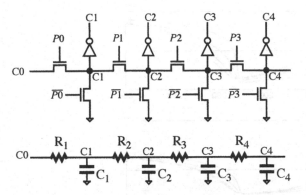

FIGURE 4-19 An Incrementer Carry Chain and RC Model

This circuit, called a *Manchester carry chain*, is widely used in modern arithmetic circuits because of its speed and low device count.[10]

For purposes of estimating delay we model the switch circuit with an RC network, as shown in the bottom view of Figure 4-19. This network corresponds to the worst case when all four Ps are high. Different networks result from different patterns on the P inputs. Although in general the waveforms on the node of this RC network are complex, the solution of a 4th-order differential equation, we can approximate an RC delay by associating each resistor with all the capacitance it must charge downstream. With this approximation, the delay to node Cn is

$$(4\text{-}17) \qquad \tau_n = \sum_{i=1}^{n} \left(R_i \sum_{j=1}^{n} C_j \right)$$

This delay is quadratic in the length of the chain. For short chains, the delay is often smaller than the rise time of the input signal, making the response of the chain essentially instantaneous. However, it grows rapidly for longer chains, limiting the maximum effective length of a carry chain to between four and eight devices.

Consider the case where the propagate devices have $W/L = 8$ and $R_{ON} = 300\ \Omega$ and the total capacitance at each intermediate carry node is 40 fF. Using these numbers, Eq. (4-17) predicts delays of 48, 84, 108, and 120 ps to the four nodes.

The curves in Figure 4-20 illustrate the limitations of this model. The upper panel shows the waveforms for the RC model driven with a square wave on $C0$, whereas the lower panel shows simulated waveforms for the actual carry-chain circuit. The RC network is faster than predicted and has a delay of 100 ps to $C4$. The actual NFET circuit shows a delay of 66 ps falling and 100 ps rising along with several qualitative differences. The NFET curves never rise above $V_{DD} - V_{Tn}$, about 1.75 V. To account for this shift, the threshold line is plotted at

---

[10] In a full-adder the Manchester carry chain includes a third transistor pulling up or *generating* the carry signal at each stage. The three transistors correspond to the three possibilities of *generating*, *propagating*, or *killing* the carry at each stage. In the incrementer shown here, there is no need to generate a carry.

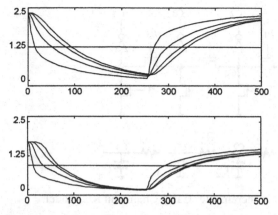

FIGURE 4-20   Simulation of Carry Chain

0.9 V. Because the FET is nearly off when the source is high, curve Ci does not begin to fall until $Ci - 1$ has fallen far enough to turn the FET on. Note that the first curve, $C1$, falls rapidly until the downstream FETs turn on, increasing its load, and then falls more slowly. The rising edges show a more characteristic series RC delay. The waveform is modified, however, by the fact that the rising source and drain nodes turn the FET off, increasing its resistance. Overall, the RC model, once calibrated, is a fair predictor of pass network performance to within 20%. It captures the quadratic nature of the delay and the effect of interstage capacitance.

4.3.2   The Static CMOS Gate

Static CMOS gate circuits, as illustrated in switch form in Figure 4-18(d), are the basic building blocks of most modern digital logic. Although the logical function of the gate can be derived from an analysis of switch networks, a more detailed circuit analysis reveals the DC and AC transfer characteristics of the gate. These detailed characteristics are important in determining the performance and noise immunity of logic circuits based on gates. In this section we derive the transfer characteristics for a CMOS inverter, illustrated in Figure 4-21, which is representative of more complex gate circuits.

4.3.2.1   Inverter DC Transfer Characteristics

Figure 4-22 shows the DC transfer characteristics of the inverter (i.e., the output voltage as a function of input voltage). At the left side of the curve, $V_{in} < V_{TN}$,

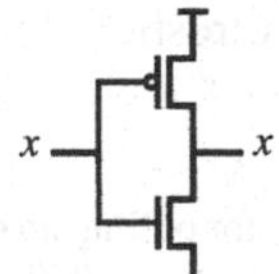

FIGURE 4-21   A CMOS Inverter

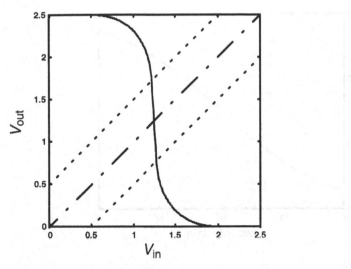

FIGURE 4-22 Inverter Transfer Curve

the NFET is off, and the PFET is in the resistive region with $V_{DS} = 0$. When V_{in} reaches $V_{TN} = 0.5$ V, the NFET comes on as a current source. In this region the output voltage is calculated by equating the NFET and PFET current and solving for V_{out}. When the transfer curve crosses the upper dotted line, the PFET becomes saturated. At this point both devices are acting as current sources and, as we shall see in Section 4.3.2.2, the gain is set by the channel-length modulation of the devices λ_N and λ_P. The point where the curve drops through the center line is the *threshold voltage*, V_{inv}, of the inverter – the point at which $V_{in} = V_{out}$. This should not be confused with the threshold voltage of the FETs in the inverter. When the curve crosses the lower dotted line, the NFET enters the resistive region. Finally, when $V_{DD} - V_{in} > V_{TP}$, the PFET cuts off and V_{out} remains steady at 0 V. As we shall see in Section 7.5.3, the transfer characteristic of a logic gate or line receiver defines its *noise margins*. What is important, however, is not the absolute value of these margins but rather the *noise immunity* of the system.

We can calculate the threshold voltage of the inverter by setting $V_{in} = V_{out}$ and solving for the resulting voltage. Ignoring channel-length modulation, we get

$$(4\text{-}18) \qquad V_{inv} = \frac{V_{TN} + \left(\frac{\beta_P}{\beta_N}\right)^{\frac{1}{2}}(V_{DD} + V_{TP})}{1 + \left(\frac{\beta_P}{\beta_N}\right)^{\frac{1}{2}}}$$

Figure 4-23 shows how inverter threshold varies with beta ratio (β_P/β_N) for an inverter with $V_{DD} = 2.5$ V and $V_{Tn} = -V_{Tp} = 0.5$ V. With the NFET sized much stronger than the PFET, V_{inv} approaches V_{Tn}. Enormous PFETs, on the other hand, cause V_{inv} to approach $V_{DD} + V_{Tp}$. Asymmetric beta ratios are often used in digital circuits to improve the speed of one edge (rising or falling) at the expense of the other.

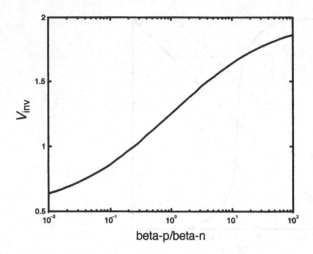

FIGURE 4-23   Inverter Threshold as a Function of Beta Ratio

4.3.2.2   Inverter Gain

In circuits where we use an inverter, or other gate, to amplify a small signal, the gain of the inverter in its *linear region* is important. This gain, the slope of Figure 4-22 between the two dashed lines, is determined largely by the channel-length modulation parameters of the devices, λ_n and λ_p. If the FETs were ideal current sources, the gain would be infinite in this region.

The gain can be calculated by writing an expression for V_{out} as a function of V_{in} and differentiating. However, more insight comes by computing the gain using a *load-line analysis*, as illustrated in Figure 4-24. The figure shows simplified (bilinear) V_{DS} versus $|I_{DS}|$ curves for the NFET and PFET for two input voltages, V_1 (black lines), and $V_2 = V_1 + \Delta V_{in}$ (gray lines). Note that for an inverter, $V_{DSn} = V_{DD} - V_{DSp} = V_{out}$. In equilibrium, $I_{DSn} = -I_{DSp}$, and so, for a given V_{in}, V_{out} must coincide with the intersection of the NFET I–V curve with the PFET I–V curve. This happens at point A in the figure for $V_{in} = V_1$.

For purposes of analysis, suppose that with the circuit operating at point A we increase the gate voltage on the NFET by ΔV_{in} to V_2 while keeping the PFET

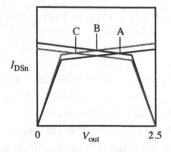

FIGURE 4-24   Load-Line Analysis of Inverter Gain

gate voltage constant. The NFET current increases to the I–V curve shown by the gray line, and the output voltage moves to point B.

To quantify this, note that we can find the incremental change in current with terminal voltages for a saturated FET by differentiating the third case of Eq. (4-5)

(4-19)
$$\frac{\delta I_{DS}}{\delta V_{GT}} = 2\beta V_{GT}$$

$$\frac{\delta I_{DS}}{\delta V_{DS}} = \lambda\beta V_{GT}^2$$

Therefore, to get from point A to point B in Figure 4-24, the increase in NFET current is approximately

(4-20)
$$\Delta I = \Delta V_{in}\frac{\delta I_{DS}}{\delta V_{GT}} = \Delta V_{in}(2\beta_n V_{GTn})$$

This puts us on the gray line directly over point A. To get to point B, V_{out} must decrease so the combined decrease in NFET current and increase in PFET current due to channel-length modulation match this amount. Consequently, V_{out} must decrease by

(4-21)
$$\Delta V_{out} = \Delta I\frac{\delta V_{DS}}{\delta I_{DS}} = \frac{\Delta I}{\lambda_p\beta_p V_{GTp}^2 + \lambda_n\beta_n V_{GTn}^2}$$

If we assume that $V_{GTp} \approx V_{GTn}$ and the beta ratio is unity, we get

(4-22)
$$\frac{\Delta V_{out}}{\Delta V_{in}} = \frac{2\beta_n V_{GTn}}{\lambda_p\beta_p V_{GTp}^2 + \lambda_n\beta_n V_{GTn}^2} \approx \frac{2}{V_{GT}(\lambda_p + \lambda_n)}$$

Of course, this just gets us to point B. If we now increase the PFET gate voltage, its current decreases to the gray line, and the circuit moves to point A. The incremental analysis above is repeated, and we are left with the following final expression for gain:

(4-23)
$$\frac{\Delta V_{out}}{\Delta V_{in}} = \frac{4}{V_{GT}(\lambda_p + \lambda_n)}$$

If we assume $\lambda_p + \lambda_n = 0.2$, and $V_{GT} = 1$, we get a DC gain of about 20. Figure 4-25 shows a plot of gain as a function of input voltage. This is just the derivative of Figure 4-22. The gain peaks at nearly -30. However the region of this peak is very narrow, for it is just a few tens of millivolts either side of V_{inv}.

4.3.2.3 Transient Response

In digital circuits we are usually more concerned with how fast a gate switches than with the details of its DC transfer function. The switching time is largely determined by the amount of charge that needs to be moved and the current available to move it. Consider the case of a $W = 1\text{-}\mu$m NFET discharging a capacitance, C, initially charged to V_{DD}, as illustrated in Figure 4-26(a). If we assume that the NFET switches on instantaneously, the capacitor voltage, V_C,

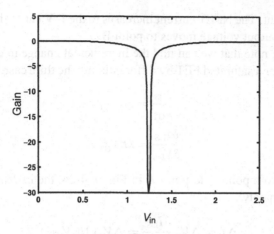

FIGURE 4-25   Inverter Gain as a Function of Input Voltage

ramps down linearly while the FET is in saturation and then becomes exponential, asymptotically approaching zero, when the FET enters the resistive region. If we extrapolate the linear portion of the curve, we get an estimate of the discharge time

$$(4\text{-}24) \qquad\qquad \tau(C) = \frac{V_{DD}C}{I_{DSS}}$$

If the NFET is driving the gate of an equal-sized NFET, as illustrated in Figure 4-26(b), we have an I_{DSS} of about $600\,\mu A$ and about 2.5 fF of capacitance,[11] giving a device time constant, τ_n, of about 10 ps.

The device time constant, τ_n, can be used to estimate the delay of more involved circuits by scaling the delay as the capacitance and saturation current change.

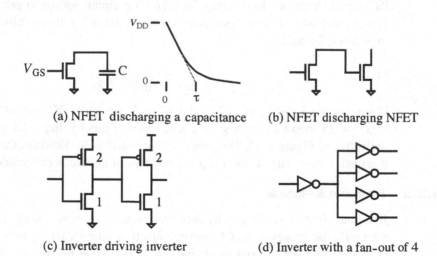

(a) NFET discharging a capacitance   (b) NFET discharging NFET

(c) Inverter driving inverter   (d) Inverter with a fan–out of 4

FIGURE 4-26   Transient Response

---

[11] The capacitance here is 1.3 fF of C_{ox}, 0.2 fF of gate overlap capacitance, and 1 fF of drain junction capacitance on the driving device.

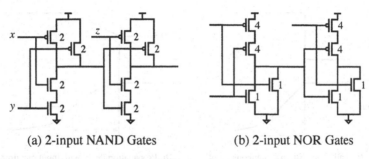

(a) 2-input NAND Gates (b) 2-input NOR Gates

FIGURE 4-27 Delay with Fanin

Figure 4-26(c) shows the case of a $W_p/W_n = 2$-μm/1-μm inverter[12] driving another equal-sized inverter. Here the current is the same, but the capacitance is roughly tripled,[13] for we have 3 μm of gate and drain rather than 1 μm; the time constant for the falling edge of the inverter is $\tau_{inv} = 3\tau_n = 30$ ps.

When the fan-out of the inverter is increased, as in Figure 4-26(d), the delay increases in proportion to the added capacitance. The delay with a fan-out of 4 is not quadrupled, however, because the drain junction capacitance does not increase. The ratio of gate capacitance to drain capacitance when the fan-out is 1 is $\eta = 1.5$. Thus, when the fan-out is N, the capacitance, and hence the delay, scales as

(4-25)
$$C_N = \frac{1 + N\eta}{1 + \eta} C_1$$

$$\tau_N = \frac{1 + N\eta}{1 + \eta} \tau_{inv}$$

Thus, for the case of Figure 4-26(d), we have $\tau_4 = 2.8\tau_{inv} = 85$ ps. This fan-out–of–four inverter delay, τ_4, is a good estimate of the delay of a typical logic gate (fan-in = 2) driving a typical load (fan-out = 2) over relatively short wires.

Fan-in also increases delay as illustrated by the case of a 2-input NAND gate driving an identical gate as shown in Figure 4-27(a). Here we have sized the gates 2/2 so that the output drive current matches the 2/1 inverter of Figure 4-26(c).[14] To first approximation,[15] our output load has increased by 4/3, to 4 μm of gate from 3 μm for the inverter. Thus, the falling delay is about 4/3 that of the inverter or 40 ps. Sutherland and Sproull call this increase in delay for a logical function

---

[12] We choose a 2:1 $W_p : W_n$ ratio to roughly balance the saturated drain currents, I_{DSS}, of the two devices. This tends to give equal rise and fall times. We do not use a uniform β ratio because this would give an enormous PFET and with velocity saturation, a shifted V_{inv} would result.

[13] Here we are ignoring the Miller effect of C_{GDO} on the second inverter. Because the drain terminal of this capacitor is swinging in the direction opposite the gate, the capacitance is effectively doubled.

[14] We get identical results if we size the NAND gate 1.5/1.5, which gives an input load identical to the 2/1 inverter but with reduced output current.

[15] The approximation here ignores the drain capacitance. For both the NAND and NOR gates, we have 6 μm of drain versus 3 μm for the inverter, ignoring the junction capacitance between the two series devices.

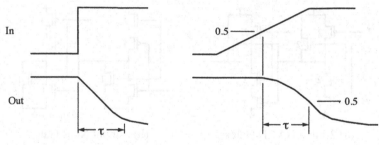

(a) Fall time with instantaneous input   (b) Propagation delay with input rise time.

FIGURE 4-28   Propagation Delay

the *logical effort* of a gate [SuthSpro91]. For 2-input NOR gates, as illustrated in Figure 4-27(b), the load is 5 μm of gate, and hence the delay is 50 ps and the logical effort 5/3.

4.3.2.4   Propagation Delay and Nonzero Rise Time

So far we have been calculating the fall time of a gate with a zero rise time on the input. For real digital logic circuits, we are concerned with the propagation delay of a gate, the time from when the input reaches 50% of its swing (usually $V_{DD}/2$) to when the output reaches 50% of its swing (see Section 9.3.1.1) and the input rise–fall time has a significant effect on this delay. Fortunately, as we shall see, the time constants we have calculated above also describe the propagation delay of a gate when the input and output rise–fall times are the same.

Suppose we have an input rise time $t_r = 2\tau$, as shown in Figure 4-28(b). The output does not begin to change until the input reaches V_{inv}, which is assumed to be $V_{DD}/2$ here for simplicity. Assuming the device is velocity saturated, the output current increases linearly with input voltage for the second half of the rise time, reaching a maximum of I_{DSS} when the input reaches the positive rail. This gives a quadratic voltage profile to the halfway point. Beyond this point the current is constant and voltage linear with time until the device enters the resistive region and the curve becomes exponential.

Intuitively we know that it takes the quadratic curve in Figure 4-28(b) twice as long to reach the 50% point as the linear curve in Figure 4-28(a) because the average current of the linear ramp (b) is half that of the step (a). More formally, if we start time when the input slope reaches 50% we have

(4-26)
$$I_O = -\left(\frac{2I_{DSS}}{t_r}\right)t$$

$$\Delta V_O = \frac{1}{C}\int_0^{t_r/2} I_O\, dt = -\left(\frac{I_{DSS}}{Ct_r}\right)t^2\Big|_0^{t_r/2} = -\left(\frac{I_{DSS}t_r}{4C}\right)$$

Now this change in voltage is equal to half the supply, and thus we have

(4-27)
$$\frac{I_{DSS}t_r}{4C} = \frac{V_{DD}}{2}$$

Rearranging and substituting Eq. (4-24) gives

(4-28) $$t_r = \frac{2V_{DD}C}{I_{DSS}} = 2\tau$$

Therefore, the propagation delay, the time to reach the midpoint, is

(4-29) $$t_d = \frac{t_r}{2} = \tau$$

If we assume that the exponential portion of the curve at the end of the output transition extends the fall time by an additional $\tau/2$, this situation gives us equal input-rise and output-fall times.

Notice that if the device is not velocity saturated, the current is quadratic, the voltage is cubic, and we get $t_d = 4\tau/3$. Also, even though the rise and fall times are roughly the same, the shape of the output curve will affect the delay of the next stage of logic by a small amount. These constant factors are not important because they can be calibrated out. What is important is that, modulo a constant factor, the propagation delay of the gate can be accurately predicted by the time constant given in Eq. (4-24).

4.3.2.5 The Effect of Input Rise Time on Delay

In general, input and output transition times are not equal, and, as illustrated by Figure 4-28, input rise time has a very strong effect on delay. Figure 4-29 illustrates the effect of fast (a) and slow (b) rise times on delay. In both cases the nominal rise time of 2τ has been multiplied by a factor, r. Consider first the case of a fast rise time, as shown in Figure 4-29(a). The input curve, and hence the pulldown current, reaches peak value in time $r\tau$ after crossing the midpoint. In this time the output falls a fraction r of the way to the midpoint. From this point on, the output is saturated and thus falls the remaining distance to the midpoint in time $(1 - r)\tau/2$. This gives a delay that varies linearly with r:

(4-30) $$t_d = \frac{\tau}{2}(1 + r)$$

Now consider the case shown in Figure 4-29(b) where $r > 1$. Here the input and pulldown current do not reach peak value before the output has reached the

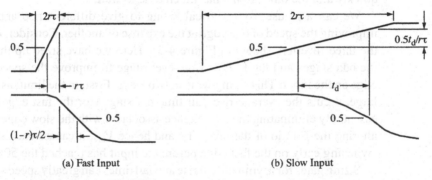

(a) Fast Input   (b) Slow Input

FIGURE 4-29   The Effect of Input-Rise Time on Delay

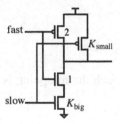

FIGURE 4-30 Asymmetrical Input Delays

midpoint. The peak current value at the midpoint is a fraction $t_d/(\tau r)$ of the normal value. Because delay is inversely proportional to peak current, we have

$$t_d = \tau \left(\frac{\tau r}{t_d} \right)$$
(4-31)
$$t_d = \tau r^{1/2}$$

In summary, delay increases linearly, from $\tau/2$ to τ as the input rise time factor, r, goes from zero to one, and increases as the square root of r thereafter.

4.3.2.6 Asymmetrical Sizing

By asymmetrically sizing our gates, as shown in Figure 4-30, we can make one input fast at the expense of the other. As the big transistor driven by the slow input approaches infinity, the speed of the fast input approaches τ_{inv}. The fast input is presented with the input load of an inverter and generates an output current approaching that of an inverter. The delays of the fast and slow inputs driving identical gates are

$$\tau_{fast} = \tau_{inv} \left(1 + \frac{1}{K_{big}} \right)$$
(4-32)
$$\tau_{slow} = \tau_{inv} K_{big}$$

The penalty here is large because the slow input pays a linear increase in delay to reduce the delay of the fast input by a small amount. Asymmetrical sizing is a valuable technique when one signal absolutely and positively needs to get there quickly and the other signal has much time to wait.

We can also use asymmetrical sizing to give different rise and fall times, improving the speed of one edge at the expense of another. Consider, for example, the three inverters shown in Figure 4-31. Here we have sized up the NFETs of the odd stages and the PFET of the even stage to improve the speed of a rising edge on the input. This sizing wins in two ways. First, in the limit, as K gets very large, it cuts the average rise–fall time per stage (for the fast edge) in half, by essentially eliminating the capacitance associated with the slow edge. Second, by altering the β ratio of the inverters, and hence V_{inv}, it causes each stage to start switching early on the fast edge before the input has reached the 50% point.

Sizing gates for asymmetrical rise and fall times can greatly speed some circuits where one of the edges is critical. The speed of a memory decoder, for example,

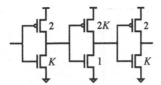

FIGURE 4-31   Asymmetrical Rise–Fall Times

can be nearly doubled by sizing the gates so that the edges that turn on a word line are favored. There is usually plenty of time to turn off the word line, and thus those edges are less critical. Sizing gates in this manner requires careful attention to noise budgets because, by shifting V_{inv}, the high and low noise margins are made asymmetric as well.

4.3.2.7 Miller-Effect Capacitance

The capacitance between the input and output of a switching gate, primarily the gate-drain overlap capacitance, appears twice as large as its nominal value. This is because sufficient charge must be transferred not just to discharge the capacitor but also to charge it to the opposite polarity. When the inverter in Figure 4-32(a) switches, for example, the voltage, V_C, across the Miller capacitance, C_M, goes from V_{DD}, when the output is low, to $-V_{DD}$ when the output is high. This shift of $\Delta V_C = 2V_{DD}$ results in a transfer of charge $Q_M = \Delta V_C C_M = 2V_{DD}C_M$. This is the same charge that would be transferred if capacitors of value $2C_M$ were tied from both the input and output to ground, as shown in Figure 4-32(b).

The circuit of Figure 4-32(c) gives an intuitive development of Miller capacitance. The feedback capacitance is replaced by a series connection of two capacitors, each of value $2C_M$. The middle node of this series capacitor, V_x, starts and ends each transition at the same voltage. Thus, for purposes of analyzing large-signal (full-swing) behavior, we can consider V_x to be an AC ground and split the two series capacitors apart, as in Figure 4-32(b).

Over the entire signal transition the Miller capacitance appears to be doubled; however, incremental value varies with the gain of the inverter. If we assume that the input changes slowly compared with the time constant of the inverter, the apparent input capacitance due to the Miller capacitance is

(4-33)
$$C_{iM}(V_{in}) = \frac{\delta Q_M}{\delta V_{in}} = C_M[1 - A(V_{in})]$$

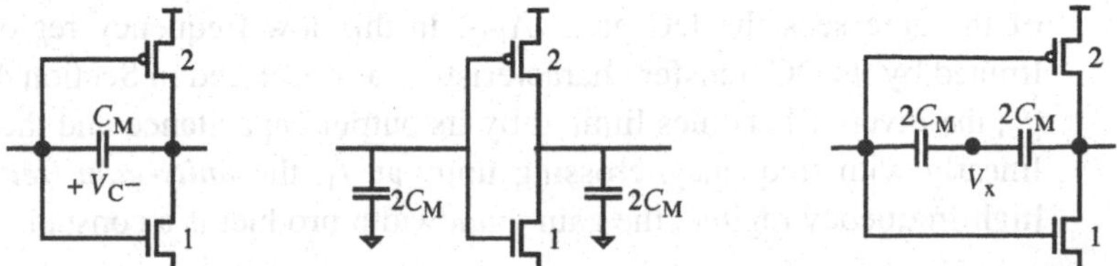

(a) Miller Capacitance   (b) Equivalent Input and Output Capacitance   (c) Intuitive Model

FIGURE 4-32   Miller-Effect Capacitance

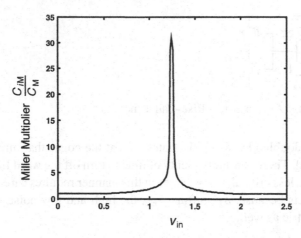

FIGURE 4-33   Small-Signal Miller Capacitance As a Function of Input Voltage

where $A(V_{in})$ is the gain of the device (dV_{out}/dV_{in}) when the input is at V_{in}. The peak value of A, given by Eq. (4-23), is typically in the range of 20–100, depending on transistor parameters. Thus, although the average input capacitance for a full-swing signal is $2C_M$, for a slowly varying signal in the high-gain region of the inverter, the instantaneous input capacitance may be $20C_M$ or more. Moreover, this capacitance is voltage and frequency dependent.

As the input voltage varies, the Miller capacitance follows the gain curve, as illustrated in Figure 4-33. The multiplier is 1 across nearly the whole input range and rises to about 30 in a narrow range about V_{inv}.

This behavior is particularly relevant when the inverter or gate is used as a transmission line receiver. At the point where the Miller capacitance peaks, the input impedance of the inverter drops dramatically, making it difficult to terminate the line in a matched impedance.

4.3.2.8   Gain–Bandwidth Product

At high frequencies, the gain of a static CMOS gate is much smaller than that shown in Figure 4-25. Above a certain frequency, the output swing becomes dominated by the ability to pump charge into the output capacitance rather than the DC transfer characteristics of the device. The frequency response for most gates has the single-pole characteristic, as shown in the log–log sketch of Figure 4-34. Below a cutoff frequency, f_c, a small signal centered in the high-gain region of the gate sees the DC gain, A_{DC}. In this low-frequency region, the gate is limited by its DC transfer characteristics, as described in Section 4.3.2.1. Above f_c, the inverter becomes limited by its output capacitance and the gain rolls off linearly with frequency, crossing unity at f_1, the *unity-gain frequency*. In this high-frequency regime, the gain–bandwidth product is a constant

$$(4\text{-}34) \qquad\qquad f A(f) = f_1 \qquad (f > f_c)$$

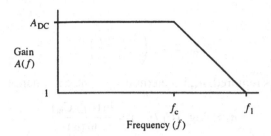

FIGURE 4-34   Frequency Response of a Gate

We can calculate f_1 by observing that for a small-signal sine wave

(4-35)
$$\frac{dv_{\text{out}}}{dt} = \frac{i}{C} = \frac{g_m v_{\text{in}}}{C}$$

If we approximate the small-signal transconductance by $I_{\text{DSS}}/V_{\text{DD}}$, at the point of unit gain we have

(4-36)
$$\omega_1 = \frac{g_m}{C} = \frac{I_{\text{DSS}}}{V_{\text{DD}}C} = \frac{1}{\tau}$$

$$f_1 = \frac{1}{2\pi\tau}$$

Thus, we see that the basic time constant derived in Section 4.3.2.3 gives us our gain–bandwidth product as well. For our basic inverter with $\tau_{\text{inv}} = 30$ ps, we have $f_1 = 5.3$ GHz.

From a design perspective, gain–bandwidth product is an important concept in that it tells us that we can operate circuits at high speed or with high gain but not both at once. In the design of high-speed signaling systems we will see that we can operate circuits faster than f_1 by operating at less-than-unity gain. In building receive amplifiers, we will see that a low-frequency system can get by with a single-stage amplifier with high-gain, but a high-speed system needs either a multistage amplifier, with low per-stage gain, or a regenerative amplifier.

4.3.2.9   **The Exponential Horn**

The delay of a gate, as expressed in Eq. (4-24), depends linearly on the ratio of load capacitance to driver size, and hence gate input capacitance. To overcome this linear dependence we drive large loads with a series of gates of exponentially increasing size, *an exponential horn*, as illustrated in Figure 4-35.

Each stage is a scale factor, α, larger than the previous stage. In the figure, $\alpha = 4$. If the ratio of input capacitance to output capacitance $\eta = 1.5$, the delay

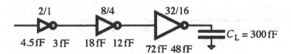

FIGURE 4-35   An Exponential Horn

per stage is

$$(4\text{-}37) \qquad t_{ds} = \tau_{inv}\left(\frac{1 + \alpha\eta}{1 + \eta}\right)$$

The number of stages required, n_s, is determined by the capacitance ratio

$$(4\text{-}38) \qquad n_s = \log_\alpha\left(C_L/C_{in}\right) = \frac{\ln\left(C_L/C_{in}\right)}{\ln\left(\alpha\right)}$$

Thus, the total delay is

$$(4\text{-}39) \qquad t_d = n_s t_{ds} = \left[\frac{\tau_{inv}\ln\left(C_L/C_{in}\right)}{1 + \eta}\right]\left(\frac{1 + \alpha\eta}{\ln\left(\alpha\right)}\right)$$

Taking the derivative with respect to α and solving for the minimum delay gives

$$(4\text{-}40) \qquad \alpha = \exp\left(1 + \frac{1}{\eta\alpha}\right)$$

which, while not solvable in closed-form, is easily solved iteratively. It tends toward $\alpha = e$ as γ goes to zero. For our example process, $\eta = 1.5$, we get $\alpha = 3.3$.

The normalized delay of an exponential horn is plotted as a function of α in Figure 4-36. The figure shows that, although the optimal α for our process is 3.3, our using $\alpha = 4$ or 5 gives just a few percent more delay.

4.3.2.10   SPICE Simulations of Gates

The SPICE results shown in Figures 4-37 and 4-38 validate the hand calculations we have made so far in this section. Figure 4-37 shows the results of an HSPICE DC analysis of a 2-μm/1-μm inverter. The plot closely matches our calculated transfer curve in Figure 4-22. The peak gain here is -20 and agrees exactly with Eq. (4-23).

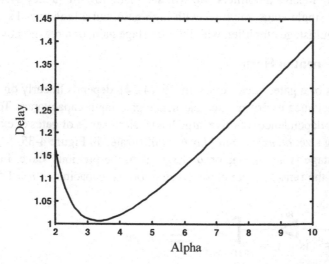

FIGURE 4-36   Normalized Delay of an Exponential Horn As a Function of Stage Ratio, α

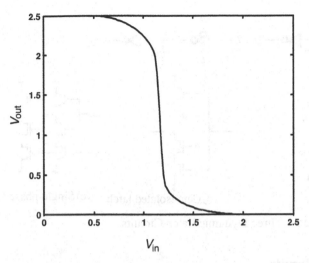

FIGURE 4-37 Simulated DC Transfer Characteristics of an Inverter

Figure 4-38 shows the HSPICE transient response of (top) a chain of 2-μm/ 1-μm inverters, (middle) a chain of these inverters with a fan-out of four on each stage, and (bottom) a chain of 2-input NAND gates. The simulated circuit is shown to the right of each panel in the figure. For the inverter chain, Figure 4-38(top), the delay, both rising and falling, is 30 ps and agrees exactly with our calculation of τ_{inv}. The rise and fall times between the 25 and 75% points are also 30 ps. Extrapolating the linear parts of these curves between 0 and 100%, we validate our assumption that, for equal-sized stages, $t_r = 2\tau_{inv}$. The simulated delay for the fan-out–of–four inverters, Figure 4-38(middle), is 66 ps for the output falling and 83 ps for the output rising. These are both a bit faster than our estimate of $\tau_4 = 85$ ps. The NAND gates (bottom trace) have output rising and falling delays of 50 and 40 ps, respectively, as compared with our calculation of 40 ps, given the 2-input NAND logical effort of 4/3. In general, once calibrated, τ-model calculations of delay tend to agree with simulation results to within 20%.

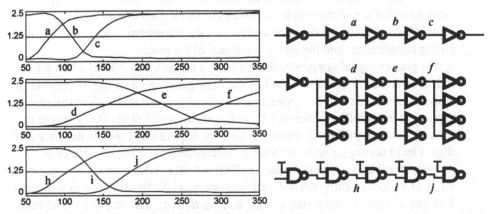

FIGURE 4-38 Simulated Transient Response of Inverters (top), Loaded Inverters (middle), and 2-Input NAND Gates (bottom)

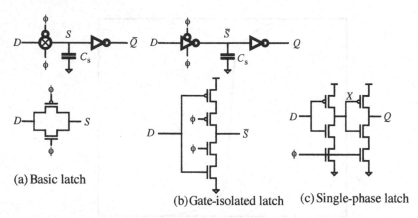

(a) Basic latch

(b) Gate-isolated latch   (c) Single-phase latch

FIGURE 4-39   Three Dynamic Latch Circuits

4.3.3   Dynamic Circuits

We often regard parasitic capacitance (gate, diode, and wire) as a nuisance because it slows down our circuits. However, it also serves a useful function by *holding* the state of a node when it is not being driven. We exploit this property as the basis for building storage elements and *dynamic* gate circuits. As we shall see in Chapter 6, capacitance on a node also provides resilience against several types of noise.

4.3.3.1   The Dynamic Latch

The simplest dynamic circuit is the basic latch, illustrated in Figure 4-39(a). The latch consists of a complementary transmission gate, denoted by a crossed circle, and an inverter. The transmission gate consists of a PFET and an NFET, as shown at the bottom of the figure. When the clock, ϕ, is high, the complementary transmission gate conducts and the storage node, S, follows the input D with a small RC delay. The inverter follows the signal on the storage node to generate the inverted output, $\bar{Q}$, and isolates the storage node from the output node. When ϕ is low, the transmission gate is off and the voltage on S remains constant, thus storing the value. Physically, the value is stored as charge on the parasitic capacitance of the storage node shown as C_s. There is no explicit capacitor here; rather C_s consists of the drain capacitance of the transmission gate, the parasitic wiring capacitance, and the gate capacitance of the inverter.

For proper digital operation, S must be at a reliable 0 or 1 level when ϕ falls. If it is at some intermediate level in the high-gain region of the inverter, large amounts of current will be drawn, and any noise coupled into S, for example, by capacitive cross talk (Section 6.3.1), will appear amplified on $\bar{Q}$. To ensure that S has a stable digital level when ϕ is low, we require that input D have a stable digital level during an *aperture* time, t_a, referenced to the falling edge of ϕ.

Consider the situation illustrated in Figure 4-40 in which a narrow 1 pulse on input D is successfully latched onto storage node S. To charge S to a reliable 1 before ϕ falls, D must rise at least a *setup time*, t_s, before ϕ falls. The setup time is usually a small multiple of the RC time constant set by the resistance of the transmission gate and the capacitance of the storage node. To prevent S from

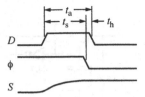

FIGURE 4-40   Aperture, Setup, and Hold Times for a Dynamic Latch

discharging until the transmission gate is completely off, D is not allowed to fall until after *hold time*, t_h, after ϕ falls. Because the transmission gate is fully off once ϕ falls below V_{Tn}, the hold time is largely determined by the fall time of the clock signal. It is not unusual for dynamic latches to have zero or even negative hold times. The sum of the setup and hold times sets the width of the aperture, t_a. These concepts of setup, hold, and aperture time are discussed in more detail in Section 9.3.4.

The signal stored in a dynamic latch is ephemeral (or dynamic) in nature and must periodically be refreshed. If ϕ is low for a long period, charge will leak off of C_s, degrading the signal on S. After a certain period, t_{rfsh}, the signal will be degraded beyond the allowable noise margin and must be refreshed by raising ϕ for the latch output to remain reliable. The primary mechanism for charge leakage is subthreshold conduction through the transmission gate. Refresh periods are calculated by dividing the storage capacitance by the subthreshold current.

The difficulty of distributing complementary clock signals can be avoided by replacing the complementary transmission gate in Figure 4-39(a) with a single NFET. This also reduces the area required to implement the latch. In such an n-only latch the voltage on S never rises above $V_{DD} - V_{Tn}$ (about 1.75 V for our example process). This is compensated by setting the inverter ratio to give a low threshold, V_{inv}, as in Eq. (4-18). In some cases a PFET *keeper* device is added, as described below, to pull up the storage when $\bar{Q}$ is low.

A gate-isolated latch, as illustrated in Figure 4-39(b), is used in cases where it is desirable to isolate the input node, D, from charge injection. When the simple dynamic latch switches on, the storage capacitor is connected to the input node. If the two nodes, S and D, are at different values, the resulting charge sharing disturbs node D by an amount dependent on the capacitance ratio. If node D is driven, this disturbance is momentary; however, in some circuits the resulting *glitch* from this *dynamic charge sharing* can be problematic.

Dynamic charge sharing is eliminated entirely by using a *tristate* inverter (circuit detail shown at bottom of Figure 4-39(b)) for the input stage of the dynamic latch. This inverter operates like a normal inverter when ϕ is high and isolates its output in a high-impedance state[16] when ϕ is low. Thus, when ϕ rises, the storage node is driven by this inverter with no charge injection back into the input

---

[16] This third state gives rise to the name *tristate*. Although most digital signals have two states, 0 and 1, the output of a tristate circuit has a third state, high impedance, sometimes denoted Z.

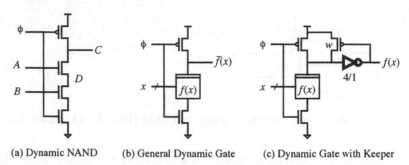

(a) Dynamic NAND   (b) General Dynamic Gate   (c) Dynamic Gate with Keeper

FIGURE 4-41   Precharged Gates

signal. The result is identical to adding an inverter to the input of Figure 4-39(a) for isolation.

A single-phase latch, or Svensson latch [YuanSven89], provides gate isolation and requires only a single polarity of the clock signal, ϕ. When ϕ is high, the circuit simply acts as two back-to-back inverters, passing D to Q. When ϕ is low, the intermediate signal, X, is monotonically rising – it can no longer fall. Thus, the output is stable. It cannot fall because the series NFET is off, and it cannot rise, for that would require that X fall to switch the PFET on. In practice, keepers on X and Q are added to this circuit to enhance its noise immunity.

4.3.3.2   Precharged Gates

Logic functions can be built using dynamic circuits, as illustrated in Figure 4-41. A two-input dynamic NAND gate is shown in Figure 4-41(a). When clock ϕ is low, the storage node, C, is *precharged* to a high state while the NFET switch logic is disabled by the bottom NFET. When ϕ rises, the gate evaluates and pulls node C low if the logic function is true. In this case, if $A = B = 1$. Precharged gates can be implemented using an arbitrary switching logic function, $f(x)$, as illustrated in Figure 4-41(b).

Precharged logic shares the advantages of sizing for asymmetrical rise and fall times (Section 4.3.2.6).[17] The input capacitance is reduced by eliminating the PFETs, and the gate begins switching as soon as the inputs rise above V_{Tn}. This can give a factor of 2 to 3 performance advantage in some cases compared with static CMOS gates.

The cost of this performance improvement is a loss of noise immunity and a serious timing restriction on the inputs of the gate. For proper operation, the inputs of a dynamic gate must be *monotonically rising* while ϕ is high. That is, after ϕ goes high, a low input is allowed to rise, but once it rises it must remain high, and a high input is not allowed to fall. If an input were to violate this rule, it might discharge the storage node while high. The storage node would then remain low after the input falls because there is nothing to pull it up, giving an incorrect logical result.

---

[17] In a sense, a precharged gate is the extreme case of sizing for asymmetric rise and fall times in which the ratio, K, is made infinite.

Even with this rule, dynamic gates must be carefully laid out to avoid dynamic charge sharing between internal nodes (e.g., node D in Figure 4-41(a)) and the storage node. If input A goes high while input B is low, node D shares charge with output C. For proper operation, node C must have significantly greater capacitance than node D. This problem could be overcome by requiring that the inputs be completely stable while ϕ is high. However, this would restrict the use of dynamic logic to one gate per clock phase, thus severely limiting its utility.

To restore charge lost from the storage node due to charge sharing with internal nodes and to prevent cross talk from capacitive coupling to nearby signals, most dynamic gates use a *keeper* circuit, as illustrated in Figure 4-41(c). The dynamic gate is followed by a high-ratio inverter (to shift V_{inv} up for speed) that generates a noninverted output, $f(\mathbf{x})$. This output is fed back to the gate of a PFET that restores a logic 1 on the storage node as long as the node remains above the inverter threshold. The keeper PFET must be weak, as denoted by the w, so that it can be overpowered by the NFET pulldown network. The use of the keeper greatly increases the reliability and noise immunity of dynamic logic.

4.3.3.3   Domino Logic

A dynamic gate followed by an inverter, as shown in Figure 4-41(c), has the property that monotonically rising inputs give rise to monotonically rising outputs. Thus, an acyclic composition of these noninverting dynamic gates will obey the input timing rule on all gate inputs as long as the inputs to the composition obey this rule. Figure 4-42, for example, shows a three-stage dynamic circuit that exploits this property. A cascade of dynamic gates is often called *domino logic* because the operation of the circuit resembles a line of falling dominoes. The discharge of the first gate triggers the discharge of the second gate, and so on.

Note that because inputs B and D to the second and third stage cannot rise until after ϕ rises, there is no need for the series NFET to disable the pulldown except on the first stage. The absence of this NFET, however, increases current draw during precharge (ϕ low) because the precharge PFET must pull up against a conducting NFET switch network until the preceding stage precharges. The absence of the series NFET also increases the time required to precharge the circuit, for, without this device, the precharge must ripple stage-by-stage from input to output. With a series pulldown device on each stage, all stages can precharge

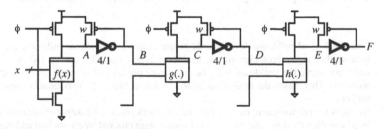

FIGURE 4-42   Domino Logic

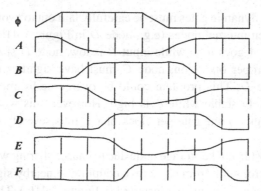

FIGURE 4-43   SPICE Simulation of Domino Circuit

simultaneously. For these reasons, many domino circuits use clocked pulldowns on every stage.[18]

Alternatively the excessive current during precharge can be reduced by delaying the precharge to later stages (e.g., with an inverter pair).

The domino action of this circuit is illustrated in the simulation waveforms of Figure 4-43. The figure shows the waveforms for the three-stage domino circuit of Figure 4-42 where each stage consists of a 3-input NOR gate, $f(x) = x_1 \vee x_2 \vee x_3$. For a timing reference, the vertical lines in the figure are spaced on 50-ps intervals. The waveforms show that when ϕ rises, a chain reaction is set off, with A falling, B rising, C falling, and so on, until F rises. The entire sequence takes 150 ps, with the first stage being slowest (65 ps from ϕ to B) because of its series pulldown device.

With the absence of series NFETs on the later stages, the precharge sequence also proceeds in domino fashion. When ϕ falls, the first stage begins to precharge, and the two later stages, C and E, rise to an intermediate level with the PFET fighting the pulldown network. Only when $B(D)$ falls is $C(E)$ able to rise above the inverter threshold. Considerable current flows during these intervals when the precharge PFET is fighting the pulldown network.

The output of a domino chain is only valid for a short period at the end of the phase that enables the chain and thus must be captured in a latch for use during the next phase while the chain precharges. The monotonic properties of domino gates can be exploited to simplify the required latch,[19] as shown in Figure 4-44. The figure shows a chain of domino logic enabled by $\phi 1$, a latch (shaded region), and the first stage of a $\phi 2$ domino chain. At the end of the evaluate phase, when $\phi 1$ falls, the value on signal B must be held steady while the $\phi 1$ chain precharges. The latch is simplified by observing that at this point signal A is monotonically

---

[18] A single clocked pulldown device can be shared across several stages without loss of performance because the stages draw current one at a time. When a pulldown is shared in this manner, the node just above the pulldown must be separately precharged to avoid dynamic charge-sharing problems. This makes the design equivalent to connecting $\bar{\phi}$ to the bottom terminal of the NFET network.

[19] If there is a small amount of overlap between the clock phases, the output of a domino chain clocked by ϕ_1 can directly drive the inputs of a domino chain clocked by ϕ_2 without an intervening latch.

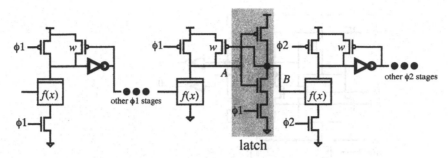

FIGURE 4-44   Two-Phase Domino Logic with Integral Latch

rising. Thus the PFET in the latch can only turn off, and no gating PFET clocked by $\bar{\phi}1$ is required. This is the same trick played in the Svensson latch of Figure 4-39(c) with the monotonicity of the domino logic obviating the need for the first stage of the Svensson latch.[20]

4.3.3.4   Dual-Rail Domino

At this point the astute reader will be questioning the utility of domino logic. After all, domino logic can only implement monotonic functions, and many important logic functions, such as almost all arithmetic functions, are nonmonotonic.

In fact, nonmonotonic functions can be implemented using domino logic by simply computing both polarities of each signal. Such circuits are called *dual-rail* because each logical variable is represented by two wires, one that goes high if the signal is true and one that goes high if the signal is false. With this encoding, an input variable going true can cause an output variable to go true or false (nonmonotonic behavior), and yet all signals are monotonically rising. Such dual-rail domino circuits represent one of the fastest ways to implement a given logic function and thus are widely used today in the arithmetic units of the fastest microprocessors. As we shall see in Section 10.4, dual-rail signaling also facilitates asynchronous design.

As an example of this design style, a dynamic dual-rail, two-input exclusive-or (XOR) gate is shown in Figure 4-45. A three-input version of this circuit is the mainstay of many commercial adder and multiplier designs. The circuit accepts four input signals that represent two input variables. Input signal $a1(a0)$ is high if input variable a is true (false). Similarly, the circuit generates two output signals that encode a single output variable, c. If input signal $a1$ rises, the output variable c may become true or false, depending on the state of variable b. However, in either case one of the two output signals will rise, preserving the monotonic circuit behavior.

Instead of keepers, this circuit employs cross-coupled PFETs to restore high-level signals on internal nodes $\overline{x0}$ and $\overline{x1}$. In general, keepers around the inverters are actually preferred because they reduce the capacitive load on these internal

---

[20] For noise immunity, a pulldown keeper on node B, possibly gated by $\phi2$, should be used with this circuit.

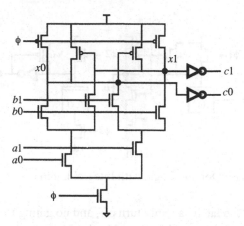

FIGURE 4-45   A Dynamic Dual-Rail XOR Gate

nodes. However, with the cross-coupled PFETs, this circuit can be converted for static use by simply tying ϕ high or by removing the precharge transistors and shorting the clocked NFET. This form of static gate is called a differential cascode voltage switch (DCVS) logic [Heller84].

Although it is possible to share some transistors between the two sides of a dual-rail circuit (e.g., the $a0$ and $a1$ transistors in Figure 4-45), the dual-rail circuits are usually nearly twice the size of their single-rail counterparts (nearly the size of a static CMOS circuit). They are, however, substantially faster than static CMOS circuits.

4.3.3.5   Bootstrap Circuits

A bootstrap circuit exploits capacitive coupling to drive a dynamic node to a voltage that exceeds the power supply. This sounds like a risky proposition, and it is. If the voltage across a device exceeds the supply by more than a small amount, permanent damage may occur. However, if done carefully, bootstrapping can be performed so that all the terminals of a device rise together and the device is not overstressed. Bootstrap circuits are rarely used today – partly because of the danger involved and partly because there are easier ways to qualify clocks with CMOS. For many years, however, they were widely used in NMOS and CMOS circuits to qualify clocks and to drive the word lines of RAM arrays.[21]

The staple bootstrap circuit is the clock-AND driver illustrated in Figure 4-46. This circuit passes the input clock, ϕ, to the qualified output clock, ϕq, when the enable signal, en, is high, and holds ϕq low when en is low. The circuit in effect ANDs ϕ with en, as illustrated in the logic symbol on the right side of the figure. Compared with a static gate, the bootstrap clock-AND is very fast and takes very little chip area.

Operation of the clock-AND is shown in the SPICE waveforms of Figure 4-47. The figure shows two pulses of the input clock, ϕ. During the first pulse, $en = 1$,

---

[21]   The word lines of DRAMs are typically driven V_{Tn} above the power supply so that a full swing signal can be passed through an n-only transmission gate and stored on the bit-cell capacitor.

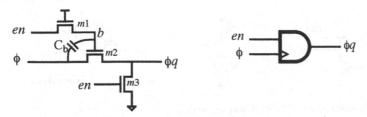

FIGURE 4-46   A Bootstrap Clock-AND Circuit

and the pulse is passed to the output clock with just a 15-ps delay (the driver is 8-μm wide, and the load is 50 fF). The enable is low during the second pulse, and the output remains low. For reference, the vertical lines are spaced on 50-ps intervals and run from 0 to 2.5 V.

The key to the operation of the circuit is the waveform on signal b. When en is high and ϕ is low, b rises to $V_{DD} - V_{Tn}$ or about 1.75 V. At this point, isolation transistor m1 is off and node b is floating. When ϕ rises, the gate-drain and gate-source capacitance of the pass transistor, m2, drawn as C_b in the figure, capacitively couple the rising clock signal onto this floating node, driving b well above the power supply to about 4 V. This process of capacitively driving up the gate-node is called *bootstrapping*, for the gate appears to be pulling itself up by its bootstraps. Because node b, the gate of m2, is always about 1.5 V above the source and drain, m2 passes the full amplitude of the clock signal. It does not attenuate it by V_{Tn}, as with a conventional n-only transmission gate. When ϕ falls, the capacitive coupling to the falling clock returns node b to its previous state. Throughout this process, there is never more than 2 V across any device except the drain diode of m1.

When the second pulse arrives on ϕ, gate node b is low. In this state almost all of the gate capacitance is to the body terminal (Section 4.2.1.1). Thus, capacitor C_b is greatly diminished (just C_{GDO}), there is little capacitive coupling from ϕ to b, and the small isolation device has no trouble holding b at GND.

4.3.4   Source Followers and Cascodes

As shown in Figure 4-48, we can construct an FET amplifier by tying any one of the three main terminals of an FET (not the body) to a power supply. Tying the source to ground gives a common source amplifier (Figure 4-48(a)), which forms

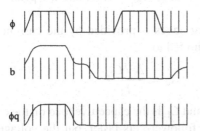

FIGURE 4-47   SPICE Simulation of a Bootstrap Clock-AND

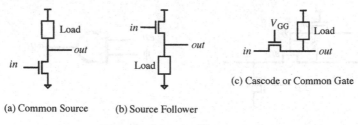

(a) Common Source (b) Source Follower

(c) Cascode or Common Gate

FIGURE 4-48 Three Basic FET Amplifier Forms

the basis for the static CMOS gate (Section 4.3.2). The load here can be a resistor, a current source, or, as in the case of a CMOS gate, a complementary PFET. A source follower results if the drain is tied to V_{DD}, as shown in Figure 4-48(b). Finally, tying the gate to a bias supply, V_{GG}, gives the cascode or common-gate amplifier shown in Figure 4-48(c).

Each of these three configurations has its uses. The common source amplifier is the most widely used because it provides a high-impedance input and both voltage gain and current gain. We have already analyzed it thoroughly in the guise of a CMOS gate. The source follower, in contrast, provides no voltage gain. The output *follows* the input a V_{Tn} drop below. It does, however, provide a high-impedance input, and it is very fast. Finally, the cascode amplifier provides no current gain. When the input is below $V_{GG} - V_{Tn}$, the input and output are effectively connected, and the input receives the entire output load. The cascode does, however, provide voltage gain.

4.3.4.1 Source Follower

A source follower is most often used with a current-source load, as shown in Figure 4-50(a). It is used as a level shifter or as a buffer for a small-swing signal driving a large capacitive load. In this configuration, the output signal follows the input signal with a drop given by

$$(4\text{-}41) \qquad V_{out} = V_{in} - V_{Tn} - \left(\frac{I_S}{\beta}\right)^{1/2}$$

Because the output voltage varies, the body effect modulates V_{Tn} in the same direction, as described by Eq. (4-6), giving the source follower slightly less than unity voltage gain. This effect is illustrated in Figure 4-49, which shows the DC transfer characteristics of a source follower with a $W = 8\text{-}\mu m$ FET and a $100\text{-}\mu A$ current bias. The gain for this circuit is $A_{sf} = 0.88$, and the peak voltage drop from input to output is 0.9 V.

Because all current for falling edges is provided by the current source, the speed of the source follower is limited to

$$(4\text{-}42) \qquad t_d = \frac{\Delta V C_L}{I_S}$$

where ΔV is the voltage swing, and C_L is the capacitive load on the output. Thus, as I_S is made larger, the source follower gets faster, but the voltage drop for a given transistor size gets larger.

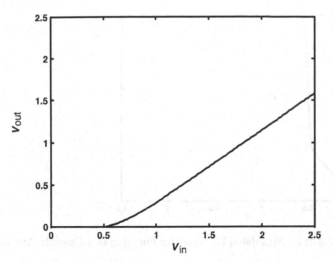

FIGURE 4-49 Simulated DC Transfer Characteristics of a Source Follower

The good news about a source follower is that it presents almost no capacitive load to its input. Because the FET is in saturation, almost all of the gate capacitance is to the source, which is moving in the same direction as the input. Thus, the charge across C_G in Figure 4-50(a) remains nearly constant across the operating range of the circuit, and the effective input capacitance is very small. This is, in essence, the flip-side of the Miller effect. When the gain is positive and nearly unity, Eq. (4-33) shows that the effective feedback capacitance vanishes – no gain, no capacitive pain. Because of this effect, the FET in a source follower can be made quite wide without excessively loading its input.

Logic of a sort can be built out of source followers, as shown in Figure 4-50(b). This circuit computes the function $D = (A \wedge B) \vee C$ with three caveats. First, the circuit is not *composable*. Because output D is a voltage drop, V_{GT}, and has a slightly smaller swing than the input signals, it must be amplified and level-shifted before it can be used as an input to a similar circuit. Second, the reduced input capacitance of the source follower is seen only by the input that causes the output to switch.[22] For example, if A, B, and C are all high, and B swings low, it sees the full C_G of its FET because the output D remains roughly constant

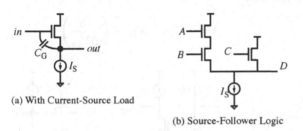

(a) With Current-Source Load

(b) Source-Follower Logic

FIGURE 4-50 Source Follower

---

[22] Many would argue that this is not a problem, for we only care about the delay of the signal that causes the output to switch.

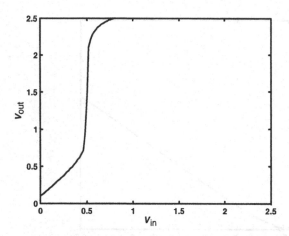

FIGURE 4-51 Simulated DC Transfer Function of a Cascode Amplifier

and is held high by input C. Finally, the fan-in of such a gate is limited because, as the current divides over differing numbers of high inputs, Eq. (4-42) shows that the voltage on D varies as well. Despite these limitations, there are a few applications where this represents an attractive way to sneak a bit of logic into a circuit.

4.3.4.2 Cascode

Figure 4-52(a) illustrates a cascode amplifier with a current-source load, and the simulated DC transfer function for this circuit is shown in Figure 4-51. The circuit has two main regions of operation. When V_{in} is less than a threshold voltage, V_x, the FET is on and the output follows the input with a small upward voltage shift due to the voltage drop, V_{DS}, across the resistive FET. When V_{in} rises above V_x, the FET turns off, and the current source pulls the output high. Between these two main regions of operation is a narrow, high-gain region in which the gain is set by the channel-length modulation factor, λ, of the device and the impedance of the current source (see Exercise 4-15). The curve is rounded at the top of this region because the current source, a PFET current mirror, turns itself off as it runs out of headroom.

If we define the threshold, V_x, as the point where the output drops through V_{GG}, then V_x is given by

(4-43) $$V_x = V_{GG} - V_{Tn} - \left(\frac{I_D}{\beta V_{Tn}} \right)$$

(a) Cascode Amplifier   (b) Bias Generation   (c) Cascode Logic

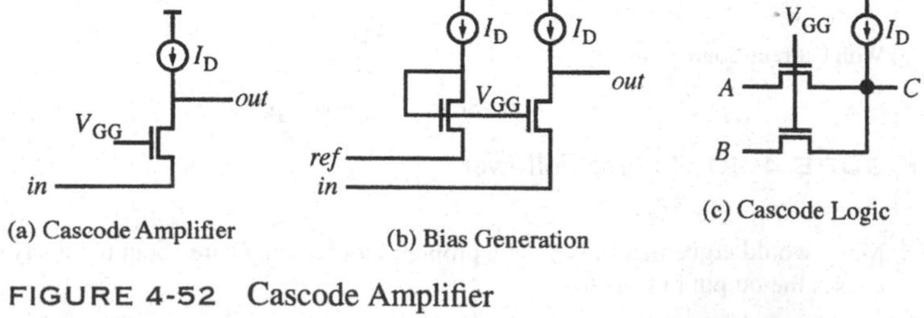

FIGURE 4-52 Cascode Amplifier

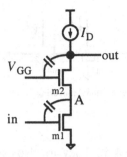

FIGURE 4-53 Cascode Isolates Miller Capacitance

and the voltage drop across the FET in the linear region is

$$(4\text{-}44) \qquad V_{DS} = \frac{I_D}{\beta(V_{GG} - V_{Tn} - V_{in})}$$

The threshold voltage, V_x, in Eq. (4-43) depends strongly on device parameters β and V_{Tn}. Variation in these parameters can be compensated by generating V_{GG} using a *replica-bias* circuit, as shown in Figure 4-52(b). A bias cascode, with input V_{ref} and output tied to V_{GG}, sets V_{GG} to a level that makes the threshold equal to a reference input, V_{ref}. When $V_{in} = V_{ref}$, the two cascodes are identically biased, and $V_{out} = V_{GG}$, our definition of threshold.

As with most amplifiers, logic can be folded into the cascode, as shown in Figure 4-52(c). Here the output C is the logical AND of inputs A and B. This cascode logic is not composable because it provides no current gain. A low input must sink current I_D; yet, the output is not capable of sinking any substantial amount of current.

Because a cascode amplifier has no current gain, it is commonly used in conjunction with another amplifier to enhance its performance. A cascoded common-source amplifier is shown in Figure 4-53, for example. Here a cascode-connected FET, m2, is placed in the drain circuit of a common-source amplifier, m1. The cascode provides two advantages. First, by holding node A at a nearly constant voltage (about $V_{GG} - V_{Tn}$), the effective output impedance of m1, and hence the DC gain of the circuit, is greatly increased. Second, the cascode isolates the input from the Miller-effect capacitance, greatly increasing the AC input impedance in the high-gain region. As shown in the figure, the feedback capacitance from the output is to V_{GG}, an AC ground. The drain of the input FET, node A, is held at a nearly constant voltage and thus the gate-drain capacitance of ml is not multiplied. For these two reasons, both the AC and DC performance of the common-source amplifier are greatly enhanced by adding a cascode stage. As we shall see in Section 4.3.5.2, cascoding can also improve the performance of current sources.

4.3.5 Current Mirrors

A current mirror, as the name suggests, is a circuit that produces a replica or image of a reference current. Current mirrors are widely used in circuits where we need two nearly identical currents, for example for the two current sources in

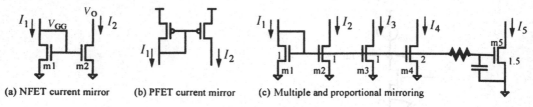

FIGURE 4-54   Current Mirrors

the replica-biased cascode amplifier of Figure 4-52. They are also used as a high-impedance differential load, and because we can mirror one reference current into a large number of copies, as utility current sources.

4.3.5.1   The Basic Current Mirror

The basic current mirror configuration is illustrated in Figure 4-54(a). Input current I_1 biases diode-connected FET m1, generating gate voltage, V_{GG}. An identically sized FET, m2, also has its gate tied to V_{GG} and its source grounded. As long as the drain of m2 remains above V_{GT}, a threshold drop below V_{GG}, m2 is saturated and acts as a current source. With identical sizing and identical gate voltages, m1 and m2 have identical saturation current; thus current I_2 is nominally equal to I_1.

Mathematically, we have

$$(4\text{-}45) \qquad\qquad V_{GG} - V_{Tn} = \left(\frac{I_1}{\beta}\right)^{1/2}$$

Therefore, as long as m2 remains in saturation

$$(4\text{-}46) \qquad I_2 = \beta(V_{GG} - V_{Tn})^2(1 + \lambda V_O) = I_1(1 + \lambda V_O)$$

Consequently, the output impedance of the basic current mirror is largely determined by the channel length modulation

$$(4\text{-}47) \qquad\qquad r_o = \frac{\partial V_O}{\partial I_2} = \frac{1}{\lambda I_1}$$

To increase the output impedance of the current mirror, it is often advantageous to use longer than minimum length devices. The longer length reduces the effects of channel-length modulation.

The DC transfer curve for the simple current mirror is shown in Figure 4-55. This curve is identical to one line from the device's I–V characteristics (Figure 4-15). From 0 to about 0.3 V, the FET is in the triode region, and the current ramps roughly linearly up. Above about 0.3 V the FET enters the saturation region and acts as a current source with the output impedance determined by λ, as described by Eq. (4-47). This curve is for a 2-μm FET biased with a 100-μA current source, giving $V_{GG} \approx 0.9$ V.

Current mirrors can also be constructed referenced to the positive supply using PFETs, as illustrated in Figure 4-54(b).

Once a bias voltage, V_{GG}, has been generated, it can be used to bias any number of FETs to generate multiple replica currents, as illustrated in Figure 4-54(c). It is

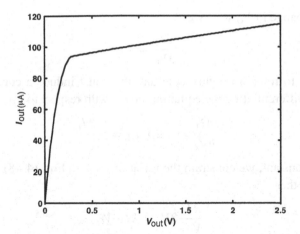

FIGURE 4-55 DC Transfer Curve for a Simple Current Mirror

not unusual to have a single current mirror generate the bias voltage for all of the NFET (or PFET) current sources on a chip. When distributing V_{GG} over a chip, however, it is important that the bias be low-pass filtered close to the point of use, as illustrated with m5 in Figure 4-54(c), to prevent supply noise from corrupting the current source.

By varying the width of the transistors biased with V_{GG}, one can generate proportional current mirrors. For example, in Figure 4-54(c) transistor m4 is sized twice as wide as m1. Thus $I_4 = 2I_1$.

4.3.5.2 The Cascode Current Mirror

The output impedance of a current mirror can be increased at the expense of operating range, sometimes called *headroom*, by adding a cascode stage, as illustrated in Figure 4-56. Here reference current I_1 is used to bias two diode-connected FETs in series generating a pair of gate bias voltages, V_{G1} and V_{G2}, which in turn bias a series-connected pair of FETs in the output leg, m1 and m2. Here m1 is the current source and m2 is a cascode that serves to hold the drain of m1, V_x, at a roughly constant voltage.

To derive the output impedance of the cascode current mirror, we first determine how a change in V_O affects V_x, assuming constant current through m2, and then determine the change in current through m1 caused by this variation in V_x. If we

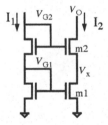

FIGURE 4-56 Cascode Current Mirror

make a small change in V_O we have

(4-48)
$$\frac{\partial I_2}{\partial V_O} = \lambda I_1$$

Now if I_2 is to remain roughly constant, this must induce a corresponding change in V_x. Differentiating the equation for I_{DS} with respect to V_{GT} gives

(4-49)
$$\frac{\partial I_2}{\partial V_x} = -2\beta V_{GT} = \frac{-2I_1}{V_{GT}}$$

To keep I_2 constant, we constrain the variations due to Eqs. (4-48) and (4-49) to cancel each other

(4-50)
$$\frac{2I_1}{V_{GT}}\partial V_x = \lambda I_1 \partial V_O$$
$$\frac{\partial V_x}{\partial V_O} = \frac{\lambda V_{GT}}{2}$$

Substituting V_x for V_O in Eq. (4-47) then gives the output impedance for the cascode current source

(4-51)
$$r_O = \frac{\partial V_O}{\partial I_2} = \left(\frac{2}{\lambda V_{GT}}\right)\left(\frac{1}{\lambda I_1}\right) = \frac{2}{\lambda^2 V_{GT} I_1}$$

To first approximation, the cascode increases the output impedance by more than a factor of $1/\lambda$. The cost paid for this is operating range or headroom. The circuit only operates properly when V_O is large enough to keep both m1 and m2 in saturation. With low-voltage power supplies this can be a serious restriction.

Figure 4-57 shows the I–V characteristics of a cascoded current mirror biased with $I_1 = 100\ \mu A$. The curve shows three regions of operation. From $V_O = 0$ to about 0.3 V, both devices are in the triode region, and the current ramps up nearly linearly from 0 to about 95 μA. From $V_O = 0.3$ to 1.1 V, the current source device, m1, is in saturation, but the cascode device, m2, is still in the triode

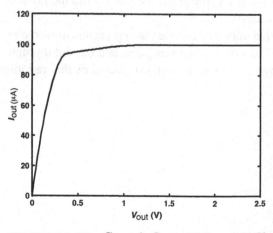

FIGURE 4-57   Cascode Current Mirror I-V Characteristics

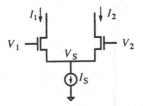

FIGURE 4-58   A Source-Coupled Pair

region. In this region, the cascode acts as a resistance, causing V_x to follow V_O. Thus, the circuit acts as a simple current mirror with the current in this region matching the profile of Figure 4-55. Finally above $V_O = 1.1$ V, both devices are in saturation, and current becomes very flat, reflecting a high-output impedance, about 2 MΩ compared with 100 kΩ for the simple current mirror. However, this high impedance is achieved over a range of only slightly more than half the supply voltage, whereas the simple current source operates over all but 0.3 V of the supply voltage. A nice feature of the cascode current mirror is that its output impedance degrades gracefully. When the cascode device comes out of saturation, it resorts to operation as a simple current mirror.

4.3.6   The Source-Coupled Pair

A source-coupled pair, as shown in Figure 4-58, converts a differential voltage, $\Delta V = V_1 - V_2$ into a differential current $\Delta I = I_1 - I_2$ and is the basic building block of differential circuits: circuits in which the difference of two quantities, not their *common-mode* value, carries information. Differential circuits are widely used to compare two voltages or to amplify a signal with respect to a voltage reference.

The pair consists of two NFETs sharing a common source node, V_S, biased with a current source, I_S. The source node, isolated from ground by the high impedance of the current source, floats a V_{GT} drop below the higher valued of V_1 or V_2. The two NFETs *steer* the current from the current source, dividing it between I_1 and I_2 in proportion to the voltage difference between V_1 and V_2.

4.3.6.1   V–I Characteristics of the Source-Coupled Pair

For an FET biased in the saturation region, a small variation in V_G will generate a change in drain current given by differentiating Eq. (4-4)

(4-52) $$\frac{\partial I}{\partial V} = \beta V_{GT} = \frac{2I_S}{V_{GT}} = g_m$$

We refer to this ratio of current change to voltage change as the forward transconductance of the device, g_m. It depends on both the device transconductance, β, and the bias conditions, V_{GT}.

Applying Eq. (4-52) to a pair that is initially balanced with $\Delta V = 0$ and $I_1 = I_2 = I_S/2$, we get

(4-53) $$\Delta I = g_m \Delta V$$

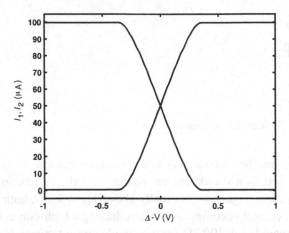

FIGURE 4-59   DC Transfer Characteristics of a Source-Coupled Pair

The DC transfer characteristics of a source-coupled pair built from 2-μm wide FETs biased with 100 μA is shown in Figure 4-59. The curve is fairly linear for $|\Delta V| < 0.25$ V with only a small nonlinearity just before the pair saturates at $|\Delta I| = 100\,\mu$A. The transconductance of this pair, g_m, is about 360 μA/V.

4.3.6.2   Differential Circuit Analysis

When analyzing differential circuits, it is usually best to separate the input and output signals into their *differential* and *common-mode* components and analyze them independently. The differential behavior of the circuit describes how it handles signals, whereas the common-mode behavior of the circuit determines its bias conditions, operating range, and how well it rejects noise. For the differential pair of Figure 4-58, we define two differential variables and two common-mode variables

$$\Delta V = V_1 - V_2 \qquad \Delta I = I_1 - I_2$$

(4-54)

$$V_C = \frac{V_1 + V_2}{2} \qquad I_C = \frac{I_1 + I_2}{2} = \frac{I_S}{2}$$

We can then derive the large-swing operating characteristics as

$$I_1 = \beta\left(V_{CT} + \frac{\Delta V}{2}\right)^2 = \beta\left(V_{CT}^2 + V_{CT}\Delta V + \Delta V^2/4\right)$$

(4-55)

$$I_2 = \beta\left(V_{CT} - \frac{\Delta V}{2}\right)^2 = \beta\left(V_{CT}^2 - V_{CT}\Delta V + \Delta V^2/4\right)$$

$$\Delta I = 2\beta V_{CT}\Delta V$$

where $V_{CT} = V_C - V_S - V_{Tn}$.

This equation shows that, if channel length modulation is neglected, Eq. (4-53) applies across the entire operating range of the circuit as long as both devices remain in the saturation region.

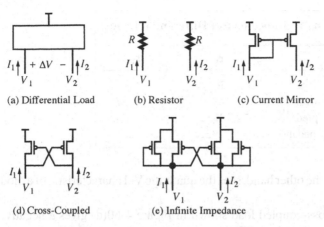

(a) Differential Load   (b) Resistor   (c) Current Mirror

(d) Cross-Coupled   (e) Infinite Impedance

FIGURE 4-60   Some Differential Load Circuits

4.3.6.3   Differential Loads

After a source-coupled pair has converted a differential voltage into a differential current, we typically use a *differential load* to convert the differential current back to a voltage. As shown in Figure 4-60(a), a differential load is a three-terminal circuit. One terminal is a reference terminal, the positive supply in the figure. A pair of voltages, V_1 and V_2, applied to the other two terminals give rise to a pair of currents, I_1 and I_2, or vice-versa. The currents are drawn oriented into the load so that a simple resistor gives a V–I relationship with a positive sign.

We characterize a differential load by its differential impedance, r_Δ, and common-mode impedance, r_C.

(4-56)

$$r_\Delta = \frac{\partial \Delta V}{\partial \Delta I}$$

$$r_C = \frac{\partial V_C}{\partial I_C}$$

The differential impedance determines how much the differential current changes when the voltages on the two terminals are varied in opposite directions. The common-mode impedance determines how much the average or common-mode current changes when both voltages are varied together in the same direction. There are also two cross-impedances (Eq. (4-57)) that we will ignore for now.

Figure 4-60 shows several commonly used differential loads. The differential and common-mode impedance of these loads is tabulated in Table 4-5. Although these loads are all drawn as PFET loads referenced to the positive supply, the same results apply to NFET loads referenced to ground. The simplest differential load is just a pair of equal-valued resistors, as shown in Figure 4-60(b). The resistors must be linear and closely matched to avoid mode coupling, as discussed below. In this case, the differential and common-mode impedances are both just R. A current mirror, Figure 4-60(c), resists any difference in the two currents and provides a high differential output impedance given by Eq. (4.47). The common-mode

TABLE 4-5   **Impedance of Differential Loads**

Load	r_C	r_Δ
Resistor	R	R
Current mirror	$1/g_m$	$1/\lambda I_1$
Cross-coupled	$1/g_m$	$-1/g_m$
Infinite impedance	$1/2g_m$	∞

signal, on the other hand, sees the quadratic V–I characteristic of a diode-connected FET.

The cross-coupled load shown in Figure 4-60(d) gives a negative differential impedance. With both FETs in saturation, an increase in V_1 causes an increase[23] in I_2 or, stated differently, an increase in ΔV causes a decrease in ΔI. This negative impedance causes amplifiers with cross-coupled loads to exhibit hysteresis due to the positive feedback they represent. Placing this negative impedance in parallel with an equal and opposite positive impedance, as shown in Figure 4-60(e), gives a differential load with infinite differential impedance.

4.3.6.4   Mode Coupling

To reject common-mode noise from the differential signal and to avoid having signal levels shift the common-mode operating point of the circuit, we would like to avoid coupling between the common and the differential modes of operation. Unfortunately, mismatches and nonlinearities in the loads couple the modes. To describe this coupling, we define two cross impedances[24]

(4-57)

$$r_{C\Delta} = \frac{\partial \Delta V}{\partial I_C}$$

$$r_{\Delta C} = \frac{\partial V_C}{\partial \Delta I}$$

We are usually more concerned with $r_{C\Delta}$ because it affects the common-mode rejection of a circuit using the load. This coupling impedance can be caused by either a mismatch or a nonlinearity in the load. Consider the case of the resistor load, Figure 4-60(b), where the right-hand resistor is increased to $R + \Delta R$. In this case, an increase in common-mode voltage increases I_1 more than I_2, and we have

(4-58) $$r_{C\Delta} = \left(\frac{1}{R} - \frac{1}{R + \Delta R} \right) = \frac{\Delta R}{R(R + \Delta R)} \approx \frac{\Delta R}{R^2}$$

---

[23] Note that, given the direction of the current arrows into the load, I_2 is usually negative. Hence an increase in V_1 reduces the negative current, resulting in an increase in I_2. The signs work out more conveniently with NFET loads; however, PFET loads more commonly used in practice.

[24] It is often more convenient to think of differential circuits in terms of vectors $V = [V_C \Delta V]^T$ and $I = [I_C \Delta I]^T$. In this case the load is described by a Jacobian matrix with the diagonal terms given by Eq. (4-56) and the cross terms by Eq. (4-57).

An effective mismatch can result from a nonlinearity. Suppose, for example, that our load consists of two perfectly matched diode-connected FETs. If $\Delta V = 0$, the FETs have identical I–V characteristics, $I = \beta V^2$, and there is no mode coupling.

With a nonzero ΔV, however, the two FETs are biased into different operating points, which results in different transconductances, as follows:

$$\partial V_1 = \frac{\partial I_C}{\beta V_1}$$

$$(4\text{-}59) \qquad \partial V_2 = \frac{\partial I_C}{\beta(V_1 - \Delta V)}$$

$$r_{C\Delta} = \frac{\partial \Delta V}{\partial I_C} = \frac{1}{\beta V_1} - \frac{1}{\beta(V_1 - \Delta V)} = \frac{-\Delta V}{\beta V_1(V_1 - \Delta V)} \approx \frac{-\Delta V}{\beta V_1^2}$$

4.3.6.5 FET Resistors

There are many ways to construct load resistors on a MOS integrated circuit. Polysilicon resistors are perfectly linear but are poorly controlled. In most processes their absolute resistance may vary by a factor of 2:1 or more. Resistor-to-resistor tracking is often acceptable, however. Diffusion or N-well resistors are also fairly linear but suffer from a large junction capacitance.

The most popular method of constructing load resistors is to build FET resistors. Four variations of FET resistors are illustrated in Figure 4-61. The first two and the last are intended to be used as loads, with one terminal tied to V_{DD}, whereas the third can be used as a general-purpose resistor with both terminals tied to signal nodes. Although inherently nonlinear, FET resistors have the advantage of compact size, good tracking between components, and the ability to be *digitally trimmed*.

The simplest load resistor is a PFET with its gate grounded as shown in Figure 4-61(a). This device operates in the resistive or *triode* region with the quadratic I–V characteristics of Eq. (4-3). As illustrated by the middle curve of Figure 4-62, the relationship is close to linear for small V, but the quadratic component becomes too large to ignore for $V > 1$ V. To extend the linear region of operation the triode-connected FET may be combined with a diode-connected FET, as shown in Figure 4-61(b). When the I–V curves of the two FETs (two lower curves in Figure 4-62) are added together, the positive quadratic diode curve largely cancels the negative quadratic portion of the triode curve, giving a nearly linear composite curve (top curve of Figure 4-62). The dashed line in the figure shows a perfectly linear resistor for comparison.

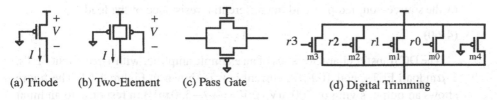

(a) Triode (b) Two-Element (c) Pass Gate (d) Digital Trimming

FIGURE 4-61 FET Resistors

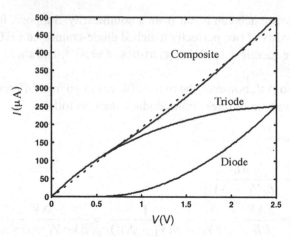

FIGURE 4-62   I–V Characteristic of Two-Element FET Resistor

When the voltage on both terminals of the resistor may vary over a wide range, a pass-gate resistor, Figure 4-61(c), is often employed. As the common-mode terminal voltage rises, the conductance of the PFET is reduced, whereas the conductance of the NFET increases. If the two devices are correctly sized, these two effects nearly cancel one another and yield a relatively constant resistance over a range of terminal voltages.

When a very precise resistance is required, any of these circuits can be digitally trimmed, as illustrated for the triode resistor in Figure 4-61(d). The digital values on lines $r0$ through $r3$ select the subset of transistors $m0$ through $m3$ that are on. If $m0$ through $m3$ are exponentially sized (1x, 2x, 4x, and 8x), this gives sixteen equally-spaced values of variable conductance to be added to the fixed conductance of $m4$. Transitions are problematic with exponential sizing. For example, in switching $r_{3:0}$ from 7 to 8, all transistors may be momentarily off, giving zero variable conductance. To avoid such glitches in conductance values, one can size the variable devices $m0$ to $m3$ equally, giving four equally spaced values of variable conductance. In this case, $r_{3:0}$ are usually driven with a thermometer code in which $r_i \Rightarrow r_{i-1}$.

4.3.6.6   A Simple Differential Amplifier

Combining a source-coupled pair with a load gives a differential amplifier, as shown in Figure 4-63(a). This circuit takes a differential voltage input ($in+$, $in-$). The source-coupled pair converts this to a differential drain current (I_1, I_2), and the load converts this current back to voltage, giving a differential output voltage ($out+$, $out-$). The gain of the amplifier is just the product of the transconductance of the source-coupled pair and the differential resistance of the load

$$(4\text{-}60) \qquad\qquad A_\Delta = g_m r_\Delta$$

The DC transfer characteristics of an example amplifier with 4-μm input FETs, 1-μm load FETs, and 100-μA current bias is shown in Figure 4-64. The figure shows an output swing of 700 mV ($\Delta V = +/-350$ mV) in response to an input

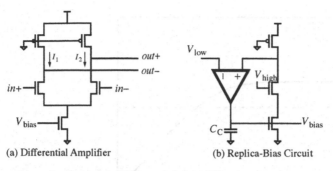

(a) Differential Amplifier (b) Replica-Bias Circuit

FIGURE 4-63   A Differential Amplifier

swing of 400 mV, a gain of about 1.8. The swing is limited by the 350-mV drop across a 3.5 kΩ output resistor carrying the full 100 μA. To achieve the observed gain, the differential pair has a transconductance, g_m, of about 510 μA/V at this operating point.

Variation in the load resistance can be compensated by setting the bias current to give a fixed output swing using a *replica-bias* circuit, as shown in Figure 4-63(b). The three-FET stack is a replica of the on-side of a differential amplifier with one input tied to the high side of the output range, V_{high} (usually V_{DD}). The operational amplifier closes a feedback loop that adjusts the bias current so that the voltage dropped across the load gives a drain voltage equal to the low end of the range, V_{low}. A compensation capacitor, C_C is needed to stabilize the feedback loop.

Logic can be built into a differential amplifier by replacing either or both of the input transistors with arbitrary NFET switching networks. There are two general approaches. Both transistors can be replaced by complementary networks, or one input can be tied to a reference voltage, usually half way between V_{high} and V_{low}, and a single network replaces the other input transistor.

A differential amplifier has a first-order low-pass response with time constant

$$\tau_\Delta = r_\Delta C_d \tag{4-61}$$

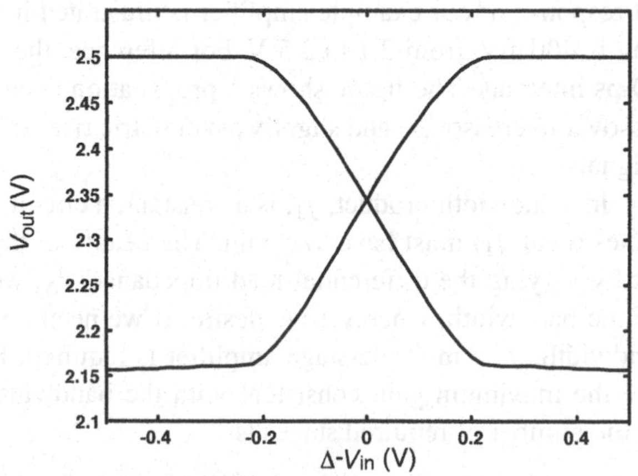

FIGURE 4-64   DC Transfer Characteristics of Differential Amplifier

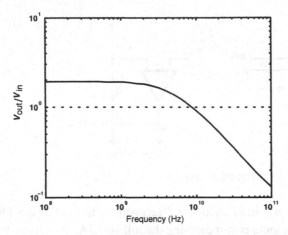

FIGURE 4-65   AC Response of Differential Amplifier

where C_d is the capacitance on the drain nodes of the source-coupled pair. This includes the junction capacitance of the drains of the pair and load devices as well as any output load. To derive Eq. (4-61), observe that the output circuit consists of a parallel combination of a current source (the pair), a resistor (the load), and a capacitor, C_d. When the current source switches, the output settles to the new steady-state value with a time constant determined by the resistor and capacitor.

Varying r_Δ trades off gain (Eq. (4-60)) against bandwidth (Eq. (4-61)). As with static CMOS gates, the product of gain and bandwidth remains constant.

$$(4\text{-}62) \qquad f_1 = A_\Delta f_\Delta = \frac{A_\Delta}{2\pi\tau_\Delta} = \frac{g_m}{2\pi C_d}$$

This is essentially the same equation as Eq. (4-36). The only difference is that g_m varies, depending on bias conditions, and C_d varies with circuit topology.

Figure 4-65 shows the simulated frequency response of our example amplifier. The figure shows a gain of 1.8 that rolls off and reaches the unity-gain point at $f_1 = 9$ GHz.

The transient response of our example amplifier is illustrated in Figure 4-66. The signal swing is 400 mV, from 2.1 to 2.5 V. For reference, the vertical lines are placed at 20-ps intervals. The figure shows a propagation delay of just over 20 ps (from crossover to crossover) and slightly asymmetric rise and fall times of the individual signals.

Because the gain–bandwidth product, f_1, is a constant, a circuit that operates at high frequencies (near f_1) must have low gain. The beauty of the differential amplifier is that by varying the differential load impedance, r_Δ, we can set the gain, and hence the bandwidth, wherever we desire. If we need both high gain, A, and high bandwidth, f, a multiple-stage amplifier is required. Each stage is designed to give the maximum gain consistent with the bandwidth constraint, $A_s = f/f_1$, and the number of required stages is

$$(4\text{-}63) \qquad n = \log_{f/f_1}(A)$$

If what we really want is to amplify a sample of a high-bandwidth signal, we are often much better off using a regenerative circuit.

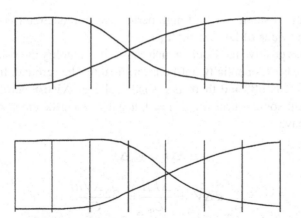

FIGURE 4-66 Transient Response of Differential Amplifier

4.3.7 Regenerative Circuits and Clocked Amplifiers

Suppose we have a small (≈ 50 mV), high-bandwidth differential signal, ΔV, and we need to determine at a given instant in time if it is positive or negative. We could do this in two stages: first by amplifying the signal up to full-swing with a multistage differential amplifier and then sampling it with a latch. However, it is much more efficient to combine the two functions in a clocked regenerative amplifier. Moreover, by building clocked amplifiers with small *aperture* times, we can amplify samples of signals with frequency components above the unity-gain frequency, f_1, of our process.

The simplest regenerative circuit is the *n*-only sense amplifier shown in Figure 4-67(a). The circuit consists of a cross-coupled, source-coupled pair biased by a current source, usually a clocked NFET. The capacitance on each drain node is shown as C_d. This includes the gate capacitance of the other FET and any output

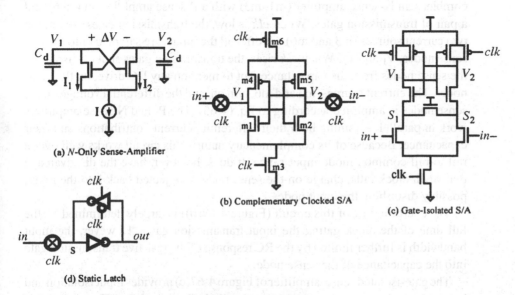

(a) *N*-Only Sense-Amplifier

(b) Complementary Clocked S/A

(c) Gate-Isolated S/A

(d) Static Latch

FIGURE 4-67 Some Regenerative Circuits

load. Because of its small size and high performance, this circuit is commonly used to sense the value of DRAM bit lines.

The circuit has positive feedback, which causes it to amplify the voltage across the drain terminals exponentially until one terminal reaches ground. Initially, the current source, I, is off, and there is a small voltage, $\Delta V(0)$, across the pair. When the current source turns on, at $t = 0$, usually when the clock rises, using Eq. (4-53) we have

$$\Delta I = g_m \Delta V$$

(4-64)

$$d\Delta V = \frac{\Delta I dt}{C_d} = \frac{g_m \Delta V dt}{C_d}$$

Solving this differential equation gives the transient response of all regenerative circuits

(4-65)
$$\Delta V(t) = \Delta V(0) \exp\left(\frac{t g_m}{C_d}\right) = \Delta V(0) \exp\left(\frac{t}{\tau_r}\right)$$

where $\tau_r = C_d/g_m$ is the time constant of the regenerative circuit. Equation (4-65) shows that the positive feedback increases ΔV exponentially, with the voltage increasing by a factor of e each τ_r until the gate of one of the FETs drops below V_T and the FET cuts off.

Another way to derive this behavior is to realize that Figure 4-67(a) is just the negative resistance circuit of Figure 4-60(d). Combining a negative resistance with a capacitor gives a pole in the right-half plane and hence an exponentially increasing voltage.

Figure 4-67(b through d) show three commonly used regenerative circuits. Although these circuits differ in details, they all share the dynamics of Eq. (4-65).

A complementary clocked sense amp is shown in Figure 4-67(b). This circuit combines an N-sense amplifier (m1–m3) with a P-sense amplifier (m4–m6) and a pair of transmission gates. When *clk* is low, the transmission gates are on, the two current sources (m3 and m6) are off, and the inputs are sampled onto the two sense nodes, V_1 and V_2. When *clk* rises, the transmission gates shut off, isolating the sense nodes from the capacitance, not to mention any DC drive, on the input nodes. The current sources, m3 and m6, turn on, and the differential voltage on the sense nodes is amplified according to Eq. (4-65). The P- and N-sense amplifiers work in parallel, summing both their differential current contributions and their capacitance. Because of its complementary nature, this circuit works well over a rail-to-rail common-mode input range. It does, however, have the disadvantage that when clock falls, charge on the sense nodes is injected back into the input, possibly disturbing the input nodes.

The aperture time of this circuit (Figure 4-67(b)) is largely determined by the fall time of the clock gating the input transmission gates. However, the input bandwidth is further limited by the RC response of the resistive transmission gate into the capacitance of the sense node.

The gate-isolated sense-amplifier of Figure 4-67(c) provides input isolation and better charge injection than the conventional clocked amplifier (Figure 4-67(b))

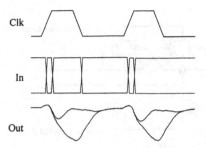

FIGURE 4-68 Transient Response of a Gate-Isolated Sense Amplifier

but has limited common-mode range. When the clock is low, all internal nodes of the gate-isolated amplifier are precharged high.[25] When the clock first rises, all of the devices in the cross-coupled inverters are cut off, and the input pair is in the saturation region. The input pair converts the differential input voltage into a differential current. This current is integrated on source nodes S_1 and S_2, causing these nodes to fall, with one falling faster than the other. When the source node corresponding to the high input, say S_1, reaches a threshold drop below V_{DD}, the transistor above this node begins conducting, transferring the charge imbalance to V_1 and V_2, which starts the regenerative action. At about the same time, the NFET connecting S_1 and S_2 starts conducting. This shorts the source nodes together, ending the influence of the input FETs on the differential signal. The time to reach this point sets the aperture time of this amplifier.

The static latch shown in Figure 4-67(d) is also a regenerative circuit. When the clock falls, the voltage on the storage node, S, relative to the inverter threshold, V_{inv}, is regeneratively amplified when the feedback inverter turns on.

Figure 4-68 shows the transient response of a gate-isolated sense amplifier. The top two traces show the clock and data inputs, respectively, and the bottom trace shows the differential output. To illustrate the short (20-ps) aperture of the amplifier, the data input is held in the correct state for only a 20-ps window aligned with the later half of the rising edge of the clock. The input has the reverse polarity both before and after this aperture. As shown in the bottom trace, the sense nodes have about a 100-mV difference at the end of the aperture. Regeneration exponentially amplifies this small voltage with a time constant $\tau_{gsa} = 22$ ps. The sense nodes reach full swing in about 100 ps. All of the regenerative circuits in Figure 4-67 share this exponential amplification.

All regenerative circuits must be laid out in a manner that exactly matches the capacitance of the two sense nodes. Because these circuits integrate current on the capacitance of the sense nodes, an imbalance in capacitance translates into an offset in the voltage amplified. If only one node of a sense amplifier drives an output load, for example, an equal *dummy load* must be placed on the other sense node. Because the capacitance of different layers varies from wafer to wafer, good matching can only be achieved by exactly duplicating the layout for the two sense

---

[25] In practice, a third precharge transistor should be used, shorting V_1 and V_2. It is omitted here to avoid cluttering the figure.

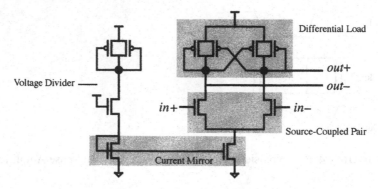

FIGURE 4-69   Qualitative Analysis of a Differential Amplifier

nodes and their loads. It is not sufficient to just attach an equivalent capacitor to the other node.

4.4   CIRCUIT ANALYSIS

4.4.1   Qualitative Circuit Analysis

Identifying the basic circuit forms described in the preceding sections is the key to analyzing circuits qualitatively. Consider, for example, the circuit of Figure 4-69. We will analyze this circuit using the following procedure:

1. Break all feedback loops and assign a direction to any bidirectional circuit elements.
2. Identify basic circuit forms in the circuit and partition the circuit into these components.
3. Identify region(s) of operation for each device.
4. Describe the open-loop behavior of the circuit.
5. Describe the closed-loop behavior of the circuit.

Most of qualitative analysis is pattern matching, recognizing familiar circuit forms, and seeing how they fit together. Only after the qualitative behavior of the circuit is understood does one solve for the quantitative behavior by calculating bias currents, operating points, gains, and delays. Circuit synthesis proceeds in the same manner. First we develop an overall circuit topology[26] as a composition of basic forms. Then we solve for the operating points, bias currents, and device sizes.

4.4.1.1   Qualitative Analysis of a Differential Amplifier

Because the circuit in Figure 4-69 has no feedback loops, we begin by breaking it into basic circuit forms as denoted by the shaded regions of the figure. The

---

[26] A good designer will actually develop several circuit topologies and select the best from among them.

circuit consists of a voltage divider, a current mirror, a source-coupled pair, and a differential load. Note that the NFET at the lower left belongs to both the voltage divider and the current mirror.

We are now prepared to understand the basic operation of the circuit by seeing how the basic circuit forms interact. First, the voltage divider, a series connection of a PFET diode, an NFET resistor, and an NFET diode, determines the amount of current required to develop a reasonable voltage across the common-mode load (the PFET diode).[27] In short, the voltage divider is a bias generator, simpler and less precise than the replica-bias circuit shown in Figure 4-63(b). Next, the current mirror, which shares a device with the voltage divider, mirrors this current to bias the source-coupled pair. The source-coupled pair then steers this current, generating a differential current into the load, ΔI, that depends on the differential input voltage, ΔV, with a gain given by the transconductance, g_m. Finally the differential load converts ΔI to an output voltage with gain due to the differential resistance, r_Δ.

Once this qualitative behavior is understood, it is easy, given device sizes, to solve for the bias current, the gain, and the common-mode operating point. These are left as an exercise for the reader.

4.4.1.2   Qualitative Analysis of a Voltage-Controlled Oscillator

The circuit of Figure 4-70 consists of three inverters with a current-source controlled by the input in series with the source of each inverter FET. A current mirror is used to make the current of the PFET current sources track that of the NFET current sources. To analyze this circuit, we first remove the feedback connection. Next we identify the current sources and the inverters and partition the circuit into these elements. We observe that the current source devices remain mostly in the saturation region. The inverter devices, on the other hand, act as switches operating almost entirely in the resistive region.

We are now prepared to sketch the open-loop transient response of the circuit. Suppose node a switches from high to low. When node a passes through V_{inv},

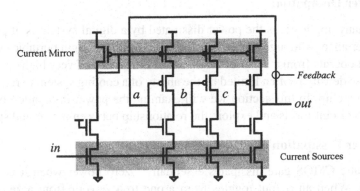

FIGURE 4-70   VCO Using Current-Starved Inverters

---

[27] The exact amount of voltage drop will vary with process, voltage, and temperature; however, with appropriate device sizing it can be made to stay within the desired region.

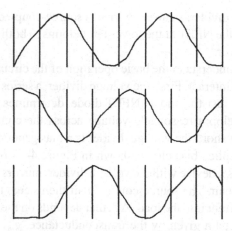

FIGURE 4-71   Simulated Waveforms for Current-Starved Inverter VCO

the inverter will *switch* and start charging node b from the current source. The result will be a near-linear rise on node b, taking $t_r = V_{DD}C_{inv}/I_{bias}$ to swing from rail to rail. For example, if the capacitance of the 4-μm/2-μm inverter is 15 fF per stage and the current bias is 50 μA, then $t_r = 750$ ps. Stage b will begin switching at the midpoint for a stage-to-stage delay of $t_d = 375$ ps.

When we close the feedback loop, we create an oscillator because a high value on a leads to a high value on c, which in turn causes a to fall. Each half-cycle takes three stage delays, 1,125 ps, for a period of 2.25 ns. It is easy to see that this period is inversely proportional to the bias current.

For comparison, simulated waveforms for the VCO are shown in Figure 4-71. The figure shows the waveforms at nodes a, b, and c in Figure 4-70. For timing reference, the vertical lines are spaced at 500-ps intervals. The charging and discharge ramps are not perfectly linear, and the period is 2 ns rather than 2.25 ns; however, in general our qualitative analysis closely predicts the simulated behavior.

4.4.2   Power Dissipation

In many applications the power dissipated by a digital system is of penultimate importance. Although this is obviously true for lightweight portable systems that must operate from a small battery pack, it is also true of very high-speed circuits whose density is often limited by the ability of a cooling system to remove power from a chip. In this section we will examine the power dissipation of common MOS circuit forms and explore the relationship between power and speed.

4.4.2.1   Power Dissipation of a Static CMOS Gate

A static CMOS gate dissipates essentially[28] zero power when it is in a stable state. When an output toggles from a one to a zero or from a zero to a one,

---

[28] There is a small amount of dissipation due to subthreshold conduction and leakage current. However, in most applications this is small enough to ignore.

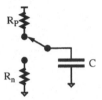

FIGURE 4-72 Power Dissipation in a Static CMOS Gate

however, power is dissipated in the transistors that charge and discharge the load capacitance. Consider the circuit of Figure 4-72, which models the power dissipation of a static CMOS gate. When the output switches from zero to one, the capacitor is charged through resistor R_P. The switching energy, E_{sw}, dissipated in this process is given by the integral

$$(4\text{-}66) \qquad E_{sw} = \int_0^{V_{DD}} (V_{DD} - V_C)I \, dt = \int_0^{V_{DD}} (V_{DD} - V_C)C \, dV_C = \frac{CV_{DD}^2}{2}$$

An identical amount of energy is dissipated in the pulldown resistor R_N when the gate output switches from one to zero. Thus, for a full cycle, from zero, to one, and back to zero, a charge $Q = CV_{DD}$ is transferred from the power supply to ground dissipating energy $E_{cy} = QV_{DD} = CV_{DD}^2$. For example, a 2-$\mu$m/1-$\mu$m inverter in our example process driving an identical inverter has a switching energy, E_{sw}, of about 25 fJ or a dissipation per cycle, E_{cy}, of 50 fJ.

The power dissipation of a CMOS gate depends on its output signal frequency

$$(4\text{-}67) \qquad P_{sig} = E_{cy}f_{sig} = CV_{DD}^2 f_{sig}$$

Often the signal frequency, f_{sig}, is expressed in terms of a duty factor, K_D, and the clock frequency, f_{ck}, as follows:

$$(4\text{-}68) \qquad P = CV_{DD}^2 f_{tog} = CV_{DD}^2 K_D f_{ck}$$

For most sequential logic, the worst possible case is that a node toggles every cycle, going through a full cycle every other cycle, for $K_D = 0.5$. More often, one assumes a much lower value for K_D (typically about 0.15) based on statistical measurements from actual circuits.

Equation (4-68) shows that the power dissipated by a static CMOS circuit increases linearly with frequency and depends quadratically on voltage and linearly on capacitance and duty factor. To build low-power circuits we strive to keep capacitances small, operate slowly with low-duty factor, and use as small a supply voltage as possible.

4.4.2.2 Energy-Delay Product of a CMOS Gate

As we decrease the supply voltage, V_{DD}, of a static CMOS gate, power decreases quadratically and the speed of the gate decreases approximately linearly. If the gate is not velocity saturated, $I_{DSS} = \beta(V_{DD} - V_T)^2$ and we can rewrite

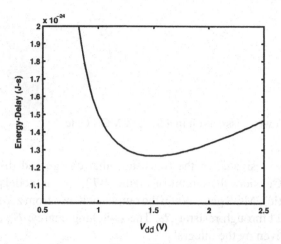

FIGURE 4-73   Energy-Delay Product as a Function of Supply Voltage

Eq. (4-24) as

$$(4\text{-}69) \qquad \tau = \frac{V_{DD}C}{I_{DSS}} = \frac{C}{\beta}\left[\frac{V_{DD}}{(V_{DD} - V_T)^2}\right] = \frac{C}{\beta}\left(V_{DD} - 2V_T + V_T^2/V_{DD}\right)^{-1}$$

Thus, the *energy-delay product*[29] of the CMOS gate, a useful figure of merit, is given by multiplying Eqs. (4-68) and (4-69) to give

$$(4\text{-}70) \qquad E_{cy}\tau = \frac{C^2 V_{DD}}{\beta}\left(1 - 2V_T/V_{DD} + V_T^2/V_{DD}^2\right)^{-1}$$

The energy delay product for a minimum-sized inverter in our example process is plotted in Figure 4-73 as a function of V_{DD}. For a large V_{DD} compared with V_T, the expression in parentheses in Eq. (4-70) is nearly one, and the energy-delay product increases linearly with V_{DD}. As V_{DD} becomes smaller, however, this term begins to dominate with the energy-delay product and reaches a minimum of about 1.5 V, asymptotically increasing to infinity at $V_{DD} = V_T$. In this region, switching energy is still decreasing quadratically with voltage; however, delay is increasing faster than quadratically.

This curve suggests that lower energy-delay products can be realized by reducing the threshold voltage of the devices, V_T. This is true up to a point. However, if V_T is made too small, power due to static subthreshold leakage current will begin to dominate the dynamic switching power.

4.4.2.3 AC Versus DC Power

Because a static CMOS gate dissipates no power when it is not switching, most of the power it dissipates is AC power. For example, consider an inverter that has a fan-out of four with a delay of 85 ps and a rise time of 170 ps (see Section

---

[29] Many texts use *power*-delay product rather than *energy*-delay product. This is a less meaningful measure, however, for the power dissipated by a static CMOS gate is determined by the frequency at which the gate is operated, f_{sig}, whereas the energy is determined only by the properties of the gate and its load.

4.3.2.3). Suppose this gate is used in a system with a 400-MHz clock cycle, $t_{cy} = 2.5$ ns, and that the signal toggles, on average, once every three cycles, completing a full cycle every six cycles. During each switching event, the gate draws an average AC current of about 300 μA, (2.5 V)(21 fF)/170 ps. Averaged over time, however, the DC current is only 3.5 μA. This 85:1 ratio of AC to DC gives CMOS a tremendous power advantage over logic families such as NMOS or SCFL that draw DC current. However, it also makes the job of power distribution (see Chapter 5) more challenging because the power network must deliver substantial AC current at frequencies comparable to the clock.

4.4.2.4 Power Dissipation of Source-Coupled FET Logic

In contrast to the static CMOS gate, a source-coupled FET gate, such as the differential amplifier or buffer shown in Figure 4-63, draws constant DC current from the power supply. The power here is easy to calculate, $P = I_{bias}V_{DD}$. The switching energy of the source-coupled gate is reduced because the output swings over a narrow range, ΔV, rather than from rail to rail, as in the static gate. This gives

(4-71) $$E_{cy} = CV\Delta V$$

However, even a 10:1 reduction in signal swing cannot compensate for the 85:1 ratio of idle to switching periods for our typical gate. Thus, source-coupled circuits like the emitter-coupled circuits they are derived from are at a serious disadvantage in terms of power.

By varying the bias current of a source-coupled stage, we can, within limits, linearly trade off delay against power. If we rewrite Eq. (4-61) using $r_\Delta = \Delta V / I_{bias}$, we find that the *power-delay product* is independent of I_{bias}

(4-72) $$P\tau = (I_{bias}V_{DD})\left(\frac{C\Delta V}{I_{bias}}\right) = CV_{DD}\Delta V$$

Thus, reducing bias current by a factor of two, while holding ΔV constant, cuts power dissipation in half at the expense of doubling delay.

4.5 BIBLIOGRAPHIC NOTES

The classic text on digital MOS circuit design is Hodges and Jackson [Hodg-Jack83]. A more modern treatment can be found in Rabaeye [Rabaey96]. The texts by Glasser and Dobberpuhl [GlasDobb85] and Uyemura [Uyemura92] also give good treatments of the subject.

There are many mathematical models of the MOSFET. The one we develop here is derived from Schichman and Hodges [ShicHodg68]. The concept of logical effort was developed by Sutherland and Sproull [SuthSpro91]. Yuan and Svensson describe the family of single-phase latches and flip-flops [YuanSven89]. Differential cascode voltage switch logic (DCVSL) is described by Heller et. al. [HellGriff84]. A good treatment of replica-biased amplifiers used for delay elements is [Maneat96]. The linearized MOSFET resistor was first proposed in

[BabaTeme84], which describes a variant based on depletion-mode FETs. Modern CMOS processes have only enhancement-mode devices, and the form of this load that we use in this text was first analyzed in [MoonZagh90]. Gabara and Knauer first described digitally trimmed MOSFET resistors [GabaKnau92]. The amplifiers in Exercises 4-21 and 4-22 are described in [Char88] and [Bazes91].

4.6 EXERCISES

4-1 **Switch Logic:** The circuit in Figure 4-74 computes a four-bit output, $y_{3:0}$, from a three-bit input, $a_{2:0}$. What function does it perform? How would you perform the same function using logic gates (NANDs and NORs)? How many transistors would the gate implementation require? How does that compare with the switch implementation? (optional) Estimate the relative delays of the gate implementation and the switch implementation.

4-2 **Logical Effort:** Calculate the logical effort (see Section 4.3.2.3) of a 3-input NOR gate.

4-3 **Gate Decoders:** Draw the logic diagram for a 3-to-8 decoder (a circuit that drives output y_i high when the input pattern is the binary representation of i) using only NAND gates and again using only NOR gates. Use logical effort to compare the performance of a NAND decoder and a NOR decoder.

4-4 **Pseudo-NMOS Gate (DC Response):** Consider the inverter circuit in Figure 4-75(a). Compute its DC transfer function (V_{out} as a function of V_{in}). What is V_{OL}, the output voltage when V_{in} is equal to V_{DD}? How much power is consumed by this gate compared with a static CMOS gate? Suppose the resistor is implemented as a PFET with a grounded gate (as is common practice) and that the ratio of I_{DSSn}/I_{DSSp} varies by a factor of 1.5 across process corners. What does this do to V_{OL}?

4-5 **Pseudo-NMOS Gate (AC Response):** Compute the approximate rising and falling delay of the gate shown in Figure 4-75(a) driving an identical gate. Assume that $V_{OL} = 0.1V_{DD}$. How does its delay compare with that of a static CMOS gate?

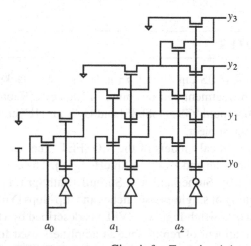

FIGURE 4-74   Circuit for Exercise 4-1

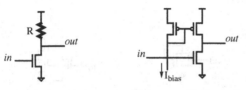

(a) Pseudo-NMOS Inverter   (b) Inverter with Current-Source Load

FIGURE 4-75   Circuits for Exercises 4-4

4-6 Current-Source Load (DC Response): Consider the inverter circuit in Figure 4-75(b). Compute its DC transfer function (V_{out} as a function of V_{in}). What is V_{OL}, the output voltage when V_{in} is equal to V_{DD}? Not counting the bias current (I_{bias}) to the current mirror, how much power is consumed by this gate compared with a static CMOS gate? Suppose that I_{bias} is generated by an appropriately sized NFET with its gate tied to V_{DD}. How does variation of 1.5 in the ratio of I_{DSSn}/I_{DSSp} affect this circuit?

4-7 Current-Source Load (AC Response): Compute the approximate rising and falling delay of the gate of Figure 4-75(b) driving an identical gate, assuming that $V_{OL} = 0.1V_{DD}$. How does it compare with a static CMOS gate and with the pseudo-NMOS gate of Figure 4-75(a)?

4-8 Logic in Latches: The area and performance of a circuit can often be improved by combining logic with a latch or flip-flop. Take the three latch circuits shown in Figure 4-39 and modify them to combine a 2-input NAND gate with the latch. How does your combined circuit compare with concatenating a NAND gate with a separate latch in terms of transistor count and delay?

4-9 Sizing Static Gates: Figure 4-76 shows one path through a two-stage 6-to-64 decoder. The first stage decodes the true ($a_{5:0}$) and complement ($\bar{a}_{5:0}$) inputs two bits at a time in three 2-to-4 decoders using twelve 2-input NAND gates. The fan-out (FO) of each input signal is two. The outputs of the first-stage decoders are labeled $\bar{b}_{3:0}$, $\bar{c}_{3:0}$, and $\bar{d}_{3:0}$, respectively. The second stage combines one output from each of the three decoders (one signal from each of b, c, and d) in sixty-four 3-input NOR gates (AND gates with low-true inputs) to produce the output, $y_{63:0}$. Each output drives a fan-out of 32. All gates are sized 2/1 (2-μm PFETS over 1-μm NFETS). What is the delay of this decoder? What is the total effort of the decoder (the product of logical effort and electrical effort)? Resize the decoder and add inverter stages as necessary to keep the total effort per stage six or less. Convert NANDs to NORs using DeMorgan's law as required. What is the delay of your resized decoder? What is its total effort?

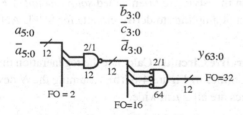

FIGURE 4-76   Path through a two-Stage 6-to-64 Decoder for Exercise 4-9

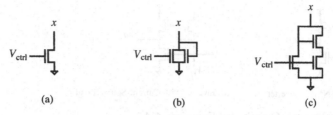

FIGURE 4-77   Voltage-Controlled FET Resistors

4-10   **Current-Mirror Sizing:** Figure 4-55 shows the transfer curve for a 2-μm NFET biased to act as a 100-μA current source. Suppose this 100-μA current source were made from a 0.5-μm-wide NFET? What would happen to the transfer curve? How would the current source's sensitivity to V_{Tn} variations change? What would happen if the current source were made from an 8-μm-wide FET?

4-11   **Setup and Hold Time of Svensson Latch:** Estimate the setup and hold time of the Svensson latch shown in Figure 4-39(c). Are these times different for rising and falling data inputs?

4-12   **Negative-Clock Svensson Latch:** Modify the Svensson latch of Figure 4-39(c) so it passes its input when the clock is low and holds its output when the clock is high.

4-13   **Svensson Edge-Triggered Flip-Flop:** Concatenating the negative-clock Svensson latch of Exercise 4-12 with the positive-clock Svensson latch of Figure 4-39(c) gives a four-stage circuit that realizes an edge-triggered flip-flop. Show how this circuit can be manipulated to give a 3-stage edge-triggered flip-flop using nine devices.

4-14   **Speed of Domino Logic:** How much faster is the three-stage 3-NOR domino circuit simulated in Figure 4-43 than an equivalent static circuit?

4-15   **Gain of Cascode Amplifier:** Calculate the DC gain of a cascode amplifier in terms of the transistor parameters. What is its gain–bandwidth product?

4-16   **Voltage-Controlled Resistors:** Figure 4-77 shows three methods for varying the resistance of a FET resistor using a control voltage. Using SPICE, compute the I–V curves for the three resistors for values of V_{cntl} between 1 and 2.5 V in 0.5-V increments. Which resistor would you use for small voltage swings above GND? Which would you use if the voltage swing is large and constant? Which would you use if the voltage swing is between GND and V_{cntl}?

4-17   **Source-Coupled FET Logic:** The differential amplifier of Figure 4-63 can be thought of as a buffer (or inverter if the outputs are swapped) for low-swing differential logic signals. Logic gates built in this style are often called *source-coupled FET logic* or SCFL. Modify the differential amplifier to derive circuits for SCFL AND, OR, and XOR gates.

4-18   **Time Constant of Regenerative Circuits:** Calculate the regeneration time constant, τ_r, of the clocked sense amplifier of Figure 4-67(b), assuming the N-devices are all 1 μm wide and the P devices are all 2 μm wide.

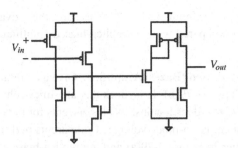

FIGURE 4-78 Supply Insensitive Buffer Amplifier

4-19 **Sizing of Source-Coupled Circuits:** Determine the appropriate device sizes to bias the differential amplifier of Figure 4-69 for a 700-mV output swing with a source current of 100 μA. What is the small-signal gain of the circuit at this operating point? (optional) Simulate your sized circuit using SPICE to confirm your results.

4-20 **Supply Voltage and Delay:** It is desirable to build timing circuits from logic elements that have delays that are relatively insensitive to power supply variations to reduce timing jitter due to supply noise. Source-coupled circuits are often used in these circuits because of their low delay sensitivity to supply noise (dt_d/dV_{DD}). To see this first hand, compute the sensitivity of delay to supply voltage for a static CMOS inverter and a differential amplifier (or alternatively make this comparison using SPICE). The low-swing output of a differential amplifier must usually be amplified up to a full-swing signal to clock circuits. If an inverter is used for this final amplifier, the supply sensitivity of the overall timing circuit is increased. Consider using the circuit of Figure 4-78 to perform this amplification. Give a qualitative analysis of this circuit's operation and compute its delay sensitivity to supply voltage. How does its sensitivity compare with that of a static CMOS inverter?

4-21 **Self-Biased (Chappell) Amplifier:** The circuit of Figure 4-79(a) generates its own current source bias. Explain qualitatively how this circuit operates. How does it adjust its bias current in response to device parameter variations and in response

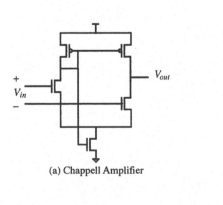

(a) Chappell Amplifier

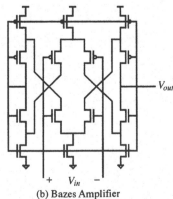

(b) Bazes Amplifier

FIGURE 4-79 Self-Biased Amplifiers

to a change in common-mode input voltage? What are the advantages and disadvantages of this circuit compared with the replica-biased amplifiers of Figures 4-63 and 4-69?

4-22   **Wide Common-Mode, Self-Biased (Bazes) Amplifier:** Give a qualitative analysis of the Bazes amplifier of Figure 4-79(b). How does this amplifier achieve its wide common-mode input range? How does it adjust its bias currents for parameter variations and variations in input common-mode voltage? Compare its performance with that of the Chappell amplifier in Figure 4-79(a) and the replica-biased amplifier of Figure 4-63.

5 POWER DISTRIBUTION

Digital logic requires a stable, quiet, DC supply voltage while drawing a large AC current with very high-frequency components comparable to signal rise times. It is not unusual for a high-performance digital circuit board to draw over 200 A from the primary power supply with the derivative at the point of use over 200 GA/s. However, with careful design, a power supply network can tolerate large variations in current draw while holding the supply voltage within a specified range (typically ±10% or less).

    In this chapter we discuss the characteristics of power supply networks and their loads and explore several methods for providing quiet supplies for high-performance digital systems. We begin by examining the primarily inductive, off-chip power supply network in Section 5.1. The supply and ground are distributed over a network with inductive and resistive components. The current causes IR drops across the resistive components, and the derivative of the current causes $L di/dt$ drops across the inductive components. In this section we look at the most commonly used passive method to provide load regulation: bypass capacitors, which supply the high-frequency components of the current demand and thus smooth the current load carried by the inductive components of the distribution network.

Section 5.2 examines active methods to control the power supply. Clamps and shunt regulators smooth the current profile of the load by adding an additional current in parallel with the load current. Local series regulators step down a distribution voltage to the local supply voltage and use the *headroom* between these two voltages to absorb voltage variations on the distribution supply. When switching regulators are used for local regulation, there is also a significant reduction in the current required for the distribution supply.

In Section 5.3 we examine the problem of on-chip power distribution. We start by looking at the current profiles drawn by individual logic gates and typical logic functions. Using these load models, we then examine the problem of distributing the load current across the primarily resistive thin-film on-chip distribution networks. We see how the on-chip logic itself aids this process by providing *symbiotic* bypass capacitance.

The next two sections address noise control methods. Section 5.4 describes how supply isolation can be used to isolate sensitive circuits from the supply noise created by noisier parts of the system. Bypass capacitors are examined more closely in Section 5.5. We see how the parasitic resistance and inductance of bypass capacitors limit the frequencies of current they can handle. A hierarchy of bypass capacitors is thus needed, and each level of the hierarchy must provide enough capacitance to limit the ripple across the inductance of the next level.

We close the chapter in Section 5.6 by bringing all of this material together in an example power distribution system for a high-performance digital system. Our example uses on-chip linear regulators and clamps, a hierarchy of bypass capacitors, on-chip and off, and board-level regulation with switching power supplies to reduce distribution current.

Power supply noise is a major factor in the design of a digital signaling system. By examining the characteristics of supply networks and the sources of supply noise this chapter lays the groundwork for our examination of the effects of supply noise in Section 6.2 and our design of signaling systems insensitive to supply noise in Chapter 7.

5.1   THE POWER SUPPLY NETWORK

Figure 5-1 shows a typical power distribution network. Power is supplied by voltage sources (V_P) at one or more points on the network. This power is distributed in a network composed of cables, backplanes, and PC boards to several integrated circuit packages. Each package supplies power to one or more chips. Power is supplied to circuits on each chip through a hierarchy of distribution networks.

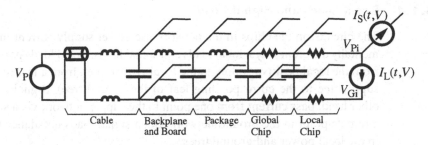

FIGURE 5-1   A Typical Power Supply Network

Usually the network is a tree; however, it is not unusual to short the leaves and intermediate nodes of the tree, resulting in a power network with loops. Despite commonly misunderstood fears of ground loops (see Exercise 5-1), such shorting usually improves the performance of the power distribution network by lowering the impedance presented to a typical load.

The upper level of the power distribution grid is primarily inductive with distributed capacitance, whereas the on-chip portion of the grid is mainly resistive with distributed capacitance. The inductances are due to the bus bars, cables, powerplanes, connector pins, and package pins used to distribute the power from the supply to the integrated circuit. One or more *bypass* capacitors are typically inserted between the power and ground networks along the path from supply to load. These capacitors supply AC current to the load faster than the inductor can respond with reasonable voltage ripple. Because there are both distributed (parasitic) and lumped (bypass) capacitors in the inductive portion of the network, it has properties that are intermediate between those of an LC circuit and a transmission line.

Although we are primarily concerned with the inductance of the upper levels of the supply network, they do have a nontrivial resistance. This resistance results in local heating of the lines and drives the requirement for cable gauge or bus-bar cross section. Also, without local regulation or a remote sense feature, the IR drop across the resistance of the distribution network can result in a significant voltage drop.

Each inductive section of the network acts as an undamped, second-order low-pass filter. The bypass capacitors downstream (toward the load) from a section must be large enough to supply AC current above the cutoff frequency of the section without an excessive $i/j\omega C$ drop. The downstream portion of the network must also be sufficiently resistive at the resonant frequency of the section, $\omega_c = (LC)^{-1/2}$, to damp any oscillations.

The major resistance in the network is due to the on-chip power distribution wiring. These wires are sized both to limit the iR drops to reasonable levels and to avoid metal migration or local heating due to excessive current density. Both explicit bypass capacitors and symbiotic capacitors due to "quiet" circuits and wiring capacitance are distributed throughout this network. Each section of this network acts as a first-order RC lowpass filter. Local capacitance acts to smooth out the current profile carried by the resistive network to lower the peaks of the iR drop.

5.1.1   Local Loads and Signal Loads

The circuits on the chips in the network use power supply current in two fundamentally different ways: local loads and signal loads. Local loads pass current, I_L, from the local positive supply to the local ground (i.e., from a leaf of the positive supply tree to the corresponding leaf of the ground tree). Signal loads, on the other hand, pass current from one point in the supply network via a signal lead to a remote point in the ground network. Such signal loads unbalance the currents in the local power and ground trees.

5.1.1.1   Local Loads

The iR drops and $L\,di/dt$ due to local loads cause the differential supply voltage at point $i\,(V_{Pi} - V_{Gi})$ to vary. However, because the supply and ground currents are balanced, if the distribution networks are also balanced, local loads do not affect the common mode supply voltage $(V_{Pi} + V_{Gi})/2$ between two leaves of the network. The balanced and local nature of these loads makes it easy to address the AC portion of the noise they generate by placing either a bypass capacitor or a shunt regulator, or both, from V_{Pi} to V_{Gi} or by using local conversion as described in Section 5.2.

5.1.1.2   Signal Loads

Signal loads are more problematic, for they affect the common-mode voltage between two points in the network. A signal load passes a current, I_S, from the positive supply V_{Pi} at one point in the network to the negative supply V_{Gj} at a different point in the network. Because, to first order, the bypass capacitors act as AC shorts between corresponding points of the power and ground network, we consider a single network composed of the parallel combination of the power and ground networks when analyzing signal loads. In this combined network, a signal load passes current, I_S, from point i to point j, and this current returns through a path in the power supply network with impedance Z_{ij}, which induces a voltage

(5-1) $$V_{ji} = V_j - V_i = Z_{ji}I_S$$

When a transmitter at point i sends a single rising signal with amplitude V_S over a line with impedance Z_0, the return current causes the receiver's supply to shift by

(5-2) $$V_{ji} = \frac{V_S Z_{ij}}{Z_0 + Z_{ij}}$$

This causes the receiver to see a rising waveform with amplitude

(5-3) $$V_R = V_S\left(1 - \frac{Z_{ij}}{Z_0 + Z_{ij}}\right)$$

If the return impedance is comparable to the signal impedance, the receiver sees a half-amplitude signal because the voltage is evenly split between the line and signal return. If a 1-V signal is sent at the transmitter, the receiver sees the signal rise by 0.5 V, and the transmitter supplies (both power and ground) momentarily drop by 0.5 V. If voltage-mode signaling is used (Section 7.4.1.1), all unswitched signals from the transmitter also drop by 0.5 V, possibly causing high signals to be incorrectly detected as low signals.

Because variation in signal load current causes both receiver supplies to shift relative to the transmitter, remedies that control the differential voltage at one point in the network (e.g., bypass capacitors or local conversion) do not address the spatial common-mode supply voltage shift caused by signal currents.

There are several approaches to reduce supply noise due to signal currents. A brute-force method is to reduce supply impedance. This is costly and difficult to do in practice. A more effective method is to balance signal currents so the net current between two points in the supply network is DC, for example by using differential signaling (Section 7.3.5) or N of M signaling (Section 8.4).

It is useful to provide a signal return path separate from the power supplies to isolate signal return noise from power supply noise due to local loads. However this does not solve the problem of signal return noise; it simply moves the problem from the power supply network to a signal return network. The problem of signal return cross talk in such a network is addressed in more detail in Section 6.3.3.

5.1.2 Inductive Power Supply Noise

To simplify our analysis we will start by considering a single section of the inductive (off-chip) portion of the supply network. As shown in Figure 5-2, a section of the supply network can be modeled either as a transmission line (with impedance Z_S and length t_1) or as a pair of inductors (L_P and L_G). Both models connect a voltage source, V_P, to a bypass capacitor, C_B, and a variable current load, I_L. Because the impedance of the line is high compared with the load, we will model it as a lumped inductance and consider only the inductive model on the right side of the figure.

The nature of the differential noise caused by a section of the inductive (off-chip) power supply network depends on the frequency spectrum of the load current, I_L. The natural frequency of a section of the network is

$$(5-4) \qquad \omega_c = \frac{1}{\sqrt{LC}}$$

where $L = L_P + L_G$.

Load currents at frequencies well below ω_c see primarily the inductive impedance, whereas high-frequency currents see primarily the capacitor, giving a

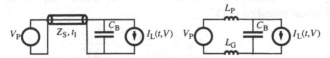

FIGURE 5-2   Two Models for an Inductive Section of the Supply Network

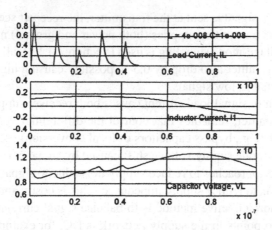

FIGURE 5-3   Response of LC Section to a Transient Load

voltage drops, respectively, of

(5-5) $$V_{\text{NL}} = I_{\text{L}}Z = I_{\text{L}}j\omega L$$

and

(5-6) $$V_{\text{NH}} = \frac{I_{\text{L}}}{j\omega C}$$

At the natural frequency, the impedance is infinite. Even a small current at ω_{c} will cause large voltage oscillations.

Figure 5-3 gives an example of the response of an LC section of a power distribution network to a typical transient load. The section is a 40-nH inductor with a 10-nF bypass capacitor ($f_{\text{c}} \approx 8$ MHz). For the first five $t_{\text{ck}} = 10$-ns cycles, the load draws an average of 0.12 A with a current profile that peaks at 1 A and varies from cycle to cycle. After the fifth cycle, the load current is shut off to accept the step response of the LC network.

A typical CMOS chip has a current profile that is quasiperiodic with a period equal to the clock period, t_{ck}. Each cycle, the clock edge switches a set of flip-flops, which in turn cause several stages of logic gates to switch states. Switching these stages (clock driver, flip-flops, and logic) draws supply current. After the last logic stage settles, the supply current returns to zero until the next cycle. The left half of the top row of Figure 5-3 gives an example of such a current profile. The figure shows five cycles of operation. In each cycle, the current ramps to a peak value and then decays to zero as the logic circuits reach their final values.

Because the clock cycle is usually short compared with the period of the LC, the inductor carries the average (DC) current, and the bypass capacitor must be sized to supply the instantaneous (AC) current profile while keeping supply variation less than some threshold ΔV.

(5-7) $$C_{\text{B}} > \frac{k_i Q_{\text{ck}}}{\Delta V} = \frac{k_i I_{\text{avg}} t_{\text{ck}}}{\Delta V}$$

Here $Q_{\text{ck}} = I_{\text{avg}} t_{\text{ck}}$ is the average charge transferred in one cycle, the average area under one cycle of the top curve in Figure 5-3. The inductor provides a current of I_{avg}, and the capacitor provides the difference. As seen in the second curve of Figure 5-3, this causes a small ripple (of magnitude ΔV) about the average voltage because the capacitor discharges when the current drawn by the load exceeds I_{avg} and is charged by the inductor when the load current is less than I_{avg}.

The factor k_i is given by

$$(5\text{-}8) \qquad k_i = \max_t \frac{\left| \int_0^t (I - I_{avg}) \, dt \right|}{I_{avg} t_{ck}}$$

Thus, k_i reflects the maximum fraction of total charge transferred each cycle, Q_{ck}, that must be supplied by the capacitor at a given instant, t. It is a function of the waveshape and varies from a maximum of 1 for a delta function, to 0.25 for a triangle wave, to 0 for a DC current. A value of 0.25 to 0.5 is typical.

As illustrated in Figure 5-3, there is usually some variation in the current profile from cycle to cycle. Depending on data patterns, different logic may switch, drawing more or less current. For example, when a counter toggles all of its outputs, considerably more current is drawn than on average when only two bits switch. This variation represents a current with a spectrum that has nonzero components up to the clock frequency.[1] On average it does not significantly increase the ripple. However, if the variation is truly random, the worst-case ripple can be worse than the step response of the power supply section, for bad patterns can *pump* energy into the resonant circuit. Adding clamps to a supply, as described in Section 5.2.1, eliminates the potential for pumping and makes the worst case equivalent to the step response.

The right half of Figure 5-3 illustrates the step response of the LC section. After five cycles of operation, the load current is shut off. The inductor current continues to flow, and the LC circuit oscillates with the voltage overshooting by 40%. Regardless of the stage of the supply network, the oscillation is passed unattenuated to the load because downstream sections usually have higher cutoff frequencies than upstream sections. The voltage oscillation due to a step change in current in the LC section is given by

$$(5\text{-}9) \qquad \Delta V = \frac{I_{avg}}{C_B \omega_c} \sin(\omega_c t) = I_{avg} \sqrt{\frac{L}{C_B}} \sin(\omega_c t) = I_{avg} Z_s \sin(\omega_c t)$$

To keep the ripple within a prescribed ΔV, the capacitor must be sized so that

$$(5\text{-}10) \qquad C_B > L \left(\frac{I_{avg}}{\Delta V} \right)^2$$

In the absence of shunt regulators or clamps (see Section 5.2.1), Eqs. (5-7) and (5-10) together constrain the size of C_B. The capacitor chosen must be large enough to cover the sum of the transient during a clock cycle (Eq. (5-7)) and the

---

[1] The spectrum of the supply current includes harmonics of the clock frequency as well.

step response (Eq. (5-10)), the worst case of cycle-to-cycle variation. Therefore, the total bypass capacitance required is given by

$$(5\text{-}11) \qquad C_B > \frac{k_i I_{avg} t_{ck}}{\Delta V} + L\left(\frac{I_{avg}}{\Delta V}\right)^2 = \frac{I_{avg}}{\Delta V}\left(k_i t_{ck} + \frac{L I_{avg}}{\Delta V}\right)$$

Step variations in load current are not unusual in digital systems. They occur, for example, in a processor when a memory system is activated after a long string of cache hits. Also, in systems that provide for "hot-plugging" of modules, the insertion or removal of a module causes a significant current step plus an additional transient while the power supply network charges the module's bypass capacitors.

Oscillations in the LC power distribution network are damped by a resistive component of the load. If we assume that the current depends on the supply voltage linearly as

$$(5\text{-}12) \qquad I_L(t, V) = I_L(t, V_n)\left(k\frac{V}{V_n} + 1 - k\right)$$

where V_n is the nominal voltage and k is the resistive fraction of the load, then the equivalent parallel resistance is

$$(5\text{-}13) \qquad R_L = \frac{V_n}{k I_{avg}}$$

and the quality factor of the LRC is

$$(5\text{-}14) \qquad Q = \frac{R_L}{\pi}\sqrt{\frac{C}{L}} = \frac{V_n}{\pi k I_{avg}}\sqrt{\frac{C}{L}} = \frac{V_n}{\pi k I_{avg} Z_S}$$

For the example of Figure 5-3, $I_{avg} = 0.12$, $V_n = 1$, and $Z_S = 2\,\Omega$ if we assume $k = 0.5$, R_L is $17\,\Omega$, and the Q of the section is 5.3. That is, oscillations are attenuated by a factor of e after 5.3 cycles.

Circuits with either local regulation or constant-current source-coupled FET stages, or both, tend to draw a constant current regardless of supply variations. Thus, they have a very small resistive fraction of the load and a high Q. These circuits will tend to oscillate owing to power supply variations unless parallel resistance or active dampening is employed.

5.2   LOCAL REGULATION

5.2.1   Clamps and Shunt Regulators

Supply overshoot can be reduced by clamping the local supply so that it cannot exceed the nominal voltage by more than a small amount. The clamp can be a

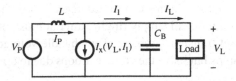

FIGURE 5-4   General Form for Clamp and Shunt Regulator

zener diode or a feedback circuit that gates a load device. In effect the clamp clips off the top half-cycle of the LC oscillation by directing the inductor current into the clamp rather than the capacitor. This prevents overshoot when the load current is rapidly decreased as well as pumping of the supply due to pathological patterns of current variation. A clamp, however, cannot prevent the supply voltage from drooping when the load current rapidly increases as the clamp cannot supply current to the load.

A shunt regulator keeps the supply current seen by the LC distribution network at a constant DC value, $I_P = I_{max}$, by making up the difference between I_{max} and the filtered load current, I_1. The difference current, $I_x = I_{max} - I_1$, is bypassed by a dependent current source directly from the local supply node to the local ground node. From the AC point of view, the shunt regulator looks like an infinite-valued bypass capacitor. The regulator handles arbitrary variation in load current (within the bounds of I_{max}) with negligible voltage variation.

Figure 5-4 shows the general circuit form for both a clamp and a shunt regulator. They vary in the control law used to govern I_x as a function of V_L and I_1. For a clamp, I_x is

$$(5\text{-}15) \qquad I_X = \begin{cases} 0 & \text{if } V_L < V_n \\ k_s(V_L - V_n) & \text{if } V_L > V_n \end{cases}$$

where k_s is the transconductance of the clamp. For a shunt regulator, the control law is

$$(5\text{-}16) \qquad I_x = \max[0, I_{max} - I_1 + k_s(V_L - V_n)]$$

The first term of the shunt regulator equation (Eq. (5-16)) attempts to keep the current constant, and the second term regulates the voltage. The transconductance k_s determines the relative importance of the two goals and also determines the Q of the resulting LRC

$$(5\text{-}17) \qquad Q = \frac{1}{\pi k_s}\sqrt{\frac{C}{L}}$$

Because rounding the triangular current profiles of Figure 5-3 up to their peak values would dramatically increase power dissipation, shunt regulators typically regulate the current upstream of a bypass capacitor.

Clamps and shunt regulators have very different characteristics and hence are used under different conditions. Clamps are inexpensive and draw no power except during voltage overshoots. Thus, clamps can be extensively used and can even be placed on-chip. They eliminate all supply ringing after at most one half-cycle and solve half of the current transient problem. They handle voltage overshoots due to downward current steps but leave the voltage droops due to upward current steps unsolved.

Shunt regulators dissipate considerable average power and tend to be expensive (owing to the high-power components and cooling requirements). Thus, they are almost never used on chip. Even off-chip they tend to be a method of last resort in handling the voltage droop due to large upward current transients. There are cases, however, where regulators are an attractive alternative to the large, low ESR[2] bypass capacitors that would otherwise be required.

5.2.2   Series Regulators

The problem of differential $IZ(iR + Ldi/dt)$ power supply noise due to the inductance and resistance of the off-chip supply network can be largely eliminated by using a local series regulator to control the supply voltage locally on each board or even on each chip or part of a chip. Local regulation does not, however, address common-mode supply noise due to signal currents.

If the local regulation includes a significant step-down in the supply voltage, it has the added advantage that supply power can be distributed at a higher voltage, which requires less current and hence smaller cables and lower iR losses in distribution. Although in theory any voltage and frequency could be used for distribution, for convenience and regulatory reasons, the most common distribution systems use 120 V, 60 Hz AC or 48 V DC.

Figure 5-5 shows a simplified power supply network using local regulation. A distribution voltage source, V_D, supplies the distribution voltage (e.g., 48 V DC) and ground to the distribution network. The inductance and resistance of the typical distribution tree network are abstracted here as a pair of impedances, Z_D and Z_G. A converter or regulator located near the load converts the possibly noisy local distribution voltage, V_{LD}, to the supply voltage, V_P (e.g., 3.3 V DC). Because the converter is located near the load, I_L, the impedances between the converter and the load Z_{LP} and Z_{LG} are small, resulting in minimum IZ power supply noise between V_{LP} and V_P.

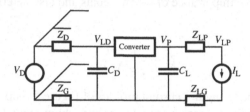

FIGURE 5-5   Power Supply Network Using Local Regulation

---

[2] Effective series resistance. See Section 5.5 for more information on bypass capacitors.

Signal loads, I_S in Figure 5-1, still see the point-to-point impedance of the parallel combination of the power and ground networks. Thus, the power supply noise due to unbalanced signal currents is not affected by local conversion.

Using a distribution voltage higher than the final supply voltage gives a quadratic reduction in IZ noise relative to V_D. If we choose

$$(5\text{-}18) \qquad\qquad V_D = k_D V_P$$

then

$$(5\text{-}19) \qquad\qquad I_D = \frac{I_L}{k_D}$$

and thus the relative noise $Z I_D / V_D$ is reduced quadratically as expressed by

$$(5\text{-}20) \qquad\qquad \frac{Z_D I_D}{V_D} = \frac{Z_D \frac{I_L}{k_D}}{k_D V_P} = \frac{Z_D I_L}{k_D^2 V_P}$$

This quadratic improvement is augmented by the line regulation of the converter, which typically provides considerable attenuation of voltage noise on V_D.

With local regulation, the load sees a small distribution impedance along with the output impedance of the local converter instead of a large (mostly inductive) distribution impedance back to a central power supply. Thus, local conversion trades the problem of building a low-noise power distribution network for the relatively easier problem of building a converter with good load regulation (low output impedance).

5.2.2.1 Linear Regulator

On-chip local regulation is usually performed with a linear regulator, as shown in Figure 5-6, owing to the complications involved in attaching an off-chip inductor. A typical on-chip regulator converts a noisy 3.3-V off-chip supply to a quiet 1.5- to 2.5-V on-chip supply. Linear regulators can be used off-chip as well. However, switching regulators, which dissipate less power, especially for large step-downs, are usually preferred.

As shown in Figure 5-6, the noisy off-chip supply, V_D, is connected through the local distribution impedances (e.g., package pins, bond wires, and resistive on-chip wires), Z_{LP} and Z_{LG}, to an on-chip bypass capacitor, C_B, which absorbs some of the current transients from I_L. The on-chip distribution voltage, V_{LD}, across

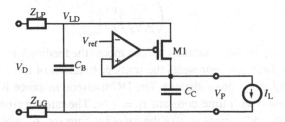

FIGURE 5-6 Linear Regulator for On-Chip Local Regulation

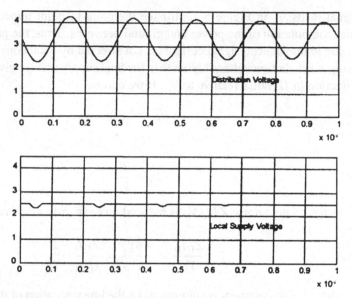

FIGURE 5-7   Local Regulation Waveforms

C_B is then dropped across PFET M1 to give the supply voltage, V_P. A feedback loop controls the gate of M1 to attempt to keep V_P equal to a reference voltage, V_{ref}. A compensation capacitor C_C stabilizes this feedback loop and absorbs small current transients that are faster than the feedback loop can respond to. If a bipolar device is available, the amplifier and PFET can be replaced by an emitter follower with some increase in output impedance.

If the feedback loop had infinite bandwidth, the voltage, V_P, would remain constant as long as V_{LD} did not drop below V_{ref}. Thus, the linear regulator increases the allowable ripple, ΔV_D, across C_B by the voltage headroom, $V_{HR} = V_D - V_{ref}$. This significantly decreases the required size of C_B, as given in Eq. (5-11). This effect is illustrated in Figure 5-7. The top trace shows a noisy 3.3-V distribution voltage. A current transient has excited a 2-V peak-to-peak 5-MHz ripple on this supply. The bottom trace shows a quiet 2.5-V supply generated from the upper trace. Only those portions of the ripple that drop below 2.5 V appear on the output.

To first order, the compensation capacitor, C_C, is sized to keep the ripple, ΔV_P, within bounds during the response time of the feedback loop. If the loop response time is τ_f, then

$$(5\text{-}21) \qquad\qquad C_C > \left(\frac{\tau_f^2}{\Delta V_P}\right)\frac{di}{dt}\bigg|_{max}$$

To see the effect of C_C on loop stability, we can model the feedback loop, as shown in Figure 5-8. The first box represents the transfer function of the amplifier and PFET in converting ΔV_P into a current. The DC transconductance is K, and the response is first-order with time constant $\tau_f = 1/a$. The current from the PFET is summed with the load current to give the capacitor current, I_C, which is in turn integrated to give ΔVP.

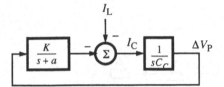

FIGURE 5-8 Model of Linear Regulator Feedback Loop

From Figure 5-8 we can calculate

(5-22)
$$V_P(s) = I_L(s)\left[\frac{s+a}{C_C\left(s^2 + as + \frac{K}{C_C}\right)}\right]$$

which is overdamped as long as

(5-23)
$$C_C > \frac{4K}{a^2} = 4K\tau_f^2$$

The term in brackets in Eq. (5-22) is the output impedance of the local regulator.

Because the circuitry required to realize a linear regulator is relatively simple and the size of the devices scales with the required current, it is possible to provide independent linear regulators for individual modules on a chip. This has the advantage of isolating modules requiring a quiet power supply from modules generating high AC load current.

The disadvantage of a linear regulator is high power dissipation in the series device (the PFET in Figure 5-6). The average power dissipated in this device is the headroom voltage times the average current. Thus, the overall power dissipation is increased by the percent of headroom plus a small amount of additional power needed to bias the amplifier. For example, dropping a 3.3-V external supply to a 2.5-V internal supply increases power dissipation by 32%. Because of this power inefficiency, linear regulators are not practical with large stepdowns in voltage. To achieve a large stepdown efficiently, a switching regulator must be used.

5.2.2.2 Switching Regulator

For off-chip local regulation, where inductors can be used, a switching regulator is typically employed to permit larger voltage stepdowns and greater power efficiencies.

Figure 5-9 shows a *buck-type* switching regulator used to convert a 48-V distribution supply, V_D, to a 3.3-V local supply, V_P. An intuitive model of this regulator is shown in Figure 5-10. The control circuit switches M1 and M2[3] to give a fixed-frequency rectangular wave on V_S with amplitude, V_D, and steady-state duty factor of V_P/V_D. In effect these components form a pulse-width modulator that

---

[3] Transistor M2 is not strictly needed in this circuit because parallel diode D1 conducts whenever M2 would be switched on. The extra transistor serves to improve efficiency by avoiding the losses across the diode drop of D1.

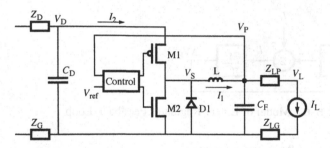

FIGURE 5-9   A Buck-Type Switching Regulator

generates a pulse-train with amplitude, V_D. The LC low-pass formed by L and C_F filters the pulse train on V_S to generate V_P. The control circuit compares V_P to a reference voltage, V_{ref}, and adjusts the duty factor to regulate V_P. The duty factor is varied during current transients to adjust the average inductor current, I_1.

Figure 5-11 shows the steady-state current and voltage waveforms for two cycles of operation of a buck-type regulator running at 100 kHz. The top trace shows the switch voltage, V_S. Each $t_{cy} = 10$-μs cycle, the switch voltage pulses to 48 V for about 700 ns (a duty factor of 3.3/48 or 7%) and remains at zero for the rest of the cycle. The second trace shows the inductor current, I_1 in Figure 5-9. The inductor integrates the switch voltage to give a sawtooth current waveform. During the pulse on V_S, the inductor current increases rapidly with a slope of $(V_D - V_P)/L$ ($\sim$4.5 mA/s in the example); the current then decreases gradually with a slope of $-V_P/L$ ($\sim$−0.33 mA/s) during the remainder of the cycle. The difference between the inductor current and the load current is in turn integrated by the filter capacitor, C_F, to give the regulated supply voltage, V_P. The final trace shows the input current, I_2, in Figure 5-9, which is equal to I_L during the pulse and zero at all other times.

With a constant load current, the ripple on the supply voltage, V_P, is calculated by integrating twice as

$$(5\text{-}24) \qquad \Delta V_P = \frac{V_P\left[t_{cy}\left(1 - \frac{V_P}{V_D}\right)\right]^2}{8LC_F}$$

For our example, the ripple is 360 mV.

The cycle time of a switching regulator is set to trade off the switching power lost from switching the gates of M1 and M2 and switching diode D1, which increases with frequency, against the increased cost of larger inductors and capacitors. As shown in Eq. (5-24), both the inductor and capacitor must be increased linearly with t_{cy} to maintain a given voltage ripple.

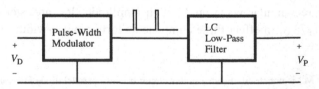

FIGURE 5-10   Intuitive Model of a Switching Regulator

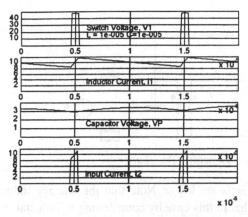

FIGURE 5-11 Waveforms for Buck-Type Switching Regulator

Because the controller responds by changing the voltage on the supply side of the inductor, the output voltage disturbance due to a current transient is smaller for a switching regulator than for the passive LC section discussed in Section 5.1.2. Assuming an immediate response by the controller, the voltage change due to a step change in current is given by

$$(5\text{-}25) \qquad \Delta V_P = \begin{cases} \dfrac{L \Delta I^2}{2 C_F V_P} & \text{if } \Delta I < 0 \\[2mm] \dfrac{L \Delta I^2}{2 C_F (V_D - V_P)} & \text{if } \Delta I > 0 \end{cases}$$

If we assume that $V_D > 2V_P$, then C_F is constrained by

$$(5\text{-}26) \qquad C_F > \frac{L \Delta I^2}{2 \Delta V_P V_P}$$

which differs from Eq. (5-10) by a factor of $V_P / \Delta V_P$.

The buck regulator has a number of problems stemming from its high peak input current that limit its use in practice. Although the average input current is reduced by V_P / V_D, the peak input current is equal to the peak output current. The inductor and switching components (M1, M2, and D1) must all be sized to handle this current, which increases their size and the switching losses. Also, the high, narrow pulses of input current place heavy demands on the distribution network. Either distribution capacitor C_D must be sized to handle these pulses or large IZ voltage transients will be induced across Z_D and Z_G.

These limitations of the buck regulator can be overcome by using a switch-mode regulator employing a transformer. A simple approach is to place a transformer between the inductor and capacitor of Figure 5-9, resulting in a *flyback* regulator, illustrated in Figure 5-12. The primary of transformer, T1, is connected between the inductor and ground and the secondary is connected between V_P and ground. The $N:1$ turns ratio of the transformer results in an N-times higher duty factor with N-times smaller peak current demands on the switching components and the distribution network. The inductor, being upstream of the transformer, carries this smaller current as well. The inductor could be placed on either side of the transformer; however, it is more economical to place it in the primary circuit,

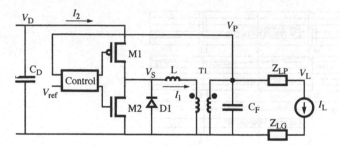

FIGURE 5-12   Flyback Switching Regulator

where the current demands are lower. Note that the leakage inductance of the transformer actually helps in this case by contributing to inductance L.

Because current is only passed through the transformer in one direction, the flyback regulator only uses half of the B–H curve of the transformer core. For a given power level this design requires a larger core to avoid saturation than a regulator, which uses both sides of the B–H curve.

A smaller, and hence less expensive core, can be used with an *inverting* switch-mode regulator, as shown in Figure 5-13. An H-bridge formed by FETs M1–M4 applies alternating positive and negative pulses of distribution voltage, V_D, across the primary circuit of step-down transformer T1. These FETs *invert* the DC input voltage, making it AC. The diodes across the FETs return energy stored in the inductor to the power supply when the transformer is switched off. The secondary of T1 is rectified by a diode bridge and filtered by capacitor C_F. To reduce the power lost by dropping voltage across the forward-biased diodes, the diode bridge can be replaced (or paralleled) by four FETs that are switched at appropriate times. A controller (not shown) switches the H-bridge FETs, modulating the pulse width to regulate the output voltage, V_P.

In both the flyback and inverting regulators, transformer T1 has a step-down turns ratio, $N:1$, slightly smaller than the voltage ratio, V_D/V_P. A current of I_1 in the primary results in a current of $I_2 = NI_1$ in the secondary. Thus, the switching components can be sized for $1/N$ of the peak output current, and the distribution network carries current pulses that are N times broader with $1/N$ the peak amplitude compared with the buck regulator.

A capacitor is often placed in series with inductor L to make the primary circuit of the transformer resonant. In this case the H-bridge *pumps* energy into

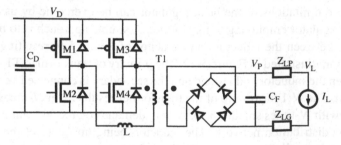

FIGURE 5-13   Inverting-Type Switching Regulator

the resulting tank circuit. Resonant circuits are also often used in the gate drive of transistors M1–M4 to reduce gate drive losses.

5.3 LOGIC LOADS AND ON-CHIP POWER SUPPLY DISTRIBUTION

The on-chip load current is consumed primarily by logic gates and other circuits (memory arrays and datapath blocks) with similar load characteristics. Most of these circuits draw current from the power supply only when switching to charge or discharge their capacitive output loads.[4] This switching takes only a small fraction (usually 5–10%) of a clock cycle, and only a fraction of the gates on a chip (typically 5–20%) switch during a given cycle. Except for tristate gates, a logic gate that is not switching connects its output load capacitance to either the positive supply or ground. Thus, most of the time these output loads serve as *symbiotic bypass capacitors* that help maintain the supply voltage during current transients.

5.3.1 Logic Current Profile

Figure 5-14 shows the voltage and current waveforms for a logic gate switching. The waveforms are for a 0.35-μm inverter with P and N widths of 4 μm and 2 μm, respectively. The inverter is driving two identical inverters and 200 μm of wire for a total load (including self-load) of 62 fF. The four traces show the input voltage, output voltage, overlap current, and charging current from top to bottom. The left side of the figure shows a low-to-high transition and the right side shows a high-to-low transition. The overlap current is shown on a 100-μA scale, whereas the charging current is shown on a 1-mA scale. The inverter has

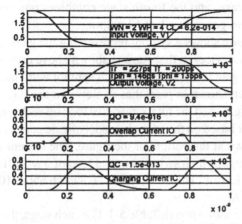

FIGURE 5-14 Logic Switching Waveforms

---

[4] The exception is circuits, such as source-coupled amplifiers and delay lines, that draw constant current whether the output is switching or not. In modern CMOS integrated circuits, such constant current circuits are rare.

rising and falling propagation delays of 146 and 135 ps, respectively, and rise and fall times of 227 and 200 ps, respectively.

Figure 5-14 shows that overlap current is negligible. Recall that overlap current is the current that flows directly from the positive supply to ground through the two FETs of the inverter during the time that both are partially on. For this circuit, 160 times as much charge is transferred charging the output node as is consumed during overlap.

The major source of power supply current, the charging current, has an approximately triangular shape with area $Q_{ch} = C_{ld}V_P$. Empirically the base of the triangle is about, $1.8t_r$, giving a peak current of

$$(5\text{-}27) \qquad I_{pk} = \frac{2Q_{ck}}{1.8t_r} = \frac{1.1C_{ld}V_P}{t_r}$$

For the example circuit, $t_r = 227$ ps and Eq. (5-27) predicts a peak current of about $750\ \mu\text{A}$, which is in close agreement with the simulation. To study the current draw of functions composed of gates, we model the current draw of each gate as a triangle. In contrast, the average current drawn by a gate is given by

$$(5\text{-}28) \qquad I_{avg} = \frac{k_s C_{ld}V_P}{t_{ck}}$$

where k_s is the fraction of gates switching in each direction each cycle.

The current profile of a logic block depends on its function. For some functions we can derive exact current profiles, whereas for others we statistically estimate the current profile. Decoders, for example, have very flat current demand because, although they have high fan-out, only a few outputs at each level switch. Consider, for example, a 6-to-64 decoder, as shown in Figure 5-15. The decoder has four gain stages. The first stage inverts the six inputs. Pairs of inputs and their complements are decoded in three $2 \rightarrow 4$ predecoders in the second stage. The third stage boosts the drive of the second stage, and the fourth stage combines one output of each of the three predecoders to generate a 1 of 64 output.

For each stage, the figure shows a symbol representing the gates at that stage. The width of the P and N devices in that stage is shown above each symbol. The number of copies of that gate is shown below each symbol with the number that can simultaneously switch shown in parentheses. Between the stages, the figure shows the fanout of each gate and the total capacitive load on each gate. A current waveform for the decoder based on the triangle model of gate current and a worst-case input pattern is shown at the bottom of the figure. The current waveform is dominated by the third stage, which switches a total load of $3 \times 350\ \text{fF} = 1.05\ \text{pF}$, giving a peak current of 13 mA. The other stages all switch about 100 fF, giving currents of less than 2 mA.

This information is also tabulated in Table 5-1. For each stage, the table shows the number of gates in that stage (N), the number that can simultaneously switch in the same direction (S), the load capacitance per gate (C_{ld}), the total switched load for the stage ($C_{tot} = SC_{ld}$), the unswitched capacitance for the stage ($C_{us} = (N - S)C_{ld}$), the rise time for the stage (t_r), and the peak current for the stage (I_{pk}).

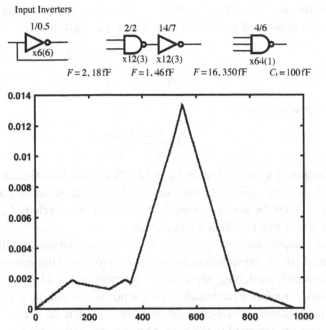

FIGURE 5-15 Schematic and Worst-Case Current Profile of a 6 → 64 Decoder

The C_{us} column also indicates the supply to which the unswitched capacitance is connected. The decoder has over 6.7 pF of symbiotic bypass capacitance attached to the positive supply and over 3.1 pF attached to ground.

Current profiles for most regular functions (memories, arithmetic units, data selectors, etc.) can be estimated in the same manner as the decoder by calculating the switched and unswitched load per stage and assuming a triangular current profile for each stage.

For less regular (random) logic, where the number of gates per stage and the fraction of gates switching is unknown, statistical estimates are used to arrive at a current profile. For example, suppose we have a random logic block with $N_G = 50,000$ gates with an average load of $C_{ld} = 100$ fF per gate arranged in $d = 10$ levels (stages) of logic. We assume some fraction $2k_s$ of the logic gates switch each cycle, half in each direction, and that the $N_S = k_s N_G$ gates switching

TABLE 5-1   Parameters for Decoder of Figure 5-15

Stage	N	S	C_{ld} (fF)	C_{tot} (fF)	C_{us} (fF/dir)	t_r (ps)	I_{pk} (ma)
1	6	6	18	108	0/X	153	1.9
2	12	3	46	138	414/1	201	1.9
3	12	3	350	1050	3150/0	218	13.4
4	64	1	100	100	6300/1	217	1.3

in one direction are distributed in a triangular manner over the d stages. Assuming d is even, the number of gates switching in stage i is given by

$$(5\text{-}29) \qquad N_i = \begin{cases} \frac{4N_s i}{(d^2 + 2d)} & \text{if } i \le \frac{d}{2} \\ \frac{4N_s(d-i)}{(d^2 + 2d)} & \text{if } i > \frac{d}{2} \end{cases}$$

and the current in stage i is

$$(5\text{-}30) \qquad I_i = \frac{1.1 N_i C_{\text{ld}} V_{\text{P}}}{t_{\text{r}}}$$

For example, if $k_s = 0.25$, then $N_s = 12{,}500$ for our 50,000-gate module, and the peak N_i is 2,083, giving a peak current of 2.9 A. If we assume a clock cycle of $t_{\text{ck}} = 5$ ns, then the average current over a worst-case cycle is $I_{\text{aw}} = 624$ mA, about a factor of five less than the peak value.

For power supply noise calculations it is important that the selection of both k_s and the profile for N_i be sufficiently conservative to bound the *worst-case* amount of simultaneously switching capacitance. Average values of N_i, often collected through logic simulation, although good for power estimation, are not sufficient for noise calculations. Worst-case values of N_i are often many times the average values. A system designed to the average value may fail under data patterns that draw more current.

5.3.2   IR Drops

The current pulses from on-chip logic and memory blocks cause voltage drops across the resistive on-chip power distribution network. These IR voltage drops are the major source of on-chip power supply noise.

An on-chip power distribution network for a chip with peripheral bonding is illustrated in Figure 5-16. The left side of the figure shows a caricature of the entire chip. Power and ground are brought onto the chip via bond pads located along the four edges of the die and then routed horizontally on metal buses to the remainder of the chip. A blowup of the area near the left edge of the chip is shown in the right half of Figure 5-16. Two metal layers are shown. The upper metal layer is colored lighter than the lower metal layer. The blowup shows four pads: a power pad, a ground pad, and two signal pads that will not be discussed

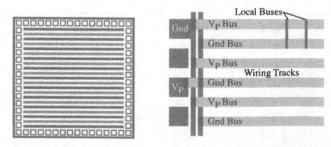

FIGURE 5-16   Simplified Sketch of On-Chip Power Distribution

further. The power and ground pads are tied to two vertical metal buses that are part of power and ground *rings* circling the chip to supply power to I/O pads and to tie together common supply pads. Typically there will be more than two rings (e.g., to provide separate supplies for the I/O pads and chip internals). The supply rings are used to feed a set of alternating horizontal power and ground buses that carry the supplies across the chip. These buses use a substantial fraction of the area on the top metal layer. The remaining area, between the buses, is left for wiring tracks. These global power buses in turn feed a set of local power buses that carry the power to the point of use.

The resistance of the network is calculated by counting the *squares* of metal and the vias along the path. A typical 1-μm-thick aluminum wire has a resistivity, r_w, of 0.04 Ω/square, and a via has a resistance of about 1 Ω. For example, suppose the global power buses are 15-mm long and are 30-μm wide on 40-μm centers (VP buses and ground buses each on 80-μm centers). A half a power bus, from the edge to the center, is 250 (30- $\times$ 30-μm) squares or 10 Ω. A 1.8-μm wide local bus of thinner metal, 0.07 Ω/square, spans the 50 μm between adjacent power buses of the same polarity. Half of this bus is about fourteen squares or roughly 0.93 Ω.

A simplified equivalent circuit model of half of one pair of power buses is shown in Figure 5-17. Power is supplied to the left side of the figure. The buses are then divided into N segments, each with resistance

$$(5\text{-}31) \qquad R_P = \frac{L_P r_w}{2N W_P}$$

The current source associated with each segment supplies power to circuits in an area of

$$(5\text{-}32) \qquad A_P = \frac{L_P W_P}{2N k_P}$$

where k_P is the fraction of the metal layer devoted to the power buses of one polarity. For our example in Figure 5-16 of 15-mm-long 30-μm buses on 80-μm centers, $k_P = 0.375$, and $A_P = 0.6/N$ mm^2.

The peak current drawn by a segment is the product of the peak current density and the area supplied. Consider a peripherally bonded 0.35-μm chip with a working area of 15 $\times$ 15 mm containing 1 M gates ($\sim$4,444 gates/mm^2). If we assume logic depth, switching fraction, and current profile numbers similar to those in Section 5.3.1, this translates to a peak current density of $J_{pk} = 0.26$ A/mm^2 and

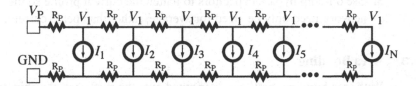

FIGURE 5-17 Simplified Circuit Model of On-Chip Power Distribution

an average current density of $J_{aw} = 56$ mA/mm^2. Thus, the peak current drawn by each segment in our example is $J_{pk} A_P = 0.78/N$ A.

Each resistive segment carries a current equal to the sum of all downstream current sources, and thus the drop across the segment i_{th} from the end is $iJA_P R_P$. Summing these drops gives the total IR drop from the edge to the center of one of the two buses:

$$(5\text{-}33) \qquad V_{IR} = \sum_{i=1}^{N/2} i J_{pk} A_P R_P = \sum_{i=1}^{N/2} \frac{i J_{pk} L_P^2 r}{4 N^2 k_P}$$

Taking the limit as N goes to infinity gives

$$(5\text{-}34) \qquad V_{IR} = \int_0^{L_P/2} \frac{J_{pk} r_w x}{k_P} dx = \frac{J_{pk} r_w L_P^2}{8 k_P}$$

For our example 1M gate chip, $V_{IR} = 0.78$ V. This amount is dropped by both power buses, and thus in the center of the chip the local supply voltage would be down by 1.56 V! This is clearly an unacceptable voltage drop. Even if we devote all of a metal layer to the power supply, $k_P = 0.5$, the combined drop is still 1.17 V or almost half of a 2.5-V supply.

Equation (5-34) shows that the voltage drop across the global buses is dependent only on the fraction of a metal layer devoted to each bus, k_P, and not on the width of the individual buses. Thus, the individual buses should be made as narrow as possible, without making the overhead associated with spaces excessive, to reduce the length over which local power buses must run. In practice, setting the width of each bus at thirty times the top-level metal-to-metal spacing works well. For example, if top-metal spacing is 1 μm, lower metal width, spacing, and thickness are 0.6 μm each, and $k_P = 0.375$, then setting the top metal bus width at 30 μm gives a local bus run of about 50 μm. If the local bus is 1.8-mm wide (two tracks and the intervening space), the 25-μm run from one end to the center is about 14 squares at 0.07 Ω/square (higher resistivity for the thinner layer) or about 0.93 Ω.

There are three common approaches to reduce the voltage drop across the global power buses to acceptable levels:

1. Use an area-bonded chip so that power need not be distributed from the chip edge.
2. Use more or thicker metal layers to distribute the power to reduce the effective resistivity r_w.
3. Use on-chip bypass capacitors to flatten the current profile so the distribution network need only be sized for average, rather than peak, current.

5.3.3   Area Bonding

With area bonding, pads are distributed over the surface of the chip, typically on about 10-mil (250-μm) centers. The chip is then flipped over and bonded to a substrate with solder balls. Power and ground pads are distributed on a regular basis so that no point on the chip is farther than 1 mm from a source of power and ground. This largely eliminates IR drops due to global power buses. However, local power buses must still be designed carefully.

The area pads move the power distribution out to the next level of packaging in which thick metal films are used to distribute power with negligible IR drops. A 0.7-mil (17-μm)-thick 0.5-oz copper film, for example, has a resistivity of 0.001 Ω/square – a factor of 40 better than a 1-μm-thick on-chip wire. Area bonding also greatly reduces $L di/dt$ supply noise due to bond-wire inductance. The inductance of a solder ball is on the order of 100 pH, whereas a wire bond is usually several nanohenrys.

5.3.4 Metal Migration

Area bonding is also a solution to the problem of metal migration due to excessive current density. If a metal layer is subjected to an average current density of greater than about 1 mA/μm^2 (10^9 A/m^2) the layer will slowly fail over time as the high current causes portions of the material to *migrate* and thus form voids. To avoid metal migration the fraction k_P of metal devoted to each power bus must satisfy

$$(5\text{-}35) \qquad k_P \geq \frac{10^{-3} J_{aw} L_P}{2H}$$

where H is the thickness of the metal layer, J_{aw} is in A/mm^2, and L_P and H are in the same units. For our example, the minimum k_P is 0.417. We must widen our 30-μm power buses to 34 μm to meet this number.

5.3.5 On-Chip Bypass Capacitors

On-chip bypass capacitors reduce the peak current demand on the distribution network. A capacitor sized according to Eq. (5-7) reduces the current load on the distribution network to the average value. In our example, if we require a ripple, ΔV, no larger than 0.25 V, Eq. (5-7) dictates that we distribute 12.5 nF of local bypass capacitance with each 50K gate module. This capacitance will smooth out the current draw over a cycle so that the power distribution network carries the average current density of $J_{avg} = 0.056$ A/mm^2, giving a voltage drop of about 0.25 V across each supply network. If we also use local regulation to allow a 0.8-V ripple, the required size of the bypass capacitor is reduced to 3.9 nF.

Thin-oxide MOS capacitors are most often used for on-chip bypass because they give the highest capacitance per unit area. Well and diffusion junction capacitors and metal and polycrystalline silicon parallel plate capacitors can also be used for this purpose. A thin-oxide capacitor is essentially an MOS transistor with its source and drain tied together. As long as the voltage across the capacitor is greater than the threshold voltage, its capacitance is well approximated by

$$(5\text{-}36) \qquad C_{ox} = \frac{\varepsilon_r \varepsilon_0 WL}{t_{ox}} = \frac{3.45 \times 10^{-13} WL}{t_{ox}}$$

where W and L are the width and length of the capacitor, respectively, in μm and t_{ox} is the oxide thickness in angstroms. For example, a 0.35-μm process with $t_{ox} = 70$ Å has a C_{ox} of about 5 fF/μm^2. In our example above, a 50K gate module occupies about 11.2 mm^2 of chip area. An MOS capacitor with an area of 2.5 mm^2 (23% the area of the logic) is required to provide the 12.5 nF required to bypass this logic with a 0.25-V ripple. With local regulation to tolerate a 0.8-V ripple, the required area is reduced to 0.8 mm^2 (7% the area of the logic).

Thin-oxide capacitors must be laid out with a short length, no more than four times the minimum gate length[5] (e.g., 1.4 μm for a 0.35-μm process), to keep their series resistance low.

5.3.6   Symbiotic Bypass Capacitance

A significant amount of symbiotic bypass capacitance is present in any logic circuit because only a small fraction of gates are switching at any one time and all gates that are not switching connect their output load to a power supply. Consider, for example, the three inverters shown in Figure 5-18. In the case where the circuit is quiescent, $A = C = 1$, and $B = D = 0$, transistors M2, M3, and M6 are on. Transistor M2 provides a low resistance path from node B to GND, effectively placing C_{B1} and the gate capacitance of M3 between V_P and GND, thus making them bypass capacitors. Similarly, M3 connects C_{C0} and M6 as bypass capacitors, and M6 connects C_{D1} as a bypass capacitor. Consequently, when the circuit is in the quiescent $A = 1$ state, M3, M6, C_{B1}, C_{C0}, and C_{D1} all serve as bypass capacitors. In this state, the other elements (M4, M5, C_{B0}, C_{C1}, and C_{D0}) do not serve as bypass capacitors because both ends of these capacitors are connected to the same supply. In the quiescent $A = 0$ state, the roles reverse with M4, M5, C_{B0}, C_{C1}, and C_{D0} serving as bypass capacitors. In general, about half the load capacitance of any quiescent circuit is connected as bypass capacitance.

Even a logic gate that changes state during a cycle serves to connect its load as a bypass capacitor, except during the short time that it is actually switching. For example, consider the circuit of Figure 5-18 when node A switches from a 0 to a 1. While node B is in transit, the loads on nodes B and C are removed from the pool of symbiotic bypass capacitors: B because it is in transit and C because

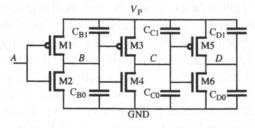

FIGURE 5-18   Example of Symbiotic Bypass Capacitance

---

[5] This relationship remains constant with improving technology, for both the logic gates and the bypass capacitors get faster at the same rate.

the transistor connecting it to the supply is turning off. However, the loads on node D and later stages are still connected between the supplies and add to the charge available for bypassing supply loads. After node B completes its transition and is at a steady 0 value, the load on node B is added back into the bypass pool, but on the other side of the supply. Thus, even in active logic, except for the one or two stages right at the switching wavefront, about half of all of the load is serving as symbiotic bypass capacitance.

In our example of a 50K gate module with $C_{ld} = 100\,\mathrm{fF}$ and a maximum of about 2,000 gates switching simultaneously in each direction, the remaining 46,000 gates all connect about half of their output load across the power supplies. This gives a symbiotic bypass capacitance of 2.3 nF. If the fraction of gates switching simultaneously can be guaranteed to be sufficiently small, this symbiotic bypass capacitance is adequate to average the supply current over a clock cycle.

5.4 POWER SUPPLY ISOLATION

Unless the load draws a constant DC current, even the most carefully designed power distribution system will have some amount of supply noise. The effect of this noise on system operation can be reduced by isolating sensitive circuits from the power supply.

5.4.1 Supply-Supply Isolation

As illustrated in Figure 5-19, the power supply of a circuit, A, can be isolated from supply noise generated by another circuit, B, by providing separate distribution networks back to a common point, X. Most of the ZI noise generated by B is dropped across the impedance of its private distribution impedance, Z_{PB} and Z_{GB}, and thus does not affect circuit A. The portion of I_B that remains after filtering by C_{BB} and C_B generates a small amount of noise at point X due to the common supply impedance, Z_P and Z_G.

Supply isolation can be used to isolate either very noisy or very sensitive circuits from the common power supply. If circuit B is a noisy circuit, such as a clock driver or a full-swing output pad, isolation serves to keep the large AC current generated by the circuit, I_B, from corrupting the common power supply shared by the remaining circuits (circuit A). Alternatively, if circuit A is a very

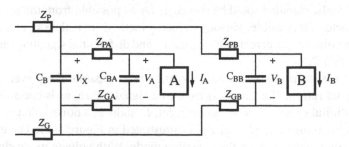

FIGURE 5-19 Power Supply Isolation

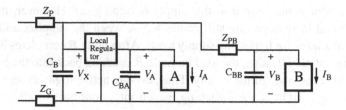

FIGURE 5-20   Single-Ended Supply Isolation

sensitive circuit, such as a receive amplifier or a low-jitter delay line, supply isolation serves to keep the AC supply current, I_B, generated by the remaining circuits (circuit B) from producing noise on the sensitive circuit's supply, V_A.

Because circuit boards typically have very low differential supply noise, supply isolation is most commonly used on-chip. In this case, point X is at the connection to the power and ground network of the circuit board, and the supply networks for circuits A and B have separate package pins, package planes or wiring, bond wires, and on-chip distribution networks.

All circuits on a single chip share a common substrate, and substrate noise is coupled between circuits even if power supplies are isolated. The substrate serves as one end of all field capacitors and as a signal return for all on-chip signals. Thus, unbalanced signal switching induces current in the substrate supply leads. The substrate is also often tied to a power supply (ground for a P-type substrate) and thus also carries all IZ noise from this supply. The supply IZ portion of substrate noise can be reduced by isolating the substrate supply from a noisy ground; however, the noise induced by substrate current remains.

One approach to dealing with substrate noise is to isolate only the nonsubstrate supply using a local series regulator, as illustrated in Figure 5-20. The figure assumes an N-well process with a grounded P-type substrate. Sensitive circuit A shares a noisy ground and substrate with the remaining circuits B. A local regulator and bypass capacitor, C_{BA}, make the positive supply of circuit A track the noisy ground and substrate to maintain a quiet differential voltage, V_A, across circuit A.

5.4.2 Signal-Supply Isolation

To avoid corrupting signals with power supply noise, supplies should be isolated from both signals and signal returns. To minimize direct coupling of supply noise into signals, signals should be routed as far as possible from the power supplies and shielded if possible. Various signaling methods to isolate signals from power supply noise (e.g., current mode signaling and differential signaling) are discussed in Chapter 7.

The first step in signal return isolation is to separate the power supply from the signal return. If a supply is used as a signal return, as is commonly done in many digital systems, AC supply current, I_P, induces a noise voltage, $V_N = I_P Z_R$, across the return impedance, Z_R, as illustrated in Figure 5-21. The effect of this noise voltage depends on the signaling mode. With voltage mode signaling (left

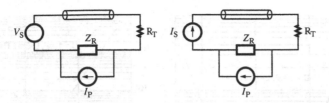

FIGURE 5-21   Supply Noise Coupling via the Signal Return

side of Figure 5-21) the noise voltage appears unattenuated at the receiver. With current mode signaling (right side of Figure 5-21) the noise voltage induces a noise current $I_N = V_N/(R_T + Z_0)$ through the termination resistor.

Ideally signals should be run over a dedicated signal return plane that carries no supply current and isolated from the noisy supplies by a shield plane that is grounded at a single point. Such supply isolation precautions are common in analog system design but are the exception in contemporary digital systems.

5.5   BYPASS CAPACITORS

Bypass capacitors at the system, backplane, board, package, and chip level are key elements in a power distribution system. At each level the bypass capacitor must be sized according to Eq. (5-11) to handle the expected current variation while keeping ripple within limits. In addition, the type of capacitor used at each level must be selected to have adequate bandwidth to filter the expected current variations.

Figure 5-22 shows an equivalent circuit for a bypass capacitor. All capacitors have some amount of parasitic lead inductance, L_C, and effective series resistance (ESR), R_S, that limit the bandwidth of the capacitor. The overall impedance of the capacitor is

$$(5\text{-}37) \qquad\qquad Z_C = j\omega L_C + R_S + \frac{1}{j\omega C}$$

The capacitive and resistive components of this impedance cancel at

$$(5\text{-}38) \qquad\qquad f_{LC} = \frac{1}{2\pi\sqrt{LC}}$$

FIGURE 5-22   Equivalent Circuit of a Bypass Capacitor

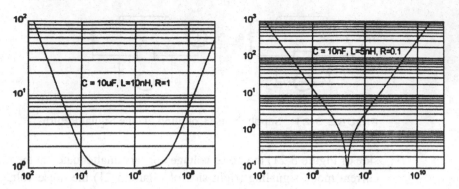

FIGURE 5-23 Impedance Magnitude for 10-μF and 10-nF Capacitors

If the resistance is large enough to damp the series LC, then there are two frequency breakpoints at

$$(5\text{-}39) \qquad\qquad f_{RC} = \frac{1}{2\pi R_S C}$$

$$(5\text{-}40) \qquad\qquad f_{LR} = \frac{R}{2\pi L}$$

Above either of these frequencies, the impedance of the capacitor becomes dominated by either the lead inductance (f_{LC}) or the series resistance (f_{RC}), and the capacitor loses its effectiveness. For proper operation bypass capacitors must be operated well below both of these frequency breakpoints.

Figure 5-23 shows the magnitude of Z_C for two capacitors: a 10-μF electrolytic (left) and a 10-nF ceramic disk (right). The electrolytic, with a lead inductance of 10 nH and a series resistance of 1 Ω, shows the two breakpoints of an overdamped RLC. The device acts as a capacitor up to $f_{RC} = 160$ kHz, at which point it behaves like a 1-Ω resistor. Above $f_{LR} = 16$ MHz, the lead inductance dominates. If the inductive and capacitive curves were extended, they would meet at f_{LC}. In practice this capacitor would not be used above 100 kHz.

The 10-nF ceramic disk (right side of Figure 5-23) shows the response of an underdamped LC with a resonant frequency of $f_{LC} = 23$ MHz. Below this frequency, the device acts as a capacitor, and above this frequency it appears as an inductor. Right at 23 MHz, the impedance of the inductor and capacitor cancel, leaving only the 0.1-Ω series resistance. In practice, such a capacitor would be used at frequencies under 10 MHz.

A power distribution network uses a hierarchy of capacitors, and each stage of the hierarchy filters a frequency band of current transients. Typical types are shown in Table 5-2 along with their characteristics and breakpoint frequencies. To catch the fast, 200-ps, current transients associated with individual gate switching,[6]

---

[6] The high-frequency components of the signal rise time ($f_s = 1/2\pi t_r$) determine the required bandwidth of the first-tier bypass capacitors independent of clock frequency. Lowering the clock rate does not ease the constraints on these capacitors.

TABLE 5-2 **Characteristics of Typical Bypass Capacitors**

Description	C	R_S	L_C	f_{RC}	f_{LC}	f_{LR}
On-chip MOS (0.35 × 114 μm)	250 fF	10 Ω	0	64 GHz		
On-chip MOS (1.4 × 114 μm)	1 pF	40 Ω	0	4 GHz		
SMT ceramic	1 nF	0.1 Ω	1 nH		160 MHz	
SMT ceramic	10 nF	0.1 Ω	1 nH		50 MHz	
Ceramic disk	10 nF	0.1 Ω	5 nH		23 MHz	
Aluminum electrolytic	10 μF	1 Ω	10 nH	160 kHz		16 MHz
Aluminum electrolytic	1000 μF	0.05 Ω	10 nH	3 kHz		800 kHz

there is no substitute for on-chip bypass capacitors (symbiotic or explicit). The lead inductance of these capacitors is negligible, and in a 0.35-μm process, a capacitor with the minimum gate length has a cutoff frequency of 64 GHz. In practice, a capacitor four times this long (1.4 μm) is more area efficient and has an adequate bandwidth of 4 GHz.

After on-chip bypass capacitors have smoothed the current demand over a cycle, small ceramic surface-mount (SMT) and disk capacitors filter current transients in the next frequency band. These capacitors have negligible series resistance but have lead inductances that limit their bandwidths to 0.1 to 1 times a typical clock frequency of 200 MHz. Because lead inductance is to first order independent of capacitance, high bandwidth is achieved by using many small capacitors in place of one large capacitor. Small ceramic chip capacitors are typically used on the package to filter transients on the order of one clock cycle, whereas larger chip or disk capacitors on the PCB filter larger but slower transients.

At the bottom of the capacitance hierarchy are aluminum electrolytic capacitors that provide large capacitance but have high series resistances that limit their application to the kilohertz range. These capacitors are used in power supplies to store energy between AC line or switch-mode cycles and for bulk bypass capacitors for entire PC boards and backplanes.

At each level of the hierarchy, the size of the required capacitor goes up while its bandwidth goes down. A capacitor at a given level must be sized to handle a current transient until the capacitor and associated distribution wiring at the next level of the hierarchy can respond.

5.6 EXAMPLE POWER DISTRIBUTION SYSTEM

To illustrate the concepts introduced in this section, consider a digital system with parameters as shown in Table 5-3. At each level of the distribution hierarchy the table shows the distribution voltage, the average and peak supply current, and the time scale on which current transients must be handled. The characteristics

TABLE 5-3 **Power Demand Parameters for an Example Digital System**

Description	V	I_{avg}	I_{peak}	τ
Gate	2.5 V	13 μA	1.4 mA	200 ps
Module (50,000 gate equivalents)	2.5 V	624 mA	3 A	5 ns
Chip (20 modules)	3.3 V	12 A	30 A	10 ns
PC board LV (20 chips)	3.3 V	240 A	240 A	10 μs
PC board HV	48 V	18 A	30 A	10 μs
Chassis DC (8 PC boards)	48 V	144 A	144 A	10 μs
Chassis AC (3Φ)	220 V	276 A	552 A	10 μs
System AC (3Φ)	220 V	67 A	67 A	8.3 ms

of the conductors used at each level of the distribution hierarchy are listed in Table 5-4.

The demand for current begins with the individual gate, as described in Section 5.3.1. The average and peak current demands of an individual gate are calculated from Eqs. (5-28) and (5-27) to be 13 μA and 1.4 mA, respectively. The 250:1 ratio of peak to average current reflects the low duty factor of a gate in a typical logic system. The rise time of the current transient when a gate switches is comparable to the rise time of a gate (about 200 ps for our example technology).

Power is supplied to individual gates over local power buses that are 1.8 μm wide and span the 60 μm between global power buses. A 30-μm-long half-section supplies 16 gates (about eight 3-track [3.6 μm] 2-input gates on either side of the bus). If all sixteen gates switch simultaneously, the maximum IR drop across the local bus is 13 mV.[7] The current transients from individual gates are handled by local bypass capacitors (symbiotic and explicit) and by aggregation of the current demand of many gates to spread the demand over time.

At the next level a group of about 50K gates (or the equivalent) forms a module. This might be a simple CPU, a floating-point arithmetic unit, a memory array, a group of I/O pads, and so on. The average module current is determined by

TABLE 5-4 **Characteristics of the Distribution Network**

Description	L	R	I_{avg}	I_{pk}	IR	$L di/dt$
Local power buses (1.8 × 60 μm)	0	1.1 Ω	104 μA	23 mA	13 mV	
Global power buses (34 × 15 mm)	0	15 Ω	33 mA	82 mA	361 mV	
Bond wire	5 nH	0	120 mA	240 mA		0.5 V
Power plane	80 pH	0	240 A	240 A		0
Bus bar	2.5 nH	14 $\mu\Omega$	144 A	144 A		0

---

[7] This is half the value of $I_{pk}R$ because the average gate sees half of the total resistance of the bus.

summing over the gates in the module. The peak module current is estimated using Eqs. (5-29) and (5-30). The roughly 5:1 ratio of peak to average current at the module level reflects the temporal distribution of logic switching that distributes the current load in time. The current transient has a time constant comparable to a clock cycle, $t_{ck} = 5$ ns.

In our example system, the IR drop due to current transients at the module level is managed using local linear regulators, as described in Section 5.2.2.1. The local bypass capacitors form the compensation capacitor of the regulator. If we assume a regulator time constant of $\tau_f = 1$ ns and a peak di/dt of 3 GA/s (3 A in 1 ns) and allow a maximum ΔV_P of 10% or 0.25 V, then Eq. (5-21) gives 12 nF as the required size of the compensation capacitor. Symbiotic bypass capacitors account for 2.3 nF, and thus 9.7 nF of explicit MOS bypass capacitors must be added to each module. Equation (5-23) is used to calculate the maximum K for which the loop is stable.

Because the required compensation capacitor scales quadratically with τ_f, making a faster regulator pays big dividends in reducing the size of the required compensation capacitor. Halving τ_f to 500 ps reduces the required capacitance to 3 nF, all but 700 pF of which is covered by symbiotic bypass capacitors.

Current is supplied to the local power buses of the modules on a chip over an array of 34-μm-wide global power and ground buses on 40-μm centers using 85% of the top metal layer. A half-section of each of these buses supplies power to a 0.6-mm^2 (80 μm $\times$ 7.5 mm) strip of chip, which, on the basis of the numbers from Section 5.3.1 contains about 2,700 gates, consumes an average current of 33 mA, and has about 640 pF of bypass capacitance.

If there were no local regulator, the RC time constant of this level of the distribution network would be 5.6 ns, about one clock cycle, and the local bypass capacitors would smooth out the load current, reducing the ratio of peak current to average current from 5:1 to 1.6:1, as shown in Figure 5-24. This reduction in peak current (from 150 to 48 mA) reduces what would otherwise be a 660-mV peak drop across the global bus to a drop of only 212 mV.

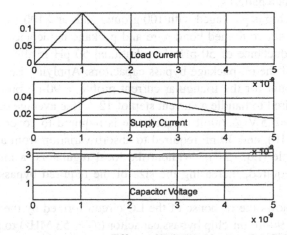

FIGURE 5-24   Effect of RC Filtering on On-Chip Global Supply Current

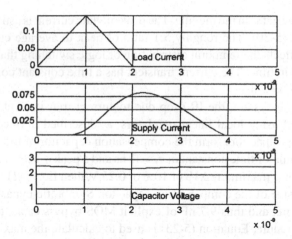

FIGURE 5-25   Effect of Local Regulation on On-Chip Global Supply Current

The current profile on the on-chip global supply buses with a downstream local regulator is shown in Figure 5-25. This simulation was run using a regulator with a time constant of 1 ns and a regulator gain, K/a in Eq. (5-22), of 1 A/V. The figure shows that the regulator limits the drop in supply voltage to 132 mV while drawing a peak current of 82 mA. The resulting 361-mV drop across the supply bus is absorbed by the regulator's headroom. The regulator reduces the required bypass capacitor size for a given ripple to that required to supply charge to the circuit during the response time of the regulator. As we will discuss in the next paragraph, the regulator's headroom also allows us to absorb the supply droop due to lead inductance on a positive current transient.

The Ldi/dt noise due to the package and bond-wire inductance is managed through a two-pronged approach. Voltage droop caused by increasing current is absorbed by the headroom of the local regulator, whereas voltage spikes due to decreasing current are clipped by an on-chip clamp. By clipping the top half of the oscillation, the clamp also acts to damp oscillations and thus to prevent pumping by pathological data patterns.

Our example chip is packaged with 100 ground pads and 100 V_{dd} pads. Each of these pads sees a combined bond-wire and package inductance of 5 nH for a total supply inductance of 50 pH. An additional 50 pH is alloted to the series inductance of the on-package bypass capacitors. Applying Eq. (5-11) with $k_i = 0.25$ to account for the triangular current profile, a 90-nF on-chip bypass capacitor is required to handle a current step of 12 A (the average current) with a ripple of $\Delta V = 0.5$ V. A 60-nF capacitance is required to cover the turn-on transient, Eq. (5-10), and 30 nF required to absorb variation from average current within a cycle (Eq. (5-7)). Without the local regulators, a much smaller ΔV would be required, increasing the size of the required bypass capacitors proportionally.

Figure 5-26 shows the response of the LC circuit formed by the 100-pH inductance and the 90-nF on-chip bypass capacitor ($f_c = 53$ MHz) to a triangular

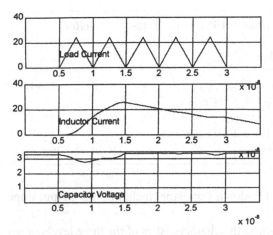

FIGURE 5-26 *LC* Response of Bond Wires and Package

load current with a turn-on and turn-off transient. The simulation shows seven cycles of operation with zero load current during the first and last cycles and a triangle-shaped load current peaking at 24 A during the middle five cycles. Average current during cycles 2–6 is 12 A.

The combination of the turn-on transient and the per-cycle current variation causes the capacitor voltage to dip about 0.54 V during the second cycle because the capacitor supplies current until the lead inductance can respond. The voltage overshoot in cycle 4 (at 15 ns) is clipped by the clamp to 0.1 V over the nominal value of 3.3 V. The clamp prevents this oscillation from continuing into subsequent cycles and possibly being reinforced by subsequent current transients. Using a clamp to halt oscillation is particularly important on a chip that uses local regulators because, to first approximation, the local regulators make the incremental load resistance infinite (current draw is independent of capacitor voltage), giving a very high Q LC circuit. Cycles 4–6 show a maximum ripple due to intracycle current variations of about 0.1 V. Voltage overshoot during the turn-off transient that starts in cycle 7 is also limited by the clamp.

The on-chip bypass capacitor was sized assuming a 50-pH series inductance for the next level bypass capacitor. To achieve this low inductance, twenty surface-mount ceramic capacitors are connected in parallel between the power planes of the chip package. As shown in Table 5-2, each capacitor has a series inductance of about 1 nH, and thus the parallel combination of twenty capacitors gives a series inductance of 50 pH. If we use 100-nF surface-mount capacitors, we get a total capacitance of $2\,\mu$F. Applying Eq. (5-11) allows up to 3 nH of inductance at the next level.

The second-level off-chip capacitors are five 22-μF low-ESR electrolytic capacitors placed on the PC board close to the chip. The five capacitors in parallel have a capacitance of 110 μF, a lead inductance of 2 nH, and an ESR of about 0.01 Ω. They are placed close to the chip and distributed around its periphery to keep the wiring inductance small compared with the lead inductance. This final rank of per-chip capacitors can tolerate up to 200 nH of inductance back to

TABLE 5-5   **Summary of Per-Chip Bypass Capacitors**

Stage	Description	C	L	f_c
1	On-chip thin oxide capacitors	90 nF	100 pH	53 MHz
2	Twenty 100-nF SMT ceramics on the package	2 μF	2 nH	2.5 MHz
3	Five 22 μF low ESR electrolytics on the PCB	110 μF	200 nH	48 kHz

the circuit-board's step-down regulator (including the output impedance of the regulator).

Table 5-5 summarizes the characteristics of the three levels of per-chip bypass capacitors. For each level the table shows the total capacitance, the inductance to the next level of capacitance, and the resonant frequency of the LC section. For the last row, the maximum inductance that can be tolerated while handling a 12-A current step with no more than a 0.5-V droop is used. At each level the dominant factor is lead inductance, which determines the number of capacitors that must be connected in parallel. The total resulting capacitance then determines the allowable lead inductance for the next stage according to Eq. (5-10).

Because the frequencies of the LC sections at each stage are very different, the voltage droops allocated to the stages do not sum. The transient of stage i is over before stage $i + 1$ has drooped by an appreciable amount. Thus, allocating 0.5 V to each of three stages gives us a total droop[8] of 0.5 V, not 1.5 V!

After stage 1, one third of which handles the intracycle transient, all of the capacitance is acting to handle the 12-A turn-on transient. The alternative to this large capacitance is to design the chip to limit the size of the transient by making it always consume nearly its maximum current, possibly by using an on-chip shunt regulator. In most cases the costs of the increased power dissipation associated with forcing a DC current profile is more expensive than the bypass network described above. An off-chip shunt regulator will only reduce the required size of the third stage of bypass capacitors because its lead and wiring inductances will be greater than the inductance that can be tolerated by stages 1 and 2.

The PC board combines twenty chips on a 30- $\times$ 30-cm glass–epoxy board. Power is distributed to the chips over a pair of power planes separated by $h = 6$ mils (150 μm). The inductance of the power plane is calculated by treating it as a parallel plate transmission line with a tapered width, $w = 2\pi r$, where r is the distance from the center of the chip. Integrating from the outer rim of the chip to the edge of the board gives the inductance as follows:

$$(5\text{-}41) \qquad L_{\text{plane}} = \int_{r_{\min}}^{r_{\max}} \frac{h\mu_0}{w} \, dx = \int_{r_{\min}}^{r_{\max}} \frac{h\mu_0}{2\pi x} \, dx = \frac{h\mu_0}{2\pi}(\log r_{\max} - \log r_{\min})$$

---

[8] This assumes a single transient. A second, high-frequency transient in the middle of the droop of the second stage of bypass capacitors would cause the droops of successive stages to sum.

For 6-mil plane separation, the constant term is 3×10^{-11}. Therefore, if we model our chip as a circle with a 1-cm radius and the board as a disk with a 15-cm radius, the inductance is about 80 pH, which is negligible compared with the series inductance of the bypass capacitors.

In fact, as long as we have a signal return plane, full planes are not required to distribute power and ground. A 30-cm-long, 1-cm-wide, 6-mil-thick parallel plate transmission line used to distribute power from one edge of the board to the opposite edge is about 6 nH. This is a key point: planes found in modern PC boards serve primarily to control the impedance of signal lines and act as signal returns. They are not needed for power distribution.

An inverting-type switching regulator, Section 5.2.2.2, is used on each circuit board to step down a 48-V DC distribution voltage to provide 240 A at the 3.3-V DC board supply. The regulator must handle a 240-A turn-on transient with, at most, an 0.5-V supply droop. The regulator uses a transformer with an $N = 8{:}1$ turns ratio to make the effective V_D 6 V. Assuming a 100 kHz switching frequency and applying Eq. (5-24) with the constraint of a 0.1-V ripple and Eq. (5-25) with the constraint of a 0.5-V droop will result in required component sizes of $L = 250\,\text{nH}$ and $C = 40\,\text{mF}$. The 250 nH of inductance is the primary inductor, L, (plus the leakage inductance of the transformer) referred to the secondary. At the primary this appears as $N^2 L = 16\,\mu\text{H}$ of inductance.

If 90% efficiency is assumed, the regulator reduces the peak current draw to 30 A and the average current draw to 18 A. This greatly reduces the required size of the cabling in the distribution network and the IR losses due to distribution. It also makes the inductances in the distribution network appear quadratically smaller. Any inductance that is substantially smaller than the $16\text{-}\mu\text{H}$ primary-referenced regulator inductance is negligible. There is no input capacitor on the step-down regulator. Such a capacitor is unnecessary because the distribution inductance will be much lower than the regulator inductance and is undesirable, for it will cause a current surge if a board is hot plugged.

At the next level of our system, eight circuit boards are stacked on 2-cm centers and combined in a chassis. By synchronizing the regulators on the eight boards so that they operate with phases evenly distributed between 0 and 180 degrees, the current variations are averaged out, and at peak demand the chassis imposes a steady 144-A current draw on the 48-V DC supply. On a 144-A current transient, the $2\text{-}\mu\text{H}$ parallel combination of the eight local regulators dominates the distribution inductance.

Power is distributed to the eight boards in a chassis over a pair of 16-cm-long 12.5- $\times$ 1.5-mm (0.5- $\times$ 0.062-in.) copper bus bars (aluminum could be used as well). The resistivity of each bus bar is $14\,\mu\Omega$ and, if the two bars are stacked with a 6-mil insulator, the inductance is 2.5 nH. Tabs on the bus bar can be fabricated to directly contact power connectors on each board. The boards can be "hot plugged" without a special startup supply, for the power system has been designed to handle a peak transient.

The chassis accepts 3-phase 220-V 60-Hz AC power and converts this, using another switching regulator, to 48 V DC. If the converter is 90% efficient, the AC current draw is 35 A (about 12 A per phase). Power is distributed between chassis

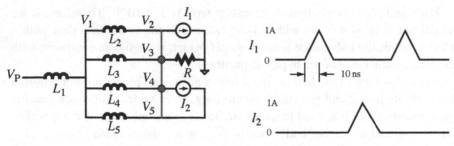

FIGURE 5-27   Example Power Distribution Network

as 220-V AC. If the chassis switching converter is designed to operate with 50% input voltage, the converter can be built without an input filter by operating directly from rectified three-phase supply. An input filter may be required, however, both for power factor correction and to allow the converter to ride through short transient outages on the AC supply.

At peak current draw, a chassis of the type described above dissipates about 7 kW of power in a 13.5-liter volume. Cooling such a chassis is a nontrivial exercise that we will not deal with here.

5.7   BIBLIOGRAPHIC NOTES

Power distribution and management of power supply noise are critically important to the proper operation of a high-performance digital system. Unfortunately, it has received little attention in the literature. A good overview of the power distribution problem is given in Chapter 7 of [Bakoglu90]. The problem of power distribution in mixed-signal ICs is discussed in [StanRute96].

5.8   EXERCISES

5-1   **Ground Loops:** Consider the example power distribution network[9] of Figure 5-27. For this exercise, all inductors are 10 nH, $V_P = 2.5$ V, and R = 10 Ω. The current waveforms for sources I_1 and I_2 are as shown in the figure. What is the worst-case supply noise on nodes V_2 through V_5 when the leaves of the network are left unconnected (gray lines removed)? How does this supply noise change if the leaves are shorted with zero-inductance wires (gray lines)? Is there any downside to shorting the leaves of the distribution network? (Optional) Calculate the supply noise under the more realistic assumption that each gray link in the figure has an inductance of 5 nH.

---

[9] Any real power distribution network has inductance in the return path to V_G as well as in the path to V_P, as shown. Thus, drawing the triangular ground symbol in this figure is a bit misleading. If we assume that the ground inductance is equal to the power inductance, the differential supply noise due to logic loads is doubled, and the single supply noise due to signal loads is halved.

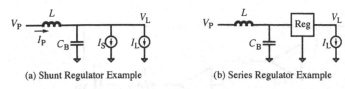

(a) Shunt Regulator Example   (b) Series Regulator Example

FIGURE 5-28   Shunt and Series Regulator Examples

5-2   **Inductive Distribution:** Consider the power supply network of Figure 5-27 where the leaves are unconnected (gray lines removed), $L_1 = 100$ nH, the remaining inductors are 10 nH, and the current profiles are as shown. Select bypass capacitors C_1 through C_5 to be added to the network just to the right of the corresponding inductors to keep voltage ripple on V_2 through V_5 to less than 5% as a worst case.

5-3   **Shunt Reglator:** Consider the circuit of Figure 5-28(a) where $L = 10$ nH and the load current, I_L, has the profile shown for I_1 in Figure 5-27. How large a bypass capacitor, C_B, is required to limit ripple on the 2.5-V supply at the load, V_L, to $\pm 5\%$? If a shunt regulator, I_S, is added to keep the total supply current, I_P, above half the peak value of I_L, what happens to the required size of C_B? What happens to the total power drawn from the supply?

5-4   **Series Regulator:** Consider the circuit of Figure 5-28(b), where $L = 10$ nH and I_L has the profile shown for I_1 in Figure 5-27. How large a bypass capacitor, C_B, is required to keep variation in V_L to 5% if there is no series regulator? How large a bypass capacitor is required if a series regulator drops a 3.3-V distribution supply down to a 2.5-V load supply? What happens to the total power drawn from the supply in this case?

5-5   **Series Regulator Output Impedance:** Consider the series regulator circuit model shown in Figure 5-29. The operational amplifier used for feedback is modeled as an ideal amplifier with a gain of A and a single pole in its output circuit. Assume that the output of this operational amplifier is centered on $V_{DD}/2$. In terms of the gain, A, the time constant of the pole ($\tau = RC$), and the transconductance of the PFET ($g_m = K_p W/L$) calculate the output impedance of this circuit. (Hint) Assume that the PFET is in the resistive region. For $A = 100$, $\tau = 500$ ps, and $g_m = 200$ mA/V^2, what is the impedance?

5-6   **Series Regulator Compensation:** Calculate the size of compensation capacitor, C_C, needed on the output of the circuit of Figure 5-29 to make it stable. What value of C_C is needed for $A = 100$, $\tau = 500$ ps, and $g_m = 200$ mA/V^2?

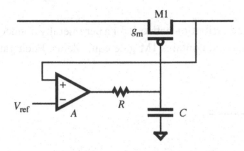

FIGURE 5-29   Series Regulator Circuit

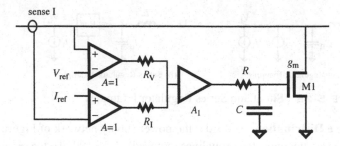

FIGURE 5-30   Shunt Regulator Circuit

5-7   **Shunt Regulator Circuit:** Figure 5-30 shows a circuit model for a shunt regulator. As with the series regulator model in Figure 5-29, we have modeled the control circuit using ideal amplifiers with gain as shown and a single pole in the output circuit. As in Exercise 5-5, assume that the output of the amplifiers is centered on $V_{DD}/2$. How do the resistors R_V and R_I affect the control law of the regulator? How do they correspond to the parameters in Eq. (5-16)? In terms of the circuit parameters, how fast a current pulse (width of a triangular pulse) can the regulator track to within 10%? Give a numerical answer for $\tau = RC = 500$ ps, $A_1 = 100$, and $g_m = 400$ mA/V^2.

5-8   **Switching Regulator Output Impedance:** Calculate the output impedance of the flyback switching regulator shown in Figure 5-12.

5-9   **Switching Regulator Current Profile:** Sketch and dimension the input current waveform for the inverting switching regulator of Figure 5-13.

5-10   **Switching Regulator Voltage Ripple:** Give an equation similar to Eq. (5-24) for the output voltage ripple of the flyback switching regulator of Figure 5-12 with a constant current load.

5-11   **Logic Current Profile:** Calculate the logic current profile of (a) a 32-bit ripple-carry adder (assume worst-case carry propagation); (b) of a carry-lookahead adder; and (c) a 64-Kbit (256 × 256) ROM with full-swing bit-lines.

5-12   **Bypass Capacitor Selection:** Using the parameters of Table 5-2, derive a parallel combination of bypass capacitors that is able to supply the current needs of a load with the periodic triangular waveform sketched in Figure 5-31 that may start and stop abruptly. Your combined capacitor should hold voltage ripple to within 5% of the supply voltage. Assume that your capacitors are fed from a DC supply through an inductance of 1 μH.

5-13   **IR Drops:** Design a power distribution network for a peripherally bonded ASIC. Your chip is 15 × 15 mm in area and contains 1M gate equivalents. Each gate equivalent

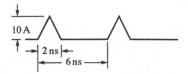

FIGURE 5-31   Current Waveform for Exercise 5-12

drives a 200-fF load (40 fF of gate and 160 fF of wire) and switches on average every third cycle of a 100-MHz clock. What is the total power dissipation of your chip? Assuming a peak current to average current ratio of 4:1, what fraction of a metal layer (or how many metal layers) do you need to distribute power so the overall supply fluctuation of a 2.5-V supply is ±250 mV?

5-14 **IR Drops and Module Placement:** You are designing a custom chip that has a few dense arithmetic units that demand very high current density from the power supply (500 mA/mm^2 peak) and a larger number of units with modest current demands (20 mA/mm^2 peak). If power were the only concern, where on your die should you locate the power hungry arithmetic units?

5-15 **On-Chip Bypass Capacitors:** Consider the chip of Exercise 5-13 but with a very high inductance (1 μH) power connection to the next level of bypass capacitors. If you choose to solve your supply noise problems due to this lead inductance by converting logic gates to symbiotic bypass capacitors, what fraction of the gates must be converted to keep the supply variation within ±10%? Does this change the requirements on the on-chip distribution network?

6 NOISE IN DIGITAL SYSTEMS

Noise is the deviation of a signal from its intended or ideal value. The intended signal, V_S, may be corrupted by a number of noise sources resulting in a received signal, $V_R = V_S + V_N$, where V_N represents additive noise. To transmit information reliably, we manage the noise either by having a large signal-to-noise ratio (SNR), V_S/V_N, or by predicting or measuring the noise and rejecting it, or both.

In the latter case, we estimate the received signal as $V_R = V_S + V_N - V_r$, where V_r is a reference that estimates V_N, and the effective SNR is $V_S/(V_N - V_r)$. With either approach we need to understand the noise sources. Only by understanding the noise can we devise methods to overpower or cancel it.

Most noise in digital systems is created by the system itself. Typical digital systems operate at such high energy levels that thermal (Johnson) noise, shot noise, and electromagnetic interference from external sources are usually negligible. Noise in digital systems is due to internal sources such as current flowing through parasitic components in the power supply network, parasitic coupling between signal lines, signal line ringing, shared signal returns, and device parameter variation.

A good fraction of the system-created noise is induced by the transmission of signals and scales with the signal magnitude. This signal-induced noise cannot be overpowered because increasing V_S proportionally increases this component of noise. For this reason it is useful to represent noise as having two components:

$$(6\text{-}1) \qquad\qquad V_N = K_N V_S + V_{NI}$$

The first component, $K_N V_S$, represents those noise sources that are proportional to signal magnitude such as cross talk, intersymbol interference, and signal-induced power supply noise. The second component, V_{NI}, represents noise sources that are independent of signal magnitude such as transmitter and receiver offsets and unrelated power supply noise.

6.1 NOISE SOURCES IN A DIGITAL SYSTEM

Figure 6-1 illustrates typical sources of noise in a digital system. Each source is briefly explained here and dealt with in more detail later in this chapter. The figure shows two transmitters (labeled Xmit) driving lines A and B and a single receiver (Rcv). The transmitter is connected to a power supply, V_{xp}, that is corrupted by power supply noise, and the transmitter may have an offset voltage, V_{xo}, due to process variation. Each transmitter has a source impedance, Z_S, that may include an inductance that could lead to ringing and intersymbol interference. A mismatch between the characteristic impedance of the lines and the termination impedance, Z_T, could also lead to intersymbol interference. Lines A and B are coupled by

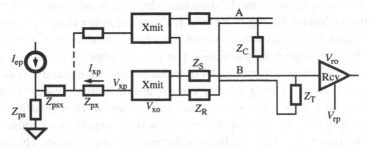

FIGURE 6-1   Noise Sources in a Digital System

mutual inductance and capacitance (both loosely denoted by Z_C), and lines A and B share a signal return with impedance Z_R leading to cross talk between the lines. Finally, the receiver also is fed a corrupted power supply, V_{rp}, and has an input-referenced receiver offset, V_{ro}.

Power Supply Noise: Each transmitter power supply, V_{xp}, and each receiver power supply, V_{rp}, differ from the reference power supply voltage, V_p, because of voltage dropped across the parasitic impedances of the power supply network. The noise induced by the currents I_{xp} from all of the transmitters is proportional to signal swing and thus contributes to K_N, whereas the noise induced by the current from other components of the system, I_{ep}, is independent of signal swing and contributes to V_{NI}. In some systems, the power supply network includes resonant circuits that oscillate and thus add to the directly induced noise. Depending on the designs of the transmitter and receiver, the total power supply noise may be coupled into the transmitted signal or affect the receiver threshold.

Transmitter and Receiver Offsets: Parameter mismatch in the transmitter may lead to the transmitted voltage differing from the ideal voltage by a transmitter offset, $V_T = V_S + V_{xo}$. Similarly, imperfections in the receiver may lead to an input offset in the detected voltage, $V_{det} = V_R + V_{ro}$. These noise sources tend to be fixed. The transmitter offsets are usually proportional to signal swing, whereas the receiver offsets are usually independent of signal swing.

Cross Talk: Noise caused by one signal, A, being coupled into a different signal, B is called cross talk. Cross talk can occur over many paths. Parasitic capacitance and mutual inductance between nearby signal lines (Z_C in Figure 6-1) directly couple a fraction of one signal into another. The impedance of a shared signal return, Z_R, couples energy between the signals sharing the return. The fraction of the power supply noise due to signal A switching is actually cross talk.

Intersymbol Interference: A symbol X sent over a line B at time, t_1, interfering with a symbol Y transmitted over B at a later time, t_2, is called intersymbol interference. This interference is caused by residual energy from X being stored in the transmission system. A mismatched line termination, Z_T, may cause energy from X to reflect back down the line and corrupt Y. A resonant output circuit, Z_S, may oscillate and thus spread the energy from X over several bit cells. Internal storage in the nodes of the transmitter and receiver circuits and even power supply modulation may also lead to intersymbol interference.

Timing Noise: Timing noise affects the phase rather than the magnitude of the signal. It changes *when* a signal transition is detected rather than the *value* of the signal after the transition. The DC component of timing noise is called *skew* and is usually caused by mismatched line lengths and variations in device parameters. *Jitter* is the AC component of timing noise, the cycle-to-cycle variation in when a signal transition occurs. Jitter is usually due to power supply noise modulating the delay of active components or additive noise such as cross talk or intersymbol interference moving the point when the transition is detected.

The remainder of this chapter discusses some of these noise sources in more detail. Section 6.2 discusses power supply noise in more depth and builds on the development of Chapter 5. Cross talk is covered in Section 6.3, and intersymbol interference is covered in Section 6.4. Other noise sources, including alpha-particle strikes, Johnson noise, shot noise, $1/f$ noise, electromagnetic interference, and process variations, are addressed in Section 6.5. We defer discussing transmitter and receiver offsets until Chapter 11 and timing noise until Chapter 9. The chapter closes in Section 6.6 with a discussion of how noise is managed in a digital system. This section introduces the relationship between Gaussian noise margins and bit error rate and describes how a designer can budget for noise to ensure reliable operation.

6.2   POWER SUPPLY NOISE

One of the largest noise sources in a typical digital system is the power supply. Although we often think of a power supply as an ideal voltage source and ground as a universal voltage reference, in practice neither is the case. As described in Chapter 5, the voltage dropped by power supply current and unbalanced signal current across the impedance of the power and ground distribution networks (*IZ* drops) and the ringing of the *LC* components of these networks cause the ground voltage to vary significantly from one point in the system to another and over time. The *IZ* drops and supply ringing also cause the local differential voltage between power and ground to vary in both time and space. It is not unusual to find digital systems with several volts of peak common-mode noise between distant points of the system and local differential noise of 0.5 V peak between power and ground at a single point.

Power supply noise can affect signaling in several ways. Large common-mode voltage shifts between supplies in different parts of the network can cause signals to fall outside the operating range of the receiver. Voltage shifts, as well as *IZ* drops and ringing, corrupt signals that use a power supply as either a transmit or receive voltage reference, or both. Variation in the local differential power supply voltage can adversely affect the operation of circuits, resulting in transmitter and receiver offsets and jitter in timing circuits.

Most digital systems have two primary power supplies: a negative supply and a positive supply. The voltage between these two supplies is used to power circuits. Signals are usually referenced to one supply, and that supply is denoted GND. The GND is the negative supply for CMOS and TTL logic families, which reference their signals to the negative supply. For ECL logic families, signals are referenced to the positive supply (GND). For the remainder of this section we make no distinction between the positive and negative supply networks.

In a well-designed digital system, power supply noise is managed through a combination of reduction and isolation. The noise is minimized by careful design of the distribution network and the use of bypass capacitors, clamps, shunt regulators, and local series regulators, as described in Chapter 5. Appropriate application of these techniques can keep both the local differential noise and point-to-point single-supply and common-mode noise within reasonable limits.

Isolation is used to keep the remaining noise from affecting the operation of the system. The effect of supply noise is minimized by choosing a signaling convention that is insensitive to power supply noise (e.g., current-mode differential signaling, Section 7.3.5). In some cases, the signal return should be distinct from the power supply network to prevent supply currents from causing signal offsets. Critical circuits such as receive amplifiers and timing delay lines can be designed to make them insensitive to local power supply noise (Chapters 11 and 12).

In Chapter 5 we examined in detail the sources of power supply noise. In this section we abstract these details and model supply noise as one or more independent voltage sources. Depending on the analysis we are performing, we may use these sources to represent either single-supply or differential supply noise.

6.2.1 Single Supply Noise

Single supply noise is the spatial variation in a single supply (e.g., GND or V_{DD} in a CMOS system) between two points in the system. As illustrated on the left side of Figure 6-2, differences in the IZ drop[1] between a common point, i, and points j and k in a supply network result in a voltage between j and k of $V_{Njk} = I_{ik}Z_{ik} - I_{ij}Z_{ij}$. For purposes of noise analysis, we abstract the I_s and Z_s and model this noise with a single voltage source, as shown on the right side of Figure 6-2.

The single supply noise between two points, j and k in a supply network is generally an increasing function of the distance between j and k because the supply impedance between these points increases with distance.

Table 6-1 gives some typical values for single supply noise as a function of distance. These values are calculated from the example in Section 5.6 by making some assumptions about balanced currents between PC boards and rounding to the nearest 10 mV. The table shows that circuits that are very close to one another have very small single supply noise, 10 mV for circuits 30 μm apart, and 50 mV for circuits 1 mm apart. From the center to the edge of a chip with peripheral bonding, however, the IR noise on a single supply is quite large (350 mV in our example). This large noise requires a more conservative approach to signaling

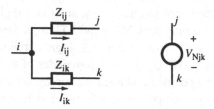

FIGURE 6-2   Single Supply Noise

---

[1] The IZ drop includes both the resistive (IR) and inductive ($L\,di/dt$) components of supply noise.

TABLE 6-1   **Typical Values for Single Supply Noise versus Distance**

Distance	$V_{Nij}(mV)$
On-chip, local bus, 30 μm	10
On-chip, global bus, 1 mm	50
On-chip, global bus, 7 mm	350
Between chips on PC board	250
Between PC boards, 1 m	500

across a chip than in a local region of a chip. The table lists 250 mV for noise between chips. Much of this value represents Ldi/dt drop across the package and lead inductance of the chips. With clamps, this noise represents only drop and not overshoot; otherwise, this value would be doubled. Assuming that only balanced currents are sent between PC boards, we estimate 500 mV difference between supplies on different boards. If unbalanced currents are sent between boards (the signal loads described in Section 5.1.1.2), this value would be much larger.

Single supply noise is directly added to the signal when voltage mode signaling is employed using a supply as a reference, such as with static CMOS logic, as depicted in Figure 6-3. The figure shows that when the first inverter sends a one to the second inverter, the logic high value differs by the amount of the positive supply noise. When a zero is sent, the logic low value differs by the amount of the negative supply noise. This effect is quite pronounced across a chip and is particularly serious in situations where circuits are sensitive to low-voltage swings, as with most dynamic logic. Use of dynamic logic is usually restricted to small areas of a chip for this reason and to limit the effects of cross talk.

When an explicit reference is used or differential signaling is employed (Sections 7.3.1.5 and 7.3.5), the single supply noise is made common-mode and is largely rejected. The magnitude of the noise is still a concern, however, because if the noise exceeds a limit, it will drive the signal and reference out of the common-mode range of the receiver.

One approach to dealing with single supply noise is to operate with current-mode signaling (Section 7.3.1.1), as illustrated in Figure 6-4. The left side of the figure shows a simple MOSFET current-mode signaling system. A simplified equivalent circuit is shown at the right. To first approximation, the NFET acts

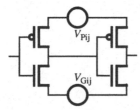

FIGURE 6-3   Effect of Single Supply Noise on CMOS Logic

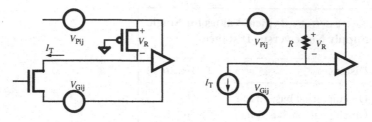

FIGURE 6-4   Current-Mode Signaling to Reject Supply Noise

as a current source, causing I_T to be unaffected by the negative supply noise, V_{Gij}. At the receiver, the PFET acts as a resistor and converts the transmitted current, I_T, to a receive voltage, V_R, that is referenced to the positive supply at the receiver. Because the receiver uses the positive supply at the same point as a voltage reference, the received voltage is unaffected by V_{Pij}.

6.2.2   Differential Supply Noise

Differential supply noise is the variation between two supplies (e.g., GND and V_{DD} in a CMOS system) at a single point in the system. Although it is caused by IZ drops in both supply networks back to a reference point, for purposes of noise analysis we model differential supply noise by a voltage source in series with the normal supply voltage. Figure 6-5 illustrates the noise source (left) and its model (right). The voltage dropped by the supply and ground currents, I_{Pi} and I_{Gi}, across the distribution impedances, Z_{Pi} and Z_{Gi}, from point i in the network back to the reference point causes the local differential power supply voltage, V_{Pi}, to vary from the nominal value, V_P. We model this variation by a voltage source,

$$V_{Ni} = -I_{Gi}Z_{Gi} - I_{Pi}Z_{Pi}.$$

Differential supply noise is determined by the properties of the distribution network, as described in Chapter 5. It can be controlled through a combination of reduced supply impedance, bypass capacitors, supply isolation, and local regulation. In a typical system, these methods are used in some combination to keep the differential supply noise to ±10% of the supply voltage.

Because most signals are referenced to a single supply, they are less sensitive to differential supply noise than they are to single supply noise. However, when signals referenced to one supply are capacitively coupled to the other supply, differential supply noise is coupled into the signal. In the circuit of Figure 6-4, for

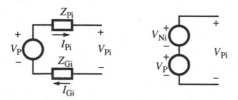

FIGURE 6-5   Model of Differential Supply Noise

example, the gate-to-drain capacitance of the PFET capacitively couples ground noise into the supply-referenced input of the receive amplifier.

Delay is a major concern with differential supply noise. As described in Section 4.3.2, to first order the delay of a gate varies linearly with supply voltage. For reliable operation, the circuit must be designed to operate with the worst-case local supply voltage. For example, if a 2.5-V supply varies by ±0.25 V, the circuit must be designed to operate 10% faster than required at the nominal supply voltage of 2.5 V so that it will meet timing specifications with the worst-case voltage of 2.25 V. Similarly, we must make sure that minimum delay, peak current, and cross talk constraints are satisfied at the worst-case high supply voltage of 2.75 V.

For critical timing circuits, such as delay lines and clock drivers, a ±10% variation in delay would cause unacceptable timing jitter. In Section 12.2, we discuss several techniques for building circuits with delay that are less sensitive to supply variation.

6.2.3 Internal and External Supply Noise

To determine the required signal swing or analyze the noise immunity of a signaling system, we must separate the power supply noise (both differential and single supply) generated by the signaling system from that generated by other sources. The former contributes to K_N in Eq. (6-1), whereas the latter contributes to V_{NI}. A well-designed signaling system contributes very little to the supply noise by using small signal swings and either drawing a constant DC current from the supply or controlling rise times to minimize interaction with the supply inductance. A poorly designed, brute-force signaling system, however, can generate significant amounts of supply noise by driving large voltage swings into large capacitive loads with short rise times in an unbalanced manner.

6.3 CROSS TALK

Cross talk is noise induced by one signal that interferes with another signal. On-chip cross talk is caused primarily by capacitive coupling of nearby signals. A transition on a signal injects charge into adjacent signals, disturbing their voltage. Off-chip transmission lines are coupled by mutual inductance as well as capacitance. A signal propagating down such a line induces signals traveling in both directions along nearby lines. Signals also interfere with one another when they share current return paths. This signal-return cross talk occurs when return current due to one signal develops a voltage across the return impedance, which corrupts the other signals that share the return path.

Cross talk between signals of comparable voltage levels is a proportional noise source. That is, it contributes to K_N in Eq. (6-1) rather than V_{NI}. Thus, cross talk cannot be reduced by scaling signal levels to increase noise margins. Instead, we address cross talk by controlling line geometry to reduce coupling between signals and arranging our circuits and signaling conventions to be less susceptible to coupled energy.

The remainder of this section describes three forms of cross talk in detail: cross talk between capacitive lines, such as those found on-chip; cross talk between transmission lines; and signal return cross talk. For each of these forms of cross talk we describe the phenomena, derive formulas to quantify the cross talk, and discuss countermeasures.

6.3.1 Cross Talk to Capacitive Lines

Cross talk between on-chip lines and short off-chip lines is primarily due to parasitic capacitance between the lines. A transition on a signal, A, causes a transition on an adjacent signal, B, scaled by a capacitive voltage divider. If line B is floating, the disturbance persists and may be worsened by the switching of other adjacent lines. If B is driven, on the other hand, the signal returns to its original level with an RC time constant. If the signal rise time is comparable or longer than the RC time constant, the peak magnitude of the disturbance is reduced by the restoration. In cases where adjacent signals are driven in opposite directions, capacitive cross talk increases delay because twice as much charge must be transferred across the coupling capacitance than in the case where only one line is switching.

6.3.1.1 Coupling to a Floating Line

Cross talk from a driven line, A, to a floating line, B, is illustrated in Figure 6-6. A is coupled to B by a parasitic coupling capacitance, C_C. The total capacitance from B to lines other than A, including ground, is C_O. Applying superposition, we model C_O as a capacitor to ground. Any incremental voltage waveform on A will appear on B attenuated by the capacitive voltage divider.

$$(6\text{-}2) \qquad\qquad \Delta V_B = k_c \Delta V_A$$

where the capacitive coupling coefficient, k_c, is given by

$$(6\text{-}3) \qquad\qquad k_c = \frac{C_C}{C_O + C_C}$$

Cross talk with floating lines is particularly important when a high-swing signal passes near a low-swing precharged signal. This can occur, for example, in dynamic domino circuits, RAMs, and low-voltage on-chip buses. Because of the difference in signal swings, a small amount of coupling capacitance can create a significant amount of noise.

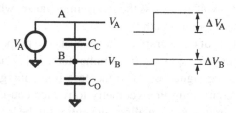

FIGURE 6-6   Capacitive Coupling to a Floating Line

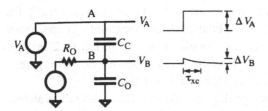

FIGURE 6-7 Capacitive Coupling to a Driven Capacitive Line

6.3.1.2 Coupling to a Driven Line

If line B is driven with an output impedance of R_O, a step on line A results in a transient on line B, as illustrated in Figure 6-7. This transient decays with a time constant, $\tau_{xc} = R_O(C_C + C_O)$. This circuit models coupling between two on-chip driven signals and the case of a precharged cicuit with a feedback "keeper."

Taking Laplace transforms, the response of B to a signal on A is

$$(6\text{-}4) \qquad V_B(s) = V_A(s)\left(\frac{R_O C_C s}{R_O(C_C + C_O)s + 1}\right)$$

The response to a unit voltage step is

$$(6\text{-}5) \qquad V_{B1}(t) = k_c \exp\left(-\frac{t}{R_O(C_C + C_O)}\right) = k_c \exp\left(-\frac{t}{\tau_{xc}}\right)$$

and the response to a unit magnitude signal with rise time t_r is

$$(6\text{-}6) \qquad V_{B2}(t) = \begin{cases} k_c\left(\dfrac{\tau_{xc}}{t_r}\right)\left[1 - \exp\left(-\dfrac{t}{\tau_{xc}}\right)\right] & \text{if } t < t_r \\[4mm] k_c\left(\dfrac{\tau_{xc}}{t_r}\right)\left[\exp\left(-\dfrac{t - t_r}{\tau_{xc}}\right) - \exp\left(-\dfrac{t}{\tau_{xc}}\right)\right] & \text{if } t \geq t_r \end{cases}$$

The peak of V_{B2} is at $t = t_r$.

Consider, for example, the case of a dynamic domino circuit with a keeper (Section 4.3.3.3) disturbed by cross talk from a signal routed over the circuit, as illustrated in Figure 6-8. Node B is precharged by device M1. The signal on line A falls 2.5 V with transition time $t_r = 300$ ps pulling signal B downward through C_C. As long as B remains above the threshold of the high-ratio inverter, keeper device M2 restores B by resistively pulling it back toward V_P. The 0.5-μm/0.35-μm

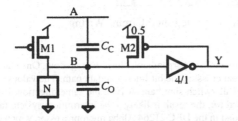

FIGURE 6-8 Cross Talk to a Precharged Circuit with Keeper

keeper is in the resistive region with a resistance of about $4.6\,k\Omega$. The parasitic capacitance of node B, C_O, is about $20\,fF$, and the coupling capacitance, C_C, is $10\,fF$.

Without the keeper, ΔV_B would be given by Eq. (6-2) as $0.83\,V$. With the keeper, which has a time constant of $\tau_{xt} = 138\,ps$, Eq. (6-6) gives the maximum ΔV_B as $0.34\,V$, which is a significant reduction.

For on-chip driven signals, the major effect of cross talk is an increase in delay. If lines A and B are switching simultaneously in opposite directions, as commonly occurs with parallel outputs of a logic circuit, the cross talk increases the delay of the circuit because twice as much charge, $2\Delta V C_C$, must be transferred across C_C. The effect is as if a capacitor of twice the size ($2C_C$) were connected to a fixed voltage. For purposes of estimating delay, two signals switch simultaneously if they switch within τ_{xc} of one another.

The effect of cross talk on delay in modern integrated circuits can be significant. For signals on middle metallization layers, most capacitance is to other signal lines. In the worst case of all of these, switching simultaneously in the opposite direction, the delay is doubled. Except for adjacent signals in the same direction, most designers ignore this effect and assume that most signals do not switch simultaneously and that those that do switch equally in both directions. This is a rather dangerous assumption that, if incorrect, can lead to system failure due to excessive cross talk.[2]

6.3.1.3 Typical Capacitance Values

Figure 6-9 depicts a cross section of the wiring layers of a typical integrated circuit. There are five levels of metallization. Layers 1–4 carry 0.6-μm square wires with 1.2-μm centers. Layer 5 has coarser, 1.2-μm thick wires, making it well suited for power distribution. As drawn, the odd layers carry signals in a direction perpendicular to the page, whereas the even layers carry signals horizontally across the page. Parasitic capacitors are shown schematically in the second column from the right. Each signal has a significant parasitic capacitance to its neighbors above,

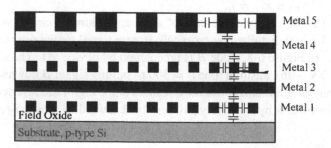

FIGURE 6-9   Cross Section of Integrated Circuit Wiring

---

[2] Many designers assume that cross talk to perpendicular lines averages out. One place this assumption is definitely false is a signal crossing the bit lines of a data path. The values on the bit lines are highly correlated and may all switch simultaneously in the same direction. If this cross talk is not anticipated and accounted for, the result is likely to be intermittent system failure. A novel approach to this problem is found in the DEC 21264 Alpha microprocessor, which places on-chip power planes between pairs of signal layers to shield signals from interlayer cross talk.

TABLE 6-2   **On-Chip Parasitic Capacitance**

Description	Capacitance	Units
Vertical parallel-plate capacitance	0.05	$fF/\mu m^2$
Vertical parallel-plate capacitance (minimum width)	0.03	$fF/\mu m$
Vertical fringing capacitance (each side)	0.01	$fF/\mu m$
Horizontal coupling capacitance (each side)	0.03	$fF/\mu m$

below, and to either side. Except for metal 1, which is coupled to the substrate, almost all of the parasitic capacitance is to other signals, not to the substrate.

Table 6-2 gives values for parasitic capacitance between metal layers in a hypothetical 0.35-μm process with 0.6-μm square wires on 1.2-μm centers. They are calculated by assuming a dielectric constant of 3.9 (SiO_2) and are rounded to one significant figure.

Consider, for example, a set of 1-mm-long minimum width wires running in parallel. Each of these wires has a capacitance of 50 fF to the signals on the layer above, 50 fF to the signals below, and 30 fF each to the signals on either side for a total parasitic capacitance of 160 fF. These lines run in an environment where the signals on perpendicular lines are uncorrelated, and thus we will assume that transitions on the signals above and below average out and consider this 100 fF as if it were to ground. The capacitive coupling coefficient, k_c, to each of the two adjacent signals on the same layer is 0.19, and in the worst case, in which these two signals switch simultaneously, the combined coupling is 38% of the signal value.

6.3.1.4   Capacitive Cross Talk Countermeasures

There are several approaches to dealing with cross talk between capacitive transmission lines:

1. Wiring ground rules should be put in place to limit the magnitude of the capacitive coupling between any pair of signals. Wherever possible signals on adjacent wiring layers should be routed in perpendicular directions to minimize the vertical coupling. A limit should be placed on the maximum parallel run allowed between two signals on the same layer to minimize horizontal coupling.
2. Floating signals should be avoided, and keeper devices should be placed on dynamic signals to reduce susceptibility to cross talk and restore values after a disturbance.
3. Signal rise time should be made as long as possible, subject to timing constraints, to minimize the effect of cross talk on driven nodes, as described by Eq. (6-6).
4. If signals are sent differentially (e.g., like the bit lines in a SRAM), cross talk can be made common-mode by routing the true and complement lines close to each other and (optionally) periodically reversing their positions.

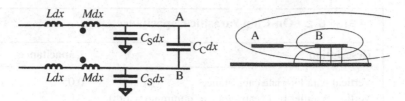

FIGURE 6-10 Incremental Section of a Pair of Transmission Lines

5. Sensitive signals (e.g., those that operate at a low voltage) should be well-separated from full-swing signals to minimize the capacitive coupling from signals with large ΔV.
6. In extreme cases, a sensitive signal can be shielded by placing conductors above, below, and on either side of it that are tied to the reference supply (V_P or GND, depending on the signal) at a single point.
7. Sensitive DC signals (e.g., a current source gate bias) should have capacitance to the appropriate supply (e.g., GND for an NFET current source) added to reduce the coupling coefficient. Capacitance to the opposite supply should be avoided, for it will couple power supply noise into the sensitive node.

6.3.2 Cross Talk Between Transmission Lines

A signal transition on a transmission line may induce traveling waves on nearby transmission lines owing to parasitic capacitance and mutual inductance between the lines. Figure 6-10 shows a cross section of a pair of transmission lines, A and B, over a signal return plane (right) and a circuit model of an incremental length, dx, of line (left). The cross section shows a few electric field lines and magnetic flux lines from conductor B.

The electric field lines illustrate the capacitance affecting line B. Most field lines terminate at the return plane and contribute to the self-capacitance, C_S, which has both parallel plate and fringing components. A few lines, however, terminate on the adjacent transmission line and contribute to the coupling capacitance, C_C. Similarly, many lines of flux (one shown) couple only line B and contribute to the self-inductance, L, and a few flux lines (one shown) couple both A and B and contribute to the mutual inductance, M.

6.3.2.1 Capacitive and Inductive Coupling of Transmission Lines

A transition on line A has two effects on line B. The capacitance couples the time derivative of voltage, whereas the inductance couples the spatial derivative of voltage. The time derivative of voltage $dV_A(x)/dt$ at a point, x, on A couples through the capacitive voltage divider and induces a scaled change in voltage $dV_B(x)/dt$ at position x on B, as expressed by

(6-7)
$$\frac{dV_B(x, t)}{dt} = k_{cx}\frac{dV_A(x, t)}{dt}$$

where k_{cx}, the capacitive coupling coefficient, is given by

$$(6\text{-}8) \qquad\qquad k_{cx} = \frac{C_C}{C_S + C_C}$$

Thus, a positive time derivative of voltage on line A, which could be caused by a wave traveling in either direction, induces a positive time derivative of voltage on line B, which in turn generates positive forward and reverse traveling waves as if line B were driven at the point of coupling. Half of the coupled energy goes in each direction.

The spatial derivative of voltage on A $dV_A(x)/dx$ induces a change in current across the self inductance of line A. If current going in the forward direction (to the right) is positive, then

$$(6\text{-}9) \qquad\qquad \frac{\partial I_A(x,t)}{\partial t} = -\frac{\partial V_A(x,t)}{L\partial x}$$

This time derivative of current in turn induces a spatial derivative of voltage in the adjacent line through the mutual inductance.

$$(6\text{-}10) \qquad \frac{dV_B(x,t)}{dx} = -M\frac{dI_A(x,t)}{dt} = \frac{M}{L}\left[\frac{dV_A(x,t)}{dx}\right] = k_{lx}\frac{dV_A(x,t)}{dx}$$

where the inductive coupling coefficient, k_{lx}, is given by:

$$(6\text{-}11) \qquad\qquad k_{lx} = \frac{M}{L}$$

Thus, a spatial derivative on A induces a spatial derivative on line B scaled by the ratio of mutual to self-inductance. This in turn generates a negative forward traveling wave and a positive reverse traveling wave as if a current source had been inserted in line B at the point of coupling. This is easy to see by recalling the relation between spatial and time derivatives of traveling waves. For a forward traveling wave, V_f,

$$(6\text{-}12) \qquad\qquad \frac{dV_f(x,t)}{dt} = -v\frac{dV_f(x,t)}{dx}$$

whereas for a reverse-traveling wave, V_r,

$$(6\text{-}13) \qquad\qquad \frac{dV_r(x,t)}{dt} = v\frac{dV_r(x,t)}{dx}$$

In a homogeneous medium (e.g., a microstripline sandwiched between two return planes) the mutual inductance and capacitance are duals, and $k_{cx} = k_{lx}$. As we will see, this causes the positive forward-traveling wave due to the capacitive cross talk to exactly cancel the negative forward-traveling wave due to the inductive cross talk.

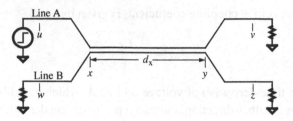

FIGURE 6-11   Line Geometry for Cross Talk Example

6.3.2.2   Lumped Inductive Coupling

Inductive coupling is particularly important between signals in an integrated circuit package. It is not unusual in a package to have mutual inductance between adjacent signals be half the amount of the self-inductance. For example, in a package with a combined bond-wire and lead inductance of 5 nH, the mutual inductance to adjacent lines would be about 2.5 nH each. Because the package is small, we treat this inductive coupling as a lumped circuit element and separate it from the transmission-line coupling problem. The primary countermeasures for lumped inductive coupling are routing signals near their returns to minimize differential-mode coupling and increasing signal rise time to minimize the voltage generated in the coupled line.

6.3.2.3   Near- and Far-End Cross Talk

The capacitive and inductive coupling between lines A and B results in cross talk at both ends of line B. Consider the situation illustrated in Figure 6-11. A rising signal propagates down line A from a driver at point u to a receiver at point v. For distance d_x from point x to point y, this signal is coupled onto line B. The reverse-traveling wave induced on line B arrives at point w at the *near end* of line B, the end near the driver on A, whereas the forward-traveling wave induced on line B arrives at point z at the *far end* of line B.

Figure 6-12 shows the waveforms at points x and y on lines A and B. The near-end cross talk at Bx, point x on line B, is a wide pulse with amplitude k_{rx}. It begins as soon as the edge on line A reaches x and continues for a round-trip delay until the reverse-traveling wave induced by the edge on A reaching y gets

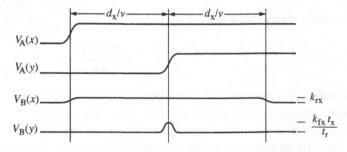

FIGURE 6-12   Waveforms for Cross Talk Example

back to x. Section 3.7.2 gives experimental measurements of this type of cross talk in Figures 3-44 and 3-45.

As the signal on A propagates, its derivative is coupled to line B, as described in Eqs. (6-7) and (6-10). The reverse-traveling wave that arrives at point x at time t, $V_{Br}(x, t)$, sums these contributions during the time, $t_x = d_x/v$, taken to propagate from y back to x

$$(6\text{-}14) \qquad V_{Br}(x, t) = \frac{(k_{cx} + k_{lx})}{2} \int_0^{t_x} \frac{dV_A(x + \tau v, t - \tau)}{d(t - \tau)} d\tau$$

Referencing the signal, V_A, to point x, and substituting $u = 2\tau$ gives

$$V_{Br}(x, t) = \frac{(k_{cx} + k_{lx})}{2} \int_0^{t_x} \frac{dV_A(x, t - 2\tau)}{d(t - 2\tau)} d\tau$$

$$= \frac{(k_{cx} + k_{lx})}{4} \int_0^{2t_x} -dV_A(x, t - u)$$

$$(6\text{-}15) \qquad = k_{rx}[V_A(x, t) - V_A(x, t - 2t_x)]$$

where the reverse coupling coefficient, k_{rx}, is given by

$$(6\text{-}16) \qquad k_{rx} = \frac{(k_{cx} + k_{lx})}{4}$$

The four in the denominator of Eq. (6-16) has two components. One factor of two is due to the division of energy between the forward- and reverse-traveling waves. A second factor of two is due to the energy from coupling for time t_x being spread over a pulse width of $2t_x$.

The far-end cross talk seen at point y on line B is the time derivative of the signal on line A scaled by the forward-coupling coefficient, k_{fx}, and the coupling time, t_x. As the signal propagates along line A and couples its derivative into line B, the forward-traveling cross talk on line B travels with it. Each part of the forward-traveling wave sums the same portion of A's derivative over the time interval, t_x. Mathematically

$$(6\text{-}17) \qquad V_{Bf}(x, t) = \frac{(k_{cx} - k_{lx})}{2} \int_0^{t_x} \frac{dV_A(x - \tau v, t - \tau)}{d(t - \tau)} d\tau$$

Referencing V_A to point x gives

$$V_{Bf}(x, t) = \frac{(k_{cx} - k_{lx})}{2} \int_0^{t_x} \frac{dV_A(x, t)}{dt} d\tau$$

$$(6\text{-}18) \qquad = k_{fx} t_x \frac{dV_A(x, t)}{dt}$$

where the forward-coupling coefficient, k_{fx}, is given by

$$(6\text{-}19) \qquad k_{fx} = \frac{k_{cx} - k_{lx}}{2}$$

TABLE 6-3   Typical Transmission Line Parameters and Coupling Coefficients

Dimensions			Electrical Parameters					Coupling Coefficients			
W	S	H	C	C_m	L	M	Z	k_{cx}	k_{lx}	k_{fx}	k_{rx}
8	8	6	88	6.4	355	57.5	63	0.068	0.162	−0.047	0.058
8	8	3	137	3.0	240	18.5	42	0.021	0.077	−0.028	0.025
8	16	6	87	2.0	356	28.7	64	0.023	0.081	−0.029	0.026
8	16	3	136	1.0	240	8.2	42	0.007	0.034	−0.013	0.010
8	8	6*	148	6.6	302	13.4	45	0.043	0.044	0.000	0.022
8	8	3*	233	1.2	191	1.0	29	0.005	0.005	0.000	0.003
8	16	6*	147	1.3	302	2.6	45	0.008	0.009	0.000	0.004
8	16	3*	233	0.3	191	0.2	29	0.001	0.001	0.000	0.001

Reverse or near-end cross talk is the major concern because in most systems k_{cx} and k_{lx} are nearly equal and forward or far-end cross talk is negligible. If the near-end of line B is not properly terminated, the near-end cross talk will reflect and appear at the far end of the line as well. With some care about line geometry, near-end cross talk from a single adjacent line can be held to 5% or less. Because in the worst case[3] two adjacent lines may switch simultaneously, twice this value would be used for the cross-talk term of a noise budget.

6.3.2.4   Typical Coupling Coefficients

In practice, coupling coefficients are calculated from either circuit-board or cable cross sections, or both, using CAD programs and then checked via experiments on actual circuit boards and cables. Table 6-3 gives values for coupling coefficients for some common board geometries.[4]

The first three columns of Table 6-3 give the dimensions of the transmission lines: the width of each line (W), spacing between lines (S), and height of each line above the return plane (H), as illustrated in Figure 6-13. All dimensions are in mils. The first four rows give the parameters of microstrip lines where the conductor lies at an air–dielectric interface (Figure 6-13, left). The last four rows (with

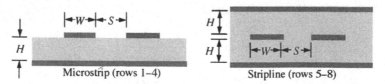

Microstrip (rows 1–4)   Stripline (rows 5–8)

FIGURE 6-13   Transmission Line Geometry for Table 6-3

---

[3] If the coupling coefficients are very high, lines farther away than the immediately adjacent ones may need to be considered, which will lead to a larger multiplier than 2.

[4] The data in this table were computed using LinPar, a two-dimensional field solver program.

an asterisk in the H column) give the parameters of striplines (Figure 6-13, right). For these lines, H also refers to the the height of a top return plane above each line.

For each of the two types of lines, we list the parameters for four variations. The nominal case is 8-mil width, 8-mil space, and 6-mil height. The three variations are to double the spacing, halve the height, and to double the spacing and halve the height.

After the dimensions, the next five columns give the electrical parameters for the lines. The capacitance to the return plane, C, and coupling capacitance, C_m, are given in picofarads per meter, whereas the self-inductance, L, and mutual inductance, M, are given in nanohenrys per meter. The line impedance, Z, is given in ohms. The final four columns give the capacitive, inductive, far-end, and near-end coupling coefficients.

The table illustrates several points:

1. Unless there is a compelling reason to do otherwise, the stripline geometry should be used if cross talk is a concern. The stripline geometry constrains the wave to travel entirely in the dielectric, a homogeneous medium, and thus the capacitive and inductive coupling coefficients exactly cancel, resulting in no far-end cross talk. Because it more tightly constrains the fields, the stripline geometry also has much lower near-end cross talk than the microstrip (about 40% for the nominal case), and the coefficient drops off much faster with increased spacing and decreased height.
2. The height above the ground plane should be made as small as can be economically fabricated. For the stripline geometry, cutting this height in half reduces cross talk by nearly an order of magnitude. Of course, reducing the height also reduces the line impedance.
3. For very sensitive lines, cross talk can be further reduced by increasing the spacing between lines. Doubling the spacing decreases cross talk by about a factor of 2 for microstrip and 5 for stripline. Even more effective than doubling the spacing is surrounding a line with shield conductors that are grounded at one end.

6.3.2.5 Transmission Line Cross Talk Countermeasures

There are several approaches to reducing cross talk between transmission lines and its effects:

1. High-swing signals should not be routed on lines immediately adjacent to low-swing or other sensitive signals. Spacing and shielding should be used to keep the coupling coefficient times the scale factor within a noise budget.
2. The capacitive and inductive coupling coefficients should be matched to eliminate forward (far-end) cross talk. This is most easily done by placing all signal lines between a pair of return planes to keep the signal energy in a homogeneous medium (the board).
3. If the forward-coupling coefficient is nonzero, avoid long parallel runs of transmission lines on circuit boards or in cable assemblies. A maximum parallel

length should be calculated to keep the total cross talk contribution within a noise budget.

4. If the signaling convention permits, both ends of all transmission lines should be terminated in the characteristic impedance of the line. In particular, the near end of lines should be terminated to prevent reverse or near-end cross talk from reflecting and appearing at the far end of the line.

5. Signal rise times should be made as long as possible subject to timing constraints. This reduces far-end cross talk, which is directly proportional to signal derivative and thus is reduced directly as the derivative is reduced. Near-end cross talk is proportional to the maximum difference in signal level across the coupled length and thus is reduced proportionally once the rise time is greater than t_x, the coupled time.

6. Signals on adjacent layers of a circuit board should be routed in perpendicular directions. This results in zero inductive coupling and negligible capacitive coupling.

7. Where differential signals are sent on a pair of adjacent lines, their positions should be periodically reversed, or twisted, in a manner to make coupling to adjacent lines common-mode.[5]

8. The two lines of a differential pair should be spaced close together and far from the lines of other pairs to keep the fields local to the pair. Where possible, a symmetric transmission line (Section 3.4.2) should be used.

6.3.3   Signal Return Cross Talk

Whenever a pair of signals, A and B, share a return path that has finite impedance, a transition on signal A induces a voltage across the shared return impedance that appears as noise on signal B. In a typical system, shared wire bonds, package pins, board planes and traces, connector pins, and cables all contribute to the impedance (largely inductance) of the signal return. Unless differential signaling is used, or each signal is supplied with its own return (nearly the same thing), signals share returns, and cross talk over these returns is a major source of noise.

The effect of signal-return cross talk depends on the signaling convention. Figure 6-14 illustrates the situation for the transmitter side of a voltage-mode signaling system. Signal-return cross talk at the receive side and for current-mode signaling is discussed in Sections 7.3.2.2 and 7.3.1.3. Figure 6-14 shows two signals, A and B, sharing a portion of the return path with impedance Z_R. A positive transition on line A with magnitude ΔV and rise-time t_r causes a current $I_A = \Delta V / Z_0$ to flow in line A. A corresponding return current flows through Z_R, generating a voltage

$$(6\text{-}20) \qquad\qquad V_{xr} = \Delta V \frac{Z_R}{Z_0} = k_{xr}\Delta V$$

---

[5] Adjacent signal pairs must be "twisted" at different points. If all pairs are reversed at the same point, the differential coupling remains unchanged. The simplest approach is to use a set of evenly spaced "twist" points and to "twist" even signal pairs at even points and odd signal pairs at odd points.

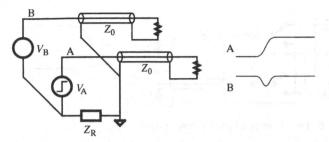

FIGURE 6-14   Equivalent Circuit for Signal-Return Cross Talk

where $k_{xr} = Z_R/Z_0$ is the return cross talk ratio. The return cross talk voltage, V_{xr}, is added to the normal signal voltage on line B and any other lines sharing the return. If Z_R is mostly inductive, the result is a downward glitch on B, as shown on the right side of Figure 6-14. If N lines sharing a return with line B switch simultaneously, their effects are additive, and k_{xr} is multiplied by N.

Consider, for example, a case where Z_R is a 5-nH lead inductance shared by four 50-ohm signal lines with 1-V signal swings and 1-ns rise times. If three of the lines switch simultaneously, the return current ramps 60 mA in 1 ns, generating a 300-mV $V_{xr}(k_{xr} = 0.3)$ across the inductor. A typical noise budget will require k_{xr} to be no more than 0.1, which can be achieved by lowering the return inductance or slowing the rise time. Sending balanced currents, as with differential signaling, completely eliminates signal-return cross talk. In cases where the supply and ground are used as signal returns, the increase in local ground voltage due to signal-return cross talk across lead inductance is sometimes referred to as "ground bounce."

If the characteristics of the transmission lines and the shared return impedance are known, signal-return cross talk can in priniciple be predicted and canceled at the sending end. When waveform A switches in Figure 6-14, the pulse on B is predicted, and an equal and opposite pulse is injected into B by a high-pass RC circuit, for example, to compensate. At the time of this writing, I am unaware of any system that cancels return cross talk. It is difficult in practice to predict accurately the timing and shape of the pulse on B. If the compensating pulse is not adequately matched with the noise pulse, it can make the problem worse.

Signal-return cross talk is a particular problem when unbalanced signals are sent over cables between boards where the return impedance is comparable to the signal impedance. Consider, for example, the case shown in Figure 6-15 where two boards are connected by a bundle of twisted-pair cable (two shown). The return

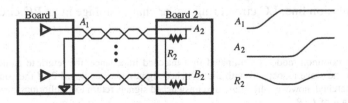

FIGURE 6-15   Signal Return Cross Talk Between Boards

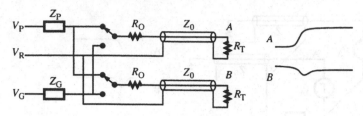

FIGURE 6-16   Power Supply Cross Talk

inductance of a single twisted-pair is identical to the signal inductance. Thus if M of N signals on the cable switch simultaneously in the positive direction, the signals will rise by $\Delta V(1 - M/2N)$, whereas the return and any unswitched signals will fall by $\Delta V M/2N$. The unswitched lines then return to equilibrium.[6] In the worst case, where all but one of the signals switches in the same direction, the disturbance on the unswitched signal is $\Delta V(N - 1)/2N$.

Because it is impractical to provide very low return inductance between boards, this type of signal-return cross talk must be avoided by limiting signal current imbalance. This can be accomplished either via differential signaling or through some form of limited imbalance coding, as discussed in Section 8.4.3.

Signal-return cross talk is even a factor on-chip, where it takes the form of substrate current and additional IR drops across the power distribution network.

6.3.4   Power Supply Cross Talk

Signals can also affect one another via a shared power supply, as illustrated in Figure 6-16. The figure shows two output drivers using underterminated signaling (Section 7.3.4) that share power and ground impedances. When signal A switches high, the current it draws through Z_P creates a voltage drop that appears on line B, as shown at the right side of the figure.

Strictly speaking, this is a form of cross talk because one signal is affecting another. In our noise analyses we will classify this effect as signaling-induced power supply noise.

6.4   INTERSYMBOL INTERFERENCE

A value or symbol on a channel can corrupt another symbol traveling on the same channel at a later time. This intersymbol interference occurs as a result of energy from one symbol being stored in the channel so that it sums with a later unrelated signal. This stored energy can take the form of reflections off discontinuities in a transmission line, LC circuit ringing, or charge storage in an RC circuit.

---

[6] If the common mode is terminated in a matched impedance, the return to equilibrium occurs when the wave associated with the switched signals reaches Board 2. If the common mode is mismatched, however, the return and unswitched signals return to equilibrium slowly with a time constant of L/R

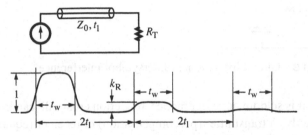

FIGURE 6-17   Intersymbol Interference Due to Mismatched Termination

6.4.1   Impedance Mismatch and Reflections

Reflections of a signal on a transmission from a mismatched termination resistor or a discontinuity in the line can interfere with signals traveling on the line later. Consider the situation illustrated in Figure 6-17. The current source drives a unit amplitude pulse with width t_w on a line with impedance Z_0 and length t_1. At time t_1, the pulse reaches the termination resistor, R_T. The reflection from the far end of the line has an amplitude given by the Telegrapher's Equation (Eq. (3-37)), which we repeat here for convenience as

$$(6\text{-}21) \qquad k_R = \frac{R_T - Z_0}{R_T + Z_0}$$

where k_R is the reflection coefficient.

The reflected wave, with amplitude k_R, arrives back at the current source at time, $2t_1$, where it is completely reflected off the infinite impedance of the source. The reflected wave reaches the termination at time $3t_1$ and is reflected again with amplitude k_R^2. The cycle continues indefinitely with the signal at the source having amplitude k_R^n at time $2nt_1$.

If the impedance is mismatched by some fraction ε, $R_T = Z_0(1 + \varepsilon)$ where $\varepsilon \ll 1$, then it is easy to see that

$$(6\text{-}22) \qquad k_R = \frac{Z_0(1+\varepsilon) - Z_0}{Z_0(1+\varepsilon) + Z_0} = \frac{\varepsilon}{2 + \varepsilon} \approx \frac{\varepsilon}{2}$$

For small values of impedance mismatch, the reflection coefficient is about half the amount of the mismatch. For example, if a $50\ \Omega$ line is terminated in a $45\ \Omega$ resistor, a 10% mismatch, the reflection coefficient will be about -5%.

The reflected pulses on the line in Figure 6-17 are a noise source that later corrupts symbols on the line. In the worst case, the prior symbols on the line will have had values making the series of reflections sum coherently and giving a reflection interference coefficient of

$$(6\text{-}23) \qquad k_{ir} = \sum_{i=1}^{\infty} k_R^i = \frac{k_R}{1 - k_R}$$

For $k_R \ll 1$, only the first reflection is relevant, and $k_{ir} \approx k_R$.

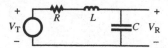

FIGURE 6-18   Circuit for Resonant Intersymbol Interference

Although it is seldom done in practice, reflection cross talk can in principle be canceled exactly. A transmitter (precompensation) or receiver (equalization) can measure the reflection coefficient and round-trip delay on actual signals or a series of test pulses and then, knowing the history of symbols on the line, subtract the expected reflection cross talk from the transmitted or received signal. In practice, however, it is easier to control termination resistance and line impedance to keep the reflection cross-talk coefficient less than 5%, thus obviating the need for such extreme measures.

6.4.2   Resonant Transmitter Circuits

A transmitter driving a lumped LC tank circuit can store energy in the tank that rings out over time and corrupts later signals. Consider, for example, the circuit shown in Figure 6-18. On a signal transition, the voltage source applies a unit step to the series inductor. This step pumps energy into the LC circuit and starts an oscillation that decays over time, depending on the damping from the parallel resistor, R. These oscillations are described in Section 7.4.2 and illustrated in Figure 7-32. From Eq. (7-34) we see that if the bit cell is t_b, the envelope of the oscillation at the start of the next bit cell is

$$(6\text{-}24) \qquad k_X = \exp\left(-\frac{t_b R}{2L}\right)$$

In the worst case, that oscillations from all preceding bits sum coherently, the resonant interference coefficient is given by

$$(6\text{-}25) \qquad k_{ix} = \sum_{i=1}^{\infty} k_X^i = \frac{k_X}{1 - k_X}$$

Section 7.4.2 discusses several methods for reducing resonance interference. These include using a current-mode driver, controlling the rise time of the signal, and adding a parallel termination to the line to reduce signal swing and damp the oscillations. In practice, resonance interference is a serious effect that can lengthen the required bit-cell time to allow oscillations to damp.

Because the resonance interference is linear, in theory it could be corrected by building an equalizing filter at the receiver. However, difficulties in building a filter with the required transfer function accurately matched to the characteristics of the transmitter make this approach impractical.

6.4.3   Inertial Delay and Hidden State

If an internal node of a logic circuit does not reach steady state at the end of each cycle, the value and timing of subsequent outputs of the circuit will depend on the

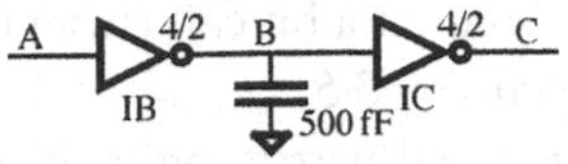

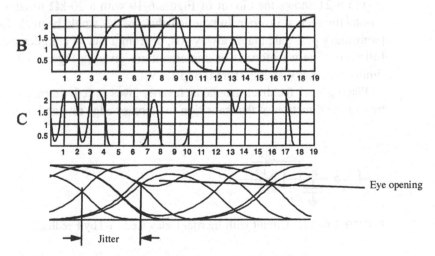

FIGURE 6-19 Circuit with Inertial Delay

residual state and hence on the history of inputs to the circuit. These phenomena can cause narrowing or even loss of isolated pulses and jitter in signals because rising and falling delays are a function of past inputs.

The time required for a node in a logic circuit to reach steady state[7] is often called the *inertial delay*,[8] t_i, of that node. As long as transitions on a circuit's input are spaced by at least t_i, the circuit will always reach steady state before the next transition, and circuit delays will be independent of history. A rising or falling pulse narrower than t_i may leave the node in an intermediate state and thus affect its response to subsequent transitions.

In Figure 6-19 the large capacitive load on node B gives the inverter IB a large inertial delay, about 2 ns, to settle within 10% of its steady state. If we operate this circuit in a system where a new value is placed on node A every 1 ns, node B will not have time to settle before the next value is applied to A. A string of ones or zeros on A will drive B to the supply rails, whereas alternating ones and zeros will leave B at an intermediate voltage. The response seen at C depends on this residual voltage on node B and thus on the history of inputs on A.

Figure 6-20 shows the response of this circuit to the bit sequence 1 0 1 0 0 0 1 0 0 1 1 1 0 1 1 1 0 0 0 applied at A with a 1-ns cell time. The top two traces show the voltage on nodes B and C over nineteen bit times. The bottom trace shows an eye diagram for node C. This trace overlays all of the bit-cell waveforms from the

FIGURE 6-20 Waveforms for Inertial Delay Circuit

---

[7] For the purpose of determining inertial delay we will consider a signal to be in *steady state* when it is less than 10% of the signal swing from its final value.

[8] Some texts refer to the inertial delay of a gate as the minimum pulse width required to cause the output to switch, which is a closely related but slightly different dinition [BreuFrie 76].

second trace for a two-bit-cell period centered on a bit cell (from 0.5 to 2.5 ns). Eye diagrams are described in detail in Section 9.3.5.

Figure 6-20 shows duty factor distortion and narrowing of isolated 1 and 0 pulses. During the first four bit cells, the value on node B never reaches steady state. It has a sawtooth waveform that swings about 1.15 V between 0.45 and 1.6 V. This waveform in combination with the asymmetry of the P and N devices in the second inverter gives a 63% duty factor on node C (1,250 ps high, 750 ps low). During bit cells 4–6, node B is charged up to V_{dd}. As a result of this precharging, node B only gets down to 0.8 V in cell 7, which results in a narrowed output pulse (600 ps) on C that only gets up to 2 V. The narrowing of the isolated zero pulse in cell 13 is even more severe. Node B is fully discharged at the beginning of this cell and only gets up to 1.45 V. This results in a "runt" pulse on C that only gets down to 1.5 V.

The eye diagram at the bottom of Figure 6-20 shows the effect of inertial delay on signal reception. The runt pulse results in a vanishingly small eye opening in which the signal can be detected. Even if we ignore the runt pulse, the inertial delay results in edge jitter of 450 ps or almost half of the cell time.

Inertial delay in the circuit of Figure 6-19 could be dealt with by sizing up the first inverter. However, in many high-speed circuits that are operating at near the limits of the process technology, such an approach will simply move the problem back to node A. The inertial delay of the first inverter can be reduced without changing its size by limiting the swing on node B.[9] This can be accomplished either by clamping node B to a reference voltage, resistively or with diode-connected FETs, or via negative feedback around the second inverter.

Figures 6-21 and 6-22 illustrate how feedback limits the magnitude of a signal, centers it on the switching threshold of the inverter, and sharpens its edges. Figure 6-21 shows the circuit of Figure 6-19 with a 20-kΩ resistor connected around the second inverter. In practice, this resistor would be made from a complementary pass gate that is always on, or from a pair of complementary source followers. The waveforms for this circuit are given in Figure 6-22. Node B is limited to a 1.1-V swing, from 0.6 to 1.7 V.

Placing weak feedback around an inverter gives an active termination that pulls first in the direction of the transition to increase edge rate and later pulls in the

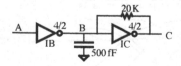

FIGURE 6-21   Circuit with Inertial Delay Reduced by Feedback

[9] Here we are taking advantage of the fact that the gain–bandwidth product (Section 4.3.2.8) for IB with a 500 fF load is constant. By reducing the gain, we get more bandwidth. We must be careful, however, not to demand too much gain from IC, or we will move the problem forward to node C.

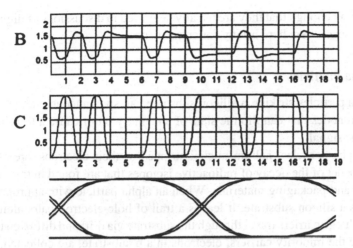

FIGURE 6-22 Waveforms for Inertial Delay Circuit with Feedback

opposite direction to limit swing. This technique is a form of underterminated signaling, which is described in Sections 7.3.4 and 7.4.1.3. From the time node A switches until node C switches, the resistor is pulling in the same direction as IB, resulting in a faster transition. After node C switches, the resistor pulls in the opposite direction of IB, limiting the swing by the voltage divider formed by R and the output resistance of IB. The delays of B and C need to be reasonably well matched to make the resistor "turn around" at the right time. In the figure, B is completing its transition before C, resulting in a small overshoot on B before the resistor starts pulling the other way. The net result is a 50% duty factor, negligible jitter (25 ps), and less delay (600 ps versus 1.2 ns).

With or without feedback, node B is a low-swing signal, and noise must be budgeted appropriately for its swing. In particular, care must be taken to limit cross talk in full-swing signals.

6.5 OTHER NOISE SOURCES

In the preceding sections, we have dealt with noise caused by the operation of the system itself: power supply fluctuations, cross talk, and intersymbol interference. Strictly speaking, these phenomena are internal *interference* rather than *noise*. In this section, we discuss six noise sources that are independent of system operation. Electromagnetic interference results when external fields disturb signals within the system. Alpha particles, emitted as a byproduct of radioactive decay, can spontaneously discharge a circuit node. Variations in-process parameters can cause offsets in the input and output voltages of circuits. Johnson (or thermal) noise is a potential that is generated any time power is dissipated by a resistive element. Shot noise results from the quantization of current to individual charge carriers. Flicker or 1/f noise results from fluctuations in device parameters. These last four noise sources are truly noise as opposed to interference. The last three are small enough that they are usually neglected in discussions of digital systems. We discuss them here briefly for completeness.

6.5.1 Alpha Particles

Alpha particles striking a silicon substrate can spontaneously inject charge into circuit nodes that can flip the state of a memory bit or cause a transient error on a logic signal.

Alpha particles, helium nucleii stripped of their electrons, are emitted as a byproduct of the decay of radioactive isotopes that are found in trace amounts in chips and packaging materials. When an alpha particle with appropriate energy enters a silicon substrate, it leaves a trail of hole-electron pairs along its track. The charge carriers travel through the substrate via drift and diffusion to junctions where the minority carriers, electrons in a p-substrate, are collected, disturbing the charge on a circuit node.

Figure 6-23 shows an alpha particle striking a silicon substrate in an n+ region (the source or drain of an FET), crossing the n+/p− junction, and traveling for some distance in the p-substrate. Along this entire path, the particle is generating hole-electron pairs. We divide the minority carriers into two groups. Electrons within a collection length $l_c = l_1(1+\mu_n/\mu_p)$ of the junction [Hu82] are collected at the junction by drift. Carriers generated farther along the track travel by diffusion and thus are distributed over an area proportional to the depth at which they are generated and may be collected at junctions other than the one struck by the particle. Thus, the amount of diffusion charge collected by a junction is proportional to the area of a junction. For particles that strike the substrate between junctions, all of the charge is transported by diffusion.

We model noise due to alpha particles with a pulsed current source [McPartland 81], as shown in Figure 6-24. The source decays exponentially with a time constant of 1 ns and transfers a total charge of

$$(6\text{-}26) \qquad\qquad Q_\alpha = Q_{\alpha c} + Q_{\alpha d}(A)$$

where $Q_{\alpha c}$ is the charge collected from drift at the space-charge layer and $Q_{\alpha d}(A)$ is the amount of charge collected as the result of diffusion. The diffusion charge increases linearly with area up to the point that all of the charge associated with

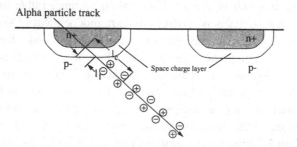

FIGURE 6-23 Alpha Particle Generation and Collection

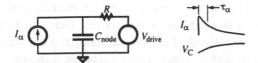

FIGURE 6-24   Current Source Model of Alpha Particle Noise

one alpha particle is collected. The current source in Figure 6-24 has a value of

$$(6\text{-}27) \qquad I_\alpha = \frac{Q_\alpha}{\tau_\alpha} \exp\left(-\frac{t}{\tau_\alpha}\right)$$

where τ_α is typically about 1 ns.

If the time constant of the circuit, $\tau_{node} = RC_{node}$, in Figure 6-24 is large compared with τ_α, then the disturbance on the node is given by

$$(6\text{-}28) \qquad \Delta V_C = Q_\alpha / C_{node}$$

This is the case for floating or dynamic nodes, where R is infinite and the disturbance is permanent until the node is recharged.

For driven or dynamic nodes where $\tau_{node} < \tau_\alpha$, the maximum disturbance of the node voltage is given approximately by

$$(6\text{-}29) \qquad \Delta V = \left(\frac{Q_\alpha}{C_{node}}\right)\left(\frac{\tau_{node}}{\tau_\alpha}\right)\left[1 - \exp\left(-\frac{\tau_\alpha}{\tau_{node}}\right)\right]$$

If a circuit can tolerate a certain ΔV without an error, then the critical charge, the smallest amount of charge that will cause an error, is given by

$$(6\text{-}30) \qquad Q_{crit} = C_{node}\Delta V \left(\frac{\tau_\alpha}{\tau_{node}}\right)\left[\frac{1}{1 - \exp(-\tau_\alpha/\tau_{node})}\right]$$

where the terms in parentheses are replaced by 1 if the node is floating or if $\tau_{node} > \tau_\alpha$.

For example, a typical 6-T SRAM cell has $R = 6\,\text{k}\Omega$, $C_{node} = 10\,\text{fF}$ for a τ_{node} of 60 ps and can tolerate a ΔV of 1 V. The critical charge for this circuit is given by Eq. (6-30) to be 170 fC. Most logic circuits have more capacitance than this and thus are even less susceptible to alpha particle noise.

If Eq. (6-28) or (6-29) indicates that the node will be sufficiently disturbed to cause an error, the error rate can be calculated from the area of the circuit and the alpha particle flux, which ranges from 0.1 cm^{-2}h^{-1} for unprotected chips to 1×10^{-4} cm^{-2}h^{-1} for chips with a polyimide coating and highly purified aluminum [Juhnke 95]. For chips with area bonding, circuits near lead-tin solder balls may be subjected to a much higher flux.

Alpha particles typically are produced by decay processes that give them an initial energy of about 5 MeV. If all this energy is absorbed by the silicon, which generates a hole-electron pair for each 3.6 eV, then 1.4 M hole-electron pairs are generated, giving a total charge, $Q_{\alpha T}$, of 220 fC. This charge is distributed along

The distribution of charge depends on the geometry of the collision. If the alpha particle strikes the silicon at a high angle, nearly perpendicular to the surface, most of the charge is generated deep in the substrate, and a diffusion process distributes it in both time and in space with a Gaussian distribution about the point of impact. A low angle of incidence, on the other hand, results in most of the charge being generated near the surface along a line. In this case, the charge is distributed linearly and nearly instantaneously.[10]

6.5.2 Electromagnetic Interference

Large external electric and magnetic fields can couple into circuit nodes and cause noise. For both types of fields, susceptibility is reduced by keeping a minimum distance between a signal and its return. For E fields, the induced voltage is proportional to the distance between the signal and return, whereas for B fields, the amount of flux coupled is proportional to the area of the loop between the signal and the return.

Electromagnetic interference is rarely a problem in digital circuits unless they are operated near large sources of fields. Usually, the larger concern is the interference created by the digital system. Reciprocity tells us that the same techniques that reduce susceptibility to external fields also reduce emissions by the digital system. Most digital systems can be made "quiet" naturally by keeping signals and returns close together, balancing currents in external cables, controlling rise time on signals, and properly terminating lines. Lots of shielding and large ferrite beads on external lines are band-aid solutions that are applied when care is not taken to limit emissions in the first place.

6.5.3 Process Variation

Variations of process parameters create fixed offsets in the input and output voltages of receivers and transmitters, respectively. We treat the worst-case offsets as a static DC noise source. Process variations also cause variations in delay of circuits, such as delay lines. Often we can compensate for process variations by building circuits that measure their characteristics and adjust accordingly. For example, in Section 12.2 we describe how to compensate a delay line to match the clock period across a wide range of process parameters.

The largest process variations occur between different chips and between different types of devices on a single chip. Instances of the same type of device on the same chip (e.g., two NFETs on the same chip) track more closely. We often exploit this tracking of like devices to build circuits that are less sensitive to variations and to *compensate* for process variations by closing a control

---

[10] The fraction of the 730 fC that is collected at a single node depends on the geometry of the collision, the size and shape of the node's diffusion region, and the proximity of other collectors that can serve to attract charge away from the node. For a typical small (5-μm square) diffusion, the maximum chrage collected is usually about 50 fC or less.

TABLE 6-4   Variation in Process Parameters for a Typical 0.35-μm Process*

Parameter	Symbol	Typical	On-Chip	Between Chips
N threshold voltage	V_{TN}	0.5 V	± 10 mV	± 50 mV
P threshold voltage	V_{TP}	-0.5 V	± 10 mV	± 50 mV
N transconductance	K_N	200 μA/V^2	$\pm 5 \mu$A/V^2	$\pm 20 \mu$A/V^2
P transconductance	K_P	50 μA/V^2	$\pm 2 \mu$A/V^2	$\pm 8 \mu$A/V^2
Gate width	W		$\pm 0.03 \mu$m	$\pm 0.06 \mu$m
Gate length	L		$\pm 0.03 \mu$m	$\pm 0.06 \mu$m

loop around a reference circuit and using the control signals to operate similar circuits.

6.5.3.1   Typical Process Variations

Table 6-4 shows how some critical process parameters might vary, both on one chip and between chips, for our representative 0.35-μm process.

6.5.3.2   Inverter Offset

To see the effect of process variation on input offset noise, consider using an inverter as a receiver. The threshold voltage of the inverter is given by Eq. (4-18). Table 6-5 shows how the process variations from Table 6-4 cause inverter thresholds to vary. The table assumes off-chip variation of all parameters, except for L and W, for which the on-chip numbers are used. The inverter thresholds differ by 280 mV, from 1.07 V at the fast-n/slow-p (Fn–Sp) corner to 1.35 V at the slow-n/fast-p (Sn–Fp) corner. If a $\pm 10\%$ variation of the supply voltage, V_P, is taken into account as well, the maximum difference in inverter thresholds is 520 mV from the fast-n/slow-p/low-voltage (Fn–Sp–L) corner to the slow-n/fast-p/high-voltage (Sn–Fp–H) corner.

The inverter has a large variation in its input threshold because it depends on the ratio of an N-device to a P-device. Except for T_{ox}, the parameters of these devices are determined by separate process steps and thus do not track well.

TABLE 6-5   Effect of Process Variations on Inverter Threshold

	V_{tn}	V_{tp}	K_n	K_p	W_n	W_p	L_n	L_p	B_n	B_p	V_I
Typical	0.5	0.5	150	60	1	2	0.35	0.35	429	343	1.21
Fn–Sp	0.45	0.55	170	52	1.03	1.97	0.32	0.38	547	270	1.07
Sn–Fp	0.55	0.45	130	68	0.97	2.03	0.38	0.32	332	431	1.35
Fn–Sp–L	0.45	0.55	170	52	1.03	1.97	0.32	0.38	547	270	0.97
Sn–Fp–H	0.55	0.45	130	68	0.97	2.03	0.38	0.32	332	431	1.48

* Rather than use the absolute tolerances given in Table 6-4, most designers uses a statistical model of process variation based on [PelgDuin89]. With this model, variations are considered to have a normal distribution with a standard deviation that varies inversely to the square-root of the area of the device. That is,

$$\Delta V_{Tn} = \frac{A_{VT}}{\sqrt{WL}} \quad \text{and} \quad \frac{\Delta \beta}{\beta} = \frac{A_{\beta}}{\sqrt{WL}}$$

For a typical 0.35 μm process, $A_{VT} = 10$ mV/μm and $A_{\beta} = 0.03/\mu$m.

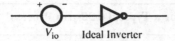

V_{io} Ideal Inverter

FIGURE 6-25   Equivalent Circuit for Inverter Threshold Variation

We model the combined effects of process and power supply variation as a ±260 mV input–offset voltage source in series with the input of an ideal, zero offset but finite gain inverter, as shown in Figure 6-25. Although it is fixed, such a large voltage offset figures prominently in any noise budget.

6.5.3.3   Inverter Compensation

Figure 6-26 illustrates how the fixed portion (the portion due to process variation, not the portion due to supply variation[11]) of the inverter's input offset voltage can be canceled by charging an input capacitor with an offsetting voltage. To charge the capacitor to the appropriate voltage, switch S_f closes and switch S_i switches to the lower position. In this position, the inverter ties one side of the capacitor to its threshold voltage, V_{inv}, whereas the other side is tied to the desired threshold, V_r, so the capacitor charges to $V_{io} = V_{inv} - V_r$ (positive to the right). In operation the switches are as shown, switch S_f open and S_i in the top position. In this configuration the capacitor acts as a series voltage source exactly canceling V_{io} and making the inverter look as if it had a threshold voltage of V_r. The input capacitor must be made fairly large because it does form a voltage divider with the gate capacitance of the inverter somewhat reducing the gain of the inverter.

In addition to being used as a line receiver and an inverter, the circuit of Figure 6-26 is often employed as a high-speed voltage comparator (e.g., in *flash* A/D converters).

6.5.3.4   Differential Pair Offset

Because it depends on matching of like devices on the same chip, a differential source-coupled pair has a relatively small input–offset voltage given by

$$(6\text{-}31) \qquad V_{io} = \Delta V_{Tn} + 0.5(V_{GS} - V_{Tn})\left(\frac{\Delta\beta}{\beta}\right)$$

Usually W is large enough that we can ignore ΔW. For the values in Table 6-4, and a bias voltage, $V_{gs} - V_{tn}$, of 600 mV, Eq. (6-31) gives us a ±20-mV input–offset voltage. Half of this is due to the 10-mV on-chip variation in threshold

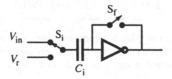

FIGURE 6-26   Canceling Inverter Offset

---

[11]   This compensation method corrects for slow supply variation but not fast supply variation (within one calibrate–sample cycle).

voltage of like devices and half is due to the 3% variation in length multiplied by the bias voltage.

6.5.4 Thermal (Johnson) Noise

The next three noise sources we will deal with (thermal, shot, and $1/f$ noise) are negligible in the context of digital systems. These microvolt sources are swamped by tens of millivolts of system-induced interference. They are primarily of concern in instrumentation and radio receivers in which the signals of interest are in the microvolt range. We discuss them here for completeness.

Any component in the system that dissipates power generates thermal noise. We model this thermal noise as a Gaussian white noise source with an rms voltage of

$$(6\text{-}32) \qquad\qquad V_{jR} = (4k_B TRB)^{1/2}$$

where k_B is Boltzmann's constant (1.38×10^{-23} J/K), T is the temperature in Kelvin, R is the resistance of the dissipative element, and B is the bandwidth in Hertz. At room temperature (300 K), this reduces to

$$(6\text{-}33) \qquad\qquad V_{jR} = 1.29 \times 10^{-10}(RB)^{1/2}$$

For example, an FET with a resistance of 1 kΩ generates an rms noise voltage of 129 μV in a bandwidth of 1 GHz.

This noise is Gaussian. Thus, the probability density function of the noise voltage, V_j, is given by

$$(6\text{-}34) \qquad\qquad p(x) = \frac{1}{V_{jR}\sqrt{2\pi}} \exp\left(-\frac{x^2}{2V_{jR}^2}\right)$$

and the probability that the noise exceeds a given amount, x, is bounded by

$$(6\text{-}35) \qquad\qquad P(|V_j| > x) < \exp\left(-\frac{x^2}{2V_{jR}^2}\right)$$

For example, the probability that the thermal noise from our 1-kΩ FET exceeds 1.29 mV is 2×10^{-22}.

6.5.5 Shot Noise

Shot noise is caused by the quantization of current to individual charge carriers. For a current, I, the average number of carriers arriving during time, t, is

$$(6\text{-}36) \qquad\qquad N = \frac{It}{q}$$

where q is the charge of an electron (1.6×10^{-19} C). Because N must be an integer, there is a fluctuation of the current as N is rounded up during one time interval and rounded down during the next. We can model the arrival of electrons over time as a Poisson process. By the central limit theorem the statistics become

Gaussian as N becomes large. Thus, for most practical purposes, we can model shot noise as a Gaussian white noise source with rms value as follows:

$$(6\text{-}37) \qquad\qquad I_{sR} = (2qIB)^{1/2}$$

For example, for a 1-mA current and a 1-GHz bandwidth, the shot noise is 566 nA, which induces a voltage of 28 μV across a 50-Ω impedance.

6.5.6 Flicker or $1/f$ Noise

Random variations in components give rise to a noise that has equal power per decade of frequency. The amount of $1/f$ noise ranges from 10 nV/decade to 1 μV/decade, depending on the quality of the component. Flicker noise is primarily a concern when handling small signals in a band at or near DC, where a small bandwidth can cross several decades.

For example, suppose we have a termination resistor with flicker noise of 100 nV/decade. From 0.1 Hz to 1 GHz, 10 decades, the total flicker noise will be 1 μV.

6.6 MANAGING NOISE

A system designer manages noise by budgeting signal swing against noise sources. Separate noise budgets are prepared for signals with different levels of locality and for signals that employ different signaling conventions within the same region of locality because these signals are affected differently by noise. In a well-designed system, the noise budget includes all relevant noise sources and leaves a comfortable margin for safety. The absolute value of the margin is not relevant; instead, the ratio of the margin to the anticipated noise is the relevant measure of noise immunity.

In most digital systems we budget for noise using *worst-case analysis*. That is, we consider all of our bounded noise sources as if they were simultaneously at the worst possible extreme value. A budget is then arrived at to give adequate margins even when all of the noise sources are summed.

In cases where an unbounded noise source, like Johnson or shot noise, is large enough to be important, we perform *statistical noise analysis*. That is, we combine the probability distributions of the statistical noise sources to estimate the probability that the total noise will exceed our margin. This technique is also often applied to systems with bounded noise sources when the summed magnitude of uncorrelated bounded noise sources is too large to use worst-case analysis.

In this section we see how a digital designer manages noise through a combination of worst-case analysis (Section 6.6.1) and statistical noise analysis (Section 6.6.2).

6.6.1 Bounded Noise and Noise Budgets

To perform a worst-case noise analysis of a digital system, a designer prepares a *noise budget* for each signaling scenario in the system. Each budget sums up the

TABLE 6-6 **Proportional Noise Budgets (K_N)**

Region	Convention	XT	Atn	EXT	RXT	IPS	ISI	Tx 0	Total K_N
Local (0.1 mm)	Domino	0.2	0.5	0.1		0.01		0.1	0.21
Module (1 mm)	CMOS	0.1	0.2	0.02		0.03		0.1	0.15
Module (1mm)	Diff LV	0.1	0.1	0.01		0.01		0.1	0.12
Chip (20 mm)	CMOS	0.4	0.2	0.08		0.05		0.1	0.23
Chip (20 mm)	Diff LV	0.4	0.1	0.04		0.01		0.1	0.15
Board	CM	0.05	1	0.05	0.05	0	0.05	0.1	0.25
System	Diff CM	0.05	0.1	0.005	0	0		0.1	0.1	0.21

magnitude of all the bounded noise sources that apply to a given scenario. Each scenario corresponds to a different noise situation, a different signaling method, or a different region of communication.

In preparing noise budgets, proportional sources of noise, those that contribute to K_N, are handled separately from the independent noise sources, those that contribute to V_{NI}. Proportional noise sources scale with the signal swing and thus consume a fixed fraction of signal swing. A proportional source that is too large must be dealt with through isolation. Independent noise sources, on the other hand, consume a fixed amount of signal swing and can be dealt with either by isolation or by increasing signal swing.

Tables 6-6, 6-7, and 6-8 give examples of noise budgets for a typical system. The tables consider seven different signaling scenarios. For each scenario, Table 6-6 lists the proportional noise sources, Table 6-7 tabulates the independent noise sources, and Table 6-8 summarizes the overall noise budget and calculates the signal-to-noise ratio.

6.6.1.1 Proportional Noise Sources

In Table 6-6, the first row shows the proportional noise for dynamic Domino logic (the signaling convention) with wire lengths limited to 0.1 mm (the region). The XT column gives the raw cross talk component of 0.2. This is the capacitive

TABLE 6-7 **Budgets for Independent Noise Sources (V_{NI})**

Region	Convention	Rx O	Rx S	PS	Atn	E PS	Total V_{NI}
Local (0.1 mm)	Domino	0.05	0.2	0.01	1.0	0.01	0.26
Module (1 mm)	CMOS	0.25	0.25	0.05	1.0	0.05	0.55
Module (1 mm)	Diff LV	0.01	0.01	0.05	0.1	0.01	0.03
Chip (20 mm)	CMOS	0.25	0.25	0.25	1.0	0.25	0.75
Chip (20 mm)	Diff LV	0.01	0.01	0.25	0.1	0.03	0.05
Board	CM	0.01	0.01	0.5	0.05	0.03	0.05
System	Diff CM	0.01	0.01	0.5	0.05	0.03	0.05

TABLE 6-8   **Overall Noise Budgets**

Region	Convention	Swing	K_N	V_{NI}	ΔV_{min}	ΔV	Margin	V_N	SNR
Local (0.1 mm)	Domino	1 V	0.21	0.26	0.88	1.00	0.06	0.47	1.08
Module (1 mm)	CMOS	2.5 V	0.15	0.55	1.55	2.50	0.48	0.91	1.37
Module (1 mm)	Diff LV	300 mV	0.12	0.03	0.06	0.30	0.12	0.06	2.52
Chip (20 mm)	CMOS	2.5 V	0.23	0.75	2.78	2.50	−0.14	1.33	0.94
Chip (20 mm)	Diff LV	300 mV	0.15	0.05	0.13	0.30	0.09	0.09	1.67
Board	CM	10 mA	0.25	0.05	0.18	0.50	0.16	0.17	1.47
System	Diff CM	10 mA	0.21	0.05	0.15	1.00	0.43	0.25	2.00

coupling coefficient K_c multiplied by the ratio of signal swings. This raw cross talk is attenuated by 0.5 (the Atn column) to give an effective cross talk (EXT) of 0.1 or 10%. This attenuation is achieved by a keeper with a time constant slightly faster than the rise time of the coupling signals. Adding internal power supply noise (IPS) of 1% and a 10% transmitter offset gives a total K_N of 21% for Domino logic.

The second scenario covers CMOS logic operating with 1-mm wires, and the fourth scenario describes CMOS logic operating across a chip with 20-mm wires. The raw cross talk number is lower for the 1-mm wires because the increase in coupling is more than offset by the ratio of signal swings; for the 20-mm wires the cross-talk number is higher because wire capacitance dominates load capacitance at this distance. The cross-talk attenuation for the two CMOS scenarios is achieved by adding to the effective delay of the signal so the driver has time to replace the charge removed as the result of cross talk.

The third and fifth scenarios give budgets for an on-chip, low-voltage differential signaling convention. Here cross talk is attenuated without delay by "twisting" the two wires associated with a signal periodically in a staggered manner to make any coupling common-mode.

The last two scenarios in the table give budgets for current-mode, off-chip signaling conventions that operate by sending ±5 mA of current into 50-Ω lines. On a circuit board, a single-ended signaling method is used that shares a signal return pin over four signal lines, resulting in 5% signal return cross talk (RXT). Between boards, differential signaling is used, and a pair of wires is devoted to each signal. These methods budget an additional 5 and 10%, respectively, for intersymbol interference (ISI) due to resonances in the packaging and impedance mismatches.

Overall, the signaling methods have proportional noise between 12 and 25% of the signal swing. Because, without hysteresis, noise cannot exceed half of the signal swing, between a quarter and half of the available signal magnitude is consumed by proportional noise.

6.6.1.2   Fixed Noise Sources

Table 6-7 lists the noise sources that are independent of signal swing. For the Domino logic we budget 50 mV for receiver offset (Rx O) and 200 mV for receiver sensitivity[12] (Rx S) to reflect the high-ratio inverter used to sense the dynamic node. The two regular CMOS lines budget 250 mV for offset and 250 mV for sensitivity. The Domino and CMOS schemes have raw, single-supply, external power supply noise (PS) that depends on the size of the region over which they signal: 10 mV in a local region, 50 mV over 1 mm, and 250 mV across this chip. Because *IR* drops develop over distance in the power supply network, circuits that are near one another have less relative supply noise. The excursions in their power supplies track one another. Because these three signaling methods are voltage-mode and use the supplies as the transmitter references, there is no attenuation of power supply noise.

The on-chip differential schemes and off-chip current mode conventions all use differential amplifiers to sense the signal and thus have 20 mV budgeted for offset and sensitivity combined. In addition, all four of these conventions have good rejection of power supply noise, although the current mode schemes have slightly better rejection.

6.6.1.3   Overall Noise Budgets

The overall noise budgets, combining both proportional and independent sources, are given in Table 6-8. For each case, this table gives the proportional noise, K_N, from Table 6-6 and the independent noise, V_{NI}, from Table 6-7. From these two columns, the minimum signal swing, ΔV_{min}, is calculated as

$$(6\text{-}38) \qquad\qquad \Delta V_{min} = \frac{2V_{NI}}{(1 - 2K_N)}$$

Half the difference between the actual ΔV and ΔV_{min} is the noise margin, the amount of absolute voltage between the signal and the noise. This number is not particularly meaningful by itself, for it does not account for isolation or attenuation of noise. Thus, a larger margin does not imply better noise immunity. By dividing the margin by the attenuation for each independent noise source, however, one can get an indication of the headroom available to tolerate greater than expected noise from that source. For example, the module-level CMOS system with a margin of 0.48 V can tolerate power supply noise up to 0.48 V, whereas the board-level current-mode signaling system with a margin of 0.16 V can tolerate supply noise up to 3.2 V.

The column V_N shows the total noise according to Eq. (6-1). Dividing ΔV by twice this number gives the signal-to-noise ratio (SNR). This is the best overall measure of noise immunity because it accounts for isolation as well as margins. The SNR indicates the amount by which all of the noise sources can scale before overwhelming the signal.

There is a certain amount of conservatism built into these numbers. We assume, for example, that an excursion below the Domino gate's inverter threshold, even for a few picoseconds, will result in an error, whereas in fact, the dynamics of the gate permit it to tolerate small excursions of several hundred picoseconds.

---

[12] The sensitivity of a digital receiver is the voltage swing on the input required to give a full-swing output. Mathematically, sensitivity $\Delta V_{in} = \Delta V_{out}/|A|$, where A is the gain of the receiver.

This conservatism, however, is offset by an uncertainty about the exact values and distributions of several noise sources.

Noise budgets are intimately related to ground rules. For example, budgeting 5% of signal swing for cross talk with the off-chip signaling conventions sets constraints on the geometry of transmission lines. The 10% allocation for inter-symbol interference with the system-level signaling sets constraints on the types of connectors and cables that can be used. The attenuation values for cross talk in the CMOS signaling systems result in delay multipliers that must be applied to all signals when critical-path analysis is performed. The raw cross-talk factor for the Domino logic determines the maximum coupling allowed into a dynamic node.

Determining ground rules and noise budgets is an iterative process. If the budget is set too tight, it becomes difficult to achieve. For example, lines may need to be spaced so far apart to get cross talk less than 1% that board density becomes unacceptably low. In practice, one sets a budget, derives a set of ground rules, and then iterates, relaxing the budget where the ground rules are onerous and tightening it where there is room.

Noise budgets are based on estimates of the type and magnitude of different noise sources in a system. Early in the development of a system or of a new set of ground rules it is prudent to actually measure the noise sources to validate these estimates. This is usually done using test chips and test boards. The chips contain examples of the on-chip and off-chip signaling systems along with suitable generators of power-supply noise and cross talk and on-chip instrumentation (sample and hold amplifiers on key nodes) to measure the noise. The boards include various geometries of transmission lines, candidate cabling systems, and power distribution networks and are used to measure the off-chip noise sources with conventional instrumentation.

Often a designer forgoes the type of noise analysis described here, reasoning that what he or she is doing worked the last time. This type of complacency is very dangerous and has caused the failure of more than one system. Technology is advancing at a sufficient rate that it is likely that even if the same signaling conventions are employed, many key parameters such as clock rate, rise times, supply current, and so forth, will have changed significantly, thus potentially pushing a noise budget over the edge. In Table 6-8, for example, the CMOS sig-naling scheme works well over small distances but is over budget when operated across the entire chip. Either delay must be added to reduce cross talk, or better receivers must be used to make this signaling method operate reliably across the entire chip.

6.6.2 Gaussian Noise and Bit Error Rates

When unbounded Gaussian noise sources account for a significant fraction of sys-tem noise, worst-case analysis is not appropriate. There is always some probability that the Gaussian noise source will exceed the margin. The question is not if this will happen, but rather how often.

To calculate the frequency with which the noise exceeds the margin, we account separately for the bounded and unbounded noise sources. For the bounded noise sources we perform the analysis described above in Section 6.6.1 and compute the total noise, V_N, as tabulated in Table 6-8. From the total noise we can calculate the *net noise margin*, V_M, as

(6-39) $V_M = \Delta V/2 - V_N$

The net noise margin V_M is the amount of voltage margin available to tolerate unbounded noise when all of the bounded sources combine in a worst-case manner. Most of the time, the situation is not nearly this bad, and there is considerable additional margin to tolerate unbounded noise.

Unbounded noise sources are usually approximated as Gaussian sources, with a normal distribution, and described by their *standard deviation* or root mean square (rms) value. We will denote the rms voltage of the ith noise source as V_{Ri}. We can model several Gaussian noise sources as a single combined source with rms voltage V_R by summing the *variance* (V_{Ri}^2) of each source and taking the square root as follows:

(6-40) $V_R = \left(\sum_i V_{Ri}^2 \right)^{1/2}$

The effective voltage signal-to-noise ratio[13] is calculated from V_M and V_R as

(6-41) $VSNR = \dfrac{V_M}{V_R}$

From Eq. (6-35) we know that the probability of the instantaneous noise voltage exceeding the margin is

(6-42) $P(\text{error}) = \exp\left(-\dfrac{VSNR^2}{2} \right)$

In a typical signaling system we sample this probability distribution once each bit. In this case, Eq. (6-42) gives the probability of a given bit being in error, or viewed over time, the *bit error rate* (BER). For example, suppose we have a VSNR of 10 (20 dB); then, Eq. (6-42) gives us a BER of 2×10^{-22}.

Calculating BER in this manner often gives an excessivly conservative estimate. Because the worst-case combination of the bounded noise sources almost never occurs, the real margin (and hence the real VSNR) is much higher than that estimated by V_M.

A more realistic estimate of BER can be achieved by applying statistical noise analysis to some of the bounded noise sources as well. This technique can only be applied to noise sources that are time-varying and uncorrelated with one another. Fixed sources, such as transmitter and receiver offsets and sensitivities, should

---

[13] Signal-to-noise ratio (SNR) normally refers to the ratio of signal power to noise power. To make it clear that we are referring to a voltage ratio, not a power ratio, we use the unambiguous acronym VSNR. The two ratios are related because $SNR = VSNR^2$.

always be handled with worst-case analysis. However, cross talk with many un-correlated signals and uncorrelated power supply noise can be handled with sta-tistical analysis.

For purposes of statistical analysis we model the sum of several uncorrelated, bounded noise sources as a single Gaussian source with an rms voltage that is calculated by taking the square root of the sum of the variance of the individual sources. With statistical analysis, N unit noise sources give an rms noise source with magnitude $N^{1/2}$. For comparison, a worst-case analysis of the same N sources gives a peak noise with magnitude N. The latter is often excessively conservative.

Care must be taken when doing statistical noise analysis to ensure that the independent sources truly are uncorrelated. This is not the case, for example, for cross talk from datapath bit lines for which it is not unusual for all 64 lines to switch simultaneously from 1 to 0. When some noise sources are correlated and some are not, we sum each group of correlated noise sources linearly (using worst-case analysis) to give a single source and then sum the variances of the resulting uncorrelated noise sources.

It is very difficult in practice to measure very low bit error rates directly. For example, a 1-Gb/s channel with a VSNR of 15 has a BER of about 10^{-47} and produces an error about once every 10^{38} seconds (about 10^{30} years). To measure the error rates of such channels, we accelerate the error rate by adding a known amount of Gaussian noise to the signal and measure the BER of the degraded channel. To estimate the BER of the raw channel, we take two or more measurements of this type (with different amounts of additive Gaussian noise) and extrapolate the results. The extrapolation also gives an estimate of the fixed component of the noise, V_N (see Exercise 6-16). For meaningful estimation of BER or V_N, such measurements must be made on a statistically significant sample of channels because noise components, such as receiver and transmitter offsets, may vary significantly from sample to sample.

6.7   BIBLIOGRAPHIC NOTES

Many noise issues, including cross talk and power supply noise, are covered by Bakoglu [Bakoglu90]. Glasser and Dobberpuhl give a good treatment of on-chip noise in Section 4.3 of [GlasDobb85]. Thermal and shot noise are discussed in the context of analog circuits in [HoroHill86]. Alpha particles were first identified as a noise source in the context of DRAMs by May and Woods [MayWood79]. A circuit model of alpha particles was introduced in [McPartla81]. The funneling of charge along the particle track is described in [Hu82]. A modern update on alpha particles is given in [Juhnklar95]. A slightly different definition of inertial delay is given in [BreuFrie76] in the context of logic simulation.

6.8   EXERCISES

6-1   **Single-Supply Noise:** Consider a 16 × 16-mm chip that uses full-swing CMOS signaling. The gates have the input–output transfer characteristic shown in Figure

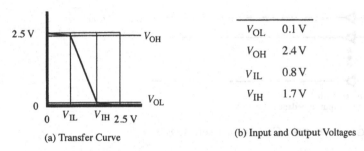

(a) Transfer Curve

(b) Input and Output Voltages

V_{OL}	0.1 V
V_{OH}	2.4 V
V_{IL}	0.8 V
V_{IH}	1.7 V

FIGURE 6-27 Transfer Function of a Static CMOS Gate

6-27(a). This corresponds to the input and output high and low voltages shown in Figure 6-27(b) and yields high and low noise margins of 700 mV. The chip is populated with a density of 10^4 gates/mm². The *average* gate has an output load of 100 fF and toggles every third 5-ns cycle. Power (V_{DD}) and ground are distributed to the gates from peripheral pads over a single metal layer using 25% of the layer for power and 25% for ground. The current profile is triangular each clock cycle with a peak value of four times the average current.

1. What components of noise are accounted for in the input and output voltages and noise margins listed in Figure 6-27?
2. What is the magnitude of single-supply noise between a CMOS gate on the edge of the chip and another gate 1 mm away in the direction of the power distribution network? Repeat this calculation for gates that are 2, 4, and 8 mm distant.
3. Now consider a gate in the center of the die. What is the magnitude of the single supply noise between this gate and gates located 1 and 8 mm away in the direction perpendicular to the power distribution network?
4. Over what distances will the CMOS signaling convention operate reliably?

6-2 Power Supply Noise: You are building an integrated circuit where the clock driver shares 1-mm-long by 2-μm-wide power and ground wires with full-swing driver and receiver circuits. Suppose the clock driver and its 100-pF clock load are modeled as shown in Figure 6-28 by a switch, a 5-Ω resistor, and 100-pF of capacitance to "ground." Assume that the switch toggles every 2.5 ns to generate a 200-MHz "square" wave on the clock network.

Sketch and dimension the local power and ground voltages, V_{LP} and V_{LG}, in Figure 6-28. How does this noise affect connection A in the figure? Connection B?

6-3 Capacitive Cross Talk and Delay: You are designing a chip that has a 2-mm-long data bus of 0.6-μm wires on 1.2-μm centers (see Figure 6-29). Assume the capacitance

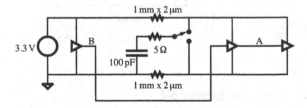

FIGURE 6-28 Circuit for Exercise 6-2

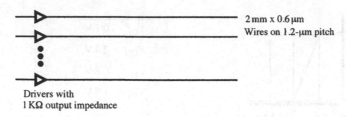

2 mm x 0.6 μm
Wires on 1.2-μm pitch

Drivers with
1 KΩ output impedance

FIGURE 6-29   Circuit for Exercise 6-3

numbers from Table 6-2 and assume that the perpendicular wires on adjacent layers are all grounded. You are driving each bus line with a static driver that can accurately be modeled as a voltage source in series with a 1-kΩ resistor. Assuming that all lines switch simultaneously to random states, what is the worst-case maximum and minimum delay of a line (give an *RC* time constant)? (Hint: What combination of transitions on adjacent lines will speed up or slow down a transition on a given bit?)

6-4   **Capacitive Cross Talk to Dynamic Circuits:** Consider the 2-mm-long on-chip bus from Exercise 6-3. In this case, however, you are precharging the bus and selectively discharging each bit with the circuit shown Figure 6-30(a). What happens to the voltage on bit 2 if, after precharging, adjacent bits 1 and 3 are pulled low whereas bit 2 is allowed to float (draw a dimensioned sketch). Assume that the selected pulldown chain can be modeled by a 1-kΩ resistor and ignore the capacitance of the pulldown chains. What happens if bit 2 is pulled up with a "keeper," as shown in Figure 6-30(b), which you can model as a 2-kΩ resistor? Draw a second sketch.

6-5   **Transmission-Line Cross Talk:** Your printed-circuit layout contractor has inadvertently run a full-swing (3.3-V) CMOS signal with a fast 500-ps rise time right next to a low-swing (300-mV) signal for a 10-cm run of microstrip line. The lines are each 8 mils wide spaced 6 mils above a ground plane and spaced 8 mils from one another, a geometry that matches the first line of Table 6-3. Both lines are parallel terminated at the receiving end only. What is the magnitude of the noise induced on the low-swing line? Is this a concern?

6-6   **Transmission Line Cross Talk Using Propagation Modes:** Another way to analyze cross talk is to consider the differential and common-mode impedances of a coupled pair of lines. Putting a unit step into line 1 while holding line 2 at a steady value, $V_1 = U(t)$, $V_2 = 0$, is the equivalent of sending a differential voltage of

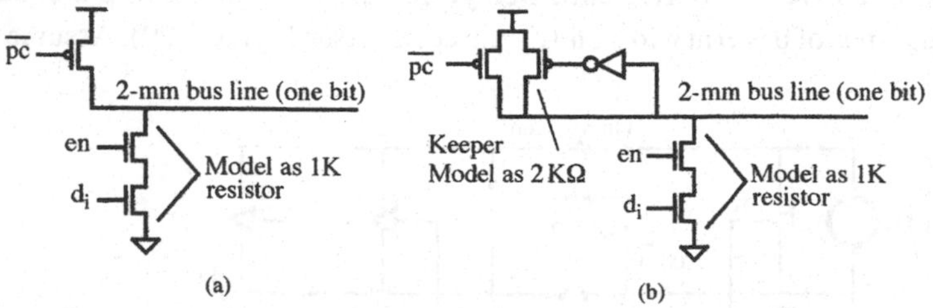

$\overline{pc}$
2-mm bus line (one bit)

en
d_i
Model as 1K resistor

(a)

$\overline{pc}$
Keeper
Model as 2 KΩ
2-mm bus line (one bit)

en
d_i
Model as 1K resistor

(b)

FIGURE 6-30   Circuit for Exercise 6-4

$V_D = -0.5 \, \Delta V = -0.5 \, U(t)$, and a common-mode voltage of $V_C = 0.5 \, U(t)$ into the *quiet* line, line 2. The cross talk can then be calculated as the superposition of the even and odd mode responses of the quiet line.

Using Eqs. (3-59) and (3-60), calcuate the differential and common-mode impedances of the coupled line assuming the geometry from the first line of Table 6-3. Compute the differential and common-mode response of the quiet line to a step on the driven line assuming a source impedance and a termination impedance of Z_0. From these responses compute the near-end and far-end coupling coefficients.

6-7 **Signal-Return Cross Talk:** You have an integrated circuit package that can be accurately modeled as a lumped 5-nH inductor for each pin. You plan to use this package to house a chip that drives 128 full-swing (3.3-V) outputs into 50-Ω lines with 1-ns rise times. How many return pins do you need if the drop across the returns must be kept less than 300-mV in the worst case? How many returns are needed if the rise time is slowed to 3-ns?

6-8 **Reflections:** Consider a signaling system that uses a 5-mA current-source driver into a 50-Ω transmission line terminated into a 45-Ω resistor (a 10% mismatch). What is the worst-case magnitude of intersymbol interference due to impedance mismatch in this system? The transmission line is 5 ns long, and the data rate is 500 Mb/s.

6-9 **Resonant Circuits:** A signaling system drives a 500-mV step into a parallel-terminated 50-Ω line via a package that can be modeled as a 5-nH series inductor followed by a 2-pF capacitor to ground. If the data rate is 500 Mb/s, what is the maximum intersymbol interference due to oscillations of the package parasitics?

6-10 **Alpha Particles and Critical Charge:** Consider a storage device composed of a pair of back-to-back inverters sized $W_p / W_n = 2 \, \text{mm}/1 \mu\text{m}$. What is the *critical charge*, Q_c, that, when removed from the high node of the circuit, causes the state of the circuit to flip? If the circuit is slowed by halving the current drive of the inverters without changing their capacitance, what happens to Q_c?

6-11 **Alpha Particles:** A typical alpha particle has an energy of 5 MeV, and the band-gap of silicon is 1.1 eV (at room temperature). Therefore, one alpha particle excites about 4.5 million electrons (680 fC) to the conduction band (also creating 4.5 million holes) as it loses its energy hitting a piece of silicon. Suppose the alpha particle enters the silicon normal to its surface and generates these charge carriers uniformly distributed across a 50-μm track straight into the silicon. Also assume that only diffusion, not drift, affects the motion of the carriers and ignore recombination. To simplify this problem, we will approximate the density of the charge where it is collected on the surface with a Gaussian distribution with a standard deviation of 50 μm. (Alternatively, to simplify the calculation, you may assume that the density decreases linearly from a peak at the center to zero at a radius of 50 μm.)

Given this model, is a circuit with a critical charge of 100 fC having a junction area of only 20 μm^2 more susceptible to upset by an alpha particle than a circuit with a critical charge of 200 fC but a much larger junction area of 4,000 μm^2? Explain.

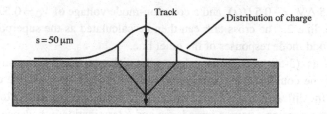

FIGURE 6-31   A Perpendicular Alpha-Particle Strike

6-12   **Thermal Noise:** What is the magnitude (rms voltage) of the thermal noise across a FET operating in the resistive region with a resistance of 1 kΩ where the bandwidth of interest is from DC to 2 GHz? How does the noise voltage change if the impedance is reduced to 50 Ω?

6-13   **Worst-Case Noise Analysis:** Suppose you are starting with a signaling system with the following parameters:

Signal swing	500 mV
Receiver offset	±100 mV
Receiver sensitivity	±100 mV
Transmitter offset	±100 mV
Cross talk coefficient	20%
Termination mismatch	20%

With a worst-case noise analysis, will this system work? Why or why not?
To improve this system you are considering the following changes:

1. Increasing signal swing to 1 V.
2. Using an improved reciever with ±10-mV offset and ±10-mV sensitivity.
3. Improving layout ground rules to reduce cross talk to 5%.
4. Using a self-compensating terminator to reduce termination mismatch to 5%.
5. Using an improved transmitter with ±30-mV offset.

To meet the shipping date you have scheduled for your system you only have time to implement two of these changes. Which two should you pick? What is your signal-to-noise ratio after implementing these changes? Will your system pass a worst-case noise analysis now?

6-14   **Statistical Noise Analysis:** Consider a system with $\Delta V = 500$ mV. The signal is corrupted by fixed-noise sources with total $V_{NI} = 100$ mV and $K_N = 0.2$. In addition, there is additive Gaussian noise with a magnitude of 10-mV rms. Calculate the BER for this system.

6-15   **Statistical Analysis of Bounded Sources:** Consider a system with $\Delta V = 250$ mV. Fixed-noise sources have a magnitude of $V_{NI} = 50$ mV. Correlated-noise sources (datapath bits that may all switch simultaneously) are modeled by $K_N = 0.20$. In addition, the signal crosses 100 perpendicular signals whose transitions are uncorrelated. The worst-case noise due to capacitive cross talk from each of these perpendicular signals is $K_N = 0.005$ (or 1.25 mV). If you perform a worst-case analysis, will the system work? If you model the 100 perpendicular signals as a statistical source, what is its rms voltage level? What is the predicted BER using the statistical model?

6-16 **Measuring Bit-Error Rate:** You are attempting to measure the BER of a channel with a nominal signal swing, ΔV, of 500 mV. The BER is too low to be measured directly. However, when you add 15 mV rms and 25 mV rms of Gaussian noise to the channel, you are able to measure BERs of 10^{-8} and 10^{-4}, respectively. What is the BER of the channel with no additive noise? What is the fixed component of noise, V_N?

7

SIGNALING
CONVENTIONS

Signaling, the method used to transmit digital information from one location to another, is central to the design of digital systems. A signaling convention involves encoding information into a physical quantity (typically current or voltage), generating a reference against which this quantity is measured, providing terminations to couple signal energy into the transmission medium and absorb energy to prevent unwanted reflections, and controlling signal transitions to limit the spectrum of transmitted energy. To a large extent, the signaling convention determines the reliability, speed, and power consumption of a system. A good signaling convention isolates a signal from noise to provide noise immunity. It does not attempt to overpower the noise with noise margin. Most signaling conventions in common use are actually quite poor because they are based on standards that are accidents of history rather than on careful design to isolate noise sources. For this reason, many modern systems define their own signaling conventions rather than employ these standards.

A major factor in the design of a signaling convention is the output impedance of the driver. A very low-output impedance (nearly zero) gives voltage-mode signaling, whereas a very high impedance (nearly infinite) gives current-mode signaling. An output impedance matched to the line gives source-terminated signaling, whereas a higher, but not infinite, impedance gives underterminated signaling. Current-mode or underterminated signaling is usually preferred because these conventions obviate the need for accurate transmitter and receiver voltage references. It is very difficult to provide accurate voltage references isolated from power supply noise for the small signal swings used in efficient signaling systems.

A measure of efficiency for a signaling system is the amount of energy expended per bit. The energy requirement is determined by the approach used to provide noise immunity. With careful isolation from power supply noise and compensation of parameter offsets, signal energies around 1 pJ per bit can be achieved with good reliability. A current-mode system with a ±2.5-mA signal swing into $50\,\Omega$ and a 2-ns bit time, for example, gives 0.63 pJ per bit with 250-mV signal swings. Generating this signal from a 2.5-V supply requires 6.3 pJ per bit. In contrast, full-swing 3.3-V signaling into the same impedance with a bit time of 10 ns gives a signal energy of over 2 nJ per bit. This brute-force approach to signaling uses over three orders of magnitude more energy than is needed to move the information reliably and consumes more than two orders of magnitude more energy from the power supply. Signaling accounts for a large fraction of the power dissipation in many chips that use such crude signaling methods.

Clean references are the key to good noise immunity. Transmitter references are used to determine the current sent to represent a given symbol, whereas receiver references are used to detect the received current. Noise in either reference directly corrupts the signal. With bipolar signaling, zero is used as the receive reference, and the transmitter sends positive or negative current to denote the two symbols. Alternatively, an explicit reference can be sent with a signal or group of signals, or the signal can be sent differentially, as a pair of signals whose difference represents the signal. Generating a reference locally in the receiver generally results in poor noise immunity because parameter mismatches offset the reference, and the reference fails to track AC noise coupled into the signal.

Good signaling performance requires *incident-wave switching*. The first wave arriving at the receiver after a signal transition must be of sufficient amplitude to be detected reliably, and there should be no significant reflections or oscillations. This gives a wire delay equal to the time-of-flight over the wire. In contrast, many conventional signaling systems either require several round-trip wire delays to charge up the wire with reflections or excite oscillations that must be allowed to die down before the signal can reliably be detected. To achieve incident-wave switcing requires control of the signal transition (to avoid exciting oscillatory modes of the transmission medium) and matched terminations to eliminate reflections.

This chapter describes basic signaling conventions for use with LC transmission lines and lumped LRC circuits. Particular attention is given to noise and signal energy. Chapter 8 describes more advanced topics in signaling, including methods for dealing with lossy (RC and LRC) transmission lines, simultaneous bidirectional signaling, and AC signaling. In Chapter 11 we describe how to design the circuits required to implement these signaling conventions.

We start in Section 7.1 by comparing conventional full-swing, voltage-mode CMOS signaling with low-swing current-mode signaling. This example illustrates many of the issues associated with designing signaling conventions and their effect on noise, power, and delay. Section 7.2 summarizes the considerations involved in designing a transmission system. Signaling conventions for transmission lines are discussed in Section 7.3, including current-mode and voltage-mode signaling, series termination, undertermination, source references, and differential signaling. Section 7.4 describes signaling methods for lumped, capacitive, and LC transmission media. This section includes discussions of pulsed signaling, return-to-zero signaling, and rise-time control. Section 7.5 addresses the issue of signal encoding. Binary and multilevel signaling are compared, expressions are derived for required signal magnitude, and pulsed signaling is introduced.

7.1   A COMPARISON OF TWO TRANSMISSION SYSTEMS

In this section, we illustrate many of the issues involved in designing a signaling convention by comparing two solutions with a common transmission problem: the communication between two 3.3-V CMOS circuits in a 100-MHz synchronous digital system separated by about 1 m (6 ns) of a 50-ohm transmission line with noise parameters as shown in Table 7-1.

Our first solution (CMOS) is a conventional supply-referenced, voltage-mode, full-swing CMOS transmission system, as shown in Figure 7-1. The driver uses the two supply voltages to represent a 1 and a 0, respectively, and has an output impedance, R_O, of 200 Ω. The receiver is a CMOS inverter that compares

TABLE 7-1	**Noise Parameters for Example System**	
Parameter	**Description**	**Value**
V_{en}	External power supply noise	300 mV
K_{xt}	Cross talk from adjacent lines	10%
K_{zr}	Termination mismatch	10%
K_{in}	Self-induced power-supply noise	10%
K_{cm}	Common-mode gain	.01

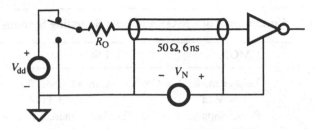

FIGURE 7-1 Full-Swing CMOS Transmission System

the received voltage with a power-supply-derived reference. The inverter has a sensitivity[1] of 300 mV and an input–offset voltage of ±250 mV across process corners.

A low-swing, current-mode CMOS transmission system (LSC), as shown in Figure 7-2, is our second solution. The driver injects a current of +3.3 mA for a 1 and −3.3 mA for a 0. The injected current induces a voltage wave of 330 mV (2 × 3.3 mA × 50 Ω) in the transmission line. All but 5% of the incident wave is absorbed in the parallel termination resistor. A differential amplifier is used to sense the voltage across the termination resistor. The amplifier has a sensitivity of 10 mV and an input–offset voltage of ±10 mV. The signal and the signal return are both isolated from the power-supply noise, making any supply noise common-mode to the differential receiver.

Table 7-2 compares the properties of these two systems. The first three rows of the table describe the signaling convention: how binary values are represented, the reference used by the receiver to discriminate between a 0 and a 1, and how the line is terminated. The remaining rows compare the performance of the two systems. The table shows that the LSC system represents a signal with much less energy than the CMOS system and, accordingly, dissipates less power. Although the LSC operates at lower signal levels, and hence has lower absolute noise margins, it has better noise immunity. Finally, because LSC switches the receiver with the first wave that traverses the transmission line (incident-wave switching) and requires less transmitter amplification, it operates with lower delay than CMOS.

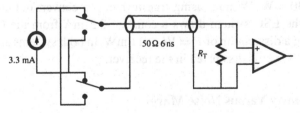

FIGURE 7-2 Low-Swing Current-Mode Transmission System

---

[1] Recall that receiver sensitivity is the amount of input voltage swing required to get ΔV output voltage swing. That is, sensitivity or $\Delta V_{in} = \Delta V/|A|$, where A is the gain of the receiver.

TABLE 7-2	Comparison of CMOS and LSC Signaling Systems	
	CMOS	**LSC**
Signaling	Voltage mode: 0 = GND, 1 = Vdd	Current mode: 0 = −3.3 mA, 1 = +3.3 mA
Reference	Power supply: $V_r \sim V\text{dd}/2$	Self-centered: $I_r = 0$ mA.
Termination	Series terminated in output impedance of driver	Parallel-terminated at receiver with R_T within 10% of Z_0
Signal energy	1.3 nJ	22 pJ
Power dissipation	130 mW	11 mW
Noise immunity	1.5:1 actual:required signal swing (with LSC receiver)	3.6:1
Delay	18 ns	6 ns

The remainder of this section describes the derivation of the performance values shown in the table.

7.1.1   Signal Energy and System Power

The energy required to send an event across a transmission line is

$$(7\text{-}1) \qquad\qquad E_{sw} = \frac{\Delta V^2 t}{Z_0} = \Delta I^2 t Z_0$$

For the series-terminated CMOS system, t is the length of the line (6 ns), and the signal energy is 1.3 nJ. Even though the underterminated driver takes longer than 6 ns to charge the line, the energy is the same as if the line were charged on the incident wave because the same amount of charge is moved through the same voltage.

For the parallel-terminated LSC system, t is the length of time current is applied for each event. For a simple system this corresponds to the clock period (10 ns), and the signal energy is 22 pJ.

Because the CMOS system operates full-swing, its power dissipation is $P = E_{sw} f_{ck}$ or 130 mW. Without using transformers to convert output voltage and impedance, the LSC system draws a constant 3.3 mA from the CMOS power supply, giving a dissipation of $P = VI$ or 11 mW. In both systems a small amount of additional power is dissipated in the receiver.

7.1.2   Noise Immunity Versus Noise Margin

The reliability of a digital system depends on the *noise immunity* of the signaling system, which is its ability to transmit information correctly in the presence of various noise sources of specific amplitudes. As described in Chapter 6, most noise in digital systems is internally generated, and the most significant components are power-supply noise, cross talk, reflections, and transmitter and receiver offsets.

TABLE 7-3 Noise Margins
for CMOS and LSC Signaling

	CMOS (V)	LSC (mV)
V_{OH}	3.3	165
V_{OL}	0.0	−165
V_{IH}	2.05	15
V_{IL}	1.25	−15
V_{MH}	1.25	150
V_{ML}	1.25	150

For noise sources that are not related to signal levels such as external power supply noise, we express noise levels directly in volts or amperes. For noise sources that are a function of signal levels (e.g., cross talk), we express noise level as a fraction or percentage of signal level.

Many texts on digital systems discuss *noise margins* rather than noise immunity. The noise margin of a transmission system is the difference between the highest (lowest) output signal that represents a 0 (1), V_{OL} (V_{OH}), and the highest (lowest) input signal that will be reliably detected as a 0 (1), V_{IL} (V_{IH}). Usually noise margin is specified from the transmitter and receiver data sheet and accounts for transmitter and receiver offsets and internal power-supply noise. This margin does not account for external power-supply noise, cross talk, and reflections due to unmatched termination. More importantly, noise margin does not account for noise rejection. Many signaling systems with very low noise margins have very good noise immunity because they reject a noise source rather than overpower it. A high noise margin is neither necessary nor sufficient to ensure good noise immunity.

Table 7-3[2] shows the output and input high- and low-voltage limits for the CMOS and LSC signaling systems along with the high- and low-noise margins. These numbers do not account for any noise sources. They are simply a function of the signal swing, receiver sensitivity, and receiver offset. The table shows that the CMOS system has 1.1-V high- and low-noise margins, whereas the LSC system has only 155-mV noise margins. At first glance it appears that the CMOS system should have better noise immunity than the LSC system because it has seven times the noise margin. However, the analysis that follows shows that this is not the case.

To see the true noise immunity of each system, we prepare a noise budget that allocates the available margin to various noise sources. The signal swing is $\Delta V = V_{OH} - V_{OL}$. Assuming that the detection threshold is centered[3] between

---

[2] This table is calculated by setting $V_{OH} - V_{OL}$ to ΔV (no transmitter offsets considered). The input voltages are set to $V_{OL} + \Delta V/2 \pm (V_{ro} + V_{rs}/2)$, taking into account receiver offset and sensitivity.

[3] Unless there are asymmetric noise sources, this is the optimum location for the threshold, for any other threshold would give a lower minimum noise margin.

TABLE 7-4   Swing-Independent Noise Sources for CMOS and LSC

Symbol	Description	CMOS (mV)	LSC (mV)
V_{rs}	Receiver sensitivity	300	10
V_{ro}	Receiver offset	250	10
V_{en}	Uncanceled external power-supply noise	300	3
V_{NI}	Total swing-independent noise	700	18

the high and low output voltages,

$$(7\text{-}2) \qquad V_T = \frac{V_{OH} + V_{OL}}{2},$$

we start with a noise margin of half the signal swing, $V_M = \Delta V/2$. The total of all uncanceled noise sources must be less than V_M. We divide the noise into the part that is independent of signal swing, V_{NI}, and the part that is proportional to signal swing, $K_N \Delta V$. To operate properly, the noise margin must be greater than the sum of the noise components, which is true when

$$(7\text{-}3) \qquad \Delta V > \frac{2V_{NI}}{(1 - 2K_N)}$$

Table 7-4 shows the calculation of V_{NI} for CMOS and LSC. The table shows that the CMOS system allocates 700 mV, almost half, of the 1.65 V between the output voltage level and the receiver threshold to noise sources independent of threshold. Most of this, 400 mV, is due to the receiver properties, and the remainder is uncanceled power supply noise. By using a good receive amplifier and canceling all but 1% of the power supply noise as common-mode across the termination, the LSC system uses only 15% of its signal swing on these independent noise sources. Even if the CMOS system used a good receive amplifier, it would still use 20% of its signal swing dealing with external power supply noise.

Table 7-5 shows that 35% of the signal swing or 70% of the noise margin for CMOS must be allocated to noise sources that are proportional to the signal

TABLE 7-5   Swing-Dependent Noise Sources for CMOS and LSC

Symbol	Description	CMOS (%)	LSC (%)
K_{in}	Self-induced power supply noise	10	0
K_{xt}	Cross talk from other signals	10	10
K_r	Reflections of the same signal from previous clock cycles	large (>5)	5
K_{to}	Transmitter offset	10	10
K_N	Total proportional noise fraction	>35	25

swing. By isolating power supply noise, LSC reduces this amount to 25% of signal swing.

Applying Eq. (7-3) shows that the CMOS system does not provide immunity to the forecast noise sources. The required signal swing for CMOS is 4.7 V, which exceeds the available 3.3 V. Thus, with the worst-case combinations of noise sources the CMOS signaling system will fail.

The CMOS system can be made to work by improving the quality of the receive amplifier. Using the LSC receive amplifier, the required signal swing for CMOS is reduced to 2.1 V. The LSC system with a required signal swing of 72 mV has 4.6 times the signal swing required for immunity to forecast noise sources. Even with an equal receive amplifier, the CMOS system has only 1.5 times the signal swing required to tolerate the same noise environment. Although the CMOS system has larger signal swings and hence larger noise margins, its noise immunity is inferior to that of the LSC system.

One aspect of noise we have not considered here is signal-return cross talk (see Sections 6.3.3 and 7.3.1.3). Both the CMOS and LSC signaling systems require some ratio of signal-return pins (supply pins for the CMOS system) to signal pins be maintained to keep signal-return cross talk within a noise budget. By operating in the current mode, the LSC system attenuates this cross talk by a factor of two (compare Eq. (7-8) with Eq. (6-20)) and thus could operate with about half the return pins if all other things were equal. A well-designed LSC system would also use rise-time control (Section 7.4.2.1), further reducing the requirement for return pins. As described here, the CMOS system enjoys one advantage in terms of required return pins. Because the CMOS system cannot drive its full amplitude on the first traversal of the transmission line, it spreads its signal-return cross talk out over time as the line rings up. This reduces the peak amplitude of the cross talk and hence the ratio of required return pins. However, this reduction in cross talk comes at the expense of delay, as we will see in the next section. A CMOS system with a low enough output impedance for incident-wave switching will require more return pins than an LSC system because it operates in the voltage mode and because most CMOS drivers do not employ rise-time control.

7.1.3 Delay

There are three major components of delay in a transmission system: transmitter delay, transmission time, and receiver delay. Transmission delay is the major factor in comparing the CMOS and LSC transmission systems. Because it injects enough current into the transmission line to induce its full 330-mV swing in a single step, the transmission delay of the LSC system is the one-way delay of the transmission line or 6 ns.

The CMOS driver, because of its high (200-ohm) output impedance, is unable to drive its full 3.3-V output swing onto the line in one step as a single incident wave. Instead, the driver must wait for the line to ring up to the full voltage, as shown in Figure 7-3. At time 0, the driver initially places 3.3 V across 250 Ω (the 200-ohm output impedance in series with the 50-ohm line), which injects

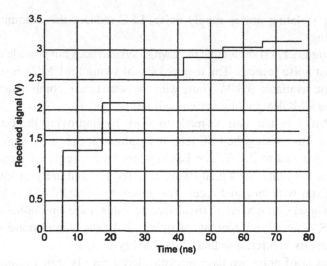

FIGURE 7-3   Received-Voltage Waveform for CMOS Transmission System

13.2 mA into the line, inducing a 660-mV incident wave. After 6 ns this wave reflects off the open end of the line at the receiver, doubling its amplitude to 1.32 V. This is seen at the receiver as a single 1.32-V step. The 660-mV reflected wave arrives back at the driver at 12 ns, where it is partially reflected (396 mV) back to the receiver. Not until 18 ns, when this wave reflects off the open end of the line and the receiver input voltage reaches 2.11 V, does the signal cross the detection threshold (V_{IH}). As designed, the CMOS system will not work with a 10-ns clock because the first wave of the next bit arrives before the first bit has caused a detectable transition.

In addition to increasing delay, this ringing up of the line also seriously degrades the noise immunity of the CMOS system for two reasons. First, transient noise may cause spurious multiple transitions across the detection threshold while the line is at an intermediate voltage. This increases power dissipation and causes logical errors on edge-sensitive lines such as clocks. Second, because the line is underterminated, continuing reflections of one transition interfere with subsequent bits on the same line. The wave continues to reflect back and forth indefinitely and is attenuated by 40% after each 12-ns round trip.

7.1.4   Discussion

The basic CMOS transmission system considered here is the most common system in use today. Yet it is far from optimal in almost any application. Large energy signals are used in an environment that does not require them. The transmitted signal is not isolated from transmitter power-supply noise, and the receiver uses a reference that changes significantly with manufacturing process variations. The line is not properly terminated and thus may take several "rings" to cross the receiver threshold, thus increasing the signal delay.

This signaling system is a remnant of the era of catalog part design when logic, not communications delays, dominated system performance. The CMOS system is still used largely for reasons of compatibility. However, in today's systems, where most chips (except for memories) are system-specific, there is no need to adhere to an obsolete, suboptimal signaling convention. The modern digital systems designer can tailor a transmission system to the needs of the system under design.

7.2 CONSIDERATIONS IN TRANSMISSION SYSTEM DESIGN

The design of a transmission system is influenced by demands, constraints, and costs. The communications demand is characterized by a required bandwidth (b/s), latency (s), and error rate (s^{-1}). The solution is constrained by the physical distance to be traversed, the noise environment, the parameters of the available transmitters and receivers, the power available, and the size and weight requirements for the overall system.

Cost considerations involve pin and wire counts: the number of pins required on chips, the number of tracks and vias required on modules and boards, the number of wires in a cable. Cost is also affected by the quality of the components. A low-permittivity dielectric will reduce time-of-flight but at considerable increase in cost. Similarly, a lower-gauge (thicker-wire) cable reduces attenuation at a cost of increased size and weight. Increasing the density of circuit boards and connectors beyond standard values carries a significant cost premium.

To fit these goals and constraints, the system designer has several variables to choose from:

Reference: The signal and reference can be isolated from noise by sending differential signals (Section 7.3.5), explicit references (Section 7.3.1.5), or by using the DC component of the signal as a reference (Section 8.4).

Signal energy: The signal energy should be set at the minimum level required to achieve the desired error rate and latency in the presence of the expected noise energy (Section 7.5.2). With proper noise isolation, this level can be made quite low. Typical energies range from 0.1 to 1 pJ on a chip, 1 to 10 pJ on a board, and up to 50 pJ or higher over cables, depending on distance and noise. Recall that the energy dissipated in the driver is usually much greater than the signal energy because the voltage swing of the line is less than the power supply voltage.

Static power: If power dissipation is a concern, a method that uses power only on signal transitions, such as pulsed signaling (Section 7.4.1.4) or series termination, (Section 7.3.3) is preferred.

Voltage versus current mode: The signaling convention can involve forcing either current or voltage on the line (Section 7.3.1). Current-mode signaling has the advantage that the line voltage is largely isolated from the transmitter power supply and thus rejects power supply noise.

Bipolar versus unipolar signaling: The drive can either be bipolar or push–pull (e.g., +5 mA for a 1, −5 mA for a zero) or unipolar (e.g., +10 mA for a 1, 0 ma for a zero). Bipolar signals are easier to sense because it is easy to make comparisons against a zero threshold. Unipolar drivers are generally easier to build but often have asymmetric output impedance.

Signal bandwidth (rise time): The signal bandwidth (Hz), not to be confused with the information bandwidth (b/s), should be kept as low as possible to avoid introducing noise via transmission line irregularities and power supply parasitics (Section 7.4.2.1). Unless latency is an overriding concern, a rise time of 1/2 to 1/3 of a bit time is adequate.

Number of signal levels: It is possible to encode more than one bit per transition by defining more than two signal levels (Section 7.5.1). Although binary signaling is generally preferred, there are cases where multilevel signaling makes sense.

Point-to-point versus multidrop: Point-to-point signals with a single transmitter and a single receiver are electrically simpler and easier to operate at high speed than signals that may have multiple receivers, multiple transmitters, or both.

Synchronization: A signal may carry its own synchronization information, may be accompanied by a transmit clock, or may be received with a receive clock. Different overheads and timing margins apply to each approach.

Unidirectional versus bidirectional signaling: A transmission line can send signals in both directions simultaneously without interference (Section 8.1). This potentially doubles the effective bandwidth per pin and per wire. However, cross talk between the transmitted and received signals adds to the noise level.

The remainder of this chapter along with the next few chapters will examine several techniques for signaling and the circuits to support them.

7.3 SIGNALING MODES FOR TRANSMISSION LINES

The signaling mode, the method used to encode a signal on a transmission line, determines the transmitter output impedance, the termination method, and the receiver reference. A good signaling mode is one that provides good noise immunity while minimizing power dissipation and delay.

Figure 7-4 shows a typical transmission line signaling system. A transmitter, with output impedance R_O, injects a signal onto the transmission line. At the far end of the line, the signal energy is absorbed into termination R_T, and the

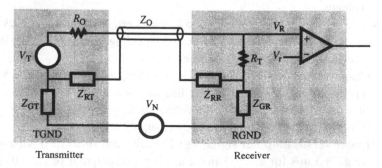

FIGURE 7-4 Basic Transmission Line Signaling System

transmitted value is detected by comparing the received voltage, V_R, with a reference voltage, V_r. At both ends of the system nonzero signal return impedance[4] (Z_{RT} and Z_{RR}) and coupling to the local power supply (Z_{GT} and Z_{GR}) introduce noise that distorts the signal.

To simplify the discussion, we analyze the transmitter (Section 7.3.1) and the receiver (Section 7.3.2) separately. We can separate these components if the transmission system is terminated into a matched impedance ($R_T = Z_0$) so that there are no reflections. Source-terminated systems, with an open circuit at the end of the line, are discussed in Section 7.3.3. We close the section with a discussion of differential signaling in Section 7.3.5.

7.3.1 Transmitter Signaling Methods

There are four major variables in the design of the transmitter:

1. The output impedance, R_O.
2. The coupling between the signal level and the local power supply (or ground), Z_{GT}.
3. Whether the signal is bipolar or unipolar.
4. The signal amplitude.

The first two of these variables, R_O and Z_{GT}, are closely related. If the transmitter employs current-mode signaling, the output impedance is high and may be completely isolated from the local power supply. With voltage-mode signaling, on the other hand, the output impedance is low and, for implementation reasons, the transmitted voltage is usually referenced to one of the local power supplies.

7.3.1.1 Current-Mode Transmission

Current-mode transmission is depicted in Figure 7-5(a). The transmitter consists of a current source that injects a current $I_T(t)$ into a transmission line with impedance Z_0. Different current levels are used to represent the symbols of the transmitter's alphabet (usually 0 and 1). This current induces a forward-traveling wave in the transmission line with amplitude

$$(7\text{-}4) \qquad\qquad V(t, x) = I_T\left(t - \frac{x}{v}\right)Z_0.$$

where x is the position along the line and v is the propagation velocity.

Current-mode transmitters usually provide isolation of both the signal and current return from the local power supplies. Thus, these transmitters typically have a very large Z_{GT} that is due almost entirely to parasitic supply coupling. This provides good isolation of signals from single-supply power-supply noise

---

[4] Any real transmission line also has some return impedance and, in particular, return inductance, which adds to Z_{RT} and Z_{RR}.

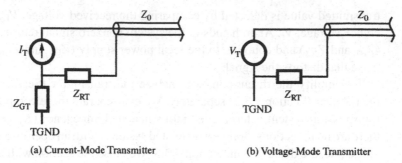

(a) Current-Mode Transmitter   (b) Voltage-Mode Transmitter

FIGURE 7-5   Current-Mode and Voltage-Mode Transmitters

(V_N in Figure 7-4). Circuits to realize current-mode transmitters are discussed in Section 11.2.3.

7.3.1.2   Voltage-Mode Transmission

As shown in Figure 7-5(b), a voltage-mode transmitter consists of a voltage source referenced to the local power supply (TGND). The transmitter directly forces a voltage, $V_T(t)$, onto the transmission line, inducing a forward-traveling wave in the line $V(t, x) = V_T(t - x/v)$. Circuits to implement voltage-mode drivers are discussed in Section 11.2.1.

If we choose $V_T = I_T Z_0$, we can generate exactly the same traveling wave with voltage-mode signaling as with current-mode signaling. The two signaling methods differ, however, in their output impedance and their coupling to the local power supply. The analysis in this section shows how these two factors make a significant difference in their ability to isolate the signal from two major noise sources: signal return cross talk, and single-supply power-supply noise.

The two driver circuits illustrated in Figure 7-5 represent extremes. Any real driver has some finite output impedance, as illustrated in Figure 7-4, and, as we shall see in Section 7.3.3, there are particular advantages in having the source impedance matched to the line. For purposes of analysis, however, we will consider transmitters with output impedance much less than Z_0 as if they were voltage-mode transmitters, and transmitters with output impedance much greater than Z_0 as if they were current-mode transmitters.

7.3.1.3   Transmitter Signal-Return Cross Talk

A signal return path is typically shared among a group of N signals (typically 2 to 8) to amortize the cost of the return pins and interconnect. This sharing occurs at both ends of the line; however, for the present analysis we confine our attention to the transmitter return path. We approximate the parasitics of this return path (lead inductance, resistance, transmission line) as a transmitter return impedance, Z_{RT}. An equivalent circuit is shown in Figure 7-6. The figure shows N Thévenin-equivalent transmitter circuits with output impedance R_O driving N transmission lines, each modeled by a resistor with value Z_0. The return current from all N transmission lines passes through impedance Z_{RT}.

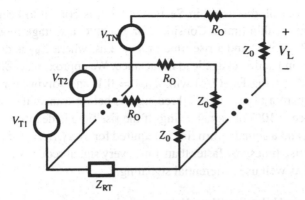

FIGURE 7-6 Equivalent Circuit for Transmitter Signal Return Cross Talk

We analyze this circuit using superposition. To consider the contribution from a single signal, V_{T1}, we replace the other voltage sources with shorts. The current $I_{T1} = V_{T1}/(Z_0 + Z_X)$, sees the shared return impedance in parallel with the series combination of the line and output impedances from the other signals. The total return impedance is

$$Z_X = Z_{RT} \left\| \left(\frac{R_0 + Z_0}{N - 1} \right) \right.$$

(7-5)

$$Z_X = \frac{Z_{RT}(R_0 + Z_0)}{(N - 1)Z_{RT} + R_0 + Z_0}$$

The multiple return paths form a current divider. The current flowing through each of the $N - 1$ line impedances in this divider is given by

(7-6) $$I_X = I_{T1}\left(\frac{Z_X}{Z_0 + R_0}\right) = I_{T1}\left[\frac{Z_{RT}}{(N - 1)Z_{RT} + R_0 + Z_0}\right]$$

This induces a voltage across the line impedance of

(7-7) $$V_X = I_X Z_0 = V_{T1}\left(\frac{Z_0}{Z_0 + Z_X}\right)\left(\frac{Z_{RT}}{(N - 1)Z_{RT} + R_0 + Z_0}\right)$$

Considering the worst case, where $N - 1$ signals switch simultaneously, and dividing by the transmitted voltage, V_{T1}, gives the transmitter signal return cross talk ratio

$$K_{XRT} = \frac{(N - 1)V_X}{V_{T1}} = \left(\frac{(N - 1)Z_{RT}}{(N - 1)Z_{RT} + R_0 + Z_0}\right)\left(\frac{Z_0}{Z_0 + Z_X}\right) \leq \frac{(N - 1)Z_{RT}}{R_0 + Z_0}$$

(7-8)

Because Z_{RT} is usually much smaller than $R_0 + Z_0$, the rightmost expression in Eq. (7-8) is a good estimate of the cross talk ratio.

Equation (7-8) shows the advantage of high output impedance. With voltage-mode signaling, $R_0 = 0$, the transmitter signal return cross talk is a maximum. As the output impedance is increased, the transmitter return cross talk is reduced. For current-mode signaling, $R_0 = \infty$, this form of cross talk is completely eliminated.

Rise-time control, discussed in Section 7.4.2.1, is critical to keeping signal-return cross talk within limits. Consider, for example, a voltage-mode signaling system with $Z_0 = 50\ \Omega$ and a rise time of $t_r = 2$ ns, where Z_{RT} is dominated by 5 nH of wire bond and package lead inductance. We approximate Z_{RT} as L/t_r or about 2.5 Ω. Applying Eq. (7-8) with $k_{XRT} = 0.1$, and solving for N suggests that we can share a return across three signals before transmitter signal-return cross talk exceeds 10% of signal swing. If the rise time is decreased to 1 ns, Z_R becomes 5 Ω, and a signal return line is required for every $N = 2$ signals to keep $k_{xr} \leq 0.1$. For rise times any faster than 1 ns, every signal requires its own return, and we might as well use differential signaling.

7.3.1.4   Bipolar Versus Unipolar Signaling

Figure 7-7 illustrates two methods for encoding binary symbols into currents. A *bipolar* signaling convention, Figure 7-7(a), encodes a binary 1 as a positive current, I_1, and a binary 0 as a complementary negative current, $I_0 = -I_1$. A *unipolar* signaling method, on the other hand, Figure 7-7(b), encodes the binary 0 as zero current, $I_0 = 0$. Although the figure illustrates the two conventions with currents, bipolar and unipolar signaling can be applied to voltages as well. Bipolar voltage-mode signaling was at one time widely used in IBM mainframes that employed a signaling convention that operated with an 800-mV swing centered on a supply voltage.

Figure 7-7 also illustrates the effects of transmitter and receiver offsets and receiver sensitivity. The nominal current to encode a 1 or 0 symbol is I_1 or I_0. However, a real transmitter may output a current that is offset from this ideal value by up to I_{xo}, the transmitter offset current. The allowable range of output currents are shown as dark gray areas in the figure. This offset current is a significant noise source that comes directly off the fixed portion of the noise budget. The receiver will accept as a 1 or a 0 the currents shown as light gray areas in the figure. The outer edges of these areas are limited by the safe operating range of the receiver, whereas the inner edges are set by the receiver offset current, I_{ro}, and sensitivity, I_{rs}. The amount by which the input ranges extend beyond the output ranges is the noise margin available to tolerate other noise sources.

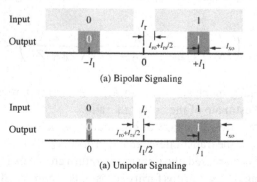

(a) Bipolar Signaling

(a) Unipolar Signaling

FIGURE 7-7   Unipolar and Bipolar Signaling

The symmetric nature of bipolar signaling gives roughly equal transmitter offsets for the 0 and 1 symbol. Unipolar signaling, on the other hand, lumps most of its total offset into the 1 symbol (it is not hard to get zero current right). For example, consider a transmitter with a dynamic range of $\Delta I = I_1 - I_0 = 5$ mA that uses a current source accurate to within 5%. A bipolar signaling system uses a pair of complementary current sources nominally sized for ± 2.5 mA. The 5% variation in these sources gives $I_{xo} = \pm 125$ μA for both the 0 and 1 symbol. A unipolar signaling system, on the other hand, uses a single 5-mA current source. The 5% variation in this source gives $I_{xo} = \pm 250$ μA for the 1 symbol and zero offset for the 0 symbol. To give equal performance, the unipolar system must reduce its detection threshold, I_r, by 125 μA to balance its high and low noise margins.

Bipolar signaling also reduces power dissipation. For a given signal swing, a bipolar system draws half the peak current from the supply as a unipolar system.

7.3.1.5 Transmitter-Generated References

To discriminate optimally between the two symbols, the receiver compares the received current to a reference, I_r. Bipolar signaling uses a zero reference, $I_r = 0$, which is particularly easy to generate accurately. Unipolar signaling, on the other hand, requires a half-scale reference, $I_r = I_1/2$. It is difficult to generate such a reference accurately in the receiver.

One method for dealing with this problem is to generate the reference in the transmitter and send it along with the signal, as illustrated in Figure 7-8. By generating the reference in the transmitter, the reference current source can be made to track the signal current source. Also, any noise added to both transmission lines will be common-mode. To conserve pins and wires, a single transmitter-generated reference can be shared by many receivers.

Transmitter-generated references can also be used with voltage-mode signaling, as illustrated in Figure 7-9.

Because much of the supply noise we are attempting to reject is very high-frequency, the delay must be carefully matched between the reference and each signal. A delay mismatch will phase shift the noise, leading to reduced cancellation or even reinforcement. As the skew between these signals, ΔT_r, approaches $1/(4 f_{max})$, a quarter of the smallest wavelength of interest, all noise canceling in this frequency band is lost. If the skew gets as large as a half a wavelength,

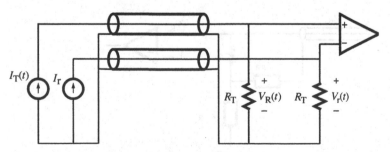

FIGURE 7-8 Transmitter-Generated Reference for Unipolar Current-Mode Signaling

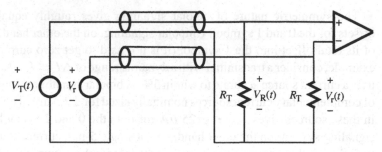

FIGURE 7-9   Transmitter-Generated Reference for Voltage-Mode Signaling

$1/(2f_{max})$ this high-frequency noise is doubled. Because of the difference in output loading between a single-drop signal line and a shared reference, it is difficult in practice to match delays accurately.

7.3.2   Receiver Signal Detection

Figure 7-10 illustrates the receiving end of a transmission line signaling system. The incident wave is absorbed in a parallel terminating resistor $R_T = Z_0$. The arriving symbol is detected by comparing the received voltage, V_R, with a reference voltage, V_r. The receiver return impedance, Z_{RR}, and the coupling to the receiver power supply, Z_{GR}, may couple noise into the signal as described in Section 7.3.2.2.

The major consideration with receiver design is the method used to generate the reference voltage, V_r. The amount of coupling with the receiver power supply, Z_{GR}, is also a factor. The remainder of the design variables are set by the transmitter, as described above in Section 7.3.1. For now we restrict the termination, R_T, to be matched. We relax this restriction below in Section 7.3.3.

7.3.2.1   Generating the Receiver Reference

The method used to generate the receiver reference voltage is a critical aspect of any signaling system. An inaccurate reference can lead to a large offset voltage, V_{ro}, and a method that couples power supply or return noise into the reference can lead to poor noise rejection. Three commonly used methods to generate the receiver reference voltage, V_r are as follows:

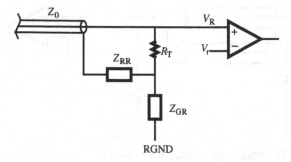

FIGURE 7-10   Transmission Line Termination and Receiver

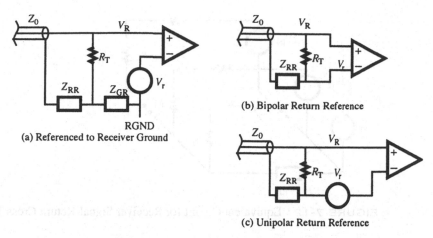

(a) Referenced to Receiver Ground

(b) Bipolar Return Reference

(c) Unipolar Return Reference

FIGURE 7-11   Methods for Generating the Receiver Reference

1. Derive V_r from the receiver power supplies, as illustrated in Figure 7-11(a).
2. Generate the reference in the transmitter and send it to the receiver, as illustrated in Figures 7-8 and 7-9.
3. Derive V_r from the return voltage on the opposite side of the termination resistor as illustrated in Figure 7-11(b) for bipolar signaling and Figure 7-11(c) for unipolar signaling.

The simplest of the circuits shown, the bipolar return reference of Figure 7-11(b), is also the best. The receive amplifier directly detects the polarity of the incident wave. There is no reference voltage or current to be generated locally. The only offset voltage is the input offset of the receive amplifier. When unipolar signaling is used, the best reference is one generated in the transmitter, as described above. When this is not practical, it is possible to generate a return-referenced receiver offset, as shown in Figure 7-11(c). However, it is difficult in practice to generate the small offset voltage required with the needed precision. Some form of external reference is usually employed.

Generating the reference voltage relative to the receiver supplies (AC ground) is the most commonly used method. However, this approach can be problematic unless the impedance, Z_{GR}, is kept very small. If the terminator is located off chip, for example, the bond-wire and packaging impedance between the terminator and the receive amplifier can give a large AC impedance that couples power-supply transients into the received signal. To avoid such supply coupling, the signal return should be isolated from supply current wherever possible.

7.3.2.2   Receiver Return Cross Talk

As in the transmitter, a shared return pin can generate signal return cross talk in the receiver. Figure 7-12 shows the equivalent circuit for analyzing this noise source. The figure depicts N transmission lines, each modeled as a Thévenin-equivalent source with voltage, $2V_i$, and output impedance, Z_0 (see Section 3.3.3.4), driving

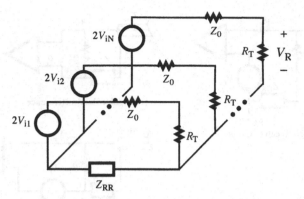

FIGURE 7-12 Equivalent Circuit for Receiver Signal-Return Cross Talk

N terminators with resistance $R_T = Z_0$. All N terminators return their current through a shared impedance, Z_{RR}.

Following the derivation of Eq. (7-8), it is easy to see that, in this case, the receiver signal-return cross talk coefficient is given by

$$(7\text{-}9) \qquad k_{XRR} = \frac{(N-1)Z_{RR}}{(N-1)Z_{RR} + 2Z_0} \leq \frac{(N-1)Z_{RR}}{2Z_0}$$

There is no advantage to current-mode signaling in terms of receiver return cross talk. The transmission line looks like a matched source regardless of how the traveling wave is generated. There is an advantage, however, to generating the reference relative to the return end of the termination resistor. If the reference is generated relative to the end of the line, on the other side of Z_{RR}, the voltage drop across Z_{RR} will be added to this cross talk value. In this case, we ignore the current divider and consider the cross talk to be just the voltage drop across Z_{RR}, which gives nearly twice the coefficient as expressed by

$$(7\text{-}10) \qquad k_{XRR} = \frac{(N-1)Z_{RR}}{Z_0}$$

7.3.2.3 Power Supply Noise

Variation in a single power supply voltage (e.g., GND) between the transmitter and receiver can inject noise into a transmitted signal. This variation is represented by source V_N in Figure 7-4. The source is coupled to the transmitter via impedance Z_{GT} and to the receiver via Z_{GR}. For the purposes of our analysis, we lump these two impedances together into $Z_N = Z_{GR} + Z_{GT}$ and draw the equivalent circuit shown in Figure 7-13.

The figure shows the Thévenin-equivalent noise source (V_N, Z_N) applied across the return of the line. The transmitter and receiver return impedances (Z_{RT} and Z_{RR}) along with the return impedance of the line itself are lumped together into Z_R. The noise source sees the termination resistor, R_T, and the impedance of the line, Z_0, in parallel with this return impedance. The voltage divider formed by Z_N with the rest of the circuit combined with the current divider formed by Z_R with

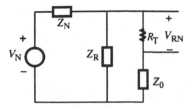

FIGURE 7-13   Equivalent Circuit for Power Supply Noise*

the terminator and line attenuate the noise voltage so that the portion across the terminator, V_{RN}, is

$$(7\text{-}11) \qquad\qquad V_{RN} = V_N \left[\frac{Z_0 Z_R}{2Z_0 Z_R + (2Z_0 + Z_R)Z_N} \right]$$

If we assume that we have a low-impedance signal return (i.e., $Z_R \ll Z_0$), this simplifies to

$$(7\text{-}12) \qquad\qquad V_{RN} = \frac{V_N Z_R}{2(Z_R + Z_N)}$$

Equation (7-12) shows that, to reject power supply noise, one wants to make the noise impedance, $Z_N = Z_{GT} + Z_{GR}$, as large as possible. This is most easily accomplished by using a current-mode transmitter completely isolated from the transmitter power supplies, $Z_{GT} \approx \infty$. A large noise impedance can also be accomplished in a voltage-mode system ($Z_{GT} = 0$) by isolating both the received signal and the return path from the receiver supply, $Z_{GR} \approx \infty$.

7.3.3   Source Termination

Matching the output impedance of the transmitter to the transmission line and omitting the far-end terminator, as shown in Figure 7-14, gives a system with no static power dissipation and avoids the difficult problem of building a transmitter with zero output impedance.

Figure 7-15 shows how the received voltage is simply a delayed copy of the transmitted waveform even though intermediate points on the line carry the superposition of two skewed, half-magnitude copies of this waveform. The figure

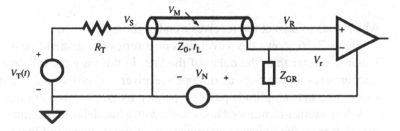

FIGURE 7-14   Series-Terminated Voltage-Mode Signaling

* Note that in Figure 7-13, we have made the assumption that R_O from Figure 7-4 is 0. Also, in Eqs. (7-11) and (7-12) we have assumed that $R_T = Z_0$.

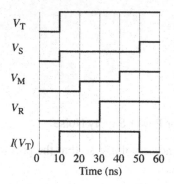

FIGURE 7-15   Waveforms for Series-Terminated Signaling System

shows the waveforms resulting from a unit step applied to the transmitter voltage source V_T at $t = 10$ ns with a $t_L = 20$ ns line and $R_T = Z_0$. Initially the 1-V step is divided between the termination resistor and the line impedance, resulting in a 0.5-V step traveling forward down the line and a transmitter source current $I(V_T)$ of $0.5/Z_0$. At 20 ns this wave reaches the midpoint, V_M of the line. At 30 ns the step reaches the open end of the line at the receiver and reflects back toward the source. The superposition of the forward-traveling 0.5-V step with the reflected 0.5-V step results in an instantaneous 1-V step on the receiver voltage V_R. The reflection travels back along the line reaching the midpoint, V_M, at 40 ns and the transmitter at 50 ns. At this point, the reflection is absorbed into the series termination and, because there is no voltage drop across the termination, no further current flows from the transmitter voltage source.

The voltage at a point x along the line is given by

$$(7\text{-}13) \qquad V(t, x) = 0.5V_T(t - x/v) + 0.5V_T(t - 2t_L + x/v)$$

The first term of this equation represents the forward-traveling wave, and the second term represents the reflection from the open end of the line. The skew between these two waveforms, which corresponds to the length of the half-voltage step on the line, is

$$(7\text{-}14) \qquad \Delta t = 2(t_L - x/v)$$

which goes to zero at the receiver's end of the line, $x = x_L$.

Figure 7-16 shows the waveforms on a series-terminated line when the pulse width is shorter than the delay of the line. In this case the full-amplitude pulse only appears within 5 ns of the open receiver end of the line. Most of the line carries two half-amplitude pulses separated by Δt, as given in Eq. (7-14).

When a series-terminated line is used with a line delay longer than a bit-cell, the waveforms on the line are superpositions of those shown in Figure 7-16, one for each high bit-cell shifted appropriately. In this case most points on the line carry the superposition of two (or more) bit positions separated by Δt. The transmitted bit pattern appears cleanly only at the receiving end.

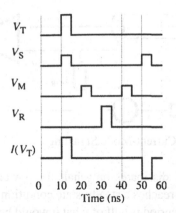

FIGURE 7-16 Waveforms for a Series-Terminated Line with a Short Pulse

Because the signal waveform appears cleanly only at the end of the line, series termination is limited to use on point-to-point links. Intermediate points on multidrop links would see distorted waveforms. Also, applying the half-voltage midline waveforms to receivers would cause them to toggle as additive noise flip-flopped the receiver about its decision voltage.

7.3.3.1 Noise Considerations

The issues of voltage references and power-supply noise are identical between series-terminated signaling and parallel-terminated voltage-mode signaling. Both signaling conventions are voltage-mode and thus directly couple power-supply noise into the received voltage. Rejection of this noise requires generating the receiver reference from the signal return with good isolation from the receiver power supply (large Z_{GR}).

A series-terminated line differs significantly from a parallel-terminated line in its response to cross talk. Any forward-traveling waves induced in the line as a result of coupling with nearby signals will be doubled at the receiver by reflecting off of the open receiver end of the line.[5] These waves will be absorbed by the series termination when they arrive at the transmitter end of the line. Any reverse-traveling waves induced on the line, on the other hand, will be absorbed by the series termination at the source. It should be pointed out that the major noise issue with source-terminated lines is that near-end cross talk appears at the far end of the line due to coupling of the reflected wave.

7.3.3.2 Power Dissipation

For signaling rates where the bit period is longer than the line delay or where signal transitions are infrequent, series termination dissipates no static power. Once the entire line is charged to the bit value, no further power is dissipated. If the bit period is shorter than the round-trip line delay and signal transitions

---

[5] The forward coupling between two source-terminated lines is, of course, the same as between two parallel-terminated lines. Although the response at the end of the line is doubled, the magnitude of the coupled wave is halved.

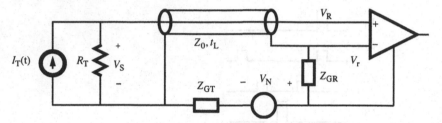

FIGURE 7-17   Source-Terminated Current-Mode Signaling

are frequent, series termination still dissipates only half the power of parallel termination. Although the line never reaches a steady-state condition, the current injected by the source during the bit period is half of what it would be for parallel termination. Thus, the energy per bit is given by

$$(7\text{-}15) \qquad E_{bs} = \begin{cases} \dfrac{t_L \Delta V^2}{Z_0} & \text{if } 2t_L \le t_B \\[2ex] \dfrac{t_b \Delta V^2}{2Z_0} & \text{if } 2t_L > t_B \end{cases}$$

whereas for parallel termination the energy per bit is

$$(7\text{-}16) \qquad E_{bp} = \frac{t_b \Delta V^2}{Z_0}$$

7.3.3.3 Current-Mode Source Termination

Parallel-source termination can be used with current-mode signaling to achieve properties similar to a series-terminated voltage-mode system. As shown in Figure 7-17, the voltage source and series-termination of Figure 7-14 are replaced by a Norton-equivalent source. This figure assumes bipolar current-mode signaling, and thus the signal return is used as the voltage reference. Source termination is also possible with a unipolar current source. The waveforms on the line are identical to those for the series-terminated case shown in Figures 7-15 and 7-16.

Source-terminated current-mode signaling provides better power supply isolation than series-terminated signaling. The source voltage, V_S, developed across the termination resistor is referenced to the signal return at the transmitter and isolated from the transmitter power supplies. In other words, impedance Z_{GT} can be made very large. To first order, all power-supply noise is common-mode to the sensed voltage difference $V_R - V_r$. In practice some power-supply noise will be coupled into the line and return. The degree of coupling can be analyzed by drawing an equivalent circuit similar to the one in Figure 7-13.

Source-terminated current-mode signaling has half the dynamic energy per bit but dissipates the same amount of static power as receiver-terminated current-mode signaling. The voltage across the current source for a short pulse is $I_T Z_0/2$, half the value as for receiver-terminated signaling. In theory this means that the dynamic power is reduced by a factor of two; however, in practice the current source is generated from a fixed power supply, and the reduction in signal swing

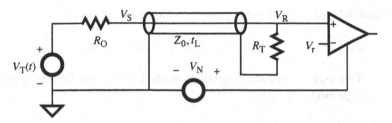

FIGURE 7-18   Underterminated Source with Parallel Termination

does not translate into a reduction in power consumption. Once the line reaches its steady-state value, the voltage across the current source, and thus the power dissipation, is the same as for receiver-terminated signaling.

7.3.4   Underterminated Drivers

A series-terminated driver may be *underterminated* by setting the output impedance, R_O, larger than Z_0. If the receiver end of the line is left open, the driver produces a damped waveform, like the one in Figure 7-3, that requires many round-trips of the line to ring up to its final voltage. If the receiver end of the line is parallel-terminated into a matched impedance, however, as shown in Figure 7-18, the result is an interesting hybrid between voltage-mode and current-mode signaling.

The voltage source is attenuated by a divider formed by R_O and the line. If we denote the attenuation coefficient as K_a, then

$$(7\text{-}17) \qquad K_a = \frac{Z_0}{Z_0 + R_O}$$

and $V_S = K_a V_T$.

Without the parallel termination this forward-traveling wave would reflect off the open end of the line and arrive back at the transmitter. The wave would then reflect off the transmitter with a reflection coefficient given by the Telegrapher's Equation (Eq. (3-37)) as

$$(7\text{-}18) \qquad \frac{V_r}{V_i} = \frac{R_O - Z_0}{R_O + Z_0} = 1 - 2K_a$$

The voltage on the line at the ith arrival of the wave at the receiver end is

$$(7\text{-}19) \qquad V_R(i) = 2V_T K_a \sum_{j=0}^{i-1} (1 - 2K_a)^j = V_T[1 - (1 - 2K_a)^i]$$

As shown in Figure 7-3, the receiver voltage slowly and geometrically converges to the correct value, traversing a fraction $2K_a$ of the remaining distance on each round trip.

This slow convergence, which leaves the line in an uncertain, pattern-dependent state for the next bit, is unacceptable in a high-speed signaling system. The slowness can be avoided by placing a matched termination at the receiver end of the line to eliminate all reflections. The received voltage is then just an attenuated and delayed copy of the transmitter voltage expressed by

(7-20) $$V_R(t) = V_T(t - t_L)K_a$$

This underterminated signaling method solves the following problems with voltage-mode signaling:

Transmitter references: It is much easier to build a full-swing driver and re-sistively attenuate it to a reasonable signaling level than to attempt to build closely spaced transmitter voltage references.

Driver impedance: It is impossible in practice to build a driver with zero output impedance, and approximating zero with a low-output impedance is costly. Here, a reasonable output impedance is turned into an advantage.

Power-supply noise: Supply noise between the transmitter and receiver is di-rectly coupled into V_T and then attenuated by a factor of K_a before appearing superimposed on V_R. This makes the power-supply noise proportional to signal swing. Of course, power supply noise directly couples into the signal, and the line does not scale with signal swing.

Receiver references: A receiver reference is still required, and a transmitter-generated reference or the use of bipolar signaling is preferred. However, a receiver-generated reference has a power supply noise component attenuated by a factor of K_a compared with straight voltage-mode signaling.

Compared with current-mode signaling, underterminated signaling has the advantage that it results in a very simple driver design (Section 11.2) that has power supply isolation nearly as good as pure current-mode signaling.

7.3.5 Differential Signaling

A binary signal can be sent *differentially* over a pair of conductors by driving one conductor with the signal and a second conductor with the complement of the signal. Figure 7-19 shows a differential voltage-mode signaling system. To send a 1, the upper voltage source drives V_1 on the upper transmission line, and the lower voltage source drives V_0 on the lower transmission line. To send a 0, the voltages are reversed.

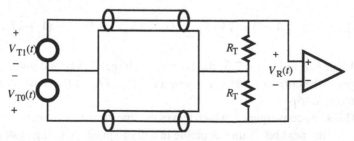

FIGURE 7-19   Voltage-Mode Differential Signaling

Differential signaling requires more pins and wires than does *single-ended* signaling. The overhead is not 2:1, as might first appear, however. Compared with a high-performance single-ended system, where a signal return is required for every 2–4 signal lines, differential signaling requires 1.3 to 1.8 times as many pins. In return for this increased pin count, differential signaling offers several advantages:

References: A differential signal serves as its own receiver reference even with unipolar signaling. The receiver compares the voltage of the two signal lines to detect the symbol being transmitted. Transmitter references are less critical because the receiver is comparing two voltage levels, both from the same transmitter, rather than comparing a voltage to a fixed reference.

As with transmitter-generated references, comparing two voltages sent over identical transmission lines from the transmitter can cancel several noise sources by making them common-mode to the receiver. However, like a transmitter-generated reference, the delays of the two lines must carefully be matched for the noise to cancel.

Signal swing: The difference in relative voltage across the two lines between a 1 and a 0 is

$$(7\text{-}21) \qquad\qquad \Delta V = 2(V_1 - V_0)$$

which is twice the value for single-ended signaling. Thus, for a given signal swing ($V_1 - V_0$) differential signaling gives twice the noise margin. This doubling of effective signal swing also gives a speed advantage inasmuch as the rise- or fall-time affecting the receive amplifier is half the transition time of a single-ended signal.

Return current: With differential signaling the return current is a constant DC value. Because a voltage of V_1 is always across one termination resistor and V_0 across the other, the return current is always

$$(7\text{-}22) \qquad\qquad I_R = \frac{V_1 + V_0}{R_T}$$

With bipolar differential signaling, $V_1 = -V_0$, the return current is always zero.

Self-induced power-supply noise (K_{in}): With most differential driver designs, there is very little AC power supply current and hence very little self-induced power supply noise, K_{in}. A change in current in the true signal's driver is compensated by an equal and opposite change in current in the complement signal's driver. The small amount of AC current that does flow is usually due to mismatches between the true and complement drivers and their connections to the power supply network. In many systems this reduction in power supply noise is a very significant advantage of differential signaling.

Other signaling modes: Differential signaling can be applied to any signaling mode, including unipolar or bipolar current-mode, series-terminated, and

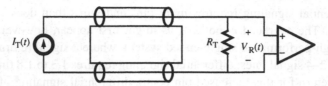

FIGURE 7-20   Differential Bipolar Current-Mode Signaling

underterminated signaling (Figures 7-5, 7-14, and 7-18) by building two copies of the transmitter, line, and terminations and comparing the two voltages at the receiving end of the line.

Differential bipolar current-mode signaling, Figure 7-20, is equivalent to providing a separate return for each signal. To send a 1, the current source injects I_1 in the upper transmission line and $I_0 = -I_1$ in the bottom transmission line. The lines are terminated to each other with an $R_T = 2Z_0$ valued resistor. Equal and opposite return currents flow in the two line's returns, which are tied together at the ends.

7.3.5.1   Symmetric Transmission Lines

With zero net return current, a bipolar differential signal, voltage- or current-mode, can be used to directly drive the two source terminals of a symmetric transmission line (return inductance equal to signal inductance, see Section 3.4.2) such as a twisted pair or twin-lead, as shown in Figure 7-21. The receiving end of the line is parallel-terminated. With current-mode signaling, this is nearly indistinguishable from having a separate return lead per signal. Because the signal and its complement are packaged closely together, cross talk with other signals is reduced. With voltage-mode signaling, this arrangement has all of the advantages listed above and requires only a single symmetric transmission line rather than a pair of asymmetric lines. Further, the symmetric line is inherently balanced with matched delays for the two components of the differential signal. This eliminates uncanceled common-mode noise due to delay mismatches between pairs of lines.

Differential signaling over a single symmetric line can be applied to unipolar signaling by splitting the termination resistor and providing a DC return path from the resistor midpoint to the transmitter, as shown in Figure 7-22. The DC return path can be shared by many signals because each signal can be inductively

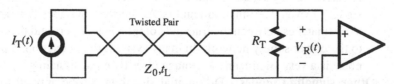

FIGURE 7-21   Bipolar Differential Signaling on a Symmetric Line

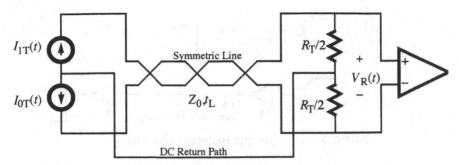

FIGURE 7-22   Unipolar Differential Signaling on a Symmetric Line

isolated[6] from the common path, and any noise on this return is common-mode to the receiver.

7.4   SIGNALING OVER LUMPED TRANSMISSION MEDIA

When lines are short compared with the signal rise and fall time or an interconnect has many impedance discontinuities, it is better to model the interconnect as a lumped circuit rather than a transmission line. The issues in designing a signaling system for a lumped circuit are similar to those for a transmission line. We wish to minimize delay, power consumption, and noise generated by signaling while providing good noise immunity.

7.4.1   Signaling Over a Capacitive Transmission Medium

On an integrated circuit chip, lines are short (a few centimeters at most), and inductances are usually small enough to ignore. The resistance of long lines (more than a few millimeters) is significant and requires a lossy transmission line model. We discuss signaling over such lossy RC lines in Section 8.1. On-chip lines shorter than a few millimeters can be modeled as a lumped capacitor. We wish to transmit bits on this capacitor reliably while minimizing delay and power dissipation. In particular, we would like to minimize both the DC and AC current draw to keep the iR and $L di/dt$ power supply noise small.

As shown in Figure 7-23, a logic family, such as static CMOS, defines a de facto signaling system. In Figure 7-23(a), a gate output drives the interconnect, and a gate input senses the signal. For short lines this is usually adequate. For long lines, however, the gate will either be very slow, or the electrical effort required to drive the line will dominate the logical effort being performed by the gate. In this case it is better to split the gates, which perform logic, from the driver and receiver, which transmit bits over the wire, as shown in Figure 7-23(b). This

---

[6] The return current is *mostly* DC. However, inductive isolation is necessary to prevent the current spikes that often occur during switching transients from coupling between lines.

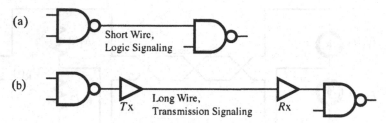

FIGURE 7-23   Signaling Between Logic Gates

allows us to optimize the signaling system for the load and noise environment rather than to use a convention optimized for the operation of logic gates.

7.4.1.1   Voltage-Mode Signaling

Most gates drive on-chip interconnects using a circuit equivalent to a voltage source with a finite output impedance, R_O, as shown in Figure 7-24. The capacitor represents the distributed capacitance between the signal line and the local ground along the line. Ground noise between the transmit voltage source and the distributed capacitor is modeled by source V_{N1}. Additional noise between the line ground and the receiver ground is modeled by V_{N2}. Source V_{N1} is in series with V_T and thus appears across C_L after being filtered by the low-pass RC. Source V_{N2} does not affect the charge on the line, but appears unfiltered at the receiver, where it may corrupt the reference voltage, V_r.

In the absence of noise, if the voltage switches instantaneously from V_0 to V_1 at $t = 0$, the line voltage has an exponential waveform:

$$(7\text{-}23) \qquad V_R(t) = V_1 + (V_0 - V_1)\exp\left(-\frac{t}{R_O C_L}\right)$$

Unlike the transmission lines considered above, voltage for the capacitive line is not a function of position. We consider the line to be an equipotential region. The time constant of this line, $\tau_L = R_O C_L$, determines the delay of the transmission system along with transmitter and receiver delay. For example if $R_O = 200\ \Omega$ and C_L is 20 pF, τ is 4 ns.

Full-swing voltage-mode signaling has most of the same problems over a capacitive line that it does over a transmission line. The signal power is excessive, and since power supplies are used to define the output levels and input reference, there is little rejection of power supply noise. A large transient current is required to switch a large capacitive line through the full supply voltage in a small amount

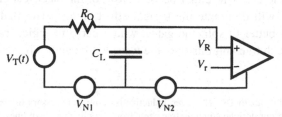

FIGURE 7-24   Voltage-Mode Signaling over a Capacitive Line

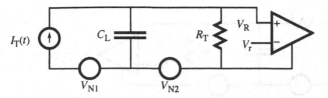

FIGURE 7-25 Current-Mode Signaling over a Capacitive Line

of time. This current generates power-supply noise, and on integrated circuits, this current can exceed the maximum rating of a minimum-width line. Making the line wider does not help,[7] for it increases capacitance at the same rate that it increases the current-carrying ability of the line. The system must either be operated slowly or, preferably, signal swing should be reduced.

7.4.1.2 Current-Mode Signaling

As with transmission lines, operating the driver in the current mode allows signal swing to be reduced without separate voltage references and isolates the received signal from power supply noise. Figure 7-25 shows a current-source driver at one end of the capacitive line and a resistor with value R_T at the other end. This arrangement is better than simply replacing the voltage source and series resistor with a Norton equivalent. Placing the resistor at the receiving end causes the received voltage to be developed referenced to the receiver ground rather than the transmitter ground.

Noise source V_{N1} is completely attenuated because it is in series with a current source. If the current source has a finite output impedance, R_O, V_{N1} is attenuated by $R_T/(R_T + R_O)$. If V_r is generated relative to the bottom terminal of R_T, V_{N2} is partially attenuated. The DC portion of V_{N2} is attenuated by the same amount as V_{N1}, $R_T/(R_T + R_O)$. The AC portion of V_{N2}, however is divided by the resistor and the line capacitance and thus is attenuated by

$$(7\text{-}24) \qquad A_{N2} = \frac{R_T C_L s}{R_T C_L s + 1}$$

Frequency components of V_{N2} that are above the cutoff of the line, $f_c = 1/(R_T C_L)$, are passed largely unattenuated, whereas frequencies below this cutoff are attenuated.

7.4.1.3 Resistive Voltage Divider

A simple method of limiting signal swing with a voltage-source driver is to place a resistor in parallel with the line capacitor at the receiver, as shown in Figure 7-26. The signal swing is reduced to

$$(7\text{-}25) \qquad V_R = \frac{V_T R_1}{R_1 + R_O}$$

---

[7] Actually, as the result of fringing effects, making the line wider helps at first because R decreases faster than C increases until the capacitance is dominated by the parallel-plate component. See Section 8.1.3.

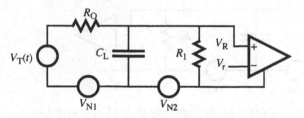

FIGURE 7-26   Reduced-Swing Signaling with a Resistive Divider

The time constant is also reduced to

$$(7\text{-}26) \qquad \tau_L = \frac{R_1 R_O C}{R_1 + R_O}$$

Noise from V_{N1} is attenuated by the same amount as the signal, whereas V_{N2} sees the same low-frequency attenuation as for current-mode signaling.

Consider for example a full-swing 3.3-V driver with $R_O = 200\,\Omega$ and $C_L = 20$ pF, as above. Without R_1, τ_L is 4 ns. Adding $R_1 = 20\,\Omega$ reduces the swing to 300 mV and τ_L to 360 ps. This reduction in τ_L both speeds up the system and reduces noise because it increases the cutoff frequency of the high-pass filter that attenuates V_{N2}. A small amount of delay is added, of course, to amplify the 300-mV signal at the receiver.

7.4.1.4   Pulsed Signaling

The signaling systems described in the preceding two sections have the disadvantage that they place a steady current load on the line and dissipate static power. On chip, the steady current draw may exceed the DC current-limit of the line. For signals that change infrequently, the static power dissipation is a disadvantage. A pulsed signaling system overcomes these disadvantages by dissipating power only during transitions and by having no DC current component.

A pulsed current-mode signaling system operates with a circuit similar to that shown in Figure 7-25 but with no resistor at the receiver. Figure 7-27 shows the source current and the receiver voltage for such a system sending the sequence 11010. When the bit being transmitted remains the same, the source current remains off and the line voltage remains constant. For each 0-to-1 transition, the source produces a current pulse of width t_r and magnitude I_p, which changes the

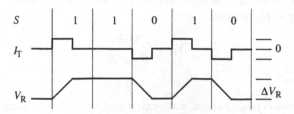

FIGURE 7-27   Pulsed Current-Mode Signaling Waveforms

voltage on the line by

$$(7\text{-}27) \qquad\qquad \Delta V_R = \frac{I_p t_r}{C_L}$$

A pulse with magnitude $-I_p$ is produced for each 1-to-0 transition, which changes the line voltage by $-\Delta V_R$.

Although this dynamic signaling dissipates less power than the methods described above, it is not as good at rejecting noise due to V_{N2}. Because the impedance across the line is infinite, the cutoff frequency of the high-pass that attenuates V_{N2} in Figure 7-25 is at zero. All of the frequency components of V_{N2} appear unattenuated at the receiver. This limitation can be overcome by using a transmitter-generated receiver reference or by using differential signaling.

In Chapter 11 we discuss circuit techniques for building signaling systems. For pulsed systems, the pulse may be produced by a fixed time delay adjusted for process variations or by a feedback system that turns off the current source when the desired voltage is reached.

If the positive- and negative-going pulses are not exactly matched in width and magnitude, the average line voltage will drift over time. To keep the line voltage in a fixed range we may precharge the line or send one symbol value by connecting the line to a supply.

7.4.1.5 Return-to-Zero (Precharged) Pulsed Signaling

One approach to pulsed signaling is to start every bit-cell by precharging the line to a known voltage, usually a power supply. A unipolar current source then conditionally drives the line with a current pulse of magnitude I_p and duration t_r. The presence of a pulse denotes a 1, whereas the absence of a pulse denotes a 0.

Waveforms for this signaling method are shown in Figure 7-28. The four traces show the transmitter current, I_T, the precharge signal, *Pre*, the line voltage, V_R, and a reference voltage, V_r. When the precharge signal is high, at the beginning of each cycle, the line is connected to a voltage reference through some resistive switch. When the precharge is complete, the precharge signal goes low, and the line floats. The reference voltage V_r is generated by precharging a matched line each cycle and then driving it with a half-magnitude current pulse, $I_p/2$. This

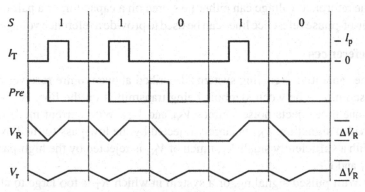

FIGURE 7-28   Waveforms for Precharged Pulsed Signaling

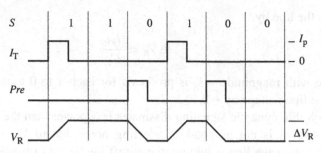

FIGURE 7-29   Band-Limited Pulsed Signaling

generates a voltage at the end of the cycle that is halfway between the voltages corresponding to a 1 and a 0 on V_R.

This method has three main advantages: (a) only a unipolar current source is needed, (b) the value of the line after the precharge is complete serves as a transmitter generated reference, and (c) setting the line voltage to a known value each cycle prevents the average line voltage from drifting over time. However, the return-to-zero method has the disadvantage that additional time is required during each bit-cell to precharge the line. If the precharge and discharge currents are comparable, the maximum bit rate at which the system can operate is nearly halved.

7.4.1.6   Band-Limited Pulsed Signaling

If the transmitted signal is band-limited so that there are no more than N consecutive ones or zeros, the signal can be encoded by precharging the line on a $1 \rightarrow 0$ transition and discharging it with a current pulse on a $0 \rightarrow 1$ transition. This gives us all of the advantages of return-to-zero signaling without paying the time penalty required to precharge the line each cycle. As long as the time constant of the line is long compared with the interval between $1 \rightarrow 0$ transitions, there will be negligible drift in the average line voltage. In effect this method is a hybrid between voltage-mode signaling and pulsed current-mode signaling. We encode a 0 with a fixed voltage reference (usually a power supply) and encode a 1 with a current pulse.

A reference can be provided with this method by precharging a matched line on odd cycles and charging it with a half-magnitude current pulse on even cycles. The reference voltage can either be stored on a capacitor, or a pair of 180-degree out-of-phase reference lines can be used to provide a reference voltage every cycle.

7.4.1.7   References

The capacitive signaling systems described above require receiver references to discriminate between symbols being transmitted on the line. A good reference is one that rejects noise sources V_{N1} and V_{N2}. With current-mode or resistively divided signaling, V_{N1} is largely rejected by the low-pass formed by R_O and C_L. With a sufficiently small R_T, much of V_{N2} is rejected by the high-pass formed by R_T and C_L.

With pulsed signaling, or a system in which R_T is too large to attenuate V_{N2}, a matched reference is required to cancel this noise, as shown in Figure 7-30. A

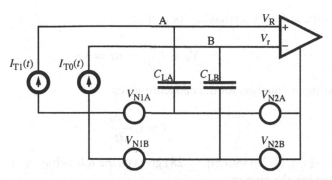

FIGURE 7-30   Matched Reference for a Capacitive Line

reference line, B, is routed beside signal line, A, so that noise source V_{N2A} matches V_{N2B} as closely as possible. In addition to power supply noise, this arrangement also cancels cross talk coupled to both the signal and the reference.

There are several methods to encode signal(s) and a reference on lines A and B. With differential signaling, a separate reference is provided for each signal and the two sources, I_{T0} and I_{T1}, drive complementary signals on lines A and B. This has all of the advantages cited for differential signaling on transmission lines. There is zero AC current, and the effective signal swing is doubled as is the effective rise time. Because of these advantages, differential pulsed current-mode signaling is used by almost all MOS SRAMs, as described in Section 8.5.2.

To reduce wire count, a single reference line can be shared by a group of signal lines if pulsed bipolar current-mode signaling is used. In this case, I_{T0} is removed, and the source end of line B is tied to a reference through an impedance that matches the output impedance of I_{T1}. In this case V_r is an estimate of the noise on line A in the absence of current drive.

With precharged unipolar signaling, a shared reference line is driven by a current source with half the amplitude of the signal source. This produces a voltage on line B that is half-way between a 0 and 1 voltage on line A.

7.4.2   Signaling over Lumped LRC Interconnect

When driving signals off-chip, the inductance of the interconnect becomes a factor. For example, a voltage source driver with output impedance R_O driving a capacitive load, C_L, through a pin with inductance L_p can be modeled by the equivalent circuit shown in Figure 7-31. The effective loop inductance includes both the output pin inductance and the inductance of the shared power supply leads multiplied by the degree of sharing.

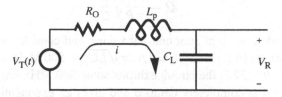

FIGURE 7-31   Driving a Capacitive Load through an Inductive Lead

Summing the voltages around the loop gives

(7-28)
$$V_R + L\frac{di}{dt} + Ri = V_T$$

The constituent equation for the capacitor gives

(7-29)
$$i = C\frac{dV_R}{dt}$$

Substituting Eq. (7-29) into Eq. (7-28) gives us the following second-order equation describing the circuit:

(7-30)
$$LC\frac{d^2V_R}{dt^2} + RC\frac{dV_R}{dt} + V_R = V_T$$

Taking Laplace transforms gives

(7-31)
$$V_R(s) = \frac{V_T(s)}{LC\left(s^2 + \frac{R}{L}s + \frac{1}{LC}\right)}$$

and factoring the denominator gives

(7-32)
$$V_R(s) = V_T(s)\frac{1}{LC\left(s + \frac{R}{2L} + i\omega\right)\left(s + \frac{R}{2L} - i\omega\right)}$$

where

(7-33)
$$\omega = \sqrt{\frac{1}{LC} - \left(\frac{R}{2L}\right)^2}$$

In the time domain, this gives a response to a step function on V_T of

(7-34)
$$V_R(t) = 1 - \exp\left(-\frac{Rt}{2L}\right)\cos(\omega t)$$

if

(7-35)
$$\frac{R}{2L} < \frac{1}{\sqrt{LC}}$$

The critical factor here is the ratio, Q, of $\omega/2\pi$ to $R/2L$, which gives the number of cycles before the waveform is attenuated to $\exp(-1)$.

(7-36)
$$Q = \frac{1}{\pi R}\sqrt{\frac{L}{C}}$$

Let $L = 10$ nH and $C = 10$ pF, not unusual values, and consider what happens as we vary R from 0 to 16 Ω. Here $f_0 = 1/(2\pi\sqrt{LC}) = 500$ MHz and $\sqrt{L/C} = 32\,\Omega$, and thus for $R < 32\,\Omega$ the circuit exhibits some 500 MHz ringing, and for $R > 32\,\Omega$ the circuit is completely damped and gives an exponential response. Figure 7-32 shows the response of this circuit for R set to 0, 2, 4, 8, and 16 Ω.

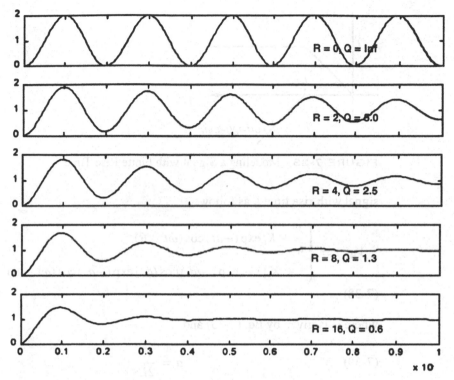

FIGURE 7-32   Response of LRC Circuit to Unit Step

The ringing associated with a high-Q output circuit is unacceptable for digital signaling. The signal oscillates in and out of the detection range for the current bit-cell, and continued oscillations create intersymbol interference that corrupts later bit-cells. Depending on the noise budget, the signal must settle to within about 10% of its final value before the center of its current bit-cell.

7.4.2.1   Rise-Time Control

Ringing of an LRC circuit can be reduced by controlling the rise time of the input waveform. By reducing the high-frequency components of the input, less energy is coupled into the tank circuit to cause the ringing.

Consider applying a signal with rise time, t_r, as the input voltage, V_T, in Figure 7-31. We model this signal as the superposition of two ramps, as illustrated in Figure 7-33: an upward ramp starting at $t = 0$, and a downward ramp starting at $t = t_r$. The slope of both ramps is set to $\pm t/t_r$. Mathematically, this is expressed as

$$(7\text{-}37) \qquad V_T(t) = U(t)\frac{t}{t_r} - U(t - t_r)\frac{t - t_r}{t_r}$$

where $U(t)$ is the unit step function.

The response to each of the two ramp signals is derived by integrating Eq. (7-34). Combining the two gives the overall response of the circuit to a

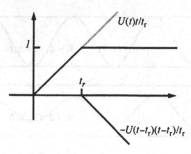

FIGURE 7-33 Modeling a Signal with Finite Rise Time

signal with rise time t_r as follows:

$$V_R(t) = \begin{cases} \dfrac{t}{t_r} + K_r \exp(-at) \cos(\omega t - \theta) & \text{if } t \le t_r \\[2ex] 1 + K_r[1 - \exp(-at_r) \cos(\phi)] \exp(-at) \cos(\omega t - \theta) & \text{if } t > t_r \end{cases}$$

(7-38)

where ω is given by Eq. (7-33) and

$$(7\text{-}39) \qquad\qquad a = \frac{R}{2L}$$

$$(7\text{-}40) \qquad\qquad K_r = \frac{1}{t_r \omega_0} = \frac{t_0}{2\pi t_r}$$

$$(7\text{-}41) \qquad\qquad \omega_0 = \frac{1}{\sqrt{LC}}$$

$$(7\text{-}42) \qquad\qquad \theta = a \tan\left(\frac{\omega}{a}\right)$$

$$(7\text{-}43) \qquad\qquad \phi = \omega t_r = \frac{2\pi t_r}{t_d}$$

$$(7\text{-}44) \qquad\qquad t_d = \frac{2\pi}{\omega}$$

Equation (7-38) shows that, compared with the response from a unit step, a controlled rise time attenuates the ringing by a factor of

$$K_{ar} = K_r K_\phi = K_r[1 - \exp(-at_r) \cos(\phi)] = \frac{t_0}{2\pi t_r}\left[1 - \exp(-at_r) \cos\left(\frac{2\pi t_r}{t_d}\right)\right]$$

(7-45)

Equation (7-45) shows that the attenuation of the ringing is determined entirely by the ratio of the damped period, t_d, and the undamped period, t_0, to the rise time t_r. The first term of Eq. (7-45), K_r, is the phase-independent attenuation, which reduces the ringing by $t_0/(2\pi t_r)$. Thus, if we temporarily ignore phase, increasing the rise time linearly decreases the ringing.

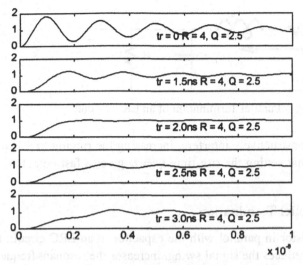

FIGURE 7-34   Response of LRC Circuit with Rise-Time Control

The phase-dependent second term of Eq. (7-45), K_ϕ, can increase or decrease the attenuation, depending on the phase difference, ϕ, between the response to the upward and downward slopes of V_T, as defined in Eq. (7-37). If t_r is an integral multiple of t_d, the two waves destructively interfere, further attenuating the ringing by $K_\phi = [1 - \exp(-at_r)]$. If t_r is an integral multiple of t_d plus one half, the two waves constructively interfere, increasing the ringing by $K_\phi = [1 + \exp(-at_r)]$. Intermediate phase differences give attenuations between the two extremes.

Figure 7-34 shows the response of a circuit with $Q = 2.5$ and $f = 500\,\text{MHz}$ to a 1-V input step with rise times of 0, 1.5, 2, 2.5, and 3 ns. The attenuation parameters for the four cases with controlled rise times are shown in Table 7-6. For the 1.5- and 2.5-ns rise times $\phi \cong 2\pi \pm \pi/4$, and thus $K_\phi \sim 1$. The two waves are in quadrature, and the damping is determined by K_r to be 0.21 and 0.13, respectively. Including the effect of the $\exp(-at_r)$ damping (0.74 and 0.61, respectively), the overall ringing at $t = t_r$ has magnitudes of 0.15 and 0.08, respectively. Rise-time control has reduced the ringing from an unacceptable level (0.74 and 0.61) to a level that can be dealt with in a noise budget (0.15 and 0.08).

The traces corresponding to rise times of 2 and 3 ns show the effect of K_ϕ. For the 2-ns case, $\phi \cong 2\pi$ and $K_\phi = 0.33$. The two waves are π radians out of phase and destructively interfere, reducing the overall ringing to 3% at $t = 2\,\text{ns}$. With the 3-ns rise time $\phi \cong 2\pi + \pi$ and $K_\phi = 1.55$. Because the two waves are in

TABLE 7-6   **Attenuation Parameters for Example of Figure 7-34**

t_r	K_r	$\phi/2\pi$	K_ϕ	K_{ar}	$\exp(-at_r)$	Ringing at t_r
1.5	0.21	0.75	0.98	0.21	0.74	0.15
2.0	0.16	1.00	0.33	0.05	0.67	0.03
2.5	0.13	1.26	1.02	0.13	0.61	0.08
3.0	0.11	1.51	1.55	0.16	0.55	0.09

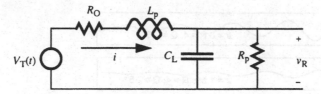

FIGURE 7-35   Parallel Termination of an LRC Circuit

phase, they constructively interfere, increasing the ringing to 9% at 3 ns. These traces show that setting the rise time $t_r = t_d$ gives a fast output with minimum ringing.

7.4.2.2   Adding Parallel Termination

Adding a resistor in parallel with the capacitor in an LRC circuit, as shown in Figure 7-35, reduces the signal swing, increases the resonant frequency, and increases the damping. Thus, adding a parallel resistor can be used to control ringing without increasing delay as long as a reduction in signal swing can be tolerated.

    With a parallel resistor R_p added, the differential equation (Eq. (7-30)) becomes

(7-46)
$$LC\frac{d^2V_R}{dt^2} + \left(\frac{L}{R_p} + RC\right)\frac{dV_R}{dt} + \left(1 + \frac{R}{R_p}\right)V_R = V_T$$

If

(7-47)
$$\left(\frac{L}{R_p} + RC\right)^2 - 4LC\left(1 + \frac{R}{R_p}\right) > 0$$

then the system is overdamped, and there will be no oscillation. Otherwise, Eq. (7-46) gives an undamped frequency of

(7-48)
$$\omega_0 = \sqrt{\frac{R_p + R}{R_p LC}}$$

and a Q of

(7-49)
$$Q = \frac{\sqrt{\frac{R_p + R}{R_p LC}}}{\pi\left(\frac{L}{R_p} + RC\right)}$$

    As an example, consider the values of L and C used above with $R_O = 8\,\Omega$ and $R_p = 4\,\Omega$. The left-hand term of Eq. (7-47) evaluates to 6.7×10^{-18}, whereas the right-hand term evaluates to 1.2×10^{-18}, and thus the system is overdamped and will not oscillate. Its time constant is approximately $(R_O \| R_p)C$ or 27 ps. This is in contrast to the $Q = 1.3$ oscillations, shown in Figure 7-32, without parallel termination.

    Figure 7-36 shows an equivalent circuit for a source V_T driving a parallel-terminated LRC circuit. The parallel termination reduces the signal swing of the source by $R_p/(R + R_p)$ and at the same time puts the resistor R_p in parallel with the

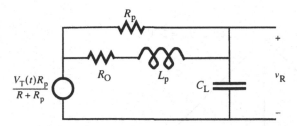

FIGURE 7-36 Equivalent Circuit for Parallel-Terminated LRC

complex output impedance, $j\omega L + R$, of the source. As with the underterminated driver of Figure 7-18 and the parallel termination of Figure 7-26, we trade signal swing for reduced source impedance.

7.4.2.3 Reducing Power Supply Noise

Several drivers on an integrated circuit typically share a common power supply terminal, as shown in Figure 7-37. If all of the N drivers switch simultaneously, the inductance of this terminal, L_P, is effectively multiplied by N because it carries N times the current of the signal terminal inductance, L. This switching current can induce a significant amount of internal (signaling-induced) power-supply noise that may be coupled into the signals. To reduce this noise to a minimum, the current waveform of the transmitter should be controlled to keep the slope of the current to a minimum.

Rise-time control, in addition to reducing ringing, quadratically reduces power supply noise due to power-lead inductance if the slope of the current waveform is also controlled. If a capacitor C is driven with a voltage ramp with rise time t_r and magnitude V, then the current is

$$(7\text{-}50) \qquad i = C\frac{dv}{dt} = \frac{CV}{t_r}U(t)U(t_r - t)$$

Without current control this step-current waveform would induce a very large voltage across the shared supply lead inductor.

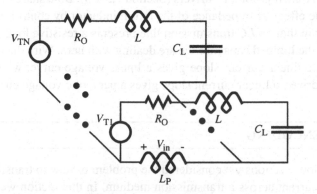

FIGURE 7-37 Multiple Drivers Sharing a Common Power Supply Lead

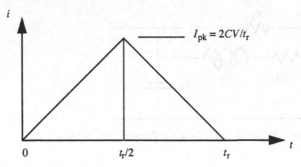

FIGURE 7-38   Triangular Current Waveform

The power supply noise due to output switching is minimized by driving the LRC load with a triangle-shaped current waveform as shown in Figure 7-38. With very large capacitive loads, a trapezoidal waveform may be used to keep the peak current, I_{pk}, within limits. The triangular current waveform leads to a parabolic voltage waveform, $V(t) = Kt^2$.

With a triangular wave, the current is given by

$$I(t) = U(t)\frac{2I_{PK}t}{t_r} - U\left(t - \frac{t_r}{2}\right)\frac{4I_{PK}(t - t_r/2)}{t_r} + U(t - t_r)\frac{2I_{PK}(t - t_r)}{t_r}$$

(7-51)

where

(7-52) $$I_{pk} = \frac{2CV}{t_r}$$

which results in a noise voltage of

(7-53) $$v_{in} = L\frac{di}{dt} = \pm\frac{4LCV}{t_r^2}$$

Circuits to produce output waveforms with controlled rise times and controlled current slopes are discussed in Section 11.2.

Power-supply noise in lumped LRC drivers is closely related to signal-return cross talk in transmission line drivers (Section 7.3.1.3). Both share the solution of reducing the effective impedance of the return inductor by controlling rise time. They differ in that an LC transmission line presents a resistive load to the driver rather than the lumped capacitor we are dealing with here. With the transmission line driver, a linear current slope gives a linear voltage curve, whereas for the capacitive driver, a linear current slope gives a parabolic voltage curve.

7.5   SIGNAL ENCODING

In the previous sections we considered the problem of how to transfer a discrete voltage or current across a transmission medium. In this section we address the problem of how best to encode digital information into discrete voltage or current levels for transmission.

7.5.1 Number of Signal Levels

To transmit digital symbols across a medium, the symbols must be mapped onto a continuous variable, usually voltage or current. Binary signaling, in which the digital symbols are drawn from a two-character alphabet, is used almost universally because of its simple implementation and favorable energetics. It is not, however, the only option. We can encode an alphabet of N input symbols, $\{a_0, \ldots, a_{N-1}\}$ on a continuous variable v with range $V_L \le V \le V_H$ by assigning each symbol a nominal value, $\{V_0, \ldots, V_{N-1}\}$, and defining $N - 1$ thresholds, $\{U_0, \ldots, U_{N-2}\}$. If noise is independent of signal level and the input signals are equally likely, it is easy to show that the optimal choices for these values are

$$(7\text{-}54) \qquad\qquad V_i = V_L + i\left(\frac{\Delta V}{N - 1}\right)$$

and

$$(7\text{-}55) \qquad\qquad U_i = V_L + \left(i + \frac{1}{2}\right)\left(\frac{\Delta V}{N - 1}\right)$$

where $\Delta V = V_H - V_L$.

Figure 7-39 graphically shows this relationship between symbols, values, and thresholds for a four-element alphabet and a two-element or binary alphabet. Each symbol, a_i, is represented by a $\Delta V/(N - 1)$ range of voltage centered on V_i. Threshold U_j separates the voltage range representing a_j from that representing a_{j+1}. Symbol a_0 is bounded below by V_{min}, and a_{N-1} is bounded above by V_{max}. Voltages outside of the range $[V_{min}, V_{max}]$ are disallowed. They are associated with no symbol and may cause physical damage to the receiver or other components of the transmission system. Note that the receiver must operate over $[V_{min}, V_{max}]$ even though the transmitter only generates voltages in $[V_0, V_{N-1}]$ or equivalently $[V_L, V_H]$.

If we optimistically assume our noise is independent of signal swing with range $[-V_{NI}, V_{NI}]$, the required signal swing ΔV is

$$(7\text{-}56) \qquad\qquad \Delta V > 2V_{NI}(N - 1)$$

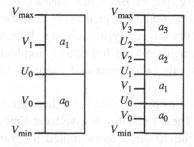

FIGURE 7-39 Symbols, Values, and Thresholds

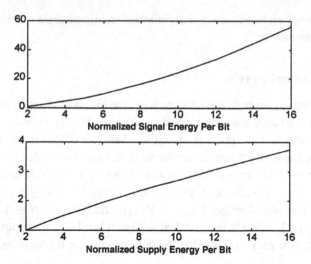

FIGURE 7-40   Signal and Supply Energy versus Number of Signal Levels

The required signal energy is

$$(7\text{-}57) \qquad E_{\text{sw}} = \frac{t_{\text{sw}} \Delta V^2}{Z} > \frac{4 t_{\text{sw}} V_{\text{NI}}^2 (N-1)^2}{Z}$$

where Z is the impedance of the transmission medium and t_{sw} is the switching time. The signal energy per bit is thus

$$(7\text{-}58) \qquad E_{\text{swb}} = \frac{t_{\text{sw}} \Delta V^2}{Z \log_2 N} > \frac{4 t_{\text{sw}} V_{\text{NI}}^2 (N-1)^2}{Z \log_2 N}$$

The top curve of Figure 7-40 plots E_{swb} versus N to show how the energy per bit increases with the number of signal levels. The figure is normalized to the energy required for binary signaling. If the signaling system uses a fixed power supply voltage, independent of the number of signal levels, the required power supply energy is proportional to ΔV rather than ΔV^2. The bottom curve of Figure 7-40 shows how the power supply energy per bit increases with the number of signal levels. Although the normalized increase in power supply energy per bit is not as great as for signal energy, the energy per bit still increases monotonically with number of signal levels.

Binary signaling, encoding two symbols 0 and 1 onto a continuous variable, results in the minimal required energy per bit. Because a substantial amount of the noise in most digital systems is proportional to signal swing, the energy required for multilevel signals is worse than this analysis indicates. In addition to its favorable energetics, binary signaling is also much simpler to implement because it requires transmitters that send only two values and receivers that compare against a single threshold.

Despite the favorable energetics of binary signaling, there are cases where multilevel signaling is preferred. These typically involve band-limited channels with high signal-to-noise ratios. If the channel is band-limited, for example a lossy LRC transmission line (Section 8.2), it is difficult to reduce t_{sw} to transmit more symbols per unit time. The only method available to increase data rate is then to send more bits per symbol. If there is very little noise on the channel, this can be done with reasonable power. Four times the supply energy of binary signaling (Figure 7-40) may be a very small value. For these band-limited channels, symbols are usually encoded by varying the phase and magnitude of the transmitted signal, as described in Section 2.10.3.

7.5.2   Signal Magnitude

Once the number of signal levels is selected, the signal swing between levels remains to be determined. To minimize power dissipation, the smallest signal level that achieves the desired bit error rate is usually selected. In some cases a larger signal magnitude than required by noise concerns will be used to avoid amplification latency.

With binary signaling the two symbols are encoded with $V_0 = V_L$ and $V_1 = V_H$, the signal swing between levels is ΔV, and the detection threshold is $U = (V_L + V_H)/2$. This gives a noise margin of $V_M = \Delta V/2$. The absolute value of this noise margin is meaningless. The noise immunity of the system is determined by the margin-to-noise ratio, K_{NM}, the ratio of margin, V_M, to the total noise, V_N.

The required noise margin, V_M, is calculated by preparing a noise budget. We divide the total noise, V_N, into a component that is independent of signal swing, V_{NI}, and a component proportional to signal swing, $K_N \Delta V$ as follows:

$$(7\text{-}59) \qquad V_N = V_{NI} + K_N \Delta V$$

The signal swing is then selected to give the desired margin to noise ratio using

$$(7\text{-}60) \qquad \Delta V > \frac{2 K_{NM} V_{NI}}{(1 - 2 K_{NM} K_N)}$$

Equation (7-60) shows that the proportional signal noise K_N limits the achievable margin to noise ratio, and thus

$$(7\text{-}61) \qquad K_{NM} < \frac{1}{2 K_N}$$

The details of a noise budget depend on the specifics of the signaling method and the environment. The comparison in Section 7.1.2 gives two example noise budgets and margin-to-noise ratios.

The subject of signal magnitude, noise margins, and bit error rate is discussed in more detail in Sections 6.6.1 and 6.6.2.

7.5.2.1   Hysteresis

A receiver with hysteresis increases the noise margin for the current state from $\Delta V/2$ to a larger fraction, K_h, of ΔV by dynamically moving the threshold away from the present signal value. This is done at the expense of the noise margin for the other state, which becomes a smaller fraction $(1 - K_h)$ of ΔV.

With binary signaling, the threshold becomes

$$(7\text{-}62) \qquad U = \begin{cases} V_{\mathrm{L}} + K_{\mathrm{h}}\Delta V & \text{if last bit was 0} \\ V_{\mathrm{H}} - K_{\mathrm{h}}\Delta V & \text{if last bit was 1} \end{cases}$$

where K_{h} is the hysteresis factor. Setting $K_{\mathrm{h}} = 0.5$ gives conventional signaling with a fixed threshold. Larger values of K_{h} move the threshold away from the last bit.

With hysteresis, Eqs. (7-60) and (7-61) become

$$(7\text{-}63) \qquad \Delta V > \frac{K_{\mathrm{NM}} V_{\mathrm{NI}}}{(K_{\mathrm{h}} - K_{\mathrm{NM}} K_{\mathrm{N}})}$$

and

$$(7\text{-}64) \qquad K_{\mathrm{NM}} < \frac{K_{\mathrm{h}}}{K_{\mathrm{N}}}$$

for the current state. Substituting $(1 - K_{\mathrm{h}})$ for K_{h} in Eqs. (7-63) and (7-64) gives the expressions for the opposite state. These reduced noise margins dominate, causing hysteresis to reduce performance unless the probability of remaining in the current state is many times higher than the probability of changing states. If the probability of the two states is equal, the effect is the same as if the threshold were offset from the center of the signal swing by $(K_{\mathrm{h}} - 0.5)\Delta V$.

Hysteresis is sometimes useful for low-speed signals where the noise bandwidth is greater than the signal bandwidth and the noise is zero mean. Under these circumstances, the high-frequency noise will eventually allow a changing signal to cross the threshold. For high-speed signals, however, symmetric noise margins give significantly better performance. Even for low-speed signals, a designer would be better off using pulsed signaling (Section 7.5.5), an integrating receiver (Section 9.6.4.2), or filtering the noise rather than using hysteresis.

7.5.3   Signal Transfer Function

Many texts on logic design describe signal levels and noise margins in relation to the signal transfer function, $V_{\mathrm{O}} = f(V_{\mathrm{I}})$. This function, $f(V)$, gives the output voltage V_{O} generated by applying V_{I} to a receiver and connecting the input of a transmitter to the output of the receiver. In this section we relate the signal transfer function to our measures of signal levels and noise immunity.

Figure 7-41 shows the signal transfer function for a typical receiver–transmitter pair or for a noninverting logic gate that serves as both a transmitter and receiver. By our definition of transmitter offset, V_{to}, and receiver sensitivity and offset, $V_{\mathrm{rs}} + 2V_{\mathrm{ro}}$, the transfer function is constrained to stay within the shaded region. One such function is shown as a solid line.

Figure 7-41 shows the relationship between conventional specifications of input and output high and low voltages and our measures of signal level. The output voltage for a high (low) signal is bounded by $V_{\mathrm{OH}} = V_1 - V_{\mathrm{to}}(V_{\mathrm{OL}} = V_0 + V_{\mathrm{to}})$. To

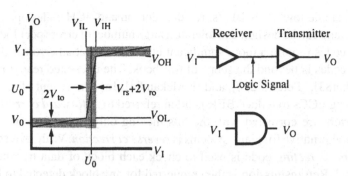

FIGURE 7-41   Signal Transfer Function

detect a 1 (0) reliably, the input level must be above (below) $V_{IH} = U_0 + V_{ro} + V_{rs}/2$ ($V_{IL} = U_0 - V_{ro} - V_{rs}/2$). The result is a positive (negative) noise margin of $V_{OH} - V_{IH} = V_1 - U_0 - V_{to} - V_{ro} - V_{rs}/2$ ($V_{IL} - V_{OL} = U_0 - V_1 - V_{to} - V_{ro} - V_{rs}/2$).

The signal transfer function shows that gain greater than unity is required to provide positive noise margins in a transmission system. To stay within the shaded region the gain of the transmission system, the slope of the transfer function, must be at least $(V_{OH} - V_{OL})/(V_{IH} - V_{IL})$.

The concept of signal transfer function captures the transmitter and receiver offsets and receiver sensitivity. We must also consider the remaining noise sources (power-supply noise, cross talk, and intersymbol interference), however, to calculate our noise immunity.

7.5.4   Error Correcting Codes

Error correcting codes (ECCs) offer a method for trading bandwidth for error rate in signals that operate with signal energies near the noise energy.

For example, a simple (38, 32) Hamming code that adds 6 check bits to each 32-bit word corrects all single-bit errors in a word and detects all double-bit errors. If bit errors are independent and uniformly distributed and the raw BER (bit-error rate) of a 100-Mb/s channel is 1×10^{-8} (one error per second), the Hamming code improves the BER to about 1×10^{-15} (five errors per year) at a cost of about 20% overhead. Undetected errors (more than two bits in the same word) will happen with a rate of about 3×10^{-17} (one undetected error in 10 years).

Incorporating ECC in a link adds logical complexity and a small amount of latency to the system. For a Hamming code, a parity tree that spans a subsets of the data bits is used to generate the check bits and to generate a syndrome from the received data bits. A nonzero syndrome indicates an error. A small ROM (often implemented from gates) decodes the syndrome to correct the error. The overall complexity is a few hundred gates with a logical depth of about 6 for the encoder and 10 for the decoder.

In the presence of impulse noise, errors typically occur in bursts. To handle burst errors, either codes with a large block size (compared with the typical burst length) must be employed, or several blocks must be interleaved to decorrelate the bursts by dividing them across several blocks, or both.

To handle lower raw BERs, Reed–Solomon and BCH codes operate on larger blocks and can be designed to tolerate a large number of errors per block. However, these codes require a more significant effort to correct an error. A discussion of these codes is beyond the scope of this book. The interested reader is referred to ([Blahut83], [Peteweld72], and [Berlekam84]) for a treatment of this topic.

Using ECCs to reduce BER is often referred to as *forward correction* because the errors are corrected with the bits moving only in the forward direction. A viable alternative for many systems is *reverse correction*. With reverse correction, an *error-detecting* code is used to check each block of data transmitted over a channel. Retransmission is then requested for any block detected to be in error.

Reverse correction offers the advantage of significantly improved efficiency if a reverse channel is available and some variability of bit rate and latency can be tolerated. If the block length is N, and the detecting code is of length R, then, assuming uniformly distributed errors and a good checking code, all single-bit errors are detected, the probability of an undetected multiple-bit error is 2^{-R}, and the overhead is $R/(N + R)$. For example, consider a system with 1K-byte blocks and a 32-bit CRC (cyclic-redundancy check) code. This code can detect all errors of 1–3 bits, and all but one in 10^9 errors of four or more bits. Its overhead is 0.4%. If the raw error rate is 10^{-8}, the probability of an undetected error is 10^{-31}.

7.5.5 Pulsed Signaling

Because many sources of noise are fixed offsets, at signaling rates less than the maximum channel bandwidth it is more efficient to send information in pulses of moderate amplitude rather than continuous signals of very low amplitude. In this situation we use pulsed signaling to concentrate signal energy over a short period of time to overcome fixed noise sources when driving a transmission line. This is in contrast to the use of pulsed signaling in Section 7.4.1 where the object is to minimize current draw when driving a capacitive load.

Suppose we have a system with $V_{NI} = 23$ mV and $K_N = 0.25$, as in Section 7.1.2, that uses a 50-ohm transmission line with parallel termination and has a bit rate of 1 Mbit/s. To achieve adequate noise immunity, we choose a signal swing of $\Delta V = 300$ mV. The signal power level is $P_{SW} = 1.8$ mW and this power is dissipated over the entire 1-μs cycle, giving a signal energy of $E_{SW} = 1.8$ nJ. This is much more energy than the 1 to 10 pJ required to transmit a bit reliably in a typical on-board noise environment.

A long bit period would allow us to use a lower signaling level if the noise were zero mean and uncorrelated with the signal. In this case we could integrate the received signal, and our signal-to-noise ratio would increase with the square root of the integration period. Unfortunately, the bulk of V_{NI}, receiver sensitivity and offset is not zero mean uncorrelated noise. Although clever receiver design can reduce these components of V_{NI}, allowing very low signaling levels, it is usually easier to operate the transmission system in a pulsed mode.

Figure 7-42 shows a waveform for a bipolar pulsed-mode system with bit period, t_{bit}. The signal is sent as a pulse with width, t_{PW}, and then the transmitter is keyed off for the remainder of the cycle. With bipolar signaling, a 1 is signaled

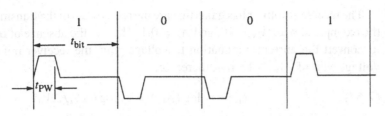

FIGURE 7-42   Pulsed Signaling

by a positive voltage or current pulse and a 0 by a negative pulse. Unipolar pulsed signaling is also possible where a 1 is signaled by the presence of pulse and a 0 by the absence of a pulse.

Pulsed-mode signaling gives a switching energy that is independent of t_{bit}. Instead, it depends on t_{PW}.

$$(7\text{-}65) \qquad E_{SWP} = \frac{\Delta V^2 t_{PW}}{Z_0}$$

For the parameters described above and a pulse width of 5 ns, the energy would be $E_{SWP} = 9$ pJ. The pulse width, t_{PW}, is typically chosen to be the smallest possible value subject to constraints of transmission system bandwidth and timing uncertainty.

The energy advantage of concentrating information in a short period of time is another reason, in addition to wire and pin savings, to favor serial communication. It is more efficient to send information on N wires operating at the maximum possible signaling rate, f, than to send them on $2N$ wires operating at a rate of $f/2$. The only disadvantage of serial communication is the latency penalty of serialization.

7.5.6   Signal Level and Delay

Because on-chip signal impedances are very high compared with off-chip impedances, to first approximation, delay is independent of off-chip signal levels.

Suppose the average on-chip logic signal has a capacitance of 100 fF and swings 3 V in 0.5 ns. This gives a current drive of 600 μA. The equivalent impedance of this signal is $Z_i = V/I = 5$ kΩ. There is a $K_Z = 100\!:\!1$ impedance mismatch between this signal and off-chip 50-ohm transmission lines.

Let the on-chip and off-chip signal swings be ΔV_i and ΔV_0, respectively. The output amplifier requires a voltage gain of $A_{OV} = \Delta V_0/\Delta V_i$ and a current gain of $A_{OI} = K_Z \Delta V_0/\Delta V_i$. For example, if $\Delta V_0 = 300$ mV, $A_{OV} = 0.1$ and $A_{OI} = 10$. Without a transformer to convert voltage attenuation to current gain, the output amplifier must step up the current by A_{OI} so that

$$(7\text{-}66) \qquad t_{dO} = \tau_A \log{(A_{OI})} = \tau_A[\log{(K_z)} - \log{(\Delta V_i/\Delta V_0)}]$$

For the example numbers above, $t_{dO} = 2.3\tau_A$, where τ_A is the amplifier time constant.

The receive amplifier has gains that are the reciprocals of the transmit gains. For the example above, $A_{IV} = 10$, and $A_{II} = 0.1$. Thus, in the absence of transformers to convert the current attenuation to voltage gain, the receiver must provide a voltage gain of $A_{IV} = 1/A_{OV}$; therefore,

$$(7\text{-}67) \qquad t_{dI} = \tau_A \log\,(A_{IV}) = \tau_A \log\,(\Delta V_i / \Delta V_0)$$

Thus, for normal ranges of signal levels ($A_{OV} < 1$, $A_{II} < 1$), the combined transmitter and receiver delay depends only on the impedance mismatch and is independent of off-chip signal level.

$$(7\text{-}68) \qquad t_{dO} + t_{dI} = \tau_A [\log\,(A_{OI}) + \log\,(A_{IV})] = \tau_A \log\,(K_z)$$

Equation (7-68) implies that we can choose our off-chip signaling levels to optimize noise immunity and minimize power dissipation without worrying about signal delay. Across a wide range of signal levels the amount of delay added to the receiver (transmitter) amplifier by using a smaller (larger) signal swing is exactly offset by a reduction in the delay of the transmitter (receiver) amplifier.

7.6 BIBLIOGRAPHIC NOTES

Most texts on digital design discuss logic signaling [HillPete93] and [WardHals90]. Methods for terminating transmission lines are discussed in Chapter 6 of [John-Grah93]. A classic, slightly dated, but still very useful text on signaling, transmission-line analysis, and termination methods is [MECL88]. Current-mode signaling has been used for many years and in many forms such as the 20-ma current-loop communications standards for electromechanical terminals ("tele-types") and industrial data links described briefly in [RoddCool81]. Differential current-mode signaling has become fashionable in the context of high-speed se-rial data links; Chapter 11 provides many references to current work in this area; [IEEE1596] describes the LVDS (Low-Voltage Differential Signaling) standard recently adopted by the industry. The problem of driving on-chip capacitive lines is discussed in [Bakoglu90], and, in the context of low-power electronics in [RabaPedr96], which also gives a treatment specific to memory arrays. Rise-time control, to solve the problem of signal-return cross talk (sometimes called *ground-bounce*) began to get considerable attention in the industry in the late 1980s, and solutions to the problem were proposed in [Raver87], [GabaThom88], [HanaDenn92], [GunnYuan92], and [SentPrin93]. These solutions are based on "analog" approaches such as controlling the voltage on the gates of driver tran-sistors. Another technique, the use of current shaping to control rise time, is discussed in [DenLeDall93]. A good example of pulsed signaling is described in [GabaThom88a]. Deciding the number of signal levels is an application of quantization theory developed in [GersGray92] and [Gray90]. Many papers have been written on the topic of multilevel logic; the topic has a fairly long history [Smith81]. The Institute of Electrical and Electronics Engineers sponsors a yearly conference on the subject [ISMVL97]. Memory with multilevel storage has also been a topic of some interest because it allows the possibility of multiple bits per storage device and thus much cheaper memory chips; this idea has been implemented, for example, in [FuruOsha89] and [MuroNari97]. Error correcting codes are a subject in their own right with several excellent texts available such as [Blahut83], [Berlekam84], and [PeteWeld72].

7.7 EXERCISES

7-1 Noise Rejection of Underterminated Signaling: Consider the underterminated signaling system (modeled after Figure 7-18, but with return inductance shown) presented in Figure 7-43. As a function of return inductance, L_R, signal rise time t_r, and parameters shown in the figure, derive an expression for the signal-return cross talk coefficient, k_{xr}. (Hint: Derive separate expressions for the return cross talk at each end of the line.)

7-2 Differential versus Single-Ended Signaling: Suppose you have a system with the following characteristics:

Line impedance	50	Ω
Lead inductance	5	nH
Pin count	32	pins
Required data rate	8	Gb/s

One approach is to implement 16 differential channels at 500 Mb/s each. An alternative approach is to implement more (but not 32) single-ended channels at a somewhat lower data rate while providing an adequate number of return pins to keep k_{xr} less than 10%. Suppose both approaches use current-mode signaling and have a fixed noise of $V_{NI} = 20$ mV (receiver offset plus sensitivity) and proportional noise (other than k_{xr}) of 15%. Assume that the signal rise time is half the bit-cell width.

Which approach is preferable? Why?

7-3 Current References: Consider a unipolar current-mode signaling system that encodes a 0 as $I_0 = 0$, and a 1 as I_1. The transmitter and receiver each generate their own current reference, and these references are each $\pm15\%$ of nominal. Suppose the fixed noise sources total 30 mV (600 μA assuming a 50-ohm load), and cross talk, ISI, and signal return noise give proportional

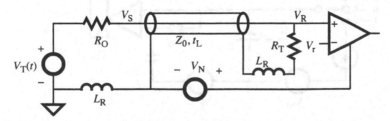

FIGURE 7-43 Underterminated Signaling with Return Inductance (for Exercise 7-1)

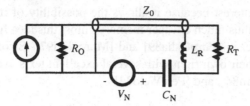

FIGURE 7-44 Signaling System with Power Supply Noise (for Exercise 7-4)

noise that totals 25%. What is the effect of this variation in current reference? What is the minimum signal swing (I_1) that will satisfy a worst-case noise analysis? What is the minimum signal swing that would satisfy a worst-case noise analysis if bipolar current-mode signaling were used ($I_0 = -I_1$)?

7-4 Power Supply Noise: A signaling system with capacitively coupled power supply noise is illustrated in Figure 7-44. Give an expression for the amount of supply noise, V_N, that appears across the termination resistor, R_T, as a function of frequency and component values. Suppose $Z_0 = R_T = 50\,\Omega$, $R_O = 1\,k\Omega$, $C_N = 5\,pF$, $L_R = 5\,nH$, and $V_N = 500\,mV$. How much signal swing is required to keep the power-supply noise less than 10% of the signal swing across the spectrum from DC to 1 GHz?

7-5 Capacitive Signaling: Consider the signaling system of Figure 7-45. A 10-pF capacitive line is pulled to V_{DD} to signal a logic 1. The line is discharged with a 1-mA, 2-ns current pulse during the first half of the clock (*Clk* high) to signal a 1 to 0 transition. The line is left floating for repeated zero bits. The receiver operates without a reference. Instead it has 50% hysteresis and compares the value on the line at the middle of a clock cycle to the value on the line at the beginning of the clock cycle. How effective is this system at rejecting the voltage noise sources shown in the figure? Why is a hysteretic receiver needed for this system? What happens to the noise margins if the hysteresis is increased or decreased?

7-6 Rise-Time Control: Consider the circuit of Figure 7-6, where Z_{RT} is a 5-nH inductor, $R_O = Z_0 = 50\,\Omega$, and $N = 4$ outputs share a return lead. What is the signal-return cross talk coefficient if the output rise time is 100 ps? What is the minimum rise time that gives a coefficient of 10% or less?

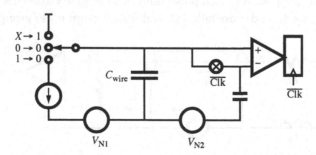

FIGURE 7-45 Capacitive Signaling with Temporal Reference (for Exercise 7-5)

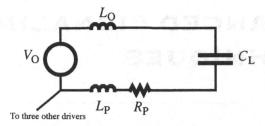

FIGURE 7-46   Lumped Output with *RL* Supply Parasitic (for Exercise 7-7)

7-7 Current-Shaping: As shown in Figure 7-46, four output drivers share a power-supply path that includes both inductive, L_P, and resistive, R_P, parasitics. Each output drives a capacitive load, C_L, through an output inductance. For parameters of $L_O = L_P = 5\,\text{nH}$, $R_P = 10\,\Omega$, and $C_L = 100\,\text{pF}$, what is the optimum current profile to switch the capacitor voltage from 1to 0 V while keeping the power supply noise less than 150 mV when all four outputs switch at once?

7-8 Multilevel Signaling: Using the noise parameters from Tables 7-4 and 7-5 for the LSC signaling system, what is the maximum number of signal levels that could be supported while maintaining proper operation under worst-case analysis? What total signal swing is required for this number of levels?

7-9 Low-Speed Signaling: A signaling system has a bit rate of only 10 bits/s and must operate over a single 10-m, 50-ohm transmission line (a transmitter reference cannot be sent along with the data). The system should dissipate as little power as possible while providing adequate margins under worst-case noise assumptions. Using the noise parameters for the LSC signaling system in Tables 7-4 and 7-5, compare the power requirements of a series-terminated voltage-mode signaling system with a pulsed, parallel-terminated, bipolar current-mode signaling system that has a pulse width of 5 ns. For the series-terminated, voltage-mode signaling system (which cannot cancel supply noise), assume the power-supply noise is 500 mV.

8 ADVANCED SIGNALING TECHNIQUES

In this chapter we continue our treatment of signaling conventions by examining several signaling techniques that are specialized for particular circumstances.

Lossy interconnect, RC or LRC, is particularly demanding on a signaling convention. RC lines have a delay that increases quadratically with length and long tails to the step response that lead to intersymbol interference. Both of these problems can be addressed by using repeaters or by overdriving the line. LRC lines have frequency-dependent attenuation that leads to intersymbol interference at high signaling rates. This frequency-dependent attenuation can be canceled by equalization, which will significantly extend the maximum signaling rate for a particular line.

The effective pin and wire density of a signaling system can be doubled by using *simultaneous bidirectional signaling* to send bits simultaneously in both directions over a single transmission line. Bits travel in one direction on the forward-traveling wave and in the other direction on the reverse-traveling wave. The line is terminated at both ends to eliminate coupling between the two bit streams. This signaling convention introduces a new noise source cross talk between the forward- and reverse-traveling waves.

For AC-coupled lines it is necessary to band-limit the signal to remove its DC components, or the resulting DC offset will degrade margins. Encoding signals using nonoverlapping codes or running-disparity codes removes the DC component of the signal and has the added benefit of limiting the maximum run length of the signal. The widely used 8b/10b code is a popular example of a running-disparity code.

A similar set of encodings can be applied spatially to restrict the Hamming weight of a group of parallel signals. Such an encoding can greatly decrease the AC return current and hence the signal-return cross talk because the return current due to rising signals is canceled by the return current due to an equal number of falling signals.

This chapter closes with a set of signaling examples that illustrate many of the points made in the last four chapters. The examples cover signaling techniques employed across a system, including on-chip logic signaling and low-voltage signaling, underterminated single-ended signaling between chips on a board, and current-mode differential signaling between boards.

8.1 SIGNALING OVER RC INTERCONNECT

On-chip metal wires over a few mm in length have a significant resistance. These wires act as distributed RC transmission lines, adding significant delay to signals and slowing edge rates. The effects are particularly pronounced on clocks and other timing critical signals.

8.1.1 Circuit Model

The circuit model for a distributed RC line is shown in Figure 8-1. As described in Section 3.3.2, the behavior of this line is described by the diffusion or heat equation

(8-1)
$$\frac{dv(x,t)}{dt} = \frac{1}{R_l C_l} \frac{d^2 v(x,t)}{dx^2}$$

where R_l and C_l are the resistance and capacitance per unit length, respectively.

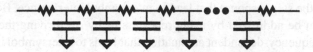

FIGURE 8-1   Distributed RC Transmission Line

For our example 0.35-μm process, minimum-width metal lines have a resistance of 0.12 Ω/μm and a total capacitance of 0.16 fF/μm, giving a time constant of 0.019 fs/μm^2. Figure 8-2 shows waveforms at each mm along a 10-mm line in this process driven by a unit step with a 200-ps rise time (shown at the top). Each waveform is plotted against a horizontal line at 50% with timing marks every 100 ps. The three vertical lines on each waveform show the points where the signal reaches 10, 50, and 90%, respectively. The last four waveforms never reach 90% in the 2 ns simulated.

The simulated delay and rise time for the eleven waveforms are listed in Table 8-1. The overall delay for the 10-mm line is about 750 ps. The slow rise time of these signals is as serious as the delay for time-critical signals, such as clocks, since a slow rise converts a small amount of voltage noise into a large amount of jitter.

Note that the time for the 5-mm portion of the 10-mm line to reach 50% is not the same as the delay for a 5-mm line but rather is significantly slower because much of the current that reaches the 5-mm point continues downstream to charge the remainder of the line.

For hand calculations the delay of an unloaded line of length d is approximately.

(8-2)
$$t_d = 0.4\, d^2 R_l C_l$$

Table 8-2 compares simulated delays for several line lengths with the value predicted by Eq. (8-2). The numbers agree to within a few percent.

The waveforms and delays discussed above are all for unloaded lines. The situation is much worse when a line must drive a heavy capacitive load in addition to the capacitance of the line as, for example, in the case of a clock line. In this case, there are three RC components to the delay, one due to the driver resistance and

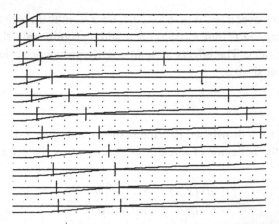

FIGURE 8-2   Waveforms for a 10-mm RC Transmission Line

TABLE 8-1 **Delay and Rise Time for Points on a 10-mm RC Line**

Distance (mm)	t_d (ps)	t_r (ps)
0	0	160
1	52	601
2	109	1112
3	201	1386
4	334	1555
5	467	1664
6	572	1729
7	650	
8	703	
9	735	
10	747	

the combined capacitance of the line and the load, one due to the line resistance and capacitance (estimated by Eq. (8-2)), and one due to the line resistance and the load capacitance.

8.1.2 Repeaters

The delay of a line can be made linear rather than quadratic with distance by breaking the line into multiple segments with repeaters between each segment, as illustrated in Figure 8-3. The figure uses a combined resistor–capacitor symbol to denote a resistive line segment with distributed capacitance.

The delay of the line with repeaters is given by

$$(8\text{-}3) \qquad t_d = \left(\frac{l}{l_s}\right)\left(t_b + 0.4 l_s^2 RC\right)$$

where the delay of a repeater is t_b, the line has length l, and each section has length l_s. The section length that minimizes delay is calculated by differentiating with

TABLE 8-2 **Simulated versus Estimated Delays of RC Lines**

Length (mm)	t_d (simulated)	t_d (Eq. (8-2))
5	199 ps	192 ps
10	747 ps	768 ps
15	1.72 ns	1.73 ns
20	3.10 ns	3.07 ns
30	6.88 ns	6.91 ns

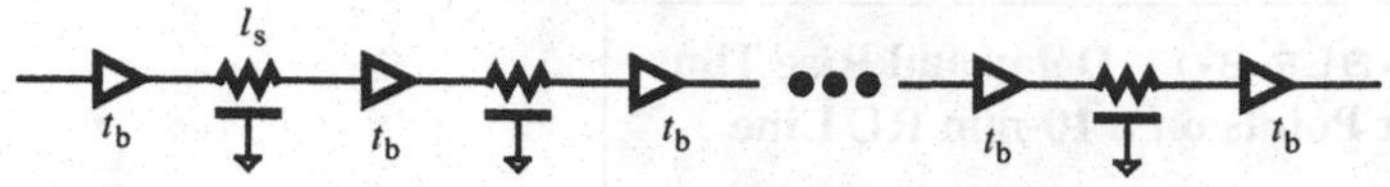

FIGURE 8-3   Inserting Repeaters into an RC Line

respect to l_s and setting the result to zero. This gives an optimal section length of

(8-4)
$$l_s = \left(\frac{t_b}{0.4RC}\right)^{1/2}$$

Not surprisingly, at this optimal section length, the wire delay exactly matches the repeater delay, giving an overall delay of $2t_b$ per section. Substituting Eq. (8-4) into Eq. (8-3) and solving for velocity gives

(8-5)
$$v = 1.3(t_b RC)^{-1/2}$$

For our typical 0.35-μm CMOS process, these equations give an optimal section length, l_s, of 3.5 mm and a velocity of 17.5 mm/ns. Inserting two repeaters at the 1/3 and 2/3 points of a 10-mm line slightly reduces the delay (from 750 to 570 ps) and significantly sharpens the rise time. For a 30-mm line, the delay improvement is more significant (from 6.9 to 1.7 ns).

Although only the longest RC lines today justify the use of repeaters, their use will become widespread in the future as line width and thickness drop and resistance per unit length increases quadratically.

8.1.3 Increasing Wire Width and Spacing

The delay of heavily loaded lines can be reduced by making the wires wider than minimum width and spacing them farther apart. This reduces the RC delay per unit length, for the resistance decreases linearly with width whereas capacitance increases more slowly because the fringing fields are not increased. Although delay remains quadratic with length, the constant factor can be reduced by about 30%.

For example, Figure 8-4 shows lines of minimum width on the left and wires that have three times the normal width on the right.[1] The horizontal component of the parasitic capacitance, $C_{h1} + C_{h2}$, remains the same, whereas the resistance decreases by a factor of three and the vertical capacitance, C_v, increases by a

TABLE 8-3   **Electrical Properties of Minimum and 3× Width Lines**

Width	R	C_h	C_v	C_{tot}	RC
0.6 μm	0.12 Ω/μm	0.06 fF/μm	0.1 fF/μm	0.16 fF/μm	0.019 fs/μm^2
1.8 μm	0.04 Ω/μm	0.06 fF/μm	0.3 fF/μm	0.36 fF/μm	0.014 fs/μm^2

---

[1] Oversized wires tend to be odd multiples of minimum width so that they use up an integral number of wiring grids plus the intervening spaces.

FIGURE 8-4   Increasing Wire Width and Spacing

factor of three. In this case, the result is a 25% decrease in RC time constant. In general, because the capacitance to adjacent wires, C_{h1}, and fringing capacitance, C_{h2}, can account for as much as half of the total capacitance, this technique can double the speed of a wire. However, this decrease in delay comes at a significant cost in power. For our example of tripling the wire width, power dissipation is increased by a factor of 2.25. Thus, this method of reducing delay tends to be much less attractive than either repeaters or overdrive.

8.1.4   Overdrive of Low-Swing RC Lines

The delay of an RC line can be reduced by using a low-voltage swing-signaling convention and overdriving the transmit end of the line with a higher-voltage pulse. In effect this technique *equalizes* the low-pass nature of the RC line by preemphasizing the high-frequency components of the signal.

Figure 8-5 shows waveforms for overdrive of two RC transmission lines. The panel on the left illustrates driving a 10-mm minimum-width line in our example 0.35-μm process. The panel on the right illustrates driving a 30-mm line in the same process. In both panels, the five traces show the voltage as a function of time at five equally spaced positions along the line. The timing marks in the left panel are spaced 100 ps apart. The right panel has a compressed scale with 300-ps timing marks.

Both lines are pulsed with five times overdrive. To realize a 300-mV signal on the far end of the line, the near end is pulsed momentarily to 1.5 V and then brought to 300 mV. As the pulse propagates down the lossy line it is attenuated by the

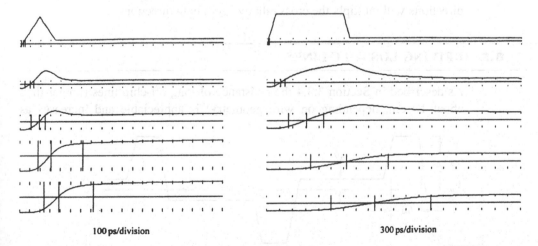

100 ps/division   300 ps/division

FIGURE 8-5   Waveforms for Overdrive of 10-mm and 30-mm RC Lines

diffusive nature of the line, resulting in no overshoot at the far end. The duration of the pulse is tailored to the length of the line to give the desired response. For the 10-mm line, a 200-ps overdrive pulse results in a delay of 350 ps as compared to 750 ps for a conventional driver. For the 30-mm line the overdrive pulse is 1.8-ns wide and results in a delay of 2.5 ns as compared with 6.9 ns for conventional drive. In practice, a closed-loop control circuit would be used to adjust the duration of the overdrive automatically.

Overdrive reduces the delay by a constant factor proportional to the amount of the overdrive; however, the delay remains quadratic. This is why the 30-mm line with repeaters outperforms the overdriven 30-mm line (1.7 ns versus 2.5 ns).

Using repeaters that overdrive line segments gives only slightly better performance than conventional receivers. Overdriving repeaters require voltage gain and hence have a larger delay than conventional repeaters. This, combined with the lower delay of an overdriven line, results in a much wider repeater spacing. Assuming a repeater delay of 200 ps, a spacing of about 7.5 mm gives a maximum velocity of about 19 mm/ns. This is not a sufficient advantage to justify the complexity of overdriving. Thus, overdrive is the method of choice for lines that are long enough for diffusive delay to be an issue but short enough that the overdriven line is faster than a line with conventional repeaters.

Bipolar signaling is required to get the advantages of overdrive for both rising and falling signals. As illustrated in Figure 8-6, this signaling is centered on a reference voltage, V_0. In the steady state, the voltage on the line is $V_0 + \Delta V$ to signal a "1" and $V_0 - \Delta V$ to signal a "0." For each positive (negative) transition on the line, the transmitter momentarily drives the line to $V_0 + k_{od}\Delta V (V_0 - k_{od}\Delta V)$, where k_{od} is the overdrive factor. The overdrive pulse has width t_{od}.

Cross talk is a major concern with overdrive signaling. The voltage swing at the transmit end of a line is k_{od} times the swing at the receive end of a line. To avoid excessive noise, it is essential to isolate the receive end of lines from high-swing signals, including the transmit ends of similar lines. Running two adjacent lines in the same direction will result in the same cross-talk coefficient as with conventional signaling. However, running two adjacent lines in opposite directions will multiply the cross talk by k_{od} in both directions.

8.2   DRIVING LOSSY LC LINES

As described in Section 3.3.4 the resistance of long off-chip lines (longer than about 10 cm, depending on wire geometry) is appreciable and increases as

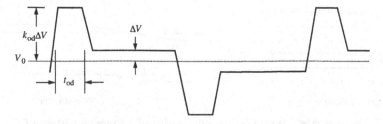

FIGURE 8-6   Bipolar Overdrive Signaling

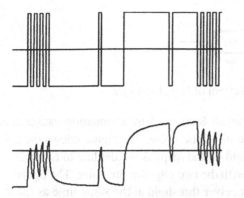

FIGURE 8-7   Response of a Lossy LC Line

the square root of signal frequency because of the skin effect. The resulting frequency-dependent attenuation results in intersymbol interference (Section 6.4) as unattenuated low-frequency signal components overwhelm the attenuated high-frequency components. This effect can be countered by equalizing the transmission line, amplifying the high-frequency components, or attenuating the low-frequency components to level the frequency response.

Figure 8-8 illustrates the problem by showing transmit and receive waveforms for a simulated lossy line (1 m of 5-mil, 0.5-oz stripguide along with package parasitics). The top trace in the figure shows the transmitted bit pattern. The lower trace shows the received waveform. The high-frequency components of the signal, both the alternating ones and zeros and the lone pulses, have been attenuated by nearly 50%, whereas the low-frequency components of the signal, the long runs of ones and zeros, are received at full amplitude. These runs shift the baseline presented to the high-frequency components. As a result, many of the high-frequency pulses barely reach the signaling threshold and are therefore undetectable.

8.2.1   The Lone Pulse

The effects of frequency-dependent attenuation are most severe in the case of a "lone" pulse, as illustrated in Figure 8-8. The figure shows how attenuation causes both a reduced eye opening and data-dependent jitter. The left side of the figure shows that a lone pulse attenuated by a factor A relative to the surrounding runs of ones or zeros results in an eye opening (the overlap of the positive- and negative-going pulses) of 1–2A. Stated differently, the effective received signal swing is reduced by *twice* the amount of the attenuation. Because of this doubling, the eye opening disappears, and the signal is undetectable, for attenuations of 50% or greater.

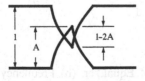
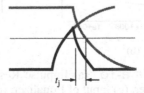

FIGURE 8-8   High-Frequency Attenuation Affects a "Lone" Pulse

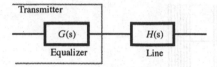

FIGURE 8-9   Block Diagram of Equalized Line

The right side of Figure 8-8 shows how attenuation causes data-dependent jitter on the trailing edge of a lone pulse. The figure shows the response of the line to a lone pulse overlaid on the response of the line to rising and falling steps (shown in gray) aligned with the two edges of the pulse. The figure shows that the rising edge crosses the receiver threshold at the same time as the step response. However, because the trailing edge starts closer to the threshold, it crosses the receive threshold, t_j, ahead of the falling step.

The reduced eye opening and data-dependent jitter caused by frequency-dependent attenuation are forms of intersymbol interference (Section 6.4). Because the line does not reach a steady state after each bit, the residual history of previous bits affects the response of the line to the current bit.

8.2.2   Equalization of LRC Lines

Frequency-dependent attenuation can be canceled by equalization. A block diagram of an equalized line is shown in Figure 8-9. An equalizing filter in the transmitter has a transfer function, $G(s)$, that approximates the inverse of the line transfer function, $H(s)$. The concatenation of the equalizer and the line thus has a transfer function $G(s)H(s)$ that approximates unity. Note that although this figure illustrates transmitter equalization (also called Tomlinson precoding), the equalizer could also have been placed in the receiver or split between the two ends.

With digital technology it is convenient to realize the equalizer as a finite-impulse response (FIR) digital filter. Figure 8-10 shows the impulse response

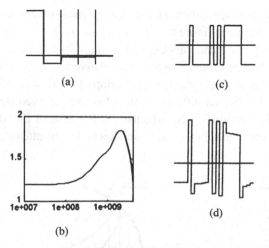

FIGURE 8-10   (a) Impulse Response of Equalizer, (b) Frequency Response of Equalizer, (c) Input of Equalizer, (d) Output of Equalizer

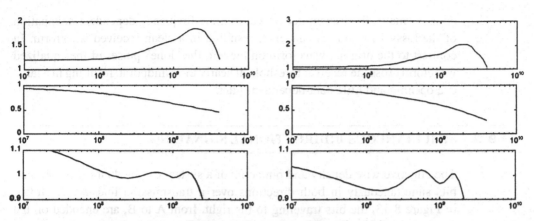

FIGURE 8-11 Frequency Response of Equalized Line

(a) and frequency response (b) of an FIR high-pass filter designed to approximate the reciprocal of the frequency response of a 1-m, 5-mil stripguide. Also shown in the figure are a digital input to the equalizer (c), and the output of the equalizer for this input (d). Note that the high-frequency components of the equalizer output are preemphasized. This precompensates for the expected attenuation of these components.

The result of equalizing two lines is illustrated in Figure 8-11. The three curves on the left correspond to a 1-m, 5-mil stripguide, and the curves on the right correspond to the same line along with a 1-pF load capacitor. In each column the top curve shows the frequency response of the equalizer, $G(s)$, the middle curve shows the frequency response of the line, $H(s)$, and the bottom curve shows the frequency response of the equalized line, $G(s)H(s)$. The scale on the bottom curves is compressed to show detail. Across the frequency band of most interest, from 100 MHz to 1 GHz, the frequency response of the equalized line is flat to within a few percent.

The effect of equalization in the time domain is illustrated in Figure 8-12. The left panel, repeated from Figure 8-7, shows the transmitter and receiver waveforms for our example 1-m stripguide without equalization. The curves on the right show the waveforms with equalization. By preemphasizing the high-frequency

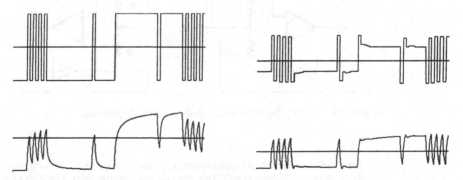

FIGURE 8-12 Transmitted (Top) and Received (Bottom) Waveforms Without Equalization (Left) and with Equalization (Right)

components of the transmitted waveform, the frequency-dependent attenuation of the lossy LRC line is canceled, resulting in a clean received waveform. In contrast to the original waveform on the left, the "lone" pulses of the equalized waveform cross the receiver threshold at nearly their midpoint, resulting in a large eye opening and little data-dependent jitter.

8.3 SIMULTANEOUS BIDIRECTIONAL SIGNALING

The effective wire density and pin count of a system can be doubled by sending bits simultaneously in both directions over a transmission line. As illustrated in Figure 8-13, the bits traveling to the right, from A to B, are encoded on the forward-traveling wave, whereas the bits traveling to the left, from B to A, are encoded on the reverse-traveling wave. The line is terminated at both ends to prevent reflection of the bits in either direction. The voltage on the line is the superposition of the forward- and reverse-traveling waves, $V_L = V_f + V_r$. At the left end of the line, transceiver A, the receiver constructs a copy of the forward-traveling wave, V_{f1}, and subtracts this copy from the line voltage to recover an estimate of the reverse-traveling wave, $\tilde{V}_r = V_L - V_{f1}$. A similar process is used to construct an estimate of the forward-traveling wave, $\tilde{V}_f$, at point B.

This technique of simultaneously sending information in both directions over a transmission line has long been used in telephony. A telephone subscriber loop sends analog voice information in both directions simultaneously over a single pair of wires. In an old telephone the forward-traveling wave is subtracted from the combined signal using an electromagnetic device, called a hybrid, that sums the flux generated by coils of wires wound in opposite directions to generate a difference signal that is converted back to an electrical potential by a third coil.[2] The hybrid converts the two-wire, simultaneous, bidirectional interface to the subscriber loop into a four-wire, unidirectional, interface to the handset.

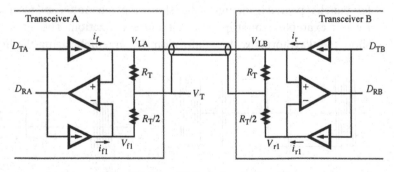

FIGURE 8-13 Simultaneous Bidirectional Signaling

---

[2] The hybrid is purposely designed to couple a small amount (−20 dB) of the forward signal into the recovered difference signal. This *sidetone* lets a person using a handset hear his or her own voice, significantly attenuated, in the speaker. This feedback permits them to adjust their volume accordingly.

8.3.1 Current-Mode Bidirectional Signaling

Figure 8-13 shows a single-ended, current-mode, bidirectional signaling system. The upper current driver at transceiver A generates a forward current, i_f, which divides equally between the terminator, R_T, and the line. The portion of forward current that enters the line causes a forward-traveling wave with amplitude $V_f = i_f Z_0 / 2$. Similarly, the upper current driver at B injects a reverse-traveling wave with amplitude $V_r = i_r Z_0 / 2$. The voltage at position x on the line is the superposition of the forward- and reverse-traveling waves

$$(8\text{-}6) \qquad V_L(t, x) = V_f \left(t - \frac{x}{v} \right) + V_r \left(t - \frac{l - x}{v} \right)$$

In particular, the voltage at the two ends of the line are

$$(8\text{-}7) \qquad \begin{aligned} V_{LA}(t) &= V_f(t) - V_r(t - l/v) \\ V_{LB}(t) &= V_r(t) - V_f(t - l/v) \end{aligned}$$

To separate the contributions of the two waves, the lower current driver at transceiver A generates a replica of the forward-traveling wave. This driver generates a current, i_{f1}, that matches the current from the top driver.[3] This current is driven into a resistance, $R_T/2$, that matches the combined line-terminator system seen by the upper driver. The result is a voltage, relative to the signal return, of $V_{f1} = i_{f1} R_T / 2$, which matches V_f to within the tolerances of current and impedance matching.

The differential amplifier subtracts the estimate of the forward-traveling wave, V_{f1}, from the combined line voltage, V_{LA}, to generate an output that to first order reflects only the reverse-traveling wave.

$$(8\text{-}8) \qquad \tilde{V}_r = V_{LA} - U_f = i_f Z_0 / 2 + i_r Z_0 / 2 - i_{f1} R_T / 2 \approx V_r$$

At first glance, simultaneous bidirectional signaling appears to have a clear two-to-one advantage over unidirectional signaling: twice as many signals transferred over the same number of wires. Things are not quite this good, however, for two reasons. First, bidirectional signaling requires that the line be terminated at both ends. Although this helps attenuate cross talk and intersymbol interference, it also doubles the transmitter power required to achieve a given signal swing.

Second, and most importantly, simultaneous bidirectional signaling introduces a new noise source, *reverse-channel cross talk*. Because of component and delay mismatches, a certain portion of the forward-traveling wave will remain in the estimate of the reverse-traveling wave, $\tilde{V}_r$. Also, the forward-traveling wave generates return current, and hence return noise, that is seen by the reverse-traveling wave. This coupling between the forward- and reverse-traveling signals, which is discussed in Section 8.3.5, makes the noise situation somewhat worse

---

[3] In practice the replica source usually generates a scaled current, $k_s i_f$, where k_s is typically 0.1, into a resistance of $R_T/2k_s$. This saves power while producing the same replica of V_f.

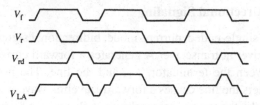

FIGURE 8-14   Simultaneous Bidirectional Signaling Waveforms

for simultaneous bidirectional signaling, particularly for attenuating lines where the transmit signal levels are significantly greater than the receive signal levels.

8.3.2   Bidirectional Signaling Waveforms

Figure 8-14 illustrates the superposition of forward- and reverse-traveling waves characteristic of simultaneous bidirectional signaling. The top two traces show the forward-traveling wave at point A, V_f, and the reverse-traveling wave at point B, V_r, respectively. The third trace shows V_{rd}, the reverse-traveling wave as received at transceiver A after having been delayed by the length of the line (1.5 bit-cells in this case). The final trace shows the voltage on the line at transceiver A, V_{LA}. This voltage is the superposition of V_f with V_{rd}.

The line voltage, V_{LA}, has three levels. When both V_f and V_{rd} are low, V_{LA} is at its minimum level, V_0. When one signal is low and the other high, V_{LA} is at its midlevel, $V_1 = V_0 + \Delta V$. When both signals are high, V_{LA} is at its maximum level, $V_2 = V_0 + 2\Delta V$.

Although the line voltage has three levels, bidirectional signaling should not be confused with multilevel signaling (Section 7.5.1). This is still binary signaling. From the point of view of the receiver, there are just two signal levels, corresponding to 0 and 1, and the detection decision is made with a single threshold. It is just that the received signal is superimposed with a predictable noise source, the output bitstream, that is canceled with a reference. Thus, bidirectional signaling retains the energy efficiency of binary signaling even though there are three signal levels on the line. The need to cancel the interfering output bitstream does, however, give rise to a component of *reverse-channel cross talk*, as described in Section 8.3.5.

8.3.3   Differential Simultaneous Bidirectional Signaling

When signaling over cables or other media with significant return impedance, it is usually more efficient to use two conductors to carry two simultaneous bidirectional signals *differentially* (Section 7.3.5) rather than to carry two single-ended signals that will generate significant amounts of signal-return cross talk.

Figure 8-15 illustrates a differential current-mode simultaneous bidirectional signaling system. The figure is similar to Figure 8-13 except that the single-ended current drivers have been replaced by current sources, and a four-input differential summing amplifier is used at each end to subtract the transmitted waveform from the line voltage. The upper current source in transceiver A generates current i_f, which in turn generates a forward-traveling wave, $V_f = i_f Z_0/2$. As with the

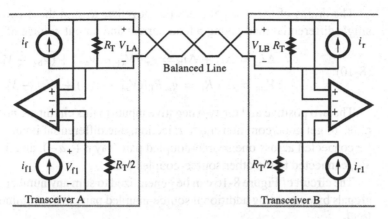

FIGURE 8-15 Differential Simultaneous Bidirectional Signaling

single-ended system, half of the transmitted power is absorbed in the source termination.[4] This forward-traveling wave is summed on the line with the reverse-traveling wave to give the line voltage, V_{LA}. The lower current source and its load resistor generate a replica, V_{f1}, of the forward-traveling wave. The four-input amplifier subtracts this differential replica from the differential line voltage to recover the reverse-traveling wave, V_r.

Unlike the single-ended system, the replica voltage, V_{f1}, and the line voltage, V_{LA}, are differential, viz. they do not share a common reference. Thus they cannot be directly compared with a two-input amplifier, or small differences in their common-mode voltage would corrupt the signal.

Two differential voltages are subtracted using a four-input differential summing amplifier, as illustrated in Figure 8-16. The circuit uses two source-coupled differential pairs. Each pair converts a differential voltage into a differential current. The difference in current flowing through the two transistors of the two pairs is described by

(8-9)
$$\Delta i_a = g_m \Delta V_a = g_m(V_{a+} - V_{a-})$$
$$\Delta i_b = g_m \Delta V_b = g_m(V_{b+} - V_{b-})$$

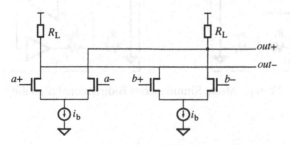

FIGURE 8-16 Four-Input Differential Amplifier

[4] In practice, each of the four resistors in the figure would have center taps tied to a common-mode voltage.

The drains of the two pairs are tied together to sum these two currents in a single differential load giving a load current and output voltage of

$$\Delta i_L = \Delta i_a + \Delta i_b = g_m[(V_{a+} - V_{a-}) + (V_{b+} - V_{b-})]$$

(8-10)

$$\Delta V_{out} = \Delta i_L R_L = g_m R_L[(V_{a+} - V_{a-}) + (V_{b+} - V_{b-})]$$

The two positive and the two negative inputs in this circuit are *not* interchangeable. To get good common-mode rejection, one differential input, say V_{LA}, must be connected across one source-coupled pair (say $a+, a-$), and the other input, V_{f1}, connected to the other source-coupled pair.

The circuit of Figure 8-16 can be generalized to sum any number of differential signals by connecting additional source-coupled pairs to the common differential load.

Differential simultaneous bidirectional signaling requires fewer pins than unidirectional single-ended signaling, because fewer signal returns are needed, and largely eliminates signal-return cross talk because the currents in both directions are balanced. The only downside is the introduction of reverse-channel cross talk as described in Section 8.3.5.

8.3.4   Voltage-Mode Simultaneous Bidirectional Signaling

A voltage-mode simultaneous bidirectional signaling system is illustrated in Figure 8-17. Transceiver A uses a voltage-mode driver[5] to generate forward signal V_{fx}, this signal is coupled to the transmission line using a series termination, R_T, which halves the magnitude of the transmitted wave, $V_f = V_{fx}/2$. A replica voltage-mode driver, V_{fx1}, along with a resistive voltage-divider[6] generates an estimate of this voltage, V_{f1}. As in Section 8.3.1, the differentialamplifier subtracts

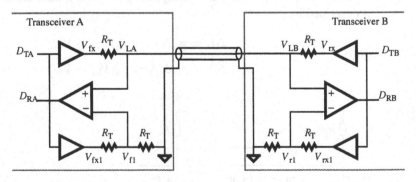

FIGURE 8-17   Voltage-Mode Simultaneous Bidirectional Signaling

---

[5] In practice the source termination is folded into the driver to obviate the need for a very low-impedance output driver.

[6] A resistor much larger than R_T is typically used in the divider to reduce power dissipation. However, the resistor must be kept small enough to prevent large time constants on the negative input to the amplifier.

the estimated forward wave from the line voltage to recover the reverse-traveling signal.

Bidirectional voltage-mode signaling inherits all of the disadvantages of unidirectional voltage-mode signaling described in Section 7.3.1.2. It does a poor job of isolating signals from power supply noise and attenuating signal-return cross talk. In addition to these problems, bidirectional voltage-mode signaling also suffers from a return ground loop. Unless the voltage-mode drivers are floating, which is difficult to implement, the signal return must be tied to a reference supply at both ends of the line, making it an alternate current path for that supply. In contrast, the return is tied to a termination voltage, V_T, at only one end of the line in the current-mode system shown in Figure 8-13. For all of these reasons, current-mode bidirectional signaling should be used unless there is some compelling reason to use voltage mode.

8.3.5 Reverse-Channel Cross Talk

Simultaneous bidirectional signaling introduces *reverse-channel cross talk*, a proportional noise source that reflects coupling between the two channels that share a conductor. This coupling occurs due to

1. Incomplete cancellation of the forward signal owing to mismatch between the replica forward voltage, V_{f1}, and the actual forward voltage, V_f. This mismatch usually involves both amplitude and delay, causing this component to peak during signal transitions.
2. Termination mismatch, and other transmission line imperfections, that cause a portion of the forward signal to reflect off of the far end of the line and combine with the reverse signal.
3. Voltage induced across the return impedance shared between the transmitter and receiver. Even with a current-mode transmitter, voltage induced by the received signal is coupled into the transmitted signal via the termination resistor.

The first two sources of reverse-channel cross talk are dealt with using conventional measures. Incomplete cancellation is minimized by careful matching of components. Reflection of the forward wave is minimized by digitally trimming the termination resistors (Section 11.1).

Reverse-channel cross talk due to the return impedance can be significantly reduced by splitting the signal return into *clean* and *dirty* paths, as illustrated in Figure 8-18. The figure uses differential current drivers (Section 11.2.3) that supply a constant DC current but provide a differential current over their two outputs. For example, assuming a zero DC current, the top current driver sources i_f over its top (bottom) output and sinks i_f into its bottom (top) input when transmitting a logic 1 (0). To balance the driver, the two outputs must drive identical impedances, $R_T/2$ for the top driver and a scaled $R_T/2k_s$ for the bottom driver. The $R_T/2$ load for the bottom output of the top driver is split into two loads of value, R_T, one each connected to the clean and dirty returns. This arrangement

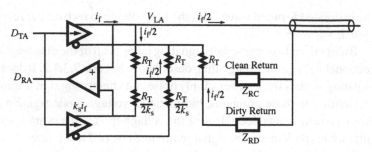

FIGURE 8-18   Splitting Signal Return into Clean and Dirty Paths

gives zero AC current across the clean return impedance, Z_{RC}, for the components from the top and bottom outputs of each driver exactly cancel. All of the $i_f/2$ transmitter return-current flows through the dirty return path.

Unfortunately, isolating the transmitter current to the dirty return path in this manner does not completely eliminate the return component of reverse-channel cross talk. It only halves the cross talk. The derivation of this result and an improved method are left as an exercise.

8.4   AC AND N OF M BALANCED SIGNALING

Signals that are AC-coupled via capacitor or transformer (Section 3.4.4.1), must be band-limited to remove the DC component of the signal. From the digital perspective, such a *DC-balanced* signal has an equal number of ones and zeros over a period of time corresponding to the longest wavelength in the passband of the transmission system. A related constraint arises in signals that use closed-loop timing (Section 9.6). These signals require a minimum frequency of transitions, to provide input to a timing loop. The transition frequency constraint is equivalent to restricting the maximum run length of repeated symbols. A band-limited signal necessarily has a maximum run length that is related to its lowest-frequency components. However, the converse is not true. A run-length-limited signal need not be DC-balanced.

8.4.1   Terminology

Before introducing some codes used to DC balance signals we must first introduce the nomenclature we will use to describe these codes.

8.4.1.1   DC Offset

The DC level of an AC-coupled signal depends on the duty factor, f_d, of the signal, as illustrated in Figure 8-19. The blocking capacitor and bias resistor in the figure will cause the DC component of the received voltage to be equal to the bias voltage, V_{bias}, which is usually also the receive threshold. A signal with a duty factor of f_d has a DC component of $(1 - f_d)V_0 + f_d V_1$. Hence, the bias

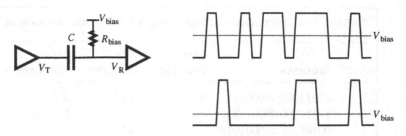

FIGURE 8-19   An AC-Coupled Signal with a Nonzero DC Component Causes an Offset in the DC Level of the Received Signal

voltage and receive threshold will settle to a level f_d of the way between V_0 and V_1. An AC signal, with equal numbers of ones and zeros, as illustrated in the upper waveform, has a 50% duty factor that centers the bias voltage on the signal swing. A signal with a 25% duty factor (three zeros for each 1), shown in the lower waveform, drifts upward so that the bias voltage is one quarter of the signal swing above V_0. If the duty factor changes, the signal level shifts to track the changes with a time constant $\tau_{bias} = R_{bias}C$. For any duty factor other than 50%, the shift of DC signal level results in a large offset of the signal relative to the receiver threshold and a serious decrease in noise immunity.

In the system of Figure 8-19, it is not sufficient for the signal to be DC-balanced. The signal must be band-limited to frequencies well above $f_{bias} = 1/\tau_{bias}$, or low-frequency components of the signal will cause drift in the receiver offset.

8.4.1.2   Run Length

The maximum (minimum) *run length* of a signal is the maximum (minimum) number of ones or zeros that may appear in sequence. Maximum run length is usually restricted in systems employing closed-loop timing, because it directly relates to the maximum amount of time between transitions that carry timing information. Minimum run length is of interest in systems with large amounts of intersymbol interference[7] because it specifies the minimum distance between transitions. Most signaling systems use a minimum run length of 1.

Limiting the maximum run length of a signal to r_{max} guarantees that the signal will have some frequency components above $f_r = 1/(2r_{max})$. However, it does not eliminate frequency components below this point. A run-length-limited signal may have a large DC component. The method of *bit-stuffing* to limit run length is discussed in Section 9.4.2.2.

A code that has a maximum run length of r_{max} and a minimum run length of r_{min} is often referred to as an $(r_{min} - 1, r_{max} - 1)$ code. For example, the 8b/10b code discussed below in Section 8.4.2.5 is considered a (0,4) code, for it has a minimum run length of 1 and a maximum run length of 5.

---

[7] High-density digital magnetic recording systems, for example, typically use codes with a minimum run length greater than unity.

TABLE 8-4   Disparity and Run Length for Example Sequences

No.	Sequence	Max Disparity	Min Disparity	Max Run Length
1	11011000 01000111	+3	−3	4
2	11110000 00001111	+4	−4	8
3	00101110 11000101	+2	−2	3

8.4.1.3   Disparity or Digital-Sum Variation (DSV)

The *disparity*, $D(a)$, of a sequence of bits, $a_0 \dots a_{n-1}$, is the number of zeros in the sequence subtracted from the number of ones.

$$(8\text{-}11) \qquad D(a) = -n + 2\sum_{i=0}^{n-1} a_i$$

The *digital-sum variation (DSV)* of a sequence is the maximum variation in disparity over prefixes of the sequence. For an arbitrary-length sequence, a constant DSV implies a DC-balanced signal, and the magnitude of the DSV is roughly half the period of the lowest frequency component in the signal. The bandwidth of an encoding scheme is often specified in terms of its DSV. A signal with a constant DSV is both DC-balanced and run-length-limited and has a maximum run length equal to the DSV.

Table 8-4 shows examples of three 16-bit sequences and tabulates their maximum disparity, minimum disparity, and run length. All three of these sequences are DC-balanced over their 16-bit length but differ considerably in their run length and DSV.

8.4.2   Codes for DC-Balancing Signals

8.4.2.1   Nonoverlapping Block Codes

A simple method of DC-balancing a signal is to take a block of n bits and encode it as a block of m bits with equal numbers of ones and zeros. Such a code will exist as long as the number of zero-disparity blocks of length m is greater than the number of blocks of length n.

$$(8\text{-}12) \qquad \binom{m}{m/2} > 2^n$$

The number of bits, m, required to encode blocks of length n is shown in Table 8-5 for several popular values of n. Each row of the table corresponds to an input block size that is a power of 2 and shows the number of bits, m, required to encode all 2^n input symbols with zero disparity, the number of resulting output symbols $N_O = \binom{m}{m/2}$, the number of extra symbols, $N_O - 2^n$, and the efficiency of the code, m/n. The simplest code, with $n = 1$ and $m = 2$, involves

TABLE 8-5 **Properties of Nonoverlapping DC-Balanced Block Codes**

n	m	$\binom{m}{m/2}$	Extra	n/m
1	2	2	0	0.50
2	4	6	2	0.50
4	6	20	4	0.67
8	12	924	668	0.67
16	20	1.8×10^5	1.2×10^5	0.80
32	36	9.1×10^9	4.8×10^9	0.89

just transmitting a bit and its complement and has efficiency 0.5. Given a block size of 32, the efficiency is almost 90%. The extra symbols that are available for all codes with $n > 1$ are useful for sending out-of-band control information over the transmission channel.

Although the codes shown in Table 8-5 achieve DC balance with reasonable efficiency, they have two problems. First, for large block sizes they are very difficult to implement unless a systematic encoding can be found.[8] Also, more efficient codes can easily be realized if we allow the present code word to depend on more than the current input word.

8.4.2.2 Running-Disparity Encoding

A simple method of encoding for DC balance is illustrated in Figure 8-20. The input is coded in n-bit blocks but uses a disparity accumulator to allow nonzero disparity in a given block. For each input block the circuit compares the sign of the disparity of this block, D_b, with the sign of the accumulated disparity on the line, D_a. If the signs are equal, signal *comp* is asserted to complement the block. If the disparity of the current block is zero, the *comp* bit is set if the running disparity is negative and cleared otherwise. This last rule acts to make the contribution of the *comp* bit on the running sum always act in the right direction in the case of a tie.

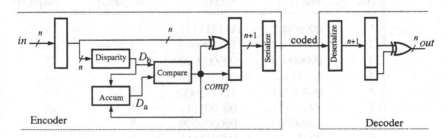

FIGURE 8-20 Running-Disparity Encoder–Decoder

----

[8] Look-up tables with 2^{32} 36-bit entries are rather costly.

The possibly complemented block and the *comp* signal form an $n + 1$-bit code-word block that is serialized and transmitted over the line. Each cycle the disparity of the code-word block is added to the accumulator to update the running disparity. The decoder deserializes each code-word block and uses the complement bit to complement the data bit recovering the original data selectively.

The running-disparity encoder DC-balances the line by closing a feedback loop on disparity. By choosing whether or not to complement each block, the encoder always guarantees that the disparity of a code-word block has a sign that is opposite that of the running disparity on the line and thus tends to force the line back to a zero disparity.

Over time, the running sum of disparity on the line will vary from a minimum of $-3n/2$ to a maximum of $+3n/2$ for a DSV of $3n$. The disparity contribution of a single block (with *comp* bit) is in the range $[-(n+1), (n+1)]$. Because the coder always makes the contribution of a block act in the direction opposite the running sum, the running disparity at the end of each block will be in the range $[-n, +n]$. The worst case occurs when a block ends at one end of this range and the next block (with *comp* bit) goes $n/2$ in the same direction before going $n/2 + 1$ in the opposite direction. Thus, at an arbitrary bit position, disparity is in the range $[-3n/2, 3n/2]$, giving a DSV of $3n$.

The maximum run length of the running-disparity encoder is $2(n + 1)$. The worst case starts with a block that reaches a peak disparity value. Suppose WLOG this is a positive peak. Then this block leaves the disparity at $n - 1$ and ends with $n/2 + 1$ zeros. If the next block has $n + 1$ repeated symbols in the same direction, the disparity is left at -2. The following block must have positive disparity but can begin with $n/2$ zeros. The result is a combined run of $2(n + 1)$ symbols.

A sequence that exhibits both maximum DSV and maximum run length for $n = 8$ is shown in Table 8-6. A plot showing running disparity as a function of bit position for this sequence is shown in Figure 8-21. The vertical grid lines

TABLE 8-6   Worst-Case Sequence for Running-Disparity Code

No.	Data Word	Code Word	Block Disparity	Running Disparity
1	00000000	111111111	+9	+8
2	00011111	111100000	−1	+7
3	00000000	000000000	−9	−2
4	00011111	000011111	+1	−1
5	00000111	111111000	+3	+2
6	00001111	000001111	−1	+1
7	00000000	000000000	−9	−8
8	00011111	000011111	+1	−7
9	00000000	111111111	+9	+2
10	00011111	111100000	−1	+1

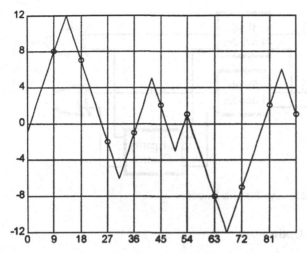

FIGURE 8-21 Running Disparity for Worst-Case Sequence

denote the end of each code word, and the disparity at the end of each code word is denoted by a circle. The sequence begins with a disparity of -1. With a negative running disparity, the first data word of all zeros is complemented to all ones, giving a block disparity of $+9$ and a running disparity of $+8$. The second data word is complemented to give a block disparity of -1 but starts with four ones, reaching the peak positive disparity of $+12$. This code word also starts the maximum-length run of 18 zeros that extends through the first four bits of code word 4. The next two code words, 5 and 6, reposition the running disparity to $+1$ to start a sequence, code words 7 through 10, that demonstrate the peak negative disparity and a maximum-length run of ones.

8.4.2.3 Framing

To decode the output of the running-disparity encoder correctly, the decoder must be synchronized to a 9-bit *frame* so that it can determine which bit to use as the complement bit in the decoding process. Similarly, to decode a nonoverlapping block code, the decoder must determine the start and end of each block. This framing is accomplished by transmitting a known synchronization pattern on the line during reset and idle periods. Ideally, this synchronization pattern, sometimes called a *comma*, should be distinct not only from every data word but also from every shift of two adjacent data words. This can be accomplished, for example, by using a comma sequence with a longer run length than any data word.

8.4.2.4 Burst-Error Length

The *burst-error length* of a code is the number of decoded data bits that can be corrupted by a single code-bit error. For example, the burst-error length of the running disparity code is 8 bits, for a single-bit error in the complement bit can cause an entire block of 8 bits to be decoded in error.

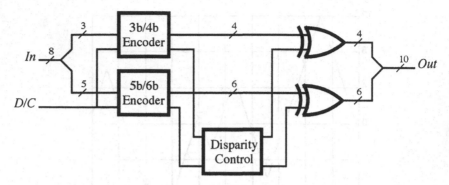

FIGURE 8-22   An 8b/10b Encoder

8.4.2.5 The 8b/10b Code

One of the most popular DC-balanced codes in use today is the 8b/10b code originally developed by IBM [WidmFran83] This code encodes 8-bit data words into 10-bit code words in a manner that gives a maximum run length of 5, a maximum DSV of 6, and a burst-error length of 5. The code includes out-of-band symbols for framing and control purposes.

As illustrated in Figure 8-22, the coder operates by partitioning each 8-bit input block into a 5-bit subfield and a 3-bit subfield, separately coding these with 5b/6b and 3b/4b coders and selectively complementing the output of each of these coders to control disparity. The 3b/4b coder emits an output code word with a disparity of either 0 or -2 (viz. there are either two zeros and two ones or three zeros and one 1). This gives ten possible code words, six with zero disparity[9] and four with disparity -2. For the 5b/6b coder there are twenty possible zero-disparity code words and fifteen possible code words with disparity -2.[10] The two coders select among their 9×33 possible outputs based both on the 8-bit input symbol and on the data/control, D/C, line that selects between normal data symbols and special out-of-band control symbols.

Of the 297 possible symbols, 256 are used for data and 12 for control. The remainder are unused. Of the twelve control symbols, three can be used as *commas* (viz. they are not equal to any data symbol or any shift of a pair of concatenated data symbols).

The disparity control block in Figure 8-22 selectively complements the outputs of the sub-block encoders to keep the running disparity in the range $[-3,3]$. It operates in a manner similar to that of the running-disparity encoder described in Section 8.4.2.2. At the end of each sub-block, the running disparity will be either

---

[9] The 3b/4b coder uses only five of the six zero-disparity code words. The code words 0011 and 1100 are used to represent the same data word. One or the other is selected, depending on the output of the 5b/6b coder to reduce both the maximum run length and the maximum DSV.

[10] In a similar manner, the 5b/6b coder uses only 19 of the 20 possible zero-disparity code words. In this case, code words 111000 and 000111 are used to represent the same data word, and the selection is made depending on the last bit of the previous code word to limit run length. Also, the 5b/6b coder uses only 14 of the 15 possible disparity -2 code words.

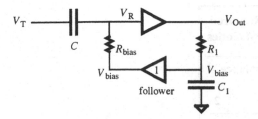

FIGURE 8-23   Simple DC Restoration

−1 or 1. The next sub-block is complemented if it has a nonzero disparity with the same sign as the running disparity. Recall that all sub-blocks have a disparity of −2 or 0. After the disparity control, the result of a block with nonzero disparity is to toggle the running disparity between −1 and 1. Of course a block with zero disparity leaves the running disparity unchanged.[11]

8.4.2.6   DC Restoration

DC restoration is an alternative to using DC-balanced coding that deserves mention. Instead of eliminating the DC offset by removing the DC component of the signal, DC restoration compensates for the offset by shifting the bias voltage or the receive threshold.

A simple form of DC restoration is illustrated in Figure 8-23. This circuit generates the bias voltage, V_{bias}, by low-passing the receiver output, V_{Out}, with an RC filter with time constant $\tau_1 = R_1 C_1$. For proper operation the filter must respond faster than the DC level drifts, and thus $\tau_1 < \tau_{bias}$. A voltage follower provides isolation between the RC filter and the bias resistor. The RC filter measures the duty factor of the received signal and adjusts the bias voltage accordingly to prevent any drift in the DC signal level. After a long string of zeros, for example, V_{bias}, will be near V_0 and thus will keep node V_R from drifting up. To avoid hysteresis, R_{bias} should be made large.

8.4.3   Spatial N of M Balanced Signaling

DC-balanced encodings can be used spatially as well as temporally. Applied across a group of signals, a balanced or nearly balanced code greatly reduces the variation in return current. This in turn reduces the signal-return cross talk (Section 6.3.3) and hence the number of required signal pins. For example, suppose an 8-bit signal group was encoded with 12 bits in a manner such that the Hamming weight of each code word was exactly 6. When switching between two equal-weight code words, the number of 1-to-0 transitions equals the number of 0-to-1 transitions. If the current draw and transition times of all of the signals are matched, the current increase from the rising transitions would exactly cancel the current decrease from the falling transitions, and such an arrangement would have only DC return current. Although exact matching is difficult to achieve in practice, the AC return

---

[11] The disparity control also acts to complement the sequences 111000 and 1100, to cause their first bit to be the complement of the last bit of the previous sub-block.

TABLE 8-7   Bits Required for Partially Balanced Codes

Data Bits	Amount of Imbalance, d		
	0	1	2
4	6	5	5
8	11	10	9
12	15	14	13
16	19	18	17

current is still far less than the unencoded case where all eight signals may switch simultaneously in the same direction.

8.4.3.1   Coding Efficiency

The number of m-bit code words with Hamming weights differing by at most d is given by

$$(8\text{-}13) \qquad |C(d,m)| = \begin{cases} \displaystyle\sum_{i=\frac{m}{2}-\frac{d}{2}}^{\frac{m}{2}+\frac{d}{2}} \binom{m}{i} & \text{if } m \text{ even} \\[4ex] \displaystyle\sum_{i=\frac{m-1}{2}-\frac{d-1}{2}}^{\frac{m+1}{2}+\frac{d-1}{2}} \binom{m}{i} & \text{if } m \text{ odd} \end{cases}$$

Using this equation, one can solve for the minimum number of bits, m, required to represent 2^n symbols with Hamming weights differing by at most d. Table 8-7 tabulates the number of bits required to represent data words of several lengths with values of d ranging from 0 to 2. For $d = 0$, the codes are *equal-weight* with equal numbers of ones and zeros in each code word. These codes are not necessarily DC-balanced. Several have odd-length code words that always have a disparity of ± 1. The table shows that one can code typical data lengths into an equal-weight code with an overhead of 2 or 3 bits.

Greater efficiency can be achieved by allowing some degree of imbalance in the code. All of the data lengths shown can be encoded with a single-bit overhead by allowing a maximum imbalance of 2 bits. For an odd-length code, the number of code words doubles when an imbalance of 1 is allowed. This allows a length-5 code, for example, to represent 20 symbols, 10 with weight 2 and 10 with weight 3, which are more than enough to represent the 16 symbols of a 4-bit data word.

8.4.3.2   Systematic Encoding

For short data lengths the data words can be encoded using small ROM lookup tables or combinational logic. For larger code words, however, brute-force encoders and decoders become prohibitively expensive. A systematic encoder algorithmically encodes the data words, giving a much simpler encoder and decoder at the expense of some efficiency. One approach to systematic encoding is to use a variant of the running-disparity encoder of Section 8.4.2.2. Very short block lengths are usually required, however, because the disparity must fall in a very narrow range at the end of each word.

8.5 EXAMPLES

In this section we illustrate many of the signaling concepts introduced in the last two chapters by examining examples of signaling conventions used in a typical digital system. Figure 8-24 is a caricature of our example system. It illustrates a chip, connections between chips on the same PC board, and connections between PC boards.

Three types of signaling are used on chip. Full-swing voltage-mode signaling is used between nearby static CMOS logic gates. Such logic gates require full-swing signals to operate. Over short distances it is more efficient to use logic signaling than to incur the delay and power overhead of conversion in a driver and receiver. When the power and delay of driving the line dominates the logic, conversion to and from a more efficient signaling convention is justified. A typical SRAM uses precharged, pulsed, differential signaling to quickly drive high-capacitance bit lines with low-current drive from the bit cells. Our example also includes a long on-chip bus that operates pseudodifferentially using precharged pulsed signaling.

Off-chip, our example uses underterminated pseudodifferential signaling between chips on a board and current-mode differential signaling across cables between boards. The on-board transmission lines employ return planes that provide very low return impedance. Hence, they can employ single-ended signaling

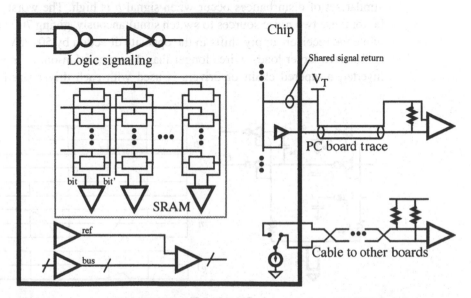

FIGURE 8-24   Signaling Conventions Employed in a Typical Digital System

without excessive signal-return cross talk. The off-board cables, on the other hand, are balanced (or symmetric) transmission lines and must employ differential signaling to eliminate the AC component of return current and the resulting large drops across the signal return.

8.5.1 Logic Signaling

Figure 8-25 illustrates several of the issues involved with a typical logic signaling arrangement. The figure shows inverter B driving signal b to inverter C over 1 mm of wire that is modeled as a capacitor $C_b = 100$ fF to ground and a capacitor $C_{be} = 60$ fF to two adjacent lines collectively denoted by signal e in the figure. The load of inverter C (10 μm/5 μm) adds an additional 75 fF. Thus, the switching energy for $V_{dd} = 2.5$ V is $E_{sw} = 1.5$ pJ. About 2/3 of this energy is used to drive the wire. The remaining 1/3 is used to drive gate C. The real power used in driving wires is a much larger fraction than 2/3, however. Gate C would be sized five times smaller if it did not need to drive a substantial load on signal c. Taking this sizing into account, the fraction of power used in signaling is well over 90%.

Gates E and H in Figure 8-25 are used to model the noise sources most important to logic signaling, capacitive cross talk, and IR power supply noise. The waveforms of these noise sources and their effect on signal b are illustrated in the waveforms on the right side of the figure. Each waveform is shown on a 2.5-V scale with vertical markers spaced on 1-ns intervals. When signal e switches high, capacitive coupling with line b causes b to momentarily rise by about 200 mV. Just as b is recovered from this disturbance, signal h falls. The large current drawn by driver H, a 200-μm/100-μm inverter driving 4 pF that is intended to represent many gates switching simultaneously, causes a 500-mV drop across the 20-ohm ground distribution resistor, R_{ga}, to the point in common with the receiver. A similar set of disturbances occur when signal b is high. The worst case would be for these two noise sources to switch simultaneously, giving 700 mV of noise while the receiver supply shifts in the opposite direction by 500 mV.

To drive larger loads, wires longer than 1 mm or a fan-out of more than one inverter, a tapered chain of drivers is used with each driver sized a constant

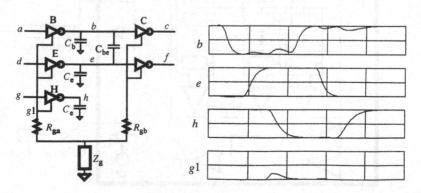

FIGURE 8-25   Logic Signaling Example

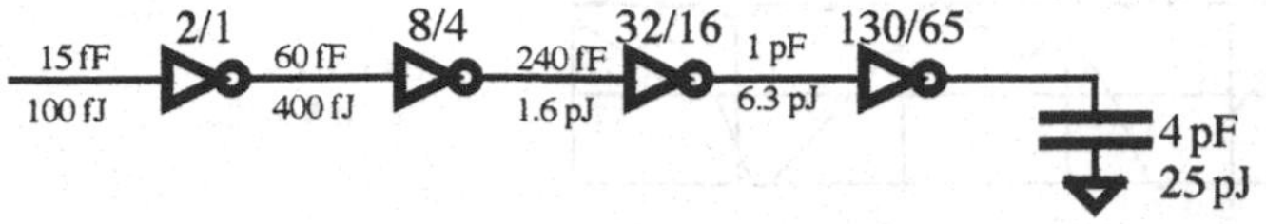

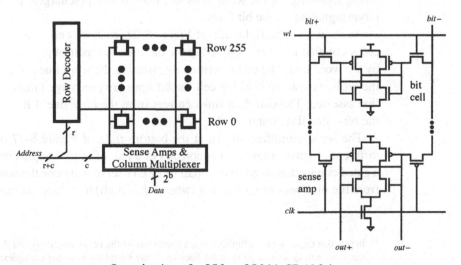

FIGURE 8-26   Using an Exponential Horn to Drive a Large Load

(typically 3 to 5) times the size of the previous driver. To drive a 4-pF load starting with a 2-μm/1-μm inverter, for example, requires four stages of drivers. The switching energy increases from 100 fJ at the input of the small inverter to 25 pJ at the load. For a transition time of 200 ps, the current required by the final stage is at least 50 mA. The driver delay is considerable, the area consumed by the driver is large, the energy consumed is excessive, and the current will cause both noise and possibly metal migration problems. Loads of this size benefit greatly from a more efficient signaling convention.

8.5.2   SRAM Bit Lines

The operation of SRAM bit lines during a memory read operation gives a good example of efficient signaling into a capacitive load. Figure 8-27 shows the organization of a typical SRAM array (left) and the circuit design of a bit cell and sense amplifier (right). Waveforms for the bit lines and outputs during a read operation are shown in Figure 8-28. The memory is organized as an array of 256×256 bit cells for a total of 64 Kbits or 8 KBytes. The address is divided into an $r = 8$ bit-row address and a $c = 8 - b$ bit-column address. The row address is decoded by the row decoder to drive the word line associated with one of the 256 rows. The selected word line enables a row of bit cells to drive the 256 pairs of differential bit lines with a differential current that reflects the contents of each cell. After a short time, the differential voltage that has developed on the bit lines is sensed by the sense amplifier. The column address is used by the column decoder to select

FIGURE 8-27   Organization of a 256- × 256-bit SRAM Array

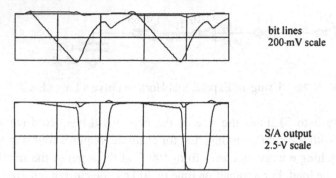

bit lines
200-mV scale

S/A output
2.5-V scale

FIGURE 8-28   Waveforms for SRAM Read Operation

one 2^b-bit output word from the 256 bits (2^{8-b} words) on the outputs of the sense amplifiers.[12]

Each word line drives 256 bit cells, giving a capacitance of about 2 pF. Each bit line has a fan-in of 256, giving a capacitance of about 1 pF mostly from the junction capacitance of the drains of the pass gates connected to the bit line. Although both lines have high capacitance, the bit line is the more difficult signaling problem. Each word line is driven from a single point, and thus a large driver can be employed. The high fan-out of the word lines also makes the use of a signaling convention that requires a complex receiver undesirable. The bit lines, in contrast, are driven from each bit cell, making the use of large drivers impractical. Not only would the area be prohibitive, but the output capacitance of each driver would increase the bit-line capacitance enormously making the problem insoluble. The bit lines are also received as only a single point, making a complex receiver acceptable. From a power perspective, only one word line is activated per cycle, making the power dissipation of a full-swing line acceptable. In contrast, 512 bit lines are activated each cycle, making the power dissipation of full-swing operation unacceptable. For these reasons, a typical RAM uses full-swing signaling for the word lines and low-voltage precharged, pulsed, current-mode signaling on the bit lines.

As shown on the right side of Figure 8-27, each bit cell consists of a pair of cross-coupled inverters coupled to the bit lines by a pair of pass gates controlled by the word line. The cell is written by asserting the word line and pulling one of the bit lines low. To read the cell the bit lines are precharged high and the word line asserted. The cell then sinks current from the *bit+* line if it contains a 0 or the *bit−* line if it contains a 1.

The sense amplifier, shown at the bottom right of Figure 8-27 is a clocked, differential sense amplifier that consists of a pair of cross-coupled inverters with a gated connection to ground. A pair of PFETs serve to isolate the sense amplifier from the bit lines during sensing (when *clk* is high) to reduce the capacitance on

---

[12] In practice the column multiplexer often comes before the sense amplifiers and shares one sense amplifier across several pairs of bit lines or it may be split with some multiplexing before and some multiplexing after the sense amplifiers.

the sense nodes. When *clk* is low, the voltage on the bit lines is coupled to the sense nodes, *out+* and *out−*. To sense, *clk* is raised, isolating the sense nodes from the bit lines and supplying current to the cross-coupled inverters. The inverters act as a regenerative amplifier (Section 4.3.7) to boost the small differential voltage across the sense nodes to full-swing.

Figure 8-28 shows the waveforms on the bit lines and the sense nodes during two successive read operations. Note that the bit lines are shown on a 200-mV scale, whereas the sense nodes are shown on a 2.5-V scale. The vertical grid lines are spaced 1-ns apart. The sequence begins with the bit lines precharged high (to 2.5 V). When a word line is asserted, the positive bit line begins to discharge. The straight-line nature of this discharge indicates that the bit-cell is acting as a current sink, and the slope indicates the current is about 200 μA. During this period the sense nodes (lower trace) also diverge by 200 mV because they are coupled to the bit lines. After 1 ns, the line has discharged by 200 mV, and the sense clock is asserted. The amplifier boosts the 200-mV signal to 2.5 V, a gain of 12.5 in about 100 ps. About 200 ps is required to give the gain of 125 required for 20-mV sensitivity. While the sensing takes place, precharge of the bit lines is started. When the sense clock goes low, the sense amplifier is reconnected to the bit lines, precharging the sense amplifier and causing a small dip in the bit-line voltage. With this arrangement the output of the sense amplifier is only valid when the sense clock is high; however it is easy to capture this state in an RS flip-flop (cross-coupled NAND gates).

The pulsed differential signaling technique employed by the SRAM drives a bit over a pair of 1-pF differential bit lines with a switching energy of 40 fJ, supply energy of 0.7 pJ, and a peak current of 200 μA (per bit). These numbers are over two orders of magnitude better than using logic signaling to drive the same load.

The SRAM signaling convention provides good noise immunity through differential, current-mode operation. Because the bit cell drives the bit line as a current source, bit-cell ground noise is isolated from the bit lines. Cross talk that is coupled equally to both the *bit+* and *bit−* lines (e.g., from signals that cross the array perpendicularly to the bit lines) is canceled by the common-mode rejection of the differential sense amplifier. Any cross talk from a full-swing signal that is coupled preferentially into one bit line, however, is a serious problem. Only a small disturbance is needed to corrupt the low-voltage signals. For this reason routing signals over RAM arrays in a direction parallel to the bit lines is usually prohibited. By isolating the signal from the noisy power supplies and making sure that any cross talk with full-swing signals is common-mode, signaling at 200-mV levels can be performed with as good or better noise immunity as full-swing logic signaling.

8.5.3 Signaling Over Long On-Chip Wires

The advantages of low-voltage signaling can be achieved without doubling the number of wires required by operating pseudodifferentially with a transmitter-generated reference voltage shared by a number of signals (typically 4 or 8).

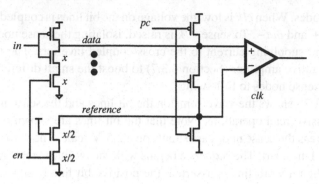

FIGURE 8-29 On-Chip, Single-Ended, Low-Voltage Signaling with a Transmitter-Generated Reference

Here the reference is generated by a half-strength driver that generates a voltage intermediate between a 1 (no discharge) and a 0 (normal discharge). To achieve the same effective signal swing as the differential signaling used by the SRAM we must swing each line twice as far (400 mV) using four times the switching energy. Pseudodifferential signals are more susceptible to noise for two reasons. First, mismatch between the reference driver and normal drivers generates a reference offset noise that is not present with differential signaling. More importantly, cross talk is a more significant problem because it is difficult to route all of the signals associated with a single reference so that cross talk with any signal is common-mode across the entire group, including the reference.

Figure 8-29 illustrates such a single-ended, low-voltage, on-chip signaling system using a transmitter-generated reference. The data and reference lines are initially precharged to a common voltage. When the enable signal, *en*, is pulsed high, the data line is then selectively discharged by a current-mode driver of size *x*. At the same time, the reference signal is discharged by a half-sized current-mode driver. Thus, at the end of the enable pulse, the reference signal takes on a voltage that is half-way between the high and low voltage on the data line. Although only one data line is shown in the figure, the reference is shared over several data lines.

Figure 8-30 shows the waveforms for the signaling system of Figure 8-29 operating over 10 mm of 0.6-μm wide wire. The top trace shows the data line (solid) and reference line (dashed) at the transmitter. The center trace shows the same two lines at the receiver, and the bottom trace shows the positive (solid) and negative (dashed) outputs of the sense amplifier. The figure shows the transmission of a 0, from 0.5 to 1.5 ns; the precharge of the line, 1.5 to 2.5 ns; and the transmission of a 1, from 2.5 to 3.5 ns.

The transmitter drives the line for 400 ps beginning at 0.5 ns. The data line driver, two 10-μm NFETs in series, pulls down the transmitter side of the line by about 1 V during this period while the half-sized reference driver pulls the transmitter side of the reference line down by 500 mV. This hard pulldown on the transmitter side of the line is a form of overdrive (Section 8.1.4). The waveform at the receive end of the line is delayed by about 0.6 ns and has a reduced amplitude (400 mV for the data line and 200 mV for the receive line). The sense lines follow the receiver side of the data and reference lines until the sense clock

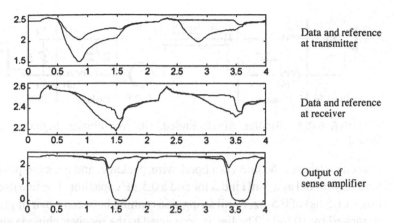

Data and reference
at transmitter

Data and reference
at receiver

Output of
sense amplifier

FIGURE 8-30 Waveforms for On-Chip, Single-Ended, Low-Voltage Signaling
with a Transmitter-Generated Reference

is asserted at 1.4 ns. At this point the sense nodes are isolated from the data and
reference lines and amplify the 200-mV difference to 2.5 V in about 100 ps. From
1.5 to 2.5 ns the line is precharged from both ends using large PFETs.

To transmit a 1, starting at 2.5 ns, the reference line discharges as before while
the data line remains high. Again, the transmitter overdrives the lossy RC line,
and the voltage at the receiver side of the line is delayed and attenuated. This
time, when the sense clock is asserted, the reference line is 200 mV higher than
the data line. This difference is amplified to 2.5 V in about 100 ps.

Although pseudodifferential signaling requires fewer lines, it is inferior in
terms of power, delay, and noise immunity. The data line must swing twice as
far to get the same voltage difference to sense, requiring four times the switching
energy and twice the supply energy as full-differential signaling. Given equal-
sized drivers, it takes twice as long to develop this larger swing; hence, delay is
doubled. Also, as described above, both reference offset and mismatched coupling
reduce the noise immunity of this signaling method. For these reasons, differential
signaling should be used for low-voltage, on-chip signaling unless wire tracks are
the limiting resource (as they often are).

8.5.4 Signaling Chip-to-Chip on a Board

As discussed in Chapter 3, a multilayer PC board provides a very low impedance
signal-return plane and good controlled-impedance stripguide transmission lines.
Our example system exploits the solid return plane of the circuit board through
single-ended operation using underterminated signaling (Section 7.3.4), as
illustrated in Figure 8-31. The transmitter is simply a 20-μm/10-μm inverter
that drives the 50-ohm line with a 450-ohm output impedance.[13] The resulting
10:1 voltage divider gives a 250-mV signal swing on the transmission line. The

---

[13] In practice this inverter would not be quite so simple. A good underterminated output driver would
     include both process compensation to control signal swing across process corners and rise-time
     control to avoid exciting impedance discontinuities and the tank circuits in the package parasitics.

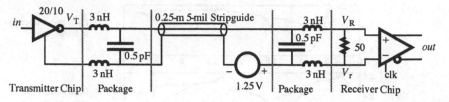

FIGURE 8-31   Bipolar, Single-Ended, Underterminated Signaling across a PC Board

transmitter drives the line via a bond-wire, package, and package-pin that we collectively model as a 3-nH inductor and a 0.5-pF capacitor. The line itself is 0.25 m (about 1.5 ns) of 0.5-oz, 5-mil stripguide running between a pair of ground planes separated by 10 mils. The line is connected to the receiver chip via another set of package parasitics. The line is parallel-terminated on the receiver chip to a 1.25-V midrail reference through a 50-ohm resistor. The received signal is detected across the termination resistor by a gate-isolated, clocked sense amplifier.

Operation of this signaling system is illustrated in the waveforms of Figure 8-32. The top trace shows the transmitter voltage, labeled V_T in the figure. The center trace shows the received voltage, V_R (solid), and the on-chip reference–return voltage, V_r (dashed). The final trace shows the output of the sense amplifier. All traces are referenced to the ground-return plane on the circuit board.

The transmitter is initially driving a logic 1 (1.375 V or 125 mV above the reference of 1.25 V). At 0.3 ns the transmitter switches to a logic 0 (1.125 V or 125 mV below reference), and at 1.6 ns it switches back to logic 1. The uncontrolled transition time on each transition gives rise to some ringing on V_T. A reflection of the transmitted pulse off of the receiver package parasitics shows up at the transmitter starting at about 3.7 ns.

The 1.3-ns low-going pulse appears at the receiver 1.5 ns later and is considerably smoothed by passing through two sets of low-pass package parasitics and a quarter meter of 7 Ω/m transmission line. The 150-ps fall-time at the transmitter has become 500 ps at the receiver. The transmitter transition time should be increased to 500 ps because the high-frequency components of the signal that do not make it to the receiver simply get pumped into noise sources.

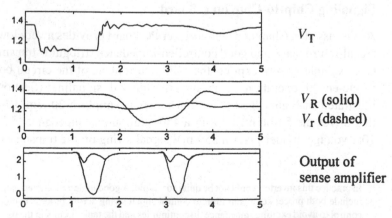

FIGURE 8-32   Waveforms for Bipolar, Single-Ended, Underterminated Signaling

The dashed curve in the center trace shows a 60-mV ripple in the reference signal at the receiver. This ripple is induced by AC current flow across the 3-nH return inductor as the signal switches. This return current and the ripple it induces are caused by just the switching of one signal. If several signals sharing the return switch simultaneously, the ripple will be proportionally larger. By sensing the signal across the termination resistor rather than relative to a receiver referenced voltage source, the effect of this ripple is halved.

The final trace of the figure shows the output of the gate-isolated sense amplifier. The amplifier is clocked twice, at 1.1 ns when the line is high, and at 2.9 ns in the middle of the low pulse. In both cases the 125-mV line voltage is amplified to full-swing in about 250 ps.

Compared with full-swing interchip signaling, the low-voltage signaling convention described here has advantages in terms of power, speed, and noise immunity. The switching energy of a 250-mV signal on a 50-ohm line with a 1.3-ns bit cell is 1.6 pJ. Operating full-swing requires 100 times the switching energy and 10 times the supply energy. The low-swing system achieves incident-wave switching, and the transmission delay is primarily the 1.5-ns delay across the wire. Without an extremely low output impedance, full-swing systems would not be capable of incident-wave switching but would rather have to *ring-up* the line over several 3-ns round trips. Finally, several noise sources are isolated from the signal by using a high-impedance output, bipolar signaling, and sensing the received voltage across the termination resistor. A typical full-swing signal would not be isolated from these noise sources and thus would likely have lower noise immunity even while it has larger noise margins.

This example illustrates the importance of return impedance. Although the signal-return plane of a typical PC board has an impedance that is low enough to be ignored, the impedance of typical package parasitics is considerable. With a single signal switching, return noise induced across the return parasitics amounts to 25% of the signal swing. With four signals switching simultaneously, return noise would swamp the signal.

Although the underterminated driver has the advantage of simplicity, a bipolar current-mode driver would be preferable to the design presented here because it retains all of the advantages of the underterminated driver while offering a higher output impedance for better transmitter signal-return and power supply noise isolation. The differential current-mode driver described in the next section can easily be adapted to single-ended operation.

8.5.5   Signaling across a Cable

When signaling over a cable, the return impedance is too high to be ignored. In this case it is often better to use a balanced cable, where the return impedance equals the signal impedance, and differential signaling. A unipolar, current-mode, differential signaling system for communicating between boards is illustrated in Figure 8-33. An NFET is biased, using a current mirror (not shown), to be a 5-mA current source. Because only DC current is drawn, the 3-nH inductor in the supply path is not an issue. The constant current is *steered* into one of the two cable conductors using a source-coupled pair of NFETs. The differential input

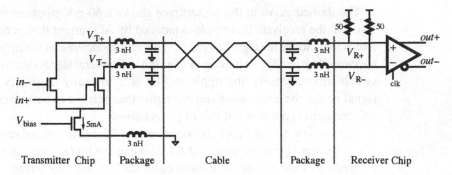

FIGURE 8-33   A Differential Current-Mode Signaling System Operating across a Balanced Cable

waveform, on $in+$ and $in-$, is controlled so that the crossover occurs with a minimum of disturbance to the voltage on the common-source node. The differential signal is coupled by a set of package parasitics to a 100-Ω balanced cable.[14]

At the receiving end, a second set of package parasitics couples the cable to the termination and receive amplifier. Each line is parallel-terminated to the receive power supply with a 50-Ω resistor. This termination provides both a 100-Ω parallel termination between the two lines and a common-mode DC bias to the line. No AC supply current is drawn by the termination because total current through the pair of resistors is always 5 mA. A gate-isolated, clocked sense amplifier detects the received signal by sensing the differential voltage across the termination.

To reduce ringing in the package parasitics and to reduce reflections from transmission-line discontinuities, the transmitter employs transition-time control, as illustrated in Figure 8-34. The current-steering transmitter is segmented into four sections. Each section contains a 1.25-mA current source along with a source-coupled pair to steer the current into one of the two output lines. The stages are sequenced on by a chain of delay buffers (cross-coupled NAND gates), and thus the overall transition time is about 1 ns.

Operation of the signaling system of Figure 8-33 is illustrated in the waveforms of Figure 8-35. The top trace shows the transmitter output, V_{T+} and V_{T-}. The center trace shows the receiver input, V_{R+} and V_{R-} (advanced in time), and the bottom trace shows the output of the sense amplifier clocked on 1.5-ns intervals (aligned in time with the middle trace).

Even with transition-time control, the transmitter output shows significant ringing in the package parasitics. This ringing is caused by abrupt switching of individual stages. The package parasitics and slightly resistive line act to low-pass this signal, giving a smooth waveform at the receiver. A small amount of intersymbol interference causes the second bit cell to have a slightly larger eye-opening than the first bit cell. With differential signaling, the 250-mV signal swing results in a 250-mV difference between the two lines as compared with a 125-mV difference with the single-ended signaling system described above.

---

[14] In practice our interconnect model would also include a connector model and a run of stripguide from the package to the connector at either end of the line.

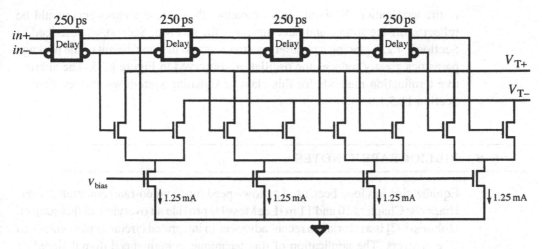

FIGURE 8-34   Transition-Time Controlled Transmitter

The signal is sampled at 1.5-ns intervals and amplified to full-swing by the sense amplifier.

The current-mode differential signaling system cancels most external noise sources. The current-mode driver isolates the line from transmitter power supply noise, and differential operation cancels most forms of cross talk and results in no AC supply or return current. The major noise source of concern with this signaling system is intersymbol interference due to the low-pass nature of the transmission system and mismatched terminations and impedance variation in the transmission system.

Both this differential current mode signaling system and the single-ended unterminated system of Section 8.5.4 may benefit from a matched source termination under certain conditions. Adding a matched parallel termination at the source end of the line doubles the power dissipation as amount of current required to give the same signal swing is doubled. However, it has two significant advantages. First, any cross talk or reflections that arrive at the source are absorbed

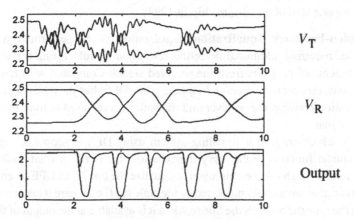

FIGURE 8-35   Waveforms for the Differential Current-Mode Signaling Example

in the termination. Without the termination, these noise components would be reflected off the source and later appear at the receiver. Second, as described in Section 7.4.2.2, placing a parallel resistance across the tank circuit of the package parasitics greatly reduces the oscillations observed in Figure 8.35. The alternative termination methods for this class of signaling system will be revisited in Section 11.5.1.9.

8.6   BIBLIOGRAPHIC NOTES

Equalization has long been used on low-speed (up to video-rate) communications channels; Chapters 10 and 11 in [LeeMess94] provide an overview of this subject. [JohnEssi97] is a tutorial on recent advances in integrated circuit implementations of equalizers. The application of this technique to high-speed digital signaling was first described in [DallPoul96] and [PoulDall97]. A different implementation is described in [FiedMact97]. Simultaneous bidirectional signaling was first described in [LamDenDa90]. More recent descriptions include [DenLeDal93], [MoonDike95], [TakaUchi95], and [LeeKim95]. Coding for spectral control, error recovery, and DC balance is an extensive subject introduced in Chapter 12 of [LeeMess94]; the 8b/10b code is described in [WidmFran83].

8.7   EXERCISES

8-1   **Optimum Repeater Spacing:** Chips in 2007 are expected to have transistors with a gate length of 0.09 μm and wires with a cross section of $0.18 \times 0.18 \, \mu$m. The capacitance per unit length of wire is expected to be unchanged. The reduction in gate length translates to a four-fold decrease in gate delay. Under these assumptions, what will the optimum repeater spacing be for these minimum-width wires in 2007? What propagation velocity does this correspond to? A large chip in 2007 is expected to be 30 mm on a side. How many "gate delays" will it take to traverse one side of a chip in 2007? How does this compare with the number of "gate delays" required to traverse one side of an 18-mm chip in 1997?

8-2   **Decision-Feedback Equalization:** Equalization can be performed in the receiver without requiring additional detection resolution by subtracting the low-frequency components of past bits from the received signal. Compared with transmitter pre-emphasis, this *decision-feedback equalization* (DFE) has the advantage that no communication between the receiver and transmitter is required to train the equalizer on a test signal.

A block diagram of a signaling system using DFE is shown in Figure 8-36. If the transfer function of the lossy transmission line is $H(s)$, what feedback transfer function, $G(s)$, should be employed to equalize the line? Can DFE be employed with receivers that are heavily pipelined or multiplexed (i.e., where it takes many bit times from the time the bit is on the line to when it is available at the output of the detector)? Why or why not?

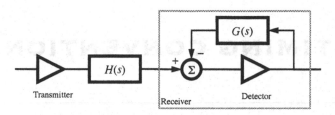

FIGURE 8-36   Decision-Feedback Equalization

8-3   **Single-Pole Equalization:** One approach to equalizing a long, lossy cable is simply to high-pass the line with a single-pole high-pass filter, $s/(s+a)$ with a cutoff at the bit frequency (half the bit rate). This can be accomplished with a single capacitor on each data line. Sketch an implementation of such a system. Describe its advantages and disadvantages.

8-4   **Simultaneous Bidirectional Signaling:** Design a differential, voltage-mode, simultaneous bidirectional signaling system. Sketch your system and describe how it operates.

8-5   **Reverse-Channel Cross Talk:** Derive the expressions for reverse-channel cross talk in a bidirectional system with (Figure 8-18) and without (Figure 8-13) split returns.

8-6   **Band-Limited Coding:** Design a 2b/3b code that is DC-balanced and has a minimum run length. Can you design other useful features such as control characters?

9 TIMING CONVENTIONS

A timing convention governs when a transmitter drives symbols onto the signal line and when they are sampled by the receiver. A timing convention may be periodic, with a new symbol driven on a signal line at regular time intervals, or aperiodic, with new symbols arriving at irregular times. In either case a method is required to encode when the symbol arrives so that the receiver samples each symbol exactly once during its valid period. With periodic signals, if the nominal data rate is known, the receiver may use a local clock source to determine when the next symbol is to arrive. In this case, an occasional transition on the signal line to correct for drift between the transmitter and receiver clocks is all that is needed to encode symbol arrival times. For aperiodic signals, an explicit transition is required to signal the arrival of each symbol. This transition may be on a separate clock line that may be shared among several signals (bundled signaling). Alternatively, this transition may be encoded on the same lines as the signal value, as with dual-rail signaling, giving a timing convention that is insensitive to line-to-line skew.

The rate at which we can send symbols over a line or through a block of combinational logic is limited by the rise time of the transmitter and transmission medium, the sampling window of the receiver, and timing noise or uncertainty. Only the uncertainty, not the absolute value, of the delay of the line or module limits the data rate. In the absence of timing noise, the minimum bit-cell width is the sum of the transmitter rise time and the receiver sampling window. The rise time of the transmitter determines how fast a new symbol can be put on the line. This signal must then remain stable during the sampling window of the receiver to be reliably detected. The minimum bit cell is widened further by timing noise in the system. Uncertainty in the arrival time of the signal at the receiver and uncertainty in the timing of the transmit and receive clocks must be compensated by widening the cell to allow for the worst-case timing plus a margin.

A good timing convention is one that manages timing noise, skew, and jitter in an efficient manner and allows the system to operate over a wide range of data rates.

Many systems, or parts of systems, use a global clock to which all signals in the subsystem are synchronized. All signals change in response to a transition on the clock and are sampled in an *aperture* region surrounding a clock transition. Using a global clock is convenient in a small subsystem because it places all signals in a single *clock domain*, obviating the need for synchronization that would otherwise be required in moving between clock domains. A global clock, however, has a number of serious limitations that limit its usefulness in larger subsystems. First, because the global clock is not usually centered on the *eye* of the signals it is sampling, this convention tends to be less tolerant of timing noise than the alternatives. Second, if any cables or logic modules have a delay longer than one clock period, the system will only operate over certain (often narrow) windows of clock frequencies. Finally, in such a subsystem the maximum data rate is limited by the maximum delay of the system rather than the uncertainty in delay.

A pipeline timing convention overcomes the limitations of a global clock by generating a clock for each data signal that is nominally centered on the eye of the data signal. The clock for the data at the output of a module is typically generated by delaying the clock used at the input of the module by the nominal delay of the module plus one-half clock cycle. This system works well as long as data are moving in one direction, as with an arithmetic pipeline or a communication channel. However, explicit synchronization is required for data to recirculate, skip a pipeline stage, or move in the other direction. At a given data rate, pipeline timing is less sensitive to timing noise than a global clock, for it maximizes timing margins by centering the clock on the eye of the data symbol. Pipeline timing gives a maximum data rate that is limited only by timing uncertainty, not maximum delay. Also, pipeline timing allows the system to operate at any clock frequency up to the maximum. However, with open-loop timing, the clock will only be centered on the eye at one frequency.

A timing convention may operate either open loop or closed loop. In an open-loop system, the frequencies and delays associated with system timing are not subject to control. The system must be designed to tolerate the worst case variation in these parameters. With closed-loop timing, on the other hand, one or more system timing parameters, delays and frequencies, are actively controlled. The system measures a timing parameter such as skew and uses feedback control to adjust the variable parameters to reduce the skew. This active control can greatly decrease the timing uncertainty in a system and hence increase the maximum data rate if pipeline timing is employed.

The remainder of this chapter discusses timing conventions in more detail. We start by comparing two typical timing conventions in Section 9.1. Section 9.2 discusses the alternatives and considerations in timing-system design. Timing fundamentals and nomenclature are introduced in Section 9.3. Methods of encoding events (when symbols change) are described in Section 9.4. Open-loop timing conventions are discussed in Section 9.5, and closed-loop timing is the topic of Section 9.6. The chapter closes with a discussion of clock distribution in Section 9.7.

A discussion of synchronization, the methods used to combine signals from different clock domains, is deferred to Chapter 10. The circuits used to implement timing systems are described in Chapter 12.

9.1   A COMPARISON OF TWO TIMING CONVENTIONS

This section introduces many of the issues related to timing-system design by comparing two approaches to timing a 16-bit-wide signal channel traveling between boards in a digital system. The constraints of the problem are summarized in Table 9-1. The system operates at 400 Mb/s (bit-cell time $t_{bit} = 2.5$ ns) over $t_{wire} = 6.25$ ns (2.5 bits) of cable. The delay of individual wires is matched to within 100 ps, the equivalent of 1.5 cm.

Approach A is a conventional open-loop, global-clock synchronous system illustrated in Figure 9-1. A 400 MHz clock is distributed to the transmitter and receiver from a master clock generator over transmission lines that are matched to ± 100 ps. A single-stage buffer at the clock generator, B1, introduces a timing uncertainty of ± 100 ps, and the four-stage on-chip clock generator, B4, adds ± 400 ps of timing uncertainty.

TABLE 9-1   **Timing Parameters**

Parameter	Symbol	Nominal	Skew (ps)	Jitter (ps)
Bit cell	t_{bit}	2.5 ns		
Transmitter rise time	t_r	1.0 ns		
Cable delay	t_{wire}	6.25 ns	100	
Receiver aperture	t_a	300 ps	100	50
Transmitter delay		500 ps	150	50
Buffer stage delay		250 ps	100	50

Approach B, shown in Figure 9-2, sends a reference clock, *RClk*, along with the data and uses a feedback loop to center the in-phase sample clock, *IClk*, on the eye of the reference clock. This approach is insensitive to the static phase difference or skew between the transmit and receive clocks. Thus, Approach B does not require matched lines for clock distribution. This approach is still sensitive to dynamic phase difference or *jitter* in the receive clock before the B4 buffer and to relative skew between the data lines and the reference clock.

The closed-loop timing controller operates using two delay lines. The first delay line, which produces *IClk*, is adjusted by the finite-state machine (FSM) to center the clock on the eye. The second delay line gives a fixed 90° (one quarter clock cycle) delay to generate a quadrature clock, *QClk*. This quadrature clock is used to sample the receive clock in flip-flop RQ. When the first delay line is properly adjusted, *QClk* will sample *RClk* right in the middle of its transition, hanging RQ in the metastable state (Section 10.2.2). If RQ is not metastable, the FSM adjusts the first delay line to move *QClk* closer to the transition. When *QClk* is right on the transition, *IClk* is centered on the eye. This type of timing loop is described in more detail in Section 9.6.4.

To further simplify clock distribution, Approach B uses a 200-MHz clock and double-edge-triggered (DET) flip-flops to give a 400-Mb/s data rate. The DET flip-flops sample their inputs on both edges of the clock. With this approach the maximum toggle frequency of the clock is identical to the maximum toggle frequency of the data. In contrast, with conventional single-edge-triggered flip-flops, the clock frequency is twice the highest data frequency, which complicates the

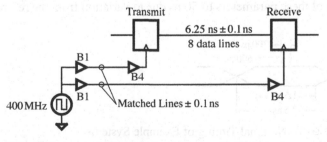

FIGURE 9-1   Approach A: A Conventional Synchronous System

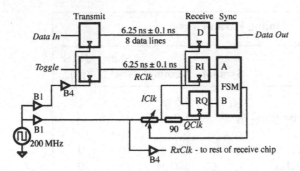

FIGURE 9-2   Closed-Loop Pipeline Timing

design of clock buffers and the clock distribution network, and, to first approximation, doubles the clock power.

9.1.1   Skew and Jitter Analysis

Our two example systems have identical nominal timing, as illustrated in Figure 9-3. Of the 2.5-ns bit cell, 1 ns is used for transition time, leaving a 1.5-ns eye opening. The 300 ps aperture or sampling window is nominally centered on the eye, leaving a 600-ps *gross timing margin* on either side. This gross timing margin is the amount of timing uncertainty, skew and jitter, that either system can tolerate.

Although the two systems have identical gross margin, they differ considerably in their timing uncertainty, as shown in Table 9-2. Approach A has a total timing uncertainty of 2.15 ns (1.55-ns skew and 0.6-ns jitter), which is far greater than the 600 ps allowed for correct operation. Approach B, on the other hand, has a total timing uncertainty of 450 ps (250-ps skew and 200-ps jitter), leaving a *net timing margin* of 150 ps.

Approach B reduces A's 1.2-ns clock skew to a 100-ps cable skew by transmitting a reference clock with the data. Approach B also bypasses the on-chip clock buffer and its 400 ps of jitter. The 100 ps of master clock buffer jitter remains. Applying these clock distribution techniques to A would bring the total uncertainty down to 650 ps, which is still over budget.

The closed-loop clock adjustment of approach B measures and cancels the transmitter delay (clock-to-output) and the receiver sampling time for the reference clock channel. This reduces the 250-ps skew due to worst-case chip-to-chip variation of these parameters to 50 ps due to variation from the reference channel

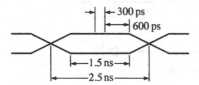

FIGURE 9-3   Nominal Timing of Example Systems

TABLE 9-2   Skew and Jitter for Approaches A and B

Description	A Skew (ps)	A Jitter (ps)	B Skew (ps)	B Jitter (ps)
Transmitter clock	600	250		50
Receiver clock	600	250		50
Transmitter	150	50	30	50
Receiver	100	50	20	50
Data cable	100		100	
Reference clock cable			100	
TOTAL	1550	600	250	200

to a data channel on the same chip. In Section 9.6.5 we will see how to eliminate this 50 ps as well by closing a separate timing loop for each data channel. Because the timing loop has a low bandwidth, it is unable to track and cancel the high-frequency jitter.

9.1.2   Allowable Clock Rates

In addition to having lower timing uncertainty, Approach B has the further advantage that it will work at any clock rate as long as the total timing uncertainty is less than the gross timing margin. The closed-loop timing control adjusts the delay of the receive clock to sample at the center of the eye regardless of how many bits long the wire is.

An open-loop timing approach, like A, on the other hand, will only sample at the center of the eye at clock rates that give an odd number of half-bits on the wire (e.g., 2.5). Particularly for long cables, this usually gives a set of narrow frequency bands at which the system will operate properly separated by frequency bands at which timing margins are not met. The range of bit periods for which the system will operate properly is given by the inequalities

$$t_{\text{wire}} - (N - 1)t_{\text{bit}} \geq 0.5(t_r + t_a) + t_u$$
(9-1)
$$Nt_{\text{bit}} - t_{\text{wire}} \geq 0.5(t_r + t_a) + t_u$$

where N is the number of bits in flight on the wire at any given time, and the total timing uncertainty (skew + jitter) is $\pm t_u$. This can be rewritten as

$$\frac{0.5(t_r + t_a) + t_u + t_{\text{wire}}}{N} \leq t_{\text{bit}} \leq \frac{t_{\text{wire}} - 0.5(t_r + t_a) - t_u}{(N - 1)}$$
(9-2)

For example, suppose the open-loop Approach A was redesigned to have a timing uncertainty of $t_u = 550$ ps. The ranges of bit periods that give correct operation with 6.25-ns nominal wire length are shown in Table 9-3. There are three allowable ranges corresponding to 1, 2, and 3 bits on the wire at a time. An

TABLE 9-3   **Allowable Bit Periods for Open-Loop Timing**

N	Minimum t_{bit} (ns)	Maximum t_{bit} (ns)
3	2.483	2.525
2	3.725	5.050
1	7.450	infinity

N larger than 3 gives nonoverlapping constraints (negative net timing margin). Note that for $N = 1$ there is no maximum bit-cell time.

9.1.3   Discussion

This example has informally introduced many of the problems of timing design, including rise and aperture times, timing uncertainty (skew and jitter), gross and net timing margins, and allowable operating frequencies. We saw that dealing with timing budgets is much like dealing with noise budgets (Section 6.6). We started with a certain amount of time, t_{bit}, and allocated it to different timing factors (t_r, t_a, and t_u).

The example comparison demonstrated many of the advantages of closed-loop timing. Closed-loop timing cancels most sources of skew in a timing system, obviating the need to match the delay of components or wires and thus considerably simplifying system design. With closed-loop timing, jitter becomes the major constraint on a timing budget.

9.2   CONSIDERATIONS IN TIMING DESIGN

There are many variables in the design of a timing convention.

Degree of synchronization: The signals in a system may be divided into disjoint sets called *clock domains*. All of the signals in a given clock domain are *synchronized* in the sense that their *events* (potential transitions) happen simultaneously. Two different clock domains may be related by having similar clocks (mesochronous or plesiochronous) or may be completely asynchronous.

Periodicity: The events in a clock domain may occur periodically, with a fixed, known delay between events; aperiodically, with a variable but possibly known interevent period; or unpredictably, with an unknown delay between events.

Encoding of events: There are numerous methods of encoding both the time and value of a signaling event onto signal lines. One may separate the problem by carrying the time information on one line, often called a clock, and the value on a distinct line. Alternatively, a group of lines can be used so that a transition on any one line signals both the time and the value of an event.

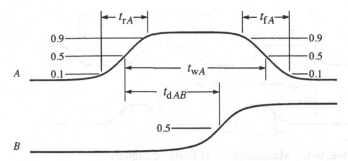

FIGURE 9-4   Rise Time, Fall Time, Pulse Width, and Delay

Open versus closed-loop timing: As illustrated in Section 9.1, timing uncertainty may be dealt with either by minimizing the sources of uncertainty (open loop) or by measuring and canceling sources of uncertainty (closed-loop).

9.3   TIMING FUNDAMENTALS

9.3.1   Timing Nomenclature

9.3.1.1   Delay and Transition Times

Figure 9-4 illustrates the terms used to describe signal transitions and delays between transitions. We measure times associated with a single transition from when the signal has completed 10% of the transition to when the signal has completed 90% of the transition.[1] The relative timing between two transitions is measured from the 50% point of one transition to the 50% of the other transition.

For example, signal A's *rise time*, t_{rA}, is the time from the start (10%) to the end (90%) of a rising transition on A. Similarly, the *fall time* of A, t_{fA}, is the time from the start to the end of a falling transition on A. We denote the time of the i_{th} transition on a signal A as t_{Ai}, the time when A crosses its midpoint for the i_{th} time after some reference time. The *delay* from a transition on A to a transition on B, t_{dAB} or just t_{AB}, is just $t_{Bj} - t_{Ai}$, for some i and j. This definition holds even when A and B have very different signal amplitudes. The *pulse width* of the signal, t_{wA}, is the time from one transition on A to the next transition on A, $t_{A(i+1)} - t_{Ai}$. Often we will distinguish between the *high* pulse width, t_{whA}, and the *low* pulse width, t_{wlA}, of signal A.

9.3.1.2   Periodic Signals

Signal A is a periodic signal of degree n if

(9-3) $$t_{cyAn}(i) = t_{A(i+n)} - t_{Ai}$$

---

[1] There is nothing magic about using 10 and 90% to define rise time. It is not unusual to find systems specified using 20 and 80% or even 25 and 75%.

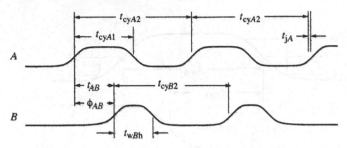

FIGURE 9-5   Measurements of Periodic Signals

the delay between the i_{th} transition and the $i + n_{th}$ transition of a signal, A, is a constant for all i. A periodic signal of degree 1 is characterized entirely by its transition *period*, t_{cyA1}, or its transition *frequency*, f_{A1} as

$$(9\text{-}4) \qquad f_{An} = \frac{1}{t_{cyAn}} = \frac{1}{t_{A(i+n)} - t_{Ai}}$$

The *duty factor* of a periodic signal of degree 2 is the fraction of time the signal is high

$$(9\text{-}5) \qquad d_A = \frac{t_{wAh}}{t_{cyA}}$$

Where it is unambiguous, we will drop the degree subscript from the cycle time or period of a signal. For example, in Eq. (9-5), we use t_{cyA} in place of t_{cyA2}.

Two periodic signals with the same period are *synchronized*.

These timing relationships are illustrated in Figure 9-5. Signal A in the figure is periodic with degree 1. However, for comparison with signal B, it is more convenient for us to think of it as a degree 2 signal with a 50% duty factor. Signal B is synchronized with signal A and has a 30% duty factor.

The average delay between two signals is often called *skew*. For example, the skew between signals A and B in Figure 9-5 is labeled t_{AB}. We are usually interested in the skew between different clocks in a system that is nominally supposed to have zero delay. Two clocks, A and B, that are synchronized with a fixed skew, t_{AB}, are often discribed as a being *mesochronous*.

When working with periodic signals it is often convenient to express a delay as the relative phase[2] between two signals and use modular arithmetic in timing calculations. For example,

$$(9\text{-}6) \qquad \phi_{AB} = \frac{2\pi t_{AB}}{t_{cyA2}}$$

Often the cycle time of a periodic signal deviates slightly from its average period. For example, the second cycle of signal A in Figure 9-5 is slightly longer than the average period. The *jitter* of a periodic signal A, t_{jA}, is the delay between

---

[2] We will express phase in either degrees or radians.

the expected transition of signal A and the actual transition on signal A. Jitter is a zero-mean random variable. When we perform worst-case timing analysis we also use the term jitter to refer to the maximum value of this random variable.

Often two signals in a system have nearly, but not exactly, the same frequency. For example, two crystal oscillators with the same nominal frequency have output frequencies that differ by about 1 part in 10^5. It is often useful to treat these nearly synchronous or *plesiochronous* signals as if they were synchronized but with slowly varying phase. For example, if two signals A and B have frequencies that differ by $\Delta f_{AB} = |f_A - f_B| \ll f_A$, then for short periods they can be treated as if they were synchronized. Over longer periods, however, the slow drift of phase

$$(9\text{-}7) \qquad \frac{d\phi_{AB}}{dt} = 2\pi \Delta f_{AB} = 2\pi(f_A - f_B)$$

must be accounted for.

9.3.1.3 Maximum Absolute Value, Peak-to-Peak, and RMS

Depending on the circumstances, we can express the value of a time-varying quantity, such as the jitter of signal A, t_{jA} in Figure 9-5, in several ways. Suppose, for example, that t_{jA} is distributed over the interval $[-1 \text{ ns}, 1 \text{ ns}]$ with the triangular density function

$$(9\text{-}8) \qquad p(x) = \begin{cases} 1 - |x| & \text{if } -1 \le x \le 1 \\ 0 & \text{if otherwise} \end{cases}$$

Table 9-4 describes three summary values we can use to describe t_{jA}: the maximum absolute value of t_{jA} is 1 ns; its peak-to-peak value, the difference between its maximum and minimum values, is 2 ns; and, its root mean square (rms) value is 0.408 ns.

Throughout this book we will refer to variables using all three of these summary values. In most cases the meaning is clear by context. Where the meaning is ambiguous, we use the notation shown in the third column of Table 9-4.

9.3.2 Timing Properties of Delay Elements

For purposes of timing analysis we model transmission lines, buffers, and delay lines as *delay elements*. Each transition on the input, A, of a delay element causes

TABLE 9-4   Definitions of Maximum, Peak-to-Peak, and RMS Values

Quantity	Definition	Example
Maximum absolute value	$\max(|x|)$	$t_{jA} = \pm 1$ ns
Peak-to-peak value	$\max(x) - \min(x)$	$t_{jA} = 2$ ns (p–p)
RMS value	$(\int x^2)^{1/2}$	$t_{jA} = 0.408$ ns (rms)

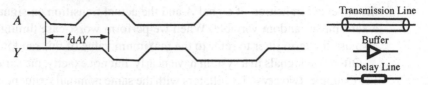

FIGURE 9-6   Delay Elements

a transition on the output, Y, after delay t_{dAY}, as illustrated in Figure 9-6. Because of component mismatch, variations in wire length and environment, and timing noise, the delay of an element can vary both from one element to the next and for a single element over time. To model this variation we consider the delay to be composed of three components: a nominal delay, the average variation or skew, and the AC variation or jitter.

$$(9\text{-}9) \qquad t_{dAY} = t_{nAY} + x_k t_{kAY} + x_j t_{jAY}$$

where t_{nAY} is the nominal delay from A to Y, x_k and x_j are random variables in the range $[-1,1]$, t_{kAY} is the maximum skew, and t_{jAY} is the maximum jitter.[3] The maximum and minimum values of t_{dAY} are thus

$$(9\text{-}10) \qquad \begin{aligned} t_{dAY_{\min}} &= t_{nAY} - t_{kAY} - t_{jAY} \\ t_{dAY_{\max}} &= t_{nAY} + t_{kAY} + t_{jAY} \end{aligned}$$

We refer to the combination of skew and jitter as the uncertainty of the delay, t_{uAY} defined as

$$(9\text{-}11) \qquad t_{uAY} = t_{kAY} + t_{jAY}$$

We are often interested in the relative delay between two signals. For example in Figure 9-7 we are interested in the maximum skew and jitter between clocks B and C, which are both generated by delaying clock A through delay elements with identical timing parameters (nominal delay, skew, and jitter). If we assume that the variations in delay are uncorrelated, then the worst-case skew and jitter between B and C are given by

$$(9\text{-}12) \qquad \begin{aligned} t_{kBC} &= t_{kAB} + t_{kAC} = 2t_{kAB} \\ t_{jBC} &= t_{jAB} + t_{jAC} = 2t_{jAB} \end{aligned}$$

The worst-case uncertainty between two identically distributed signals, in this case B and C, is twice the uncertainty of the timing path from a common reference,

FIGURE 9-7   Relative Delay Example

---

[3] Both of these quantities are expressed here as the maximum absolute value of the parameters.

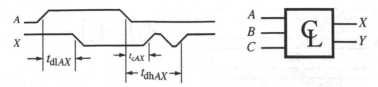

FIGURE 9-8   Propagation and Contamination Delays of Combinational Logic

A, to one of the signals, B. This is because one path, say AB, could be at minimum delay while the other, BC, is at maximum delay.

9.3.3   Timing Properties of Combinational Logic

The steady-state output of a *combinational*[4] *logic circuit* is a function only of its current inputs. Once the output reaches its final value, a combinational circuit retains no memory of previous inputs.

The timing of a combinational logic block is more involved than that of a delay element because a single input transition may cause multiple output transitions, and the delay and type of transitions produced depend on the state of the circuit's input. A set of *propagation delays*, $t_{dij}(s)$, describes the delay from an input, i, to an output, j, as a function of the state of the inputs, s. Typically we omit the input state and denote the maximum delay from i to j as t_{dij}. If the high- and low-going delays of an output are different, we denote them t_{dhij} and t_{dlij}, respectively. The delay t_{dij} is a maximum delay in three respects.

1. It is the maximum over all input states, s.
2. It is the delay to the last transition caused by an input transition, or equivalently it is the maximum delay over all active paths in the circuit.
3. It is the maximum over process, temperature, and voltage variations.

An output may make several transitions before reaching the steady state. The extra transitions are called a *hazard*. We denote the minimum time for output j to make its first transition in response to a transition on input i as the *contamination delay*, $t_{cij}(s)$. When we omit the state, we take t_{cij} to denote the minimum contamination delay from input i to output j. The contamination delay t_{cij} is a minimum over the same three sets of variables for which t_{dij} is a maximum.

Figure 9-8 illustrates the timing relationship between an input, A, and an output, X, of a combinational logic circuit. In response to a rising transition on A, X falls after falling delay t_{dlAX}. The falling transition on A causes a dynamic-1 hazard. The first transition on X occurs after contamination delay, t_{cAX}, and the final transition occurs after rising delay t_{dhAX}.

Figure 9-9 illustrates how contamination delay and propagation delay combine when combinational logic circuits are composed. In this figure we use an abstract view of a signal. Periods when the signal is stable with a known value are denoted

---

[4] Make sure not to confuse the word *combinational*, which refers to stateless logic modules, with *combinatorial*, which refers to the mathematics of counting.

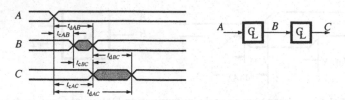

FIGURE 9-9   Abstract View and Composition of Combinational Logic Delays

by two parallel lines. The two lines cross over to denote a potential transition, and a shaded region is used to indicate that the signal is either unstable or in an unknown state.

When combinational logic circuits are composed in series, the propagation delay of the composite circuit is the sum of the delays of the individual elements. The same is true for contamination delay. As shown in Figure 9-9, because propagation delay is in general larger than contamination delay, the shaded region of uncertainty grows as circuits are combined. If combinational logic circuits are composed in a directed acyclic graph, the propagation delay from an input i to an output j is the maximum sum of element delays over all paths from i to j. Similarly, the contamination delay is the minimum sum of element contamination delays over all paths from i to j.

9.3.4   Timing Properties of Clocked Storage Elements

Synchronous sequential logic circuits are composed of combinational logic circuits and *clocked storage elements* arranged as shown in Figure 9-10. The s-bit current-state vector is held in a set of clocked storage elements (D flip-flops in Figure 9-10). The combinational logic circuit takes the current-state vector and the i-bit input vector and computes an s-bit next-state vector and an o-bit output vector. On each rising edge of the clock, the flip-flops sample their input and update their output with the new value, advancing the state vector to become the next state vector.

9.3.4.1   Edge-Triggered Flip-Flop

Figure 9-11 illustrates the timing properties of an edge-triggered flip-flop. The input, D, must have a stable[5] value (y in the figure) during the *aperture time* of the flip-flop. The aperture has width, t_a. The *aperture offset time*, t_{ao}, is the time

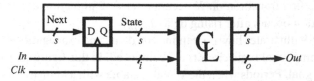

FIGURE 9-10   A Sequential Logic Circuit

---

[5] A *stable* value is within 10% of the signal swing of the nominal value.

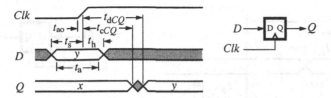

FIGURE 9-11 Timing Properties of an Edge-Triggered Flip-Flop

from the center of the aperture to the rising edge of the clock. The output remains at its previous value (x in the figure) until at least a contamination delay, t_{cCQ}, after the clock, and the output changes to its new value (y) at most a propagation delay, t_{dDQ}, after the clock.

Most data sheets and texts on logic design describe the position of the aperture relative to the clock in terms of a *setup time*, t_s, and a *hold time*, t_h. The setup time is the delay from the data's becoming valid to the rising edge of the clock. Because delays are specified from the 50% point of the waveform, whereas the aperture time is specified from the 10 or 90% point, the setup time is from $t_r/2$ before the beginning of the aperture to the rising edge of the clock. Similarly, the hold time is the delay from the clock to the data's becoming invalid. It is straightforward to convert between these two representations of the aperture interval using Eq. (9-13). The setup and hold representation is more convenient in open-loop timing systems where setup figures in the maximum delay calculation and hold figures in the minimum delay calculation. The aperture representation is more convenient in closed-loop timing systems where the width of the aperture and the uncertainty of delay are the important factors.

$$t_s = 0.5t_a - t_{ao} + t_r/2$$
$$t_h = 0.5t_a + t_{ao} + t_r/2$$

(9-13)

$$t_a = t_s + t_h - t_r$$
$$t_{ao} = 0.5(t_s - t_h)$$

The aperture time, t_a, is specified in conjunction with the delay, t_{dCQ}. The aperture characteristics are really described by a curve in (t_a, t_{dCQ}) space. A smaller input valid period may result in the correct output, but with larger delay. However, there is a minimum valid period below which the correct output will never occur. Also, for some flip-flops the aperture time for a 1 may be different than the aperture time for a 0. For present purposes we ignore this effect and consider the device to be symmetrical.

9.3.4.2 Level-Sensitive Latch

The level-sensitive latch is a clocked storage element that logically connects its input to its output when the clock is high and holds the output value stable when the clock is low. The timing properties of a latch are illustrated in Figure 9-12. In the figure, when input D changes from x to y, the output follows immediately (after a propagation delay) because the clock is high. When D changes from y to z, however, the output does not change until the clock goes high.

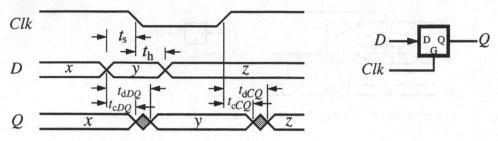

FIGURE 9-12   Timing Properties of a Level-Sensitive Latch

With a flip-flop, the aperture time and delay are both referenced to the positive edge of the clock and there is no delay property referenced to the data input. With a latch, however, the aperture and delay timing properties are referenced to different edges of the clock, and an additional delay property is referenced to the data input. The aperture time of a latch is referenced to the falling edge of the clock because this is the edge that samples the data. As illustrated in the figure, the input must remain stable with value y from t_s before the clock until t_h after the clock for the output to take on the value y reliably while the clock is low. The delay is referenced to the rising edge of the clock because this is the edge that may cause the output to change if the input changed while the clock was low.

A flip-flop can be constructed from two latches arranged in a master–slave configuration, as illustrated in Figure 9-13. The bubble on the clock input of the master latch denotes a logical inversion of the clock signal. Here the master latch samples the data on the rising edge of the clock, and the slave latch enables the data to the output on the same edge. Thus, the aperture time is determined by the master latch, and the delay is determined by the slave latch (unless the master has an unusually high t_{dDQ}). When the clock goes low, the slave latch holds the output stable. Note that for this arrangement to work, the contamination delay, t_{cCQ}, of the master latch must be greater than the hold time, t_h, of the slave latch. As we will see in our discussion of static timing analysis in Section 9.5, a more efficient and robust design results if combinational logic is placed between the master and slave latches rather than simply abutting them to form a flip-flop.

9.3.4.3 Double-Edge-Triggered Flip-Flop

A dual-edge-triggered flip-flop samples its input and updates its output on both the rising and falling edges of the clock. This generally results in a more efficient system because every power-dissipating clock edge is used to advantage.

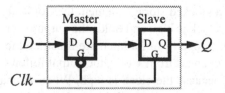

FIGURE 9-13   An Edge-Triggered Flip-Flop Realized Using Latches

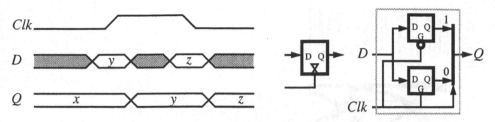

FIGURE 9-14   Double-Edge-Triggered Flip-Flop

However, it does require careful control of the clock's duty factor to ensure that the combinational logic has adequate time to operate during both the clock high and the clock low cycles.

Figure 9-14 shows (from left to right) timing waveforms, a symbol, and the construction of a double-edge-triggered flip-flop. The waveforms illustrate that each edge of the clock is associated with an aperture and a delay. The input must be stable during the aperture. The flip-flop samples the value during the aperture (y during the rising edge and z during the falling edge) and updates the output after a short delay.

To denote that the flip-flop is triggered by both edges of the clock (and to distinguish it from flip-flops that are triggered on only one edge), we put two triangles point-to-point on the clock input of the flip-flop, as illustrated on the symbol in the center of Figure 9-14 and also in Figure 9-2.

The rightmost part of Figure 9-14 shows how a dual-edge-triggered flip-flop may be constructed from two level-sensitive latches and a multiplexer. The top latch samples data on the rising edge of the clock, and the bottom latch samples data on the falling edge of the clock. The multiplexer is switched by the clock always to select the latch that is holding sampled data (not the latch that is passing its input to its output).

9.3.5   The Eye Diagram

An eye diagram of a signal overlays the signal's waveform over many cycles. Each cycle's waveform is aligned to a common timing reference, typically a clock. An eye diagram provides a visual indication of the voltage and timing uncertainty associated with a signal. It is easy to generate by synchronizing an oscilloscope to the timing reference.

A simulated noisy signal and its eye diagram are shown in Figure 9-15. The upper trace shows 100 cycles of a pseudorandom data sequence. The bottom trace shows 98 cycles of the sequence (all but the first and the last) overlaid on one another. The vertical thickness of the line bunches in the eye diagram is an indication of AC voltage noise, whereas the horizontal thickness of the bunches where they cross over is an indication of AC timing noise or jitter.[6] Fixed DC voltage and timing offsets are indicated by the position of the eye on the screen.

---

[6] Good sampling oscilloscopes (such as an HP54123 or Tek 11801) will generate a histogram of either the voltage or timing noise from which a statistical noise model can be derived.

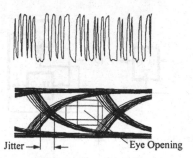

Jitter ⟶ ⟵   Eye Opening

FIGURE 9-15   A Signal and Its Eye Diagram

The size of the eye opening in the center of the diagram indicates the amount of voltage and timing margin available to sample this signal. If a *margin rectangle* with width equal to the required timing margin and height equal to the required voltage margin fits in the opening, then the signal has adequate margins. One can trade off voltage margin against timing margin, as illustrated by the two rectangles inscribed in the eye opening. One rectangle has a large timing margin that is achieved at the expense of a small voltage margin, whereas the other rectangle trades some of the timing margin to give a larger voltage margin.

Often we will draw an abstract eye diagram, as shown in Figure 9-16, to visualize a timing budget. The figure shows three superimposed waveform pairs, one each with nominal timing, worst-case early timing, and worst-case late timing. The three major components of a timing budget are labeled along the top of the waveforms. The uncertainty, t_u, is the difference between the nominal waveform and the early or late waveform.[7] The aperture time, t_a, is a property of the receiver, its flip-flops, or both. The transition time, t_r, is the time required for each waveform to switch states. These three components are stacked up along the bottom of the diagram along with a net timing margin, t_m, to round out the cycle. It is easy to see from the abstract eye diagram that it is the transition time component of the timing budget that is traded off against voltage margin when fitting a margin rectangle into the eye opening.

This diagram illustrates the fundamental equation that limits the cycle time of a logic or transmission module. The cycle time must be large enough to account for uncertainty, aperture, and rise time, as expressed by

(9-14) $$t_{cy} \geq 2t_u + t_a + t_r$$

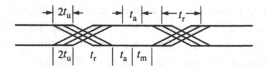

FIGURE 9-16   An Abstract Eye Diagram Illustrates a Timing Budget

---

[7] As in Eq. (9-10), t_u is a maximum value, not a peak-to-peak value. The difference between early and late, a peak-to-peak value, is $2t_u$.

9.4 ENCODING TIMING: SIGNALS AND EVENTS

At any point in time a signal carries a symbol, a digital value, between two points in a system. Over time the signal carries a stream of symbols, one after the other, in sequence. We need a source of timing information to determine where one symbol stops and the next symbol, possibly with the same value, begins. We refer to the combination of a symbol value and the time it starts as an *event*.

If events are periodic, equally spaced in time, we can use an internal time base to count out the intervals between symbols. In this case most of the events are implicit and do not require a signal transition. We need only an occasional explicit event to synchronize the time bases of the sender and receiver.

9.4.1 Encoding Aperiodic Events

For events that are not periodic, an explicit transition is required to start every symbol. Consider the case of sending an aperiodic stream of binary symbols. A binary event cannot be encoded on a single binary signal, for at any point in time there are three possibilities: continue sending the current symbol, start the next symbol with the same value, and start the next symbol with the complement value. Either a ternary signal or two binary signals are required to encode a binary event. Several methods of encoding the bitstream 101100 are illustrated in Figure 9-17.

9.4.1.1 Dual-Rail Signaling

Figure 9-17 (a) and (b) illustrate dual-rail signaling in which a binary event stream *A* is encoded as a pair of unary event streams *A*1 and *A*0. A transition on one of the unary lines signals an event. The value of the event is encoded spatially by which line switches. In Figure 9-17 (a), a transition on line *A*1 signals that

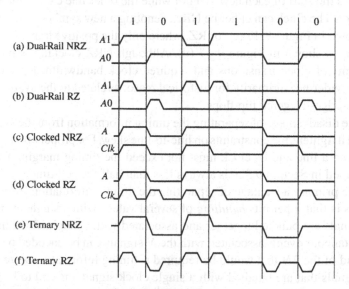

FIGURE 9-17 Encoding Events

a new 1 symbol has started on A, a transition on line $A0$ signals that a new 0 symbol has started on A, and no transition implies that the current symbol continues.

The nonreturn-to zero version of dual-rail signaling illustrated in Figure 9-17(a) is transition efficient because it requires only a single transition to encode each event. For proper operation, this approach requires only that the skew between lines $A0$ and $A1$ not exceed the minimum bit cell so that events do not get out of order.

Dual-rail signaling should not be confused with differential signaling (Section 7.3.5). Signals $A0$ and $A1$ in Figure 9-17 are not complements, and sending them single-ended between modules will result in unbalanced currents.

9.4.1.2   Return-to-Zero (RZ)/Nonreturn-to-Zero (NRZ) Signaling

With return-to-zero signaling, Figure 9-17 (b), the unary event lines return to zero after every event, and only the positive transitions are significant. This doubles the number of transitions required to encode the events. Return-to-zero signaling is advantageous in cases where power is dissipated only when the line is high. It also simplifies the decoding logic because the value of the last symbol can be generated with an RS flip-flop that looks only at the current values of the lines. Nonreturn-to-zero signaling requires remembering the old state of both lines to decode the present value. Return-to-zero dual-rail signaling is the timing convention employed by dual-rail domino logic (Section 4.3.3.4). When the clock is low, the lines are precharged to the "zero" state. One line is then selectively discharged to signal both the time and value of a binary event.

9.4.1.3   Clocked Signaling and Bundling

With clocked signaling, one line, the clock, encodes a unary event stream that denotes the start of each new symbol while the other line carries the value of the symbol. The clock can either be NRZ, denoting a new symbol on each transition, as shown in Figure 9-17 (c), or RZ, where only the positive transitions are meaningful, as shown in Figure 9-17 (d). Although NRZ clocking is more efficient in terms of clock transitions and required clock bandwidth, RZ clocking is in much wider use, primarily for historical reasons related to the availability of SSI single-edge-triggered flip-flops.

The disadvantage of separating the timing information from the symbol values is that it tightens the constraints on line-to-line skew. For proper operation the skew between a line and its clock must not exceed the timing margin. This quantity, described in Section 9.3.5, is always less than half the cell time.

The primary advantage of separating the timing information from the symbol values is that it permits *bundling* of several values with a single event stream. If N signals are bundled together and associated with a single clock line, then the simultaneous events associated with the N signals can be encoded on $N + 1$ lines instead of the $2N$ that would be required if timing information were unbundled.

Signals that are bundled with a single clock signal are said to be in the same *clock domain*. That is, all of the signals change in response to the same source of

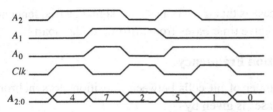

FIGURE 9-18 Example of Bundled Signaling

events. Signals in the same clock domain can be combined in combinational logic, giving an output in the same clock domain (but with greater delay). Combining signals in different clock domains, on the other hand, usually requires explicit synchronization (Chapter 10).

Figure 9-18 gives an example of bundling three lines, A_0, A_1, and A_2, with a single NRZ clock line. Each transition of the clock denotes the start of three new symbols, one on each of the three lines. Because the symbols change simultaneously we often denote their values as an octal vector, $A_{2:0}$, as shown at the bottom of the figure.

9.4.1.4 Ternary Signaling

Figure 9-17 (e) shows how a binary event stream could be encoded on a single NRZ ternary logic symbol. The three states of the logic signal are exactly what is needed to encode the three possibilities at each instant in time: staying in the current state denotes continuing the current symbol, changing to the higher of the two other states signals the start of a new 1 symbol, and changing to the lower of the two other states denotes starting a new 0 symbol.

Ternary signaling for timing information has the problem that it is difficult to distinguish a transition from state 0 (the lowest state) to state 2 (the highest state) from two transitions, one from 0 to 1 and a second from 1 to 2. Only the time interval between the crossing of the two thresholds $U0$ and $U1$ distinguishes these two cases. Also, the timing uncertainty of such a system is increased by the different-sized transitions. A two-state transition (between 0 and 2) takes more time than a one-state transition (between 1 and 0 or 2).

All of these problems are overcome by ternary RZ signaling,[8] as shown in Figure 9-17(f). This waveform is equivalent to subtracting the dual-rail RZ waveforms from one another. Because the signal returns to zero following each event, each transition crosses only a single threshold. There is no ambiguity or timing uncertainty associated with crossing multiple thresholds in a single transition; however it does require twice the number of transitions as ternary NRZ signaling.

9.4.2 Encoding Periodic Signals

If symbols are transmitted at fixed timing intervals, timing information can be determined implicitly by measuring the intervals using a local time base. All that

---

[8] Ternary RZ signaling is sometimes referred to as *duobinary* signaling.

is required in this case is that transitions on the signal be frequent enough to keep the transmit and receive time bases from drifting too far apart.

9.4.2.1   Required Transition Frequency

The maximum number of bit cells between transitions to synchronize transmit and receive time bases is given by

$$(9\text{-}15) \qquad\qquad N = \frac{t_{\phi d}}{\Delta f t_c^2}$$

where $t_{\phi d}$ is the timing margin budgeted to phase drift, Δf is the maximum frequency difference in s^{-1}, and t_c is the cell time. The denominator is the phase drift (in seconds) per cycle.

Consider, for example, a 1-Gb/s link ($t_c = 1$ ns) where we have budgeted 100 ps to phase drift and the two time bases are matched to 100 ppm ($\Delta f = 100$ kHz). For this link, N is 1,000. The link can run for 1,000 bit cells without a transition before the phase drifts by more than 100 ps. If we need to tolerate single errors on the link, we must make sure transitions happen at least twice this often so that we can miss one transition without drifting out of our phase budget.

9.4.2.2   Bit Stuffing

To ensure that a transition is present at least once every N bit cells, in the worst case we must consume $1/N$ of the channel bandwidth by inserting a transition cell that carries no data after every $N - 1$ data bits. The simplest approach is to insert this transition cell whether we need to or not. After executing a startup protocol to synchronize to the bit level, the transmitter inserts a dummy transition bit every N bits, and the receiver ignores every N_{th} bit.

If the data are uniformly distributed, or if a biased data source has been suitably scrambled, the probability that we actually need to insert a transition bit is 2^{-N}, typically a very small number. Rather than wasting bandwidth on redundant transitions, a more efficient approach is only to insert a transition after $N - 1$ cells without a transition. The transmitter and receiver both count the number of cells without a transition. When the transmitter count reaches $N - 1$, the transmitter inserts a dummy transition in the next cell. When the receiver count reaches $N - 1$, the receiver ignores the next cell. Even with this approach, the dummy transition is redundant half of the time, but that is much better than almost all of the dummy transitions being redundant.

Of course, signaling conventions that band-limit the signal as described in Section 8.4 by their very nature ensure periodic transitions in the data stream.

9.4.2.3   Phase-Encoding

If the frequency of transitions is limited but the time of a transition can be measured very accurately, it is possible to encode several bits of information in each transition of a binary signal. Consider, for example, a channel over which we can transmit a transition with a timing resolution of t_p but which is limited to at most one transition each, $t_c = N t_p$. When sending binary data encoded in voltage levels

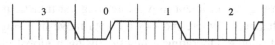

FIGURE 9-19 Phase Encoding

over this channel, our bit rate is limited to $f_c = 1/t_c$ because we can send at most one bit per transition. By encoding several bits in the position[9] of each transition, however, we can achieve bit rates approaching $lgNf_c$.

A relatively simple encoding scheme achieves a rate of $[N/(2N-1)]lgNf_c$. Consider the case where $N = 2^n$ is a power of 2. We divide our data stream into n-bit symbols. Each symbol, x, is encoded in a cell of width $(2N-1)t_p$ by placing a single transition in the cell at position $(N+x)t_p$. The encoding observes the transition frequency limit because adjacent transitions are separated by at least $Nt_p = t_c$. The data are recovered by measuring the position of the transition in each bit cell and subtracting the fixed offset. By providing a transition in each cell, this encoding scheme is naturally band-limited and places very little demand on the stability of timing sources. By using a wider cell and placing a variable number of transitions in each cell, one can come closer to the $lgNf_c$ data rate at the expense of increased complexity.

Figure 9-19 illustrates an example of this simple phase encoding for $N = 4$. The small gray lines mark time intervals of t_p, and the longer black lines mark cell boundaries at intervals of $7t_p$. The four-symbol quaternary sequence 3012 is shown phase encoded over four adjacent cells. Each symbol, x, is encoded by placing a transition at position $(4+x)t_p$ in the appropriate cell.

9.5 OPEN-LOOP SYNCHRONOUS TIMING

With a synchronous timing convention, all signals are synchronized with a common clock. Every signal potentially makes a transition within some phase range relative to a master clock signal and is sampled within a (possibly different) phase range of the clock. Such a system is open-loop if the delays or phase relationships of the signals are uncontrolled. No delay or phase adjustments can be made to compensate for measured mismatches.

In this section we describe several approaches to open-loop synchronous timing. Many subsystems operate using a single global clock to which all signals are synchronized. Global clocks are particularly convenient for implementing finite-state machines, FSMs, where the state recirculates about a loop broken by clocked storage elements. Using a single-phase global clock driving edge-triggered flip-flops (described in Section 9.5.1) gives maximum and minimum delay constraints, both of which are dependent on skew. Operating with a two-phase clock and level-sensitive latches, on the other hand, as described in Section 9.5.2, largely eliminates both the minimum delay constraint and the skew sensitivity.

---

[9] Alternatively, one can think of such a system as sending code words with a minimum run length of N (Section 8.4.2.2) at N times the bit rate.

Global-clock timing is inefficient in pipelines (e.g., arithmetic pipelines and communications channels), where most of the data move in a single direction through a series of stages. Operating a pipeline using a global clock gives a maximum data rate that is related to the maximum delay of the longest pipeline stage. Using pipeline timing, as described in Section 9.5.3, however, overcomes this limitation, giving a maximum data rate that is determined by the largest timing uncertainty of a pipeline stage. Pipeline timing places the signals for each pipeline stage in their own clock domain and thus requires explicit synchronization for signals that connect to a location other than the next pipeline stage.

9.5.1 Global Clock, Edge-Triggered Timing

Using a global clock to drive edge-triggered flip-flops is a popular approach to low-end logic design. There are three major reasons for this popularity. First, the edge-triggered flip-flop gives a simple model of sequential logic design in which all signals are in the same clock domain, the output of the flip-flop is the current state, and the input of the flip-flop is the next state (Figure 9-10). Second, edge-triggered flip-flops are widely available in most SSI logic families (CMOS, TTL, and ECL) and the gate-array and standard cell libraries that have been designed to replace SSI. Finally, most logic design courses cover only edge-triggered global clock timing, leaving designers uncomfortable with other approaches. Edge-triggered timing, however, is rarely used in high-end microprocessors and system designs largely because it results in a minimum cycle time dependent on clock skew.

An FSM is realized by feeding back the output of a combinational logic block to a bank of flip-flops that drive the input of the block, as shown in Figure 9-10. Implementing this state feedback using edge-triggered flip-flops leads to a two-sided timing constraint on the combinational logic. The maximum delay of the logic must be less than a limit for the circuit to operate with a given cycle time. The minimum delay must be greater than a limit related to the clock skew for the circuit to operate properly at any clock frequency.

Figure 9-20 shows an edge-triggered state-feedback circuit and its timing. To illustrate clock skew, the circuit shows two banks of flip-flops. A common clock, ϕ, passes through distribution delays to generate a worst-case early clock, ϕ_E, and a worst-case late clock, ϕ_L, that are separated by a skew[10] of t_k, to clock the two banks of flip-flops, producing signal vectors A and B. The signal vectors pass through a combinational logic block producing an output vector, Y that is fed back to the flip-flops.

9.5.1.1 Minimum Delay Constraint

The path from the early (top) flip-flop to the late (bottom) flip-flop gives the minimum delay constraint. The upper bank of flip-flops receives the early clock

---

[10] Clock skew is almost always specified, as we have done here, by a peak-to-peak value, t_k, that is the maximum difference between the earliest clock and the latest clock, not by the maximum difference between a single clock and nominal timing.

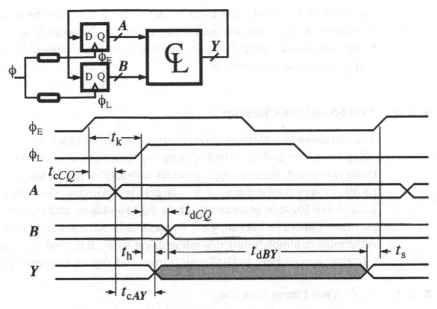

FIGURE 9-20   Edge-Triggered State-Feedback Timing

and generates a transition on signal vector A after a contamination delay (t_{cCQ}). (For simplicity Figure 9-20 shows only the contamination delay from ϕ_E to A and the propagation delay from ϕ_L to B.) After a contamination delay (t_{cAY}), this transition propagates to Y. This transition on Y must not occur until a hold time (t_h) after the transition on late clock ϕ_L, or the state of the bottom flip-flop may become corrupted. This gives the following constraint on the minimum delay of the combinational logic:

(9-16)
$$t_{cAY} \geq t_k + t_h - t_{cCQ}$$

Equation (9-16) does not involve the cycle time. If the minimum delay constraint is not met, the circuit will not work reliably at any clock frequency. Most systems solve the minimum delay problem through good clock distribution to minimize t_k (see Section 9.7). In some cases a ground rule specifying a minimum delay or a minimum number of gates in any logic path is required as well.

9.5.1.2   Maximum Delay Constraint

The maximum delay constraint is set by the other path, from the late (bottom) flip-flop to the early (top) flip-flop. The lower bank of flip-flops receives late clock ϕ_L. Signal vector B stabilizes after a propagation delay (t_{dCQ}). After the propagation delay of the combinational logic (t_{dBY}), output vector Y stabilizes. To ensure reliable sampling, this must happen at least a setup time (t_s) before the early clock, ϕ_E, rises. Summing the delays around the cycle gives the maximum delay constraint, or alternatively the minimum cycle time constraint, as follows:

(9-17)
$$t_{dBY} \leq t_{cy} - t_k - t_s - t_{dCQ}$$
$$t_{cy} \geq t_{dBY} + t_k + t_s + t_{dCQ}$$

Equation (9-17) shows that clock skew is also a factor in the maximum delay constraint on the combinational logic. However, the issue here is performance rather than functionality because the maximum delay constraint can always be met by increasing the cycle time.

9.5.2   Level-Sensitive Clocking

The two major shortcomings of edge-triggered global-clock timing, the minimum delay constraint and the effect of skew on cycle time, can both be eliminated by using two-phase, nonoverlapping clocks with level-sensitive latches. This method results in very robust timing that is largely insensitive to skew; however, it does require that logic be partitioned across the two phases, and signals from the two partitions cannot be intermingled. Because of its advantages, two-phase clocking is the most common timing discipline in use today. It is used in applications from microprocessor chips, to IBM mainframes, to Cray supercomputers.

9.5.2.1   Basic Two-Phase Clocking

Figure 9-21 shows a sequential logic circuit using two-phase nonoverlapping clocks and its timing waveforms. The circuit divides the next-state logic into two combinational logic modules, CL1 and CL2. This can be done, for example, by making a cut through a single combinational logic module along a line of constant delay. Two level-sensitive latches break the state-feedback loop: a master latch clocked by phase 1 ($\phi1$) between CL2 and CL1 and a slave latch clocked by phase 2 ($\phi2$) between CL1 and CL2. The signal vectors around this loop are labeled with superscripts that denote their period of validity. For example, A^2 is valid

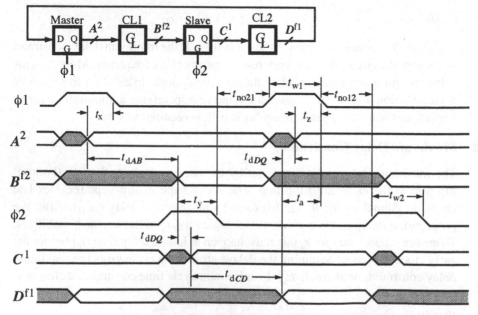

FIGURE 9-21   Two-Phase Nonoverlapping Clocks

during all of $\phi2$, whereas B^{f2} is valid by the falling edge of $\phi2$. This labeling convention is useful to prevent mixing of signals across phases and is explained in more detail below.

The two-phase clock divides the clock cycle, t_{cy}, into four periods corresponding to $\phi1$ high, t_{w1}; the $\phi1$ to $\phi2$ nonoverlap period, t_{no12}; $\phi2$ high, t_{w2}; and the $\phi2$ to $\phi1$ nonoverlap period, t_{no21}. Methods for generating periodic signals with arbitrary timing are discussed in Chapter 12.

The minimum cycle time of the two-phase circuit is limited only by the propagation delay of the combinational logic blocks and the flip-flops. This can be seen by following the timing around one cycle. Signal vector A^2 becomes stable some time, t_x, before the end of $\phi1$. Vector B^{f2} stabilizes after a propagation delay (t_{dAB}) through CL1. We assume that B^{f2} becomes stable after the rising edge of $\phi2$ and time $t_y > t_s$ before the falling edge of $\phi2$. Because vector B arrives while the slave latch is open, vector C^1 becomes valid a latch delay (t_{dDQ}) later, and D^{f1} becomes valid a propagation delay (t_{dCD}) after that at time $t_a > t_s$ before the falling edge of $\phi1$. Assuming that the master latch is open when D arrives, vector A changes a latch delay (t_{dDQ}) later at time t_z before the falling edge of $\phi1$, completing the loop. For proper operation, A must become valid during the second cycle no later than it became valid during the first cycle ($t_z \geq t_x$). This gives a minimum cycle-time constraint involving only propagation delays as expressed by

(9-18) $$t_{cy} \geq t_{dAB} + t_{dCD} + 2t_{dDQ}$$

9.5.2.2 Borrowing Time

Two-phase clocking also imposes a delay constraint on each combinational logic block individually, as illustrated in Figure 9-22. Suppose combinational logic block CL2 has a very small delay. Block CL1 can only borrow delay from CL2 up to a limit related to the width of the clock before it is limited by the time period from the rising edge of a late $\phi1$ to the falling edge of an early $\phi2$. This gives a maximum delay constraint for each phase of

(9-19)
$$t_{dAB} \leq t_{w1} + t_{w2} + t_{no12} - t_s - t_{dCQ} - t_k = t_{cy} - t_{no21} - t_s - t_{dCQ} - t_k$$
$$t_{dCD} \leq t_{w1} + t_{w2} + t_{no21} - t_s - t_{dCQ} - t_k = t_{cy} - t_{no12} - t_s - t_{dCQ} - t_k$$

Note that in the extreme case of $t_{no} = 0$, Eq. (9-19) becomes the same as Eq. (9-17). This signifies that if CL2 has no delay and there is no nonoverlap between the clock phases, the two back-to-back latches are equivalent to an edge-triggered flip-flop.

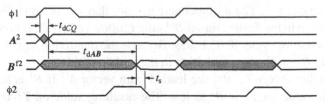

FIGURE 9-22 Single-Phase Maximum Delay Constraint

Time borrowing can be performed across clock cycles as well as between the two phases of one cycle. In general, a two-phase system will operate properly if Eq. (9-19) is observed for every combinational logic block and if for every cycle or closed loop in the logic that crosses N pairs of latches, the total delay of the combinational logic around the loop is less than N clock cycles less the latch delays

$$(9\text{-}20) \qquad t_{dN} \leq N t_{cy} - 2 N t_{dDQ}$$

To illustrate the insensitivity of nonoverlapping two-phase clocking to minimum delays, Figures 9-21 and 9-22 are drawn as if all contamination delays were zero; thus, A^2 and B^{f2} are shown changing as soon as $\phi 1$ goes high, opening the master latch.

9.5.2.3 Effect of Skew

The skew and minimum delay insensitivity of a two-phase timing system are limited by the nonoverlap period. The actual nonoverlap is reduced from the nominal amount by the amount of skew. If the skew exceeds the nonoverlap period, a late $\phi 1$ will overlap an early $\phi 2$, and a minimum delay constraint is required to meet the hold-time requirements on the falling edge of $\phi 1$.

$$(9\text{-}21) \qquad t_{cCD} \geq \max\left(0, t_k + t_h - t_{no12} - t_{cCQ}\right)$$
$$t_{cAB} \geq \max\left(0, t_k + t_h - t_{no21} - t_{cCQ}\right)$$

Similarly, the insensitivity to skew in the maximum delay calculation (Eq. (9-18)) is limited by the pulse width of each phase. If the skew exceeds the width of a phase, the sum of the worst-case timing for each phase individually, as described by Eq. (9-19), becomes less than the overall cycle time given by Eq. (9-18). We can express this overall constraint by adding a term to Eq. (9-18).

$$(9\text{-}22) \qquad t_{cy} \geq t_{dAB} + t_{dCD} + 2 t_{dDQ} + 2 \max\left(0, t_k + t_s + t_{dCQ} - t_w - t_{dDQ}\right)$$

In practice skew is usually well-controlled and the maximum term in Eq. (9-22) is almost always zero. In some cases, particularly single-phase level-sensitive clocking, the nonoverlap period is small or zero, and the minimum delay constraint of Eq. (9-21) is significant. In either case, it is important to understand that two-phase clocking tolerates some amount of skew, but there are limits.

9.5.2.4 Qualified Clocks

With two-phase clocking, it is possible to gate or qualify a clock with a logic signal, as illustrated in Figure 9-23. Signal B^1 is ANDed with $\phi 1$ to produce a qualified clock, B^{q1}. The $q1$ label here denotes that B^{q1} is a qualified version of $\phi 1$. As shown in the figure, signal B^{q1} either follows $\phi 1$, if B^1 is high, or remains low for the entire cycle, if B^1 is low. Because the qualifying signal, B^1, is stable during $\phi 1$, B^{q1} will never transition in the middle of $\phi 1$.

The latches driven by B^{q1} are loaded from vector A^{f1} if B^1 is high, and hold their prior value on Y^2 if B^1 is low. The resulting value on Y^2 is the same as if signal B^1 were used to gate an input multiplexer, as shown at the upper right

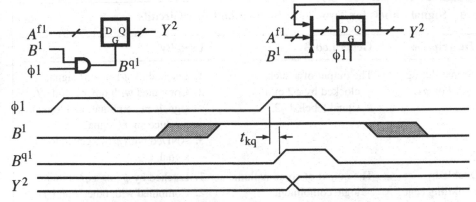

FIGURE 9-23 Qualifying a Clock

side of Figure 9-23. Using a clock qualifier, rather than multiplexers, results in reduced logic, reduced power, reduced delay, and reduced capacitive loading on signal B^1.

Qualifying a clock does result in additional skew, labeled t_{kq}, in Figure 9-23, between the original clock, $\phi 1$, and the qualified clock, B^{q1}. If the qualification is done naively, using a NAND-gate followed by buffers for example, this skew can be significant. With careful design, however, it is possible to reduce this skew to acceptable levels or eliminate it entirely.

Two common approaches to controlling qualification skew are illustrated in Figure 9-24. A low-skew clock-AND gate is shown on the left side of this figure. When the qualifying input, Q^1, is high, the complementary transmission gate is on and the clock, $\phi 1$, is resistively coupled to the output, Q^{q1}. If the RC time constant formed by the transmission gate and the load on Q^{q1} is less than the rise time of $\phi 1$, this gate introduces negligible delay. When Q^1 is low, a small NFET holds Q^{q1} low.

The right side of Figure 9-24 illustrates a path-equalizing approach to clock qualification. Here an early version of the clock, $\phi 1e$, is passed through a qualifying NAND gate that is always enabled to generate $\phi 1$. The qualified clock is generated by an identical circuit gated by Q^1. If the loads on the two inverters are comparable, there will be negligible skew between Q^{q1} and $\phi 1$.

9.5.2.5 Signal Labeling for Two-Phase Clocking

The signal labeling convention we have been using throughout this section is a useful bookkeeping tool for ensuring that two-phase sequential circuits are properly formed. In particular, this convention makes it easy to see which signals

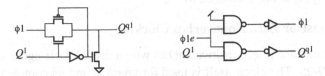

FIGURE 9-24 Minimizing Qualification Skew

TABLE 9-5   **Signal Labels for Two-Phase Sequential Logic Circuits**

Label	Description	Generated By	Used By
1	Stable during all of $\phi 1$.	The output of a latch clocked by $\phi 2$ or a signal labeled *q2*.	1. Latched by $\phi 1$ or a *q1* signal. 2. Combined with other *1* and *f1* signals in combinational logic to produce an *f1* signal. 3. ANDed with $\phi 1$ to generate a *q1* signal.
f1	Stable by falling edge of $\phi 1$.	The output of combinational logic combining *1* and *f1* signals.	1. Latched by $\phi 1$ or a *q1* signal. 2. Combined with other *1* and *f1* signals in combinational logic to produce an *f1* signal.
q1	Follows clock $\phi 1$ or remains low.	A clock and gate combining $\phi 1$ and a qualifier signal labeled *1*.	May be used as the clock input to a latch sampling *1* and *f1* signals.
2	Stable during all of $\phi 2$.	The output of a latch clocked by $\phi 1$ or a signal labeled *q1*.	1. Latched by $\phi 2$ or a *q2* signal 2. Combined with other *2* and *f2* signals in combinational logic to produce an *f2* signal. 3. ANDed with $\phi 2$ to generate a *q2* signal.
f2	Stable by falling edge of $\phi 2$.	The output of combinational logic combining *2* and *f2* signals.	1. Latched by $\phi 2$ or a *q2* signal. 2. Combined with other *2* and *f2* signals in combinational logic to produce an *f2* signal.
q2	Follows clock $\phi 2$ or remains low.	A clock and gate combining $\phi 2$ and a qualifier signal labeled *2*.	May be used as the clock input to a latch sampling *2* and *f2* signals.

can be legally combined in logic, sampled by a particular phase of the clock, or used to qualify a clock. Table 9-5 summarizes this labeling convention.

If all signals are labeled according to how they are generated and signals with a given label are only used in the manner described in the fourth column of the table, then many common errors associated with two-phase logic will be avoided. For example, signal labels make it easy to detect when a *1* or *f1* signal is being illegally combined with a *2* or *f2* signal in a combinational logic block or when a *1* or *f1* signal is being clocked by $\phi 2$.

9.5.2.6   Single-Phase or Zero Nonoverlap Clocking

Many systems use level-sensitive latches with a single clock signal, ϕ, as shown in Figure 9-25. The clock itself is used for phase 1, and its complement is used for phase 2. To avoid the skew associated with inverting the clock, low-true clock inputs are used on the slave latches. This approach decreases the nonoverlap period

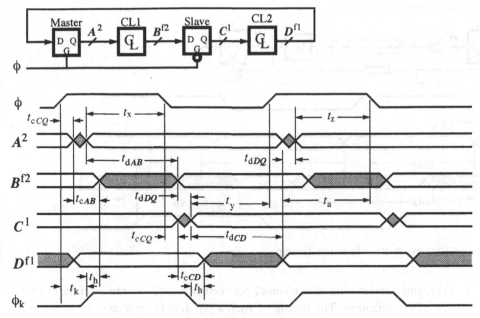

FIGURE 9-25 Single-Phase Clocking

to zero, easing the constraints on time borrowing but making minimum delays more of a concern. Single-phase clocking is widely used because, by using a single clock signal it avoids the nontrivial problems associated with distributing and deskewing two clocks. It is used, for example, in the DEC Alpha microprocessor [DobbWite92].

The timing for single-phase level-sensitive clocking, as shown in Figure 9-25, is similar to that for nonoverlapping two-phase clocking, as shown in Figure 9-21. Single-phase clocking is just the special case where $t_{no} = 0$ and $t_w = t_{cy}/2$ and its timing is still described by Eqs. (9-18) to (9-22). With the nonoverlap time reduced to zero, the minimum delay constraint becomes more significant. For this reason, the contamination delays, which were omitted from Figure 9-21, are shown in Figure 9-25, and a late version of the clock, ϕ_k, is shown at the bottom of the figure to illustrate the effect of clock skew. The figure graphically shows that to meet hold-time specifications on latches receiving the late clocks, the minimum contamination delay of the modules is given by

$$(9\text{-}23) \qquad \begin{aligned} t_{cAB} &\geq t_k + t_h - t_{cCQ} \\ t_{cCD} &\geq t_k + t_h - t_{cCQ} \end{aligned}$$

which is just a simplified version of Eq. (9-21).

As mentioned in Section 9.5.1.2, with the phase width equal to half the clock and a zero nonoverlap time, the maximum delay constraint for each combinational logic block is given by Eq. (9-17).

9.5.3 Pipeline Timing

Many digital systems use pipelines in which signals propagate in one direction through a series of pipeline stages. A processor execution pipeline, a multiplier

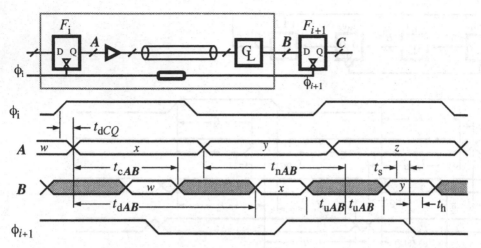

FIGURE 9-26   Pipeline Timing

array, and a communication channel between two modules are examples of this type of organization. The timing of such a pipeline is optimized by generating a clock for each pipeline stage that is centered on the valid period of the data arriving at that stage. Such a clock is easily generated by delaying the clock from the previous stage. As long as there is no feedback in a pipeline, the throughput of the pipeline is limited primarily by the timing uncertainty of each stage. The nominal delay of the stages affects latency but not throughput.

Pipeline timing is widely used on communication channels between chips and boards in digital systems where several bits are often in flight along a single wire at any given time. Because of difficulties in matching delays and distributing multiple clock signals, however, pipeline timing is rarely used for logic.

One stage of a typical pipeline is shown in the gray box in Figure 9-26. Each stage begins with a bank of clocked storage elements (double-edge-triggered flip-flops F_i) that align the data with the stage's clock (ϕ_i) to reduce the timing uncertainty of the input data signals. The outputs of F_i, A are then processed in combinational logic blocks, or transmitted over transmission lines, or both. Each of these steps involves delay, and, more importantly, increases timing uncertainty. This uncertainty stems both from timing variations over a single path due to data dependence, voltage, and so forth, and more significantly from variations between multiple paths through the pipeline stage. Note that the single line drawn along the path from A to B denotes many parallel data signals with possible fan-out and reconvergence in the combinational logic. Finally, the output of the pipeline stage, B, is sampled into the clocked storage elements F_{i+1} of the next pipeline stage by that stage's clock, ϕ_{i+1}.

The bottom part of Figure 9-26 shows the timing for the pipeline stage. Flip-flop output vector A has the value w at the start of the sequence. A short delay, t_{dCQ}, after each clock transition A takes on a new value (x, y, and z). A contamination delay, t_{cAB}, later this transition on vector A causes output vector B to enter an uncertain state, shown as a shaded region. A propagation delay, t_{dAB}, after the transition on A, vector B takes on a stable value corresponding to the value on A. In the figure, this propagation delay is greater than the cycle time, and thus A has undergone a second transition before B has settled in response to the first transition. The second cycle is labeled with a nominal delay and a timing uncertainty rather than a contamination and a propagation delay. For hazard-free logic, these times are related by

$$
\begin{aligned}
t_{nAB} &= (t_{cAB} + t_{dAB})/2 \\
t_{uAB} &= (t_{dAB} - t_{cAB})/2 \\
t_{cAB} &= t_{nAB} - t_{uAB} \\
t_{dAB} &= t_{nAB} + t_{uAB}
\end{aligned}
$$

(9-24)

This timing results in the vector B being valid for a period with width

(9-25)
$$ t_{vB} = t_{cy} - t_{uAB} - t_{rB} $$

9.5.3.1 Optimum Clock Delay

For the pipeline to operate properly, this valid period must be larger than the aperture of F_{i+1} and the receive clock, ϕ_{i+1} must be aligned to place the aperture within the valid period. To center ϕ_{i+1} on the eye of signal B, it should be delayed from ϕ_i by

(9-26)
$$ t_{n\phi_{i+1}} = t_{dCQ} + t_{nAB} + t_{cy}/2 $$

Centering the clock on the eye gives the largest timing margins. However, if latency of the pipeline stage is of concern, the overall delay can be reduced at the expense of degraded timing margins by advancing the receive clock to place the aperture in the leftmost part of the eye. This is achieved with a delay of

(9-27)
$$ t_{n\phi_{i+1}} = t_{dCQ} + t_{dAB} + t_s + t_{rB}/2 + t_{u\phi_{i+1}} $$

Note that this delay must take into account the uncertainty in the delay of ϕ_{i+1} itself.

As the cycle time, t_{cy}, is reduced, the eye of signal B is narrowed according to Eq. (9-25). The minimum cycle time at which timing margins are met is derived from Eq. (9-14) as

(9-28)
$$ t_{cy} \geq t_{uAB} + t_{u\phi_{i+1}} + t_a + t_{rB} $$

The minimum cycle time is divided up, like the abstract eye diagram in Figure 9-16, into receiver aperture, signal transition time, and timing uncertainty. The throughput of a pipeline is limited, not by the delay of any stage, but by the uncertainty of the timing and the bandwidth of the transmitter and receiver.

When the delay of the receive clock, $t_{n\phi_{i+1}}$, is greater than a cycle, one is tempted to use a shorter delay line with delay $t_{n\phi_{i+1}} - nt_{cy}$ for some integer, n. Whether this is advisable depends on the relative stability of the delay line as compared with ϕ_i. If ϕ_i has significant jitter, it is better to use the full delay, and thus the same clock edge that causes a transition on A samples its result on B. Using the full delay also permits the pipeline to be used with an aperiodic clock signal. If, on the other hand, ϕ_i, is periodic and very stable and there is significant uncertainty in the delay line, it is better to use a shorter line that gives the same phase.

A pipeline with a cycle time shorter than the maximum delay has more than one bit in flight along a combinational path between pipeline latches. Achieving such cycle times requires that timing uncertainty be kept small. This is easy to achieve for transmission lines where the delay of an individual line is quite stable, and parallel lines can be easily matched. It is often difficult, however, to achieve low timing uncertainty for logic where the delay of an individual circuit may depend on the input state, and parallel circuits may have vastly different delays. Matching logic circuits requires careful padding of delays along all paths. Logic circuits that are pipelined with several bits in flight along each path are often called *wave-pipelined*.

9.5.3.2   Level-Sensitive Pipeline Timing

It is often advantageous to construct pipelines using level-sensitive latches rather than edge-triggered flip-flops because each of these latches can be realized by just adding a pass gate to the input of the following logic block. The timing for a pipeline with a delayed clock using latches is shown in Figure 9-27. The delay elements are abstracted into a single box labeled module.

The figure shows that latches are less effective than edge-triggered flip-flops at reducing timing uncertainty. Signal A starts with a region of uncertainty that is roughly equal to half the pulse width of the clock

$$(9\text{-}29) \qquad t_{uA} = (t_w - t_{cCQ} - t_s + t_{dDQ})/2 \approx t_w/2$$

Note that $t_x = t_{dDQ} - t_s$ in the figure. The uncertainty in the delay of the module increases this so that at signal B the total uncertainty is

$$(9\text{-}30) \qquad t_{uB} = t_{uAB} + t_{uA}$$

To center the falling edge, which samples the signal, of the receive clock ϕ_{i+1} on

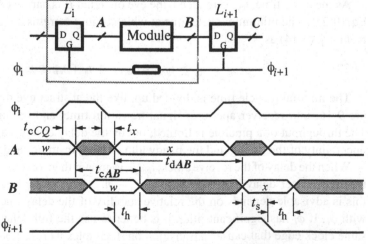

FIGURE 9-27   Level-Sensitive Pipeline Timing

the eye requires a delay of

$$(9\text{-}31) \qquad t_{n\phi_{i+1}} = t_{dCQ} + t_{nAB} + t_w + t_{cy}/2$$

This is just Eq. (9-26) with the clock width added to account for the fact that *A* starts changing with the rising edge of ϕ_i, whereas *B* is sampled by the falling edge of ϕ_{i+1}.

The minimum cycle time for this arrangement is derived from Eq. (9-14) to be

$$(9\text{-}32) \qquad t_{cy} \geq t_{uB} + t_{u\phi_{i+1}} + t_a + t_{rB}$$

which is greater than the cycle time for the edge-triggered case (Eq. (9-28)) by approximately half the clock pulse width.

9.5.3.3 Pipelines With Feedback

Often it is necessary to feed back information between pipeline stages. For example in many types of pipelines, including communications channels, flow-control information must propagate backwards from a late pipeline stage to an early pipeline stage.

In general, to connect signals from one stage of a pipeline to other than the next stage requires a synchronizer, as shown in Figure 9-28. Although all of the signals in a pipeline are synchronized to the same clock signal, they have different phase relationships. To first approximation, each pipeline stage is its own *clock domain*. If signals are arbitrarily routed between stages, it is likely that a stage will sample a signal during its uncertain period, leading to data errors or metastable states. A synchronizer, described in more detail in Section 10.3, retimes a signal to move it from one clock domain to another. For example, in Figure 9-28, the phase relationship between ϕ_{i+1} and ϕ_{i+2} may cause signal x_{i+2} to have a transition during the aperture of ϕ_{i+1}. The synchronizer ensures that signal x_{i+1} is valid during the aperture of ϕ_{i+1}.

The signal is clocked by the ϕ_{i+2} flip-flop before being fed back to reduce its uncertainty. Providing a signal with a wide valid period, such as a flip-flop output, makes it easier to synchronize the signal with a different clock. Feeding back a signal with a narrow eye, such as the output of a combinational logic block, makes the synchronization problem more difficult.

In theory it is possible to adjust the delays between pipeline stages and the overall cycle time to bring two pipeline stages into phase. However, in practice

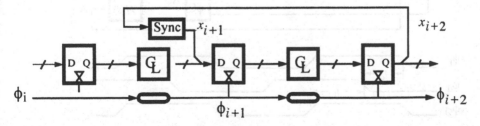

FIGURE 9-28 Pipeline Feedback Requires Synchronization

this is difficult to do reliably short of operating the entire pipeline from a single clock and resorting to state-feedback timing (Section 9.5.1) with a significant reduction in performance. Using synchronizers for feedback signals allows the timing constraints for the pipeline to flow in one direction, down the pipeline, with the synchronizers handling signals flowing in the other direction.

9.6   CLOSED-LOOP TIMING

Closed-loop timing reduces the uncertainty of signals by measuring skew, the DC portion of the uncertainty, and compensating for it. The compensation is performed by a control loop. A phase detector measures the instantaneous phase error of a signal, which includes both skew and jitter. A loop filter averages these measurements to estimate skew, and a clock adjustment is made using either a variable delay line or a variable oscillator to reduce the skew.

All sources of skew within the control loop are largely canceled by closed loop timing. All sources outside the loop are uncompensated. There are several options on control loop placement. Systems employing a global clock typically place the loop just around the clock buffer, as described in Section 9.6.1, to remove buffer-induced clock skew. Pipeline timing systems may close the loop around a reference signal, as described in Section 9.6.4, canceling all repeatable sources of skew (those that track from the reference line to the data lines). Alternatively, a pipeline system can close a separate loop about each signal line individually, as described in Section 9.6.5, to cancel the line-to-line variations in skew as well.

A well-designed closed-loop timing system largely eliminates skew as a source of timing uncertainty, leaving jitter as the major concern.

9.6.1   A Simple Timing Loop

Figure 9-29 illustrates one of the most common applications of a timing loop. A delay-locked loop is used to implement a zero-delay clock buffer. This technique is widely used in clock distribution networks to buffer a clock without introducing skew due to mismatches in clock buffer delays.

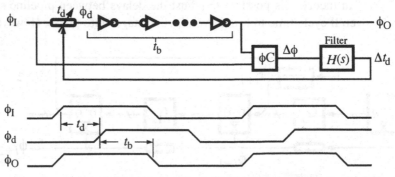

FIGURE 9-29   A Zero-Delay Clock Buffer Using a Delay-Locked Loop

The input clock, ϕ_I, is passed through a variable delay line with delay t_d. The delayed clock, ϕ_d, is then buffered by an odd number of inverters with unknown delay, t_b, to generate the output clock, ϕ_O. A phase comparator (ϕC) measures the relative phase of these two signals

$$(9\text{-}33) \qquad \Delta\phi = 2\pi(t_{\phi_I} - t_{\phi_O})/t_{cy} = \pi - 2\pi(t_d + t_b)/t_{cy}$$

For convenience, we lump any comparator gain into the filter. A loop filter, usually a low-pass with a large DC gain, smooths the result to filter noise and stabilize the loop. The output of the filter, Δt_d, is used to adjust the variable delay line about its nominal delay, t_{d0}.

$$(9\text{-}34) \qquad t_d = t_{d0} + \Delta t_d$$

Note that the transfer function of this filter, $H(s)$, has units of seconds per radian.

The feedback loop adjusts t_d to make t_d and t_b sum to exactly $t_{cy}/2$, which brings ϕ_O in phase with ϕ_I. To see how this works intuitively, suppose t_d was too small, causing ϕ_O to lag ϕ_I. Then $\Delta\phi$ would be positive, giving a positive Δt_d, which would increase t_d to decrease the lag.

9.6.1.1 Residual Error

When the loop stabilizes, a small residual phase error, $\Delta\phi_r$, remains. The amount of residual error is determined by the DC gain around the loop by

$$(9\text{-}35) \qquad \Delta\phi_r = \frac{2\pi}{t_{cy}} \left(\frac{t_{cy}/2 - t_{d0} - t_b}{1 + k_L} \right)$$

where the DC loop gain, k_L is

$$(9\text{-}36) \qquad k_L = \frac{2\pi}{t_{cy}} H(0)$$

Of course, any phase-offset in the phase comparator will also result in a residual error. We will see in Section 9.6.2.1, that by using the target flip-flop as a the phase comparator, this phase-offset can be used to advantage to compensate for the aperture offset of the flip-flop.

9.6.1.2 Loop Dynamics

The dynamics of the loop are determined by the dynamics of the individual elements and the transfer function of the loop filter. If we assume that the phase comparator gives instantaneous measurements and the delay line responds instantaneously to delay commands, the loop will respond to a perturbation, $e(s)$, with a transfer function of

$$(9\text{-}37) \qquad \frac{\Delta\phi(s)}{e(s)} = \frac{1}{1 + H(s)}$$

With simple element dynamics, loop stability is not much of an issue. In practice the loop filter should have a low-pass characteristic with a high DC gain

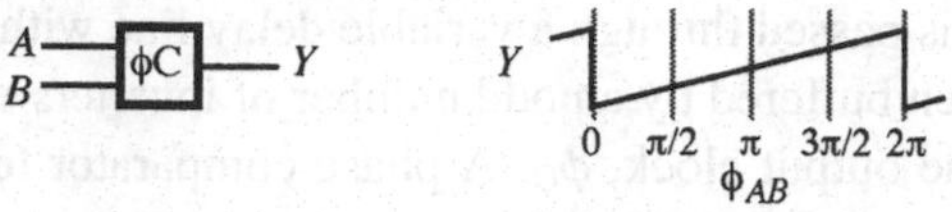

A ―――[φC]― Y   Y (waveform)

0   π/2   π   3π/2   2π
ϕ_{AB}

FIGURE 9-30   Ideal Phase Comparator

to minimize residual error and a low cutoff frequency, f_c, to attenuate jitter in the input clock.

For a simple low-pass, $H(s) = ka/(s + a)$, this gives

$$(9\text{-}38) \qquad \frac{\Delta\phi(s)}{e(s)} = \left[\frac{s+a}{s+a(k+1)}\right]$$

Equation 9-38 gives an exponential response with a time constant of $\tau = 1/a(k+1)$. In the absence of an error input, $e(t)$, $\phi(t)$ decays according to

$$(9\text{-}39) \qquad \phi(t) = \phi(0)\exp\left[-a(k+1)t\right]$$

Increasing the loop gain decreases the time constant, giving faster loop convergence. There is no danger of instability as long as the roll-off is at a low enough frequency that the delay of the phase comparator and delay line can be ignored. At these frequencies, this is a first-order system. Instability is an issue with phase-locked loops, as discussed in Section 9.6.6.3.

9.6.2   Phase Comparators

A key element of any timing loop is a phase comparator, which measures the relative delay, or phase, between two signals. Phase comparator circuits are discussed in detail in Section 12.4. Here we present a systems view of the phase comparator.

An ideal phase comparator, as shown in Figure 9-30, has two inputs, A and B, and one output, ϕ_{AB}, which reports an instantaneous measurement of the phase between the input signals.

$$(9\text{-}40) \qquad \phi_{AB} = \frac{2\pi}{t_{cy}}(t_A - t_B)$$

In some applications, both inputs A and B are periodic signals, clocks, with identical frequency. In these applications, the delay between respective transitions of A and B is measured to determine the relative phase, as shown in Figure 9-31(a). In other applications, input A is a clock, but input B is a data signal that may have zero or one transition during each clock cycle. In this case, shown in Figure 9-31(b), the phase comparator measures the relative delay between each transition on B and the *nearest* transition on A to determine the phase. In this case, there is no phase information between the transitions of B. The phase between two

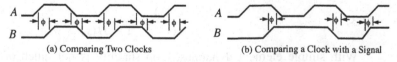

(a) Comparing Two Clocks   (b) Comparing a Clock with a Signal

FIGURE 9-31   Phase Comparison of Clocks and Signals

FIGURE 9-32   Flip-Flop Phase Comparator

synchronous signals can be measured by comparing each to a reference clock and subtracting.

In practice it is not possible to build an ideal comparator. Real phase comparators introduce offsets and have some amount of lag. They cannot provide any estimates of phase in the absence of transitions on their inputs. They also operate only over a certain range of phase and have a nonlinear gain, especially outside this range.

When referring to the range of a phase comparator we must distinguish between the *linear range* of the comparator and the *lock range* of the comparator. The linear range is the range of phase over which the comparator maintains a linear phase-to-voltage relationship. The dynamics of the timing loop will vary significantly outside the linear range. The lock range is the range of phase over which the comparator output has the proper output polarity. This is the range over which a timing loop using the comparator can acquire and lock to a signal.

Most phase comparators in use today are variants of either an exclusive–or (XOR) phase comparator (Figure 9-35) or a flip-flop phase comparator (Figure 9-32). Both of these comparators have a lock range of 2π. They have very different linear ranges, however.

9.6.2.1   Flip-Flop Phase Comparator

As illustrated in Figure 9-32, the flip-flop phase comparator has a narrow linear range of operation with high gain in the aperture time about a phase of zero and a second narrow linear range in the aperture time about a phase of π. This type of comparator operates by using input A to drive the clock of a flip-flop and input B to supply the data. If input B is early by more than t_s, the flip-flop samples B when it is high, and the output is a 1. Similarly, if B is late by more than t_h, the output is a 0. The phase-to-voltage transfer function makes a steep transition between 1 and 0 in the aperture time of the flip-flop.

The slope of this transition depends on the circuit design of the flip-flop, as described in Section 12.1. For a regenerative flip-flop, this slope is extremely steep, making this type of phase comparator essentially a digital output device. For a flip-flop without regeneration, the slope is equal to the slope of the signal transition on B times the gain of the flip-flop. In this case, the flip-flop is acting as a sample-and-hold amplifier with a narrow aperture.

When used with double-edge-triggered flip-flops or when sampling a signal on B that may make a transition in either direction, or no transition at all, as in Figure 9-31 (b), the flip-flop phase comparator must be augmented, as shown in Figure 9-33, to resolve the resulting phase ambiguity. This circuit has two outputs labeled Y and T. Output T signals if there has been a transition on B

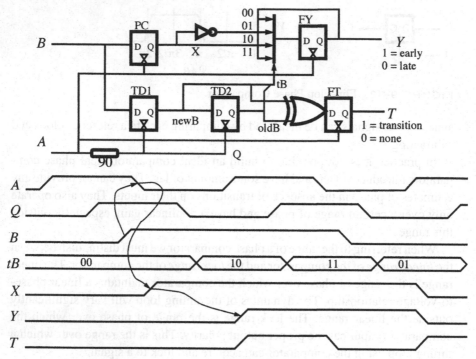

FIGURE 9-33   Resolving Phase Ambiguity with a Flip-Flop Comparator

within $\pm\pi/2$ radians of the second previous transition on A. Output Y indicates if the last transition on B was early or late. In practice, output T is usually used to gate a charge pump filter, and thus Y is ignored unless $T = 1$.

The circuit of Figure 9-33 uses five flip-flops. Flip-flop PC acts as a raw phase comparator, measuring the phase of a transition on B with respect to A. If the transition on B is falling, however, its output is incorrect, (i.e., it will signal a 1 for a late transition and a 0 for an early transition). Also, if the signal on B is steady, X will follow B and gives an erroneous early or late indication, depending on the value of B. To correct for these problems, flip-flop pair TD1 and TD2 act as a transition detector by sampling B using a quadrature clock, Q, delayed from A by $90°(\pi/2$ radians). At each transition of A, the signal $oldB$ represents the value of B $\pi/2$ before the previous transition of A, and $newB$ represents the value of B $\pi/2$ after the previous transition of A. The signal tB, the concatenation $\{newB, oldB\}$, is used to control a multiplexer that selects the source for output Y. On a rising transition of B, $tB = 10$, the signal X is selected, whereas the complement of X is selected on a falling transition, $tB = 01$. The remaining two inputs hold the output stable when there is no transition on B.

The waveforms at the bottom of Figure 9-33 illustrate operation of the circuit. The first transition on B is a rising transition that is early with respect to the second transition on A. This gives $X = 1$ and $tB = 10$, causing both Y and T to go high on the third transition of A. The arrows show the timing flow from B to A to X to Y and illustrate the one-cycle lag introduced by the circuit. The second transition of B is late with respect to the fourth transition on A, giving $X = 1$ and

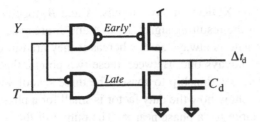

FIGURE 9-34   Driving a Charge Pump with Y and T

$tB = 01$. This time the multiplexer gates the complement of X to the input of FY, giving $Y = 0$ and $T = 1$ on the fifth edge of A.

The outputs Y and T can be combined to produce *Early'* and *Late* signals to drive a charge pump, as shown in Figure 9-34. This circuit uses a charge pump to produce an analog control voltage, Δt_d, to adjust the delay of the delay line in Figure 9-29. On an early transition, signal *Early'* goes low for one cycle, turning on the PFET, which pumps charge onto capacitor C_d, slightly increasing voltage Δt_d. Similarly, signal *Late* is asserted for one cycle on a late transition, turning on the NFET, which dumps charge off of the capacitor, decreasing control voltage Δt_d. The charge pump serves as an integrating loop filter (the transfer function can be approximated by $1/s$). If a digitally controlled delay line is used, the same effect can be achieved by using the *Early'* and *Late* signals to control a saturating up-down counter.

The flip-flop phase comparator has two significant advantages. First, the high gain of the comparator gives low phase error and jitter in the presence of voltage noise. The phase error induced by V_N of voltage noise is $\phi_N = V_N/G$, where G is the gain. Second, by using the same flip-flop for a phase comparator as is used to sample the data, the aperture offset of the flip-flop can be compensated, eliminating one source of skew. We will use this feature to advantage in Section 9.6.4.

9.6.2.2   Exclusive–Or (XOR) Phase Comparator

As shown in Figure 9-35, the exclusive-or (XOR) phase comparator has a wide (π radian) linear range of operation centered on a phase of $\pi/2$ (quadrature). The wide linear range necessarily gives a low gain. The basic circuit, as shown, only works on periodic signals with a 50% duty factor.

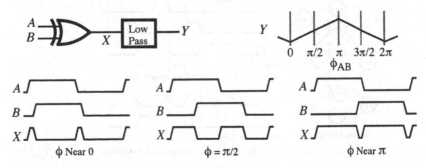

FIGURE 9-35   Exclusive-Or (XOR) Phase Comparator

The circuit operates by XORing the two inputs, A and B, together and measuring the duty factor of the resulting signal, X. If A and B are exactly in phase, the output of the XOR gate is always zero, whereas if they are out of phase by π radians, the output is always one. Between these two points, the duty factor of the output has a linear relationship to phase. The three sets of waveforms at the bottom of the figure show how the duty factor is small for a phase near zero, 50% at $\phi = \pi/2$, and large for a phase near π. The output of the XOR may be integrated over each cycle to give an instantaneous measure of duty factor. More commonly, the output is passed directly to the low-pass loop filter.

The relatively low gain of the XOR phase comparator makes it more sensitive to noise. Compared with the flip-flop phase comparator, a small amount of noise on signal Y results in a relatively large phase error. The XOR comparator, however, is widely used in applications that require a quadrature phase relationship and in applications that need a wide linear range.

9.6.2.3 Sequential Phase and Frequency Comparator

The 12-state asynchronous sequential state machine with the state diagram shown in Figure 9-36(a) is often used as a combination phase and frequency comparator. This circuit is essentially a three-state transition counter. The circuit has two inputs, a and b, two outputs, A and B, and three "counter states" $(-1, 0, \text{and } 1)$. On each positive transition of input a the counter is incremented, unless it is already at 1, in which case it stays there. Similarly, on each positive transition of input b, the counter is decremented unless it is already -1. When the counter is in state 1, output A is high, indicating that a has recently had more transitions than b, and when the counter is in state -1, output B is high, indicating that b is ahead in the saturating transition count.

The output of this circuit gives both frequency and phase information. If output B is subtracted from A, the filtered result has a phase-to-voltage transfer function similar to that shown in Figure 9-30 except that the linear range has a width of 4π centered on a phase difference of 0. The sign of the phase difference gives the sign of the frequency difference between the two signals, whereas the magnitude of the phase difference gives the phase difference, assuming the higher frequency signal is leading.

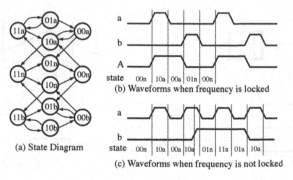

(a) State Diagram

(b) Waveforms when frequency is locked

(c) Waveforms when frequency is not locked

FIGURE 9-36   Sequential Phase Comparator

Each state in the state diagram of Figure 9-36(a) is labeled with the state of inputs a and b along with a letter (a, b, or n). The letter indicates whether a is leading (a), b is leading (b), or neither is leading (n). The three letters correspond to the three states of the transition counter. For example, in state "10a," $a = 1$, $b = 0$, and a is leading (count $= 1$). Output A is high whenever a is leading and output B is high whenever b is leading.

The waveforms and state sequence for the case where the two inputs have the same frequency are shown in Figure 9-36(b). When input a is early, output A goes high from the rising edge of a to the rising edge of b. Similarly if b is early, output B will go high for the period between the two rising edges. Thus, the duty factor of the active output determines the amount of phase difference (from 0 to 2π).

When a and b have different frequencies, this phase comparator acts as a one-bit transition counter frequency comparator. As illustrated in Figure 9-36(c), this frequency-sensitive behavior makes this type of phase comparator attractive for use in phase-locked loops (Section 9.6.6). The state sequence can best be understood by noticing that transitions between the different classes of states (a, b, and n) always happen on positive transitions of one of the inputs. A positive transition on a moves up in the diagram (from b to n or n to a), whereas a positive transition on b moves down in the diagram (from a to n or n to b). Once the state machine enters the a states, it will not enter the b states and raise output B unless there are two positive transitions on b between positive transitions on a (i.e., unless b has a higher frequency than a). Thus, the identity of the active output (A or B) determines the sign of the frequency difference (and the phase difference) between the two inputs.

If the magnitude of frequency difference is required, it can be determined by measuring the rate of change of phase difference from cycle to cycle.

Equations (9-41) describe the logic required to implement the state machine of Figure 9-36(a). Two state variables, s_0 and s_1, are required in addition to the two outputs, A and B.

(9-41)
$$s_0 = [s_0 \wedge (b \vee B)] \vee (B \wedge \bar{s}_1) \vee (A \wedge b)$$
$$s_1 = [s_1 \wedge (a \vee A)] \vee (A \wedge \bar{s}_0) \vee (B \wedge a)$$
$$A = (\bar{B} \wedge \bar{s}_1 \wedge a) \vee [A \wedge (\bar{s}_1 \vee \bar{s}_0)]$$
$$B = (\bar{A} \wedge \bar{s}_0 \wedge b) \vee [B \wedge (\bar{s}_1 \vee \bar{s}_0)]$$

The sequential phase and frequency comparator should only be used on clean periodic signals. It cannot be used, for example, to compare a data signal to a clock because the data signal may have a much smaller number of transitions than the clock. It should also not be used to compare two noisy clocks, for a spurious transition on one clock will cause it to slip an entire cycle in an effort to get an additional transition on the other clock.

A sequential phase and frequency comparator should never be used in a delay-locked loop or other application where it cannot advance the controlled clock by an entire cycle. If the comparator enters the wrong state, either because of incorrect initialization or noise, it will indicate that timing is off by an entire cycle. A DLL timing loop using such a comparator will drive the variable delay

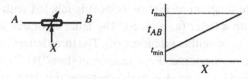

FIGURE 9-37   System View of a Variable Delay Line

line to its stops, trying to make up for the missing cycle. A sequential phase-only comparator can be used with a DLL as described in Exercise 9-6.

9.6.3   Variable Delay Line

The other key component of any timing loop is a variable delay line or variable frequency oscillator. The phase comparator serves as the sensor for the control loop and the variable delay line serves as the actuator. Delay line circuits are discussed in depth in Section 12.2. Here we give a brief systems view of variable delay lines.

As shown in Figure 9-37, a variable delay line accepts a timing input, A, and a control input, X, and produces a timing output, B, where the delay from A to B is determined by the value on X. Input X may either be an analog control voltage, or a digital control signal. Digitally variable delay lines are usually preferred because they are more immune to noise and can be constructed to operate over a wider dynamic range than their analog counterparts.

As shown on the right side of the figure, as X is varied across its range, the delay of the line varies from a minimum to a maximum value. In a closed loop timing system, the minimum value, t_{min}, determines the maximum frequency at which the loop will operate. Similarly, the maximum delay of the line, t_{max}, determines the minimum frequency at which the loop will operate. For example, in the zero-delay clock buffer of Figure 9-29, the minimum and maximum frequencies of operation are given by

(9-42)
$$f_{min} = 1/(t_{max} + t_b)$$
$$f_{max} = 1/(t_{min} + t_b)$$

The linearity of delay with X and the absolute value of the delay for a given setting of X are not critical, for a control loop is closed around the delay line. As long as the delay is monotonic with X, the loop will compensate for any offsets or nonlinearities. In addition to its delay range, the critical property of the delay line is its jitter. The control loop is not fast enough to correct for jitter in the line, and thus any high-frequency variation in the delay of the line will add to the overall jitter of the system. In Section 12.2, particular attention is paid to delay line circuits that achieve low jitter by isolating delay from power supply fluctuations.

9.6.4   Bundled Closed-Loop Timing

Although a zero-delay clock buffer like that shown in Figure 9-29 cancels one source of skew, the clock buffer, many other skew-contributing timing components are left out of the control loop. The repeatable component of the skew of the

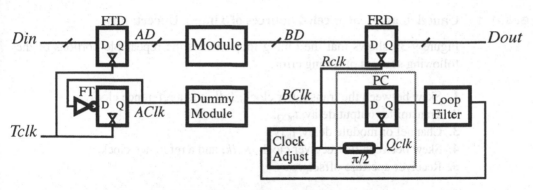

FIGURE 9-38 Bundled Closed-Loop Timing

transmitter clock, the delay of the transmission line or module, the output delay of the transmitter, and the aperture offset of the receiver can all be canceled by closing the timing loop around a replica of the data path, as shown in Figure 9-38.

In the figure, a multibit data channel, *Din*, is aligned to a transmit clock, *Tclk*, by a bank of flip-flops, FTD, passed through a module (e.g., a transmission line), and reclocked into a receiving bank of flip-flops, FRD, by a receive clock, *Rclk*, to produce output *Dout*. To provide a timing reference, a toggle flip-flop, FT, is used to generate *Aclk*, with timing identical to data signals *AD*, that has a transition on every clock edge. This signal is passed through a replica of the module that processes the data signals to generate *Bclk*, which has timing identical to the received data *BD*. A timing loop closed around a quadrature phase comparator, shown in the gray box, centers the receiving clock, *Rclk*, on the eye of signal *Bclk*. The phase comparator uses a flip-flop identical to the data-receiving flip-flop to cancel the aperture offset. Although drawn slightly differently, this circuit is identical to that of Figure 9-2.

To the extent that sources of timing uncertainty are repeatable, both from cycle to cycle and from instance to instance, the timing loop will cancel them, as illustrated in the waveforms of Figure 9-39. Signal vector **AD**, and reference *Aclk* transition t_{nCQ} after each transition on *Tclk*. Vector **BD** and reference *Bclk* transition t_{nAB} later. The timing loop locks the quadrature clock, *Qclk*, to *Bclk* with an offset lag equal to the aperture offset, t_{ao}, of the phase detector flip-flop. This places the receive clock, *Rclk*, which is offset from *Qclk* by $\pi/2$, so that the aperture is exactly centered on the eye of data vector **BD**.

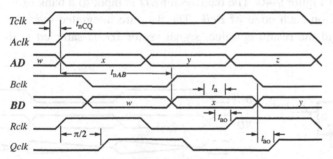

FIGURE 9-39 Waveforms for Bundled Closed-Loop Timing

9.6.4.1   Canceled and Uncanceled Sources of Timing Uncertainty

Figure 9-39 shows that the timing loop cancels the repeatable portions of the following sources of timing error:

1. Skew between the transmitter clock, *Tclk*, and a reference clock.
2. Transmitter output delay, t_{nCQ}.
3. Channel or module delay, t_{nAB}.
4. Skew between the receiver clock, *Rclk*, and a reference clock.
5. Receiver aperture offset, t_{ao}.

There are, however, several sources of timing uncertainty that are not canceled:

1. Skew in the transmitter clock between individual flip-flops, t_{kT}.
2. Jitter in the transmitter clock, t_{jT}.
3. Variations from flip-flop to flip-flop and from cycle to cycle in the transmitter output delay, t_{uCQ}.
4. Variations from flip-flop to flip-flop and from cycle to cycle in the channel delay, t_{uAB}.
5. Skew in the distribution of the receive clock, *Rclk*, to the receive flip-flops, t_{kR}.
6. Jitter in the receive clock, t_{jR}.
7. Phase error in the delay line relating *Rclk* and *Qclk*, t_{kQ}.
8. Variations from cycle to cycle and from flip-flop to flip-flop in the aperture offset time, t_{uao}.

In short, the timing loop cancels the portions of timing uncertainty that track between the data path and the reference path. Variations from channel to channel, and jitter from cycle to cycle remain. In Section 9.6.5, we will see how to eliminate the channel to channel variations. Jitter, however is a fundamental limit on the timing uncertainty of the system.

9.6.4.2   Integrating Receivers

Much of the complexity of the timing loop of Figure 9-38 is devoted to phase shifting the reference clock, *Bclk*, by $\pi/2$ plus t_{ao}. A considerably simpler timing system results if one uses a receive flip-flop that can accept *Bclk* directly. An integrating receiver, as described by [SidiHoro97a], uses *Bclk* directly, as shown in Figure 9-40. The data vector **BD** is input to a bank of integrators that are reset on each edge of *Bclk*. The data are integrated over the entire clock cycle, and the resulting value, signal vector **ID**, is sampled at the end of the cycle.

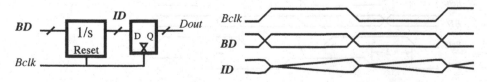

FIGURE 9-40   Integrating Receiver

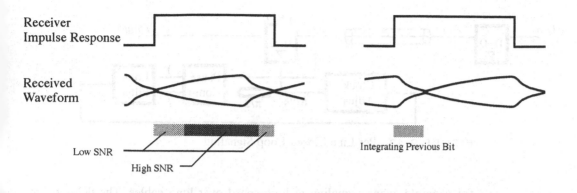

Receiver
Impulse Response

Received
Waveform

Low SNR

High SNR

Integrating Previous Bit

(a) Integrating Receiver with no Jitter   (b) Integrating Receiver with Jitter

FIGURE 9-41   Problems with Integrating Receivers

The integrators may be actual analog integrators [SidiHoro97a] or can be approximated by sampling the signal at several points during the cycle and voting the resulting digital signals as in [YangHoro96] and [LeeKim95]. The circuit design of integrating receivers is discussed in Section 11.3.3.

Integrating receivers filter out high-frequency noise at the expense of increased sensitivity to jitter and low-frequency noise. By integrating over the entire bit cell, noise at frequencies higher than the bit rate is averaged out. However, as illustrated in Figure 9-41, integrating over the bit cell has two disadvantages. With perfect timing (Figure 9-41(a)), the integration is performed over periods (light shaded regions) with low signal-to-noise ratio. Thus, the average signal-to-noise ratio over the integration period is reduced compared with a narrower aperture. When there is a timing offset (skew or jitter) between the integration period and the received waveform (Figure 9-41(b)), intersymbol interference is the result. The receiver integrates part of the adjacent bit, as illustrated by the shaded region, together with the current bit. These problems can be reduced, in part, by shortening the integration window or aperture, in effect averaging the signal over the aperture time of the receiver. However, this is what a normal receiver already does. The ideal solution is to build a receiver with an impulse response matched to the received waveform, as described in Section 11.3.3.3.

One advantage of the integrating receiver, or any receiver that uses *Bclk* directly to sample the data, is that jitter in the transmitter clock is largely canceled because the same edges used to clock data out of the transmitter are used to clock data into the receiver.

The major weaknesses of bundled closed-loop timing are (1) that it requires a reference clock, and (2) that it is vulnerable to mismatches between the timing of each data signal and the timing of the reference clock. These problems can both be overcome by closing a separate timing loop for each signal line.

9.6.5   Per-Line Closed-Loop Timing

Closing a timing loop around each signal line independently eliminates timing uncertainty due to mismatch between channels. This is a significant advantage,

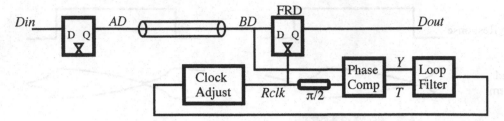

FIGURE 9-42   Per-Line Closed-Loop Signaling

for example, when signaling at high-speed over long cables. The delay of an individual pair in a cable is very stable. However, it is not unusual in an inexpensive cable to have a mismatch of several nanoseconds between the fastest and slowest pair. Although this mismatch can be eliminated by hand tuning the cable assembly on a TDR, it is more cost effective to use a timing convention that is insensitive to the mismatch.

Figure 9-42 shows the circuitry for one data line using per-line closed-loop signaling. The receive clock, $Rclk$, is locked, in quadrature, directly to the received data, BD. The phase comparator uses a flip-flop identical to FRD to compensate for aperture offset and place the sampling aperture of FRD directly on the center of the eye. Because BD may make transitions in either direction, or no transition at all, the phase comparator is constructed, as shown in Figure 9-33, to signal both if a transition occurred during the last cycle, T, and whether the transition was early or late, Y. On each transition ($T = 1$), the loop filter samples Y and adjusts the clock accordingly, as shown, for example, in Figure 9-34.

In the absence of transitions on the data line, the timing loop has no information about the relative phase between $Rclk$ and BD. If the clock source is stable such as a reference clock adjusted via a stable variable delay line, this is not a serious limitation. The delay line can be set once during a training sequence at system reset, and the system can be operated open-loop thereafter.

If the clock source is subject to drift, however (e.g., a local voltage-controlled oscillator connected in a phase-locked loop), then periodic transitions on BD are required to keep $Rclk$ centered on the eye. The minimum transition frequency is given by Eq. (9-15). These transitions can be provided, as described in Section 9.4.2.

The cost of providing separate clock generation for each signal line can be reduced by sharing a single multiphase clock source, as shown in Figure 9-43. A tapped delay line produces a set of closely spaced clock phases $\{\phi_1, \phi_2, \ldots, \phi_m\}$ that are separated in time by an amount comparable to their rise time. These clocks need only cover a range of π in phase because their complements give the remaining π. Each channel uses a multiplexer–interpolator to generate a pair of clock phases separated by $\pi/2$ in phase. The multiplexer selects the nearest two clock phases, and the interpolator mixes them to generate an intermediate phase. One of these phases is used as the sample clock, and the other is input to the quadrature phase detector. The timing loop operates as described above but with

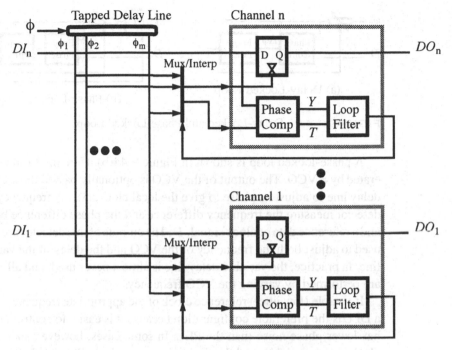

FIGURE 9-43   Clock Sharing for Per-Line Closed-Loop Signaling

the loop filter output used to control the selection of, and interpolation between, taps of the common delay line.

This organization results in considerable cost savings compared with building a stand-alone circuit for each channel. The variable delay line that would have been required for each channel is replaced by the less expensive multiplexer–interpolator. Also, the $\pi/2$ delay line required to use a flip-flop as a quadrature phase detector is eliminated by adding a quadrature output from the multiplexer.

This organization also has advantages when used in a closed-loop timing system employing a phase-locked loop. When all of the data bits of an input channel are known to have the same frequency, only a single voltage-controlled oscillator (VCO) is required to generate the clock ϕ. Each channel independently controls its phase by adjusting its multiplexer–interpolator. The outputs of the individual channels' loop filters are combined to control the frequency of the VCO. The combination of information from multiple channels reduces the noise in the VCO control voltage and results in a more stable clock.

9.6.6   Phase-Locked Loops

A closed-loop timing system may be built around either a delay-locked loop (DLL) or a phase-locked loop (PLL). As illustrated in Figure 9-44 (a), a delay-locked loop varies the phase of a reference clock, ϕ_r, to align it with a data or clock signal, D. A phase comparator is used to detect the phase difference, $\Delta\phi$, between D and ϕ_r. A filtered version of this phase difference is used to control the delay of a variable delay line.

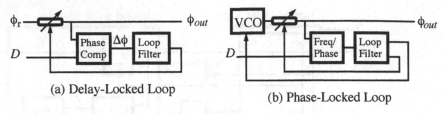

(a) Delay-Locked Loop

(b) Phase-Locked Loop

FIGURE 9-44   Delay-Locked and Phase-Locked Loops

A phase-locked loop is shown in Figure 9-44(b). Here the local clock is generated by a VCO. The output of the VCO is optionally passed through a variable delay line to adjust its phase to give the local clock, ϕ_{out}. A frequency and phase detector measure the frequency difference and the phase difference between ϕ_{out} and a reference data or clock signal, D. The outputs of this detector are filtered and used to adjust both the frequency of the VCO and the delay of the variable delay line. In practice, the variable delay line is almost never used, and all adjustments are performed by varying the VCO frequency.

If a stable (low jitter) reference clock of the appropriate frequency is available, a DLL is the preferable configuration because it is easier to control and typically has lower phase noise than the PLL. In some cases, however, such a reference clock is not available, and the timing loop must be built around a VCO.

9.6.6.1   Voltage-Controlled Oscillators

The key component of a phase-lock loop is a VCO, which takes a control input, V_f, and produces a periodic signal with frequency

$$(9-43) \qquad\qquad f = f_c + k_f V_f$$

where f_c is the center frequency of the VCO and k_f, with units of hertz per volt, is the gain. The gain determines frequency range and stability. The larger the gain, the larger the frequency range for a given range of V_f. However, a large gain also makes the VCO more susceptible to noise on V_f, giving a less stable frequency source. In general the VCO is designed with the smallest gain that gives the required frequency range.

The circuit design of VCOs is discussed in Section 12.3. Two types are in common use today: ring oscillators and resonant oscillators. A ring oscillator VCO is a ring of an odd number of inverters. The frequency is varied by either changing the number of stages, the delay per stage, or both. Often a digital coarse adjustment selects the number of stages while an analog fine adjustment determines the delay per stage. This gives a wide frequency range while keeping k_f, the gain of the analog control voltage, and hence the phase noise, low. Ring-oscillator VCOs are very popular on integrated circuits because they can be built without the external inductors, crystals, or ceramic resonators required for resonant VCOs. However, they usually give a noisier clock than a resonant oscillator.

A resonant VCO uses an LC or crystal oscillator and tunes the frequency using a voltage-variable (varactor) capacitor. Voltage-controlled crystal oscillators

(VCXOs) typically have a very narrow frequency range and provide a very stable clock source. For applications where a narrow frequency range is adequate and phase noise is an issue, a resonant VCO, or VCXO, is usually preferred.

9.6.6.2 Frequency Comparator

Although it is possible to operate a phase-lock loop using only a phase comparator, faster lock and more stable operation are achieved by using a phase comparator and a frequency comparator or a combined phase–frequency comparator. A transition counter, such as the sequential phase–frequency comparator described in Section 9.6.2.3, gives the sign of the frequency difference, which ensures that the VCO is commanded in the correct direction.

In contrast, if a phase comparator is used to control the loop, the VCO will be commanded in the wrong direction almost half the time. The output of the phase comparator is a periodic signal at the difference frequency of the two inputs. The only thing that makes the loop converge in this case is that the periodic signal spends slightly longer in the correct half of the period than in the incorrect half. This is because, when the phase difference is in the correct half of the period, the loop is acting to decrease the frequency difference and hence increase the period of the phase difference.

Figure 9-45 shows the convergence of a 100-MHz loop that is initialized at 170 MHz using both a phase-only comparator (top) and a phase–frequency comparator (bottom). In each case, a plot of both the frequency and the output of the phase comparator is shown as a function of time. The loop has a gain of 10^{10} and the filter described in the example in Section 9.6.6.3. The top two traces show that the loop with the phase comparator takes almost 5 μs to lock because its phase comparator gives a positive output only slightly more often than it gives a negative output. The bottom two traces show that the loop with the phase–frequency comparator locks in less than 1 μs because its phase comparator always gives a positive output as long as there is a frequency difference.

A frequency comparator that gives an analog or digital measure of the magnitude of the frequency difference can be built. For example, one can measure

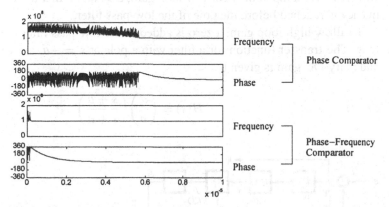

FIGURE 9-45 Dynamics of PLLs using Phase–Frequency and Phase Only

the period of the two signals by integrating a constant over a cycle. The frequency can then be derived from the periods, or the period difference can be used directly. However such comparators are rarely used in practice. A binary (sign only) frequency comparator is adequate to get the loop to lock quickly to the correct frequency. Once at the correct frequency, a phase comparator must be used to control the loop because a frequency comparator would leave a small residual error in frequency that would eventually integrate into a large difference in phase.

9.6.6.3   Loop Dynamics and Loop Filter

The VCO in a PLL acts as an integrator and gives more interesting loop dynamics than a DLL. A loop filter, with a zero as well as a pole, is usually required to stabilize the loop. A diagram showing the frequency response of each element of a PLL is shown in Figure 9-46. The VCO has a gain of k_f and integrates the frequency, f, to give phase, ϕ. The phase detector has gain k_p, and the loop filter has transfer function $H(s)$. The overall transfer function of the loop from a phase disturbance $e(s)$, to the output phase, $\phi(s)$ is given by

$$(9\text{-}44) \qquad \frac{\phi(s)}{e(s)} = \frac{s}{s + k_f k_p H(s)}$$

If a simple low-pass filter, $H(s) = a/(s + a)$, is used for the loop filter, the transfer function becomes

$$(9\text{-}45) \qquad \frac{\phi(s)}{e(s)} = \frac{s(s + a)}{s^2 + sa + ka}$$

where $k = k_f k_p$. The denominator has roots at

$$(9\text{-}46) \qquad s = \frac{-a \pm \sqrt{a(a - 4k)}}{2}$$

which is overdamped only for low loop gain, $a > 4k$, so that the unity-gain frequency is reached before the pole of the low-pass filter.

To allow high loop gain, a zero is added to the low-pass filter to stabilize the loop. The transfer function for a filter with a pole at $s = -a$, a zero at $s = -b$, and unity DC gain is given by

$$(9\text{-}47) \qquad H(s) = \left(\frac{a}{b}\right)\left(\frac{s + b}{s + a}\right)$$

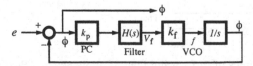

FIGURE 9-46   PLL Feedback Loop Transfer Function

Substituting this transfer function into Eq. (9-44) gives

(9-48)
$$\frac{\phi(s)}{e(s)} = \frac{s(s + a)}{s^2 + s(a + ka/b) + ka}$$

which has poles at

(9-49)
$$s = \frac{-a + k \pm \sqrt{(a + ka/b)^2 - 4ka}}{2}$$

Thus the response of the loop using the second-order filter is overdamped as long as $(a + ka/b)^2 > 4ka$. This is achieved as long as

(9-50)
$$b < \sqrt{ka}/2.$$

The damping factor, ζ, of the second order system is given by

(9-51)
$$\zeta = \frac{a + ka/b}{2\sqrt{ka}}$$

Intuitively, the loop with the simple low-pass filter oscillates because at high frequencies a low-pass looks like an integrator ($s \gg a$). An integrator gives a phase lag of $\pi/2$, so that two integrators have a lag of π, turning negative feedback into positive feedback. With a gain of k, the loop with two integrators oscillates at the unity-gain frequency, $\omega_1 = \sqrt{ka}$. Adding the zero at $b > a$ to the low-pass filter flattens its response above this frequency, canceling the phase lag and stabilizing the loop.

To illustrate the problems of loop filter design for PLLs, let us consider a 100-MHz VCO with a range of 100 MHz controlled by a flip-flop phase comparator with a linear range of 100 ps. For convenience assume that all control signals have a swing of 1 V. Then $k_f = 10^8$ Hz/V $= 2\pi 10^8$ rad/V and $k_p = (10 \text{ ns}/100 \text{ ps})(1/2\pi)$ V/rad, giving a loop gain of 10^{10}.

The pole of the low-pass filter, a, is set low enough to attenuate per-cycle noise but high enough so the feedback loop can cancel phase noise introduced by the VCO and track slow changes in the input. In practice this is a difficult trade-off, and higher-order filters with steep roll-offs and differentiators to cancel the low-pass nature of the integrator are sometimes required to satisfy both constraints simultaneously. For this example, however, we choose a 1-kHz cutoff, $a = 2\pi 10^3$ rad/s. From Eq. (9-50) the zero must be placed below 630 kHz to give an overdamped loop. We will place the zero at 1 MHz ($b = 2\pi 10^6$ rad/s), which gives a loop with a damping factor of $\zeta = 0.63$ from Eq. (9-51).

The open-loop and closed-loop frequency response of this example PLL are shown in Figure 9-47. The open-loop response, $kH(s)/s$, is shown on the left, and the closed-loop response (Eq. (9-48)) is shown on the right. In each case, the magnitude of the response (in decibels) is shown at the top, and the phase (in degrees) is shown at the bottom. The open-loop response illustrates the stability issues discussed above. Initially, the response is that of an integrator, the magnitude decreases at 6 dB per decade with a phase lag of $\pi/2$. At 1 kHz, the

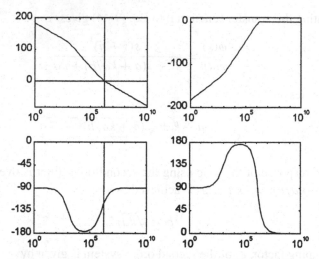

FIGURE 9-47   Frequency Response of Example Loop

pole of the low-pass takes effect, increasing the slope to 12 dB per decade and the phase shift to π. The zero takes effect at 1 MHz, bringing the phase shift back away from π before the unity gain frequency of 1.7 MHz to stabilize the loop.

The closed-loop response determines how fast the loop converges and how the loop responds to phase noise introduced by the VCO, the phase comparator, or jitter on the input signal. The loop has a high-pass response that cancels noise below the unity-gain frequency of 18 MHz with the roll-off, as shown. The response to noise at another point, x, in the loop has the profile shown in Figure 9-47 divided by the transfer function from phase to x. For example, voltage noise on the output of the phase comparator has the same profile but attenuated by k_p (24 dB). Similarly, the response to voltage noise at the input of the VCO is the profile on the left divided by $k_p H(s)$, and so on. The closed-loop response also determines how fast the loop will converge and how fast it can track frequency changes in the input signal. The loop converges with a time constant related to the unity-gain frequency (about 1 μs in this example) and will track signals slower than the unity-gain frequency.

The loop frequency response curves illustrate the trade-off between attenuating per-cycle noise and tracking lower-frequency input changes. The open-loop response should be well below 0 dB by the loop frequency to avoid tracking input jitter and to cancel noise introduced by the phase detector. On the other hand, the unity gain frequency should be as high as possible to track input changes and to cancel internal phase errors. Also, the open-loop phase must be well away from π at the unity gain frequency for stability.

9.6.6.4   Reducing Jitter with a Phase-Locked Loop

A phase-locked loop based on a stable VCO acts as a low-pass filter for phase. This causes it to attenuate the high-frequency components of jitter, those above the cutoff of the loop filter. By setting the cutoff of the loop filter appropriately,

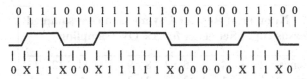

FIGURE 9-48   Oversampling Clock Recovery

a PLL can be used to clean up a noisy clock signal, significantly reducing jitter. The PLL is limited of course by the inherent jitter in its own VCO, which is high-passed by the loop filter.

9.6.7   Oversampling Clock Recovery

The methods discussed in this section so far can all be described as *tracking clock recovery*. They involve controlling a local clock, using a DLL or a PLL, to track the timing of an input clock or signal. Alternatively, one can use a free-running local clock to sample the input signal at a high rate, several samples per bit cell. This *oversampled* input is then processed digitally to recover the individual data symbols.

Figure 9-48 shows an input waveform, the sequence 1011001, being oversampled at a rate that is three times the bit rate, $3\times$ oversampling. The top sequence shows the result of sampling the input with the sample points maximally distant from the edges of the bit cells. This represents the best-case timing. The resulting sequence is just the input sequence with every bit repeated three times. The input can be recovered by selecting one of every three bits; it does not matter which one. The bottom sequence shows the worst-case timing. Here the sample clock is aligned with transitions of the input signal. As a result, those samples falling on a transition are unreliable, denoted in the figure by an X. Depending on voltage noise and jitter, these samples may be a 1 or may be 0.

With $N\times$ oversampling and worst-case timing, a string of M repeated ones will be recovered as a string of x, $NM-1 \le x \le NM+1$, ones, and similarly for zeros. Thus, as long as the oversampling rate is at least $3\times$, we can uniquely determine the input sequence from the sampled sequence. A sequence of y repeated ones (or zeros) in the sampled sequence corresponds to x repeated ones (zeros) in the input sequence where

$$(9-52) \qquad\qquad\qquad x = \lfloor (y + 1)/N \rfloor$$

Table 9-6, for example, gives the number of repeated input symbols corresponding to the number of repeated sampled symbols for $3\times$ oversampling.[11]

Although any oversampling rate greater than $1\times$ will sample every bit cell at least once, a rate of $3\times$ or greater is required to determine the timing with

---

[11] Oversampling receivers usually use a more sophisticated data recovery algorithm than just counting the number of bits between transitions. However, this sample algorithm works surprisingly well and illustrates the general concept of oversampling recovery.

TABLE 9-6 **Number of Repeated Symbols in Oversampled Sequence Versus Input Sequence for $3\times$ Oversampling**

Sample sequence	2	3	4	5	6	7	8	9	10	11	12	13
Input sequence		1	1	1	2	2	2	3	3	3	4	4	4

sufficient resolution to distinguish between different length symbol sequences with worst-case timing.

In effect, an oversampling receiver recovers the clock from the data by measuring the position of each transition. It is only able to resolve the clock position (with a single sample) to within t_{bit}/N where t_{bit} is the bit-cell width. Thus, oversampling introduces timing uncertainty in the form of *quantization jitter* with a magnitude of t_{bit}/N peak-to-peak or $\pm t_{bit}/(2N)$. With $3\times$ oversampling, for example, the quantization jitter is $1/3$ of a bit cell peak-to-peak, or $\pm 1/6$ of a bit cell, a substantial portion of any timing budget.

One might think that a tracking clock recovery system is always superior to an oversampling system because the former eliminates quantization jitter. This is usually, but not always, the case. An oversampling receiver has two significant advantages that often outweigh the disadvantage of quantization jitter. First, an oversampling receiver is extremely good at rejecting high-frequency jitter because it retains very little state. The simple algorithm of just counting the number of repeated symbols and applying Eq. (9-52), for example, rejects jitter at frequencies less than the instantaneous transition frequency. It is usually impractical to build a loop filter for a PLL or DLL tracking clock recovery system that operates above $1/10$ of the minimum transition frequency. Thus, in cases where the high-frequency jitter exceeds $\pm t_{bit}(2N)$, an oversampling receiver may be in order.

Second, by sampling first and asking questions later, an oversampling receiver can use a *noncausal* algorithm to recover clock and data (viz. one can look at transitions *after* the current bit cell as well as before the current bit cell in determining the value and timing of the current bit). Tracking clock recovery systems are restricted to use only information that is available *before* the current bit cell (usually well before) because this information is used to determine when to sample the current cell. By making more information available, noncausal algorithms often give better performance than strictly causal algorithms.

The design of a simple $3\times$ oversampling receiver is illustrated in Figure 9-49. This receiver operates by looking at a window of 37 samples, $c_{36:0}$, corresponding to 12 data bits. The receiver first finds the transitions in this window of samples by exclusive-ORing each sample with the adjacent sample (Figure 9-49(a)). The resulting signals, $e_{36:1}$, encode transition position. Signal e_i is high if a transition happened just before sample c_i. The transitions then vote (Figure 9-49(b)) to determine the best estimate of clock position. All edge signals with the same index, mod 3, vote for the same clock position. The winning clock position is used to select the bits to be output by a multiplexer (Figure 9-49(d)). The bits farthest from the estimated bit-cell edge are selected. If clock position i (mod 3) wins the election, the bit cell is estimated to start between $i - 1$ and i, and thus

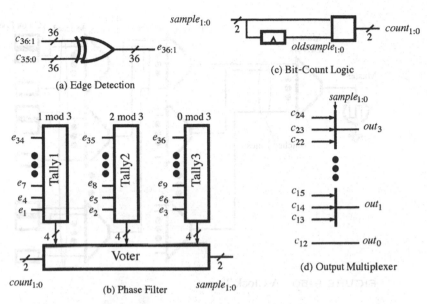

FIGURE 9-49   Data Recovery from an Oversampled Input

$i + 1$ (mod 3) is selected for output. The multiplexer shown outputs 4 bits at a time as is typical of a receiver that operates at $1/4$ the bit rate. After outputting 4 bits, the receiver shifts its sample window by 12 samples, accepting 12 new samples and dropping 12 old samples, and repeats the process.

Of course the circuit does not always output four bits each *cycle*. If the selected sample advances from 2 to 0 (mod 3) or retards from 0 to 2 (mod 3), the circuit outputs 3 bits or 5 bits. A simple circuit that compares the current sample point with the old sample point (Figure 9-49(c)) determines the number of bits to be output.

9.7   CLOCK DISTRIBUTION

Whether open-loop or closed-loop timing is employed, a clock signal must be distributed to all of the clocked storage elements in a clock domain with a minimum of skew and jitter. Whether the clock domain is an entire system spanning many cabinets or a small portion of a chip, clock distribution is a difficult problem. Variations in wire delays and driver delays, a nonuniform and possibly time-varying clock load, and noise all add to the uncertainty of the clock. Issues of circuit design for clock distribution are deferred to Section 12.6. In this section we address systems issues in clock distribution.

9.7.1   Off-Chip Clock Distribution

Off-chip clock distribution is a relatively easy problem. Off-chip wires and cables are essentially ideal delays and are particularly benign when distributing a periodic constant-frequency signal like a clock. Thus, by trimming wire lengths

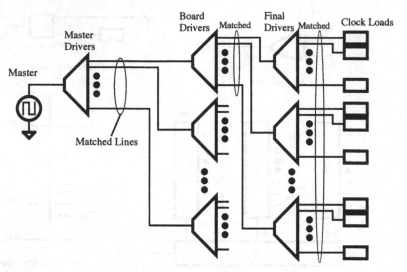

FIGURE 9-50 A Clock Tree

and matching buffer delays, a global clock can be distributed with a few hundreds of picoseconds of skew in a straightforward manner. As discussed in this section, it is also possible to distribute a clock using standing waves on the clock distribution network and by averaging the arrival time of an outgoing and incoming signal.

It is worth mentioning at this point that although it is relatively easy to distribute a global clock with low skew, it is almost never a good idea to operate an entire system off a single global clock. As discussed in previous sections, this leads to constraints on the legal operating frequencies of the system and increased sensitivity to timing noise. A more robust and efficient system usually results when the system is divided into several relatively small clock domains.

9.7.1.1 Clock Distribution Trees

A straightforward approach to off-chip clock distribution is illustrated in Figure 9-50. A master clock oscillator drives a hierarchy of clock fanout drivers. The figure shows a three-level tree. A master driver colocated with the oscillator driving transmission lines to each board; a board driver on each board distributes the signal to a set of final drivers distributed over the board. Finally, each final driver drives the clock inputs of several chips.

To control skew across all of the clock loads, the delays in the clock tree must be closely matched. This is usually accomplished by matching the driver and transmission line delays within each stage. At the first level, the lines are usually cables (twisted-pair or coaxial) that are all cut to the same length. On each board, the lines are typically printed-circuit stripguides that are routed with identical lengths, often by meandering or adding a "trombone," as illustrated in Figure 9-51(a). Where precise clock alignment is required the system may be manually tuned, either by electronically tuning the driver delays or by mechanically adjusting the length of a transmission line, for example by jumpering a trombone

(a) Matching Length

(b) Adjusting Length   (c) Binary-Weighted Adjustment

FIGURE 9-51   Matching the Length of Printed-Circuit Transmission Lines

in or out of the line using the configuration shown in Figure 9-51(b). A wide adjustment range can be achieved by using a set of such jumpered sections with binary-weighted lengths, as shown in Figure 9-51(c).

Although each path is drawn as a single line in Figure 9-50, high-performance clock distribution is almost always performed using differential signaling (Section 7.3.5) to avoid introducing phase noise as a result of shifts in a reference voltage. In most systems, the lines are single-drop (one clock load per line) because putting multiple clock loads on a line would introduce skew and impedance discontinuities. Thus, the lines may be either series- or parallel-terminated.

One approach to the fan-out driver is to distribute the signal in a carefully controlled manner on-chip to a number of output drivers, as shown in Figure 9-52(a). An alternative that often reduces skew is to build the fan-out driver using a set of zero-delay drivers (Figure 9-29), as shown in Figure 9-52(b). This still requires careful on-chip fan-out of the input signal to avoid skew but compensates for variations in delay of the output buffers. This approach can be taken one step further with series-terminated lines. Using the reflection off the open end of the line, a closed-loop output buffer can measure the length of the line (round-trip), and adjust its delay line to match the buffer plus line combination to a reference delay.

9.7.1.2   Phase-Locked Clock Distribution Networks

Clock distribution trees are vulnerable to a number of single-point failures (e.g., of the master oscillator or a high-level driver in the distribution tree) that will bring down the entire system. Where reliability is a concern, an attractive alternative is the use of a phase-locked network of clock oscillators. Each module, typically a board, has its own VCXO clock oscillator and local clock distribution tree. As shown in Figure 9-53, the entire system is phase-locked by having adjacent modules exchange clocks via cables of known length (usually a clock period).

Figure 9-53 shows a ring of four modules, each of which is phase-locked to its two neighbors. Two outputs of each module's clock tree are used to drive cables

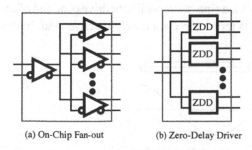

(a) On-Chip Fan-out   (b) Zero-Delay Driver

FIGURE 9-52   Fan-Out Drivers

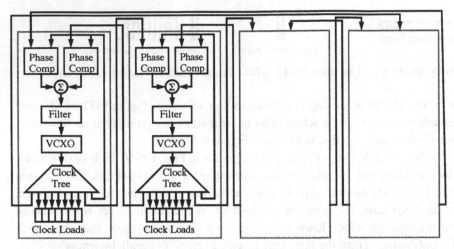

FIGURE 9-53 Phase-Locked Clock Distribution

to its two neighbors on the ring. Two phase comparators are used to compare a module's clock to that of its two neighbors, and the outputs of the comparators are summed to control the VCXO. By closing the timing loop around the local clock distribution tree, the variation of nominal tree delay from module to module is canceled. The skew of a tree within a module is not canceled, however.

Arbitrary topologies of modules are possible with the number of phase comparators required at a node equal to the in-degree of the node. The convergence properties of such networks have been studied in detail by Pratt [PratNgyu95]. If an individual module fails or a cable becomes disconnected, the remainder of the system continues in phase-lock. An individual module can even run with all cables disconnected with its VCXO operating at its center frequency. However, in this case it is no longer synchronized with the other modules.

9.7.1.3 Salphasic Clock Distribution

With a periodic waveform, such as a clock, reflections from a mismatched termination at the end of a line lead to standing waves. Normally such standing waves are considered a bug, and efforts are made to match terminations closely to eliminate standing waves. With salphasic clock distribution, as described by Chi [Chi94], however, these standing waves are exploited to distribute a clock with low skew without requiring careful matching of delays.

As shown in Figure 9-54, a sine-wave oscillator drives one end of a transmission line while the other end is terminated in a purely reactive load. In this example it

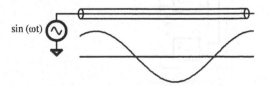

FIGURE 9-54 Salphasic Clock Distribution

is left open. Then, if the forward-traveling wave is

(9-53) $$V_F(x, t) = A \sin(\omega t + \theta - x/v)$$

the complete reflection at the open end of the line will give a reverse-traveling wave of

(9-54) $$V_R(x, t) = A \sin(\omega t + \theta - 2l/v + x/v)$$

where l is the length of the line. If we arbitrarily choose $\theta = l/v (\text{mod } 2\pi)$, then the sum of V_F and V_R gives a standing wave

(9-55) $$V(x, t) = 2A \sin(\omega t) \cos\left(\frac{x - l}{v}\right)$$

The amplitude of this signal as a function of position for a line slightly longer than a clock period is sketched in Figure 9-54. The time-varying part of this signal, $\sin(\omega t)$, has identical phase everywhere along the line with amplitude of $2A \cos[(x - l)/v]$, where A is set to match the oscillator amplitude at the source end of the line. Thus, except near the null points of the line, $x = (\pi v + l)(\text{mod } 2\pi v)$, each receiver along the line is sent a sine wave with identical phase.

There are a few sources of skew with this system. With lossy lines, the forward- and reverse-traveling waves are not exactly the same magnitude, which leads to small, but predictable, phase errors. Also some receivers will introduce a phase error due to the difference in clock magnitude at different points on the line.

Although our example has been with a linear transmission line, salphasic clock distribution can be used with a variety of geometries. For example, Chi describes a salphasic clock tree in [Chi94] and has used this technique with two-dimensional clock planes in place of one-dimensional clock lines.

9.7.1.4   Round-Trip Distribution

Round-trip clock distribution, illustrated in Figure 9-55, sends a clock along a transmission line across a set of modules and then back again across the same set of modules in reverse order. If the forward and reverse lines are matched, the average time of arrival of each edge of the forward (*FClk*) and reverse (*RClk*) clock is the same at every point on the line.

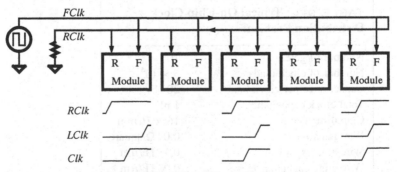

FIGURE 9-55   Round-Trip Clock Distribution

If the delay of the line is short compared with the rise time of the clock signal, *FClk* and *RClk* can be interpolated by summing (after buffering). If the delay of the line is long, however, summing will give a noisy clock, and the midpoint clock should be generated by closing a timing loop with two phase comparators.

The forward and reverse clocks may also be used themselves to provide pipeline clocks associated with left- and right-going data on a shared transmission medium such as a bus. In this case, if a module is sending data to the left (right), it synchronizes its output data with the *RClk* (*LClk*), and the receiving module uses the *RClk* (*LClk*) to sample the data. If the delays of the data and clock paths are matched, the phase relationship of data and clock will be the same at the receiver as at the transmitter. Compared with the general approach to pipeline timing, this technique has the advantage that each module in an *N*-module system must only synchronize with two clocks, rather than *N*.

9.7.2 On-Chip Clock Distribution

On-chip clock distribution tends to be a harder problem than off-chip distribution. Although the region over which the clock is being distributed is smaller (a few centimeters versus several meters), the number of clock loads is usually higher (10^5 versus 100), the on-chip wires are highly resistive, and the noise environment on-chip is more severe.

The clock distribution problem for a typical 10^6 gate logic chip is summarized in Table 9-7 below.

9.7.2.1 On-Chip Clock Trees

The most common approach to distributing a clock on-chip is to use a clock tree. These trees differ from their off-chip counterparts in the approach taken to deal with the lossy on-chip RC transmission lines. Each segment of an on-chip clock tree must be kept physically short to keep the quadratic RC delays within bounds (see Section 8.1).

The layout for one quadrant of a tree for our example clock-distribution problem is shown on the left side of Figure 9-56. The division of the chip over the levels of the tree is shown on the right side of the figure. The tree has six levels. The first five levels have fan-outs of 2, 4, 2, 4, and 4, respectively, distributing

TABLE 9-7 **Typical On-Chip Clock Distribution Problem**

Number of gates	10^6
Number of clock loads	5×10^4
Capacitance per clock load	20 fF
Total clock capacitance	1 nF
Chip dimensions	16×16 mm
Wire resistivity	0.07 Ω/square
Wire area capacitance	0.13 fF/μm^2
Wire edge capacitance	0.08 fF/μm

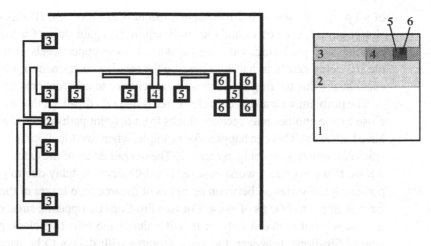

FIGURE 9-56 A Typical On-Chip Clock Distribution Tree

the clock to 256 level-6 drivers. The distribution is done first vertically and then horizontally in a manner that keeps the longest wire length 4 mm. A level-1 driver in the center of the chip drives two matched 4-mm wires to level-2 drivers, one for the top of the chip and one for the bottom (not shown). The level-2 drivers each drive four matched 3-mm wires to level-3 drivers, completing the vertical fan-out. The horizontal fan-out is similar with each level-3 driving two level-4 drivers, and each level-4 driving four level-5 drivers.

At the final level, each level-5 driver fans out both horizontally and vertically to four level-6 drivers that each drive the clock loads in a 1-mm region of the chip. On average there are 200 clock loads (4 pF) in a region. However, over the chip the load for a region can vary from a low of 0 to a high of 400 (8 pF). The drive strength of the final stage of the level-6 driver is varied to give matched delays into each driver's load.

Table 9-8 lists the properties of each level of the fan-out tree. For example, the first level of the tree drives two (fan-out) 4-mm by 3-μm wires to two level-2 drivers, which present a load of 250 fF each. These wires have a resistance of 93 Ω and a capacitance of 1880 fF, giving an overall wire delay ($0.4R_{\mathrm{W}}C_{\mathrm{W}} + R_{\mathrm{W}}C_{\mathrm{L}}$)

TABLE 9-8 Properties of the Clock Fan-Out Tree

Level	Fan-Out	Wire Length (mm)	Wire Width (μm)	C_{W} (ff)	R_{W} (Ω)	C_{L} (ff)	τ_{wire} (ps)	$C_{\mathrm{O}}/C_{\mathrm{I}}$
1	2	4	3	1,880	93	250	93	17
2	4	3	3	1,410	70	250	57	27
3	2	4	3	1,880	93	250	93	17
4	4	3	3	1,410	70	250	57	27
5	4	1	0.6	158	117	250	37	7
6	6	1	0.6	158	117	667	85	20

of 93 ps. If we assume a driver input capacitance, C_I, of 250 fF, this stage has a charge gain, C_O/C_I of 17 and thus will require two gain stages for a driver delay of about 400 ps. Using wide, 3-μm, wires for the upper levels of the tree cuts the RC delay nearly in half by reducing the relative component of the wire edge capacitance due to fringing fields and capacitance to adjacent conductors.

The problem with an on-chip clock tree is that two flip-flops that are physically close to one another may receive clocks from disjoint paths in the clock tree that have high skew. This can happen, for example, when two flip-flops are on opposite sides of the horizontal chip centerline. The overall delay of the clock tree is about 2.8 ns. If we assume a worst case $\pm 10\%$ difference in delay due to process and power supply variation between branches of the tree, two leaves of the tree could have as much as 560 ps of skew. For two flip-flops on opposite sides of the chip, this skew is of concern only in that it reduces the effective clock period. For nearby flip-flops, however, the skew requires path delays to be padded, or the system may fail at any speed owing to minimum delay constraints.

9.7.2.2   Mesh Distribution

The skew presented to nearby flip-flops can be greatly reduced by tying the outputs of the final stage drivers (and optionally one or more intermediate stage drivers) together in a two-dimensional mesh. A clock node connected to a slow driver is driven by its four neighbors, advancing its rise time. Similarly, a fast clock node is slowed by the load imposed by the neighboring nodes. The effect is to pull the timing of nearby clock loads closer together.

The dynamics of a clock mesh are governed by Poisson's equation, where the individual clock drivers are modeled as sources driving current into their respective clock nodes. Simulations are usually used to solve Poisson's equation to get accurate measurements of mesh skew. Some combination of Monte-Carlo skews and worst-case skews are usually simulated.

To approximate skew in a mesh we can use a simple RC model. A slow node (or a node with no driver for that matter) will be driven by its four neighbors with an RC delay. For our 1-mm distribution network, if we use 3-μm wires for the mesh $R_W = 23\,\Omega$, $C_W = 470$ fF, $C_L = 1$ pF (for each of the four) the effective delay is 14 ps. This approximate delay increases quadratically with distance across the mesh.

To avoid overlap currents the clock drivers of a mesh distribution network should be built using *nonoverlap pulse generators*. A nonoverlap pulse generator, illustrated in Figure 9-57, sources (sinks) current during the rising (falling) edges of its output but disables its output drivers and has a relatively high output impedance when its output is not changing. With a nonoverlap pulse generator, the node connected to a slow clock driver has high impedance and can easily be driven by its neighbors. With a conventional clock driver, this node will be pulled to the opposite supply, making it difficult for the neighbors to drive. Also, with a conventional driver, large overlap currents will flow as the two clock drivers pull in opposite directions. This leads to large power dissipation and possibly metal-migration failure of the clock mesh.

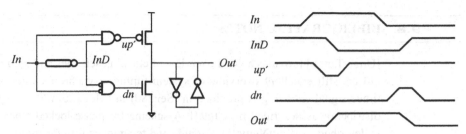

FIGURE 9-57   A Nonoverlap Pulse Generator

In the circuit of Figure 9-57, the PFET conducts only during a brief period following the rising edge of the input (while *In* and *InD* are both high), and the NFET conducts only during a period following the falling edge of the input (while *In* and *InD* are both low). At all other times, the output is held in its current state by a relatively weak inverter pair. By asymmetrically sizing the NAND and NOR gates (for fast on and slow off), this circuit can be made to have a charge gain and delay comparable to an inverter pair.

9.7.2.3   Jitter in On-Chip Clock Distribution

Jitter in on-chip clocks is usually due to power supply variations. Cross talk is also a concern but can be dealt with by isolation of the clock runs. Differential and common-mode power supply noise causes clock jitter through two different mechanisms.

Differential power supply noise modulates the delay of the clock drivers. If a clock driver has delay sensitivity to supply voltage of unity, then a $\pm10\%$ variation in differential supply voltage gives a $\pm10\%$ variation in delay. For our example in Section 9.7.2.1, the 2.4-ns of buffer delay would be modulated to give a total jitter of ±240 ps. Because much power supply noise is periodic and correlated with the clock, this effect is often reduced in practice. However, other sources of differential supply variation, such as clock-to-clock variations in IR drops and LC oscillations, still contribute to jitter. Jitter due to differential supply modulation of delay can be reduced by building clock drivers that are insensitive to supply variations, as described in Section 12.6.

Common-mode supply noise shifts the receive threshold of a clock receiver relative to the clock transmitter. This induces a jitter that is proportional to the rise time of the clock signal.

$$(9-56) \qquad\qquad\qquad t_j = \frac{V_{NP}}{\Delta V} t_r$$

To reduce this effect it is important to keep clock rise times short. This is one reason to limit the wire-delay of clock distribution networks because the diffusive RC delay of on-chip wires significantly degrades rise times. This common-mode induced jitter can be entirely eliminated by distributing the clock as a differential signal and using clock receivers with good common-mode rejection.

9.8   BIBLIOGRAPHIC NOTES

[UngerTan86] provides a good overview of clocking schemes and their analysis. An old but still excellent overview of system timing, asynchronous design, and self-timed signal encoding is provided in [Seitz80] in [MeadConw80]. Salphasic clock distribution is described in [Chi94]. A scheme for phase-locked clock distribution is described in [PrattNguy95]. Circuits and techniques for constructing latches and other storage elements, phase- and delay-locked loops, and oscillators are described in Chapter 12, which has a number of references to papers on the subject. [Gardner79], [Best84], and [Stensby97] are textbooks on phase-locked loop design. Techniques, circuits, and applications of pipelined timing are presented in [GrayLiu94]. Chapter 6 in [GlasDobb85], Chapter 8 in [Bakoglu90], Section 5.5 in [WestEshr93], and Chapter 9 in [Rabaey96], for example, provide introductions to the analysis of chip and system timing.

9.9   EXERCISES

9-1   **Aperiodic Signal Encoding:** Design a signal encoding that uses the minimum number of transitions and for which one of the signal lines always reflects the logical value of the signal.

9-2   **Bundled Signaling Without a Clock:** Events involving an alphabet of seven symbols can be encoded onto three lines without a separate clock line. The three lines encode both the value of the current symbol and the time at which each symbol starts (even if it is the same as the last symbol). Describe a signal encoding that meets this specification. What are the constraints on relative timing between the three lines?

9-3   **Operating Range for Synchronous Timing:** Consider a system that operates at 500 Mb/s using synchronous timing, as shown in Figure 9-58. A communications link in this system includes a 7-ns (3 1/2-bit-long) transmission line. The link has a rise-time of $t_r = 1$ns, an aperture time, $t_a = 300$ ps, and a timing uncertainty (skew + jitter) of $t_u = 300$ ps. Over what ranges of clock frequencies will the link operate with correct timing? Or, stated differently, over what range of frequencies will the timing constraints not be satisfied?

9-4   **Skew-Tolerant Flip-Flops:** To ensure correct operation at the expense of performance, a consultant suggests replacing all of the positive edge-triggered flip-flops in

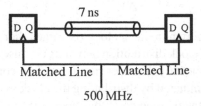

FIGURE 9-58   Synchronous Timing (for Exercise 9-3)

Symbol   Equivalent Circuit

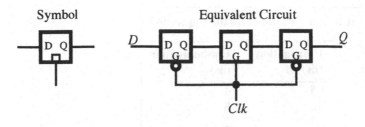

Timing Diagram

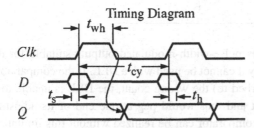

FIGURE 9-59   Skew-Tolerant Flip-Flop (for Exercise 9-4)

a design with the *skew-tolerant* flip-flop shown in Figure 9-59. This flip-flop samples its input on the rising edge of the clock and updates its output on the falling edge of the clock. The consultant claims that by adjusting the pulse width, t_{wh}, one can tolerate arbitrary amounts of clock skew.

What happens to the minimum cycle time of a system when the edge-triggered flip-flops are replaced by skew-tolerant flip-flops? How much clock skew can this system tolerate with the new flip-flops as compared with the old? Is this an effective way to tolerate skew?

9-5   Closed-Loop Timing: A friend is building a closed-looped timing system (like the one in Figure 9-38) for a communications link in his laptop computer. He has wired it up as shown in Figure 9-60. The *TxClk* and *RxClk* have exactly the same frequency, 100 MHz, but an unknown, constant phase difference. The voltage-controlled delay line has a delay range of 0 to 20 ns and has a delay that increases with an increasing control voltage. Your friend is puzzled that the system does not operate properly. Draw a timing diagram of this system. What is wrong? How would you fix it? Draw a diagram of a corrected circuit.

9-6   Sequential Phase-Only Comparator: The sequential phase–frequency comparator of Figure 9-36 is attractive because it has a linear response, possesses a wide dynamic

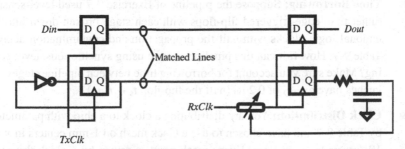

FIGURE 9-60   Closed-Loop Timing System with Bug (for Exercise 9-5)

TABLE 9-9   **Parameters for Figure 9-7**

Stage	Propagation (ns)	Contamination (ns)
1	5	4
2	10	8
3	3	2
4	4	3

range, and generates pulse-width-modulated outputs suitable for driving a charge pump. Unfortunately it cannot be used with a DLL. If the comparator's counter were to start (or be disturbed to) the wrong count, the DLL is unable to *wrap* the phase to correct the count and thus would peg at one end of its adjustment range. The advantages of this comparator can be realized without this limitation by building a sequential phase-only comparator. The following logic equations give a realization of a simple phase-only comparator:

$$
\begin{aligned}
ao &= a \wedge \bar{x} \wedge \overline{bo} \\
bo &= b \wedge \bar{x} \wedge \overline{ao} \\
x &= (a \wedge b) \vee ((a \vee b) \wedge x)
\end{aligned}
$$

(9-57)

Here a and b are the two inputs, ao and bo are the outputs that indicate that a or b came first, and x is a state variable.

Sketch an implementation of this phase comparator using only 2-input NAND gates. Simulate your circuit (by hand or otherwise) on waveforms where a comes first, b comes first, and where they come at the same time. What assumptions must you make about delay to ensure that this comparator has no *dead zone*?

9-7   Pipeline versus Sequential Timing: Consider a logic function that is broken into four pipeline stages. The propagation and contamination delay times of each stage are given in Table 9-7. The setup, hold, and clock-to-Q times of the edge-triggered flip-flops separating the stages are 0.1, 0.1, and 0.3 ns, respectively. What are the maximum throughput and minimum latency at which you could operate this pipeline using synchronous timing? What are the maximum throughput and minimum latency using pipeline timing?

9-8   Time Borrowing: Suppose the pipeline of Exercise 9-7 used level-sensitive latches rather than edge-triggered flip-flops with each stage broken down into two combinational logic blocks with half the propagation and contamination delays shown in Table 9-7. How fast can this pipeline operate using synchronous, level-sensitive timing? Make sure you account for borrowing time between pipeline stages. Assume the latches have a t_{dDQ} of 0.2 ns (half the flip-flop $t_s + t_{dCQ}$).

9-9   Clock Distribution: You are distributing a clock to a chip with parameters as given by Table 9-7 and have chosen to use a clock mesh on 1-mm centers in x and y using 10-μm-wide clock lines. Every mesh point is driven by a clock driver of the type illustrated in Figure 9-54. Suppose that the maximum clock skew to the drivers is

TABLE 9-10   **Parameters for Exercise 9-10**

Parameter	Value	Units
Intrachip clock skew	0.5	ns
Interchip clock skew	1.0	ns
Clock jitter	0.3	ns
Off-chip driver delay	0.5	ns
Off-chip receiver delay	0.5	ns
Gate delay	0.2	ns
Intrachip wire delay	0.3	ns
Interchip wire delay	0.5	ns
Flip-flop setup	0.2	ns
Flip-flop hold	0	ns
Flip-flop clock-to-Q	0.4	ns
Latch D-to-Q	0.3	ns

500 ps. Give an estimate of the worst-case skew at adjacent grid points on the mesh. State your assumptions.

9-10   **Timing Budget:** You are designing a computer system using a technology with the properties shown in the Table 9-10. Your design calls for six gate delays (and intervening wires) during a clock cycle for intrachip logic, and two gate delays plus driver, receiver, and wire delays for logic circuits that cross between two chips. No combinational circuits are allowed that involve three chips. What is the fastest clock rate you can safely (worst-case analysis) operate at using synchronous edge-triggered timing? How fast could you operate if you used synchronous level-sensitive timing? (Assume your combinational logic can be easily broken into roughly equal-sized units of three gate delays each.)

10 SYNCHRONIZATION

Synchronization involves determining or enforcing an ordering of events on signals. It is necessary to synchronize, for example, when sampling an asynchronous signal with a clock. To define the signal value unambiguously during a particular clock cycle, one must determine whether a signal transition occurred before or after a clock transition. A similar form of synchronization is required when a signal that is synchronous to one clock is sampled by a different clock. In this case we say the signal is moving between *clock domains* and must be synchronized with the new domain. If the two clocks are periodic, we will see that synchronizing signals passing between clock domains is much less expensive than synchronizing truly asynchronous signals.

Whenever synchronization must be performed in a bounded amount of time, some probability exists of *synchronization failure*. That is, if the two events happen very close together, it may not be possible for a synchronizer circuit to resolve unambiguously which occurred first in a fixed amount of time. A properly designed synchronizer can make the probability of synchronization failure arbitrarily small by waiting arbitrarily long. However, several rather common mistakes can result in very high failure probabilities. It is possible to synchronize without any probability of failure, provided one is willing to wait as long as it takes for the synchronizer to signal that it has completed the task.

The difficulty of synchronizing a signal with a clock depends on the predictability of events on the signal relative to the clock. The easiest case is when the signal is synchronized to a clock with the same frequency as the sample clock but with an arbitrary phase. In this case we say the signal and clock are *mesochronous*, and a single phase measurement suffices to predict possible transition times arbitrarily far in the future. If the signal is generated by a clock with a slightly different frequency, there is a slow drift in the phase, and we say that the signal and clock are *plesiochronous*. Even if there is a large difference in frequency, as long as the signal clock and sample clock are both periodic, we can with two measurements predict transition times far into the future. This predictability allows us to synchronize a signal generated by one periodic clock with any other periodic clock without waiting to resolve event orderings.

In most cases synchronization is not essential but rather is performed to allow us the convenience of operating on signals that are all in a single clock domain. An alternative is to use *asynchronous logic* to operate on the signals directly, obviating the need for most synchronization. In the few cases where event ordering determines the outcome of a computation, however, synchronization is still required. In addition to eliminating the need for most synchronization, asynchronous design has several fundamental performance advantages. For example, it is easy to build asynchronous arithmetic circuits that operate in the time required for the carry to propagate just the number of bits required by the current problem rather than always allowing time for the relatively unlikely ripple across the entire word.

The remainder of this chapter addresses the problem of synchronization in more detail. We begin in Section 10.1 by examining three approaches to synchronizing a simple instrumentation system to highlight some of the issues associated with synchronization. The fundamentals of synchronization are then discussed in Section 10.2, where we examine the dynamics of synchronizers and the problem of metastability and synchronization failure. Also in this section we introduce a classification of synchronization and uses of multiple clock domains. We return to pragmatics in Section 10.3 where we describe synchronizer designs for different classes of synchronization problems ranging from mesochronous to fully asynchronous. Finally, in Section 10.4 we describe asynchronous design as an alternative to synchronization. This section introduces the trajectory-map technique for designing asynchronous circuits and describes how to compose these circuits safely in combinational modules, pipelines, and cyclic state machines.

10.1   A COMPARISON OF THREE SYNCHRONIZATION STRATEGIES

To illustrate some synchronization issues we will consider an example instrumentation system that consists of a detector, a preprocessor, and a CPU. Figure 10-1

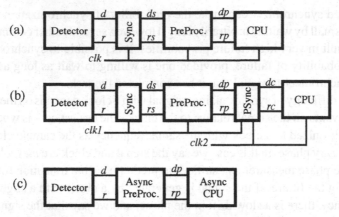

FIGURE 10-1 Three Approaches to Synchronizing a System

illustrates three approaches to synchronizing such a system: completely synchronous, separate clock domains, and completely asynchronous. In all three cases the detector produces data on its output, d, at unpredictable intervals and signals the availability of new data by toggling its request line, r. The preprocessor performs some transformations on the data and then places the result on its data output, dp, and signals availability by toggling rp. The CPU accepts the data from the preprocessor and performs final processing of the data.

Figure 10-1 (a) illustrates a completely synchronous version of the instrumentation system. A synchronizer samples the asynchronous output of the detector, d and r, and generates synchronous versions of these signals, ds and rs. The preprocessor and CPU then operate in a single clock domain without any further synchronization.

The synchronizer here is determining the ordering of events between the clock signal, clk, and the detector's request line. If these two lines toggle at nearly the same time, it must make an unambiguous determination of which came first. If it determines that the request came first, the new data will be considered to have arrived in this cycle, whereas if the clock wins the race, the data will be considered to have arrived in the next cycle. It does not matter which way the decision goes as long as it is reported consistently. If one part of the preprocessor were to see the clock arrive first and another part see the request arrive first, a malfunction would result. To synchronize the detector events unambiguously with a low probability of synchronization failure requires adding latency to the system, as we will see in Section 10.2.

Although operating the entire system synchronously is conceptually simple, it lacks modularity, constrains the signaling between modules, and requires careful clock distribution. With this arrangement, for example, upgrading the CPU to a higher clock rate would require redesigning the preprocessor to operate at a higher clock rate as well. Also, if the CPU and preprocessor were located some distance apart, the system would only operate within certain ranges of clock rates, as described in Section 9.1.2, and it would be problematic to distribute the clock with reasonable skew.

Operating the CPU and preprocessor from separate clocks, as shown in Figure 10-1(b), overcomes these problems. Now the clock rates of the preprocessor and

CPU can be changed independently of one another. There is no need to distribute a single clock globally, and signaling is simplified. Because of these advantages, this arrangement, separate clock domains for each subsystem, is the one most commonly used in practice.

In Figure 10-1(b) the output of the preprocessor is synchronized by a periodic synchronizer (PSync). Because events on the output of the preprocessor are synchronized to a periodic clock, *clk1*, the times when they may occur are predictable. The periodic synchronizer takes advantage of this predictability to synchronize the signal reliably to the CPU clock, *clk2*, without incurring the delay that would be required to synchronize an unpredictable signal, such as the output of the detector.

The system of Figure 10-1(b) still has a few disadvantages. First, the initial synchronization of the detector output adds latency to the system and carries some probability of synchronization failure. Also, operating from a periodic clock means that the system is dissipating power all the time, whether it is processing an event or not.

Operating both the preprocessor and the CPU asynchronously, as illustrated in Figure 10-1(c), overcomes these problems. In this case there are no clocks. An event on the output of the detector triggers the sequence of events in the preprocessor that operate on the data with each event triggering the next much like a line of dominos falling down. Eventually the event sequence propagates to the output, where it triggers the CPU to initiate the sequence of events that complete the processing. With appropriate design this sequence can be pipelined with the CPU processing one detector event while the preprocessor begins working on the next event.

The asynchronous approach incurs no synchronization latency and has no probability of synchronization failure because synchronization is not required. Inasmuch as the preprocessor and CPU will be in a quiescent state until triggered by an input event, they will usually dissipate less power than their synchronous counterparts.[1] Also, as we will see, asynchronous design permits lower pipeline latency and fast data-dependent arithmetic operations.

The primary disadvantage of asynchronous design is that it is unusual. One cannot buy asynchronous building blocks off the shelf, and most designers are not familiar with asynchronous design techniques. However, as we will see in later sections, these techniques are not difficult to master and often lead to superior system designs.

10.2 SYNCHRONIZATION FUNDAMENTALS

Synchronization involves imposing or recognizing an ordering of events on signal lines. An asynchronous signal, which may change at any time, must be synchronized with a clock before it can be used as an input to synchronous logic. If two asynchronous signals request a resource at nearly the same time, the order of

---

[1] With some styles of asynchronous design, such as those employing dual-rail signaling, the asynchronous modules will dissipate more power than a synchronous module when active. This can offset some of the advantage of low power dissipation in the quiescent state.

requests must be decided. In either case, synchronization failure can occur when the time taken to decide which signal came first exceeds a bound. A common use of synchronization is to take a signal synchronized with one clock and resynchronize it with a different clock. The periodic nature of the clocks can be exploited to simplify this type of synchronization.

10.2.1   Uses of Synchronization

There are three common uses of synchronization: arbiting between asynchronous requests, sampling asynchronous signals with a clock, and transmitting synchronous signals between two clock domains.

10.2.1.1   Arbitration of Asynchronous Signals

When a decision must be made concerning the ordering of two asynchronous signals, an arbitration is required to determine which signal was asserted first. Arbitration is required, for example, when the signals are requests for a shared resource such as a bus or a shared function unit.

The timing for an arbitration between two asynchronous units A and B is illustrated in Figure 10-2. The figure shows the symbol for an arbiter (left) and waveforms for two arbitration cycles (right). During the first cycle, both A and B request the resource by asserting their respective request signals. Because signal *AReq* is asserted well before *BReq*, the arbiter responds by asserting *AGrant* to grant the shared resource to A. Only after A drops its request does the arbiter grant B access to the resource by asserting *BGrant*. After B drops its request, the resource is freed.

During the second arbitration cycle, A and B request the resource at nearly the same time. This makes the arbitration problem difficult because there is no clear winner. The use of a naive arbiter (e.g., a NAND-latch) under such circumstances may result in granting the resource momentarily to both A and B. A well-designed arbiter must make an unambiguous determination of which request came first, in this case B, and grant the resource only to that requester.

10.2.1.2   Sampling Asynchronous Signals

Before an asynchronous signal can be input to a synchronous module, it must first be synchronized with the local clock to ensure that it makes transitions only during allowed portions of the clock cycle. Such synchronization is required, for example, when sampling real-world input devices such as limit switches, event detectors,

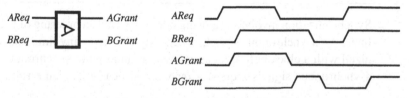

FIGURE 10-2   Arbitration of Asynchronous Signals

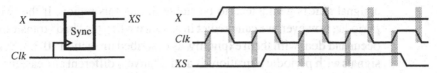

FIGURE 10-3   Sampling Asynchronous Signals

and shaft encoders whose outputs can change at any time, asynchronously. If such signals were input directly into a synchronous system, they might change during the aperture time of a flip-flop, causing a synchronization failure.

Figure 10-3 shows an asynchronous signal, X, being synchronized with a clock. The synchronizer samples signal X on the falling edge of the clock, uses the clock low time to make the synchronization decision, and updates output XS, a synchronized version of X on the rising edge of the clock. The shaded areas show the aperture times for the synchronizer input and output. The unsynchronized input to the synchronizer may or may not change during these aperture times. The synchronized output is guaranteed to be stable during the output aperture times.

The rising transition of X falls outside the synchronizer aperture. Thus, X is unambiguously detected as high by the synchronizer at the next falling edge of Clk, and the output XS is driven high following the subsequent rising edge of Clk. The falling transition of X, on the other hand, occurs during the input aperture of the synchronizer. Thus it may be detected as a 1, or a 0, or, as described in Section 10.2.2, the synchronizer input stage may enter a *metastable* state where it is momentarily unable to decide between a 1 or a 0. After waiting a half-clock for any such metastable states to decay, the synchronizer output updates XS, in this case to a 1. The input is unambiguously detected to be 0 on the next clock.

10.2.1.3   Crossing Clock Domains

A special case of sampling asynchronous inputs occurs when one synchronous module samples outputs of a synchronous module operating from a different clock. This situation is illustrated in Figure 10-4. Signal X is generated by Module A, and is synchronized with $ClkA$ so that its transitions may only occur during the darker shaded regions shown at the right side of the figure. Signal X is input to Module B, which operates synchronized with $ClkB$. Inputs to flip-flops clocked by $ClkB$ must be stable during the aperture or keep-out region denoted by the lighter shaded areas at the right side of the figure.

The situation is similar to that of Figure 10-3. Signal X may change during the keep-out region associated with $ClkB$ and thus must be synchronized to produce

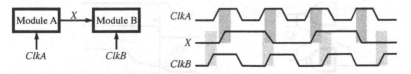

FIGURE 10-4   Crossing Clock Domains

a signal that is guaranteed to be stable during this region. If the two clocks are periodic, however, we can predict in advance when the "bad" transitions of X may occur and deal with them explicitly, as described in Section 10.3.3. Synchronizing signals with periodic transitions is a qualitatively different and easier problem than synchronizing truly asynchronous signals.

10.2.2   Synchronization Failure and Metastability

The synchronization problem is, in essence, the problem of determining which of two events came first. When sampling a changing data signal with a clock or when arbiting between two changing request signals, the order of the events determines the outcome. The smaller the time difference between events, the longer it takes to determine which came first. When two events occur very close together, the decision process can take longer than the time allotted, and a *synchronization failure* occurs.

10.2.2.1   Synchronizer Dynamics and Synchronization Time

The dynamics of the problem are illustrated for a NAND-latch in Figure 10-5. Although details differ, the fundamentals are the same for any synchronizing circuit with regenerative feedback. The NAND-latch acts as an arbiter, determining which of two request signals, A or B, rises first. If A rises first, output $AFirst'$ goes low; otherwise, if B rises first, $BFirst'$ goes low. For reliable arbitration, a circuit (such as that shown in Figure 10-7) that prevents either output from being asserted until a decision has been reached must be added to the NAND latch.

When A and B rise at nearly the same time, the dynamics are illustrated in the waveforms on the right side of Figure 10-5. During the interval, Δt, from when A rises to when B rises, the upper NAND gate sinks a current off of its output capacitance, giving a change in differential output voltage of

$$(10\text{-}1) \qquad\qquad \Delta V_1 = K_s \Delta t$$

where the constant here is approximately the reciprocal of the aperture time of the storage device $K_s = I/C \approx 1/t_a$.

Once input B rises, the two NAND gates act as a cross-coupled sense amplifier (Section 4.3.7) that amplifies the differential voltage ΔV exponentially with time.

$$(10\text{-}2) \qquad\qquad \Delta V(t) = \Delta V_1 \exp(t/\tau_s)$$

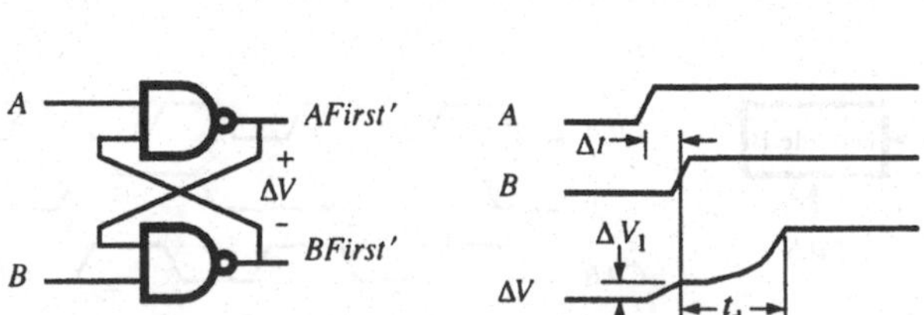

FIGURE 10-5   Synchronizer Dynamics

where τ_s is the regeneration time constant of the sense amplifier. Thus, the decision time, t_d, required for ΔV to attain unit voltage is given by

(10-3) $$t_d = -\tau_s \log(\Delta V_1)$$

Note that if ΔV_1 is zero, t_d is infinite.

10.2.2.2 Metastability

If the voltage ΔV is zero, the circuit of Figure 10-5 is in a *metastable* state. This can occur if A and B rise at exactly the same time, or if Δt is small and noise coupled into the circuit cancels the resulting ΔV_1. In this metastable state, there is no signal to be amplified to change the output, ΔV. However a small perturbation of ΔV will cause it to converge to one of the two truly stable states, $+1$ or -1. The situation is analogous to a ball balanced on the top of a hill; a slight push in either direction and the ball will fall to one side or the other.

In the absence of noise, a circuit would remain in a metastable state forever (or until the A and B inputs go low). In practice, noise tends to perturb the circuit, causing it to converge in one direction or the other. However, this convergence may take an arbitrarily long time to occur. The probability distribution of convergence time can be calculated based on the synchronizer dynamics and the distribution of noise.

10.2.2.3 Probability of Synchronization Failure

In practice, the decision time of a synchronizer is exponentially distributed. Thus, if a system is designed to wait a time, t_w, before sampling the synchronizer, the probability of synchronization failure decreases exponentially as t_w is increased.

Consider the case in which we are synchronizing two signals, A and B, with frequencies f_A and f_B, respectively, so that $f_A > f_B$. The position of an edge of the slow signal, B, is uniformly distributed across the $t_{cyA} = 1/f_A$ cycle of the fast signal, A. With probability

(10-4) $$P_a = t_a/t_{cyA} = t_a f_A$$

the edge falls during the aperture time, giving an intermediate value of ΔV_1.

If the edge of B occurs within the aperture of A, the value of $|\Delta V_1|$ is uniformly distributed between 0 and 1. Projecting this distribution of ΔV_1 through Eq. (10-3) gives an exponentially distributed t_d with mean τ_s. Thus, the probability that a given edge of B will result in a synchronizer delay longer than t_w is given by

(10-5) $$P_{sf}(t_w) = t_a f_A \exp(-t_w/\tau_s)$$

The frequency of synchronization failures is calculated by multiplying the frequency of events on B by the probability that each event results in a failure as follows:

(10-6) $$f_{sf} = t_a f_B f_A \exp(-t_w/\tau_s)$$

TABLE 10-1   **Example Synchronizer Calculation**

Symbol	Description	Value	Units
f_A	Event frequency on line A	100	MHz
f_B	Event frequency on B	1	MHz
t_a	Aperture time of flip-flop	200	ps
t_w	Waiting time	10	ns
P_{sf}	Probability of synchronization failure for each event on B	3.86×10^{-24}	
f_{sf}	Frequency of synchronization failures	3.86×10^{-18}	Hz
MTBF	Time between synchronization failures	2.59×10^{17}	s

Thus, the probability of synchronization failure depends linearly on the frequency of the events and the aperture time of the synchronizing device, and exponentially on the ratio of waiting time to regeneration time of the device.

10.2.2.4   Example Synchronizer Calculation

Table 10-1 shows the synchronizer parameters and calculated failure probability and frequency for a typical case. As illustrated in Figure 10-6, the synchronizer is composed of two flip-flops. The first flip-flop, with an aperture time and time constant of 200 ps, samples asynchronous signal B, with a frequency of 1 MHz, with a 100-MHz clock, A. After a transition on B, node BX will have an unacceptably high probability of being in a metastable state. The second flip-flop waits one clock period less t_{dCQ}, $t_w \approx 10$ ns, for any metastable states to decay. Because the waiting time is large compared with the time constant of the flip-flop, the synchronized signal, BS, has a very low probability of being in a metastable state.

Substituting the synchronizer parameters into Eq. (10-5) gives a failure probability on each transition of B of 3.86×10^{-24}. This is the probability that BX will still be in a metastable state when sampled by BS. Because these opportunities for failure occur 10^6 times per second (f_B), the failure frequency is 3.86×10^{-18}, which is equivalent to a mean time between synchronization failures of 2.59×10^{-17} s, or over 8 billion years. The cost of this synchronization is the additional 10 ns of latency introduced by waiting for node BX to settle.

10.2.2.5   Completion Detection

A synchronizer can be designed to signal completion when a decision has been made. The concept is illustrated in Figure 10-7 for the cross-coupled NAND arbiter of Figure 10-5. The circuit signals completion when the decision voltage, ΔV, has diverged beyond a decision voltage, V_d, so that noise cannot return it to

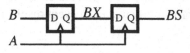

FIGURE 10-6   Example Synchronizer

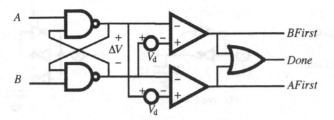

FIGURE 10-7 Completion Detection

the metastable point. The upper comparator's output goes true when $\Delta V < -V_d$, and the lower comparator's output goes true when $\Delta V > V_d$. During the time that $V_d > \Delta V > -V_d$, both outputs are low. This *excluded middle circuit* has a simple four-transistor realization, as shown in Figure 10-34.

In an asynchronous system, completion detection entirely eliminates the probability of synchronization failure, and it significantly reduces the average waiting time. Because the circuitry following the arbiter will always wait for completion to be detected before sampling the output, there is no chance of synchronization failure. Even if the output takes seconds to settle, the circuit will operate properly – slowly but properly. Most of the time the circuit never enters a metastable state or settles very quickly with completion detection, and thus the circuitry following the arbiter can start operation as soon as the decision is made rather than delaying for a worst-case waiting time.

These advantages require that the circuitry following the arbiter operate asynchronously, triggered by the completion signal. Completion detection is of little value in a synchronous system, for the completion signal itself is asynchronous and must be synchronized to the clock before it can be used.

10.2.2.6 Common Synchronizer Mistakes

The example in Section 10.2.2.4 shows that it is not difficult to build a synchronizer with a very low probability of failure. Many systems, however, suffer from synchronization failure. Some of these systems fail because they sample asynchronous signals without synchronization. Others fail, however, because they make one of two common errors in the implementation of their synchronizers. Both errors involve inadvertently slowing the regeneration of the synchronizing element.

A common synchronizer error is to implement the synchronizing element (e.g., the left flip-flop in Figure 10-6) using a dynamic latch (Figure 10-8(a)), an element without regeneration. In at least one case, this error has occurred because of lack of communication. A logic designer drew a latch on a schematic, and a circuit designer, not realizing the need for regeneration, implemented a dynamic latch. Without regeneration, the dynamic latch has an infinite τ_r and provides no synchronization. It simply samples the voltage on its input and outputs this voltage amplified by the inverter gain. Regardless of how long the waiting period is, an intermediate output voltage from a dynamic flip-flop will not change (except perhaps due to leakage) because there is no feedback.

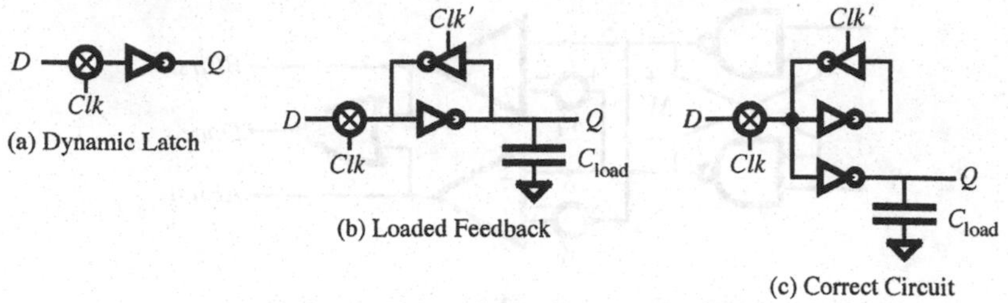

FIGURE 10-8   Common Synchronizer Errors

Another common error, shown in Figure 10-8(b), is to use a static latch but to slow the regeneration by loading the feedback loop with capacitance. This commonly occurs when a synchronizer is constructed using a library flip-flop that does not isolate the output from the feedback loop. It is not unusual for the output load to be 20 times the internal capacitance (1 pF versus 50 fF) or more, increasing the regeneration time constant, τ_s, by a proportional amount (4 ns versus 200 ps) and severely degrading the synchronizer performance ($f_{sf} \approx 10^3$ versus 10^{-18}). The same situation can occur with a NAND-latch, such as shown in Figure 10-5, if the outputs of the NANDs are not buffered before driving a load.

A correct implementation of a synchronizing element is shown in Figure 10-8(c). This design uses a static latch to provide regeneration and isolates the output from the feedback loop using an inverter. The regeneration time constant of this circuit, which is set by the transconductance of the inverters and the capacitance on the internal nodes of the latch, will be small.

10.2.3   Clock Domains

A clock domain is a set of signals that are all synchronized with the same clock signal (that is, they employ bundled clocked signaling, as described in Section 9.4.1.3). A signal in a clock domain may change only in response to an event on the clock signal, and all of the signals in a clock domain are stable during an aperture time associated with each clock event.

Grouping signals into clock domains is advantageous, for it allows these signals to be combined using logic circuits and sampled into clock storage elements without further synchronization. Membership in the clock domain is closed under simple composition rules. As long as two signals are in the clock domain, logical combinations of the signals that do not exceed maximum or minimum delay constraints are in the clock domain. Also, it is always *safe* (no probability of synchronization failure) to sample a signal in the clock domain with a clocked storage element driven by the clock signal, and the result of this sampling is also in the clock domain.

Despite the convenience of synchronous design within a clock domain, most digital systems are divided into multiple clock domains. This incurs synchronization overhead, for signals from one domain must be synchronized to the local clock before they can be used in a different domain. The sequential behavior of the system also becomes more complex because there is no longer a single stream of states to reason about. There are several advantages to such a division, however.

10.2.3.1 Independent Clock Rates

Often it makes sense for different parts of a system to operate at independent clock rates. This is particularly important in modular systems where it is desirable to permit a module, such as a CPU board, to be upgraded to a higher-frequency module without affecting the rest of the system.

10.2.3.2 Simplified Clock Distribution

Even when the entire system operates at a single frequency, there are several reasons to divide the system into separate clock domains. The clock distribution problem becomes much simpler, for the delays from the master clock oscillator to each clock domain need not be matched. Delay matching is only required within each clock domain.

10.2.3.3 Pipelined Signal Timing Eliminates Cable Delay Constraints

Consider a cable with delay $t_d > t_{cy}$. In a purely synchronous system it is convenient to express this delay as an integral number of clock delays plus a remainder delay, $t_d = N t_{cy} + t_r$. For proper operation, t_r, must satisfy maximum and minimum delay constraints. When the clock period is changed by Δt, t_r changes by $N \Delta t$, possibly violating the timing constraints. This effect results in windows of allowed clock periods, as illustrated in Table 9-3. If the modules at either end of a cable are in different clock domains, such constraints on the delay of the cable are removed.

10.2.3.4 Aperiodic Clocks

It is often advantageous for a module to have an independent, aperiodic clock. This is only possible if the module operates in a separate clock domain. One use of an independent clock is to vary the clock period of a module to be the minimum value for the operation being performed. For example, many early minicomputers used a short clock period when performing logical operations and a longer clock period when performing adds, which required a carry propagation. Aperiodic clocks are also used in low-power systems in which the clock rate and voltage may both be reduced during periods of low work to save power. Modules with stoppable clocks (Section 10.4.1) also require an independent aperiodic clock.

10.2.4 Classification of Signal–Clock Synchronization

The difficulty of synchronizing a signal so it can be safely sampled by a clock depends on the relationship between the timing of events on the signal and clock events. At one extreme, if the events on the signal are restricted to occur only during the *safe* portion of the clock phase, then the signal is synchronous with respect to the clock, and it can be used directly in the clock domain without further synchronization. At the opposite extreme, an asynchronous signal, with no restriction on event timing, must be passed through a synchronizer that samples the signal and waits for any metastable states to decay. Between these two extremes lie three interesting cases in which the events on the signal are periodic but have a phase,

TABLE 1O-2   **Classification of Signal–Clock Synchronization**

Classification	Periodic	$\Delta\phi$	Δf	Description
Synchronous	Yes	0	0	The signal has the same frequency as the clock and is in phase with the clock. It is safe to sample the signal directly with clock.
Mesochronous	Yes	ϕ_c	0	The signal has the same frequency as the clock but is potentially out of phase, with an arbitrary phase difference, ϕ_c. It is safe to sample the signal if the clock or signal is delayed by a constant amount.
Plesiochronous	Yes	Varies	$f_d < \varepsilon$	The signal is at nearly the same frequency as the clock. Thus, the phase difference between clock and signal varies slowly. It is safe to sample the signal if the clock or signal is delayed by a variable amount. The difference in frequency can lead to dropped or duplicated data.
Periodic	Yes		$f_d > \varepsilon$	The signal is periodic at an arbitrary frequency. The periodic nature of signal events can be exploited to predict in advance which events may occur during an unsafe portion of the clock.
Asynchronous	No			The signal events may occur at arbitrary times. A full synchronizer is required.

or frequency, differing from the signals in the clock domain. The vast majority of actual synchronization problems fall into one of these three periodic cases.

Table 10-2 lists five levels of synchronization between signals and clocks. Between the two extremes are three levels of periodic synchronization. A signal is *mesochronous* with respect to a clock if it is synchronized with a clock of identical frequency but with an arbitrary phase shift. Mesochronous signals arise when a master clock is distributed without controlling delays or when a signal arrives over a cable with an uncontrolled delay. A mesochronous signal can safely be sampled by a clock, with no probability of synchronization failure, as long as either the signal or the clock is delayed by a fixed amount to bring them in phase.

A signal is *plesiochronous* with respect to a clock if it is synchronized with a clock of a slightly different frequency. For example, two modules driven by separate uncompensated crystal oscillators of the same nominal frequency have clocks that differ in frequency by about 100 ppm. The relative phase of these clocks will slowly drift, covering a complete cycle every 10^4 cycles. A plesiochronous signal can be synchronized in much the same manner as a mesochronous signal with the additional requirement that the clock or data delay must periodically be adjusted. Also, when the delay adjustment crosses a cycle boundary, care must be taken to avoid dropping or duplicating data.

A signal is *periodic* if it is synchronized to any periodic clock. The phase of a periodic signal with frequency, f_s, relative to a sample clock with frequency, f_c, is itself periodic with frequency $f_\phi = |f_s - f_c|$. Because the phase changes rapidly when the frequencies differ significantly, a mesochronous synchronizer is not appropriate. However, the periodic nature of the phase difference can be exploited to predict when the signal may change during an unsafe portion of the sample clock phase. A synchronizer can use this prediction to take appropriate counter-measures.

10.3 SYNCHRONIZER DESIGN

A synchronizer is a device that samples an asynchronous signal and outputs a version of the signal that has transitions synchronized to a local or sample clock. The type of synchronizer required depends strongly on the level of asynchrony between the signal and the local clock. The higher the level of synchrony (Table 10-2), the easier the synchronization task. Synchronizing periodic signals requires significantly less delay than synchronizing completely asynchronous signals.

10.3.1 Mesochronous Synchronizers

A mesochronous signal, strictly speaking, is synchronized with the local clock. Its events occur at the local clock frequency with an arbitrary fixed phase shift. All that is required of a mesochronous synchronizer is to adjust the phase shift, if needed, to keep the signal transitions away from the unsafe regions of the local clock.

10.3.1.1 Delay-Line Synchronizer

A delay-line synchronizer is shown in Figure 10-9 along with waveforms illustrating typical operation. The synchronizer consists of a variable delay line with an adjustment range of at least a clock period and a flip-flop. The waveforms illustrate the operation of the synchronizer. The shaded areas denote the clock keep-out regions. Signal x has transitions during the keep-out regions, and thus it cannot be sampled directly. The delay line is adjusted so that signal xd has its transitions after the keep-out region and is safe to sample. The flip-flop samples xd and generates the synchronized signal xs.

The variable delay line is adjusted by measuring the relative phase of signal xd. The circuit in the figure performs this measurement using two flip-flops clocked with delayed versions of the clock that sample the signal at either end of the keep-out region, in this case with width $2t_d$ centered on the clock. When signal

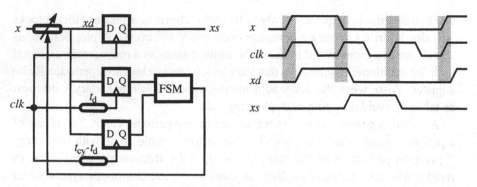

FIGURE 10-9   Delay-Line Synchronizer

xd makes its transitions in a safe region, these two flip-flops will sample the change during the same cycle. If a transition is made during the keep-out region, the lower flip-flop will sample the change of a cycle before the upper flip-flop. The FSM monitors the outputs of these flip-flops and sets the variable delay to the minimum amount that keeps the transitions of xd in the safe region. Because these two flip-flops may enter metastable states during normal operation, the FSM must resample their outputs after waiting sufficient time for any metastable states to decay with high probability.

Alternatively the synchronizer itself can be used to measure the phase of the input signal during an initial or periodic training sequence. With this approach the delay of the variable line is swept while sampling a known signal to detect the position of the signal transition. Using this phase information, the variable line is then set to the minimum value that keeps transitions on xd out of the keep-out region.

If input phases are uniformly distributed, this synchronizer has an average delay of

$$(10\text{-}7) \qquad\qquad t_z = t_{v\,min} + t_d + t_{dCQ} + t_{cy}/2$$

This is just the inherent delay of synchronization, $t_{cy}/2$, increased by the minimum delay of the delay line and the flip-flop.

The delay-line synchronizer is an expensive way to synchronize a wide, multibit signal, for it requires a variable delay line for each data bit. Also, it requires that the signal be delayed before sampling and thus cannot be used with a clocked receive amplifier (Section 11.3.2). For this reason, other methods are generally preferred for synchronizing wide signals.

10.3.1.2   Two-Register Synchronizer

For wide data paths the two-register synchronizer avoids the cost of a delay line per data bit by delaying the clock rather than the data. As illustrated in Figure 10-10, the synchronizer consists of a pair of flip-flops (registers for a multibit datapath). The upper flip-flop samples the input on positive edges of the local clock, *clk*. A delayed clock, *dclk*, that lags *clk* by the width of the keep-out region samples the input into the lower flip-flop. As long as the keep-out region of the sampling flip-flop is less than half a clock period, the keep-out regions of the two flip-flops

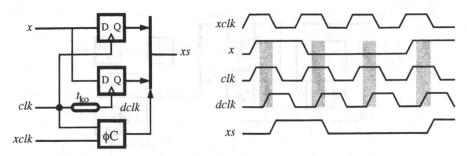

FIGURE 10-10 A Two-Register Synchronizer

do not overlap, and the input signal will be safely sampled by one of the two flip-flops. The output of the *safe* flip-flop is selected by a multiplexer and output as synchronized signal, *xs*.

The multiplexer control is a constant because the phase of *x* does not change with respect to the local clock. During system configuration, a phase comparator measures the relative phase between *xclk*, the clock from which *x* is derived, and the local clock, *clk*. The phase comparator selects the upper flip-flop unless transitions of *x* occur during the keep-out region of *clk*, in which case it selects the lower flip-flop. The waveforms at the right of Figure 10-10 illustrate this latter case. In the figure, *xclk* slightly leads *clk*, causing transitions of *x* to occur in the center of the keep-out region of *clk*. The phase comparator detects this condition during startup and selects the lower flip-flop to produce output *xs*.

The average delay of this synchronizer is given by

(10-8) $$t_z = t_{ko}^2/t_{cy} + t_d + t_{dCQ} + t_{cy}/2$$

The first term is the delay of the bottom flip-flop, t_{ko}, multiplied by the probability that the lower flip-flop is selected, t_{ko}/t_{cy}. The second term is the delay of the flip-flop, and the final term is the inherent synchronization delay of rounding up to the next clock cycle.

The two-register synchronizer places the keep-out delay into the receiver's clock cycle. This is in contrast to the delay-line synchronizer, which places this delay on the transmitter side. If the lower flip-flop is selected, *xs* is delayed by t_{ko} relative to a normal flip-flop output, reducing the amount of logic that can be performed in the first pipeline stage after the synchronizer.

10.3.1.3 FIFO Synchronizer

A FIFO synchronizer uses a small ring-buffer to decouple the transmitter and receiver timing. A FIFO synchronizer with a two-element ring buffer is shown in Figure 10-11. Waveforms for this synchronizer are shown in Figure 10-12. The transmit clock, *xclk*, is used to alternately sample the input signal, *x*, into a pair of flip-flops. A toggle flip-flop generates a transmit pointer, *xp*, that selects which flip-flop samples each symbol on input *x* via the flip-flop's clock-enable input. The outputs of the transmit flip-flops are a pair of signals, *x0* and *x1*, that are still synchronized to the transmit clock but which change only every other cycle.

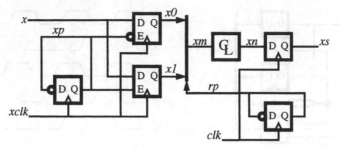

FIGURE 10-11   A FIFO Synchronizer

A toggle flip-flop driven off the local clock, *clk*, generates a receive pointer, *rp*, that drives a multiplexer to select between *x0* and *x1*. The phase of *rp* is set (by logic not shown) so that it always samples the transmit flip-flop that is guaranteed to be stable for the next clock cycle. The resulting signal, *xm*, is synchronized with the receive clock, changing in response to *rp*, and thus can be used in combinational logic and sampled by the local clock.

Figure 10-12 shows waveforms for a FIFO synchronizer operating with transmit and local clocks 180° out of phase. The first five rows illustrate how the transmit side of the synchronizer splits the input stream on signal *x* into interleaved streams on *x0* and *x1*. The last three rows show how *rp* selects the stable transmit flip-flop output. The transmit flip-flops only change state when they are not selected by *rp*.

For correct sampling, *rp* must lag *xp* by at least t_{cy}; otherwise, the changing output will be sampled. For a two-element ring-buffer, this lag in *rp* relative to *xp* by at least a clock cycle is equivalent to a lead by at most a clock cycle. Stated differently, *rp* must be high during the rising edge of *xp* so that *x1* is sampled when *x0* changes and vice versa. At startup time, *rp* is initialized by sampling *xp* with *clk*, which waits an odd number of cycles for metastable states to decay and then uses the resulting value to initialize *rp*.

The delay of the FIFO synchronizer averages a half a clock period plus latch overhead and multiplexer delay. Unlike the delay-line or two-register synchronizer, there is no penalty due to the flip-flop keep-out period because the

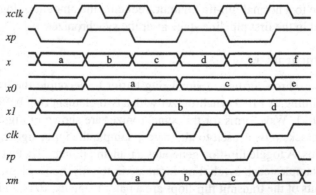

FIGURE 10-12   Waveforms for FIFO Synchronizer

transmitter clock is used to drive the flip-flops. An examination of Figure 10-12 would suggests that this delay is $1.5t_{cy}$. However, the transmitter can insert a full cycle of combinational logic between the transition on x and its being sampled into one of the two transmit flip-flops. The actual delay of the synchronization is the time from the transition on $x0$ or $x1$ to the corresponding transition on xm.

When the transmit and local clocks are nearly in phase, the two-element FIFO synchronizer cannot guarantee that output xm will be stable for the entire clock cycle. Depending on flip-flop and multiplexer delays, xm may be unstable at the beginning of the cycle or the end of the cycle. One solution to this problem is to set rp so that the instability always occurs at the beginning of the cycle (as in Figure 10-16) and reduce the maximum delay constraint on the combinational logic between xm and a flip-flop accordingly.

An alternative solution is to use more than two elements in the synchronizer ring-buffers. This relaxes the constraint on the relative phase between rp and xp so that for N elements, rp must lag xp by

$$(10\text{-}9) \qquad\qquad t_{cy} < t_{lag} < Nt_{cy}$$

The allowable range for t_{lag} must be at least t_{cy} to allow for all possible phase shifts between $xclk$ and clk. With $N = 2$, the range is exactly t_{cy}, and there is no room for margins. With more than two elements, a timing margin, t_m, can be added to this constraint as follows:

$$(10\text{-}10) \qquad\qquad t_{cy} + t_m < t_{lag} < Nt_{cy} - t_m$$

This margin allows for variations of flip-flop and multiplexer delays while keeping xm stable throughout the entire clock cycle.

Figure 10-13 shows a three-element FIFO synchronizer. A ring counter clocked by $xclk$ generates a 3-bit one-hot transmit pointer, xp, that is used to gate each symbol on input x into one of the three transmit flip-flops. A second ring counter, clocked by the local clock, generates the 3-bit one-hot receive pointer that selects the output of one of these flip-flops to drive output signal xm.

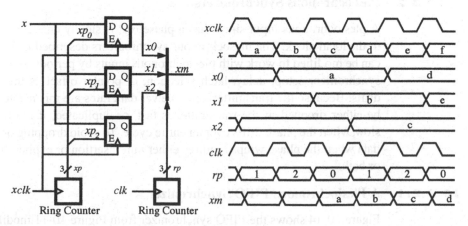

FIGURE 10-13 A Three-Element FIFO Synchronizer

The waveforms in Figure 10-13 illustrate operation of the synchronizer when the transmit and receive clocks are in phase. In cycle 3, $rp = 0$, and $x0$ is selected in the middle of its stable period with margins of t_{cy} in either direction. With a two-element synchronizer, $x0$ would change at the end of cycle 3, possibly corrupting xm at the end of the cycle, depending on delays. This instability in xm could be moved to the beginning of the cycle (as in Figure 10-16) by advancing rp and sampling $x1$ in cycle 3. Using at least three elements in the synchronizer eliminates the need for any instability by allowing adequate timing margins.

10.3.1.4 Brute-Force Synchronization

For comparison of synchronizer delay times, consider synchronizing a mesochronous signal using the circuit of Figure 10-6. This circuit does not exploit the predictability of events on the mesochronous input but rather samples x with the local clock and then waits for metastable states to decay before sampling the result with a second flip-flop. Thus the synchronization delay is

(10-11) $$t_z = t_w + 2t_{dcq} + t_{cy}/2$$

For mesochronous signals, this brute-force synchronizer has two significant disadvantages: longer delay and nonzero probability of failure. The synchronization time includes a wait, t_w, for metastable states to decay, usually a whole clock cycle. This increases the synchronization delay by a factor of three, from a half a cycle to a cycle and a half. Even with this wait, there is still a nonzero probability of synchronization failure, given by Eq. (10-6), on each transition of the input signal.

The three mesochronous synchronizers described above overcome these limitations by exploiting the periodic nature of input events to move the synchronization out of the data path. With all of these approaches, a single synchronization is performed at initialization (with some probability of failure) to set up the delay, latch selection, or pointer phase, and then data are piped through the system without further need of synchronization. After setup, the ordering of events is known.

10.3.2 Plesiochronous Synchronizers

A plesiochronous input signal has a phase that is slowly changing with respect to the local clock. The mesochronous synchronizers described in Section 10.3.1 can be modified to work with plesiochronous inputs by periodically updating the synchronizer setup, delay, latch selection, or pointer offset as the input phase drifts. Because the transmitter and receiver data rates are mismatched, data will be either dropped, if the transmitter is fast, or duplicated, if the transmitter is slow, when the phase drifts over an entire cycle. To avoid dropping or duplicating data when the phase wraps requires either null insertion or explicit flow control, or both.

10.3.2.1 A Plesiochronous FIFO Synchronizer

Figure 10-14 shows the FIFO synchronizer from Figure 10-11 modified to reset the receive pointer whenever a *resync* signal is asserted. A circuit composed of two

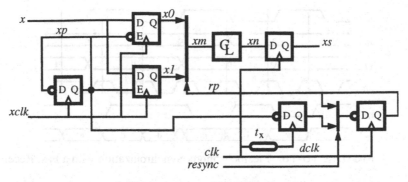

FIGURE 10-14 A Plesiochronous FIFO Synchronizer

flip-flops and a multiplexer updates *rp* with a synchronized (via a one-cycle wait for metastable decay) version of *xp* whenever *resync* is asserted. The local clock is delayed by t_x before sampling *xp* to assure that *rp* leads *xp* with adequate margin at the point of transition. When *resync* is low, the top input of the multiplexer is selected, and *rp* toggles, as in Figure 10-11. If *resync* is simply tied high, the circuit will update *rp* from *xp* on every cycle. In this case, *rp* will select the same transmitter flip-flop for two cycles in succession when *xp* slips by one cycle.

10.3.2.2 Data Rate Mismatch

The mismatch between the rate of a plesiochronous signal and the local clock used to sample it leads either to dropping or replicating data. Figure 10-15 illustrates the timing of the synchronizer of Figure 10-14 for the case in which the local clock, *clk*, is slower than the transmit clock, *xclk*. The vertical lines show the points at which the delayed local clock, *dclk*, samples *xp*. The receive pointer, *rp*, is updated with this value on the subsequent rising edge of *clk*. Because of the mismatch between the transmit and receive clock rates, the sample point occurs slightly later each clock cycle. The sample point drifts across the edge of *xp* between the second and third cycle, sampling *xp* in the high state for two consecutive cycles. This causes *rp* to remain in the high state during the third and fourth clock cycle. The result is that sample "c" of the input signal is dropped with the output advancing directly from sample "b" to sample "d." Note that if the sample clock were not delayed, the phase shift in *rp* would not occur until at least cycle 5, causing samples "c" and "d" to violate the keep-out region of the receive flip-flop.

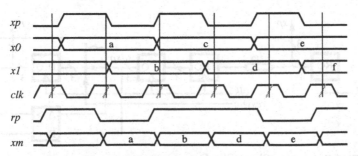

FIGURE 10-15 Plesiochronous Synchronization with Slow Receiver

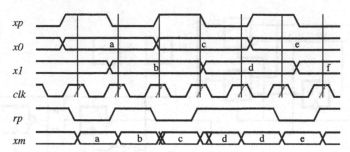

FIGURE 10-16   Plesiochronous Synchronization with a Fast Receiver

Timing of a plesiochronous FIFO synchronizer when the local clock is faster than the input signal is shown in Figure 10-16. In this case the sample points drift backward across the phase of the transmit pointer, xp. The fourth sample point drifts across the edge of xp, causing rp to remain high for two consecutive cycles. The result is that input symbol "d" is duplicated.

During cycles three and four, just before the phase of rp is flipped, output xm is unstable during the early part of the local clock cycle. This occurs because the delay of t_x between the clock and the sample point causes the phase of rp to flip only after it has drifted past 180° of lead. This is the safe direction to offset the sample point, and hence the point at which the phase of rp flips, because this direction always results in xm being stable at the end of the cycle when it is sampled by clk. The offset does reduce the amount of time available for combinational logic between the multiplexer and final flip-flop in Figure 10-14. This instability at the beginning of the cycle can be eliminated by using a FIFO, with at least three transmitter flip-flops, as shown in Figure 10-13. Using a longer FIFO also simplifies detecting the direction of slip when the phase of rp is toggled.

10.3.2.3   Detecting Phase Slip

The point at which the phase of rp should be adjusted and the direction of adjustment can be detected using the circuit shown in Figure 10-17. The figure shows the pointer portion of a plesiochronous FIFO synchronizer with a three-element ring buffer. A ring counter clocked by the transmit clock, $xclk$, generates a 3-bit, one-hot transmit pointer, xp. After a small delay to provide timing margin, as described by Eq. (10-10), the transmit pointer is sampled by the local clock, clk, and allowed to settle for a cycle to produce a synchronized, delayed transmit

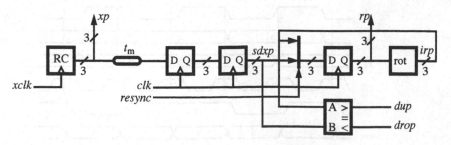

FIGURE 10-17   Phase-Slip Detector

pointer, *sdxp*. A multiplexer controlled by *resync* selects between this signal and an incremented (via a rotate) version of the receive pointer, *irp*, to be the next receive pointer.

A three-bit, one-hot magnitude comparator (three 3-input AND–OR gates) compares the two multiplexer inputs. If *irp* is greater than *sdxp*, then the receive pointer will not increment when *resync* is asserted, and the *dup* line is asserted to signal that a duplicate will occur when the pointer phase is updated. If *irp* is less than *sdxp*, on the other hand, the receive pointer will skip a state when phase is updated and the drop signal is asserted to signal this condition.

10.3.2.4 Null Symbols and Flow Control

Null symbols are used to handle the problem of duplication and dropping due to data-rate mismatch. A null symbol is the absence of data. Often nulls are encoded by adding a *presence bit* in parallel with the data signal. If the presence bit is zero, the symbol is a null; otherwise, data are present. Alternatively, if the alphabet of signal *x* is not a power of two in size, a null can be encoded using a binary data pattern not used by the alphabet.

When the phase of *rp* is retarded, repeating the same state for two cycles in a row, duplication of data can be avoided by inserting a null during the cycle following the phase adjustment. Of course, the logic downstream from the synchronizer needs to handle the null symbol appropriately.

To avoid dropping data when the phase of *rp* is advanced, skipping a state, the *resync* line is held low, postponing the phase adjustment until a null symbol appears in the transmit flip-flop that will be skipped. When the null symbol is detected, the phase is advanced and the null symbol is dropped, but no data are lost.

For correct operation, the receive phase must be updated within a certain number of cycles after the drop output of Figure 10-17 is first asserted. The maximum allowable update latency, t_u, depends on the frequency mismatch of the clocks and the amount of margin, t_m, built into the phase adjustment. Either an open-loop or closed-loop approach can be used to ensure that a null symbol will appear on input *x* within the required time. With the open-loop approach, each transmitter inserts a null periodically in the data stream with a frequency high enough to meet the t_u constraint on the receiver.

Alternatively, closed-loop flow control can be used to request a null symbol when one is needed for phase adjustment. With this approach, the receiver's drop signal is passed back to the transmitter (after appropriate synchronization) as a null request. The transmitter responds to this signal by inserting a null, allowing the receiver to adjust phase. Depending on the nature of the transmitter, it may either need an elastic buffer to hold data that arrive during the cycle that the null is inserted or the transmitter may need to request a null from its source of data.

10.3.3 Periodic Asynchronous Synchronizers

When a periodic signal is being sampled by a periodic clock of a very different frequency, a synchronizer can be constructed that exploits the periodic nature of

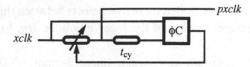

FIGURE 10-18   Clock Predictor

the signals to predict transition times arbitrarily far into the future and thus avoid synchronization failure. Because of the great frequency mismatch, however, some type of explicit flow control is required to avoid missing or duplicating events.

10.3.3.1   Clock Predictor Circuit

A clock predictor circuit is illustrated in Figure 10-18. The circuit predicts the value of an external periodic clock, *xclk*, one clock cycle t_{cy} of the local clock, *clk*, in the future. The prediction is output on line *pxclk*. Because *pxclk* is periodic and has the same frequency as *xclk*, it can be derived by phase shifting or delaying *xclk*. The amount of delay required is determined by delaying *pxclk* by t_{cy} and comparing this delayed prediction to the actual value of *xclk*. The prediction of *xclk*, a cycle in advance delayed by a cycle, should equal *xclk*. A phase comparator is used to adjust the delay from *xclk* to *pxclk* until this is the case. This technique can be extended to predict *xclk* multiple cycles in the future if required.

10.3.3.2   Periodic Synchronizer

One of several methods of exploiting the predicted clock to build a synchronizer is illustrated in Figure 10-19. The upper part of the circuit takes the external clock, *xclk*, and predicts its value one cycle in the future, *pxclk*, using the clock predictor described above. The predicted clock is then sampled by delayed versions of the clock (as in Figure 10-9) to determine if its transition lies in the keep-out region of the local clock. To avoid synchronization failure, the outputs of these flip-flops are resampled after a one-cycle delay to allow any metastable states to decay.

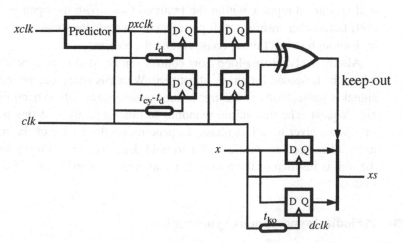

FIGURE 10-19   A Periodic Synchronizer

The outputs are then combined to generate a keep-out signal that controls the multiplexer of a two-register synchronizer (similar to that of Figure 10-10). If the predicted clock fell into the keep-out region one cycle ago, then the actual clock is in the keep-out region during the current cycle. In this case the upper flip-flop of the two-register synchronizer may be in a metastable state. To avoid sampling this flip-flop, the keepout signal controls the multiplexer to select the lower flip-flop.

In essence the circuit operates by using the time advance of the clock predictor to cancel the time delay of the synchronizer wait. The result is that a reliably synchronized keep-out signal is generated simultaneously with the sampling event it corresponds to.

10.3.4 General Purpose Asynchronous Synchronizers

The synchronization methods described in Section 10.3 cannot be applied if events on the external signal are aperiodic, or if the local clock is not periodic. In this case, the synchronization cannot be performed in advance by predicting the timing of events. Rather, synchronization must be performed explicitly in response to each event, introducing a synchronization wait into the latency of the data stream.

10.3.4.1 Waiting Synchronizer

The most straightforward method of synchronizing a truly asynchronous event stream is to use the waiting synchronizer illustrated in Figure 10-6 and discussed in Section 10.3.1.4. As described, this approach introduces a synchronization delay, t_w, typically one or more clock cycles, and has a nonzero probability of synchronization failure.

10.3.4.2 Asynchronous FIFO Synchronizer

Using a FIFO to synchronize an asynchronous data stream moves the synchronization out of the data path and facilitates flow control. As illustrated in Figure 10-20, this method involves shifting data into a FIFO using the transmit clock and shifting data out of the FIFO using the local clock. Both clocks may be aperiodic. Synchronization is performed on the transmit and receive pointers to generate an

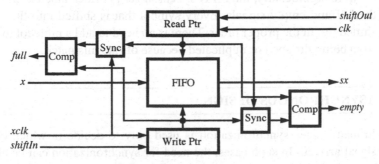

FIGURE 10-20 Asynchronous FIFO Synchronizer

"empty" signal in the local clock domain and a "full" signal in the transmit clock domain.

The FIFO in the center of Figure 10-20 can be realized as a set of flip-flops with clock enables and an output multiplexer, as in Figure 10-13. In practice, a register file or transparent latches are often used to save area. The read and write pointers are ring counters that sequence data into and out of the FIFO. The write pointer is advanced synchronously with the transmit clock, *xclk*, when the *shiftIn* signal is asserted. Similarly the read pointer is advanced synchronously with *clk* when *shiftOut* is asserted. Data are shifted into the FIFO in the transmit clock domain and shifted out of the FIFO in the receive clock domain. No synchronization is required unless the receiver attempts to read past the last word in the FIFO or the transmitter attempts to write beyond the FIFO capacity.

Synchronization is required to detect the "full" and "empty" conditions of the FIFO because this requires comparing the two pointers that are in different clock domains. In the figure, the read (write) pointer is synchronized with the transmit (local) clock, and the comparison to check for full (empty) is performed in the transmit (local) clock domain. This method is preferred to the alternative of performing the comparison directly on the two pointers without synchronization and then synchronizing the resulting asynchronous full and empty signals because the alternative delays the response of the empty (full) signal to the *shiftOut* (*shiftIn*) signal. The method illustrated in Figure 10-20 on the other hand, immediately sets empty (full) when the last word is shifted out (in), avoiding underruns (overruns). The synchronization delay is only incurred when information must be passed between the two clock domains. For example, when the transmitter shifts the first word into an empty FIFO, a synchronizer delay is required before the receiver detects empty as low.

The asynchronous FIFO synchronizer has two advantages compared with the waiting synchronizer: lower probability of synchronization failure and inherent flow-control. The probability of synchronization failure is reduced because synchronizations are performed less frequently. If the read and write pointers are encoded in a one-hot manner, then only a single synchronization is performed per word and only when the FIFO toggles between the empty and nonempty states. In contrast the waiting synchronizer performs a synchronization for every bit transmitted.

More significantly, the FIFO synchronizer provides inherent flow control via the full and empty signals. Every symbol that is shifted into the FIFO will be shifted out in the proper order. There is no need to add a protocol to prevent data from being dropped or duplicated because of rate mismatch.

10.4   ASYNCHRONOUS DESIGN

In many cases synchronization is used only to decide in which clock cycle a signal arrived. In such cases, the need for synchronization can be eliminated by processing the signal asynchronously. With asynchronous design there is no need to round the arrival time of the signal to the nearest clock edge nor to wait for a synchronizer to settle out of a possible metastable state. Processing of the signal begins as soon as the signal event is detected.

Synchronization is required in an asynchronous system when the output of the system, the type and ordering of output events, depends on the order in which input events are received. An *arbiter* is used in these cases to synchronize two (or more) asynchronous signals by deciding unambiguously the ordering of their events.

To make the number of event orderings that must be considered in an asynchronous system tractable, most asynchronous systems are designed around a protocol that constrains possible event orderings. The *weak conditions*, for example, constrain the ordering of input and output events of a module. These protocols enforce fine-grain synchronization within the modules of an asynchronous system. For example, all of the signals in a module obeying the weak conditions are loosely synchronized with one another.

The design of an asynchronous module with state involves not just ensuring that the next state function provides the required behavior, but also that transitions between the states are free of critical races and hazards. The design process is simplified by using *trajectory maps*, Karnaugh maps on which the trajectory of state transitions is superimposed. Trajectory maps also serve to identify when explicit state variables are required and when outputs and inputs can obviate the need for state variables.

Asynchronous systems are constructed by composing modules according to simple sets of rules. If the modules obey a signaling protocol and the protocol is closed under the composition rules, then the composition obeys the protocol as well. For example, the weak conditions are closed under acyclic composition, which permits large combinational asynchronous modules to be composed from smaller modules. Asynchronous pipelines are realized by inserting *align* blocks between such combinational modules, and iterative circuits can be realized by constructing cyclic pipelines.

10.4.1 Stoppable Clocks

A simple approach to handling asynchronous signals is to generate a clock that is synchronized with the arrival of the signal. With periodic signals, this can be accomplished using closed-loop timing, as described in Section 9.6. For aperiodic signals, the clock can be stopped while waiting for the arrival of a signal and started on each signal event.

A module employing such a stoppable clock is illustrated in Figure 10-21. The module accepts an input, *in*, along with its bundled event signal, *rin*. An input acknowledge line, *ain*, signals when the input has been accepted. A similar interface is implemented on the module output with signals *out*, *rout*, and *aout*. The module is operated from a local clock, *clk*, generated by a ring oscillator that runs when signal go is asserted.

Figure 10-22 shows waveforms that illustrate the operation of this circuit. The arrows between the waveforms denote the dependence of signal events. Between input events the module is in a quiescent state with *done* = 1, *go* = 0 and the clock,

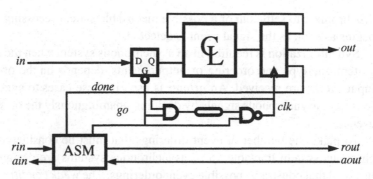

FIGURE 10-21   A Module with a Stoppable Clock

clk, stopped in the high state. Operation is initiated when input *rin* goes high. This transition causes *go* to rise, sampling *in* into the input latch and starting the clock. At the end of the first clock cycle, signal *done*, an output of the locally clocked FSM, falls to indicate that operation is to continue for another cycle. The falling edge of *done* causes *ain* to rise, which enables the environment (light arrow) to drop *rin*.

When the circuit is finished with its computation, three clock cycles in this case, signal *done* goes high, which in turn causes *go* to go low, stopping the clock. The delay from *clk* high to *go* low must be shorter than the delay of the delay line to avoid a low-going glitch on *clk*. The falling edge of *go* also triggers *rout* to rise, which in turn causes *ain* to fall, enabling the environment to make another request on *rin*. Signal *rout*, signals the availability of data on the output, enabling the environment to accept these data by raising *aout*. When the environment raises *aout*, the circuit drops *rout*, and the circuit returns to the quiescent state. If the input raises *rin* before the environment accepts the data by signaling *aout*, the circuit delays raising *go* until *rout* has fallen.

A module with a stoppable clock, like the one in Figure 10-21, has asynchronous interfaces but is internally synchronous. It avoids the need to synchronize events on its input to its local clock by instead synchronizing the local clock to input events. This has the advantages of eliminating synchronization delay and the associated probability of synchronization failure.

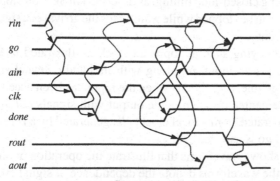

FIGURE 10-22   Stoppable Clock Waveforms

10.4.2 Asynchronous Signaling Protocols

10.4.2.1 Four-Phase Asynchronous Signaling

The request and acknowledge signals in Figures 10-21 and 10-22 (*rin*, *ain*, *rout*, and *aout*) obey the *four-phase* asynchronous signaling convention for input and output signals with bundled signaling (RZ clocked signaling, Section 9.4.1.3). An interface that conforms to this convention must perform the following four events cyclically in order:

1. All inputs are asserted.
2. Acknowledgment is asserted.
3. All inputs are deasserted.
4. Acknowledgment is deasserted.

For an input interface of a circuit, the odd-numbered steps are performed by the environment (the client), whereas the even-numbered steps are performed by the circuit (the server). For the output interface of a circuit, the roles are reversed, with the circuit acting the part of the client and performing the odd-numbered steps.

Figure 10-23 shows interface waveforms for a four-phase signaling convention for a circuit with a single input and a bundled signaling convention. The environment places data on the input lines, *in*, and signals an event by raising *req*. When the circuit has accepted the data, it responds by raising *ack*. This informs the environment that it can now lower *req* and allow the input lines to change (in that order). After *req* falls, the circuit lowers *ack*, completing the fourth phase and enabling the cycle to start over again with the environment presenting data on *in* and asserting *req*.

If a circuit has multiple, separately bundled inputs, all of the *req* inputs or their equivalents must be asserted (deasserted) before the *ack* output follows suit. Although illustrated here for bundled (clocked) signaling, this convention may be implemented for any of the return-to-zero encodings shown in Figure 9-17.

10.4.2.2 Two-Phase Asynchronous Signaling

If a nonreturn-to-zero method is used to encode input events, as illustrated in Figure 9-17 (a, c, and e), the third and fourth steps of the four-phase protocol may be omitted. The result is a two-phase signaling convention, as illustrated in

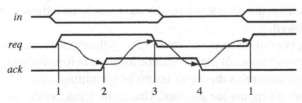

FIGURE 10-23 Bundled Four-Phase Asynchronous Signaling Convention

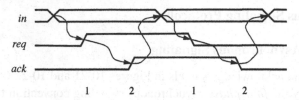

FIGURE 10-24   Bundled Two-Phase Asynchronous Signaling Convention

Figure 10-24 for bundled signaling. The environment places data in the *in* lines and toggles *req*. The circuit signals acceptance of the data by toggling *ack*, which enables the environment to start the next cycle by placing new data on *in* and asserting *ack* again.

Although illustrated here for bundled NRZ signaling, this signaling convention can be applied to any NRZ event encoding method.

10.4.2.3   The Weak Conditions

In a synchronous system, the number of input and output events is always exactly the same because all events occur in lockstep. In asynchronous systems it is often useful to constrain the relative number of input and output events by establishing a monotonicity condition on the assertion and deassertion of multiple inputs and outputs. This loosely synchronizes the system so that a group of associated input events remains together and do not mix with earlier or later events.

Consider the following events relating to the inputs and outputs of a particular module:

1. Some input is asserted.
2. All inputs are asserted.
3. Some output is asserted.
4. All outputs are asserted.
5. Some input is deasserted.
6. All inputs are deasserted.
7. Some output is deasserted.
8. All outputs are deasserted.

Figure 10-25 illustrates two constraints on event ordering: the *strong conditions* and the *weak conditions*. Each circle in the figure corresponds to an event, and each arrow denotes a precedence (occurs before) relationship. All eight events occur during each cycle of a four-phase protocol. For a two-phase (NRZ) protocol, the deassertion events do not occur, and the transitions indicated by the shaded lines are followed.

The strong conditions impose a total order on the eight events described above. Under these constraints, all inputs must be asserted before any output is asserted. The weak conditions relax these constraints by permitting some outputs to become asserted before all inputs are asserted. Under the weak conditions, however, all inputs must still be asserted before all outputs are asserted.

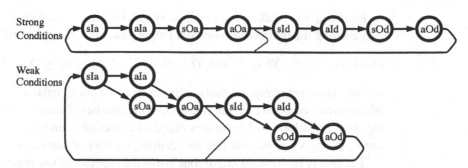

FIGURE 10-25 Event Ordering for the Strong and Weak Conditions

Figure 10-26 illustrates the weak conditions by showing input and output waveforms for two cycles of a dual-rail RZ (Figure 9-17 (b)) half-adder that obeys the weak conditions. At time 1, a zero is asserted on input A by raising line A_0. A zero carry, C, output is asserted at time 2. Even if the value of sum were known at this point, the weak conditions insist that the circuit wait for B to be asserted (at time 3) before asserting a sum, S, of one at time 4. During the deassertions of the first cycle (times 5–8), the deassertion of sum is delayed until after both A and B are deasserted. The assertion portion of the second cycle (times 9–11) actually obeys the strong conditions, for neither sum nor carry is determined until both A and B are known. The deassertion portion of this cycle (times 12–15) again uses sum as the synchronizing output, delaying the deassertion of sum until all inputs are deasserted.

The sum output (S_0, S_1) in Figure 10-26 is an example of a *completion signal*, a signal that, when asserted or deasserted, signals that its module has completed handling a set of input events. A completion signal is asserted (deasserted) only when all inputs and all other outputs are asserted (deasserted). Although not required by the weak conditions, building asynchronous modules with completion signals greatly simplifies the design of the asynchronous sequencing logic that controls the application of input events to the module. Where it is not convenient to use a data output of a module to signal completion, a single-rail output signal is often added to a module explicitly for this purpose.

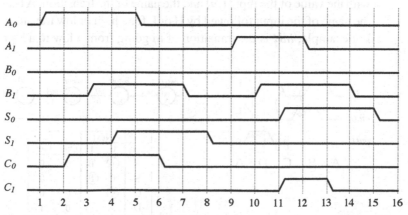

FIGURE 10-26 Dual-Rail Half-Adder Waveforms (Weak Conditions)

Enforcing the weak conditions loosely synchronizes asynchronous circuits by constraining the number of input and output assertions and deassertions so that

(10-12) $$\forall i \in I, \quad o \in O, \quad D_o \leq D_i \leq A_o \leq A_i \leq D_o + 1$$

where I is the set of input signals, O is the set of output signals, A_x is the number of assertion events on a signal x, and D_x is the number of deassertion events on a signal x. Equation (10-12) ensures that the number of events on every input and output is always equal to or one less than the number of events on any input.

The beauty of the weak conditions is that they are closed under acyclic composition. Any circuit composed from a set of modules that obeys the weak conditions without forming any cycles will itself obey the weak conditions.

10.4.3 Asynchronous Module Design Methods

10.4.3.1 State Diagrams

The process of designing an asynchronous sequential module begins with a state diagram that specifies the precedence relationship between input and output transitions. For example, Figure 10-27 shows the waveforms, state diagram, and flow table for a toggle circuit. The waveforms illustrate the behavior of the toggle circuit. Even pulses on *in* are transmitted to *out0*, whereas odd pulses are transmitted to *out1*. The vertical lines over the waveforms mark the *states* of the circuit. *Stable states*, those with no output transition pending, are labeled with a single character name, whereas *transient states* are unlabeled. A circuit leaves a stable state only when an input changes. A circuit exits a transient state owing to its own response. In general, we describe the behavior of asynchronous circuits in terms of their stable states. However, understanding of transient states is important to produce a correct implementation.

An asynchronous state diagram for the toggle circuit is shown at the upper right of Figure 10-27. Each circle in the diagram denotes a stable state of the circuit and is labeled with a single character name and the value of the outputs in that state (*out0, out1*). Each edge in the figure represents an input transition and is labeled with the value of the input (*in*) and the name of the transition. A transition name is the name of the input followed by H or L for a high or low transition, respectively. For example, *inH* is the transition of *in* going from a low to a high state. This is

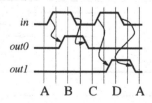

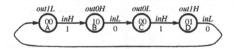

	Next			
State	0	1	Out0	Out1
A	Ⓐ	B	0	0
B	C	Ⓑ	1	0
C	Ⓒ	D	0	0
D	A	Ⓓ	0	1

FIGURE 10-27   State Diagram and Flow Table for a Toggle Circuit

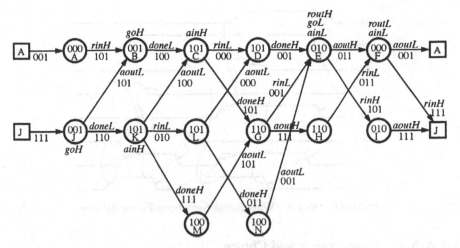

FIGURE 10-28 · State Diagram for Clock Stopper

in contrast to a synchronous state diagram in which all edges correspond to clock transitions but may be labeled with the value of inputs. In an asynchronous state machine, every input transition results in a state change regardless of the response of the circuit. This is a rather trivial state diagram because, with a single input, no branches are possible. In each state, the only possible input transition is for the single input to toggle to the opposite state.

A flow table for the toggle circuit is shown at the lower right of Figure 10-27. The table has a row for each state. For each state the table shows the next state as a function of input value and the output value in the current state. When the next state is the same as the current state, the next state value is circled to denote a stable state.

Figure 10-28 shows the state diagram for the asynchronous clock stopper module of Figure 10-21. Each state is labeled with the output (*ain*, *rout*, *go*). The edges in the figure are labeled with the input (*rin*, *aout*, *done*). The two square boxes at the right side of the figure logically connect to the corresponding boxes on the left side. The waveforms in Figure 10-22 correspond to traversal of states A through F and then J in the state diagram.

This state diagram incorporates several design decisions that represent a trade-off between performance and ease of implementation. For example, the circuit could raise *ain* in state B but defers doing so until state C to simplify implementation. For similar reasons *ain* is not dropped in D and *rout* is not dropped in H. On the other hand, complexity is increased by raising *go* in state J. If *go* were held low in J, states K through N would not be needed.

Because the clock stopper has three inputs, there are potentially several paths out of a given state. In the limit there are seven possibilities: any of the three inputs could transition, any pair could transition, or all three inputs could toggle simultaneously. In practice, the constraints on the environment limit which inputs can change. For example, in state B the transition *rinL* is not allowed by the four-phase convention because *ain* is low. In states where multiple input transitions are allowed, an *input race*, where two or more inputs change simultaneously or an additional input changes before the circuit has stabilized after the first input change, may occur.

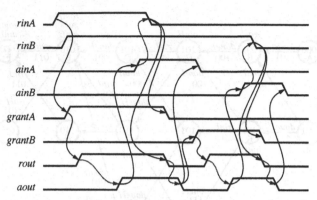

FIGURE 10-29   Waveforms for a Four-Phase Arbiter

10.4.3.2   Concurrency and Choice

When an input race may occur, the distinction must be made between *concurrency* and *choice*. An input race represents choice if the order in which the inputs change determines the outcome (i.e., if the race is critical). It represents concurrency if the order does not affect the outcome (a noncritical race). All of the forks in the state diagram of Figure 10-28 represent concurrency. For example, in state K any of the three inputs may change. Regardless of the order of the changes, the system will wind up in state E. In the waveforms of Figure 10-22, *aout* and *rin* go high simultaneously, taking the system from state E to state J. It is immaterial whether the transition is via F or I.

A four-phase arbiter is an example of an asynchronous sequential circuit with a transition that represents choice. Waveforms illustrating the behavior of this circuit are shown in Figure 10-29, and a state diagram for the circuit is shown in Figure 10-30. The circuit is used to connect two requesters, A and B, that obey a four-phase protocol to a single resource. One requester at a time is granted the resource by asserting a *grant* line and logically connecting the requester's *rin* and *ain* lines to the *rout* and *aout* lines connected to the resource. Figure 10-29

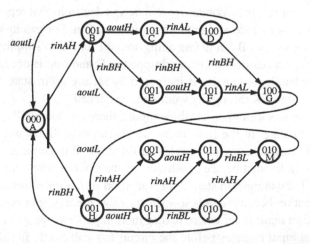

FIGURE 10-30   State Diagram of a Four-Phase Arbiter

illustrates the situation where *rinA* and *rinB* are asserted at nearly the same time, and the resource is granted to A. Only after the resource completes its four-phase protocol with A, with the transition *aoutL*, is the resource granted to B. The order in which the circuit sees transitions *rinAH* and *rinBH* clearly matters here. Whether *grantA* or *grantB* is asserted depends on the order. This is a multiple input transition representing choice.

Figure 10-30 illustrates the state diagram of the four-phase arbiter. The states are labeled with a subset of the outputs (*ainA*, *ainB*, *rout*). The vertical line crossing the two transitions out of state A denotes that this multiple input transition involves choice. If the circuit sees *rinAH* first, the transition is to the upper half of the state diagram, and A is granted the resource. Requester B is granted the resource, and a transition is made to the lower portion of the diagram if *rinBH* is seen first. The waveforms shown in Figure 10-29 correspond to the state sequence {A, B, E, F, G, H, I, J, A}.

An asynchronous state transition that represents choice requires arbitration, such as using arbiter with an excluded middle circuit, as shown in Figure 10-7, to determine unambiguously which input transition occurred first. If such a circuit is not employed, nearly simultaneous inputs may result in metastable states being inconsistently interpreted by different portions of the circuit. In effect, the arbiter synchronizes the two asynchronous signals to permit a decision to be made about the order of their events.

10.4.3.3 Trajectory Maps for Designing Asynchronous Sequential Logic

Trajectory maps are Karnaugh maps on which an asynchronous state machine's state diagram is mapped. The horizontal axis of a trajectory map is labeled with the module's inputs, and the vertical axis holds the outputs and state variables. Thus, input transitions correspond to horizontal movement in the trajectory map, whereas output and state transitions correspond to vertical movement.

The construction of a trajectory map combines the steps of state assignment and logic design. This combination provides four significant advantages of conventional asynchronous synthesis in which these steps are performed separately. First, the process makes the effect of changes in the state diagram on the logic immediately visible. This allows the state diagram to be interactively modified to give an efficient implementation (e.g., by delaying the transitions of *ain* in Figure 10-28). Second, the trajectory map reduces the number of required state variables by making it easy to use the input and output signals of the asynchronous machine as state variables. Third, showing the transitions over the Karnaugh map makes it clear which transitions between implicants must be covered to avoid hazards. Conventional approaches often cover transitions between all adjacent implicants. When multiple-state variables change in response to an input change, the degree of parallelism and order of transitions can easily be controlled to avoid critical races.

Figure 10-31 shows a trajectory map for the toggle circuit along with Karnaugh maps for the two outputs (*out0* and *out1*) and the state variable (*x*). The solid line labeled with a variable denotes that the variable is true in the area of the chart corresponding to the line. The leftmost map is the trajectory map. The arrows show the path through the space of total state during a cycle of the circuit. Because there

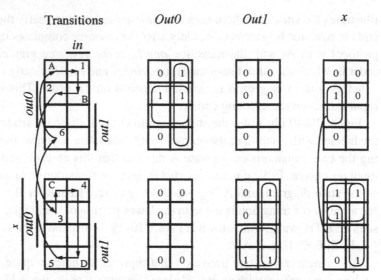

FIGURE 10-31 Trajectory Map for the Toggle Circuit

are no branches and no concurrency, the arrows form a simple cycle. There are ten states along this path: the four stable states, A–D, and six transient states, 1–6. Note that all arrows emanating from a stable state are horizontal. Only a single variable is allowed to change between two states. For this reason the stable states are all separated by at least one transient state. For example when *in* rises, the circuit moves from stable state A to transient state 1. The circuit responds by raising *out0*, entering stable state B. The transition between transient states B and C involves both *out0* and *x* changing, and hence two transient states. The trajectory map makes it clear that *x* must change first or the circuit would return to state A.

The trajectory map makes it easy to experiment with changes of state assignment. It is clear, for example, that a state variable must change no later than after state 2 to avoid returning to state A. The change could be made earlier, after state 1 or after what is currently state B, leaving $x = 1$ in state B.

Karnaugh maps for the outputs and state variables of an asynchronous circuit, such as the three at the right of Figure 10-31, are constructed directly from the trajectory map. For each state, S, in the trajectory map, enter into the corresponding position of each Karnaugh map the value of the output variable at the head of the arrow or arrows leaving S. If multiple arrows give different values, a noncritical race, enter the value at the end of the race. Logic equations are then derived from the Karnaugh maps by selecting prime implicants, denoted by the circles about groups of ones, taking care that every transition is covered by a single implicant. Logic equations (Eq. (10-13)) correspond to the prime implicants identified in Figure 10-31. These equations represent a simple realization of the toggle circuit with eleven literals.

$$Out0 = \bar{x} \wedge (in \vee Out0)$$

(10-13) $$Out1 = x \wedge (in \vee Out1)$$

$$x = (Out0 \wedge \bar{in}) \vee (x \wedge (\overline{Out1} \vee in))$$

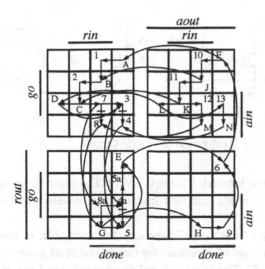

FIGURE 10-32   Trajectory Map for the Clock Stopper of Figure 10-28

The trajectory map of Figure 10-32 includes several examples of states where multiple inputs may change. In all cases these changes represent concurrency, not choice. In state C, for example, the trajectory may go left or right, depending on whether *rin* falls before *done* rises. This input race is noncritical because the circuit will get to state E in either case. Another example is state K, where a three-way input race exists.

The trajectory map also makes it clear why protocol transitions on *ain* and *rout* are delayed in states B, D, and H. In each of these cases, toggling the protocol line, and thus enabling a transition on the complementary line, would require adding a state variable to the circuit. For example, if *rin* were to fall in state B, a new state variable would be required because the square to the right of *rin* is hemmed in on all sides.

It is straightforward to derive the logic equations for the clock stopper circuit, shown in Eq. (10-14), from this trajectory map.

$$go = (go \land \overline{done}) \lor (rin \land \overline{rout} \land \overline{ain})$$
(10-14)
$$ain = (go \land \overline{done}) \lor (ain \land (\overline{rout} \lor rin))$$
$$rout = (ain \land \overline{go}) \lor (rout \land \overline{aout})$$

10.4.3.4   Set–Reset Excitation Equations

Using a set–reset (RS) flip-flop to hold each state variable or output of an asynchronous circuit often results in a more efficient implementation. This style of implementation requires the *excitation* equations for the set and reset inputs of the flip-flop.

Taking into account "don't care" input states, a state variable, a, is described by three disjoint Boolean functions: a_1, which is true for those input states where a must be a one; a_0, which is true for those input states where a must be a zero; and a_x, which is true for those input states where a may be either a zero or a one. These three functions correspond to the squares in a K-map that are labeled

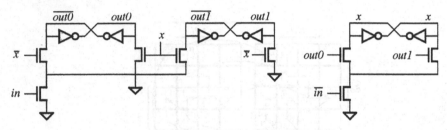

FIGURE 10-33   RS FF Realization of Toggle Circuit

1, 0, and left blank (or labeled X), respectively. The logic function used for a direct realization of a is the simplest function that covers all of a_1 and none of a_0.

The true, false, and "don't care" functions for a variable, a, can be used to derive a corresponding set of functions for the set and reset inputs of a flip-flop, as shown in Eq. (10-15). The logic is simplified because the 1 functions (a_{s1} and a_{r1}) need only cover the points in the input space where a changes state, input a is a zero, and output a is a one, or vice versa. Points where a is stable are added to the "don't care" functions.

$$a_{s1} = a_1 \wedge \bar{a} \qquad a_{r1} = a_0 \wedge a$$
$$(10\text{-}15) \qquad a_{s0} = a_0 \qquad a_{r0} = a_1$$
$$a_{sx} = a_x \vee (a_1 \wedge a) \qquad a_{rx} = a_x \vee (a_0 \wedge \bar{a})$$

For example, the application of these equations to the toggle circuit described by the K-maps in Figure 10-31 gives the following excitation equations:

$$out0_s = in \wedge \bar{x} \qquad out0_r = x$$
$$(10\text{-}16) \qquad out1_s = in \wedge x \qquad out1_r = \bar{x}$$
$$x_s = \overline{in} \wedge out0 \qquad x_r = \overline{in} \wedge out1$$

An implementation of this circuit using RS flip-flops with N-only pulldown chains for the set and reset functions is illustrated in Figure 10-33. Compared with the straightforward logic-gate realization of Eq. (10-13), this circuit requires considerably fewer devices for two reasons. First, the excitation equations, although more numerous, are considerably simpler than the direct equations for the state variables because they need to cover only the transitions. Also, building the set and reset functions into the flip-flop allows their realization with N-only switching networks, which cuts the number of devices in half.

10.4.3.5   Arbitration and Circuits with Choice

To implement an asynchronous circuit involving choice, the circuit must first be converted to a circuit without choice through the use of an arbiter. An arbiter is a two-input, two-output circuit, as illustrated in Figure 10-34. An output, a_i, is asserted only if the corresponding input, r_i, is asserted and at most one output is asserted at a time. If both inputs are asserted at nearly the same time, the output corresponding to the input asserted first is asserted. In most situations, a

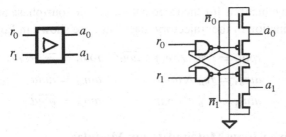

FIGURE 10-34   Arbiter Circuit

higher-level protocol requires an input to remain asserted until the corresponding output is asserted.

An arbiter can be realized by a cross-coupled pair of NAND gates followed by an excluded middle circuit, as shown in Figure 10-7. If one input rises well before the other, the output of its NAND gate goes low, disabling the other input. If both inputs rise at nearly the same time, both NAND gate outputs go to an intermediate voltage, and the excluded middle circuit prevents either output from going high until one output is a clear winner.

A simple four-transistor implementation of the excluded middle circuit is shown in Figure 10-34. The cross-coupled PFETs cause an output, say a_1, to go high only if NAND output $\bar{n}_1$ is at least a threshold voltage lower than $\bar{n}_0$.

A trajectory map for the four-phase arbiter of Figure 10-30 that uses a primitive arbiter circuit to make the two request inputs mutually exclusive is shown in Figure 10-35. A primitive arbiter accepts the two request inputs, rin_a and rin_b, and outputs two exclusive request signals, re_a and re_b. The arbiter makes the choice between the two request inputs, eliminating the critical input race. The trajectory map is then drawn in terms of these exclusive requests.

The area of the trajectory map corresponding to $re_a = re_b = 1$ is shaded to denote that this region is excluded because re_a and re_b can never be asserted at the same time. In addition to eliminating the input race between the two requests, the arbiter also eliminates states E, F, K, and L in which both request inputs are high.

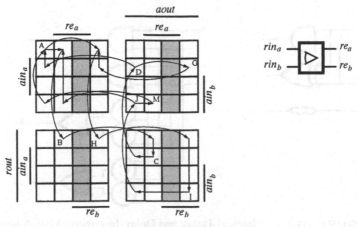

FIGURE 10-35   Trajectory Map for Four-Phase Arbiter

The excitation equations for the three outputs of the four-phase arbiter can be written by examination of the trajectory map. They are shown in Eq. (10-17).

(10-17)

$$rout_s = (re_a \vee re_b) \wedge \overline{aout} \quad rout_r = \overline{re_a} \wedge \overline{re_b}$$

$$ain_{as} = re_a \wedge aout \quad\quad ain_{ar} = \overline{aout}$$

$$ain_{bs} = re_b \wedge aout \quad\quad ain_{br} = \overline{aout}$$

10.4.3.6 Delay-Insensitive versus Matched-Delay Modules

An asynchronous module that must signal its completion (e.g., to adhere to the weak conditions), may do so in a *delay-insensitive* manner so that the timing of the completion signal will be correct regardless of the delays of circuit elements. Alternatively a completion signal can be generated using a delay line matched to the delay of the module. Such a *matched-delay* circuit is usually much simpler than the corresponding delay-insensitive circuit.

Figure 10-36 illustrates these two approaches to asynchronous modules by showing two half-adders that obey the weak conditions. The circuit on the left is a conventional combinational adder augmented by a matched delay line to generate completion signal *rout*. This circuit employs a bundled signal encoding with *rin* being asserted after the two inputs, *a* and *b*, are valid, and signal *rout* being asserted after the two outputs, *c* and *s*, are valid. The delay line is designed to be at least as long as the longest delay between inputs and outputs so that *c* and *s* are guaranteed to be valid before *rout* is asserted. When designing such circuits care must be taken to make the delay of the delay line track the combinational delay of the circuit across variations of process and voltage. Matching of 5% or better is achievable with typical processes.

The circuit on the right side of Figure 10-36 is a delay-insensitive half-adder that uses a dual-rail encoding of input and output signals and obeys the weak conditions. Waveforms for this circuit were shown in Figure 10-26. The dual-rail carry output of this circuit, c_0 and c_1, is generated combinationally from the dual-rail inputs. Because the assertion of one of the carry outputs indicates the completion of the carry computation, this circuit is insensitive to the gate

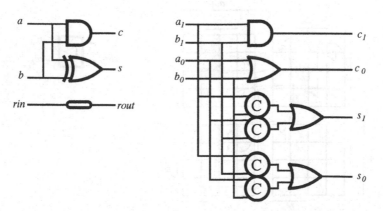

FIGURE 10-36 Matched-Delay and Delay-Insensitive Half-Adders

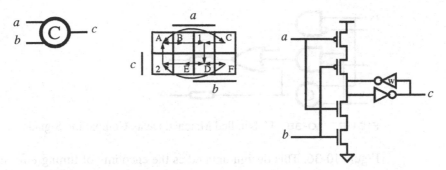

FIGURE 10-37 Muller C-Element

delays. Availability of the carry output will not be signaled until the gate output is valid.

The dual-rail sum output is computed by a circuit that employs four Muller *C-elements* to meet the requirement of the weak conditions that all inputs become invalid before all outputs become invalid. The C-element is a sequential device whose output follows its inputs when all are equal and holds its state when the inputs are not equal. Figure 10-37 illustrates the symbol, trajectory map, and a CMOS implementation of the C-element.

The sum circuit in Figure 10-36 uses four C-elements that correspond to the four possible input states of the circuit. After both *a* and *b* are asserted, the output of exactly one of these C-elements will go high, which in turn causes the appropriate sum output to be asserted. The active C-element holds its output high until both inputs are deasserted. This ensures that the weak conditions are met by holding one of the sum outputs asserted until all inputs are deasserted.

For most practical purposes the sum output of the dual-rail half-adder in Figure 10-36 can serve as a completion signal. It is not asserted (deasserted) until after both inputs are asserted (deasserted). Also, it is likely that the carry output will be asserted before the sum output because the carry is computed by a simpler circuit. The sum output, however, is not a delay-insensitive completion signal inasmuch as an arbitrary assignment of gate delays could cause the sum output to be asserted before the carry output. The addition of an OR-gate to combine the two carry outputs and an AND-gate on each sum output to delay its assertion until the output of the OR-gate is asserted would make the sum output a delay-insensitive completion signal.

One advantage of the dual-rail circuit in Figure 10-36 is that, when composed, it allows completion to be signaled in a data-dependent manner. This is particularly advantageous in an n-bit adder where the worst-case carry delay, through n stages, is much larger than the average delay, through $lg(n)$ stages. This advantage, however, is not due to the circuit being delay-insensitive, but occurs because the circuit unbundles the signal encoding, providing separate indication of the time of assertion of each input and each output.

Figure 10-38 illustrates how the same unbundled signal encoding can be applied to the matched-delay half-adder. Figure 10-38 shows only the logic for the timing signals. The logic for the sum and carry outputs is identical to that of

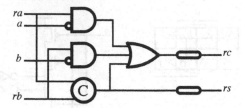

FIGURE 10-38 Unbundled Matched Delay Completion Signals

Figure 10-36. This design unbundles the encoding of timing information by replacing the single input ready line, *rin*, with separate lines, *ra* and *rb*, for each input. Similarly the output completion line, *rout*, is replaced with *rc* and *rs*. If either input is ready and low, the carry does not depend on the other input, and the circuit signals carry ready on *rc* without waiting for the other input. The C-element detects when both inputs are ready and propagates this event to both outputs. This handles the case for the carry output when both inputs are high.

10.4.4 Composition of Asynchronous Circuits

The techniques of Section 10.4.3 that convert a specification or state diagram to an asynchronous circuit are used to realize relatively small circuits. They become unwieldy when the number of states or inputs and outputs becomes too large. To overcome this complexity, large asynchronous circuits are implemented by composing smaller asynchronous circuits according to simple sets of rules.

10.4.4.1 Asynchronous Combinational Blocks

Figure 10-39 shows an acyclic composition of a number of asynchronous modules. Each line in the figure represents a signal that carries its own timing information, either dual-rail or bundled. If the composition is acyclic, the modules individually obey the weak conditions, and all of the outputs depend on all of the inputs, then the composition obeys the weak conditions.

Closure of the set of circuits obeying the weak conditions under acyclic composition can be shown by dividing the circuit into stages along cuts *x* and *y* in the figure. If A and B obey the weak conditions, then their parallel combination obeys the weak conditions at cut *x*. Some input (*a*, *b*, or *c*) must be valid before some output (*d*, *e*, *f*, or *g*) becomes valid; all inputs (*a*–*c*) must be valid before all outputs (*d*–*g*) are valid, and so on. If these conditions did not hold, then either A or B, or both, would be violating the weak conditions.

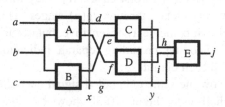

FIGURE 10-39 Composition of Asynchronous Modules in a DAG

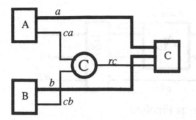

FIGURE 10-40   Fan-In to Modules with a Single Request Input

As long as all outputs at each stage are used by the following stage, the series combination of two stages also obeys the weak conditions because the partial event orderings imposed by these conditions are transitive. For example, all of the inputs must be valid before all of cut x becomes valid, and all of cut x must become valid before all of cut y becomes valid. Thus, all of the inputs must be valid before all of cut y becomes valid. This holds even for lines that pass through a stage unchanged, like g, for a wire trivially meets the weak conditions.

Repeating this analysis shows that the output, j, respects the weak conditions with reference to the inputs $(a–c)$. This closure is only true if at each stage, including the output, some signal is dependent on each signal of the preceding stage. If this were not the case, if signal g were not connected to module E for example, then all of the outputs of a stage might become valid before all of the inputs become valid, violating the weak conditions.

If the modules employ a bundled signaling convention with only a single request input, C-elements are required wherever there is fan-in to combine multiple completion signals from one stage into a single request signal. For example, Figure 10-40 illustrates two modules, A and B, whose outputs fan-in to a module C with a single request input. The bundled data signals are denoted by thick lines, and the completion–request signals are denoted by thin lines. The completion signals from A and B, ca and cb, are combined by a C-element to produce the request to module C, rc. Request line rc will only be asserted (deasserted) after both ca and cb are asserted (deasserted); thus the combination obeys the weak conditions. In effect the C-element bundles signal vectors a and b into a combined signal vector, c, with timing signaled by the request signal rc. This arrangement works for both two-cycle and four-cycle bundled signaling conventions.

Although the closure of the weak conditions under acyclic composition makes it easy to construct complex asynchronous circuits whose timing is correct by construction, this approach has the disadvantage that the throughput of the circuit is limited by the latency along the longest path through the composition. When this latency becomes large, it is advantageous to pipeline the circuit.

10.4.4.2   Align Blocks and Self-Timed Pipelines

The throughput and latency of an asynchronous circuit can be decoupled by constructing an asynchronous pipeline, as illustrated in Figure 10-41. Combinational asynchronous logic circuits, denoted by boxes labeled AL, individually obey the weak conditions and are separated by *align* blocks that decouple their timing. The align blocks latch the output data after each pipeline stage and provide an

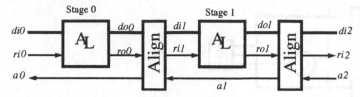

FIGURE 10-41   An Asynchronous Pipeline

acknowledgment signal so that the previous stage can place new data on the input to the stage without waiting for the original data to propagate through the entire pipeline, as would normally be required by the weak conditions. The simplest asynchronous pipeline, in which the AL blocks are just wires, acts as a first-in-first-out (FIFO) buffer with data being clocked into the align stages by the input request signal and clocked out by the output acknowledge signal. Such an asynchronous pipeline FIFO, if properly implemented, has a storage capacity equal to the number of align stages.

The timing of an asynchronous pipeline is illustrated in Figure 10-42. The diagram assumes a simple align stage that combines the request signal, ri_{i+1}, and the acknowledge signal, a_i, out of each stage into a single output signal. This combined signal cannot transition until the constraints for both the request and acknowledge signal are satisfied. Combining these signals simplifies the logic of the align stage but results in lower throughput than an align circuit that provides a quick return of the acknowledgment signal.

Initially a datum, A, is placed on the input lines, $di0$, and $ri0$ is asserted. After the delay of stage 0, data appear on the output, and $ro0$ is asserted. This causes the align circuit to latch the output data and assert both $ri1$ and $a0$. Because the align circuit latches the data and holds $ri1$ asserted, the input is allowed to drop $ri0$ as soon as $a0$ rises rather than having to wait for $ri2$ to rise. This allows several data to be injected into the pipeline before the first datum appears at the output.

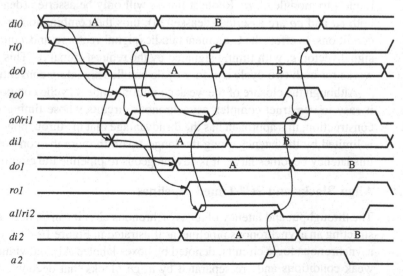

FIGURE 10-42   Timing of an Asynchronous Pipeline with a Simple Align

The asynchronous pipeline has a latency that is just the sum of the delays along the path from the data input to the data output. This is significantly lower than a synchronous pipeline (e.g., Figure 9-26), where the latency of each stage is rounded up to the nearest clock period. The latches of the asynchronous pipeline are all initially enabled, and thus the first datum just ripples through from input to output without ever waiting at a latch. Subsequent data may be latched while waiting for data ahead to be acknowledged.

The throughput of the asynchronous pipeline is limited by the delay through the longest stage plus some overhead for returning the four-phase request and acknowledge signals to their zero state. A pipeline with a simple align circuit does not achieve this bound. Its throughput is limited by the maximum delay of two adjacent stages. However, we will see below that this bound can be achieved by using a better align stage.

The effect of combining the request and acknowledge outputs of each align stage is seen in the sequence of events that enables the second request. After $a0$ is asserted, $ri0$ falls, which in turn causes $ro0$ to fall. However, because $a0$ is the same signal as $ri1$, it is not allowed to fall until completion of stage 1 is signaled by $a1$. Thus, the second datum, B, cannot be injected into stage 0 until stage 1 signals completion. In effect, combining the request and acknowledge outputs of the align stage causes the pipeline to hold valid data only in every other stage. In the case of an n-stage pipeline, where the final acknowledge, an, remains low, only $n/2 + 1$ data can be inserted before the input must wait on an. We will see later in this section how a quick-return align circuit overcomes this limitation.

A state diagram, trajectory map, and circuit for a simple align circuit are shown in Figure 10-43. Each edge of the state diagram is labeled with the input state (ro_i, a_{i+1}), and each state is labeled with the output state. The align circuit waits for the upstream data to be valid (ro_i high) and the downstream stage to be ready (a_{i+1} low) before latching the data and asserting ri_{i+1}. Then both of these signals (ro_i and a_{i+1}) must reverse their states before ri_{i+1} is returned to zero. The required functionality is that of a C-element with one input inverted. The output of the C-element serves both as the combined request–acknowledge output and as a low-true latch enable.

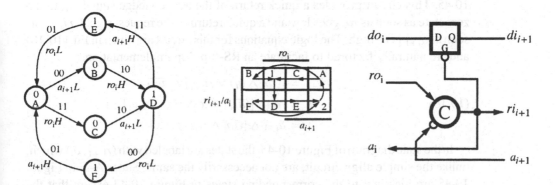

FIGURE 10-43   A Simple Align Circuit

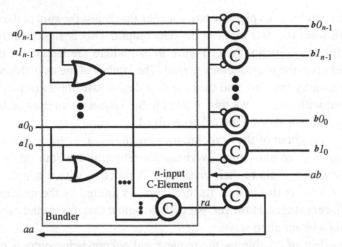

FIGURE 10-44 Dual-Rail Align Block Using a Bundler Circuit

If an asynchronous pipeline is built using a dual-rail signaling convention, a dual-rail align block, as shown in Figure 10-44, is used to decouple timing between pipeline stages. This circuit consists of a *bundler* followed by a C-element latch. The bundler, shown in a light rectangle in the figure, generates a combined request (or completion) signal, ra, that goes high only when all pairs are valid and goes low only when all pairs are invalid. The bundler converts the signal vector from a dual-rail representation, $a0_0, a1_0, \ldots, a0_{n-1}, a1_{n-1}$, to a bundled representation, $a1_0, \ldots, a1_{n-1}$ and ra.

Each bit of the input vector, $a0_i, a1_i$, is latched by a pair of C-elements enabled by the complement of the output acknowledge, $\overline{ab}$. This C-element latch allows valid signals to ripple through when ab is low and holds them valid until ab goes high. Similarly invalid signals ripple through while ab is high and are held until ab returns low. This is exactly the behavior required to enforce the weak conditions on the b inputs with respect to output ab.

The simple align circuit of Figure 10-43 results in a pipeline in which at most every other stage contains a unique datum. This limitation can be overcome by separating a_i and ri_{i+1} and using a quick-return align circuit. The state-diagram, trajectory map, and partial Karnaugh map of such a circuit are shown in Figure 10-45. This circuit provides a quick return of the acknowledge signal, a_i, to the zero state as soon as ro_i goes low and a quick return of the request signal, ri_{i+1}, as soon as a_{i+1} goes high. The logic equations for this circuit are given in Eq. (10-18) and are naturally factored to facilitate an RS-flip-flop implementation.

$$ri_{i+1} = [(ro_i \wedge \bar{a}_i) \vee ri_{i+1}] \wedge \overline{a_{i+1}}$$

(10-18)
$$a_i = ro_i \wedge [(\overline{a_{i+1}} \wedge \bar{x} \wedge ri_{i+1}) \vee a_i]$$

$$x = \bar{a}_{i+1} \wedge [(\overline{ro_i} \wedge ri_{i+1}) \vee x]$$

In the state diagram of Figure 10-45, the states are labeled with (ri_{i+1}, a_i) which, unlike the simple align circuit, are not necessarily the same. States A–E in Figure 10-45 are identical to the corresponding states in Figure 10-43 except that the two outputs have different values in states E and F. In state E, ri_{i+1} is dropped as

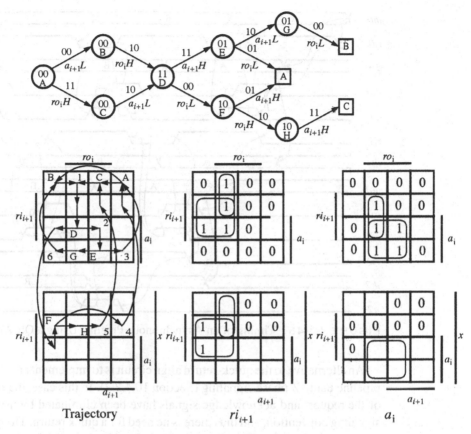

FIGURE 10-45 A Quick-Return Align Circuit

soon as a_{i+1} goes high. This in turn enables the transition $a_{i+1}L$, which requires adding a new state G to wait for the transition on ro_i before starting a new cycle in state B. Similarly, a_i, is dropped as soon as ro_i goes low in state F, enabling a rising transition on ro_i. State H is added to handle this transition and wait for the acknowledgment on a_{i+1} before dropping ri_{i+1} and starting a new cycle in state C.

Figure 10-46 illustrates the timing of a pipeline employing quick-return align stages. The figure shows that the second datum, B, can be injected into the pipeline as soon as the acknowledgment from the first align stage, a_0, returns to zero. With the quick-return circuit this event occurs as a combinational delay after the request from the first stage is valid. It is not necessary to wait for a_1 to go high before a_0 can return low, as in Figure 10-42. The input must wait for a_1 before it can inject the third datum, C, however. This is because the second align block must signal that it has latched A (with a_1H) before the first align block will open its latch to latch B (with ri_1L). By induction it is easy to see that an acknowledgment from the nth align propagates back to enable the input to inject the $n+1$st datum. With the QR align stage it is possible to have n-unique data in the latches of n align stages, whereas with the simple align circuit, only half of the align stages can hold data at any given time, the other half having their latches open while signals return to zero.

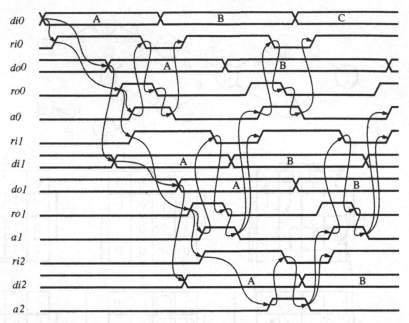

FIGURE 10-46   Timing of an Asynchronous Pipeline Using a QR Align

An alternative to the quick-return align circuit is to implement an asynchronous pipeline using 2-phase signaling (Section 10.4.2.2). In this case, the return edges of the request and acknowledge signals have been eliminated by using an NRZ signaling convention, and thus there is no need for a quick return. The align circuit of Figure 10-43 can be adapted for 2-phase signaling by replacing the latches with double-edge-triggered flip-flops.

10.4.4.3   Cyclic Asynchronous Circuits

There are many cases where it is useful to pass data iteratively through a circuit. Many arithmetic functions, such as multiplication and division, are often implemented in such an iterative manner. Asynchronous circuits are particularly well suited to implementing iterative functions because the time per iteration is limited only by the delays through the circuit. There is no need to round up delays to the nearest clock cycle. Iterative asynchronous circuits can be built whose latency is very close to that of a combinational realization.

A simple iterative asynchronous circuit is shown in Figure 10-47 along with a timing diagram for its control signals. The circuit operates in a manner similar to the clock stopper of Figure 10-21 except that the request-in and request-out interface of the asynchronous logic replaces the clock delay line. In operation data are placed on *din*, and *rin* is asserted. The multiplexer initially selects the input path to route the input data to the register, where it is latched by the rising edge of *ri*. The multiplexer then switches states to select the feedback path for the remaining cycles. As the AL block completes each iteration, *ro* rises, triggering the sequence *riL, roL, riH*, which latches the output data on *do* and starts the next iteration. On the final iteration *ack* is raised after *ro* rises. This returns the

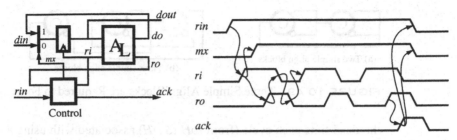

FIGURE 10-47   A Cyclic Asynchronous Circuit

multiplexer to the initial stage and inhibits *ri* from rising to start another iteration. After *rin* falls, *ack* returns to zero.

The design of the control module that produces signals *mx*, *ri*, and *ack* from *rin* and *ro* is straightforward and left as an exercise for the reader. The determination of the last cycle may be performed in the AL block, for example, by decrementing a count on each cycle. In this case, a done signal from the AL block to the control module signals the cycle in which *ack* is to be asserted, just as in the clock stopper of Figure 10-21.

A cyclic asynchronous pipeline, as illustrated in Figure 10-48, often results in greater throughput than the single-stage design of Figure 10-47, for it eliminates

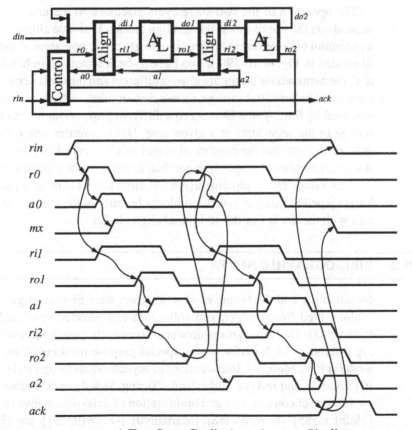

FIGURE 10-48   A Two-Stage Cyclic Asynchronous Pipeline

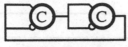

(a) Two simple align blocks

(b) Three simple align blocks

FIGURE 10-49   Three Simple Align Blocks are Required to Form a Cycle

the dead-time each cycle (from *roH* to *riH*) associated with using a single edge-triggered flip-flop as the storage element. In the two-stage design, the two align blocks act as transparent latches, allowing the data to ripple around the cycle without ever waiting for a clock edge.

The timing of the cyclic pipeline is illustrated in the lower half of the figure. After *rin* inserts an initial request into the pipeline, the multiplexer switches, connecting the data in a feedback path, and the control logic connects *ro2* to *r0* and *a0* to *a2*. This cyclic connection of request and acknowledge signals causes data to ripple around the pipeline until completion is signaled by *ack* being raised (after two cycles in this case). The completion signal breaks the feedback from *ro2* to *r0*, stopping the pipeline.

In practice, the control logic that controls the multiplexer and selectively connects *ro2* to *r0* and *a0* to *a2* is usually folded into the first align block. This reduces the delay from *ro2* to *ri1* by eliminating the intermediate signal *r0*.

The operation of the two-stage cycle discussed in the preceding paragraphs depends on the use of quick-return align blocks. If simple align blocks are used, a minimum of three stages are required to get cyclic operation of the pipeline. As illustrated in Figure 10-49(a), two back-to-back simple align blocks degenerate to C-elements whose inputs are always different and thus will never switch. Three (or more) C-elements, however, form a ring-oscillator where, once the oscillation is started by forcing one element to a different state, no more than two elements will be in the same state at a given time. Unlike inverter ring-oscillators, there is no restriction that the number of stages in a C-element ring oscillator be odd. Any even number of stages (greater than 2) will oscillate in the same manner.

A two-stage cyclic pipeline using QR align blocks is usually preferred over a longer pipeline using simple align blocks because of the cost and latency associated with the latches of the additional align blocks.

10.5   BIBLIOGRAPHIC NOTES

Metastability and the failure of synchronizers were first investigated by Charles Molnar, Fred Rosenburger, and colleagues and reported in [ChanMoln73] and [Chaney83]. This same group pioneered some early asynchronous circuits, building a series of high-performance, special-purpose machines from their *macromodules* [ClarMoln74]. Introductions to asynchronous design styles are provided in [Seitz80], and in Ivan Sutherland's Turing Award paper [Sutherla89]. Papers on the correct construction and optimization of delay-insensitive circuits include [MolnFang85], [BurnMart88], [Martain90], [DeaWilDil91], and [BurnMart91].

Martin's group at the California Institute of Technology has more recently used these techniques to build complete asynchronous microprocessors [MartLine97]. [LavaSang93] is a textbook on design and testing asynchronous circuits. [Den-DalXan95] describes a method for plesiochronous data retiming. [WillHoro87] describes an implementation of asynchronous arithmetic units.

10.6 EXERCISES

10-1 **Synchronizer Error Probability:** Consider a synchronizer built by cascading four edge-triggered flip-flops clocked by a 500-MHz clock. Each flip-flop has parameters $\tau_r = 200$ ps, $t_s = 100$ ps, $t_h = 100$ ps, and $t_{dCQ} = 500$ ps. What is the probability of synchronization failure on each input transition? What is the mean time between synchronization failures if the input toggles at 1 MHz?

10-2 **A Faulty Synchronizer:** A hapless engineer has designed a synchronizer using two flip-flops constructed from dynamic latches, as shown in Figure 10-50. The high-level schematic on the top shows asynchronous symbol x being sampled on the rising edge of the clock. After waiting a cycle for any metastable states to decay, the output of the first flip-flop is resampled by the second flip-flop to generate the synchronized output xs.

As shown on the bottom, each flip-flop is really constructed as a pair of dynamic latches, giving four dynamic latches for the synchronizer as a whole.

Given the numbers in Table 10-1, what is the probability of synchronization failure for this synchronizer? A more experienced engineer points out that the synchronizer can be greatly improved by changing just one of the four dynamic latches to a static latch. Which one does she suggest be changed? Why?

10-3 **Two-Register Synchronizer Without Delay:** The price of delay lines has gone way up. Accordingly your friend Ben Bitdiddle suggests building a two-register synchronizer (Figure 10-10) without any delay line by clocking one register with each edge of the clock as shown in Figure 10-51.

What does this change do to the average delay of the synchronizer? For what range of phases should the phase comparator select the top flip-flop? How might you build the phase comparator without using a delay line?

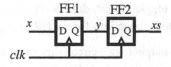

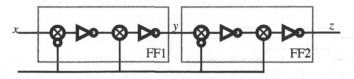

FIGURE 10-50 Synchronizer Using Dynamic Latches (for Exercise 10-2)

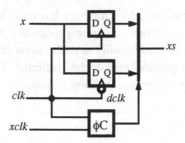

FIGURE 10-51   Two-Register Synchronizer Without a Delay Line (for Exercise 10-3)

10-4 **Synchronizer Design:** You must design an interface for a data channel where the clock frequency nominally matches your system clock but may be off by as much as 1,000 ppm (10^{-3}). The channel sends data in blocks of 10^4 symbols separated by fields of at least 20 null symbols. Describe how to design a synchronizer for this channel. Sketch your design, describe its storage requirements, and explain how it operates when the clock mismatch is at either extreme (fast or slow).

10-5 **Data Width and Rate Conversion:** Often a synchronizer combines reformatting of data with synchronization. Consider, for example, an interface that must accept 4-bit wide data at 500 MHz and output 5-bit wide data at 400 MHz. The two clocks are accurate to within 100 ppm, and a null symbol is inserted in the input stream every 10^3 symbols. Sketch the design of this synchronizer–width converter and describe its operation.

10-6 **Rational Synchronization:** The case where one clock is rationally related to another clock (e.g., clock A has N cycles for every M cycles of clock B) is a special case of periodic synchronization. Such situations often occur when both clocks are the result of dividing down a higher frequency master clock. Suppose you have two clocks that are rationally related by the ratio 3:4. Can you exploit the regularity of their ratio to design a simple synchronizer to move signals between the two clock domains?

10-7 **An NRZ Toggle Circuit:** Figures 10-27 and 10-31 describe a return-to-zero (RZ) toggle circuit for which each input pulse causes a pulse on alternate outputs. Design an NRZ toggle circuit for which each input *transition* causes a transition on alternate outputs. A timing diagram is shown in Figure 10-52.

Draw a state diagram for the NRZ toggle circuit, draw a trajectory map for the NRZ toggle circuit, and write a set of logic equations for the NRZ toggle circuit.

10-8 **Three-Output Toggle:** Design a three-output toggle circuit that routes input pulses to each of three outputs in turn. Draw a timing diagram, a state diagram, and a trajectory

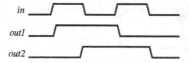

FIGURE 10-52   Timing Diagram for NRZ Toggle Circuit (for Exercise 10-7)

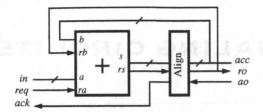

FIGURE 10-53   Faulty Asynchronous Accumulator (for Exercise 10-13)

map for your circuit. Write a set of RS FF excitation equations for your circuit and sketch its implementation using RS FF logic (as in Figure 10-33).

10-9 **Self-Timed Comparator:** Design a self-timed, 4-bit magnitude comparator that accepts two 4-bit, dual-rail RZ inputs, A and B, and generates three dual-rail RZ outputs for $A > B$, $A = B$, and $A < B$. Your circuit should obey the weak conditions using a four-cycle signaling convention.

10-10 **Self-Timed Domino Logic:** Dual-rail domino logic is naturally suited to implementing self-timed asynchronous circuits employing a dual-rail signal encoding. When an input signal becomes valid (one of its components goes high), it triggers the evaluation of any logic function that depends on it.

Sketch the implementation of a self-timed 4-bit adder using dual-rail domino. (You need not draw the transistor-level schematics. Assume that you have a domino full-adder circuit). Make sure your circuit obeys the weak conditions. How do you generate the pulldown and precharge signals?

10-11 **Pipelined Self-Timed Domino Logic:** Align circuits are also easy to dovetail into a domino circuit strategy. Show how this is so by pipelining three copies of the domino adder of Exercise 10-10 to form a two-stage pipeline that adds four numbers together.

10-12 **Concurrency and Choice:** Draw a state diagram for a two-input asynchronous circuit that has input races representing both concurrency and choice. Identify each race. Your circuit can have any function.

10-13 **Asynchronous Accumulator:** Figure 10-53 shows a faulty asynchronous accumulator designed by Sy chronous. Data are presented to the accumulator using a four-phase protocol. The accumulator is supposed to compute a running sum of the data seen so far. The input data are input to one input of a bundled asynchronous adder, and the output is fed back to the other input via a single align block. Unfortunately when Sy goes to power up his accumulator he finds that it doesn't work. What's wrong? How would you fix it?

11 SIGNALING CIRCUITS

Chapters 7 and 8 introduced techniques for constructing high-performance signaling systems. This chapter presents some of the circuit design details that must be understood to engineer a reliable high-performance signaling system in CMOS. We describe some of the details of the design of transmitters, receivers, and terminators, the building blocks of a signaling system, and also outline the problem of protecting these circuits from damage by electrostatic discharge. Because

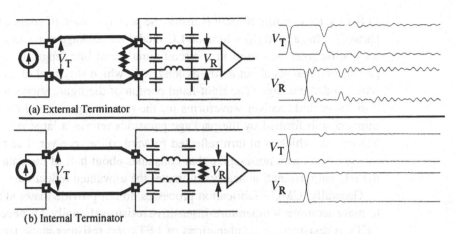

(a) External Terminator

(b) Internal Terminator

FIGURE 11-1   On-Chip Termination Avoids Unterminated Stub

clocking and timing are an integral part of of transmitter and receiver design, this chapter makes numerous references to Chapter 12, which describes timing circuits. The two chapters should be taken together as a primer on the engineering of signaling systems.

11.1   TERMINATIONS

Resistive terminations are almost always required in high-performance signaling systems to absorb traveling waves for incident-wave switching, thereby preventing unwanted reflections and their attendant intersymbol interference. Signal lines can be terminated either at the transmitter (e.g., self-series termination, as in Section 11.2.2) or at the receiver. In some signaling systems, terminations are provided at both the transmitter and the receiver. In these applications the receiver termination absorbs the signal's forward-traveling wave and guarantees incident-wave switching. The transmitter termination absorbs reflections from impedance discontinuities in the line; without this termination, backward-traveling reflections would be reflected from the transmitter in the forward direction, interfering with the signal.

11.1.1   On-Chip Versus Off-Chip Termination

In high-speed signaling between CMOS chips, it is often advantageous to build termination resistors on-chip rather than using off-chip discrete resistors. Off-chip termination always results in an unterminated stub composed of the package parasitics and the internal circuitry, and this stub generally introduces unacceptably large reflections into the signal line.

The problem is illustrated in Figure 11-1. In (a), a current-mode driver sends a signal down a symmetric line to a receiver with an external terminating resistor.[1]

---

[1] Note that the transmission line in Figure 11-1(a) is routed *past* the chip input pins to the terminating resistor. Placing the terminator across the line *before* it reaches the package pins makes the unterminated stub that much longer. The arrangement shown is almost always preferred.

In (b), the terminating resistor is inside the package, after, of course, the package parasitics. In (a) and (b) a lumped LC model for package parasitics at transmitter and receiver was used in a circuit simulation; line length is 2 ns, and the package represents about a 300-ps-long stub, which is typical of a conventional wire-bonded package. The right-hand portion of the figure shows the simulated transmitter and receiver waveforms for the two arrangements. In (a), the unterminated stub formed by the package parasitics returns a large reflection to the transmitter, which is in turn reflected forward to the receiver. The receiver sees this reflection as a noise spike that consumes about half of the data eye. In (b), the internal termination nearly eliminates the unwanted reflection.

Generally, CMOS fabrication processes do not provide material from which to make accurate, temperature-insensitive resistors. Usually it is necessary to use FETs as resistors, or combinations of FETs and resistors made from interconnect layers or wells. Because these resistors are process-, supply voltage-, and temperature dependent, on-chip terminators must be adjusted, either statically or continuously. The next sections describe some of the design considerations for on-chip adjustable terminations.

11.1.2 FET Terminations

The simplest way to implement a termination resistor in CMOS is as a single FET, either NMOS or PMOS.

Generally, PFETs have a more pronounced channel-length modulation and thus a more gradual transition from linear to saturated behavior than NFETs; they are less accurate current sources and therefore are more nearly linear resistors. In signaling systems whose signal levels are near V_{DD}, simple PFET terminators can be used effectively. A PFET terminator must be operated well below saturation to stay in the relatively linear resistive region; this argues for the highest possible gate voltage (the gate is often "triode-connected" with its gate grounded so that $V_{GS} = -V_{DD}$). The shortest channel length should be used to "enhance" the channel-length modulation effect. Short channel length also leads to the smallest physical size for the device and therefore the smallest capacitive parasitics. In most N-well CMOS processes, simple triode-connected PFET resistors are linear to within a few percent for a few hundred millivolts of signal swing below V_{DD}. The linear range of operation can be extended by using a two-element terminator that parallels a diode-connected and a triode-connected device (see Section 4.3.6.5). If a reference voltage equal to the low end of the signal swing is available to bias the triode part of a two-element terminator, the resistive characteristic can be made quite linear; improved two-element resistive loads of this sort are very useful in timing circuits and are discussed in more detail in Section 12.2.2.1.

Some of the signaling conventions we have described, for example, bipolar current-mode differential signaling (Figure 7-21), require a terminator that can be connected across a symmetric line. This type of signaling may also require

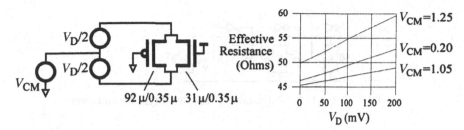

FIGURE 11-2   Resistance of Pass-Gate-Style Termination

a large common-mode voltage range.[2] On-chip terminations for symmetric lines can be built using complementary pass gates.

An example pass-gate terminator is shown in Figure 11-2, and its equivalent resistance was simulated using the example 0.35-μ technology. Resistance is a function of common-mode voltage. When V_{CM} is centered between the power supply rails, both devices in the pass gate are turned on. For V_{CM} near V_{DD}, the NFET is turned off and effective resistance is determined by the PFET, whereas near ground, the NFET provides most of the conduction. The sizes for the two transistors were chosen for about 50-Ω resistance with $V_{CM} = 1.25$ V ($V_{DD}/2$) and about equal conduction for PFET and NFET. This choice provides a resistance fairly close to 50 Ω at the extremes of common-mode voltage near the power supply rails. The resistance characteristics are, of course, symmetric with respect to V_D polarity, and thus the variation in resistance in the graph would be seen with a $2 \cdot V_D = 400$ mV differential signal swing. For larger signal swings, it may be desirable to add linearizing diode-connected elements to achieve a reasonable impedance match (diode–triode loads are discussed in Section 4.3.6.3 and Section 12.2.2.1).

11.1.3   Adjustable Terminators

Terminators built using FETs (or a combination of FETs and resistive interconnect material) have an effective resistance that is a function of the fabrication parameters, signal voltage levels, power supply voltage, and temperature. For example, the pass-gate terminator of Figure 11-2 was simulated assuming nominal FETs, power supply voltage, and temperature; best-case and worst-case limits for these parameters introduce a variation in effective resistance of nearly 2 : 1. To achieve a well-matched termination resistance, on-chip terminators are often adjustable.[3]

A typical adjustable pass-gate terminator is shown in Figure 11-3. Several resistor elements, with different resistances determined by the shape factors S_N,

---

[2] The Low-Voltage Differential Signaling LVDS (IEEE 1596) convention requires a common-mode voltage compliance over nearly the entire power supply voltage range.

[3] Adjustment of resistor values to offset parameter variations is often referred to as *trimming*. This term evolved from the process of adjusting the resistance of wire-wound resistors by trimming the length of nichrome wire used to make the resistor.

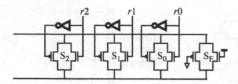

FIGURE 11-3 Adjustable Pass-Gate-Style Termination

are connected in parallel, and the resistance is varied by changing the digital value on $r\{0 : 2\}$. It is often desirable to add a fixed element in parallel with the adjustable ones so that the range of the adjustment is restricted and a more precise adjustment can be made with a given number of adjustment bits. The design process usually begins by setting the fixed element's resistance (determined by the shape factor S_F) to the high end of the adjustment range, assuming best-case values (lowest resistance) for FETs, voltages, and temperature. Next the remaining shape factors are chosen so that the total resistance with all adjustment bits turned on reaches the low end of the adjustment range under worst-case (high-resistance) conditions. Finally, the number of bits in $r\{ \}$ is chosen to achieve the necessary resistance tolerance.

11.1.3.1 Digital Versus Analog Adjustment

In the resistive region of operation, the equivalent resistance of an FET channel can be found from Eq. (4-2):

$$(11\text{-}1) \qquad R_{\text{Equiv}} = \frac{1}{\beta V_{\text{GT}}}$$

Thus, an FET's effective resistance can be varied either by changing the shape factor W/L (e.g., by switching multiple devices in or out of the circuit, implementing *digital control*, as illustrated in Figure 11-3) or by varying the gate voltage on a single device (analog control).

Analog control of terminator resistance is usually not preferred for two reasons. First, it is desirable to make V_{GT} as large as possible to allow the largest swing in V_{DS} while remaining in the linear part of the resistive characteristic of the FET. Second, the resistance controller is usually shared over several terminator resistors, requiring the control voltage to be distributed over some distance. Supply-reference voltage drops across a large circuit will move the bias point for controlled resistance elements, and in practice it may be difficult to control these voltage drops well enough to achieve sufficiently accurate resistance values. Unless the control voltage wiring is shielded, capacitive coupling to nearby digital signals can introduce dynamic variation in resistance values. A change in the termination resistance produces a change in voltage on the terminated line given by $I_{\text{signal}} \times \Delta R$, and thus resistor control voltage noise contributes to signal voltage noise.

Analog control of resistive loads is useful in other domains, however – particularly in timing circuits (Section 12.2.2.1).

11.1.3.2 Binary Versus Thermometer Digital Adjustment Codes

The most straightforward choice for a digitally adjustable resistor is binary weighted shape factors. For example, in Figure 11-3, one might choose $S_2 = 2 \times S_1 = 2 \times S_0$. The code on $r\{2:0\}$ is a binary encoding of the adjustable conductance.

Binary weighting introduces the problem of resistance glitches, which may not be tolerable in some applications. If the resistor value is adjusted by a continuously running controller, then each change in resistance ordered by the controller produces voltage noise on the signal line. In a binary weighted resistor, certain code changes (e.g., $011 \rightarrow 100$) switch all of the resistor elements at once and are likely to introduce large transient changes in resistance (and thus large noise voltages on the signal line) during the time required to change the resistance value.

This problem can be avoided by using a thermometer-coded resistor adjustment scheme. In the simplest implementation, all of the resistor elements have the same shape factor, which is chosen to meet either a noise or a resistor tolerance requirement. Legal codes into the adjustment bit-vector are of the form $r\{N:0\} = 0..00111..1$, and only one bit (at the boundary between the 0-string and the 1-string) is allowed to change on each step of resistor adjustment. The shape factors for each segment can be chosen so that the change in conductance, and thus the noise induced on the signal line, is below any desired threshold. Thermometer codes require, of course, more adjustment bits than a binary code with the same precision; therefore, there is a trade-off between resistor-adjustment-induced noise and number of control bits.

The simple thermometer-coded adjustment scheme can be improved by using shape factors that produce changes in conductance that are a fixed percentage of the *accumulated* conductance. As more elements are switched on, the total conductance increases, and larger steps in conductance can be taken while maintaining a fixed overall resistor tolerance or noise floor. This idea leads to a slowly tapering set of sizes in the resistor elements, and the total number of control bits required to achieve an overall resistor adjustment range is reduced significantly.

Digitally adjusted resistors are simple digital-to-analog converters (DACs), and the choice of binary or thermometer codings is equivalent to binary-weighted and monotonic current and voltage DAC designs.

11.1.4 Automatic Terminator Adjustment

As we have discussed, termination resistors built with available on-chip devices (FETs and interconnect) vary over changes in fabrication, supply and signal voltage, and temperature. These variations are so large that it is impossible to build satisfactory terminators with devices whose sizes are fixed at design time. In applications where only fabrication-induced variation must be accommodated, resistance values could be set at device-test time using fuses or laser-blown links. Resistors are sometimes adjusted in a static way at system initialization, often using an existing boundary scan system. However, this type of adjustment scheme

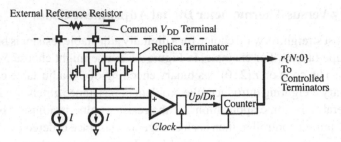

FIGURE 11-4 Termination Adjustment Servo Loop

cannot compensate for changes in supply voltage or operating temperature subsequent to initialization and requires some means of measuring the on-chip resistors in order to make adjustments.

11.1.4.1 Automated Adjustment Controllers

Most high-performance signaling systems employ continuous or periodic automatic adjustment of on-chip terminations. Usually a replica of the adjustable terminator resistor is compared with a reference resistor, and the error from this comparison drives a feedback loop that encloses the adjustable resistor.

Figure 11-4 shows an example of such a controller. In the example, a PFET-only (V_{DD}-referenced) terminator is assumed for simplicity (a controller for a pass-gate style terminator would be a bit more complex, particularly if the controller were required to compensate for common-mode voltage changes). In this scheme, an external reference resistor equal to the characteristic impedance of the transmission medium for the signaling system is used to set the resistance of the internal terminators. Both external reference and internal replica terminator share a common connection to V_{DD} (so that noise on V_{DD} is common mode for the comparison), and both carry current, I, set by identical current sources. A clocked comparator measures the voltage difference across the two resistors and drives a counter value up or down on each cycle of operation to servo the internal replica terminator toward the external reference value. All other terminators are slaved from the controls $r\{N:0\}$ from the counter. The clock can, of course, run much slower than the system clock; the power dissipated by the current sources can be reduced by turning on the current sources just long enough to perform a periodic measurement and resistor update. Further power savings can be attained by using a scaled external and internal resistor, say $N \times$ the characteristic impedance of the line; the actual line terminators are then implemented using N of these in parallel.

A simple digital servo system is shown in Figure 11-4. Such a system will exhibit "dither" between two or three adjacent states. In a current-mode signaling system, this dither will produce voltage noise on the terminated line. At the expense of a more complex comparator, a dead band can be introduced into this type of servo to avoid dither but at some expense in adjustment accuracy.

If a binary-weighted terminator element is used, a free-running adjustment machine will likely introduce unacceptable noise into the terminated signal line,

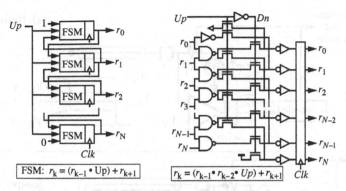

FIGURE 11-5   Thermometer-Coded FSMs

even in the absence of dither. This source of noise can be eliminated by running the resistor adjustment servo only during periods when the signaling system is idle. [GabaKnau92] discusses the fine points of this type of design.

11.1.4.2   Thermometer-Coded Controllers

Adjustment-induced noise can also be avoided, or at least reduced to acceptable levels, by using monotonically adjustable (thermometer-coded) terminators. In this case, the counter in Figure 11-4 can be replaced with a more efficient structure, an array of simple finite-state machines shown in Figure 11-5. The left side of the figure outlines a simple implementation; however, this approach requires that the registers in the FSM be initialized with all zeros to guarantee correct operation. The right-hand implementation uses a slightly stronger rule for generating each FSM's output, can be shown to initialize itself to a legal thermometer code within a few cycles, and is quite space efficient.

11.1.4.3   Self-Series Termination Control

A clever scheme proposed in [KnigKrym88] uses the characteristic impedance of an example transmission line as a reference impedance, rather than an external resistor, to servo the impedance of a self-series terminated driver. The basic scheme is shown in Figure 11-6 (a).

A replica self-series terminated transmitter launches an edge into the reference line, which is terminated in an open circuit. (The scheme described in the reference, and shown here, employs voltage-mode signaling but could easily be adapted to current-mode signaling.) Shortly after the edge is launched, the voltage at the near end of the line is sampled and compared with half the transmitter voltage. The controller servos the transmitter impedance toward the matched state in which the transmitter impedance, R_T, is equal to the line impedance, Z_0, and the initial voltage on the line, shortly after launch, is $V_T/2$.

If two chip pins can be budgeted for this function, the reference line can be terminated in a receiver on the chip. The arrival of the incident wave can be used to self-time the sampling of the line voltage at the transmitter V_L. The sample is guaranteed always to be at the center of the time interval during which V_L is partway between 0 and V_T.

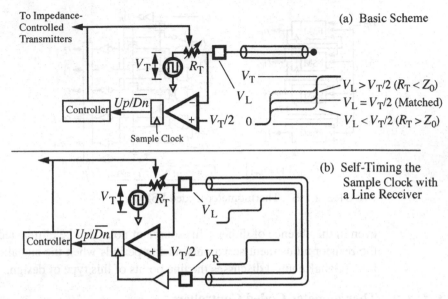

FIGURE 11-6   Self-Series Termination Control of Knight and Krymm

A somewhat different version of this scheme is described in [DeHoKnig93]. Instead of a central controller that continuously or periodically adjusts the termination, each transmitter is equipped with a receiver–sampler that examines the transmitted waveform. The sample time and transmitter impedance are controlled by a boundary scan system; additional boundary scan elements collect data from the samplers, which essentially implement a set of on-chip time-domain reflectometers (TDRs). At system initialization, the boundary scan system launches test edges from each transmitter, samples waveforms, and adjusts each transmitter's impedance to best match its line.

11.2   TRANSMITTER CIRCUITS

A transmitter circuit encodes a symbol into a current or voltage for transmission over a line. A good transmitter has an output impedance optimized for the selected transmission mode, rise-time control to avoid injecting energy into tank circuits or reflecting it off of line discontinuities, and clean signal levels without offset errors.

Different transmission modes require different transmitter output impedances. Voltage-mode transmitters have a very low output impedance and hence are implemented using large FETs operated in the resistive region. At the opposite extreme, current-mode transmitters have a very high output impedance and are implemented using FETs operated in saturation. Intermediate between these two extremes are self-series terminated transmitters that have an output impedance matched to the line and are implemented with moderate-sized FETs operated in the resistive region.

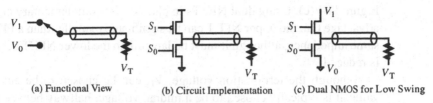

(a) Functional View   (b) Circuit Implementation   (c) Dual NMOS for Low Swing

FIGURE 11-7 A Voltage-Mode Driver

Most transmitters require one or more forms of compensation to correct for the effects of variation in process, supply voltage, and temperature. For series terminated transmitters, the output impedance is compensated by segmenting the driver devices as described in Section 11.1.4 for termination resistors. The delay lines used for rise-time control are compensated to give consistent rise time across process and voltage corners. Finally, transmitters that derive their own signal levels, such as most current-mode transmitters, require process compensation to keep signal levels constant across process corners.

Very high-speed signaling systems may employ multiplexing transmitters that multiplex several low-speed data channels on the output line under control of a multiphase clock. By reducing the signal swing in the multiplexing output stage, these transmitters can be made to operate at frequencies above the gain–bandwidth product of the process. Multiplexing transmitters require care in generating and distributing timing signals to avoid pulse distortion, skew, and systematic jitter.

11.2.1 Voltage-Mode Driver

As illustrated in Figure 11-7(a), a voltage-mode driver acts as a switch selectively connecting a signal line to one of two (or more) voltages with very low impedance. In practice this is usually accomplished, as illustrated in Figure 11-7(b): large complementary MOSFETs are switched to connect the output line selectively to supply voltages that serve as the transmitter references V_0 and V_1.

To approximate voltage-mode switching the driver transistors must be made very large. For example, for the initial step to be 90% of DV, the FETs must have an on resistance of no more than 10% of Z_0 (5 Ω for a 50-Ω line).[4] In our example 0.35-μm process, this corresponds to an N-device with a W/L ratio of 320, or $W = 112\,\mu$m. The P-device would be about 2.5 times this size, 280 μm. The large devices in a voltage-mode driver have significant gate capacitance (200 fF for the N-device and about 500 fF for the P-device). A predriver circuit, often an exponential horn (Section 4.3.2.9), is needed to amplify a small signal to drive these large capacitive loads.

When voltage-mode signaling is used with a small voltage swing, it is advantageous to have both transistors be NFETs with the upper transistor connected to a dedicated voltage reference (supply) for V_1. This configuration is shown in

---

[4] An FET with a resistance of 10% of Z_0 is only needed if the line is terminated to the opposite supply. In this case the "other" FET is not needed at all – an open drain output. If the line is terminated to midrail, a resistance of 20% of Z_0 will give 90% swing.

Figure 11-7(c). Using dual NFETs in place of the complementary circuit has the advantage that the upper NFET can be significantly smaller than a PFET with the same impedance, although it must be larger than the lower NFET because its V_{GS} is reduced.

Although the termination voltage, V_T, can be chosen to be any convenient value, it is typically chosen to be a midrail voltage, halfway between V_1 and V_0. This makes the amount of current sourced by the PFET in the one state equal to the current sunk into the NFET in the zero state and gives the minimum driver current for a given signal swing and line impedance, $I = \Delta V/(2Z_0)$.

The large size of MOS voltage-mode drivers and the large amount of delay and energy consumed by the required predrivers are a significant disadvantage of voltage-mode signaling. The current mode and self-series terminating drivers described in Sections 11.2.2 and 11.2.3 are significantly smaller, faster, and more power efficient than a low-impedance voltage-mode driver.

11.2.1.1   Break-Before-Make Action

The low impedance of the output devices makes it essential that the driver have a *break-before-make* action during switching. For example, during a high transition, the NFET must turn off before the PFET turns, or the power supplies will be shorted by a small resistance (10 Ω in our example above). This short can cause large overlap currents to flow (250 mA with a 2.5-V supply), causing power supply noise and possibly leading to failure of supply lines.

Large overlap currents can be avoided by using a break-before-make circuit such as the one shown in Figure 11-8. Circuit operation is illustrated in the waveforms at the right of the figure. When the input goes high, the conducting NFET immediately switches off, breaking the output circuit. With no drive, the line swings to V_T, illustrated here midway between GND and V_{DD}. Two gate delays later the PFET turns on, making the new circuit, and the line swings to V_{DD}. When the input swings low, the process is repeated with the PFET switching off two gate delays before the NFET switches on.

This circuit has two disadvantages: noise susceptibility and delay. First, depending on the spacing between break and make, the line has a noticeable plateau in the middle of the transient that can cause problems in edge-triggered circuits. Noise coupled onto the line during this period may present spurious signal transitions to the receiver. Second, the delay of the circuit is increased by the delays between the break and the make points. This delay is usually made as small as possible without generating overlap current.

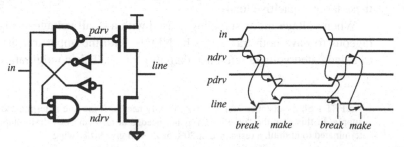

FIGURE 11-8   Break-Before-Make Predrivers

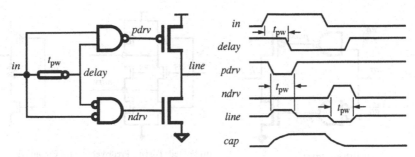

FIGURE 11-9   Pulse-Generator Predriver

11.2.1.2   Pulse-Generating Driver

An alternative method of avoiding current overlap is to pulse the output. This avoids the delay of the break-before-make circuit and reduces power dissipation by only drawing current on transitions. However, it has the disadvantage that, for DC parallel-terminated lines, the line remains in a valid state for only the width of the pulse. For capacitive loads and AC-terminated lines, this is not a problem.

A pulse-generating driver is shown in Figure 11-9 along with waveforms illustrating typical operation. An inverting delay line generates a signal, $\overline{delay}$, that follows the complement of the input after a pulse-width delay, t_{pw}. Two gates, a NAND and a NOR, combine with $\overline{delay}$ to generate drive pulses $\overline{pdrv}$ and $ndrv$ that are asserted for a period t_{pw} following each transition of in. As illustrated on the right side of the figure, the *PFET* drive signal, $\overline{pdrv}$, goes low for a pulse width following the rising transition of in, causing the line to pulse high for the same period. On low-going transitions of in, $ndrv$ pulses high, causing the line to pulse low.

If the driver is connected to a capacitive load or an AC termination, a resistor in series with a capacitor, the driver switches the line to a steady state rather than pulsing it, as illustrated in the bottom waveform, labeled cap, in the figure.

In practice pulse-mode drivers are usually placed in parallel with a small, higher-impedance, conventional driver so that the line remains driven, albeit weakly, after the pulse.

11.2.1.3   Tristate Driver

A tristate driver has three output states, high (logic 1), low (logic 0), and undriven, often called Z. Tristate drivers are used in cases where many modules drive a common signal, such as with a multidrop bus or when a point-to-point signal is driven in both directions (but not simultaneously, as in Section 8.3).

A tristate driver can be implemented, as illustrated in Figure 11-10(a), by qualifying the PFET and NFET gate drive signals in a manner similar to the pulse-mode driver of Figure 11-9. When the enable signals are asserted, $en = 1$, $\overline{en} = 0$, the gate drive signals, $\overline{pdrv}$ and $ndrv$, are enabled and the line follows the input. When the enable signals are deasserted, $en = 0$, $\overline{en} = 1$, the gate drive signals are both deasserted and the line remains in a high-impedance state.

The NAND-gate and NOR-gate in Figure 11-10(a) can be folded together into a single six-transistor circuit, as illustrated in Figure 11-10(b). In addition to

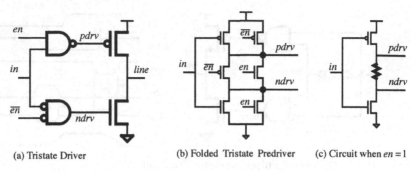

(a) Tristate Driver   (b) Folded Tristate Predriver   (c) Circuit when *en* = 1

FIGURE 11-10   Tristate Drivers

reducing transistor count, this circuit helps give the tristate driver a break-before-make action. When the enable signals are asserted, this circuit acts as an inverter with a resistive transmission gate between its two outputs, as illustrated in Figure 11-10(c). When the output switches low, for example, signal *ndrv* drops low first, switching the NFET off. The RC delay caused by the transmission gate and the gate capacitance of the PFET causes *pdrv* to fall somewhat later, switching the PFET on only after the NFET is at least partly off. In this circuit, the center two devices that form the transmission gate are sized to trade off delay against overlap current.

11.2.1.4   Open-Drain Outputs

A simpler approach for allowing multiple modules to drive a line, one at a time, is to implement an *open-drain* output driver, as illustrated in Figure 11-11. A commercial standard for this type of signaling, called GTL, has been defined [GunnYuan92]. As discussed in this section and in Sections 11.2.2 and 11.2.3, this circuit can be made to be voltage-mode, current-mode, or series-terminated, depending on the size and gate bias of the driver device. Voltage-mode operation is achieved by using a large device (e.g., a $W = 112$-μm NFET with an on-resistance of $5\ \Omega$).

The pull-only open-drain circuit has a number of advantages over the push–pull circuits illustrated above. The pull-only circuit is significantly smaller and requires only a single device. It dissipates power only when the line is in the low state. There is no chance of overlap current, for there is no complementary drive. Also, logic can be performed by shorting two enabled drivers together, giving a line voltage that is the logical-AND of the two signals.[5]

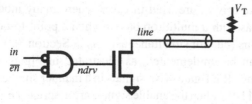

FIGURE 11-11   An Open-Drain Output

---

[5] This is often referred to with a negative logic convention (low is true) as a wire-OR connection because the signal line will be low if either driving device is on, the OR of the two low-true inputs.

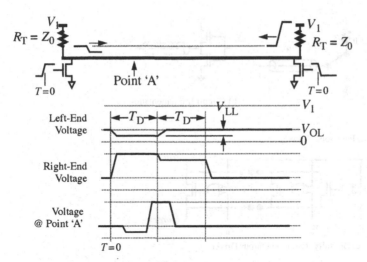

FIGURE 11-12   Wired-OR Glitch

The circuit has two principle disadvantages. The most important is that the output impedance is a function of the state of the logic signal, giving a data-dependent reflection coefficient that can lead to intersymbol interference. The driver has an infinite output impedance when the signal is high and a low, near zero, impedance when the signal is low. The reflection of a reverse-traveling signal on the line thus depends on the state of the output. A second disadvantage is that, although a push-pull circuit can be terminated to a midrail V_T (midway between V_1 and V_0), an open-drain driver must be terminated to V_1, doubling the drive current for the same signal swing and line impedance.

A particularly nasty consequence of this dynamic impedance mismatch is the *wired-OR glitch*, illustrated in Figure 11-12 and described in [ChenYuan93]. Suppose that at time $T = 0$, a driver at the right-hand end of a wired-OR bus turns off, and at the same instant a driver at the left-hand end of the bus turns on. Logically, the voltage on the bus should be steady at V_{OL}, but because time T_D, the signal propagation time, is required for changes at one end of the line to be felt at the other, the following events occur before this condition obtains: At $T = 0$, the voltage at the right-hand end of the line rises to V_1, and a wavefront of this voltage propagates to the left down the line. At $T = 0$, the left-hand end of the line falls below V_{OL} to V_{LL} because the left-hand driver sees a load composed of the terminating impedance to V_1 in parallel with the line impedance, which instantaneously is at V_{OL}. After a time, T_D, has passed, the positive edge from the right reaches the left-hand end; now, the left-hand driver feels both terminators and the voltage at the left end rises to V_{OL}. This event produces a negative edge, whose amplitude ($V_1 - V_{OL} - V_{LL}$) is reflected toward the right; this reflection occurs because the left-hand end is not terminated in the line impedance but rather in the low impedance of the left-hand driver. At time $= T_D$, the negative edge from the left-hand end reaches the right and brings the voltage down to $V_1 - V_{LL}$; at time $2T_D$, the second negative edge from the left arrives at the right, and the voltage finally reaches V_{OL}. No further reflections are generated at the right-hand end because it (at least) is properly terminated. At other points on the line, the

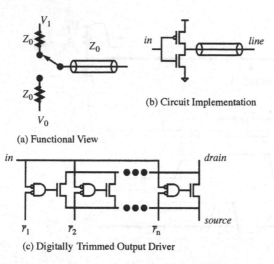

(a) Functional View

(b) Circuit Implementation

(c) Digitally Trimmed Output Driver

FIGURE 11-13   Series-Terminated Drivers

voltage changes as the forward- and backward-traveling waves pass by; point A shows an example waveform for a point about 1/3 of the way to the right.

Wired-OR bus protocols must accommodate multiple switching events at a receiver on the bus before a valid logic level is attained.

11.2.2   Self-Series-Terminating Drivers

A series-terminated signaling convention (Section 7.3.3) employs a driver with an output impedance equal to the line impedance, as illustrated Figure 11-13(a). The MOS circuit implementation, Figure 11-13(b), is no different than that for a voltage-mode driver except for device sizes. To drive a 50-Ω line, for example, requires an 11-μm-long NFET and a 28-μm PFET to give a nominal output impedance of 50 Ω. As with the voltage-mode driver, low-swing drivers with an operating range near the negative supply are typically implemented with two NFETs.

To avoid excessive reflections of reverse-traveling waves from the source requires that the output impedance be closely matched to the line, usually to within 10% or better. The on-resistance of a FET, however, may vary by 2:1 or more across process, voltage, and temperature. To achieve adequate matching, a series-terminated driver of this style, which uses the resistance of the driver FETs to set the output impedance, requires process compensation. Process compensation is most easily accomplished by digitally trimming the resistance value, as discussed in Sections 4.3.6.5 and 11.1.3. With this approach, each of the driver transistors is replaced by a segmented driver (Figure 11-13(c)). The segments are switched in or out by control lines $\bar{r}_{1:n}$ to match the driver impedance as closely as possible to the line impedance.

These control lines are usually driven by a feedback control circuit that compares a reference driver transistor to a fixed external reference resistor. After each comparison, a finite-state machine in the circuit sets $\bar{r}_{1:n}$ to adjust the resistance of the driver up or down as required to match and track the resistance of the external resistor. The adjustment process is exactly the same as for a self-adjusting termination resistor constructed from a segmented FET (Section 11.1.3 and Section 11.1.4).

This technique of building a controlled output impedance driver can also be used to build an underterminated driver (Section 7.3.4) by setting the resistance of the output FETs to a value that is significantly greater than the line impedance. In this case a parallel termination at the far end of the line is required to achieve incident-wave switching. As described in Section 7.3.4, the signal swing is determined by the voltage divider formed by the output driver resistance and the line impedance. With the parallel termination, the underterminated driver can be implemented in a pull-only or open-drain configuration, as illustrated in Figure 11-11. This is not possible in a purely source-terminated configuration because, without the parallel termination, the line would be undriven, open at both ends, when the pull-down devices switch off.

11.2.3 Current-Mode Drivers

11.2.3.1 Saturated FET Driver

The simplest current-mode driver is just a single FET operated in the saturation region, as illustrated in Figure 11-14(a). When the input signal, $\overline{in}$, is high, the FET is on, with $V_{GT} = V_{DD} - V_{Tn}$. As long as the line voltage remains above V_{GT}, the device is in saturation and acts as a current source with output impedance determined by the channel-length modulation coefficient of the device, λ. When the input signal is low, the FET is off, no current flows, and the output impedance is effectively infinite. Thus, the FET acts as a unipolar current-mode driver with the on-current being set by the saturation current of the device.

Unfortunately the amount of current sourced by a saturated FET can vary by 2:1 or more across process, voltage, and temperature, making this simple current-mode driver rather inaccurate. This variation can be partly compensated by varying the effective width of the current source device in the same manner that FET resistors are compensated. In this case the current source device is built in a segmented manner, and segments are turned on or off to set the current to the desired value. As with resistor compensation, the process is controlled by a FSM that compares a reference current to the current sourced by a typical driver. The segment settings for this driver are then distributed to all other drivers on the same chip.

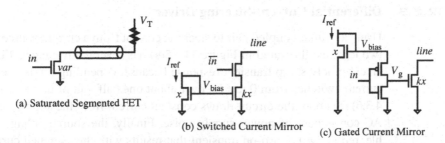

(a) Saturated Segmented FET

(b) Switched Current Mirror

(c) Gated Current Mirror

FIGURE 11-14 Current-Mode Driver Circuits

11.2.3.2   Current-Mirror Drivers

A current mirror can also be used to compensate an output driver for process, voltage, and temperature variations, as illustrated in Figure 11-14(b and c). In both configurations, a stable reference current, I_{ref}, is applied to a diode-connected FET of size x to generate a bias voltage, V_{bias}. In the first configuration, Figure 11-14(b), V_{bias} is applied to the gate of a scaled FET, size kx, to realize a current source with magnitude kI_{ref}. This current source is then switched by placing a FET in series with the drain controlled by the input, $\overline{in}$. When $\overline{in}$ is high the driver sinks current kI_{ref} from the line. When $\overline{in}$ is low, the series device is off and no current flows. When $\overline{in}$ switches, the current is set by the V–I characteristics of the upper device, quadratically following the input slope until the current limit of the lower device is reached.

Placing two devices in series requires that the devices be made large and V_{bias} be made small to provide enough headroom on the current source to allow for the voltage drop across the resistive switching device. The series connection can be eliminated by gating the bias voltage at the current source, as shown in Figure 11-14(c), instead of switching the output current. In this configuration an inverter with V_{bias} as its supply voltage is used to drive the gate of the current-source device. When input, in, is low, the gate voltage, V_g, is driven to V_{bias}, and the driver sinks a current of kI_{ref} from the line. When in is high, V_g is driven to ground, and no current flows into the driver.

With this input-gated configuration the output device can be made about half the size of each of the two series devices in the output-switched driver without running out of headroom across process corners. This results in a driver with one-quarter the area and one-half the output capacitance of the switched driver.

This small size is not without cost. The gated driver has the disadvantage of a slow transient response compared with the output switched driver. With the gated driver, the gate voltage, V_g, rises to V_{bias} exponentially with an RC time constant set by the predriver output resistance and the current source gate voltage. Several time constants are required for the output current to settle within a small percentage of kI_{ref}. With the switched driver, on the other hand, as soon as the gate voltage of the switch device reaches the point where the current source enters saturation, the transient is over, except for the effects of channel-length modulation. For this reason, switched-current drivers are employed in applications where a sharp transient response is important.

11.2.3.3   Differential Current-Steering Driver

Using a source-coupled pair to steer the current from a current source into one of two legs, as illustrated in Figure 11-15(a) has several advantages. First, it gives an extremely sharp transient response because, depending on device sizing, the current switches from 0 to kI_{ref} over about one half volt of input swing (Section 4.3.6). Second, the circuit draws constant current from the supply, reducing the AC component of power supply noise. Finally, the source voltage, V_s, is stable, reducing the turn-on transient that results with the switched current-source

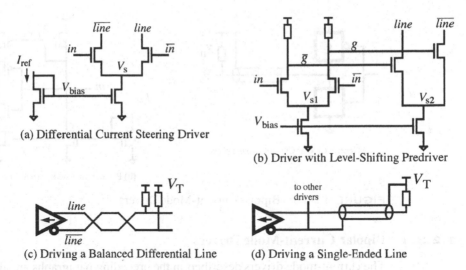

(a) Differential Current Steering Driver

(b) Driver with Level-Shifting Predriver

(c) Driving a Balanced Differential Line

(d) Driving a Single-Ended Line

FIGURE 11-15 Differential Current-Steering Driver

configuration (Figure 11-14(b)) when the switch device turns on and draws a momentary current surge from the line to charge up the capacitance of its source node.

To reduce output delay, the current-steering driver should be used with a limited-swing predriver, as shown in Figure 11-15(b). The predriver converts the full-swing differential inputs, *in* and *$\overline{in}$*, to limited swing gate drive signals, *g* and *$\overline{g}$*. The loads of the predriver are set so that the swing of the gate drive signals is limited to the amount needed to fully switch the differential output pair. This gives minimum output delay, because current starts to switch as soon as *g* and *$\overline{g}$* begin to swing. There is no *dead band* at the beginning or end of the signal swing.

As we noted in Section 4.3.6.6, the gain–bandwidth product of a differential stage is constant. This driver gets its speed by virtue of its *fractional* stage gain (full-swing to limited-swing in the predriver; limited swing to very small signal swing in the driver). With gain less than unity, bandwidth (speed) can be very high. In practice, drivers of this type can be made to switch in just a few τ.

The current-steering driver is naturally suited to drive a balanced differential line, as shown in Figure 11-15(c). The complementary outputs of the driver are attached to the two conductors of the line. The other end of the line is parallel-terminated into a positive termination voltage, V_T. The driver provides a balanced AC current drive to the line superimposed on a steady DC current of kI_{ref}. The termination supply, V_T, sees only the DC current.

The differential driver is also effective in driving a single-ended line, as shown in Figure 11-15(d). In this case, the complementary, *$\overline{line}$*, outputs of several drivers are tied together and to the signal return. The signal return in turn is AC-shorted to the termination supply. The net result again is that the termination supply sees only DC current because the sum of the signal and return current for each driver is a constant. Owing to the shared signal return, this configuration is susceptible to signal return cross talk, as described in Section 7.3.1.3.

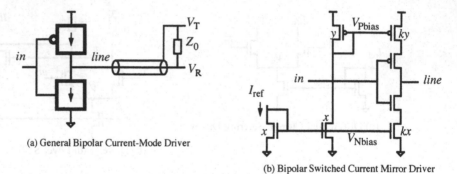

(a) General Bipolar Current-Mode Driver

(b) Bipolar Switched Current Mirror Driver

FIGURE 11-16   Bipolar Current-Mode Drivers

11.2.3.4   Bipolar Current-Mode Drivers

The current-mode drivers described in the preceding paragraphs are all unipolar; that is, they drive current in only one direction, sinking it from the line. With a unipolar driver, the two logic levels are denoted by the presence and absence of current, respectively. This requires that, for single-ended operation, the line receiver have an accurate current reference, typically half the full-scale drive current, to compare the received current against.[6] Providing an accurate reference is difficult and represents a source of noise.

A bipolar current-mode driver both sources and sinks current from the line. In this case the two logic levels are denoted by equal amounts of current flowing in opposite directions. The receiver can discriminate between these two states by comparing the received current to zero, and thus no reference is required.

A bipolar driver can be constructed from any of the unipolar drivers described in the previous section by connecting two complementary unipolar drivers together, as illustrated in Figure 11-16(a). When the input, $\overline{in}$, is high, the lower driver sinks current kI_{ref} from the line, and the upper driver is off. In the opposite state, $\overline{in}$ low, the upper driver sources kI_{ref} into the line, and the lower driver is off. The result is a bipolar drive current, $\pm kI_{ref}$. Bipolar drivers are usually terminated into a midrail termination voltage, $V_T \approx V_{DD}/2$, to provide adequate headroom for both drivers. The drive current develops a voltage of $\pm kI_{ref}Z_0$ across the termination. The received voltage, V_R, is compared against V_T to detect the signal. No reference is required.

Figure 11-16(b) shows the specific example of a bipolar switched current mirror driver. The output stage of this circuit is a pair of complementary current sources switched by a pair of complementary switch devices. When $\overline{in}$ is high, the NFET switch is on and the NFET current source sinks a current of kI_{ref} from the line. When $\overline{in}$ is low, the PFET switch is on and the PFET current source sources kI_{ref} into the line. A pair of current mirrors is used to generate the bias voltages, V_{Nbias} and V_{Pbias}, to control the complementary current sources. Similar methods can be

---

[6] With unipolar differential signaling, the complementary signal lines are compared against one another, and no reference is required.

used to construct bipolar current drivers from the other driver designs shown in Figures 11-14 and 11-15.

11.2.4   Rise-Time Control

The rise time of an output driver must be carefully controlled to avoid excessive intersymbol interference. Too fast a rise time couples energy into parasitic tank circuits (Section 6.4.2 and Section 7.4.2.1) and results in reflections off short impedance discontinuities (Section 6.4.1). As a result, systems with rise times that are too fast require interconnect that is *cleaner* and hence much more expensive than would be needed with rise-time control. On the other hand, a rise time that is too slow eats heavily into a timing budget (Section 9.3.5) and in extreme cases can cause intersymbol interference (Section 6.4.3) by not reaching a steady state by the end of a bit cell.

Like Goldilocks's porridge, the rise time needs to be just right. Usually a rise time that is between 1/3 and 1/2 the bit-cell time strikes a good compromise between demands on the timing budget and demands on the quality of interconnect. Because the rise time of a typical CMOS gate can vary by 2:1 or more across process, voltage, and temperature, active control of rise time is usually required.

11.2.4.1   Segmented Current Driver

An effective method of rise-time control is to divide the driver into segments that are sequenced on with a tapped delay line, as illustrated for a current-mode driver in Figure 11-17. The driver is divided into four current-mode drivers, each with one-quarter of the peak current. The segments of the driver are sequenced on by the taps of a delay line so that each segment turns on $0.25\,t_r$ after the previous segment. Waveforms for the rise-time-controlled driver are shown at the right side of the figure. If the current drivers turned on instantaneously, the line current, I_{line}, would have a stair-step profile that reaches full amplitude in $0.75\,t_r$, as shown in the center trace. To avoid this, the individual current drivers are designed to turn on with a linear ramp over a quarter of the rise time, giving a smoothed current on the line with the desired rise time, as shown in the bottom trace. Depending on the degree of accuracy needed in the rise time, the delay lines may need to be compensated, as described in Section 12.2.

11.2.4.2   The Problem with RC Rise-Time Control

Many designers have attempted to control output rise time by adding delay to the predriver. Because of the gain of the output stage, however, a predriver rise

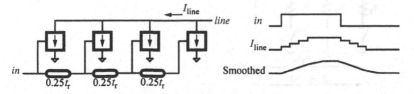

FIGURE 11-17   Rise-Time Control with a Segmented Current-Mode Driver

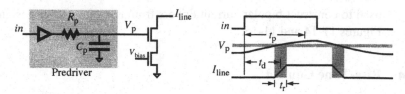

FIGURE 11-18   The Problem with RC Rise-Time Control

time, t_p, of many times t_r is required to get an output rise time of t_r. When t_r is a substantial fraction of the bit cell, the large t_p leads to large delay, jitter, and intersymbol interference.

The situation is illustrated in Figure 11-18. The figure shows an ideal predriver with an RC output circuit driving a switched current-source output driver. Waveforms of the circuit are shown at the right side of the figure. The RC output of the predriver gives a long predriver rise time, t_p. Until the slowly rising predriver output reaches the threshold voltage of the output stage, no output current flows. This results in a long output delay, t_d, and substantial jitter because various noise sources modulate this delay. Once the predriver voltage reaches the output threshold, it rapidly sweeps through the active region illustrated by the shaded area. This results in a relatively fast output rise time; t_r is substantially less than t_p. To get a t_r of half a bit cell, for example, t_p would have to be made much larger than a bit cell, resulting in intersymbol interference because the predriver output would not reach steady state by the end of a bit cell.

Because of the delay, jitter, and intersymbol interference, RC rise-time control is not a viable technique for rise times that are greater than about one-tenth of the bit cell.

11.2.4.3   Segmented Voltage Driver

The rise time of a voltage-mode driver can also be controlled by sequencing a segmented driver with a delay line. In this case, however, the segments are not equal sized but rather are sized so that the voltage divider formed by the on segments of the driver and the termination resistor give even voltage steps.

Consider the abstract voltage-mode driver circuit shown in Figure 11-19. The driver is segmented into four stages with each output FET represented by a switch

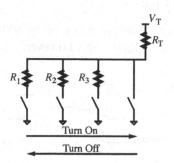

FIGURE 11-19   A Segmented Voltage-Mode Driver

TABLE 11-1 Component Values for a Four-Stage Voltage-Mode Driver			
Stage	G_i/G_T	G_i	R_i
1	0.333	0.00667	150
2	0.667	0.0133	75
3	2.00	0.0400	25

and a resistor. On a falling output, the switches are turned on from left to right, and on a rising output they are turned off from right to left. Suppose there are n stages, then, when stage i turns on, the output voltage should be $i\,V_T/n$. Thus, the total output conductance should be

$$(11\text{-}2) \qquad \sum_{j=1}^{i} G_i = G_T\left(\frac{i}{n-i}\right)$$

Thus the conductance of stage i should be

$$(11\text{-}3) \qquad G_i = \frac{nG_T}{(n-i)(n-i+1)}$$

For example, Table 11-1 shows the values of conductance and resistance for a four-stage voltage-mode driver with a 50-Ω termination. Only three stages are shown because the fourth stage, ideally, has zero resistance.

11.2.4.4 Segmented Self-Series Terminated Driver

The rise time of a self-series terminated driver (Section 11.2.2) can be controlled, as illustrated in Figure 11-20. The pull-up and pull-down drivers are segmented into four smaller drivers with equal output impedance. Each driver is illustrated here as a pair of resistors selectively connected to the output by a switch. When the input switches from low to high, a delay line (not shown) sequences the four switches so that each in turn disconnects from the bottom resistor and connects to the top resistor. When the driver switches from high to low, the process is repeated but with the switches moving in the opposite direction.

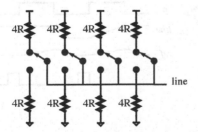

FIGURE 11-20 Rise-Time Control for a Self-Series Terminated Driver

The output impedance remains constant throughout the switching process because, at each point, the same total conductance is connected to the output. At
each intermediate point during the switching process the connected resistors form
a voltage divider so that the switching linearly ramps the open-circuit output voltage between the two supplies. To see that the ramp is linear, we see that at stage
i of an n-stage driver, the up and down conductances are

(11-4)
$$G_u = \frac{i}{n}$$
$$G_d = \frac{n-i}{n}$$

Thus, for a unit supply voltage, the open-circuit output voltage is given by

(11-5)
$$V_{oc} = \frac{R_d}{R_u + R_d} = \frac{\frac{n}{n-i}}{\frac{n}{i} + \frac{n}{n-i}} = \frac{i}{n}$$

11.2.5   Drivers for Lumped Loads

11.2.5.1   On-Chip Drivers for Capacitive Loads

The pulsed-precharged driver shown in Figure 11-21 is typical of efficient, low-
swing, on-chip driver circuits. As shown in the waveforms at the right side of
the figure, the circuit operates in three phases. First, the line is precharged to
a common voltage, usually the positive supply. Second, the drivers are pulsed,
selectively discharging the line for a short period of time. Finally, the voltage on
the line is sensed by the receiver.

To reject noise primarily due to IR supply variations, low-swing signaling
systems such as this are almost always operated differentially or with a transmitter-
generated reference. Figure 11-21 shows the latter approach. A reference signal,
ref, is discharged every cycle but with half the current of a normal driver. Thus,
during a cycle when the line is discharged, such as the first cycle shown in
the waveforms, the line will be lower than the reference. When the line is not
discharged, as in the second cycle in the figure, the half-discharged reference line
will be lower than the line. Often such a reference line will be shared across several

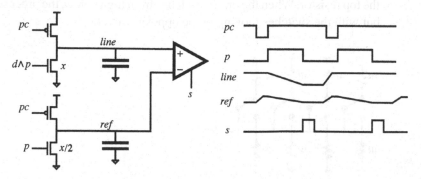

FIGURE 11-21   Pulsed Precharged Driver

data lines. Care is required in routing the reference signal to keep its capacitance balanced with that of the line and to make most noise couple equally into the line and the reference so it can be canceled.

The voltage swing on the line is set by the width of the discharge pulse, p. This pulse is usually generated by a circuit that tracks the characteristics of the driver and the line so that the voltage swing remains constant across process, voltage, and temperature variations. In some cases feedback from the line (or reference) is used to terminate the pulse once the line has been discharged to the desired voltage.

11.2.5.2 Off-Chip Drivers for LRC Loads

Short lines, particularly when they are unterminated, appear as lumped LC or LRC loads. As described in Section 7.4.2, rise-time control and output current shaping are desirable in driving these loads to reduce Ldi/dt noise in the power supply and to reduce ringing of the output tank circuits.

Adaptations of the drivers described above for terminated transmission lines can achieve both of these functions. For example, the rise-time-controlled current driver shown in Figure 11-17 performs exactly the current shaping required to reduce Ldi/dt noise. The driver gives a linear ramp on *in* current and the ramp off is usually controlled by the driver devices dropping out of saturation as the voltage approaches the supply. When operated as bipolar, push-pull drivers, a fast-off circuit is usually employed so that on a rising edge, for example, all of the pull-down sources are first shut off, and then the pull-up sources are ramped on. This gives the circuit a break-before-make action that eliminates overlap current.

When driving LC loads, a rise-time-controlled self-series-terminated driver performs the desired function. Its output impedance damps the tank circuit, and the controlled rise time reduces the amount of energy coupled into the tank in the first place.

11.2.6 Multiplexing Transmitters

The output swing of a transmitter designed to drive a low-impedance (50- to 75-Ω) transmission line is typically smaller than its input swing by about an order of magnitude. Stated differently, the transmitter has a gain less than unity (typically about 0.1). A transmitter with gain less than 1 can have bandwidth greater than the gain–bandwidth product of the technology by multiplexing several output signals together in the transmitter under control of a multiphase clock.

A simple multiplexing transmitter is illustrated in Figure 11-22. The transmitter multiplexes a four-bit input, $d_{0:3}$, onto a single output line under control of a four-phase clock, $\phi_{1:4}$. Note that $\phi_1 = \bar{\phi}_3$ and $\phi_2 = \bar{\phi}_4$; therefore, these clocks can be generated from a complementary clock with a single 90° phase shift. Each input is tied to one gate of a stack of three NFETs that form a clocked current source tied to the line. The other two gates are tied to two clocks. The current source drives the line only when both clocks are high. It is useful to think of the earlier of these two clocks as the *on-clock* because it turns the current source on and the later clock as the *off-clock* because it turns the current source off. For example,

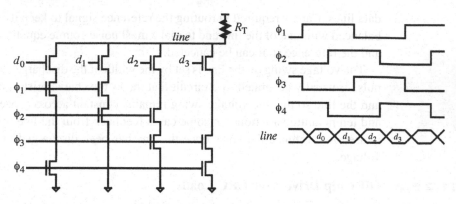

FIGURE 11-22   A Multiplexing Transmitter

the d_0 stack has ϕ_1 as the on-clock and $\phi_4(\bar{\phi}_2)$ as the off-clock. Thus, the d_0 stack starts driving the output on the rising edge of ϕ_1 and stops on the rising edge of ϕ_2 (the falling edge of ϕ_4).

The circuit of Figure 11-22 introduces timing offsets because the transistors at different positions in the stack have different threshold voltages (due to the body effect) and thus switch at different points in time. Because the on-clock and off-clock drive transistors at different positions in the stack, their effects will be slightly phase-shifted. This effect can be eliminated by replacing the clocked part of each stack in Figure 11-22 with a two-input symmetric gate, as shown in Figure 11-23. This circuit is the parallel combination of two stacks with the transistor positions reversed between the two stacks. The result is that the two input clocks see the same effective threshold and thus switch without relative phase shift.

The circuit of Figure 11-22 uses a stack of three FETs to combine the two clocks with the data signal. Better performance and reduced area can be achieved by qualifying the off-clock with the data and driving a stack of two FETs with the on-clock and this qualified off-clock as illustrated in Figure 11-24. The figure shows one multiplexer input. The off clock, ϕ_{off}, is combined with the data, d_i, in a NOR gate so that the upper device in the stack will be on if d_i is low until ϕ_{off} rises. The lower device in the stack turns on when ϕ_{on} rises. This arrangement causes current to flow in the line from the rising edge of ϕ_{on} to the rising edge of ϕ_{off} only if d_i is low. If d_i is high, no current flows.

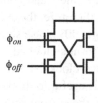

FIGURE 11-23   Symmetric Two-Input Gating

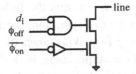

d_i
ϕ_{off}
$\overline{\phi}_{on}$ ——line

FIGURE 11-24   A Multiplexed Output Using a Qualified Clock

To avoid stretching or narrowing the current pulse, an inverter delays the rising edge of the on-clock by an amount that matches the falling delay of the NOR gate. Because it is difficult to match the rising delay of a gate (which depends on a PFET) to the falling delay of a gate (which depends on an NFET), two-stage circuits are usually employed here with the rising and falling delays of the on-clock matched to the corresponding delays of the off-clock.

A multiplexed transmitter can also be implemented by multiplexing before the predriver and output stage, as illustrated in Figure 11-25. This arrangement requires less circuitry and puts a smaller capacitive load on the output than the output-multiplexed circuit of Figure 11-22. However, it requires that the gain–bandwidth product of the unity-gain source-coupled output stage be high enough to keep up with the bit rate.

The circuit of Figure 11-25 consists of three stages: a differential input multiplexer, a source-coupled predriver, and a source-coupled output stage. The input multiplexer accepts full-swing inputs $d_{0:3}$ and generates a full-swing multiplexed signal, m and $\overline{m}$. Each input of the multiplexer consists of a series pair of NFET pass gates controlled by an on-clock and an off-clock. The multiplexer must be fast enough for its output, $m/\overline{m}$, to go full swing by the end of a bit cell, or inter-symbol interference will result. The swing of the $m/\overline{m}$ nodes can be limited by a parallel termination to V_{DD} or negative feedback around the predriver if needed to increase its operating frequency.

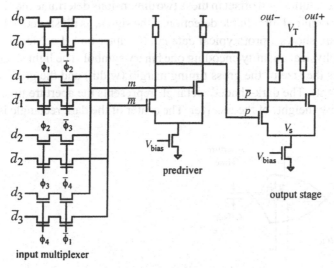

FIGURE 11-25   Multiplexing Before the Predriver

The predriver stage acts as a level shifter that converts the full-swing $m/\overline{m}$ signals into the low-swing $p/\overline{p}$ signals. For proper operation, the loads of the predriver must be adjusted so that they swing from V_{DD} down to just under a threshold voltage above the source voltage of the output stage, $V_T + V_s$. Operating the predriver over this voltage range ($V_T + V_s$, V_{DD}) eliminates dead time in the operation of the output stage. Shortly after the predriver starts switching, the output stage starts switching.

A multiplexing transmitter may exhibit systematic jitter if the phases of the multiphase clock used to control the multiplexer are not evenly distributed or if delays between the clock signals and the output are not carefully matched. Systematic jitter occurs when the duration of the output bits is uneven in a repeatable manner. For example, in a 4:1 multiplexing transmitter, every fourth bit cell may have its leading edge advanced by 50 ps owing to delay mismatches. This systematic error can be a factor in an overall timing budget.

11.3   RECEIVER CIRCUITS

A receiver detects an electrical quantity, current or voltage, to recover a symbol from a transmission medium. In this section we will be concerned with receivers that detect voltage, because most current-mode receivers detect the voltage across a termination resistor.

A receiver should have good resolution and low offset in both the voltage and time dimensions. In the voltage dimension, the resolution of the receiver is given as the receiver *sensitivity*, the amount of input voltage needed to generate a full-swing output, and the offset is expressed as an input offset voltage. In the time dimension, the resolution is expressed in terms of the *aperture time* of the receiver, and the offset takes the form of timing skew and jitter between the receiver and some reference timing marker.

The resolution and offset in these two dimensions determine the size of the *eye-opening* required for reliable detection of the signal, as illustrated in Figure 11-26. The figure shows a prototypical data *eye* (Chapter 6 in [LeeMess94]) representing the physical quantity encoding one binary symbol. The light shaded rectangle indicates the size of the gross timing margin (width) and the gross voltage margin (height). The dark-shaded rectangle represents the aperture time (width) and sensitivity (height) of the receiver. The center of the dark rectangle is offset from

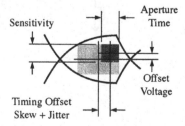

FIGURE 11-26   Eye Diagram Showing Time and Voltage Offset and Resolution

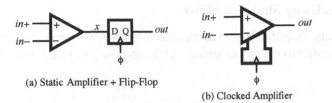

(a) Static Amplifier + Flip-Flop

(b) Clocked Amplifier

FIGURE 11-27   Separate and Combined Detection and Sampling

the center of the light rectangle by the offset time (skew and jitter) and the offset voltage. Only if the dark rectangle remains entirely within the light rectangle, and hence the data eye, will the system work reliably under worst-case combinations of offset and resolution.[7]

In designing a receiver we can choose to separate the tasks of discriminating voltage (detection) from discriminating time (sampling) or we can combine them, as illustrated in Figure 11-27. Figure 11-27(a) shows the two tasks separated. A static amplifier continuously compares the value of the two inputs ($in+/in-$) and outputs a digital value, x, if one exceeds the other by more than the sensitivity of the amplifier. The signal x is then sampled by an edge-triggered flip-flop with a clock, ϕ. As shown in Figure 11-27(b), these two functions can be combined by using a clocked amplifier (Section 12.1.2.3).

There are four main advantages to combining the functions of detection and sampling into a single circuit. First, less power is dissipated because we need only detect the signal at the moment of sampling. With the functions separated, the static amplifier dissipates considerable power as it detects the input signal continuously. Only during the aperture time of the flip-flop is the detected value, x, used. The second advantage is reduced timing uncertainty. The separate design adds two elements to the timing budget: variation in the delay of the amplifier, and delay in the wiring between the amplifier and the flip-flop. With the single-clocked amplifier, these two components of timing uncertainty are eliminated. Third, a clocked amplifier usually has much better sensitivity than a static amplifier. A regenerative clocked amplifier can amplify the smallest signals up to full swing, given sufficient time. A static amplifier, on the other hand, has fixed gain and requires several gain stages to achieve good sensitivity. Finally, a static amplifier with high gain is limited in speed by a fixed gain–bandwidth product per stage. A bank of clocked amplifiers operating as a demultiplexing receiver (Section 11.3.4) can usually be made to operate at significantly higher signaling rates than a static amplifier because each amplifier in the bank has a long time interval, the product of the bit-cell time times the number of amplifiers, to resolve its input.

For these reasons, separate detection should only be used when necessary (e.g., if the received signal is a clock or is an edge-sensitive, self-timed signal). For completeness, both types of receivers will be discussed here.

---

[7] We have chosen arbitrarily to show both offsets as positive, causing the dark rectangle to be offset to the upper right. By choosing one or both offsets to be negative, the dark rectangle can be offset to any of the four corners of the light rectangle.

11.3.1   Receivers Using Static Amplifiers

When a static amplifier is used as the detection portion of a receiver, its sensitivity, ΔV_{in}, is related to the output swing, ΔV_{out}, and the gain of the amplifier, A.

$$(11\text{-}6) \qquad\qquad \Delta V_{in} = \frac{\Delta V_{out}}{|A|}$$

With an output swing of 2.5 V, for example, a gain of 50 is required to achieve 50-mV sensitivity. A gain of this magnitude usually requires 2–3 stages of amplification.

11.3.1.1   The Inverter As a Receiver

The simplest amplifier is an inverter. For this reason inverters are in widespread use as receivers on CMOS chips. Unfortunately, inverters also have the worst sensitivity and offset voltage of any of the amplifiers we will examine here. Also, when operated in their high-gain region, inverters dissipate considerable static power due to overlap current.

Recall from Section 4.3.2.2 that the DC gain of a our prototypical inverter is about 20, giving a relatively poor sensitivity of about 125 mV. For some processes with lower DC gains, the sensitivity is even higher. For a tight noise budget, we would prefer receive amplifiers with a sensitivity of 20 mV or less.

More importantly, as discussed in Section 6.5.3.2, the inverter threshold, V_{inv}, can vary by nearly 300 mV with process variation and by over 500 mV if supply variation is considered as well. Combining the sensitivity with the offset, a vertical eye opening of more than 600 mV is required before considering any noise sources other than the receiver itself.

This analysis should not imply that the inverter is without merit for use in a static receiver. There are two ways inverters can be used effectively in receivers. First, an inverter makes a good final-stage amplifier for a multistage static receiver. Multiplying the inverter gain (20) by the gain of the earlier stages gives a high overall gain and hence a sensitive amplifier. The input-referenced offset voltage of the inverter is reduced by the gain of the input stages and hence is less of a problem in this configuration.

Inverters can also be used effectively by compensating for their variations. One approach is to use a switched capacitor circuit to measure and cancel the offset voltage of the inverter, as discussed in Section 6.5.3.3. This technique in effect turns the inverter into a sequential differential amplifier with the primary source of offset becoming the variation in the reference over time.

Another approach to compensating for the variation in the threshold voltage of inverter receivers is illustrated in Figure 11-28. A reference inverter, with input and output tied together, is used to generate V_{inv}, which is then used as a termination voltage. This references the received signal to V_{inv}. As long as the threshold voltage of the receiver inverter tracks the threshold voltage of the reference inverter, variations in V_{inv} will be compensated.

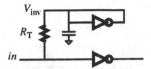

FIGURE 11-28 Using an Inverter to Generate the Termination Voltage

11.3.1.2 Source-Coupled FET Receivers

Static differential amplifiers are generally preferred for use as unclocked receivers. Their primary advantage is a relatively low offset voltage compared with an inverter. The offset voltage for these circuits depends primarily on the matching of two identical components (e.g., an NFET matched to an NFET). This matching tends to be much better than the matching of an NFET to a PFET that sets the threshold voltage, V_{inv}, of an inverter. Static differential amplifiers also are largely insensitive to power supply variation in contrast to the inverter, whose threshold voltage varies directly with variations in either power supply.

Static differential amplifiers can be built using either a source-coupled pair (Section 4.3.6) or a differential cascode circuit (Section 4.3.4.2), depending on the input impedance desired and the common-mode input range.

Most source-coupled differential amplifiers have a limited common-mode operating range. The input voltage must be high enough to bias the current source on and put the input transistors into the saturation region. At the same time, the common-mode input range must be kept below the point where V_{DS} drops below V_{GT} and the input transistors enter the resistive or triode region, or the gain of the device will be spoiled.

The current-source bias must be set to balance output voltage swing against input common-mode range. If the current bias is too low, the output voltage swing will be too small for proper operation. An excessive bias, on the other hand will pull down the common-mode output voltage, causing the input devices to drop out of saturation unless the input range is limited. The proper bias depends on process variation, supply voltage, and temperature.

One approach to biasing a source-coupled amplifier is to use a replica-biased circuit, as described in Section 4.3.6.6. This circuit sets the bias voltage to give the desired output swing into a given load circuit. An alternative approach is to use a self-biasing amplifier such as the Chappell amplifier [Chap88] shown in Figure 11-29. The single-ended Chappell amplifier (Figure 11-29(a)) is a source-coupled

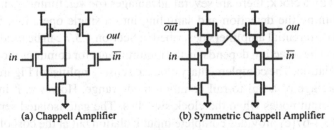

(a) Chappell Amplifier   (b) Symmetric Chappell Amplifier

FIGURE 11-29 Chappell Self-Biased Source-Coupled Amplifiers

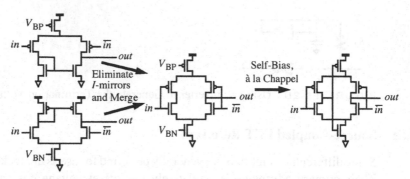

FIGURE 11-30   The Self-Biased Complementary Differential Amplifier of Bazes

amplifier with a current-mirror load that uses the gate signal from the PFET load to bias the NFET current source. This results in negative feedback that drives the bias voltage to the proper operating point. If the bias current is too low (high), the drain voltages rise (fall), increasing (decreasing) the bias voltage.

The single-ended Chappell amplifier is not suitable for driving subsequent stages of differential amplifiers, and its asymmetry leads to less than optimal common-mode rejection. A symmetric variation on the Chappell design that we have found useful is shown in Figure 11-29(b). This circuit uses two current mirrors for the load, the infinite impedance load of Section 4.3.6.3, with each mirror driving one of two current source devices. The negative feedback control of the bias current is the same as for the straight Chappel amplifier; however, the symmetric design gives better common-mode rejection and provides a differential output suitable for driving subsequent gain stages.

One approach to increasing the input dynamic range of a source-coupled amplifier is to combine an NFET source-coupled pair with a PFET source coupled-pair, as shown in [Bazes91]. Figure 11-30 shows how this is done in two steps: first, N- and P-sourced differential amplifiers are merged, eliminating the current-mirror loads; second, the bias voltages are combined and generated in much the same was as in the Chappel amplifier. The resulting amplifier has a large common-mode range, for its bias condition adjusts itself to accommodate the input swing.

11.3.2   Receivers Using Clocked Differential Amplifiers

As described at the beginning of Section 11.3, if the received data are to be sampled by a clock, there are several advantages (power, timing, gain, and speed) to combining the detection and sampling into a single operation. Either of the clocked differential amplifiers described in Section 4.3.7 can be used in a clocked receiver. The selection depends on the requirements for common-mode range and input isolation. The complementary clocked sense-amplifier of Figure 4-67(b) has the advantage of a rail-to-rail common-mode range. However, it injects charge into the input nodes when the clock switches. The gate-isolated sense-amplifier of Figure 4-67(c) provides complete input isolation but at the cost of limiting the input common-mode range.

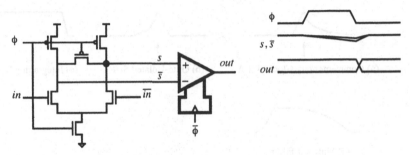

FIGURE 11-31   An Integrating Amplifier

11.3.3   Integrating Amplifiers

In most applications we want to design a receiver with a minimum aperture time so we can sense the input voltage in a narrow time window that gives us the largest possible timing and voltage margins. This gives good rejection of timing noise and low-frequency (compared with the data rate) voltage noise. In the presence of high-frequency noise of significant amplitude, however, it is advantageous to *integrate* the signal over the bit cell. This has the advantage of rejecting high-frequency noise that will tend to average out over a bit cell but has the disadvantage of reducing immunity to low-frequency noise because the low-frequency noise is being integrated across times where the signal amplitude is reduced, particularly in the presence of significant timing noise.

11.3.3.1   An Integrating Amplifier

A simple integrating amplifier is shown in Figure 11-31. When the clock, ϕ, is low, the amplifier precharges sense nodes s and $\bar{s}$ to V_{DD} (the PFET between s, $\bar{s}$ is not strictly necessary but is often included to ensure that these nodes arrive at the same voltage during precharge). During the period when ϕ is high, the source-coupled input stage converts the differential input voltage into a differential current that is integrated on the capacitance of the sense nodes (which must be precisely balanced). At the end of the integration period, ϕ goes low and a clocked sense amplifier senses the differential voltage on the sense node. Because this amplifier is integrating only half the time and precharging the other half, it is usually used together with a second amplifier operating from the complementary clock in a demultiplexing receiver.

11.3.3.2   Receiver Impulse Response

The impulse response of a clocked receive amplifier is the input weight as a function of time. We can describe the operation of the amplifier as sensing the convolution of the impulse response, $h(t)$, with the input signal, $x(t)$, as follows:

$$y(t) = \int h(\tau)x(t - \tau)\,d\tau$$

(11-7)
$$out = \begin{cases} 0 & \text{if } y(0) < 0 \\ 1 & \text{if } y(0) \geq 0 \end{cases}$$

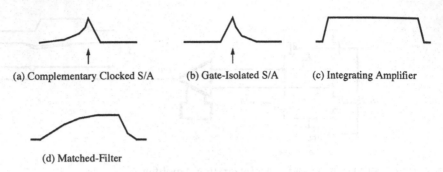

(a) Complementary Clocked S/A   (b) Gate-Isolated S/A   (c) Integrating Amplifier

(d) Matched-Filter

FIGURE 11-32   Reversed Impulse Responses of Common Receive Amplifiers

Approximate impulse responses for some typical receive amplifiers are shown in Figure 11-32. These are all shown time reversed ($h(-t)$) so that they correspond to the weight applied to the input signal at a given point in time. For the first two waveforms, the arrow denotes the point at which the sense clock rises. A complementary clocked sense amplifier (Figure 4-67(b)) has the impulse response shown in Figure 11-32(a). The sense node lags the input because of the RC delay of the transmission gate. This gives a reversed impulse response that exponentially falls off to the left with the RC time constant of the transmission gate. When the clock rises, the transmission gates are shut off, zeroing the impulse response. The ramp from the peak of the response to zero is set by the rise–fall times of the clocks controlling the transmission gates.

Figure 11-32(b) shows the impulse response of a gate-isolated sense amplifier (Figure 4-67(c)). This response is almost exactly the reverse of the pass-gate input sense amplifier. The response is zero until the clock rises. It ramps up with the rise time of the clock to a peak value and then falls off exponentially with the time constant of the regenerative circuit as the sense nodes of the amplifier diverge, reducing the sensitivity to the input.

As shown in Figure 11-32(c), the integrating amplifier has a box-filter impulse response. It responds with equal weight to the input signal during the entire integration period.

Optimal filtering theory tells us that the ideal impulse response is that of a *matched filter*. A filter matched to the impulse response of the data has a time-reversed impulse response that has a shape identical to that of the data eye, as shown in Figure 11-32(d). Intuitively, this filter provides the best signal-to-noise ratio because it integrates the signal over the entire bit cell (no wasted signal), and the gain is proportional to the signal amplitude. Thus, this filter preferentially amplifies the signal at the points where the signal-to-noise ratio is highest. In the presence of timing noise, it is advantageous to narrow the matched filter so that it completely overlaps the bit cell at either extreme of timing uncertainty.

11.3.3.3   A Matched-Filter Receive Amplifier

A matched-filter receive amplifier, or an amplifier with any desired impulse response, can be realized by modifying the integrating amplifier of Figure 11-31 to use a time-varying current source. One method for shaping the current pulse is

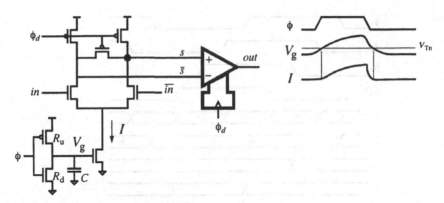

FIGURE 11-33 An Integrating Receive Amplifier with a Tailored Impulse Response

illustrated in Figure 11-33. Here the gate voltage for the current-source transistor, V_g, is driven by an inverter that is sized to give exponential rising and falling delays with time constants $\tau_u = R_u C$, and $\tau_d = R_d C$ respectively. The current pulse is foreshortened, for current does not flow until $V_g > V_{Tn}$, and follows the square-law $I-V$ characteristics for an NFET in saturation. With the appropriate choice of parameters, the resulting current waveform can be made to approximate the shape of the data eye. In practice, the values of R_u and R_d would need to be adjustable to compensate for process variation. Alternatively, one can shape the current pulse as a piecewise linear approximation by dividing the current source transistor into a number of stages and sequencing them on and off using a tapped delay line, as described for rise-time control of a current-mode driver (Section 11.2.4.1).

11.3.4 Demultiplexing Receivers

Clocked sense amplifiers can be used to build receivers for channels with bit cells much shorter than the sense time of each amplifier by operating several amplifiers in sequence in a demultiplexing receiver. As illustrated in Figure 11-34, a demultiplexing receiver is the complement of a multiplexing transmitter. A clock with n equally spaced phases sequences an array of n sense amplifiers to take n equally spaced samples of an input signal each clock cycle.

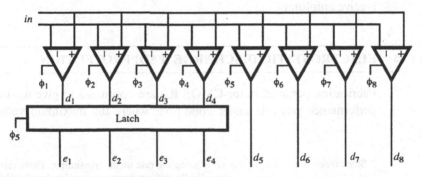

FIGURE 11-34 A Demultiplexing Receiver

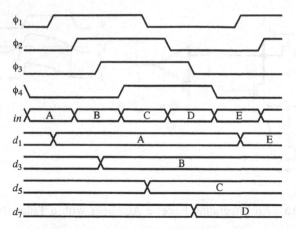

FIGURE 11-35   Waveforms for a Demultiplexing Receiver

A high-speed signaling system typically uses an n:1 multiplexing transmitter together with a demultiplexing receiver with a higher sampling rate, 1:2n or 1:3n. The higher rate is required on the receiver to recover timing information as well as data.[8] Tracking receivers, for example, usually require two samples per bit cell, one to recover the data and one to sample the edge between data bits for clock recovery. *Oversampling* clock receivers require at least three samples per bit cell.

Figure 11-34 shows a 1:8 demultiplexing receiver. A single input signal, *in*, is demultiplexed into eight signals, d_1 to d_8, by an eight-phase clock, ϕ_1 to ϕ_8. Waveforms illustrating typical operation of this circuit are shown in Figure 11-35. The waveforms show the situation where the even phases are used to sample cell edges for clock recovery and the odd phases are used to sample the data. The eight outputs of the receive amplifiers, $d_{1:8}$ are each in their own clock domain displaced 45° from each other. They are all valid simultaneously only for a single 45° clock phase. To stretch the period during which all eight signals are valid, the *early* four outputs, $d_{1:4}$, are latched by ϕ_5. This stretches the valid period to five phases, or 225°, from ϕ_8 to ϕ_5.

With a multiplexing receiver, the bit rate of the receiver is not limited by the sense time of the receiver or by the gain–bandwidth product of a receive amplifier. Instead, the bit rate is limited primarily by the ability to generate the equally spaced clock phases with low jitter and by the aperture time of the clocked receive amplifiers.

11.4   ELECTROSTATIC DISCHARGE (ESD) PROTECTION

Fabrication parameters for CMOS ICs are optimized to give the best electrical performance possible under conditions where the maximum voltage between

---

[8] Some receivers operate at the same sampling rate as the transmitter. These receivers typically recover timing information by periodically shifting their sample points by a half bit cell to sample the timing and then shifting the sampling back to resume data sampling.

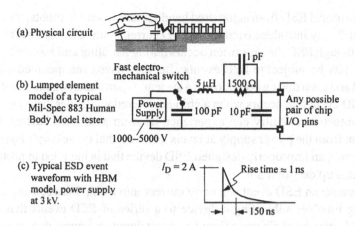

(a) Physical circuit

(b) Lumped element model of a typical Mil-Spec 883 Human Body Model tester

(c) Typical ESD event waveform with HBM model, power supply at 3 kV.

FIGURE 11-36 Human Body Model for Electrostatic Discharge

any two points in a circuit is the power supply voltage, typically 1–3 V for modern processes. The circuits on a chip that are connected to the chip's external interface (the bond pads for input, output, and power supply) may see voltages several orders of magnitude higher than this for brief periods. These high-voltage stressing events almost always occur when a chip is being handled by a person or a robot during test, packaging, and assembly onto a circuit board. This is particularly true in dry climates and air-conditioned environments in which a test–assembly technician can easily acquire a static body charge, raising his body potential to several thousand volts with respect to local ground. As the technician's hand closely approaches a chip, itself at ground potential, the air between human finger and chip lead becomes ionized and is rapidly transformed from insulator to conductor. A spark, essentially a tiny lightning bolt, jumps across the gap to the chip, and for a few hundred nanoseconds or so, the chip's internal circuitry may be exposed to a voltage source of several thousand volts and currents of several amperes. The goal of electrostatic discharge (ESD) protection circuitry is to allow such an event to occur without damage to the chip's internals.

Figure 11-36(a) shows a common situation in which an electrostatic discharge from a technician's finger causes current to flow into an ungrounded I/O pin through the chip's internal circuitry to a grounded pin. Many IC fabricators use an instrument that simulates this type of event, a human body model (HBM) tester. A lumped circuit equivalent for an HBM tester, described in Department of Defense specification 883, is shown in Figure 11-36(b). An adjustable high-voltage power supply charges a capacitor to a preset voltage; then, an ESD event is simulated by closing a fast electromechanical switch, usually a mercury-wetted relay, that dumps the charge on the capacitor into the device under test through a network that crudely models the impedance of a human finger. A typical current waveform is shown in Figure 11-36(c). The ESD protection circuitry in the chip clamps the voltage between any pair of pins to a few volts, and thus essentially all of the 100-pF capacitor's voltage drops across the series impedance during the event. For a typical ESD test, in which the capacitor voltage is set to 3,000 V, peak current is about 2 A, and the event lasts a few hundred nanoseconds. Rise time is usually very fast compared with the event duration. Other types of testers are used to model ESD from automated handlers and assembly robots; these "machine models" may introduce oscillatory ESD currents into devices under test.

Although ESD damage often occurs during handling and assembly operations, chips may be subject to ESD events after they have been mounted onto a circuit board and even during operation in a system. A particularly unpleasant scenario is an ESD event that occurs when a chip is powered up. Under these circumstances, the protection circuitry can experience latch-up and, once latched, can absorb current from the power supply at levels that are lethal to the chip's internal wiring. Ironically, an improperly designed ESD device that is intended to protect the chip may end up destroying it.

Because an ESD event can drive current into a chip between any pair of pins, testing involves subjecting a device to a series of ESD events that stress each possible pairing of pin types (input-to-input, input-to-output, output-to-V_{DD}, etc.). All of these tests are performed at a particular stress level set by the initial voltage on the tester's storage capacitor. After the series of stresses has been applied, the chip is tested for functionality and checked for excessive leakage currents on each signal pin. The DoD 833 standard defines various classes of ESD protection according to failure voltage threshold. Class 1 devices are allowed to fail at 2 kV; Class 2 devices fail between 2 and 3 kV; Class 3 devices must withstand up to 4 kV; and Class 4 devices must survive stresses over 4 kV.

As we will see, ESD protection circuitry uses large-area parasitic devices of various kinds attached to the bond pads and series impedances between pads and internal circuitry. During normal chip operation these devices are never energized and simply represent low-pass filters between pad and internal circuitry. Ensuring higher levels of ESD protection therefore inevitably compromises performance, and thus the designer of a high-performance signaling system is faced with a trade-off between signaling speed and robust protection against damage in handling and manufacture.

11.4.1   ESD Failure Mechanisms

Electrostatic discharge failures are of two types: electric-field-induced failures resulting from the large voltages generated in an event and thermally induced failures resulting from local heating caused by the large currents that flow.

11.4.1.1   Field-Induced Failures

The primary field-induced failure mechanism is breakdown in the thin oxide under the gate of a FET; if breakdown occurs, the FET is destroyed. The critical voltage for breakdown in SiO_2 is about 7×10^8 V/M. In our example 0.35-μm technology, T_{OX} is 70×10^{-10} M, and thus breakdown occurs for voltages greater than about 5 V. As fabrication technology scales down, oxide breakdown voltages are typically about twice the power supply voltage. FET gates can also be stressed in a secondary way by large fields between source and drain; this situation generates rapidly moving "hot" electrons that can tunnel into the gate oxide, where they are trapped. The result is a permanent shift in the device's threshold voltage and consequent degradation of performance.

11.4.1.2   Thermally Induced Failures

The large currents that flow during an ESD event can damage both devices and wiring in the chip. Electrostatic discharge currents, shunted away from the chip's internal circuitry by the ESD protection circuitry, must be carried away from these devices by metal interconnect. The interconnect wiring, vias, and contacts are rapidly heated during the event and may be destroyed if not robustly designed.

Field-effect transistors can be thermally damaged by more complex mechanisms. The source and drain diffusion terminals of an FET form diodes with their associated substrate material. These diodes are normally lightly reverse biased and are considered parasitic elements during normal chip operation. During ESD events, these diodes can become either forward biased or heavily reverse biased. Under reverse bias, diodes exhibit two forms of breakdown. At high reverse voltages, the thermally generated carriers that form the reverse leakage can acquire enough energy to disrupt covalent bonds in silicon lattice atoms. The hole–electron pairs that are generated themselves become carriers, collide with additional lattice atoms, and generate yet more carriers. The multiplication of carriers is called *avalanche breakdown* and leads to rapidly increasing conduction. Even in the absence of carriers with sufficient energy to ionize lattice atoms, the intense electric field near the junction can break lattice atom covalent bonds, releasing new carriers; this process is called *Zener breakdown*. Neither of these breakdown processes is necessarily fatal to the parasitic diode, although local heating due to large reverse currents may induce thermal failure in the metal interconnect system that supplies current to the diode.

If the junction is a FET source–drain terminal, the close proximity of a second junction increases the potential in the region between source and drain and thereby lowers the barrier seen by carriers. This phenomenon leads to a third breakdown mechanism, called *punchthrough*, a mode of FET operation that, like diode reverse breakdown, is not necessarily fatal to the device. A plot of breakdown drain current for an FET is shown in Figure 11-37.

Assuming $V_{GS} = 0$, when the drain voltage reaches some critical value (V_{CRIT} is typically about twice the expected supply voltage), the FET exhibits breakdown, with current rapidly increasing from a combination of punchthrough and avalanche processes. This breakdown phenomenon is not necessarily destructive (aside from the likelihood of hot-electron wear-out, should this mode of operation be sustained). The voltage, V_{crit}, is a function of channel length and is higher for longer channels. When the drain current reaches a critical value, I_{CRIT}, device heating produces more thermally generated carriers, which in turn increases the drain current and produces additional heating. This positive feedback process, called *thermal runaway*, very rapidly drives the drain current upward and

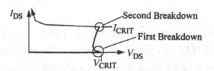

FIGURE 11-37   Drain Breakdown Current in FETs

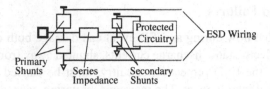

FIGURE 11-38   ESD Protection Circuitry Components

destroys the device by melting it. The critical current I_{crit} is a function of channel width (wider devices distribute the current over a larger area) and is of the order of a milliampere or so per micrometer of channel width for short-channel devices.

11.4.2   ESD Protection Devices

The goals of ESD protection device design are to avoid field-induced failures (mainly for the FET gates of signal receivers) by clamping voltage excursions well below the gate breakdown voltage and to limit the current that flows into FET drain–source terminals (mainly a concern for signal transmitters) to values well below the second breakdown current.

An ESD protection network is usually composed as shown in Figure 11-38 and consists of four elements.

1. The primary shunt devices are the first line of defense against ESD damage; their job is to clamp the voltage at the pad to a safe value and to divert essentially all of the ESD current away from the internal circuitry. The power supply networks are the most robustly wired nodes in a chip, and thus most ESD protection strategies attempt to force the ESD current to flow into one of the supply networks, usually ground, though the V_{DD} net is often co-opted as well.
2. Because ESD currents are quite large, many designs provide special wiring connected to, but separate from, the power supply networks to carry ESD currents from the primary shunt devices.
3. The series impedance, usually a resistor, has two functions. First, taken together with the capacitance of the secondary shunt and the protected circuitry, it forms a low-pass filter that slows down the very rapid initial edge of a typical ESD event. Second, the series impedance limits the current that must be handled by the secondary shunt.
4. The secondary shunt further limits the voltage excursion presented to the protected circuitry. The current that flows through these shunts is usually quite small and is limited by the series element. The secondary shunt is referred to the local power supply of the protected elements to minimize the voltage across individual devices.

11.4.2.1   Primary Shunt

The primary shunt is built from one or more of the parasitic diodes, FETs, and bipolar transistors inherent in CMOS processes. It must handle very large currents; therefore, it generally occupies a large area near the pad and is connected to the pad using short, wide metal straps and many vias and contacts.

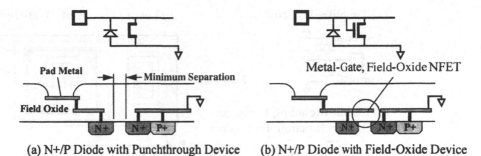

(a) N+/P Diode with Punchthrough Device   (b) N+/P Diode with Field-Oxide Device

FIGURE 11-39   A Primary Shunt Using Only *N*-Type Diffusion

One popular implementation of the primary shunt is a combination of an N+/P-substrate diode and a punchthrough device, as shown in Figure 11-39(a). The pad is connected to a large N+ diffusion, which, together with the substrate, forms the diode. Another large N+, a minimum distance away, forms a *punchthrough device*, essentially a FET with no gate. The two N+ diffusions are drawn so that the "channel" of the punchthrough device is very wide. During negative-going ESD events, the diode conducts current into the ground network (the substrate is robustly connected to ground through a nearby P+ ohmic diffusion). During a positive-going ESD event, current is conducted between the two N+ diffusions via a combination of avalanche and punchthrough processes and again carried away through the ground network.

The punchthrough phenomenon is enhanced by the presence of a gate terminal, and thus a common variation on this theme employs a metal-gate FET (shown in Figure 11-39(b)), where the gate is formed over the thick field oxide between first-level metal and substrate. Such *field devices* are usually considered unwanted parasitics, but their threshold voltage can be fairly well characterized, and they are often effective for this purpose. Current from positive ESD events is carried by normal FET drain current for low-voltage events and by punchthrough for larger ones.

Note that this strategy works even if the ESD current flows into one signal pad and out another. The ESD ground network carries the current between the two pads through the complementary devices in each pad, as shown in Figure 11-40.

This approach has the advantage that only N+ diffusions are needed for the primary device, so (as we will see) the primary device cannot latch up. Unfortunately, punchthrough devices are increasingly problematic as device geometries

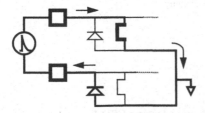

FIGURE 11-40   An ESD Event Between Two Signal Pads

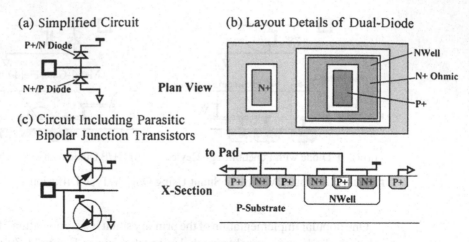

(a) Simplified Circuit

(b) Layout Details of Dual-Diode

(c) Circuit Including Parasitic Bipolar Junction Transistors

FIGURE 11-41   Dual-Diode Primary Shunt

shrink. First, the punchthrough voltage may not be particularly well controlled and cannot always be set independent of other process optimizations. Second, for very short channel lengths, localized heating due to statistical variations in substrate doping may bring about a second breakdown, permanently shorting the protection device.

A very effective primary shunt can be built using a combination of the N+/P and P+/N diodes available in the process. Both V_{DD} and ground supply networks are co-opted to carry ESD currents away from these devices. The clamp voltage for these junction devices is essentially independent of other CMOS process variables. A typical arrangement of layers is shown in Figure 11-41(b). By examining the cross section of the dual-diode arrangement, note that the N+/P diode is actually the base–emitter (BE) junction of a lateral parasitic NPN bipolar transistor, whose collector is the N-well. Likewise, the P+/N diode is the BE junction of a vertical PNP transistor, whose collector is the substrate.

These bipolar devices are critical to the correct operation of the dual-diode primary shunt for signal-pad-to-signal-pad ESD events, as shown in Figure 11-42. The leading edge of the event forward biases the BE junction of the PNP protection device in the upper pad, which raises the voltage on the V_{DD} network. The large capacitance represented by the chip's core circuitry couples the rising V_{DD} voltage

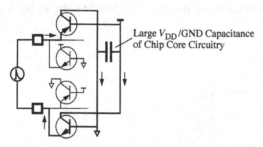

Large V_{DD}/GND Capacitance of Chip Core Circuitry

FIGURE 11-42   Bipolar Conduction During ESD Event

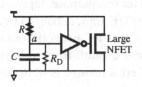
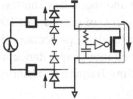

(a) Power Supply Shunt Circuit   (b) Shunt Conduction During ESD Event

FIGURE 11-43   Encouraging Diode Conduction with a Power Supply Shunt

onto the ground network, forward-biasing the BE junction of the NPN device in the lower pad. With both devices on, the diode (BE) conduction of one device is carried by the collector circuit of the other through both V_{DD} and ground networks.

The two parasitic bipolar devices inherent in CMOS fabrication conspire to form a PNPN latchable structure. Because latchup during circuit operation is usually fatal to the chip, process engineers work hard to make *both* parasitic bipolar devices fairly ineffective, to reduce the possibility of latchup. To avoid depending on the purposely poor bipolar (emitter-collector) conduction to carry ESD currents, most of the current must be forced to flow through the BE diodes.

A power supply shunt, shown in Figure 11-43(a), can be used to encourage diode conduction. The shunt contains a very wide, minimum-length NFET connected between V_{DD} and ground whose gate is driven by a large inverter. The inverter's input is an RC delay circuit with a time constant of 10 μs or so, which is much shorter than the fastest turn-on time for the system power supply but very long compared with the rise time of an ESD event. (A very large resistance R_D discharges the capacitor during power-down, resetting it for another possible ESD event.) During normal power-up, node a follows V_{DD}, and the output of the inverter remains low, holding the large NFET off. However, during a fast-rising ESD event, the voltage on V_{DD} rises abruptly, a remains low for some period of time, and the large NFET is turned on, effectively clamping V_{DD} near ground. This shunt current encourages ESD currents to flow mainly in the BE junctions of the protection devices, as shown in Figure 11-43(b), eliminating the need for substantial bipolar conduction. Generally, several shunts are provided on a chip, and they can often be tucked into the otherwise useless space in the corners of the die. The C and R_D functions can conveniently be implemented as a large N+ diode whose junction capacitance is C and whose leakage current performs the discharge.

Some IC manufacturers provide more exotic primary shunt devices. For example, as mentioned in the preceding paragraphs of this section, CMOS provides a PNPN latchable device. This device (also called a *silicon-controlled rectifier* [SCR] or *thyristor*) is usually undesirable, but it can be used to advantage as the primary shunt in protection circuitry.

11.4.2.2   Series Resistor

Pads that drive FET gates in receiver input amplifiers require additional measures to ensure that the oxide breakdown voltage is never exceeded. A combination of series resistor and secondary shunt is used for this purpose. Input capacitance for a typical receiver is of the order of 100–1,000 fF; thus, although larger resistances ensure higher levels of protection, the low-pass RC network formed by protection resistor and input capacitance must have a cutoff frequency higher than the highest signaling frequency. Usually the series resistor is of the order of a few hundred ohms.

Older designs sometimes used polysilicon resistors. Poly (without silicide) has resistance of a few tens of ohms per square, allowing relatively compact resistors to be fabricated with low parasitic capacitance. Polysilicon resistors are not a particularly good idea in new designs, however. Most modern IC processes apply a silicide to poly (and the N+ and P+ diffusions), reducing the resistance to an order of 1 Ω/square, and therefore many squares of material would be required to form a suitable resistor. Poly is also completely surrounded by a thick field oxide whose thermal conductivity is low (1.4 W/m/°C). Heat generated in the resistor is not easily shed and could lead to failure of the device.

A better option is to place the resistor in the silicon substrate, whose thermal conductivity is two orders of magnitude higher (141 W/m/°C). Although diffusion resistors are possible, salicidation makes them less attractive, because many squares of material would be required. N-well resistors are a good option in processes in which the N-well resistance is well controlled and characterized. Some processes offer a "silicide blank" mask layer that allows the designer to remove the silicide on poly and diffusion in selected areas. This feature allows resistors to be built using poly, for example.

11.4.2.3   Secondary Shunt

The secondary shunt is mainly a voltage clamp and, thanks to the primary shunt and the series resistor, carries a relatively small current. Secondary shunts are usually built using a combination of N+/P diodes and NFETs.

A typical circuit is shown in Figure 11-44. Wide, minimum-length, diode-connected NFETs form shunts to the two local power supply terminals. If the protected node tries to swing below ground, the lower NFET turns on once the voltage exceeds the NFET threshold; N+/P diode conduction provides some additional shunting current. If the signal tries to swing above the local V_{DD} voltage, the upper device clamps the input to within an NFET threshold of V_{DD}.

11.4.2.4   Protecting Output Drivers

The drain terminals of output driver FETs are themselves N+/P and P+/N diodes. In older CMOS processes, these parasitic diodes were often sufficient to protect

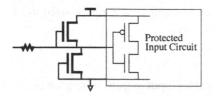

FIGURE 11-44   Typical Secondary Shunt Circuit

against ESD damage – particularly because relatively wide devices are required for voltage-mode, full-swing output drivers. In modern processes and especially for low-swing, high-speed output drivers, the driver FETs themselves have drain areas too small to serve as adequate protection diodes. Most fabricators require the addition of primary shunt diodes on outputs.

Special layout rules are usually required for FETs that drive pads. During an ESD event, some of the current will inevitably flow through the drivers, generating significant local heating in the FET channels. This can result in overheating nearby metal-to-silicon contacts; therefore, contacts to pad-connected source–drain regions are usually stepped away from junction edges by considerably larger distances than in internal circuitry, and thus source–drain diffused areas are much larger than for core transistors. Robust, large-area substrate and well ohmic diffusions, liberally contacted to metal power rails, are usually required around output drivers as well.

As previously mentioned, second breakdown is a problem for short-channel FETs and will become a greater problem as devices continue to shrink. Because NFETs in N-well processes are usually more susceptible to second-breakdown damage than PFETs, some fabricators require special measures to protect against this type of thermal damage. These measures include the addition of small-value resistors in series with the drain of each FET connected to a pad. In some cases, pad drivers must be drawn at larger than minimum channel length. These and other measures tend to reduce the speed of output drivers, which is a serious concern for the design of high-performance signaling. Future signaling system designs will not be able to take full advantage of device scaling because of these problems.

11.4.2.5 Guard Rings

Protection devices are intended to be forward-biased only during an ESD event. They may, however, become inadvertently forward-biased during normal chip operation when, for example, an input signal swings below ground or above V_{DD} owing to ringing on an improperly terminated line. In the case of a below-ground signal excursion, the N+/P diode in a primary shunt may become forward-biased and release minority carriers (electrons) into the substrate. These carriers can propagate for some distance, and thus for a fairly large radius around the ESD device the substrate may become significantly negatively biased. If the burst of electrons produced during such an event gets collected on the N-well of a normal CMOS circuit within the chip, there is the possibility that an N+/P base-emitter junction in the well may become forward-biased, turning on one of the PNPN latchable structures in the chip.

Two measures are usually employed to prevent the minority carriers injected at N+ emitters of ESD protection devices from starting a latchup process. First, ESD primary shunts (and the FETs in pad output drivers) are spaced some distance away from chip internal circuitry. It is often advantageous to place the primary shunt devices out at the die perimeter, leaving the entire width of the pad between shunt devices and chip internals. The extra distance between emitter and possible

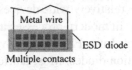
Metal wire

ESD diode

Multiple contacts

(a) An effective way to arrange
multiple contacts

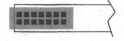

(b) A much less effective arrangement

FIGURE 11-45 Arrangement of Multiple Vias–Contacts in ESD Devices

latchup site allows minority carriers to be collected before they can do harm. Second, a series of electrical barriers, called *guard rings*, is erected between emitters and internal circuitry. N+/N-well rings connected to the V_{DD} network are usually drawn around N+ emitters. These are very effective collectors of wandering minority carriers, particularly in epitaxial ("epi") CMOS processes. They are often interspersed with grounded P+ guard rings, which serve to hold the local substrate as close to ground potential as possible. Guard rings are always heavily contacted and robustly wired to the power supply networks in continuous metal.

11.4.2.6 Wiring and Contacting

Many, perhaps hundreds, of contacts or vias are required to carry ESD currents with low series resistance and with sufficient robustness to thermal failure. Care is required in the layout of conductors and via–contact arrays that carry these currents. Some of these considerations are outlined in Figure 11-45. The illustration shows a metal-to-silicon connection typical of an ESD protection diode. In Figure 11-45(a), a wide metal wire carries current to two rows of contacts; more rows would probably not reduce the resistance of the contact array because most of the current is peeled off in the first row or two. This arrangement leads to a uniform current distribution across the contacts in the horizontal direction. The arrangement shown in Figure 11-45(b) should be avoided. Current is delivered from one side of the contact array; this arrangement promotes current crowding in the first few columns of contacts on the right.

Ensuring uniform current distribution is especially important in FETs whose drains are connected to a pad. Sources and drains for driver FETs should be contacted uniformly and as densely as possible along the full width of the device. Failure to do so could lead to current crowding in the FET channel, thereby promoting localized second breakdown.

This section is intended merely as an introduction to a complex topic. In particular, IC fabrication vendors differ substantially in their recommendations for the construction of effective ESD protection devices. The written guides for this part of the design process tend to be hard to obtain from vendors and difficult to understand, once obtained. However, a designer who wishes to build high-performance signaling systems must be intimately familiar with the problem and its solutions to design effective signaling circuits that are also ESD robust and, therefore, access to full information about the target IC fabrication process is an absolute requirement.

11.5 AN EXAMPLE SIGNALING SYSTEM

In this section we will outline the design of a 1-Gbit/s signaling subsystem intended to replace conventional signaling in a system composed of multiple CMOS chips on multiple boards interconnected by cables or a backplane within a single enclosure. A single, central clock source is assumed for this system, implying a mesochronous timing regime. The example subsystem will be composed entirely of point-to-point links that use current-mode differential signaling. Autoadjusted on-chip terminators are used, and receivers include per-pin timing recovery.

11.5.1 Transmitter

The transmitter is outlined in Figure 11-46. It uses V_{DD}-referenced current mode signaling with source-coupled current steering. Three termination schemes (transmitter-only or self-source-terminated, receiver-only, or both ends terminated) will be explored.

Transmitter and receiver chip internals are assumed to be clocked at 250 MHz, and the transmitter's input clock *TxClk* is derived from its internal chip clock. The transmitter accepts 4 bits of data from the chip internals each clock cycle and transmits them over a differential pair at 1 Gbit/s.

A multiphase clock generator using a delay-locked loop (DLL) controls high-speed operation of the transmitter. Edge-rate control is employed in the transmitter to limit rise and fall times on the output to about half a bit-cell time. An automatically adjusted bias control sets the signal current level. Terminators are built exclusively with PFETs and are automatically adjusted using a thermometer code by a controller that uses an off-chip reference resistor. This termination scheme was described in some detail in Sections 11.1.2 through 11.1.4 and will not be discussed further here.

11.5.1.1 Multiphase Clock Generator

Figure 11-47 outlines the multiphase clock generator. The *TxClk* is converted to differential form (if necessary) and driven into a delay-locked loop. The loop is locked around four delay stages in such a way that the phase shift between output clocks $c0$ and $c3$ is 180°. The DLL is implemented with source-coupled,

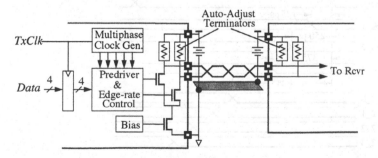

FIGURE 11-46 Block Diagram of Transmitter

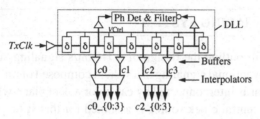

FIGURE 11-47   Block Diagram of Transmitter Multiphase Clock Generator

differential delay elements and stabilized using the replica-bias technique. An array of buffers drives out the four differential clocks $c\{0:3\}$. The even-numbered clocks are on 1-ns boundaries and become the bit-cell clocks for the transmitter. Finer control is needed, however, to set the edge rate; therefore, neighboring clocks, 0.5 ns apart, are interpolated with proportions $c(n):c(n+1)=0:4$, $1:3, 2:2, 3:1$ to generate groups of differential clocks $c(n)_-\{0:3\}$ spaced 125 ps apart. These closely spaced clocks are used to drive a segmented transmitter, as described above in Section 11.2.4.

Timing of the clocks is outlined in Figure 11-48. Clocks $c0_-\{0:3\}$ are responsible for the cell edge timing of data bits 0 and 2, and $c2_-\{0:3\}$ are responsible for bits 1 and 3. Clocks $c0_-\{0:3\}H$ and $c2_-\{0:3\}H$ (active-high half of these differential clock pairs) time bits 0 and 1, and $c0_-\{0:3\}L$ and $c2_-\{0:3\}L$ (active low halves) time bits 2 and 3.

The circuits needed to implement the multiphase clock generator are discussed in Chapter 12 in some detail.

11.5.1.2   Output Driver

The output driver is a source-coupled current steering pair that sinks current out of one or the other of the output pads. The driver is segmented into four equal-sized pieces for edge-rate control, as shown in Section 11.2.4. A 5-ma signaling current will be assumed, and therefore each of the four segments must sink 1.25 ma.

Design considerations for the output driver are determined partly by the ESD rules for the process and by related issues of layout convenience. We will assume that, for the example process, ESD rules include the restrictions that NFETs

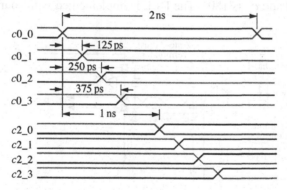

FIGURE 11-48   Multiphase Clock Generator Waveforms

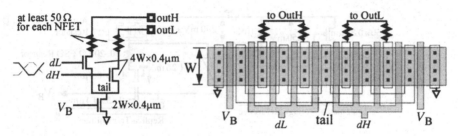

FIGURE 11-49 Convenient Layout for Output Driver Segment

connected to pads must be drawn at least 0.4 μm long, and individual NFETs must have at least 50 Ω of resistance between drain and pad. We will assume that these 50-Ω resistors are made from N-well and that their maximum resistance under process and temperature variation is 200 Ω.

Figure 11-49 shows the details of a possible layout that is particularly convenient. It remains to choose a suitable value for W. The current tail transistor must be well into saturation at the desired signaling current, with a fraction of the power supply voltage dropped between tail and ground. As a first cut, assume that V_{tail} is half the supply voltage, the signaling current (per section) is 1.25 ma, and that V_B must be well below the supply voltage, say also $V_{DD}/2$ (for convenience in the design of the bias generator), all under worst-case conditions. Simulation shows that $W = 5 \mu$m satisfies these conditions.

11.5.1.3 Bias Generator

The tail current set by the bias generator is not critical in this application. The tail current sets the maximum signal voltage swing across the terminators, and we would like to guarantee that this is large compared with the fixed sources of noise in the system. A total transmitter current of 5 ma gives 250 mV of signal (500-mV differential) if only one termination is used, and a 250-mV differential signal if both ends are terminated. In either case the signal is about an order of magnitude larger than the fixed sources of noise we estimated for this type of signaling system in Section 6.6. Because the tail current is not critical, it is most convenient to generate its reference locally at each transmitter to avoid having to distribute a bias voltage (or a digital representation of the tail current).

One of many possible ways to generate the tail bias is to produce a reference voltage equal to the intended signaling voltage and then servo the tail bias voltage in a replica transmitter circuit.

One possible circuit implementation is shown in Figure 11-50. A "poor man's" voltage reference, shown on the right, biases a large PFET just at saturation, producing a voltage of around 500 mV. The physical basis for the reference is the threshold voltage of the PFET, a reasonably well-controlled parameter. This voltage is dropped across a resistive voltage divider conveniently built using N-well resistors or perhaps triode-connected PFETs; the divider's ratio is important, but absolute resistance value is noncritical. It is relatively easy to control the voltage to better than 10%, and thus this circuit is good enough for the purpose. On the right-hand side of the figure is a replica transmitter scaled down to one-quarter

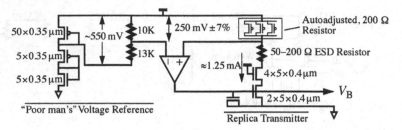

FIGURE 11-50   Bias Generator

size. An autoadjusted termination resistor is included, and the voltage generated across this termination by the current through the replica is compared with the voltage reference. The tail current is servoed to maintain this voltage. (A real design would have to consider loop stability; see Section 12.2.3.1). The ground return for the replica transmitter should be the same as that for the driver segments; V_B is bypassed using an NMOS capacitor to the transmitter-local ground so that the bias voltage will ride up and down with any ground noise that is generated, holding the bias condition in the tail transistors nearly constant.

11.5.1.4   Predriver

The predriver's job is to switch the gate voltages on the two current-steering transistors in each driver segment in such a way that current is steered smoothly from one output pad to the other. This requires a make-before-break action in the current-steering transistors to avoid allowing the current tail transistor to fall out of saturation and the tail voltage to collapse. Ideally, the voltage on the tail node should remain undisturbed during a switching event; otherwise, the changing tail voltage will inject charge into the signal paths.

To obtain this behavior, the predriver's outputs must switch between V_{DD} and a voltage just slightly less than $V_{tail} + V_{TN'}$ ($V_{TN'}$ is the body-effected NFET threshold). The outputs should switch as a complementary pair, and thus a differential predriver is preferred. This choice for V_{LOW} out of the predriver optimizes several aspects of driver behavior. The voltage crossover between rising and falling outputs of the predriver holds both steering devices on at the midpoint of the switching event, and thus the tail voltage will be held approximately constant. The rising predriver output almost immediately begins turning on its steering transistor; therefore, there is no delay waiting for the signal to exceed V_{TN} before switching begins. The signal swing out of the predriver is minimized, and consequently the predriver can be made small and fast.

Figure 11-51 shows an implementation of a predriver using the methods described in Section 11.2.3.3 and the pass-gate multiplexing methods of Figure 11-25. Note that the current tails are all drawn at 0.4-μm length to help track the behavior of the output driver. All other FETs are minimum length. The voltage swing on dH, dL depends on the ratio of the PFET loads in the predriver to the NFET current tails. Ratioing a PFET against an NFET is generally not a desirable circuit construction, but adequate current steering can be achieved with only moderately accurate tracking of the driver's tail voltage, and thus this implementation works well in practice.

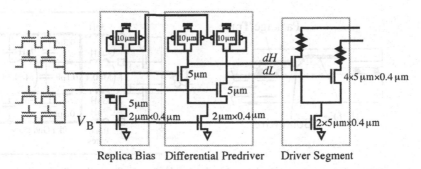

Replica Bias | Differential Predriver | Driver Segment

FIGURE 11-51 Predriver with Driver Segment

11.5.1.5 Latches and Pass-Gate Clocking Network

The remaining transmitter circuitry (Figure 11-52) latches in the 4 data bits (delaying the most significant 2 bits by half a cycle) and, using the groups of interpolated clocks, drives the four transmitter segments to implement edge rate control.

The group of clocks $c0_{-}\{0:3\}H$ is assumed to be sufficiently later than the rising edge of *TxClk* that $d0$ can be gated into the transmitter driver immediately. Signals $d0$ and $d1$ are sent during the first half of the *TxClk* cycle; $d2$ and $d3$ are delayed by a half-cycle so that they remain stable through the next rising edge of *TxClk*. Each data bit is gated into the predriver by an "*On*" clock; this path is disabled by an *Off* clock at the end of the bit-cell time. The *Off* clock for each bit is the complement of the *On* clock for the next data bit.

11.5.1.6 Package Model

For simulation purposes we will assume a type-2 BGA package. The transmitter's differential output pads are interspersed with ground pins (pin order: gnd, sig+, sig−, gnd, sig+, sig−, gnd, ...). Figure 11-53 outlines the package model. Two 1-pF capacitors model the bond pads and ESD diodes, and 4- and 3-nH inductors model the effects of unequal length bond wires. The package is assumed to have an internal ground plane with no additional inductance between package ground and board ground. The package's internal signal traces are assumed to be 3-mil-wide, 1/4-oz copper traces sandwiched between two ground planes and surrounded by FR4 dielectric. Inductance and capacitance values were computed using LINPAR [LINPAR89]. As for the bond wires, unequal-length package traces are modeled with 7- and 5-nH inductances. Two 1-pF capacitors model the board's solder pad

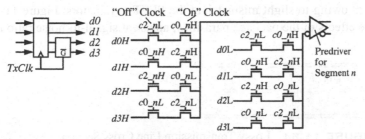

FIGURE 11-52 Input Latches and Passgate Clock Network

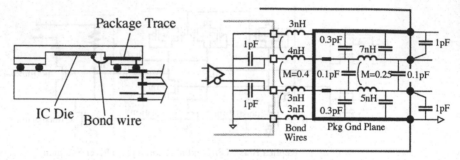

FIGURE 11-53   Package Model for Example Signaling System

and the via to the signal trace within the board. Identical package models are assumed for both transmitter and receiver, and the *outH* signal travels over the longer path in both cases.

11.5.1.7   Transmission Line Model

To evaluate the example signaling system in simulation, the follwing three transmission line models are used:

1. Simple, lossless line model; two uncoupled 50-Ω elements, 2.8 ns long (to model about 1 ft of interconnect). This model is for reference purposes only.
2. Lossy model, using HSPICE's "lossy-U" physically based model. The layer stackup assumed in this model is shown in Figure 11-54, and the line is 305 mm (1 ft) long. Frequency-dependent attenuation is included in the model.
3. Lossy-U model with two connector interfaces (e.g., to model communication between two daughter cards over a backplane). Connectors are handled with a vendor-supplied model for a standard 2-mm backplane connector.

11.5.1.8   Simulation Results for Package and Transmission-Line Models

Figure 11-55 shows eye diagrams for various simulation conditions. The transmitter was simulated using a pseudorandom bit pattern for about 80 bit-cell times. Nominal fabrication models, power supply voltage, and temperature are assumed for transmitter and receiver, and both transmitter and receiver are terminated. The transmitter's clocks are driven by voltage sources rather than the DLL. Figure 11-55(a) shows the differential signal seen at the receiver when modeled with a lossless line and no package parasitics. A small amount of overshoot is evident owing to slight mismatch at the PFET terminators. Figure 11-55(b) shows the effects of the package parasitics; apparent signal-to-noise ratio is about 17:1

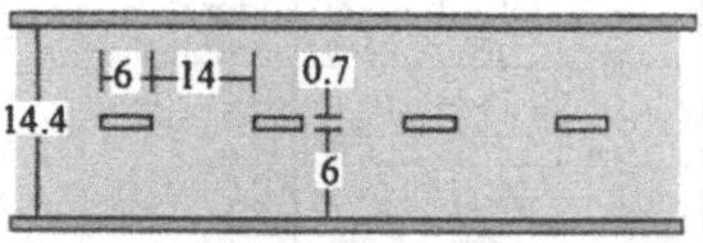

FIGURE 11-54   Lossy Transmission Line Cross Section

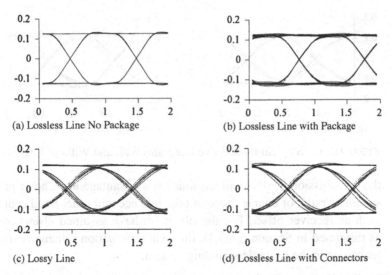

FIGURE 11-55   Simulated Eye Diagrams for Example Signaling System

and a very small amount of timing jitter has been introduced by reflections and frequency-dependent attenuation in the package. Figure 11-55(c) shows the effects of the lossy transmission line model. The frequency-dependent attenuation has introduced both noise and timing jitter, as discussed in Section 8.2; SNR has been reduced to about 10:1 and about 100 ps of jitter has been introduced. Figure 11-55(d) shows the additional effects of a pair of connectors inserted into the line; SNR has been degraded to about 7:1, and jitter has been increased slightly.

11.5.1.9   Termination Schemes

As mentioned in Section 11.2.4.4, this signaling system could be configured as a self-source terminated system (terminator at transmitter only), an underterminated system (terminator at receiver only), or with terminators at both transmitter and receiver. Figure 11-56 shows eye diagrams for each of these cases, where the transmission line is the lossy U-model with connectors. The magnitude of the signal at the receiver is twice as large for both transmitter-only and receiver-only termination schemes, but SNR for the twin-termination case is nearly twice as large (10:1 versus 5:1) as for either of the single-termination schemes, and jitter is reduced as well. Generally, if there are significant impedance discontinuities in

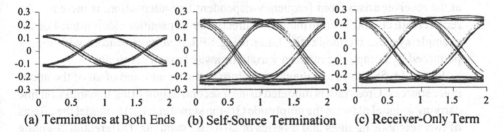

(a) Terminators at Both Ends   (b) Self-Source Termination   (c) Receiver-Only Term

FIGURE 11-56   Simulated Eye Diagrams with Three Termination Schemes

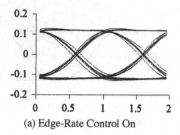
(a) Edge-Rate Control On

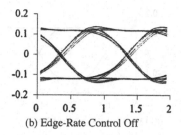
(b) Edge-Rate Control Off

FIGURE 11-57   Simulated Eye Diagrams with and Without Edge Rate Control

the transmission media, twin termination is advantageous. Choice of termination scheme would, of course, have to take into account other fixed sources of noise such as receiver offset. For the offset we have assumed elsewhere (±20 mV, as discussed in Section 6.5.3.4), the twin-termination scheme is still a superior technique in the example signaling system.

11.5.1.10   Effectiveness of Slew-Rate Control

As shown in Figure 11-57, edge-rate control provides only slight improvement in SNR (about 10:1 versus about 8:1). Both simulations use the transmission line model with lossy line and connectors. Improvement would also be larger for a best-case simulation, where FET switching speed is maximized. Edge-rate control might be expected to yield greater benefit in situations where package and connector parasitics are larger than in this example signaling system, for which the benefits of edge-rate control are modest.

11.5.1.11   Noise Modeling

To verify the noise and timing margins for the signaling system in simulation requires modeling various sources of noise, both fixed and proportional. Fixed noise sources include line attenuation (already included in the transmission line model) and receiver offset, which we will model simply by adding an offset voltage for the example system. Proportional noise sources include cross talk (from neighboring comparable signals) and noise induced by continuous adjustment of terminators as well as the intersymbol interference from line reflections already handled by the line and package models. It is also necessary to include power supply and substrate voltage fluctuations; these are mainly common-mode noise sources but are converted to differential noise by nonlinearities in the terminators and by mixing of even- and odd-mode propagation on the transmission line. Jitter at the receiver arises from frequency-dependent line attenuation, is increased by receiver offset, and is contributed to directly by transmitter clock jitter. For the example system, we model the latter using SPICE voltage sources with timing perturbed by computing random variations away from ideal timing.

Figure 11-58 shows eye diagrams before and after addition of all of the above noise sources. Cross talk is modeled using a second neighboring transmission line carrying a signal of twice the amplitude (10-ma signal current) to model the effects of two neighboring lines and a series of ..01010.. symbols. Differential coupling coefficients are generally quite low (one of the many benefits of differential signaling), and for the interconnect model used here, $k_{rx} = 0.006$, $k_{fx} = 0.001$.

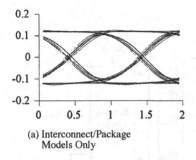 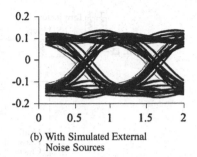

(a) Interconnect/Package
    Models Only

(b) With Simulated External
    Noise Sources

FIGURE 11-58   Eye Diagrams with and Without External Noise Sources

Backward cross talk is the dominant source of noise in two coupled lines with both ends terminated, though forward cross talk can become a far-end problem owing to impedance mismatches. For the simulation in the figure, a backward cross talk source is assumed. Termination resistors are continuously adjusted by 5% steps at a rate slightly different than half the bit-cell frequency (much more often than would be needed in practice). Fast-rise ±10% excursions were added to the external power supply voltages also at a frequency slightly different from the clock frequency. A 20-mV offset is introduced at the receiver. Transmitter clocks are perturbed randomly by ±100 ps to simulate worst-case jitter in the transmitter multiphase clock generator.

The eye diagram has an apparent SNR of about 3:1 and jitter of about 300 ps. Most of the additional noise in Figure 11-58(b) results from power supply noise; cross talk and resistor adjustment noise components are relatively small. In some designs, transmitter offset may also be a factor. In this example, the transmitter's gain is so low that offset is not an issue.

With the simulated noise sources we have used here, the eye opening is adequate for a receiver with the 10-mV sensitivity we have estimated elsewhere in the text. It is relatively easy to build receiver sense amplifiers with apertures of 50 ps or so in the example technology, and therefore the horizontal eye opening allows a reasonable margin for timing jitter in the receiver's clock.

Design of a "real" high-performance signaling system requires much greater attention to the details of the transmission line system than outlined in this example. Whether hand-generated or commercial interconnect and packaging models are used, they should be verified so far as possible against physical measurements. In a "real" design, it would also be necessary to consider the problem that transmitter and receiver chips may have different fabrication parameters, supply voltages, and temperatures, which are effects not taken into account in the results outlined above. Variation in the PC board trace impedance over manufacturing tolerances should also be included.

11.5.2   Receiver

In this section we outline an implementation for a receiver suitable for recovering data from the transmitted bit stream and delivering 4 bits of data to the chip internals retimed into the internal clock's regime. A block diagram of the receiver is shown in Figure 11-59.

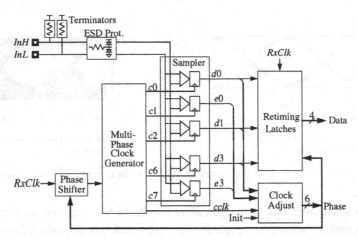

FIGURE 11-59   Receiver Block Diagram

Electrostatic-discharge-protected versions of the differential inputs $In\{H, L\}$ are sampled in eight latching sense amplifiers. When the receiver has been initialized and allowed to lock, these eight samples represent the four data bits sent during a transmitter clock cycle and four samples of the data transition edges. Timing of the eight samples is controlled by a multiphase clock generator that produces clocks $c\{0:7\}$ on 0.5-ns (half bit-cell) intervals. A phase shifter between the receiver chip's internal clock $RxClk$ and the multiphase clock generator is used for two purposes. First, it adjusts the gross phase shift in such a way that data bit $d0$ from the transmitter is latched by the top sampler and clocked by $c0$. Second, it adjusts the phase shift on a fine scale so that the edge samples (clocks $c1$, $c3$, $c5$, $c7$) are aligned with the data-cell boundaries, placing the data samples (clocks $c0$, $c2$, $c4$, $c6$) at the center of the data cells. The clock adjust module processes data and edge samples and generates a digital representation of the required phase shift, Phase$\{5:0\}$. A set of retiming latches brings the data samples into the $RxClk$ domain.

11.5.2.1   Phase Shifter and Multiphase Clock Generator

The receiver's clock generator is diagrammed in Figure 11-60 and consists of a phase shifter capable of smooth continuous adjustment over a full 360° range and a multiphase clock generator. The phase shifter is built using a DLL similar to the transmitter's clock generator and is locked so that four delay stages generate half of a (4-ns) clock period of delay, or 0.5 ns per stage. A pair of multiplexers selects two neighboring taps on the delay line (0,1; 1,2; 2,3; 3,0'; etc.), and an interpolator adjusts the output delay between the two adjacent taps with 3-bit (62.5-ps) resolution. The decoder is constructed so that the 6-bit code on *Phase* is interpreted as a digital representation of the phase shift between 0 and 360°. This general approach is advantageous for clock alignment applications and is described in more detail in Section 12.6.4.

A second delay line gets the output of the phase shifter and generates the eight sample clocks. It uses the same control voltage as the DLL and is built with identical delay elements, and thus its delay per stage is also 0.5 ns. A control clock,

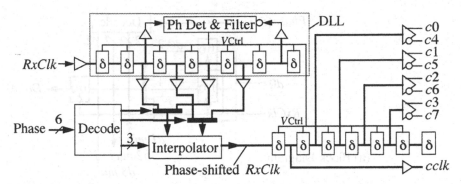

FIGURE 11-60 Block Diagram of Receiver Clock Generator

cclk, is also generated in this delay line and is used to sequence the activities of the clock phase adjuster block of the transmitter.

11.5.2.2 Samplers

The samplers could be implemented with any of the techniques discussed in Sections 11.3.2 and 11.3.3. For this example, we will assume an integrating amplifier, which, in particular, may help locate the data-cell edges more precisely in the presence of noise and jitter.

11.5.2.3 Retiming Latches

The block diagram of the retiming latch module is shown in Figure 11-61(a). The retiming latches, select multiplexer, and output latch are shown for data bit 0; the other data bits are identical. Two example timings are shown at the bottom of the figure. In Figure 11-61(b), sampler 0 produces its output just after the rising edge of *RxClk*. The object is to retime the output *Data* on the rising edge of *RxClk*. To accomplish this, the MUXs for data bits 0 and 1 are set to select the positive edge-triggered resamples $d\{0, 1\}\_2$, whereas the MUXs for data bits 2 and 3 are set to accept the negative-edge sampled data $d\{2, 3\}\_1$. Figure 11-61(c) shows the situation when the timing of sampler 0 is somewhat later. Here, the 0-bit MUX is set to select the positive-edge resampled data, the negative-edge resampled bits 1 and 2 are selected, and bit 3 is taken directly from the sampler.

In any case, the correct setting for the multiplexers can be determined unambiguously from the value on *Phase* because this determines the timing relationships between the samplers and *RxClk*. A decoder embodies these choices and sets the multiplexers appropriately for each value of *Phase*. As we will see, the value on *Phase* can change only monotonically and thus, when the multiplexers are switched from one setting to the next, both previous and new settings of each multiplexer select data samples with the same value; consequently, no timing glitches are introduced.

11.5.2.4 Clock Adjuster

Figure 11-62 sketches a design for the clock adjuster. A set of edge detectors examines two successive data samples and a corresponding edge sample; if the data bits differ and if the edge sample is equal to the next data sample, the sampling

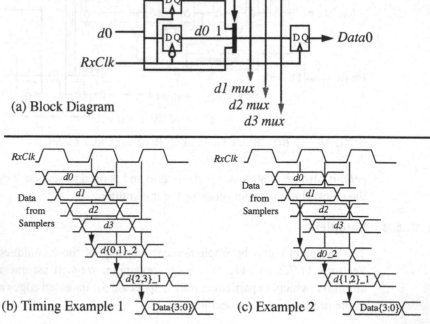

(a) Block Diagram

(b) Timing Example 1   (c) Example 2

FIGURE 11-61   Receiver Retiming Latches

clocks are inferred to be late. If the edge sample differs from the following data bit, the clocks are inferred to be early. Early and late bits are retimed and counted in a tally circuit. The tally asserts *Up* if there are more *Early*'s and *Late*'s, asserts *Dn* if *Late*'s predominate, and neither if the number of *Early*'s and *Late*'s is the same. These *Up/Dn* controls drive a counter that generates the digital representation of *Phase*. Because there are several cycles of delay between sampling *Early*'s and *Late*'s and generating the corresponding *Up/Dn* controls, the counter is allowed

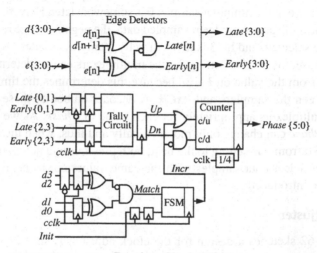

FIGURE 11-62   Receiver Clock Adjuster

to increment only every four cycles. In other words, a delay is required to stabilize the digital control loop of the phase adjuster.

There remains the problem of assuring that *Phase* is set so that the transmitted 0th data cell is sampled in the 0th data sampler at the receiver, which is often called data *framing*. This problem arises because, although by assumption the receiver and transmitter clocks are at the same frequency, their relative phase is unknown; likewise, the transmission delay between transmitter and receiver is unknown. In this example, we assume that a system initialization mechanism is available to establish the correct framing at each receiver. This mechanism, when enabled, causes all transmitters in the system to emit a "training" sequence of bits; in this example, we assume that this sequence is . . . {0010 1101} . . .. During initialization, the *Init* input to the receiver is asserted, and a coarse phase adjustment mechanism is enabled. Simple XOR logic examines the four data samples just recovered and asserts *Match* if the two *MSB*s are the same and the two *LSB*s differ. A finite state machine asserts *Incr*, which constantly advances the phase of the receiver's sampling clocks until *Match* is asserted. For safety, the FSM examines *Match* for a number of successive cycles to ensure that it remains asserted, lest it produce another increment of the sampler clock phase. Once *Match* has been determined to be stable, *Incr* is deasserted, and the clock adjuster begins its normal mode of operation, servoing the edge samplers to track data-cell transitions.

11.6 BIBLIOGRAPHIC NOTES

Most references for this chapter are embedded in the text. Some other useful references include the following: Bidirectional signaling was pioneered at MIT and reported in [LamDenDa90] and [DenLeDal93]. More recent implementations include [LeeKim95] and [MoonDike95]. An early oversampling multiplexed receiver design is described in [BassGlass86]; a more recent example is [YangHoro96]. One of the earliest serial data links to achieve gigabit per second speed was the Bull Serial Link Technology; it used multiplexed transmitters and receivers and is described in [MarbCofl93].

11.7 EXERCISES

11-1 **Adjustable Terminators:** A terminator is required with a 2:1 adjustment range and 5% precision. List the number and value of resistors required to implement this terminator as (a) a binary-weighted FET resistor, (b) an equal-weighted thermometer-coded FET resistor, and (c) a proportionally weighted thermometer-coded FET resistor.

11-2 **Wired-OR Glitch.** In Section 11.2.1.4 we described the problem of the wired-OR glitch that occurs when a driver at one end releases the bus (high) and a driver at the far end simultaneously drives low. What happens in the simpler case when drivers at both ends are initially driving low and then one of them drives high. Sketch the waveforms for this situation.

11-3   **Break-Before-Make Transmitter:** The break-before-make circuit of Figure 11-8 has a large delay because the circuit waits for the drive signal to the NFET to fall below an inverter threshold before starting to slew the drive signal to the PFET. Modify this circuit so that the amount of overlap between NFET and PFET conduction can be traded off against delay.

11-4   **Switched Current Mirror Glitch:** The switched current-mirror drivers shown in Figures 11-14 and 11-16 often glitch during turn-on. The glitch occurs because the drain of the current-source device is discharged when the current source is switched off. When the switch device turns on, the drain node (between the current-source device and the switch device) charge shares with the output, injecting a glitch of current. Once the drain node is charged up, the current reduces to its steady-state value. Suggest at least two ways to eliminate this current-mirror glitch.

11-5   **Arbitrary-Waveform Driver:** By weighting the taps nonuniformly on a segmented current-source driver, an arbitrary rising-edge (or falling edge) waveform can be created. Is a linear ramp the best choice? What advantages or disadvantages do other waveforms have? For example, is there any advantage to approximating a half-cycle of a sine wave?

11-6   **RC Rise-Time Control:** To illustrate the problems with RC rise-time control (Figure 11-18), design a unipolar current-mode driver using this technique. Assume you are working with the example 0.35-μm process from Section 4.2.4. The bit-cell width is 2 ns and the rise time should be 1 ns. Can you make this method work reliably? Why or why not?

11-7   **Output Multiplexing Transmitters:** Design and simulate an output multiplexing transmitter (Figure 11-22) in the example 0.35-μm process. How fast can you get this transmitter to operate before intersymbol interference between bit cells becomes a problem? Can you relate this rate to the device parameters?

11-8   **Input Multiplexing Transmitters:** Design and simulate an input multiplexing transmitter (Figure 11-25) in the example 0.35-μm process. How fast can you get this transmitter to operate before intersymbol interference between bit cells becomes a problem? Can you relate this rate to the device parameters?

11-9   **Static Receive Amplifier:** Design and simulate a Chappell amplifier (Figure 11-29). Determine its sensitivity and bandwidth. If you add an inverter after the amplifier, how do these two parameters change?

11-10   **Complementary Differential Amplifier:** Determine the useful common-mode range of the complementary amplifier shown in Figure 11-30. How does this compare to the common-mode range of the folded amplifier of Figure 4-79(b)? Compare the gain and bandwidth of these two amplifiers as well.

11-11   **Matched Filter Receiver:** A matched filter provides the optimum signal-to-noise ratio for a receiver in the absence of jitter. Suppose a circuit has jitter that is always exactly $+100$ ps or -100 ps (i.e., the distribution is two delta functions). The bit cell is 300 ps wide. Is the matched filter still the optimum impulse response for this configuration? If not, what is?

12 TIMING CIRCUITS

This chapter presents circuit and design details for clocked circuits (latches and flip-flops) and clock-generating circuits (controlled delay lines and oscillators). We show how the basic circuit elements presented in Chapter 4 can be combined to produce robust timing and clocking elements to implement the timing and synchronization systems of Chapters 9 and 10.

12.1   LATCHES AND FLIP-FLOPS

In Section 9.3.4 we discussed the timing properties of clocked storage elements (latches and flip-flops). In this section we will explore various CMOS circuits that implement these elements. Flip-flops are often composed of pairs of latches that are transparent on opposite phases of a single clock; therefore,we will first describe the design of level-sensitive latches and then show how these are arranged into flip-flops.

12.1.1   Level-Sensitive Latches

A latch passes its input to its output (with a small delay) when its clock is asserted; when the clock is deasserted, the input is ignored, and the output presents the most recent value on the input sampled during a narrow window in time around the asserted-to-deasserted clock transition. The fundamental component of a latch is a storage device, and CMOS latches are generally built on the basis of one of two distinctly different storage techniques: capacitive and regenerative, as illustrated in Figure 12-1.

Latches that use capacitive storage are actually sample-and-hold devices that store a continuous (analog) value, and they are said to be "dynamic" because, if the input switch is left open for too long, parasitic leakage currents present in CMOS circuits will eventually corrupt the data stored on the capacitor. Latches based on regenerative storage are "static" because data are continuously restored by the positive feedback around the storage loop, even in the absence of a toggling clock.

12.1.1.1   Dynamic Latches

Figure 12-2 shows the pass-gate-style CMOS dynamic latches introduced in Section 4.3.3.1 and some common variations on the theme. In these latches, the storage capacitor is the inherent capacitance of FET gates together with parasitic junction and wiring capacitances.

The clocked switch can be a full-complementary CMOS pass gate, as shown in Figure 12-2(a), or an NFET-only pass gate, as shown in Figure 12-2(b) and (c). The CMOS pass gate has the advantage that data on the D input are passed to the storage node without the threshold drop of an NFET-only pass gate. However, both *clk* and *clk'* are required for this type of latch, necessitating either global wiring for both clock polarities or local generation of one of the clocks.

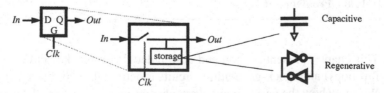

FIGURE 12-1   Level-Sensitive Latches

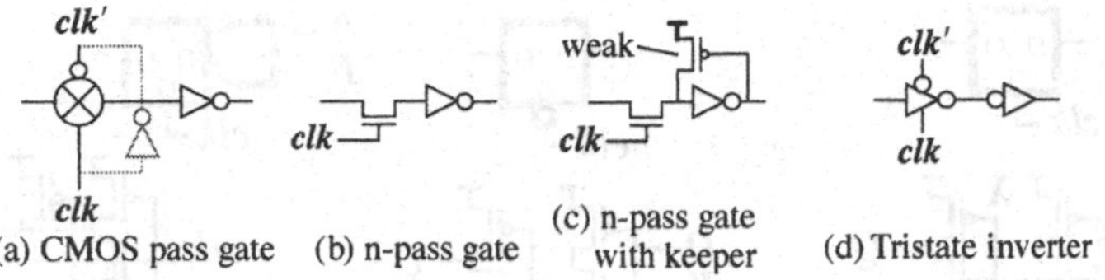

(a) CMOS pass gate   (b) n-pass gate   (c) n-pass gate with keeper   (d) Tristate inverter

FIGURE 12-2   CMOS Dynamic Latches Built with Pass Gates

The N-pass-gate latch (Figure 12-2(b)) is smaller and simpler and requires only one clock polarity, but a 1 input is passed to the storage node with voltage $V_{DD} - V_{TN'}$ (where the prime reminds us that the threshold voltage is elevated because of the body effect). When the latch is storing a 1, the inverter's NFET is turned on strongly, but the PFET is turned on weakly as well, and thus the inverter dissipates some static power. This problem is often remedied by adding a keeper (Figure 12-2(c)) to eliminate the static current flow. This complicates the design of the latch and surrounding circuitry, however: when D is driven to 0, the series combination of NFETs in the stage that sources the data, in series with the clocked NFET pass gate, must have a low enough impedance to pull the storage node down to a solid 0 against the PMOS pullup transistor. A restored N-pass-gate latch is actually a hybrid dynamic–static latch because a stored 1 is restored indefinitely by the feedback.

Pass-gate latches of the types shown in Figure 12-2(a)–(c) exhibit charge injection. When the clock is energized, the driving stage must source the current required to charge the storage capacitance and to overcome a restoring device, if one is used. This difficulty can be avoided by using a *gate-isolated* latch, such as the tristate-inverter-style latch shown in Figure 12-2(d). In this example, the tristate (first) inverter transfers data onto the input capacitance of the second inverter when the clocks are asserted. The transistors in the tristate inverter can be sized to charge the storage node safely, thereby ensuring correct behavior of the latch regardless of its data source.

Another type of gate-isolated dynamic latch was described briefly in Section 4.3.3.1. Two variations (Figure 12-3) of this latch are possible: a positive latch (Figure 12-3(a)), which is transparent when the clock input is *HI*, and a negative latch (Figure 12-3(b)), which is transparent when the clock input is LO. Both latches depend on the internal node *X* behaving monotonically rising (falling) for the positive (negative) version when the clock is deasserted.

This type of latch has a number of advantages over pass-gate latches. Both polarities of latch can be driven by a single clock polarity. Since no *clk'* is required, there is no need to distribute *clk, clk'* with low skew or provide a local clock inverter. The input stage can be enhanced with simple logic functions, improving speed and circuit density; a simple example, a latched AND function, is shown in Figure 12-3(c). First described by Yuan and Svensson [YuanSven89,AfghSven90], these latches were used in the first DEC Alpha microprocessor [DobbWite92], a trailblazing design.

Single-phase dynamic latches have drawbacks, however. The output of the latch is a dynamic storage node; consequently, care must be taken in the next

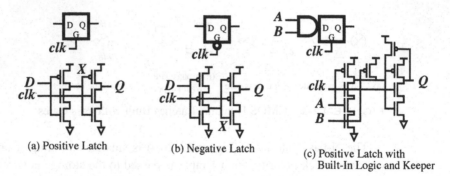

(a) Positive Latch   (b) Negative Latch   (c) Positive Latch with
                                                            Built-In Logic and Keeper

FIGURE 12-3   Single-phase Dynamic Latches

(driven) stage of logic to avoid disturbing the charge on this node by noise on the power supply nets, for example. The internal node X is also dynamic and subject to a particularly nasty problem that we will discuss in more detail in Section 12.1.3. In most applications, a keeper is added to avoid noise problems, as shown in Figure 12-3(c).

12.1.1.2   CMOS Static Storage Element

Static latches use regenerative feedback to hold a stored value indefinitely. The basic storage element is a pair of cross-coupled inverters whose steady-state behavior can be explored with the help of the transfer characteristics shown in Figure 12-4.

The voltage $V1$ is the input of the upper inverter, and $V2$ is its output; if we plot the upper inverter's transfer characteristic we get the S-shaped curve of Figure 4-22. The terminals are reversed for the lower inverter; we draw its transfer characteristic with the axes reversed. The steady-state solutions for this circuit are the three points where the curves intersect. There are two stable points with $V1$, $V2$ pinned at the power rails and a metastable point where $V1 = V2$. As we discussed in Section 10.2.2.2, any small perturbation away from $V1 - V2 = 0$ will cause the circuit to converge rapidly to one of the stable points.

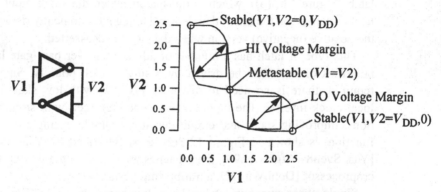

FIGURE 12-4   Cross-Coupled Inverter Steady-State Conditions

D — clk' / clk — ▷ — Q'   clk — clk'   (a) Pass Gate Static Latch   S' R — Q Q'   S' Q Q' R'   (b) R-S Flip-Flop

FIGURE 12-5 Static Latches

The area enclosed between the curves on either side of the metastable point is a measure of how strongly the circuit resists being pulled out of a stable state and its ability to retain data in the presence of noise. The *voltage margin* or *static noise margin* is a more convenient measure of this resistance to inadvertent change [AnamYosh83,Uyemura92]; it is the largest diagonal distance between the two transfer curves and is thus the largest voltage that can be applied between the two storage nodes without changing the state of the storage cell. A necessary condition for the cell to retain data is that the voltage margin(s) be positive under all conditions. The example shown in Figure 12-4 is for a pair of identical inverters. In general, if the inverters are not identical or if we include effects such as offset voltage, the metastable point may lie some way off the $V1 = V2$ diagonal, and the two voltage margins, one for storing a 1 and the other for storing a 0, may not be equal.

12.1.1.3 CMOS Static Latches

Building a static latch from a regenerative storage cell requires a method to overcome the potential "hill" between the two stable states of the cell so that it can be overwritten. One method is to break the feedback loop when the latch is transparent (D passed through to Q) and reestablish it when the latch is opaque (storing). Static latches based on pass gates perform this function by adding a switch in the signal feedback path, as shown in Figure 12-5(a), whereas latches based on R-S flip-flops (Figure 12-5(b)) break the feedback by interrupting one of the supply-current paths.

There are two canonical forms of the R-S flip-flop shown in Figure 12-6(a) and (b) along with their truth tables. The state of an R-S flip-flop represents which of the two inputs was most recently pulsed LO(HI) in the case of the NAND(NOR)

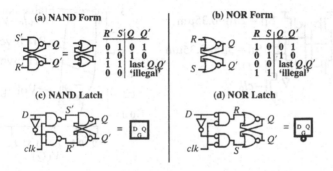

(a) NAND Form

R'	S	Q	Q'
0	1	0	1
1	0	1	0
1	1	last Q,Q'	
0	0	'illegal'	

(b) NOR Form

R	S	Q	Q'
1	0	0	1
0	1	1	0
0	0	last Q,Q'	
1	1	'illegal'	

(c) NAND Latch

(d) NOR Latch

FIGURE 12-6 R-S Flip-Flops and R-S Based Latches

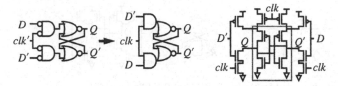

FIGURE 12-7   Compound Gate R-S Latch

forms. There is an "illegal" state for the inputs of the two forms shown in the truth tables. The state is illegal in the sense that the outputs will not be complementary in this state.

As shown if Figures 12-6(c) and (d), additional gating can be added to an R-S flip-flop to avoid the possibility of an illegal input; this gating yields static latches of both clock polarities. In Figure 12-7, a simple DeMorgan transformation on the NOR R-S-based latch yields a compound-gate latch with opposite clock polarity. The transistor-level schematic for this latch is shown at the right of the figure; clk disables the regeneration in the storage cell (shaded box) by interrupting its V_{DD} connections and enables writing data into the latch via the series NFETs.

It is possible to implement more compact, faster latches simply by overpowering the regenerative feedback in the storage cell. This approach introduces some additional complexity in the design process, as illustrated in the differential static latch of Figure 12-8. In this example, the NFETs driven by $D' = clk = V_{DD}$ pull down the Q node, perhaps against an initially-on PFET, and regeneration causes Q' to go high; D is low. The graphical analysis of the statics of this situation is shown at the right of Figure 12-8. The transfer characteristics of the left-hand inverter, with its output pulled strongly low by the clk, D' series NFETs, are modified so that there is only one stable point.

The voltage margin in the example is now negative. A necessary condition for successfully overpowering and writing the regenerative cell is that the voltage margin under the conditions of a write be less than zero. The transfer characteristic for the latch above is redrawn in Figure 12-9 with variously sized data and clock transistors. When these transistors are drawn 1.0 μm wide, the cell is not writable, the voltage margin is still positive, and there are two stable points. If the width is

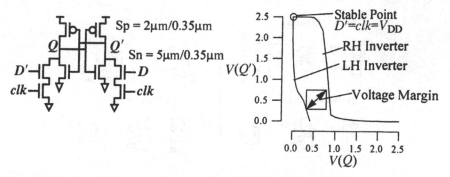

FIGURE 12-8   Writing a Differential Static Latch

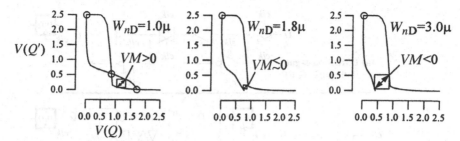

FIGURE 12-9   Writability

increased to $1.8\,\mu$m, the voltage margin becomes slightly negative, and the cell becomes writable, though with little current left over to charge the capacitances in the cell the write may be rather slow. At $W = 3.0\,\mu$m, the cell is easily writable.

Further economies in transistor count can be had by building regenerative circuits with only one of the FET types. In the CVSL (for cascode voltage switch logic) latch [HellGriff84], the storage cell has only cross-coupled PFETs. The regenerative cell is written by means of a differential pair whose current source is clocked. The internal nodes are precharged high, and thus one of Q, Q' goes monotonically high when clk goes high. This form is closely related to the clocked sense amplifiers of Section 4.3.7 and is shown in Figure 12-10(a).

As shown in Figure 12-10(b), the data-driven NFETs in the CVSL-style latch can be replaced with a pair of NFET networks, one of which computes some desired logic function (an AND is shown as an example), whereas the other computes the complement of the function. Endless variations on this theme are possible, and many have been published [ChoeRigb97, YuanSven97, PartBurd96, RenshLau90].

12.1.2   Edge-Triggered Flip-Flops

Edge-triggered flip-flops are widely used in conventional globally clocked systems with open-loop timing. Their popularity, as we discussed in Section 9.5.1, is due in large part to the conceptual simplicity of referencing all events and timing parameters to a single transition of the clock.

Edge-triggered flip-flops are frequently composed of two level-sensitive latches in series that operate on opposite phases of a clock or are otherwise arranged so

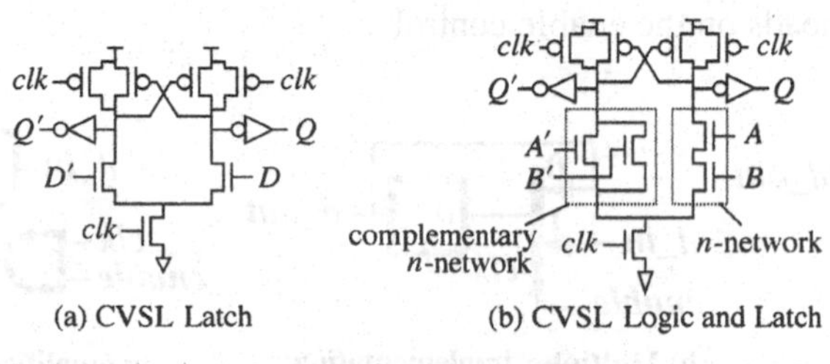

(a) CVSL Latch   (b) CVSL Logic and Latch

FIGURE 12-10   CVSL Logic and Latch

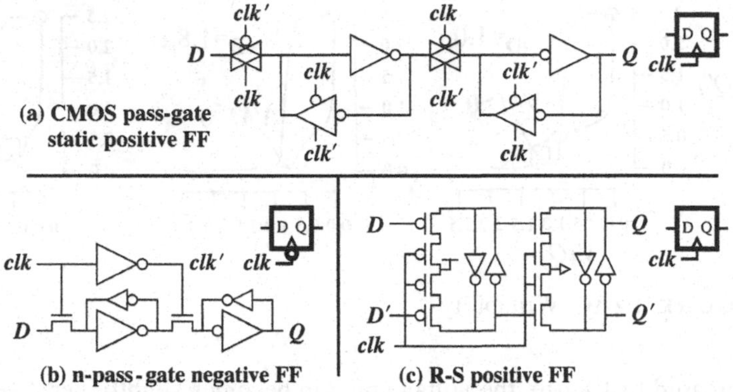

FIGURE 12-11   Example Edge-Triggered Flip-Flops

that they are never both transparent at the same time. Three edge-triggered flip-flops that illustrate various design approaches are shown in Figure 12-11.

A complementary pass-gate, static, positive edge-triggered flip-flop is shown in Figure 12-11(a). This flip-flop requires both clk and clk'; to avoid distributing two clocks, most implementations of this kind have a local clock inverter for each flip-flop or perhaps shared by a small group of flip-flops.

A more area-efficient n-pass-gate flip-flop, triggered on the falling edge of a single distributed clock, is shown in Figure 12-11(b). For correct operation the delay through the clk' inverter must be less than the delay through the master latch or else the flip-flop may fail owing to "race-through" on the rising clock edge, as we will discuss in Section 12.1.3.

An R-S style positive edge-triggered flip-flop is shown in Figure 12-11(c). This approach avoids the problems of multiple clock phases or polarities by employing a circuit technique that allows both positive and negative latches to be constructed for one clock polarity.

12.1.2.1   Auxiliary Control Inputs

Auxiliary controls are often added to flip-flops and latches, for example, to qualify register loads or to initialize state. Figure 12-12 shows the two approaches for the clock-enable function discussed in Section 9.5.2.4. Qualified clocks can be used to reduce the complexity of the flip-flops in a register bank but require careful control of skew between the qualified clock and its parent. Multiplexer implementations are usually safer and easier to design but require more area and present heavier loads on the enable control.

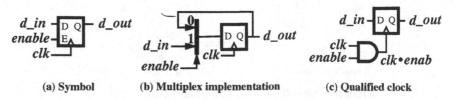

(a) Symbol   (b) Multiplex implementation   (c) Qualified clock

FIGURE 12-12   Clock Enable

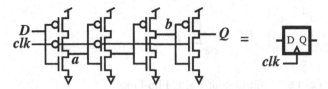

FIGURE 12-13   A Possible Flip-Flop Construction

Qualified clocks should be applied with considerable caution to dynamic latches and flip-flops; the designer must ensure that dynamic storage nodes are adequately refreshed.

Set and reset functions are often needed to initialize latches in a know state prior to normal operations. A synchronous set–reset can be added using an input multiplexer, as shown in Figure 12-12(b). When asynchronous functions are required, the reset input must disable the normal clocked functions of the latches and independently establish the state in the master and slave.

12.1.2.2   True Single-Phase-Clocked (TSPC) Flip-Flops

It is possible to cascade the negative and positive dynamic latches of Yuan and Svensson to form an edge-triggered flip-flop, as shown in Figure 12-13.

Note, however, that the node a inside the master latch is monotonically low when clk is high (the node cannot make a low to high transition). Node b is monotonically high when clk is low; it must be to preserve the data on Q. We can take advantage of the properties of node a and satisfy the requirements for node b by replacing the middle two stages of the flip-flop with a single precharge–evaluate inverter, as shown on the left in Figure 12-14.

We could, of course, have reversed the order of the latches in Figure 12-13, leading to a negative edge-triggered flip-flop, as shown on the right of Figure 12-14.

As with the single-phase latches of Figure 12-3, the TSPC flip-flops have some drawbacks. In addition to the previously mentioned caveat about dynamic output storage nodes, these flip-flops have a particularly unpleasant sensitivity to clock slope, as discussed in Section 12.1.3.4.

Another form of TSPC flip-flop is shown in Figure 12-15; this version has a fully restored output (the output has paths to V_{DD} and to ground, one of which always carries current).

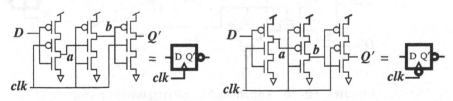

FIGURE 12-14   TSPC Flip-Flops of Yuan and Svensson

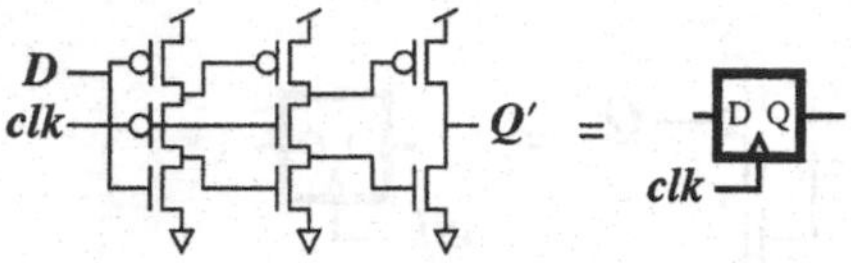

FIGURE 12-15   Split-Output TSPC Flip-Flop

12.1.2.3   Differential Edge-Triggered Flip-Flop

A single-clock-phase edge-triggered flip-flop can be built by combining a gate-isolated clocked sense amplifier of Figure 4-67(c) and an R-S flip-flop, as shown in Figure 12-16.

In this flip-flop, the slave is clocked by the master, and thus only one clock phase is needed. This flip-flop is used, for example, in DEC's StrongARM microprocessor [MontWite96]. It is quite useful in communications circuits (see examples in Chapter 11) where the input swing on D, D' is small, provided the input high voltage is well above V_{TN}. When sensing and latching small-swing inputs, it may be prudent to include the sense amplifier balancing PFET between S, S', as shown in Figure 12-16, to ensure proper equalization of the sense amplifier. An always-on NFET can also be added between the two current steering nodes, as shown in the figure. This device ensures that, once sense is well advanced, large-swing changes on D, D' cannot overpower the regenerative sense amplifier and corrupt the output data.

12.1.2.4   Double-Edge-Triggered Flip-Flops

Some timing conventions (see, for example, Sections 9.5.3, 9.6.5) require flip-flops that capture data on both edges of a clock. A block diagram of a double-edge-triggered flip-flop is shown in Figure 9-14. A positive and a negative edge-triggered flip-flop both sample the D input, and the appropriate flip-flop is selected for output on Q by means of a clocked multiplexer.

Although any of the design techniques we have discussed can be used to build a double-edge-triggered flip-flop, the 9-transistor flip-flops of Yuan and Svensson offer a particularly tidy solution to this problem [AfghYuan91]. As shown in Figure 12-17, the outputs of a negative and a positive edge-triggered flip-flop can

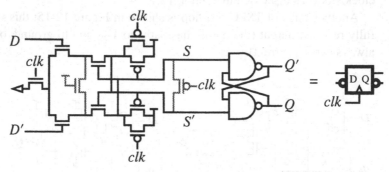

FIGURE 12-16   Differential Edge-Triggered Flip-Flop

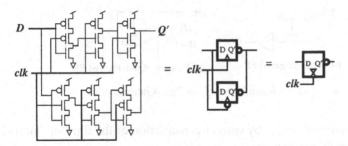

FIGURE 12-17 TSPC Flip-Flops of Yuan and Svensson

be tied together directly, and the multiplexer function is obtained for free. This works because the outputs of the two flavors of TSPC flip-flop store dynamically during opposite clock phases. The double-edge version of the TSPC flip-flop drives its output actively on both clock phases (the output is fully restored), thereby avoiding the aforementioned problem of dynamic storage on an output node.

12.1.3 Failure Mechanisms in Flip-Flops and Latches

12.1.3.1 Race-Through

This failure mode for edge-triggered flip-flops built using a pair of latches driven on opposing clock phases was mentioned briefly in Section 9.3.4.2. We will examine the problem in a bit more detail here to develop criteria for construction of safe flip-flops. Consider the model of an edge-triggered flip-flop shown in Figure 12-18.

Ideally, the flip-flop should exhibit the setup and hold times of its master latch (t_{sM}, t_{hM}) with respect to the rising edge of clk, and should cause data to appear on the Q output with the contamination and delay times of the slave latch (t_{cCQS}, t_{dCQS}) with respect to the same clk edge. The latch is supposed to hold the value sampled on the rising clock edge until the next rising clock edge. It will do so, however, only if the contamination time of the master latch is greater than the hold time of the slave ($t_{cCQM} \geq t_{hS}$). If this condition is not met, data on D will "race through" to Q, changing Q on the inactive clock edge. This condition must

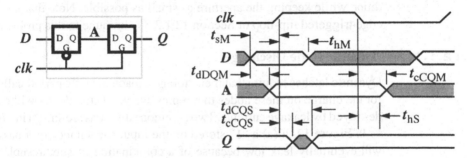

FIGURE 12-18 Internal Timing in Edge-Triggered Flip-Flop

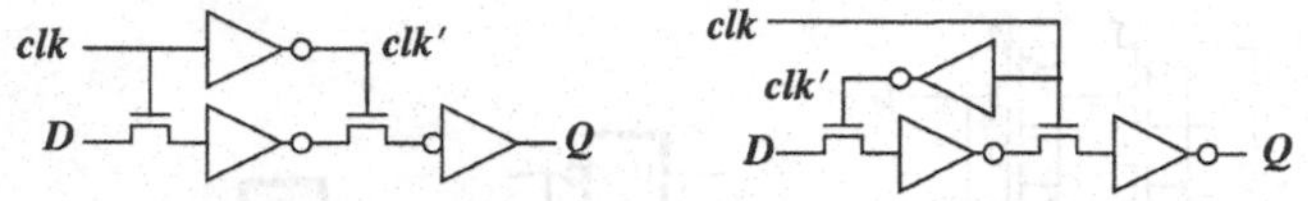

(a) Negative edge-triggered FF   (b) Positive edge-triggered FF

FIGURE 12-19   Race Through in Pass-Gate Latches

be guaranteed solely by correct construction of the flip-flop and is independent of external parameters.

The flip-flop can fail in a more subtle way. If t_{sM} is small and t_{dDQM} is large, then the behavior of the Q output may no longer be governed solely by the properties of the slave latch. Data can "race through" both latches on the active clock edge and may even cause multiple transitions on Q. At best this behavior is undesirable, for it breaks the simple behavioral model for the flip-flop output that is its presumed advantage. At worst, if a circuit driven by Q requires a monotonic signal transition, the driven circuit may fail. To avoid this behavior, the setup time for the flip-flop may have to be larger than the setup time of the master latch, at the cost of increased cycle time.

Avoiding race-through is slightly more complicated in designs where multiple versions of a single clock are used to control the master and slave latches. The pass-gate-style flip-flops shown in Figure 12-19 will serve to illustrate this point.

In the negative edge-triggered flip-flop shown in Figure 12-19(a), clk' is delayed from clk by an inverter delay. This has the effect of increasing the hold time of the slave with respect to clk, increasing the likelihood of race-through failure on the inactive edge. In practice, flip-flops of this kind can be made to work reliably by guaranteeing that $t_{dCC'} < t_{cCQM}$. The amount of margin that is needed in this inequality must be determined by careful and thorough simulation.

The positive flip-flop shown in Figure 12-19(b) is almost certainly immune to inactive-edge race through, but it may require significantly increased setup time and will therefore have a larger aperture than the latch from which the flip-flop is constructed.

In summary, the design of a flip-flop in which both master and slave are controlled by the same clock is something of a balancing act. The designer must ensure that the flip-flop cannot race through under any possible operating condition while keeping the aperture as small as possible. Note that the differential edge-triggered flip-flop of Section 12.1.2.3 is immune to this problem.

12.1.3.2   Dynamic Node Discharge

Dynamic latches require that their storage capacitances be periodically refreshed, for the charge on these nodes that represents valid stored data will otherwise be destroyed by leakage currents. Two common situations are shown in Figure 12-20.

In Figure 12-20(a) a "1" stored on the input capacitance of a pass-gate latch will eventually leak low because of a combination of subthreshold leakage in the pass-gate NFET and the reverse leakage current of its N+/P source–drain

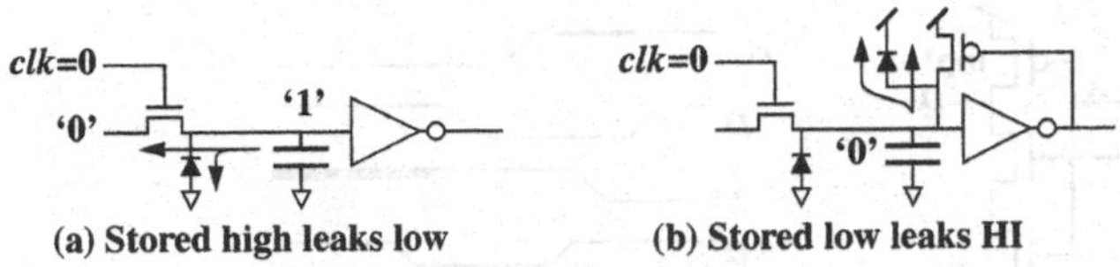

(a) Stored high leaks low   (b) Stored low leaks HI

FIGURE 12-20 Loss of Data in Dynamic Latches

junction. In Figure 12-20(b), in which a weak PFET keeper is used, a stored "0" will leak high because of leakage in the keeper. Of course, once the voltage on the storage node reaches the inverter's switching threshold, the feedback will rapidly complete the task of wiping out the stored data. (The positive-going leakage current will compete with a current to GND through the NFET pass gate's source–drain junction, and therefore the final result is dependent on the relative magnitudes of the various leakage currents.)

Subthreshold leakage in these examples varies exponentially with V_{GS} in pass-gate and keeper FETs. Even a few tenths of a volt between gate and source, arising, for example, from noise or power supply network voltage drops, can give rise to large subthreshold currents. From Eq. (4-11), even if V_{GS} is held exactly at 0, sub-threshold leakage (which scales up with decreasing threshold voltage) will cause loss of dynamic data. At elevated die temperatures commonly encountered in chip operation, junction leakage can become comparable to subthreshold leakage. Junction leakage establishes a floor for leakage current that sets the maximum time a dynamically stored value can be retained. For typical process parameters and for small storage nodes, worst-case storage times are no more than a few milliseconds.

Source–drain junction leakage currents are usually modeled by considering the area and perimeter of the diffusion terminal separately. For modern processes, currents are in the range of a few $fA/\mu m^2$ for the area leakage and a few $fA/\mu m$ for the perimeter at room temperature. Leakage current increases by roughly a factor of two for each $10°C$ temperature increase, and thus it is two orders of magnitude higher for typical junction operating temperatures.

Millisecond storage retention time is usually not a problem when operating a chip at speed, but it may be a serious problem for testing. In many modern foundries, I_{DDQ} tests are required (measurements of quiescent chip power supply current can be used creatively to perform a variety of tests [Rajsuma95]). These tests require stopping the clocks, and all other activity in a chip, for many milliseconds at a time.

The consequences of dynamic charge decay can become much more serious than simply a loss of correct logic values. As charge leaks in a purely dynamic circuit, the voltage on a CMOS input, such as the input to the inverter in Figure 12-20(a), may spend considerable time in the range where both NFET and PFET in the inverter are turned on. Under these circumstances, the inverter, and perhaps stages driven by the inverter, will consume considerable static current. I_{DDQ} tests will, of course, yield no useful information if the quiescent supply current is dominated by overlap currents in large numbers of leaky dynamic latches. Worse yet, if a stage designed to source large currents, such as a pad output

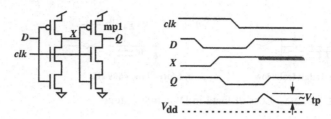

FIGURE 12-21   Stored Charge Loss Due to Power Supply Noise

driver, finds itself in this situation for long periods, metal-migration limits in power supply conductors may be exceeded and the chip destroyed.

There is considerable evidence that subthreshold leakage varies considerably from one part of a semiconductor die to another, and there is some probability of finding highly localized areas where leakage currents are much larger than average. The statistical variation in subthreshold leakage is particularly large for devices drawn at minimum channel length; consequently, when designing dynamic circuitry it may be prudent to draw devices slightly longer than minimum when their source–drain circuits include a dynamic storage node.

12.1.3.3 Power Supply Noise

Dynamic storage suffers from another potential problem illustrated, for example, in the single-phase dynamic latch discussed in Section 12.1.1 and shown in Figure 12-21.

In this scenario, D makes a transition while the clock is asserted that causes the internal node X to go HI, pulling Q LO. Once the clock goes LO, however, D returns HI, leaving X storing its high dynamically, as indicated by the dashed line. If a noise spike arrives on V_{DD} while X is a dynamic HI, and if the spike is greater than the PFET threshold, $mp1$ will turn on and pull Q HI. This situation is likely to be worse when the circuitry ahead of the latch is running at its highest speed; then D may make its HI-to-LO transition just before the setup time of the latch, perhaps leaving X only partly charged HI. In this case the noise spike need not even be as large as V_{TP} to destroy the data stored dynamically on the latch output. This failure can be prevented by a keeper transistor attached to the X node, as shown in Figure 12-3(c).

Unrestored dynamic latches that use only N-pass gates are particularly susceptible to supply noise because a stored high of $(V_{DD} - V_{TN})$ typically leaves the inverter PFET above threshold and slightly turned on. It may take only a small excursion of the supply voltage to turn the PFET on sufficiently to override the NFET pulldown and snag the latch output.

12.1.3.4 Clock Slope

Flip-flops are subject to failure if the slope of the clock waveform is degraded beyond a certain point. As with the other failure mechanisms we have discussed, dynamic flip-flops are particularly susceptible to this failure mode. The dynamic N-pass-gate flip-flop will again serve as an example, as shown in Figure 12-22. Here a high has been latched on the previous low-going active edge of the clock;

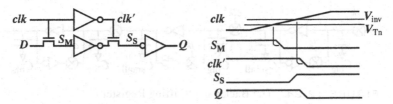

FIGURE 12-22   An Example of Clock-Slope Failure

then D goes low. As the clock begins its low-to-high (inactive) transition, it exceeds V_{TN} before reaching the clock inverter's switching threshold. The input pass gate turns on, removing the high stored on S_M, before the slave pass gate can be turned off, and thus the new data races through. In short, the latch fails because the slow clock edge extends the master latch's contamination time beyond the slave's hold time.

The TSPC flip-flop exhibits a slightly different form of clock–slope failure [LarsSven94]; consider the negative TSPC edge-triggered flip-flop in Figure 12-23.

Assume that clk is low, node b is high, and Q' is low. On the next rising (inactive) edge, node b is precharged low by $mn1$ in preparation for the next transfer of data from master to slave. However, if the clock's rising edge is slow, there is the possibility that node b may go low before $mp2$ is fully shut off, and the low that is supposed to be held dynamically on Q' will be destroyed by current flowing through $mp1, mp2$. A design requirement for this flip-flop is, then, to make $mn1$ only large enough to discharge node b fully during $clk = $ high; this strategy will improve the flip-flop's resistance to clock-slope failure but cannot eliminate it entirely.

In general, static flip-flops are more robust to clock-slope degradation than dynamic ones. For example, in a static pass gate flip-flop the restoring feedback introduces hysteresis in the switching characteristics. By adjusting the amount of feedback, it is possible to make this circuit reasonably immune to clock-slope failure, at least in the absence of noise.

The most important means of avoiding this failure mode is correct design of the clock distribution network for a chip. The wires that deliver clocks across a chip region are RC delay lines that not only introduce skew between different parts of a clock network but also attenuate the high-frequency components of the clock waveform, degrading edge rates. Fortunately, measures we described to reduce skew in Section 9.7.2 also tend to preserve edge rates. The design of latches and flip-flops and of clock distribution networks must be carefully coordinated.

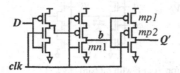

FIGURE 12-23   Fast-Precharge Failure in TSPC Flip-Flop

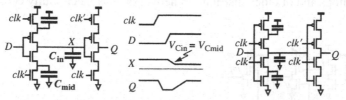

FIGURE 12-24   The Backward-Shifting Register

It is worth noting that clock-slope failures are often most pronounced under conditions of high supply voltage, low temperature, and best-case fabrication. These conditions give the fastest switching transistors and highest FET gate capacitances on RC lines. Wiring parasitics are usually uncorrelated with transistor fabrication, and therefore it is necessary to consider worst-case RC delays along with best-case FETs.

12.1.3.5   Charge Sharing

Perhaps the best-known cause of failure in dynamic latches (and other dynamic structures) is *charge sharing*, a phenomenon that occurs when two capacitors at different voltages become connected, for example, by turning on an FET. This problem was described briefly in the discussion of precharged and domino logic gates (Sections 4.3.3.2 and 4.3.3.3). Charge sharing can lead to unexpected, even bizarre, behavior in dynamic circuits.

A famous example, described in [GlasDobb85], is outlined in Figure 12-24. This shift register is composed of stages that include clocked restoring feedback. By assumption, the layout has been executed in such a way that the input capacitance of each stage is much larger than the output capacitance of the previous stage. Examination of the middle stage in the figure reveals that when *clk* goes high, data are supposed to be transferred into the right-hand stage, and at the same time the feedback path around the center stage is enabled to store the data at that stage. However, if the pass gates along the signal path are drawn wide, $C_{big} \gg C_{small}$, and the inverters are relatively weak, then the process of equilibrating the voltages on C_{big} and C_{small} can cause the data on the output of the center stage to be overwritten by the data previously stored on the input of the third stage, and the restoring feedback path carries the new data back to the input of the center stage. Under these circumstances, the shifter shifts data backwards!

Another example of a charge-sharing failure mode for dynamic latches is revealed in Figure 12-25, which shows two ways to construct a flip-flop from tristate inverters. Logically, it makes no difference whether the clocked FETs in the tristate inverters are outboard (as shown in Figure 12-25(a)) or inboard, as shown

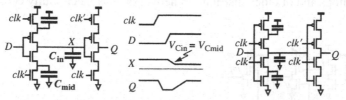

(a) Tristate inverter FF with   (b) Waveforms for   (c) FF with inboard clocked
    outboard clocked FETs   circuit (a)   FETs immune to this fault

FIGURE 12-25   Two Forms of Flip-Flop Built from Tristate Inverters

in Figure 12-25(c). However, the outboard form has a potential charge-sharing hazard, as illustrated in the waveforms in Figure 12-25(b). Suppose that D is low as clk goes high and that X is high, driving the Q output low. After the master latch has become opaque, D makes a low-to-high transition, which turns on the NFET between X and the clk-NFET in the master latch. If the parasitic capacitance on this in-between node C_{mid} is large compared with the input capacitance C_{in} of the slave latch, then charge sharing can bring X's voltage down low enough to reach the switching threshold of the slave, corrupting the output data. If the clocked FETs are placed inboard, as in Figure 12-25(c), the flip-flop is immune to this problem; this arrangement is always preferred.

As we have discussed, latch failures from dynamic node decay, power supply noise, clock slope sensitivity, and charge sharing are especially problematic for dynamic latches and flip-flops. This perhaps explains why dynamic storage, once popular in MOS design, has largely fallen out of favor. Dynamic circuits offers significant advantages for performance-driven designs, however, and should not be rejected out of hand without first considering various ways of coping with their infirmities.

12.2 DELAY LINE CIRCUITS

The clock-generation circuits we will discuss in the remainder of this chapter and have discussed in Chapter 11 all require generation of adjustable, low-jitter delayed clocks and often groups of equally spaced delayed clocks. Adjustment is needed so that delay elements can be placed inside control loops that stabilize delays (or edge placement, or phase) by comparing a delayed clock against a reference. Generally it is desirable to have a wide adjustment range to accommodate, for example, a wide range of clock frequencies. All practical delay elements are susceptible to noise injection from power supplies, both directly from supply terminals to signal outputs and indirectly through delay-control inputs to signal outputs. Both direct noise and delay modulation are sources of jitter in delay elements. In this section we will explore circuit techniques for constructing delay elements that provide widely adjustable clock edge placement, introduce as little jitter as possible, and reject noise from power supplies.

12.2.1 Inverter Delay Lines

A CMOS inverter can be used as a simple delay element, and a delay line can be built by cascading a number of inverters. An adjustable delay line could be constructed as shown in Figure 12-26.

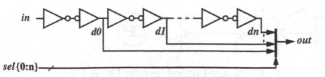

FIGURE 12-26 Inverter Delay Line

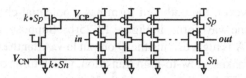

FIGURE 12-27   Current-Starved Inverter Delay Line

Here *pairs* of inverters are used so that all of the delayed versions of in have the same polarity. A multiplexer selects one of the delayed signals for output and sets the overall delay. There are several difficulties with this implementation.

1. Large delay range and fine-grain adjustment are mutually incompatible goals; if the difference in delay between two taps on this delay line is small, then many stages will be needed to realize a long overall delay, and jitter introduced at each stage will increase the jitter at the output as the square root of the number of stages.
2. The minimum delay adjustment step that is possible in a given technology, about two inverter delays, is often too coarse for high-precision, low-jitter applications. This problem can be solved with a more complex design in which inverter pairs with slightly different delays are used for vernier adjustment of the overall delay.
3. The digital delay adjustment of the delay line favors a digital control system to set the delay; as we will see, analog control systems are often more compact, power efficient, and accurate than their digital counterparts.

For all of these reasons it is desirable to find a delay element that has an analog control input.

The fundamental circuit elements that generate delay in an inverter delay line are FET current sources charging FET gate capacitances. Because FETs are voltage-controlled current sources, the most obvious way to add a voltage-mode control input is to add current control transistors in series with the switching transistors in the inverters. The current-starved inverter delay element we introduced in Figure 4-70 is used to form a delay line in Figure 12-27.

Another type of voltage-controlled inverter delay line is shown in Figure 12-28. Instead of controlling the charging current, this approach controls the capacitive load or, more precisely, the fraction of each 1-to-0 and 0-to-1 transition during which each inverter must charge its load capacitor. On a 0-to-1 transition at a delay stage, charging current flows into the load capacitor until the voltage on the capacitor reaches $V_{CN} - V_{TN}$, whereas on a 1-to-0 transition, the inverter must supply discharge current when the inverter output falls below this value. The load

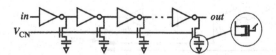

FIGURE 12-28   Capacitor-Loaded Inverter Delay Line

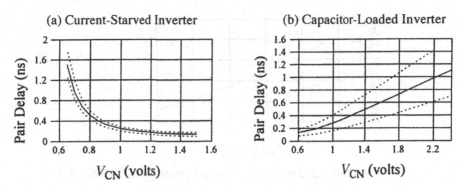

FIGURE 12-29   Delay Adjustment Range for Example Delay Elements

capacitors in this type of delay line are usually MOS capacitors. One possible implementation is shown in the inset of Figure 12-28, an NMOS capacitor with its gate connected to V_{DD} to ensure that its channel is biased well above V_{TN} (see Section 4.2.1.1). The source–drain junctions add some additional useful capacitance.

12.2.1.1   Delay Adjustment Range

Figure 12-29 shows the delay adjustment range from simulation of examples of the current-starved inverter delay line (a) and the capacitor-loaded delay line (b). Devices in the current-starved delay line are sized at $Sp = 2 \cdot Sn = 5.6\,\mu\text{m}/0.35\,\mu\text{m}$, $k = 10$ (S is the shape factor W/L for a device, k is the ratio used to size the current mirror that generates V_{CP} from V_{CN}). Switching FETs are drawn the same size as the current sources. The capacitor-loaded line uses devices of the same size and an NMOS capacitor drawn $28\,\mu\text{m}/2.8\,\mu\text{m}$. Delay for a pair of stages is shown, in order to sum the (typically different) rise and fall delays.

The solid lines in each graph represent simulated pair delay with the nominal FET parameters, $V_{DD} = 2.5$ V, and $T = 85°$C. Adjustment range is about 11:1 for the current-starved inverter delay element. Delays even larger than those plotted are possible, but the delay time's sensitivity to control voltage becomes so large that it becomes difficult to control jitter adequately. The capacitor-loaded delay element example gives about an 8:1 adjustment range; again, the delay range could be made larger but at the expense of an unreasonably large loading capacitor.

Although these delay ranges are obtainable for a particular set of FET models, power supply voltage, and temperature, we must usually design for worst-case behavior. The dotted curves represent our simulation of these conditions. The maximum delay is obtained under conditions of slow FET models, low supply voltage (2.25 V), and high temperature ($T = 110°$C). Minimum delay is found for conditions of fast FET models, high supply voltage (2.75 V), and low temperature ($T = 25°$C). The actual delay range we can count on lies between the largest delay we can get under best-case conditions and the smallest delay under worst-case conditions (about 7:1 for the current-starved inverter and only about 3.8:1 for the capacitor-loaded inverter).

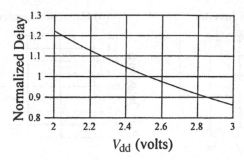

FIGURE 12-30 Power Supply Sensitivity of CMOS Inverter

12.2.1.2 Power-Supply Rejection in Inverter Delay Elements

Current-starved, capacitor-loaded, and simple inverter delay elements were used extensively in early designs (1980s) for on-chip phase-locked and delay-locked loops and are described in several of the references. These approaches have fallen out of favor in more recent designs because high-performance delay elements require much better power supply noise rejection than can be obtained in CMOS inverters.

To examine the inverter delay power supply sensitivity, we simulate a string of identical inverters and measure the delay through a pair of them. Figure 12-30 plots normalized inverter pair delay versus power supply voltage ($Sp = 2 \cdot Sn$, as above).

The graph indicates that the fractional variation in delay is about the same as the fractional variation in power supply voltage; a CMOS inverter has rather poor power supply rejection The slope of the curve can be understood from the τ-model we developed in Chapter 4. Equation (4-24) predicts that the delay per stage in an inverter chain should be

$$(12\text{-}1) \qquad \tau_{\text{Delay}} \propto \frac{V_{DD}}{I_{DSS}} \propto \frac{V_{DD}}{(V_{DD} - V_T)^2}$$

if we assume that the driving transistor is in saturation during most of the time an inverter is charging its output load. Roughly, delay should go as $1/V_{DD}$.

Supply sensitivity for a current-starved inverter delay element is shown in Figure 12-31. In this delay element, charging current is set by the current-source

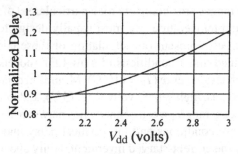

FIGURE 12-31 Supply Sensitivity for Current-Starved Inverter

FETs; consequently, our simple τ-model predicts that the delay should vary roughly as V_{DD}.

Though the slope of the power supply sensitivity curve for the current-starved inverter is opposite that of the simple inverter, the magnitude of the sensitivity is just as bad.

For purposes of this discussion, we define the supply sensitivity S_V as the fractional change in delay divided by the fractional change in supply voltage. The S_V is about 0.9 for the inverter, about 1.5 for the current-starved inverter delay element at the low end of the V_c range, and about 2.0 for the capacitor-loaded delay element. Noise on the power rails of an inverter delay line of any of the types we have described will produce large amounts of timing jitter.

12.2.1.3 Inverters with Regulated Supply Voltage

Because the main infirmity of inverter-based delay stages is power-supply sensitivity, we could attempt to improve their performance by stabilizing the power supply in some way. The simplest technique is to add a low-pass filter between the supply source and a "clean" supply dedicated to the delay elements, as shown in Figure 12-32(a). Only the high-frequency part of the supply noise is removed, but if the cutoff frequency of the filter is well within the bandwidth of the delay control loop, this may be a winning strategy. In Figure 12-32(b), an active series regulator cleans up the supply. The reference voltage V_{ref} could be generated on-chip (e.g., in a band-gap reference).

It is even possible to make a virtue of the inverter's large supply voltage sensitivity. One of the references [vonKaen96] uses the supply terminal as the delay adjustment control input; the implementation in this reference is much like Figure 12-32(b), using V_{ref} as the delay control input; the control loop filter is also incorporated into the regulator.

12.2.2 Differential Delay Elements

Delay in a CMOS stage such as an inverter is proportional to the charge that must be moved to switch the next stage and is inversely proportional to the current available to do the charging. In the current-starved delay line we made the charging current nearly independent of supply voltage. However, the charge movement needed to switch the next stage is proportional to the supply voltage (it appears explicitly in the switching threshold for the inverter, Eq. (4-18)).

Differential structures (Section 4.3.6) amplify the difference between two voltages rather than the difference between a voltage and built-in reference that

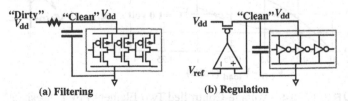

(a) Filtering   (b) Regulation

FIGURE 12-32   Supply Filtering for Delay Elements

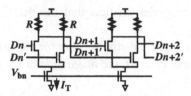

FIGURE 12-33   Differential Delay Elements

depends on the power supply voltage, and consequently a differential amplifier used as a delay element inherently has better supply-noise rejection than an inverter. An example of a delay line composed of differential amplifiers is sketched in Figure 12-33.

Each signal pair in the delay line swings between V_{DD} and $V_{LO} = I_T R$, where the differential tail current I_T is set by the bias voltage V_{bn}. In Section 4.3.6 we showed that the differential amplifier has a low-pass response given by Eq. (4-61). The stage delay is proportional to the load resistance in the stage, R, and thus we can vary the delay in a differential delay line by varying R. For ideal elements in the differential pair and for resistive loads, changes in the power supply voltage change only the common-mode voltage on the D, D' pairs; consequently, under these assumptions power supply noise will produce no jitter in stage delay. It is possible in practice to approach this ideal fairly closely. It remains to show how to construct loads that are adjustable (to control the delay) and as nearly resistive as possible (to reject power supply noise).

12.2.2.1   Adjustable PFET Resistor

In Section 4.3.6.5 we discussed the two-element FET resistor (Figure 4-61b) [BabaTeme84, MoonZagh90, GabaKnau92]. This arrangement combines the diode-like drain characteristics of a FET whose $V_{GS} = V_{DS}$ with the triode-like characteristic of a biased FET ($V_{GS} = $ constant). The opposite curvatures of the two characteristics combine to give an S-shaped, nearly resistive one. Figure 12-34

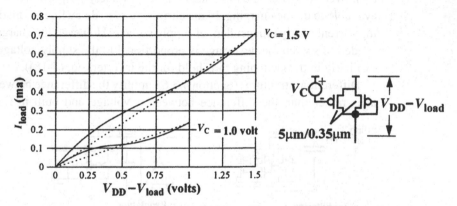

FIGURE 12-34   Voltage-Controlled Two-Element PFET "Resistor"

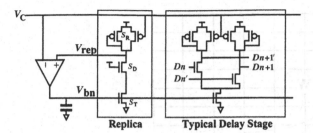

FIGURE 12-35 Replica-Biased Differential Delay Line Circuitry

shows the results of a SPICE simulation in which the "triode" V_{GS} is set by a control voltage V_C; the currents for two different control voltages are shown.

If the voltage swing across the load is limited between 0 and V_C, then the characteristic of this load is approximately resistive, and the resistance is set by the control voltage, V_C. The load is a transconductance controlled by V_C, and we can find its small-signal value by computing dI/dV at a convenient point, namely where $V_{load} = V_C$. Both FETs are in saturation, and thus if we ignore channel-length modulation, the current through each of the two FETs at this point is $\beta_P(V_C - V_{TP})^2$, and the transconductance is approximately

$$(12\text{-}2) \qquad g_m = \frac{\delta I}{\delta V_C} = 2\beta_P(V_C - V_{TP})$$

The low end of the signal swing in the differential stage can be set to any desired value by adjusting the tail current, I_T, appropriately. In a differential delay line, V_{LO} can be held at V_C by controlling I_T with a replica bias circuit like that of Figure 4-63(b).

12.2.2.2 Replica-Biased Delay Line

The circuitry for a replica-biased differential delay line is shown in Figure 12-35. Delay is set by the control input, V_C, which varies the effective resistance of the loads in the delay elements and thus varies the delay. The replica bias feedback adjusts the tail current by means of the bias voltage, V_{bn}, so that the "low" output of the replica, V_{rep}, tracks V_C. The replica is a duplicate of the "on" side of a typical delay element. This arrangement keeps the signal swing in the delay elements within the most linear part of the two-element resistor's characteristic.

12.2.2.3 Adjustment Range for Replica-Bias Delay Lines

Delay in a replica-biased delay element is proportional to C_{load}/g_{mload}, and from Eq. (12-2)

$$(12\text{-}3) \qquad T_D \propto \frac{C_{load}}{V_C - V_{TP}}$$

where C_{load} is the sum of the next-stage gate capacitance and parasitic wiring and drain capacitances. Figure 12-36 is a plot of single-stage delay versus control

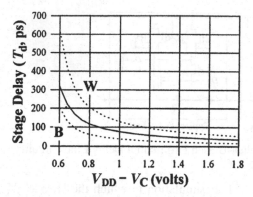

FIGURE 12-36   Delay Adjustment Range for Replica-Biased Delay Element

voltage for an example replica-biased delay line (with replica stage shape factors $S_R = 5\,\mu m/0.35\,\mu m$, $S_D = 10\,\mu m/0.35\,\mu m$, $S_T = 20\,\mu m/0.35\,\mu m$). The dotted lines show the delay at the same extrema of fabrication, V_{DD}, and temperature used in Figure 12-29. The shape of the curve is consistent with Eq. (12-3).

For control voltages less than 100 mV or so above V_{TP}, signal swings become very small and delay gain $(\delta T_d/\delta V_C)$ so large that noise on V_C, amplified by this gain, introduces unacceptable jitter. The practical range of adjustment for this stage is about 10:1 for any of the three simulations in the figure; taken across best- and worst-case operating conditions, adjustment range is about 4:1.

It should be noted that the adjustment range of a delay line can be greatly extended by having a two-tier adjustment scheme. In such a scheme, fine adjustment is accomplished by varying the control voltage, as we have discussed, but coarse adjustment is added, for example, by digitally selecting the number of delay stages in the delay line. Coarse adjustment would most likely be made only at system initialization.

12.2.2.4   Static Supply Sensitivity for the Replica-Biased Delay Stage

Figure 12-37 is a plot of stage delay versus V_C for the example replica-biased delay stage and supply voltages of 2.25 and 2.75 V ($\pm 10\%$ of nominal 2.5 V).

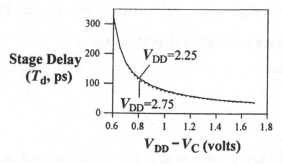

FIGURE 12-37   Static Supply Sensitivity for Replica-Biased Delay Element

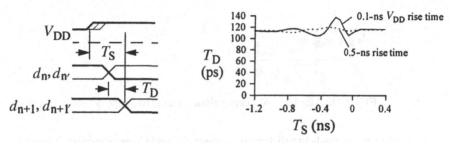

FIGURE 12-38   Dynamic Supply Sensitivity Simulation

Worst-case S_V is about 0.2 for this example, about an eightfold improvement over the current-starved inverter.[1]

12.2.2.5   Dynamic Supply Sensitivity

So far we have described the static supply sensitivity of various delay elements. Power supply noise may have significant high-frequency components, and these will introduce jitter that is worse than would be predicted from an estimate based only on static supply sensitivity. High-frequency supply noise will introduce jitter not only directly, by modulating the drain currents and switching thresholds of various devices, but indirectly through the device and wiring parasitic coupling capacitances. In a replica-biased differential delay line, supply noise at frequencies above the cutoff of the bias control loop cannot be compensated by the loop, and consequently the "resistors" will be moved away from their optimal operating range in a transient way.

Dynamic supply sensitivity is difficult to simulate because it is not easy to predict the nature of the noise on the supply rail. We can perform a far from perfect, but useful, evaluation of a delay element's resistance to transients on the supply voltage by running a simulation outlined in Figure 12-38. Using the example replica-biased delay line, with $V_{DD} - V_C$ fixed, we introduce a 0.1-ns 0.25-V step in V_{DD} at time T_S measured with respect to a signal transition within the delay line. We then determine the delay through an element as a function of T_S, marching the V_{DD} edge past the signal transition edge to find the worst-case interaction. As shown in the graph in the figure, the transient disturbance in stage delay is about 20%, which is much larger than the 2% static sensitivity. However, with a 0.5-ns V_{DD} edge, delay varies by only about 5%, as shown in the dashed line in the plot.

The results of this simulation can be understood with the model shown in Figure 12-39. R_L and R_H are the resistances of the inverting and noninverting

---

[1] Significantly better supply rejection can be obtained in practice. Our level-3 PFET model does not adequately capture the behavior of devices in real submicron processes in which PFETs have significantly worse channel-length modulation than we have shown and an extended transition region. Although these characteristics make PFETs rather poor switches, they are excellent resistors, much better than indicated in Figure 12-34. Better device modeling and more careful attention to circuit optimization will yield better results than in our example delay line. Some of the designs in the references claim supply sensitivities for replica-biased delay elements as low as 0.012.

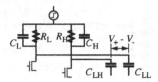

FIGURE 12-39 AC Equivalent Circuit for Supply Noise Injection

output loads in a differential stage, C_L and C_H are the capacitances across the loads, and C_{LH} and C_{LL} are the input capacitances of the next stage. The capacitances across the load devices are mostly due to the sum of the overlap capacitance, C_{GSO}, of the diode-connected PFET in the load, its channel capacitance, and C_{GDO} of the V_C-controlled PFET (the controlled PFET's gate is connected via a low AC impedance to V_{DD}). The input capacitances are the sum of the channel capacitances and (Miller-effect-enhanced) overlap capacitances. These capacitances vary with the operating point of the load device (Section 4.2.1), and their nonlinearities translate an AC voltage on V_{DD} to a differential voltage across the next stage input.

Because supply noise injection is high-passed by the load devices in a differential stage, removing the high-frequency part of the supply noise above the cutoff of the loads will mitigate the effect. Methods for dealing with the problem include careful supply network design, bypass capacitance local to the delay elements, and perhaps addition of some intentional series resistance in the supply network between noise generators and delay elements.

12.2.3 Circuit and Layout Details

This section discusses some of the details for designing delay lines and VCOs.

12.2.3.1 Replica Control Loop Stability

The replica bias circuitry is a control system that must be guaranteed stable for correct operation. A replica bias generator is shown in Figure 12-40(a) and an approximate AC equivalent circuit is shown in (b).

Typical (simple) CMOS operational amplifiers have gains of 50–100, whereas the gain of the replica stage is roughly $g_{mN}/g_{mLOAD} \approx 5$–10, and thus typical loop gain is about 1,000. Poles are introduced into the transfer function at the outputs of the two gain stages. One is formed by the output resistance of the operational amplifiers and the capacitance of the parallel collection of tail transistors, and another is formed by the conductance of the symmetric load and the input capacitance of the operational amplifier.

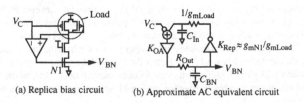

(a) Replica bias circuit   (b) Approximate AC equivalent circuit

FIGURE 12-40 Replica Bias Control Loop

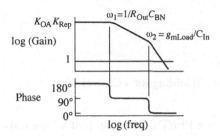

FIGURE 12-41 Bode Plot of Replica-Bias Control Loop

A Bode plot for the open-loop gain of the controller will look like Figure 12-41. If the poles are very close together, the 12 dB/octave rolloff causes the phase to reach 0°, at a frequency at which the gain is greater than unity; under these conditions, the loop will be unstable. Stability is usually ensured by moving the pole associated with the operational amplifier's output downward in frequency until there is a "safe" phase margin at unity gain. (A typical rule of thumb requires >35° or so of phase margin.) Note that loop instability will be worst at high loop gain and low ω_2, both of which conditions occur at the smallest value of $V_{DD} - V_C$ (smallest load conductance) and under best-case fabrication, high supply voltage, and low temperature.

The frequency of the operational amplifier's output pole can be reduced by increasing the output resistance of the amplifier (which generally reduces its power consumption) or by increasing the capacitance on V_{BN}. Additional capacitance lowers the AC impedance between V_{BN} and GND and helps prevent noise injection into the V_{BN} node. The lower limit on the bandwidth of the replica-bias control loop is established by the need to track changes in the timing control voltage, V_C, and thus the replica-bias loop bandwidth should at least be greater than the bandwidth of the timing control loop. Note that there may be other poles and zeros in the loop circuitry that affect loop stability; simulation with an accurate model of circuit parasitics extracted from the layout is required in this part of the design of a timing loop.

Any of a variety of operational amplifiers designs will work well in this application. The authors have successfully used simple self-biased amplifiers (like the Chappel amplifier of Section 11.3.1.2). A particularly clever approach [ManeHoro93] provides the operational amplifier's tail current bias from its own output. The scheme is outlined in Figure 12-42.

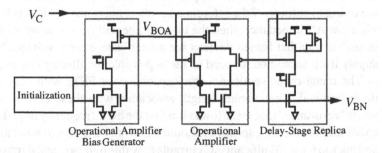

FIGURE 12-42 Self-Biased Operational Amplifier for Replica Bias Generator

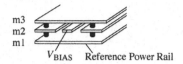

V_{BIAS} Reference Power Rail

FIGURE 12-43   Electrostatic Shielding for a Critical Bias

The operational amplifier is a PFET differential pair whose tail current is set by the bias voltage V_{BOA}. This current is, in turn, set by the replica bias voltage, V_{BN}, which establishes the current in the operational amplifier's bias generator. This arrangement allows the operational amplifier's bias to be independent of power supply fluctuations. However, there are two stable operating points for the operational amplifier bias current, and one of them is at zero current. To avoid this operating condition, a bias initialization circuit is required that, upon power-up, ensures that some current is flowing in the operational amplifier's tail transistor and that V_{BN} is high enough to sustain operation after initialization.

12.2.3.2   Power Routing and Bypassing

Generating accurate delays with controlled delay elements requires distributing precise bias voltages from a central generator to an array of delay elements. Noise on the distribution networks for these biases introduces jitter in the intended timing relationships; voltage drops introduce systematic errors.

The two lines of defense against noise injection are isolation and bypassing. Isolation attempts to reduce noise injected directly into a bias line by increasing the impedance of the coupling mechanism, usually capacitive. The layout of delay circuits should, for example, avoid passing signal wires near bias wires. Where multiple levels of metal interconnect are available, it may be possible to construct partial or full electrostatic shields around bias lines, as shown in Figure 12-43.

Bypassing reduces noise by placing a low impedance between the bias line and its reference power supply. In the delay circuits we have described in this chapter, capacitance is often required to establish a stabilizing pole in a control loop transfer function. By distributing this capacitance across the area of a delay circuit and connecting it robustly to the appropriate reference power supply, the often large area required for the capacitor does double duty as control loop and bypass capacitor.

Bypassing a critical bias voltage to its reference supply also has the benefit that noise injected into the power supply will have less effect on the bias condition we are trying to enforce. If the reference supply is noisy, but the bias is bypassed to it via a low AC impedance, then the bias voltage will tend to move with the supply in such a way that biased devices see a fixed gate–source voltage. Noise on the supply itself should be reduced as far as possible by filtering and bypassing.

The metal-oxide semiconductor capacitors are FETs with only one source–drain terminal. The channel length associated with these devices introduces a series "resistance" that sets a lower limit on the high-frequency impedance. Metal-oxide semiconductor capacitors should therefore be drawn as wide as practicable and not too long. Significant AC currents flow through loop and bypass capacitors,

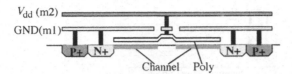

FIGURE 12-44 Cross Section of Power Bus Pair with Bypass Capacitor

and therefore they should have large-area well or substrate contacts adjacent to or abutting their source–drain terminals. A layout that efficiently combines a bypass capacitor and a power bus pair is shown in Figure 12-44; additional useful capacitance is obtained from the overlap of the metal and polysilicon wiring layers in this layout. A PMOS capacitor provides the additional well–substrate capacitance at the cost of a second P+ guard ring.

Voltage drop in the power rails is also a serious concern, because a difference in supply voltage between bias generator and biased device also changes V_{GS}. This is particularly true in circuits that consume static current. Voltage drop induced by these currents on the supply wiring series resistance introduces a systematic error in bias conditions and therefore timing. The best line of defense against this problem is robust power distribution wiring.

These points and recommendations are summarized in Figure 12-45.

1. Design robust power wiring to reduce resistance and minimize bias shifts.
2. Use metal-only wiring for bias voltages; series resistance in bias distribution may introduce additional unwanted poles in control functions.
3. Distribute loop control capacitors and tie them robustly to respective reference power supplies; capacitors do double duty as bypass elements.
4. Avoid coupling between bias and signal wiring; electrostatic shielding may be helpful.
5. Use filters and bypass power supplies to reduce noise.

12.2.3.3 Matching and Balancing

The offset voltage induced by transistor mismatches in differential timing circuits leads to systematic timing errors; therefore, care should be taken to use layout styles that promote good matching, as outlined in Chapter 11. Layouts for delay

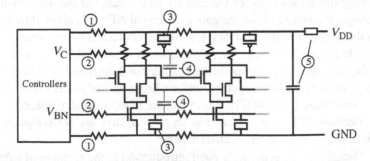

FIGURE 12-45 Layout, Wiring, and Bypassing Concerns for Delay Elements

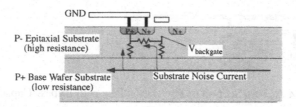

FIGURE 12-46   Substrate Noise Injection

lines that are intended to generate a set of equally spaced clocks also require very careful attention to parasitic capacitances in signal wiring. These capacitances should be balanced for each differential signal pair and be equal for all pairs. If buffering is needed for some, but not all, delay line outputs, the unbuffered delay stages require a "dummy" buffer to keep capacitive loads equal on all stages. The source-coupled node in differential timing stages also deserves careful attention in layout. Capacitance on this node shunts the current source, and thus the power supply isolation afforded by the current source's high impedance is rendered less effective at high frequency.

12.2.3.4   Substrate Noise

In addition to the power supply and bias rails, differential delay elements also share a substrate terminal. Modern "epi" CMOS processes feature a thin, relatively high-resistance P-type substrate (P−) grown epitaxially on top of a relatively low-resistance P-type base wafer material (P+), as shown in Figure 12-46. Source and drain terminals for NFETs and PFET N-wells are diffused into the epitaxial P− layer. The epi arrangement is intended to reduce the possibility of latchup by diminishing the effectiveness of lateral parasitic bipolar devices, thus allowing PFETs and NFETs to be spaced closer together to achieve higher circuit density.

The substrate terminal of an NFET is near ground potential, and an ohmic P+ diffusion into the P− epi substrate is provided so that metal ground conductors can be connected periodically to the substrate to help enforce this condition. The underlying, low-resistance P+ material is connected vertically to the ground system only through the P− substrate and unfortunately tends to acquire a voltage different from ground potential because of currents injected from many noise sources distributed over a chip. Because it has low resistance, these currents "tunnel" along under the high-resistance P− for long distances. Locally, there will be voltage difference between the underlying P+ material and the P− substrate. This voltage, measured under the gate of a typical NFET, is divided by the resistance of the epi layer to the nearest P+ substrate contact. If the substrate noise is large, the "back-gate" voltages for a collection of nearby NFETs may differ, and in a delay line this variation perturbs biasing conditions and introduces jitter. Even large, robust P+ ohmic contacts will not be particularly effective in shunting noise currents away from NFETs and in fact are likely to be detrimental.

Because PFETs are situated in an N-well, they are not seriously affected by these long-range substrate disturbances.

[VergSchm95] provides a good introduction to the problem of substrate noise. A recommendation for mixed-signal CMOS chips developed in this reference

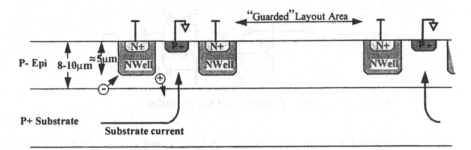

FIGURE 12-47   N-Well Noise Isolation Structure

may be useful in the context of precision delay lines. An N-well structure is used to protect analog circuits from free carriers and noise transmitted through the P+ substrate, as shown in Figure 12-47.

N+ and P+ regions are diffused only a micron or so into the epitaxial substrate, but N-wells are driven 4–5 μm into the epi, itself only 8–10 μm thick. N-wells biased at V_{DD} establish large depletion regions that trap free electrons and force free holes into the underlying P+ substrate, thereby forming a barrier against free carriers. The grounded P+ substrate contacts are "protected" by this arrangement and substrate currents terminate on these contacts. The epi substrate in the region between these guard structures should have nearly constant potential and is therefore "safe" for building well-matched NFETs; no P+ substrate contacts are allowed in the "guarded" region, for these contacts would shift the substrate potential.

12.2.4   Other Differential Timing Components

12.2.4.1   Small-Swing to Full-Swing Buffers

The signals within a differential delay line have small swings referenced to one of the supply rails. In many applications a buffer is needed to convert small-swing to full-swing signals. Such a buffer should isolate the small-swing delay-element signals from noise on the full-swing outputs, and the delay through the buffer should be as insensitive as possible to supply voltage variation. Various types of gate-isolated differential buffers can be constructed to meet both these requirements.

A simple buffer is shown in Figure 12-48. This buffer consists of two stages. The first converts the small-swing differential voltage input to a differential pair of currents that produce bias voltages $V1, V2$ in the NFET's sized Sn. These biases generate currents scaled by k in the second stage, whose current-mirror load converts the differential currents into a full-swing output. The factor k can be larger than 1 so that a large load can be driven on B while keeping the input capacitance on D, D' small. If B' is needed, a second copy of the second stage can be added, with its current mirror reversed. Because the current in the second stage is set by the voltage swing at the inputs, it might appear that the delay through this buffer has first-order supply sensitivity similar to the current-

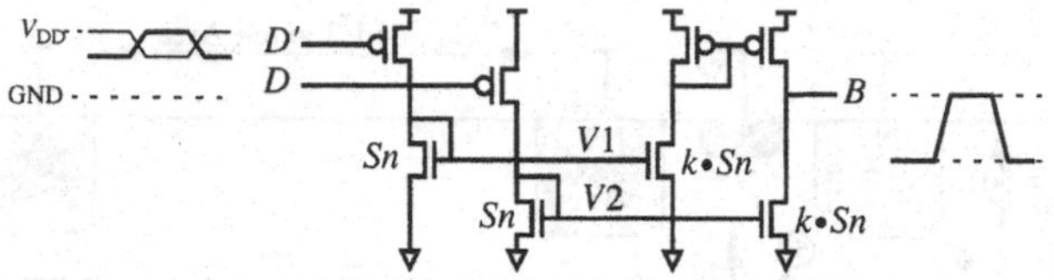

FIGURE 12-48   Differential Output Buffer

starved inverter (proportional to V_{DD}). However, the channel-length modulation in the PFETs in the circuit compensates by supplying more current at higher supply voltages; therefore, the buffer's delay is fairly insensitive to supply voltage variation.

A buffer developed in [Maneatis96] takes advantage of the replica-bias conditions established for the delay elements to construct a buffer that also uses the replica-bias tail current, thereby tracking the voltage swings within the delay elements. This approach, sketched in Figure 12-49, also uses a current-mirror load to convert a small-swing signal to a full-swing one. As in Figure 12-48, if B' is needed, a second copy of the output stage can be added with the current mirror reversed.

12.2.4.2   Interpolators

It is often useful to interpolate between two fixed delay values to generate a third. In a replica-biased delay line, an auxiliary circuit that uses the same replica-bias conditions as the delay elements can perform interpolation, as shown in Figure 12-50.

The interpolator is drawn as nearly identically to the typical delay stage as possible but has two current-tail transistors and two differential pairs. The two current-tail transistors have shape factors that are scaled down from the tail transistor in the typical delay stage, but the shape factors add up so that the total current through the load is the same as in the typical delay stage. If the inputs Da,Da' and Db,Db' are from a delay stage spaced n stages apart in a delay line, then, assuming $k1+k2=1$ and ignoring differences in parasitic capacitances between the interpolator and a typical delay stage, the output of the interpolator introduces a fixed delay of one delay stage (Td) plus a delay that is adjustable between 0 and $n \cdot Td$ by varying $k2$ (while keeping $k1+k2=1$). The example in Figure 12-50 shows a replica-biased interpolator, but any differential stage will perform interpolation weighted by the tail currents.

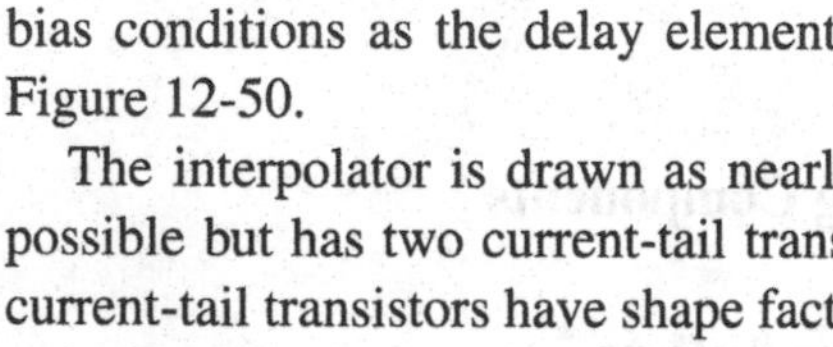

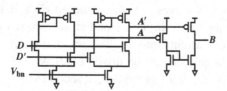

FIGURE 12-49   Replica-Biased Output Buffer

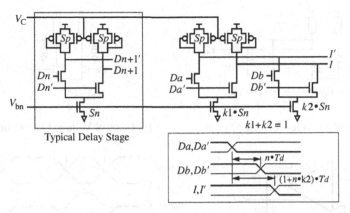

FIGURE 12-50 Replica Biased Interpolator

It is usually desirable to control the interpolation value. Two methods for digitally setting the interpolation factor are shown in Figure 12-51.

In Figure 12-51(a), the current delivered to the two differential pairs is determined by a binary-weighted set of three current tails. When $k\{2:0\} = 111$, all of the current is delivered to the left-hand differential pair, and when $= 000$ all is delivered to the right-hand pair. Other codes on k interpolate I, I' between the Da and Db inputs.

Binary weighting may present difficulties for some applications. First, it may be difficult to construct current tail transistors that are $1/(n-1)$ sized; in fact, the most accurate way to perform this sizing is to make full-sized current tails $(1 \cdot Sn)$ by paralleling $(n-1)$ identical devices. Second, the transition between certain codes (e.g., $011 \rightarrow 100$) may introduce glitches in the output. To avoid these problems, a thermometer-coded version of the adjustment variable k can be used to switch equally weighted current tails. A possible implementation for a 2-bit k is shown in Figure 12-51(b). This version uses redundant copies of the current tail transistor to establish the tail current; it is convenient for layout but may introduce some common-mode noise into the output owing to charge injection at the nodes between tail transistors and switching transistors. The two

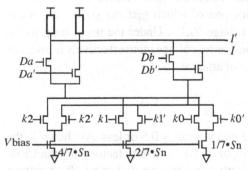

(a) Binary-Weighted Current Sources

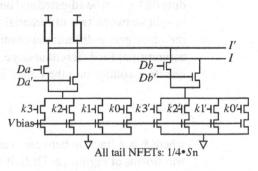

(b) Equally Weighted Current Sources

FIGURE 12-51 Digitally Adjustable Interpolators

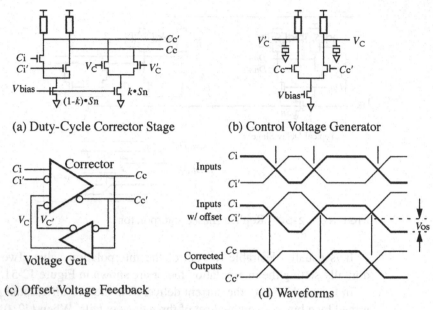

(a) Duty-Cycle Corrector Stage   (b) Control Voltage Generator

(c) Offset-Voltage Feedback   (d) Waveforms

FIGURE 12-52   Duty Cycle Corrector

implementations are, of course, binary-weighted and monotonic digital-to-analog converters.

12.2.4.3 Duty-Cycle Correctors

For applications in which the timing of both edges of the clock is critical, the duty cycle of the signals within a delay line must be held at 50%. Active control of the duty cycle may be needed to compensate for variations in switching thresholds and other asymmetries in a delay structure and for voltage offsets in a reference clock, perhaps generated off-chip. A variation on the theme of the interpolator can be used to servo the duty factor of a differential clock toward 50%. A circuit for this function is outlined in Figure 12-52.

In Figure 12-52(a), a differential stage takes as input a signal pair Ci,Ci' whose duty factor is to be adjusted and outputs a corrected signal pair Cc,Cc'. Tail current is split between two differential pairs, one of which gets the signal pair while the other gets a differential control voltage $V_c,V_{c'}$. Under the usual simplifying assumptions for differential stages, the control voltage input effectively introduces an offset voltage into the Ci,Ci' input of amount

$$(12\text{-}4) \qquad V_{OS} = \frac{k}{(1-k)}(V_c - V_{c'})$$

where k is a fraction between 0 and 1 and is usually 0.5 or less. As shown in the waveforms of Figure 12-52(d), if the input Ci,Ci' has a duty factor other than 50% and the rise and fall times are sufficiently long, we can dial in an offset voltage that will bring the output of the corrector stage to 50% duty factor.

The voltage generator in Figure 12-52(b) is a differential stage whose outputs are loaded with large capacitors (usually FETs). If the time constant $R_{load} \cdot C_{load}$ is much larger than the period of the waveform on Cc,Cc', the differential voltage between outputs $V_c, V_{c'}$ is proportional to the duty factor of Cc,Cc'. If the voltage generator is connected in a feedback loop around the corrector stage, as shown in Figure 12-52(c), the feedback tends to pull Cc,Cc' toward a 50% duty factor.

Practical considerations for designing a duty-factor corrector include ensuring small (slow) enough edge slopes that the corrector has something to work with (sinusoidal inputs work well with correctors) and obtaining sufficient feedback gain that the control voltage has enough "authority" over the corrected outputs. The feedback gain is adjustable through k but, as k is made larger, less of the corrector stage's gain is available to the signal input, and the output swing limits will become strong functions of the control voltage. A follow-on stage may be needed to "clean up" the swing offset in the Cc,Cc' outputs.

12.2.4.4 Clock Input Conditioning

A DLL receives its reference clock from a source whose signal swing and common-mode voltage generally are different from the "native" signal swing of the delay elements inside the delay line. The difference between the internal common-mode voltage and that of the external signal is amplified by the common-mode gain of the first stage. The common-mode gain is less than unity and is inverting, and thus the output swing of the first stage is generally closer to, but still not equal to, the native signal swing. This effect may persist for a few stages into the delay line, reduced at each stage by the (fractional) common-mode gain, and it is coupled through load imperfections into the timing of the differential signal crossings, thus introducing systematic jitter into the delay line.

This effect can be avoided, and the common-mode input range greatly extended, by AC coupling and DC restoration of the input clock, as shown in Figure 12-53(a). A common-mode voltage reference generator can be built using a copy of a typical delay stage with inputs shorted to outputs. Input capacitors are charged to the difference between internal and external common-mode voltages through resistors, which may be implemented, for example, with permanently on pass gates implemented with long-channel FETs. Linear capacitors should be used for this purpose. A suitable capacitor can be constructed from multiple levels of metal interconnect, thus taking best advantage of both plate and fringing capacitances, as sketched in Figure 12-53(b). The input capacitors and resistors form a high-pass filter whose cutoff frequency should be set well below the lowest frequency of the external clock.

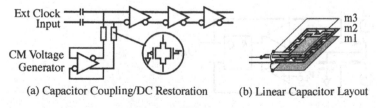

(a) Capacitor Coupling/DC Restoration (b) Linear Capacitor Layout

FIGURE 12-53 Clock Input Conditioning

12.3 VOLTAGE-CONTROLLED OSCILLATORS

This section provides a brief overview of oscillator circuits that can be integrated onto a chip. Off-chip oscillator components are outside the scope of this text but are discussed in some of the references. Oscillators are often categorized as first-order and second-order, according to the order of the differential equation that describes the behavior of the basic timing component. First-order oscillators typically develop a signal whose period is determined by the charging time for a capacitor. Second-order oscillators use a tuned (LRC) circuit, or a mechanical analog of a tuned circuit, as a timing reference.

12.3.1 First-Order Oscillators

A model of a first-order oscillator is shown in Figure 12-54.

A capacitor is charged from one of two current sources: a window comparator determines when the capacitor voltage has reached a high or low limit, or an R-S flip-flop remembers the previous direction of the capacitor charging voltage and flips the direction of charging each half cycle. The flip-flop output is, nominally, a differential pair of periodic signals with a 50% duty factor. The frequency of the oscillator can be changed by varying the strengths of the current sources; if the two current sources are set the same, the frequency is

(12-5) $$F = \frac{2C(V_{HI} - V_{LO})}{I}$$

A simpler *relaxation oscillator* can be built with only one comparator; when the capacitor voltage reaches a threshold, a reset circuit quickly reinitializes the voltage to begin a new cycle. Relaxation oscillators typically produce narrow (reset) pulses.

These ideas have been used in essentially this form for on-chip clock generators, as outlined in some of the references. However, modern designs that employ PLLs for clock generation and alignment and for clock recovery are more frequently built using ring oscillators composed of voltage-controlled delay elements of one of the types we discussed in Section 12.2. Current-starved inverter and differential delay element implementations are shown in Figure 12-55.

A VCO built from delay elements combines all of the functions of a first-order oscillator into one circuit element; the timing capacitor and its charging current are implemented directly in the delay elements, the memory function is implicit

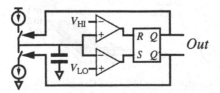

FIGURE 12-54   Conceptual Model of a First-Order Oscillator

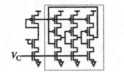 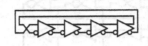

(a) VCO using I-starved inverters (b) VCO using differential delay elements

FIGURE 12-55 Voltage-Controlled Oscillators Using Delay Elements

in the delay through the chain of stages, and the toggle is explicit in the overall inversion around the loop.

The frequency of a ring oscillator is

(12-6)
$$F = \frac{1}{N(T_{DH} - T_{DL})}$$

where N is the number of stages, and T_{DH} and T_{DL} are the delays for rising and falling outputs, respectively. If the ring oscillator is built using replica-bias differential delay elements, then from Eq. (12-3)

(12-7)
$$F \propto \frac{(V_C - V_{TP})}{2N}$$

As we will see in Section 12.5, this linear dependence on control voltage is handy for constructing stable frequency control loops. Using the example delay element from Section 12.2.2.2, an eight-stage VCO has the frequency-control characteristic shown in Figure 12-56. Note that this is only a portion of the available control voltage range, and therefore the oscillator has a large frequency range. It should be cautioned, however, that the fractional change in frequency per absolute change in control voltage is very large at low frequencies, and thus noise on the control voltage will produce larger amounts of *phase noise* at low frequencies.

12.3.1.1 Array Oscillators

[ManeHoro93] describes an oscillator structure that uses the interpolator circuit (Section 12.2.4.2) as its delay element. Figure 12-57 shows a two-dimensional array of these elements that form an *array oscillator*. All signal paths in the figure are differential, and the two inputs at each element are interpolated 50–50 to generate the output.

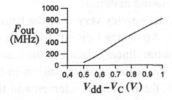

FIGURE 12-56 Frequency Versus Control Voltage for Eight-Stage Replica-Bias VCO

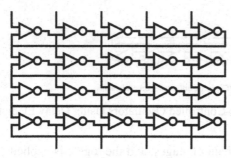

FIGURE 12-57   Array Oscillator

To complete the array oscillator, the inputs at the top are connected to the outputs at the bottom but with an arbitrary offset. The connections between horizontal rings force the rings all to oscillate at the same frequency while maintaining a fixed phase relationship to one another. The offset in the top-to-bottom connections forces the delay across the vertical dimension to be an integer multiple of the delay through an individual delay element. [ManeHoro93] describes the design criteria for this structure and its application in generating groups of signals that differ by precise delays.

12.3.2   Second-Order Oscillators

Second-order oscillators are useful in applications that require a periodic signal with very low phase noise; this *spectral purity* is traded against the ability to vary the frequency over a wide range.

12.3.2.1   Crystal Oscillators

One of the most important second-order oscillators is the "crystal" oscillator, a circuit that uses a piezoelectric crystal as a mechanical analog of an electrical LRC series resonant circuit. Piezoelectric materials support an exchange of energy between mechanical compression and applied electric field. In a bulk crystal, this effect can be used to establish mechanical vibration at a frequency that is very precisely determined by the physical dimensions of the crystal, and this mechanical vibration can be coupled into a circuit via the piezoelectric property of the crystal by applying area electrodes to two opposite faces of the crystal. The device is equivalent to a series LRC circuit whose $Q(=1/\omega RC = \omega L/R)$ is very high, typically 1,000–10,000. (Most bulk crystal resonators also exhibit a parallel resonance, sometimes used in oscillator circuits.) Resonators are usually built using quartz single crystals or ceramic materials.

An oscillator can be constructed that operates very near the natural vibration frequency of a bulk crystal resonator. An abstract circuit for such an oscillator is shown in Figure 12-58. We attach a (nonlinear) circuit to the resonator whose function is to present an impedance Z_C at the partition shown in the figure so that $Z_C = -Z_R$. Under this condition, the dissipative elements in the resonator and circuit cancel, and energy can be passed back and forth between the circuit and the resonator without loss at (or very near) the resonant frequency of the

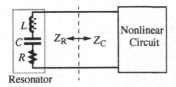

FIGURE 12-58 Crystal Oscillator

resonator, sustaining oscillation at that frequency. We introduce the common, but very useful, trick of using a transconductance to emulate a negative impedance.

The resonator's impedance is

(12-8)
$$Z_R = R + \frac{1}{j\omega C} + j\omega L = R + \frac{1}{j\omega C}\left(\frac{\omega_r^2 - \omega^2}{\omega_r^2}\right)$$

and

$$\omega_r = 1/(\sqrt{LC})$$

ω_r is the resonant frequency of the crystal. We expect that the oscillator will be operating very near this frequency so that its output will be dependent on the properties of the crystal and relatively independent of supply fluctuations and other external influences. We define the "pull" of the oscillator as the fractional deviation in frequency away from ω_r

(12-9)
$$p = \frac{\omega - \omega_r}{\omega_r}$$

Because this factor is assumed to be very small, we can perform a Taylor expansion of the imaginary term in Eq. (12-8) to give

(12-10)
$$Z_R = R + j\frac{2p}{\omega C}$$

The imaginary part of the impedance depends on how far away from resonance the resonator is operating. A circuit (AC equivalent) using an NFET as the nonlinear circuit element to supply the required transconductance is shown in Figure 12-59.

Following the treatment in [Vittoz85], we will assume that, because the oscillator will be operating very near ω_r, Z_C is a constant over the small range of frequencies; for small amplitudes, we can ignore the nonlinearities in the capacitances and g_m. With these approximations, the linear small-signal circuit

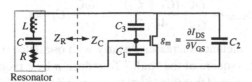

FIGURE 12-59 NFET Crystal Oscillator

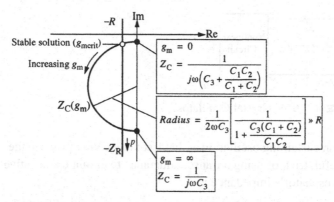

FIGURE 12-60   Approximate Small-Signal Graphical Solution to XTAL Oscillator

impedance is

(12-11)
$$Z_C = \frac{-\omega(C_1 + C_2) + jg_m}{-g_m\omega C_3 - j\omega^2(C_1 C_2 + C_1 C_3 + C_2 C_3)}$$

This is a complex bilinear expression in g_m, and thus it describes a circle in the complex plane, as sketched in Figure 12-60. Values for $g_m = 0$ and $g_m = \infty$ intersect the imaginary axis at the values shown. When $g_m = 0$, Z_C is just the series–parallel combination of C_1, C_2, C_3; when $g_m = \infty$, the transconductance cancels out C_1, C_2. The radius of the circle must be much larger than R if the circuit is to overcome losses in the resonator. If this is the case, then the condition $Z_C = -Z_R$ is met when $g_m = g_{mcrit}$, and we can calculate approximate values for g_{mcrit} and p by applying the condition on the radius of the Z_C circle.

If the radius is large, the imaginary part of Z_C is nearly unchanged from the $g_m = 0$ value, and thus

(12-12)
$$\frac{2p}{\omega C} \approx \frac{1}{\omega\left(C_3 + \frac{C_1 C_2}{C_1 + C_2}\right)}$$

$$p \approx \frac{C}{2\left(C_3 + \frac{C_1 C_2}{C_1 + C_2}\right)}$$

Setting $\text{Re}(Z_C) = -\text{Re}(Z_R)$ and again using the condition on the radius,

(12-13)
$$g_{mcrit} \approx \frac{\omega}{QC} \frac{(C_1 C_2 + C_1 C_3 + C_2 C_3)^2}{C_1 C_2}$$

Combining Eqs. (12-12) and (12-13),

(12-14)
$$g_{mcrit} \approx \frac{\omega C}{Qp^2} \frac{(C_1 + C_2)^2}{4 C_1 C_2} = \frac{\omega C}{Qp^2}(C_1 = C_2)$$

The critical transconductance increases linearly with oscillator frequency but increases as one over the square of the "pull." To reduce p by k requires a k^2 increase in transconductance and therefore k^2 more current if the NFET is operating in strong inversion.

Larger transconductance requires a larger (wider) FET and therefore higher power dissipation. For a fixed drain-current budget, FETs exhibit their highest transconductance in weak inversion; therefore oscillators are often designed with bias circuits that monitor oscillator output amplitude and feed back negatively to control drain current, holding it just above the peak weak-inversion value.

Crystal resonators are available in frequencies up to about 50 MHz (in their fundamental oscillation mode; some crystals can be operated in "overtone" modes at much higher frequencies). For a high-frequency crystal, series resistance is typically a few tens of ohms and Q is of order 10^4. If the crystal oscillator is to be operated within 0.01% of its bulk oscillation frequency, then from Eq. (12-14), we calculate g_{mcrit} of about 10^{-2}. In weak inversion, an NFET must be drawn several hundred microns wide and operated at a few milliamperes of drain current to achieve this transconductance; therefore, a 50-MHz crystal oscillator could be expected to consume several tens of milliwatts of power. [von KaVit 96] provides details about power-conserving bias circuits for crystal oscillators.

Assuming $C_1 = C_2$ and $C_3 \ll C_1$ (as it must be in order to sustain oscillation), then from Eq. (12-14) frequency deviation away from the resonator's bulk frequency varies as C/C_1. Because of the high Q of the resonator, C is very small, but it is possible to make small changes in oscillator frequency by changing C_1. This provides the possibility of building an on-chip voltage-controlled crystal oscillator (VCXO). These devices are useful in PLL applications that require a stable clock with low phase noise to be phase-locked, perhaps to another such clock.

12.3.2.2 Frequency Multiplication

Though crystal resonators are limited to frequencies of a few tens of megahertz, it is possible to multiply the frequency of the crystal oscillator output up to higher frequencies. In crystal oscillator components, this is often accomplished by buffering the oscillator output with a stage that is driven into nonlinear operation. This nonlinear stage's output will be rich in harmonic content at frequencies at an odd multiple of the oscillator frequency. Spectrally pure output at one of these harmonics can be obtained simply with a passive LC filter.

Because LC filter circuits are often not feasible on-chip, frequency multiplication is usually accomplished with a phase-locked loop, as shown in Figure 12-61. The output of the PLL's VCO is divided down in a modulo-N counter and locked to a reference at f_0. The VCO output is thus locked to $N \cdot f_0$.

12.3.2.3 Lumped-Element Oscillators

Although external high-Q resonators are often desirable because of their excellent stability and low initial tolerances, it is possible to build on-chip oscillators

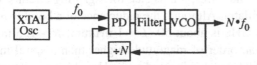

FIGURE 12-61   Frequency Multiplication Using a PLL

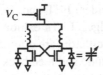

FIGURE 12-62   On-chip Variable Frequency LC Oscillator

using lumped inductors and capacitors to form LC "tank" circuits. High-quality capacitors are relatively simple to build, thanks to the oxides that are used to separate conductive layers on-chip. A metal–metal capacitor exhibits low loss, but in practice one plate always has a large capacitance to the substrate of the chip. Oscillator circuit topologies must accommodate this attribute of on-chip linear capacitors.

On-chip inductors are more problematic. Some RF integrated circuits use spiral inductors, typically fabricated on the top level of metal interconnect. Spiral inductors inevitably have fairly large capacitance to the chip substrate and between adjacent turns of the inductor, and they must be operated well below the self-resonance formed by the parasitic capacitance and inductance. The high resistance of the aluminum interconnect wiring and the resistive losses due to current induced in the substrate lower the Q of an on-chip inductor, and low Q translates into high oscillator phase noise. The resistance may be lowered somewhat by paralleling wires on multiple levels of metal interconnect, but this increases the parasitic capacitance to the substrate. It is possible to resort to exotic materials and processes to address this problem; for example, experimental chips have been built with gold interconnect wiring (to increase Q by lowering resistance) and with the substrate etched away beneath the inductor (to reduce parasitic capacitances), but these methods are not generally available to an ASIC designer.

[RofoRael96] and [Razavi97] describe oscillators built with suspended on-chip inductors. Both use the same basic circuit form shown in Figure 12-62.

A control voltage, introduced as shown, varies the drain current and thus the average voltage on the drains of the two oscillator transistors. This variable bias changes the effective capacitance of the drain junction diodes (the diodes become *varactors*) and provides frequency tuning. The second reference describes a more complex biasing network that provides improvements in tuning range over the simple scheme shown here. Two such oscillators can be cross-coupled to yield an oscillator with quadrature outputs (two sets of outputs 90° apart in phase). It should be mentioned that the varactor effect is not particularly strong in CMOS diodes, and thus this method allows a relatively small frequency adjustment range. Further, the capacitance of the diode is in series with its resistance, reducing the Q of the circuit.

The inductance of bond wires, a nuisance for signaling circuits, can be used to advantage in an oscillator. Although the inductance of a bond wire is not well controlled, the Q at 1 GHz is about 50 ($L \sim 1$ nH/mm, $R \sim 125$ mΩ/mm with skin effect included), an order of magnitude higher than a spiral inductor over substrate. [CranStey95], for example, used several bond wires connected in series

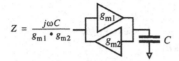

$$Z = \frac{j\omega C}{g_{m1} \cdot g_{m2}}$$

FIGURE 12-63 Fabricating an Inductor from a Capacitor with a Gyrator

in an "enhanced tank circuit" to build a voltage-controlled oscillator at about 1.5 GHz in a 0.7-μm CMOS process. They employed an oscillator configuration and tuning mechanism similar to the one depicted in Figure 12-62, except that the LC "tank" circuit bridges the drains of the cross-coupled pair. More recently, these authors have abandonded bond wires as inductors because they are difficult to manufacture repeatably and because they suffer from *microphonics*, unintentional changes in inductance and coupling caused by mechanical vibration.

Inductances can be manufactured from capacitances using a circuit called a *gyrator* shown in Figure 12-63. It is easy to show that the impedance at the left-hand terminal of this circuit looks like an inductor whose inductance is numerically equal to $C/(g_{m1} \cdot g_{m2})$. Gyrators built using CMOS devices can operate up to a gigahertz or so and are tunable by varying one or both of the transconductances. However, they consume considerable power and are complex and noisy; therefore, they are not used in modern, high-performance on-chip oscillators.

12.4 PHASE COMPARATORS

A phase comparator generates a signal proportional to the phase difference between two periodic signals; in a timing loop the phase comparator output is the error signal that, once processed by the loop filter, corrects the delay or frequency of the controlled timing component.

This section discusses various designs for phase comparators, and the next section takes up loop filters; some design approaches merge these two functions.

12.4.1 XOR Comparator

The simplest phase detector is the XOR function, whose operation is outlined in Figure 12-64.

The figure shows the logic output Q of the XOR for various phase relationships between periodic signals A and B, which have the same frequency. Output V, the low-pass filtered version of Q, varies between 0 and V_{DD} and is periodic with period 2π in the phase difference between A and B. The transfer characteristic $V(\Delta\theta)$ is shown in Figure 12-65.

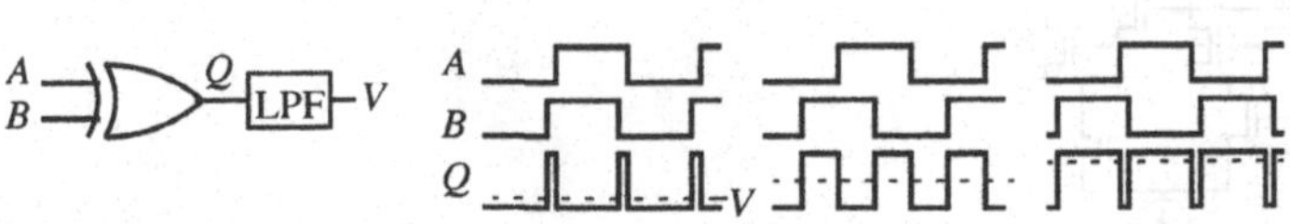

FIGURE 12-64 XOR (Quadrature) Phase Detector

FIGURE 12-65   Transfer Characteristics of XOR Phase Detector

A control loop that utilizes an XOR-type phase detector references the output to $V_{DD}/2$ and will lock when the phase difference between the controlled signal and the reference is $\pi/2$; under these conditions the two signals are said to be in quadrature.

Often a differential form of the XOR is preferred because of its superior noise rejection. An example is shown in Figure 12-66.

If the inputs to the differential XOR have very small amplitudes, the circuit will operate as a *mixer*, essentially multiplying the two inputs. Circuits of this type are often used in RF circuitry to generate the sum and difference of the frequencies of two signals (a *heterodyne*); the bipolar transistor version is called a *Gilbert cell*.

XOR phase detectors are, of course, unsuitable for timing loops that require other than $\pi/2$ phase difference at lock. Furthermore, if the two inputs have frequencies that differ substantially, the XOR's output averages very nearly to its midpoint, and thus, when XORs are used as frequency difference detectors, there will be a very slow initial convergence toward lock (Section 9.6.6.2). Phase-locked loops (PLLs) that are required to lock in quadrature usually have an auxiliary frequency detector to pull the frequency of the VCO within range of the XOR phase detector. Finally, if either of the inputs has a duty factor different from 50%, the output will exhibit an offset, which will introduce a phase error in the timing control loop (Figure 12-67). This effect can be avoided by dividing both XOR inputs by 2 with toggle cells, thus guaranteeing 50% duty factor but at the expense of lowering the control loop's cutoff frequency by 2.

Phase offsets are also introduced whenever there is an asymmetry in delay time between the phase detector inputs and the outputs. This leads to the important observation that good phase detectors are often symmetric circuits with respect to the two timing inputs. It is relatively easy to construct XORs with this property, but, as we will see, other types of phase detectors can also be built with this property.

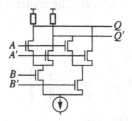

FIGURE 12-66   Differential XOR Phase Detector

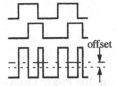

FIGURE 12-67   Duty-Factor Errors in XOR Phase Detectors

12.4.2   Edge-Triggered Flip-Flop Phase Detector

An edge-triggered flip-flop can be used as a phase detector; its properties are shown in Figure 12-68.

The edge-triggered flip-flop samples the state of clock B at the positive edge of clock A. The gain is very high; all of the gain is concentrated in a small phase angle determined by the ratio of the clock period, T_P, to the aperture time, T_A. The edge-triggered flip-flop is therefore not a "proportional" detector, and this characteristic has a significant effect on the behavior of a timing control loop, as we will see in the next section.

Because the edge-triggered flip-flop is inherently an asymmetric detector, systematic phase errors are likely. One way to avoid this problem is to build two phase detectors that exchange roles of sampling and sampled clocks and add their outputs in such a way that the systematic phase errors cancel. An implementation that is sometimes used with charge-pump loop filters (discussed in Section 12.5.2) is shown in Figure 12-69.

An analog version of this phase detector is illustrated in Figure 12-70. In this detector, the upper branch samples clock A on the rising edge of clock B, whereas the lower branch samples the complement of B on the rising edge of A. If the two clocks are exactly in phase, the voltages on the two capacitors C_1 should be exactly $V_{DD}/2$. A higher voltage corresponds to clock A leading B, a lower voltage corresponds to A lagging B. The samples of A and B', stored on capacitors C_1, are summed onto capacitor C_2; this constitutes a switched-capacitor filter with time constant set by the ratio of C_1 to C_2. The summation cancels phase offset introduced in the sampling process, assuming the A, A' and B, B' are differential pairs of signals. The switched-capacitor filter approach can be extended to the loop filter associated with this phase detector, as we will see in Section 12.5.3.2.

12.4.3   Sequential Phase Detectors

Flip-flop-based phase detectors have two states and a range of $\pm\pi$ around the lock point. It is possible to obtain a larger range by adding states to the detector.

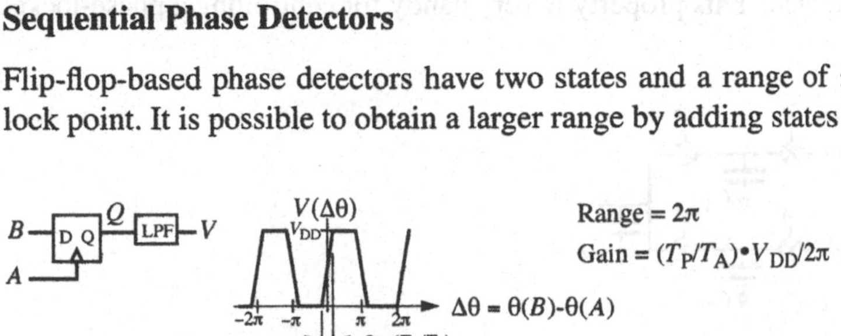

$$\text{Range} = 2\pi$$
$$\text{Gain} = (T_P/T_A)\bullet V_{DD}/2\pi$$
$$\Delta\theta = \theta(B)-\theta(A)$$

FIGURE 12-68   Edge-Triggered Flip-Flop Phase Detector

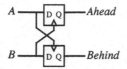

FIGURE 12-69   Symmetric Edge-Triggered Flip-flop Phase Detector

A sequential phase detector with three states can be built as shown in Figure 12-71(a). Its operation can be understood with the help of the state diagram in Figure 12-71(b). When a positive edge is received on $A(B)$, $Up(Dn)$ is latched high and held until a positive edge is received on the $B(A)$, at which point $AND(Up,Dn)$ resets both flip-flops. A brief pulse, proportional to circuit delays, appears on $Dn(Up)$ as the flip-flops are reset.

As shown in the waveforms of Figure 12-71(c), if A leads B, Up goes high for a time proportional to the phase difference between A and B. The Dn output produces a very brief pulse whose duration is roughly the sum of the delay through the AND gate and the *Reset*-to-Q delay of the flip-flops. If B leads A, the roles of Up and Dn are reversed. If the two input clocks are exactly in phase, brief pulses of equal width are output on both Up and Dn. These short pulses are important, as we will see, for avoiding a dead band in this phase detector.

If the Up and Dn outputs of this sequential phase detector are subtracted and filtered, the resulting phase detector transfer function is shown in Figure 12-72.

The addition of a third state allows a wider range of detection ($\pm 2\pi$), but the additional output doubles the voltage output range. The behavior of this detector outside the range also differs from that of the two-state detectors. Suppose A leads B and the phase angle approaches 2π. As the phase angle passes through 2π the detector continues to interpret the phase angle as positive because of the "memory" inherent in the additional state. The extended transfer function of the sequential phase detector, interpreted in this way, is shown in Figure 12-73.

This extended characteristic allows the three-state sequential phase detector to serve also as a frequency detector. For example, if clock A is at a higher frequency than clock B, Up pulses will average to a voltage proportional to the frequency difference, whereas Dn pulses will average near 0; waveforms for this situation are shown in Figure 12-74. The sequential phase detector is not subject to the false lock problem of the flip-flop phase detector when the two inputs are harmonically related. This property is very handy for controlling a phase-locked loop because

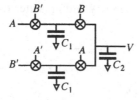

FIGURE 12-70   Switched-Capacitor Phase Detector

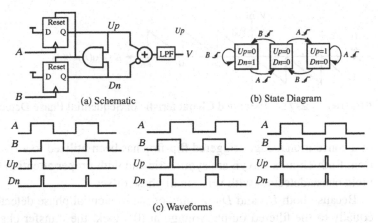

(a) Schematic (b) State Diagram

(c) Waveforms

FIGURE 12-71 Sequential Phase Detector

the sequential phase detector can issue an appropriate correction even when the VCO's frequency is far away from the reference clock's frequency. The sequential phase detector is said to have a large *capture range* by virtue of this property. In some references, this type of detector is called a *phase/frequency detector* (PFD).[2]

Although various implementations are possible, those that take advantage of the inherent symmetry of the three-state phase detector are preferred. Two example circuit realizations are shown in Figure 12-75.

The first circuit in Figure 12-75(a) is a direct realization of the gates within the venerable MC4044, a bipolar integrated circuit introduced by Motorola in the 1970s and still in use today. This version is negative-edge-triggered and produces negative-going *Up* and *Dn* outputs. It may not be obvious at first glance that the arrangement of cross-coupled NAND gates between $A'(B')$ and $Up'(Dn')$ is an edge-triggered flip-flop; we will explore the transformations between the more conventional forms (Figures 12-6 and 12-7) and this form in one of the problems at the end of the chapter. Some CMOS implementations of this phase detector use slightly different reset-generating gates.

The second realization shown in Figure 12-75(b) takes somewhat better advantage of CMOS circuits; its logic is positive. Again, a slightly tricky transformation

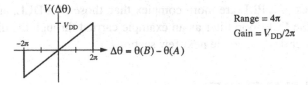

Range = 4π
Gain = $V_{DD}/2\pi$

FIGURE 12-72 Transfer Characteristics of Sequential Phase Detector

[2] The three-state sequential phase detector is sometimes called a "type 2" phase detector, and the XOR phase detector is called a "type 1."

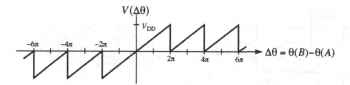

FIGURE 12-73 Extended Characteristic of Sequential Phase Detector

of a conventional edge-triggered flip-flop has been utilized to arrive at this solution. Both circuits shown are symmetric and with proper attention to layout can yield phase detectors with very small phase offset.

Because both *Up* and *Dn* outputs of the sequential phase detector contribute equally to the filtered output voltage at (0°) lock, the transfer characteristic of the phase detector near 0° depends critically on the shape and duration of these pulses, which in turn depend on the speed of the reset-generation circuit, as shown in Figure 12-76.

If the reset generator is very fast, then at lock both *Up* and *Dn* pulses will be very brief and will not reach a full V_{DD} swing. Depending on their shape and on the details of the subsequent filter, there will generally be some nonlinearity in the transfer characteristic of the phase detector, as shown in Figure 12-77. A critical part of the design of a three-state phase detector and its associated filter is the proper adjustment of the shape of the *Up/Dn* pulses to avoid a dead band in this region.

Finally it should be noted that, because the three-state sequential phase detector detects edges, either extra or missing edges on one input will produce a large change in the output. In a PLL, an extra–missing pulse will cause a persistent change in the VCO's output phase. The three-state phase detector may therefore not be suitable for applications in which the PLL is intended to track a noisy reference clock.

12.5 LOOP FILTERS

The loop filter has the dual responsibility of removing the high-frequency portion of the phase detector's output and of controlling the dynamics of the loop. The loop dynamics of a PLL are more complex than those of a DLL, and therefore we will use the PLL loop filter as an example carried through the discussion of alternative filter designs in the next few sections.

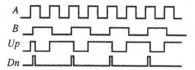

FIGURE 12-74 Sequential Phase Detector As Frequency Detector

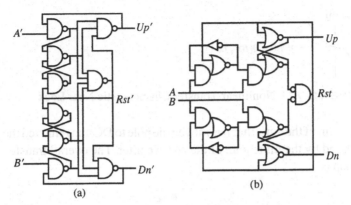

FIGURE 12-75 Two Realizations of the Sequential Phase Detector

12.5.1 RC Loop Filters

As we saw in Section 9.6.6.3, a PLL requires a loop filter with a pole and a zero to allow reasonably high loop gain and overdamped dynamics. Figure 12-78 shows a PLL with the simplest possible loop filter of this sort, one composed of discrete resistors and a capacitor.

The transfer function of this loop filter is

$$(12\text{-}15) \qquad L(s) = \frac{sR_2C + 1}{s(R_1 + R_2)C + 1}$$

This is the form we require to stabilize the loop (Eq. (9-47)), but this filter will introduce a phase offset in the output. This is so because the phase detector will output $V_{DD}/2$ at lock, but the VCO will, in general, require a control voltage input that differs from $V_{DD}/2$ by some amount. The phase detector will therefore need some phase offset at its inputs to hold the VCO input at the required voltage. A gain block is required to remove the phase offset, and the form in which this is usually applied is shown in Figure 12-79.

Assuming the operational amplifier has very large gain, this filter has the transfer function

$$(12\text{-}16) \qquad L(s) = \frac{sR_2C + 1}{sR_1C}$$

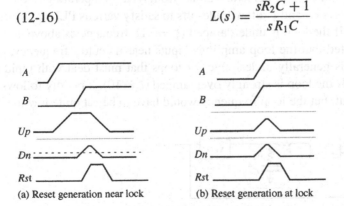

(a) Reset generation near lock   (b) Reset generation at lock

FIGURE 12-76 Reset Generation in Sequential Phase Detector

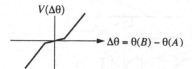

FIGURE 12-77   Nonlinear Transfer Characteristic Near Lock

The gain of the amplifier has moved the pole to DC and removed the phase offset introduced by the finite gain of the passive filter. The overall transfer function for this loop is

$$\frac{\phi_{\text{Out}}}{\phi_{\text{In}}} = \frac{\phi_{\text{Out}}}{\phi_{\text{Out}} + \phi_{\text{E}}}$$

$$\text{(12-17)} \qquad \phi_{\text{Out}} = K_{\text{PD}} \frac{K_{\text{VCO}}}{s} \left(\frac{R_2 C_s + 1}{s R_1 C} \right) \phi_{\text{E}}$$

$$\frac{\phi_{\text{Out}}}{\phi_{\text{In}}} = \frac{\frac{K_{\text{PD}} K_{\text{VCO}}}{R_1 C} (R_2 C_s + 1)}{s^2 + \frac{K_{\text{PD}} K_{\text{VCO}}}{R_1 C} R_2 C_s + \frac{K_{\text{PD}} K_{\text{VCO}}}{R_1 C}}$$

where K_{PD} and K_{VCO} are the phase detector and VCO gains, respectively, and ϕ_{E} is the phase error ($\phi_{\text{In}} - \phi_{\text{Out}}$). As is Section 9.6.6.3, the loop oscillation frequency and damping factor are

$$\omega_1 = \sqrt{\frac{K_{\text{PD}} K_{\text{VCO}}}{R_1 C}}$$

$$\text{(12-18)}$$

$$\zeta = \sqrt{\frac{K_{\text{PD}} K_{\text{VCO}}}{R_1 C}} \cdot \frac{R_2 C}{2}$$

The frequency response of this loop, with various values of ζ is shown in Figure 12-80(a); the transient response to a unit step is shown in (b) of the figure.

Recalling the dual role of the loop filter, controlling loop dynamics, and attenuating the phase detector output strongly at the operating frequency, the two parameters ω_1 and ζ allow trade-offs to satisfy various PLL application requirements. If the loop is underdamped ($\zeta = 0.1$), frequencies above ω_1 are strongly attenuated, but the loop amplifies inputs near its cutoff frequency, and this behavior is generally undesirable for loops that must deal with rapid changes in phase. If the loop is strongly overdamped ($\zeta = 10$), it rapidly follows changes at the input, but the loop frequency would have to be set quite low to attenuate the

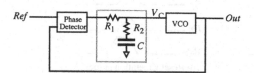

FIGURE 12-78   Discrete (Passive) RC PLL Loop Filter

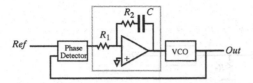

FIGURE 12-79 Active RC PLL Loop Filter

high-frequency portion of the phase detector output. For most applications the damping factor is set near unity, the best compromise between loop settling time and low-pass filtering. Noise and lock acquisition performance are also optimized for values of ζ near 1 [Gardner79].

The active RC filter is commonly used in discrete-component PLL implementations but is not very convenient for on-chip implementation. The reasons for this are several: First, it is difficult to build high-performance operational amplifiers in CMOS; amplifiers with reasonable gain and low output impedance consume a great deal of area and power. Second, most processes do not support an easy way to build high-value linear capacitors, and, as we have noted, capacitors formed by sandwiches of conducting layers tend to have one terminal with high parasitic capacitance to the substrate. Finally, and most important, it is difficult to fabricate resistors with reasonable tolerances. Interconnect layers are optimized for the lowest possible resistance and therefore require very large numbers of squares to achieve the high resistance values typically needed in a filter, at least for R_1. N-Well may be used as resistive material, but it has a large capacitance to substrate and exhibits a voltage dependence (an N-Well resistor is actually a junction FET). Both interconnect and well resistors have poorly controlled initial resistance values (often as high as $\pm 50\%$ or so) and high temperature coefficients (about 0.8%/°C for N-Well, 0.34%/°C for metal, and 0.4%/°C for salicided silicon). Variations in these parameters are not correlated with variations in FET parameters, and consequently it is very difficult to design a loop filter that will operate over all possible variations in parameters.

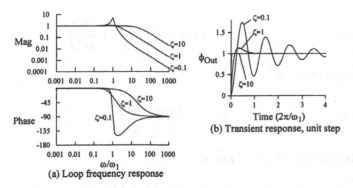

FIGURE 12-80 Frequency and Transient Response of Active RC PLL

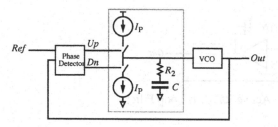

FIGURE 12-81 Charge Pump PLL Loop Filter

12.5.2 Charge Pump Filters

Charge pump loop filters provide a way to avoid some of the unpleasantness of the available resistors and capacitors in CMOS and to take best advantage of FETs. A model of a charge pump PLL loop filter is shown in Figure 12-81.

The phase detector (often a three-state sequential phase–frequency detector) meters two equal-strength current sources I_P with Up and Dn pulses. Up pulses cause I_P to add charge to the loop filter capacitor, whereas Dn pulses remove charge. The discrete resistor R_2 (so labeled to remind us of its role in the active RC filter) supplies the zero needed to stabilize the loop. The capacitor now has one terminal connected to a power supply, and thus an MOS capacitor can be employed, providing the highest capacitance per unit area available in CMOS processes (though the design must account for nonlinearities in this capacitor).

The phase detector and loop filter operate in the discrete-time domain, correcting the VCO control voltage once per cycle. However, if the loop's cutoff frequency is well below the frequency of operation of the phase detector, then the VCO control voltage can change by only a small amount on each cycle of operation, and we can approximate the behavior of the discrete-time filter as a continuous-time system by considering the currents and voltages averaged over a cycle of operation. The cycle-averaged current supplied to the loop filter is $I_P\phi_E/2\pi$ where ϕ_E is the phase difference between the phase detector inputs. Therefore, in the continuous-time approximation, the VCO control voltage is

$$(12\text{-}19) \qquad V(s) = \frac{I_P\phi_E}{2\pi}\left(R_2 + \frac{1}{sC}\right)$$

the output phase is

$$(12\text{-}20) \qquad \phi_{\text{Out}} = \frac{K_{\text{VCO}}}{s} \cdot \frac{I_P\phi_E}{2\pi}\left(R_2 + \frac{1}{sC}\right)$$

and the loop transfer function is

$$(12\text{-}21) \qquad \frac{\phi_{\text{Out}}}{\phi_{\text{In}}} = \frac{\phi_{\text{Out}}}{\phi_{\text{Out}} + \phi_E} = \frac{\frac{I_P K_{\text{VCO}}}{2\pi C}[R_2Cs + 1]}{s^2 + \frac{I_P K_{\text{VCO}}}{2\pi}R_2s + \frac{I_P K_{\text{VCO}}}{2\pi C}}$$

This expression is formally the same as Eq. (12-17) for the active RC implementation of Figure 12-79 with loop frequency and damping factor

(12-22)

$$\omega_1 = \sqrt{\frac{I_P K_{VCO}}{2\pi C}}$$

$$\zeta = \sqrt{\frac{I_P K_{VCO}}{2\pi C}} \cdot \frac{R_2 C}{2} = \omega_1 \frac{R_2 C}{2}$$

These are comparable to the expressions for the active RC loop filter (Eq. (12-18)), and thus the charge pump PLL is equivalent to a PLL with active RC filter and infinite gain, and its frequency and transient responses are identical to those shown in Figure 12-80. However, the charge-pump filter eliminates the need for a high-performance operational amplifier, substituting a relatively simple switched current source that also takes care of one of the problematic resistors. Note that if the PLL is used for frequency multiplication, the phase detector operates at $1/N$ of the output frequency, and an additional factor of $1/N$ appears inside the square root in ω_1.

Though simpler than an active RC filter, the design of a charge pump PLL in CMOS is still challenging. In many applications it is desirable to make the loop frequency, ω_1, as large as possible while not allowing the loop dynamics to become underdamped. If ω_1 is comparable to the input clock frequency, the continuous time approximation used in the preceding derivation breaks down. The reader is referred to [Gardner80], which shows the derivation of the upper limit on ω_1 in detail. A useful rule of thumb is $\omega_1 \leq 0.1\omega_{Ref}$. Because all of the factors affecting the loop frequency are process dependent, the best that can be done in a direct implementation of the charge pump shown in Figure 12-81 is to set the loop frequency to its highest allowed value at the appropriate extremes of all the parameters; for typical values of the parameters, ω_1 will be a "safe" but perhaps far from optimal value.

Ensuring proper damping under all conditions is difficult because of the remaining resistor in the circuit. If the resistor is implemented directly on one of the wiring layers of the chip, or in N-Well, both the initial tolerance in the resistivity of the wiring material and the temperature coefficient of the material must be taken into account. Often the aluminum wiring layers have the best-controlled initial value of resistivity and the lowest temperature coefficient, but metal resistors still have tolerances not much better than ±20% and then only for wire widths significantly greater than minimum. Metal resistors may therefore require unacceptably large areas. A given damping factor can be obtained with a lower resistance by increasing the size of C; there will therefore be an area-optimal solution once a loop fre quency and resistor material have been chosen.

Finally, the PLL designer is faced with the problem of setting the pump current. A precision fixed-current source, such as a band-gap reference, or one of a variety of simpler current sources, can be used for this purpose. Current references generally also require a resistor; however, this resistor is sometimes external to the chip.

In general, the design of a loop filter is a difficult multidimensional optimization problem. As we will discuss in Section 12.5.2.2, however, there are

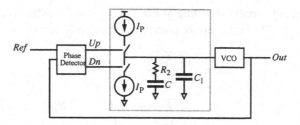

FIGURE 12-82   Improved Charge Pump PLL Loop Filter

self-biasing techniques for PLL filter design that avoid most of the difficulties we have described.

12.5.2.1 Charge Pump Control Voltage Ripple

At lock, the charge pump will introduce synchronous disturbances ("ripple") onto the control voltage arising from mismatches between the up- and down-pulling current sources, mismatches in the switching waveforms and in the switch devices themselves, and charge injection from the parasitic capacitances in the current sources. The loop filter cannot remove all of the ripple because of the resistor R_2 that provides the stabilizing zero in the loop transfer function, and thus the ripple will modulate the VCO and produce jitter on its output.

There are two ways to deal with this problem: additional filtering and improved charge pump design. A simple example of the first of these methods is shown in Figure 12-82.

The capacitor C_1 introduces a new pole in the loop transfer function that can be chosen to reduce considerably the ripple from the charge pump with little effect on the loop dynamics; the new loop is a third-order system. [Gardner80] works out the details of the design of this improved filter.

To illustrate the problems with simple charge pump implementations, consider the two designs shown in Figure 12-83.

In both examples a bias voltage sets the pump current, I_P, in an NFET current source, and in both cases the Up current is copied using a PFET current mirror. Figure 12-83(a) uses a PFET to switch the Up current directly, whereas (b) uses an NFET Up current switch ahead of the current mirror.

If only one polarity of Up/Dn pulse is available from the phase detector, circuit (a) requires inversion of one of the outputs, and this introduces two problems. First, the width and height of the Up/Dn pulses, carefully tailored to be identical (through careful design of the phase detector), are distorted in the inverter chains needed for the inversion. Second, the time of arrival of the pulses at the

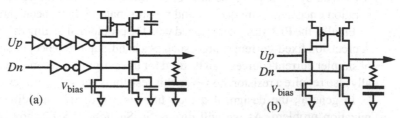

FIGURE 12-83   Simple Charge Pump Implementations

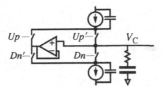

FIGURE 12-84   An Approach for Reducing Charge Injection

switches is skewed, and thus the up/down current pulses that control the charge on the loop filter are metered into the filter at slightly different times, introducing additional ripple on the control voltage. For phase detectors such as the one in Figure 12-75(b) that provide both polarities of output, this problem may not be so severe. However, it is impossible in principle to match the NFET and PFET switched current sources perfectly.

In Figure 12-83(b), because both up and down currents are initially generated in NFETs and the switching is done with NFETs as well, the switches can be matched. Only one polarity of Up/Dn pulses is needed in this pump, and thus the carefully symmetrized outputs of the phase detector can be used directly.

Both implementations suffer from charge injection. Each of the parasitic capacitances at the junctions between current source and switch FETs gets charged to its respective power rail when the switch is off. When the switch turns on, the parasitic capacitor must be charged from the control voltage node, adding to the noise on the node. It is possible to achieve an approximate balance between the parasitic capacitors in Figure 12-83(a), but (b) is fundamentally asymmetric with respect to this effect. One solution to this problem is shown in Figure 12-84. A unity gain buffer copies the control voltage and sources it with low impedance to switches that hold the current source outputs at V_C while the pump switches are off; note that both polarities of phase detector output are required. In any case, it is always desirable to minimize the parasitic capacitances in the pump through careful layout.

A more elegant approach for canceling charge injection can be applied to our example circuit Figure 12-83(b), as shown in Figure 12-85. This is one of many possible variations of a *differential charge pump*, the preferred circuit design approach for high-performance loop filters.

12.5.2.2   Self-Biased Loop Filters

The remaining resistor and current reference in the charge pump loop filter can be eliminated completely by borrowing some ideas from the replica-bias delay circuits introduced in Section 12.2.2.2.

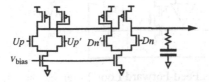

FIGURE 12-85   Differential Charge Pump

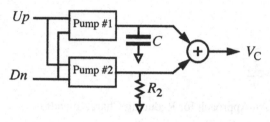

FIGURE 12-86   Feed-Forward Loop Filter

For a particular set of process parameters, the loop frequency for a charge pump PLL is proportional to $I_P^{1/2}$. In the replica-biased delay element, the tail current is servoed in the replica to the value

(12-23) $$I_T = \beta_P(V_C - V_{TP})^2$$

Because the frequency of a VCO built from replica-biased delay elements is proportional to $(V_C - V_{TP})$, ω_{VCO} is proportional to $I_T^{1/2}$. So, if the pump current is set by the replica tail current bias V_{BN}, the loop frequency can be held at a constant fraction of the operating frequency. This is a highly desirable situation, for the bandwidth of the loop, and thus the highest frequency noise it can cancel, will increase as the operating frequency increases.

Although it is very handy to have the loop frequency track the operating frequency, maintaining the damping factor at a fixed value may appear hopeless, because the resistor R_2 would have to vary as $I_T^{-1/2}$ to hold ζ fixed. However, the effective resistance of the replica-bias load device behaves in exactly this way. It remains only to show how to make use of a replica-bias load device as a loop filter component.

We will employ a trick used in several of the references. Two pumps, both driven from the same Up/Dn phase detector outputs, drive two separate circuit elements (in our case, the "resistor" load that simulates R_2, and the loop capacitor, C). A feed-forward circuit adds the voltages on the two elements and, as shown in Figure 12-86, allows both components to be referenced to a common terminal. Note that the two pumps are not required to have the same pump current, and thus we also have available another scaling parameter that may be useful in sizing the resistor and capacitor.

One implementation of this idea [Maneatis96] is shown in Figure 12-87. The replica-bias circuit is constructed as before but receives only the capacitor voltage.

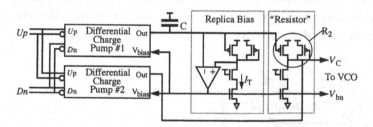

FIGURE 12-87   Replica-Bias Feed-Forward Loop Filter

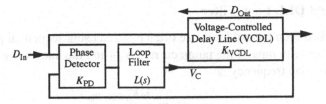

FIGURE 12-88 Delay-Locked Loop

A "resistor" cell is interposed between the replica-bias generator and the control voltage. This cell has identical (or possibly scaled) tail current, I_T, and load resistance proportional to $I_T^{-1/2}$. Without the pump current from Pump 2, this cell simply buffers the capacitor voltage onto V_C. The current from Pump 2, however, develops a voltage across R_2 that is summed with the capacitor voltage onto V_C, as required.

In real implementations of this circuit, there will be nonnegligible capacitance between V_C and V_{DD} because of the gates of the load devices in the VCO; because this capacitance is unavoidable, it may be best to make a virtue of necessity and add yet more capacitance to compose a filter like the one shown in Figure 12-82.

The self-biasing, feed-forward scheme neatly sidesteps the resistor construction issues discussed in Sections 12.5.1 and 12.5.2. The pump current, I_P, and loop control resistor, R_2, have been implemented in such a way that the loop filter design depends on ratios of currents, which are easily controlled in CMOS. Alternative versions of this idea are described in [MijuBaye94] and [NovoAust95].

12.5.3 Delay-Locked Loop Filters

This section presents filters for delay-locked loops and introduces a few additional ways to implement filters for both PLLs and DLLs. Delay-locked loops are generally much simpler to analyze than PLLs because DLLs are first-order systems. An abstract model of a DLL is shown in Figure 12-88.

The phase detector compares the desired input delay D_{In} with the delay through the delay line converting the phase difference $\omega_{In} \cdot (D_{In} - D_{Out})$ to a voltage. The control voltage out of the loop filter is

(12-24)
$$V_C = \omega_{In}(D_{In} - D_{Out})K_{PD}L(s)$$

Only a single pole is needed to stabilize a DLL, and thus $L(s)$ is typically of the form $1/sRC$, and the loop transfer function is

(12-25)
$$\frac{D_{Out}}{D_{In}} = \frac{1}{1 + s/\omega_1}$$
$$\omega_1 = \frac{K_{PD}K_{VCDL}\omega_{In}}{RC}$$

The frequency, ω_1, is the cutoff frequency for the (low-pass) loop filter, the bandwidth within which the loop can cancel noise.

12.5.3.1   Self-Biased DLL Loop Filter

Delay-locked loop control loops are often realized using sequential phase detectors and charge pumps. If the pump current is I_P and the integrating capacitor is C, then the loop frequency is

$$(12\text{-}26) \qquad \omega_1 = \frac{I_P K_{\text{VCDL}} \omega_{\text{In}}}{2\pi C}$$

It is usually desirable to hold the loop bandwidth at a constant fraction of the operating frequency. Typically $\omega_1 \leq 0.1\omega_{\text{In}}$ in order to satisfy the continuous-time approximation, as in Section 12.5.2. If the pump current and the VCDL gain are constant, this condition holds across the range of operation of the loop. However, from Eq. (12-3), replica-biased element delay is proportional to $1/(V_C - V_{\text{TP}})$, and thus

$$(12\text{-}27) \qquad K_{\text{VCDL}} \propto \frac{1}{(V_C - V_{\text{TP}})^2} \propto \frac{1}{I_T}$$

where I_T is the replica-bias tail current. We can employ a simple form of the self-biasing trick used in Section 12.5.2.2, making the pump current $I_P = k \cdot I_T$. Under these conditions, the loop bandwidth is related to the operating frequency only by constants. [Maneat96] describes the approach in detail and shows that the ratio of loop bandwidth to operating frequency is proportional to a ratio of capacitances, and consequently the loop bandwidth condition is fairly easy to set in CMOS, independent of process variations, supply voltage, and temperature.

12.5.3.2   Switched-Capacitor Loop Filters

Figure 12-70 introduced a switched-capacitor phase detector. It is easy to extend this approach to the loop filter as well, and the complete circuit is shown in Figure 12-89.

The inverter in the circuit of Figure 12-89 provides gain for the phase detector, driving its output low if input A lags input B and driving high if A leads B. At lock, the inverter's input and output are both near $V_{\text{DD}}/2$. The two additional switches and capacitors C_3 and C_4 comprise a switched-capacitor low-pass filter that provides the pole required in the control loop of a DLL. To see how this works, suppose the voltages on V_L and V_C just before A rises are denoted $[i]$, and voltages just after A rises are denoted $[i+1]$, then on each cycle of operation the voltage on V_C can be computed from its value on the previous cycle by

$$(12\text{-}28) \qquad V_{C[i+1]} = V_{C[i]} + \frac{C_3}{C_4} V_{L[i]}$$

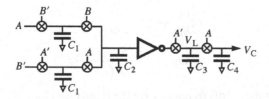

FIGURE 12-89   Switched-Capacitor Phase Detector and Loop Filter

In the frequency domain, delaying a signal by one clock period is equivalent to multiplying it by e^{-sT}, where T is the clock period; therefore

$$(12\text{-}29) \qquad V_C(s) = V_C(s)e^{-sT} + \frac{C_3}{C_4}V_L(s)e^{-sT}$$

and the filter transfer function is

$$(12\text{-}30) \qquad \frac{V_C(s)}{V_L(s)} = \frac{C_3}{C_4}\left(\frac{1}{e^{sT}-1}\right)$$

If we want the transfer function at frequencies much less than the clock frequency, the second term reduces approximately to $1/sT$, and the transfer function is

$$(12\text{-}31) \qquad \frac{V_C(s)}{V_L(s)} = \frac{\omega_1}{s}$$

$$\omega_1 = \frac{FC_3}{C_4}$$

where F is $1/T$, the clock frequency. This has the form of a low-pass filter with $1/(FC_3)$ performing the role of a discrete resistor.

In a DLL that uses this filter, the overall transfer function is

$$(12\text{-}32) \qquad \frac{D_{Out}}{D_{In}} = \frac{K_{PD}K_{VCDL}\omega_{In}^2(C_3/C_4)}{4\pi^2}$$

where K_{PD} includes the gain of the first switched-capacitor filter and the inverter. If the delay line is implemented in the replica-bias style,

$$(12\text{-}33) \qquad K_{VCDL} \propto \frac{1}{(V_C - V_{TP})^2} \propto D_{Out}^2 \propto \frac{1}{\omega_{In}^2}$$

and thus the loop has a bandwidth that is fixed by transconductances and capacitance ratios and is independent of operating frequency.

12.5.3.3 Loop Initialization

In some DLL applications it is necessary to initialize the VCDL control voltage before allowing the loop to lock up. If the range of the delay line spans more than T_{In} to $2 \cdot T_{In}$ and the loop happens to be initialized at a delay value greater than $2 \cdot T_{In}$, then it will attain a *false lock* at that delay value. This may not be a problem in less demanding applications, but under conditions of false lock, the loop bandwidth will be half the value at the correct lock, and thus the loop's ability to reject noise will be severely compromised. If the DLL is intended to generate a set of equally spaced multiphase clocks, a false lock condition may be disastrous. Usually, this problem is handled by initializing the delay line at its minimum delay value using an external system *Reset* signal. In the replica-biased delay lines we have used as examples in this chapter, initialization could be handled simply by adding a large NFET that grounds V_C whenever *Reset* is asserted.

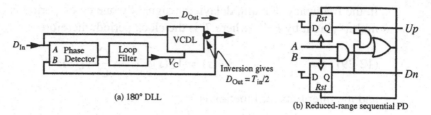

(a) 180° DLL

(b) Reduced-range sequential PD

FIGURE 12-90   180° Delay-Locked Loop

Although the phase detectors we have described in this section lock at 0° phase difference, it is sometimes convenient to build DLLs that provide only half a clock period of delay. If the delay line is a differential one, the inverted output can be used to supply one of the inputs to the phase detector. Such a loop (Figure 12-90a) will lock with $D_{Out} = T_{In/2}$ (180° phase difference between input and output).

Delay-locked loops of this type that use a sequential phase detector require a separate initialization for the phase detector because the large phase input range of the detector leads to an ambiguity about which input is "leading" the other. Suppose the VCDL is initialized at minimum delay, and the phase detector happens to start in the reset state (center state in Figure 12-71). Now suppose that the first edge presented at D_{In} is a negative one; then the phase detector will see its first positive edge on input B and produce a Dn pulse. Successive cycles of operation will continue to generate Dn pulses, but the VCDL has been initialized at its minimum delay, and thus the loop will remain wedged in this state. This problem can be avoided either by ensuring that the phase detector starts in the "correct" state or by limiting the range of the phase input difference, for example, by adding an additional reset term, as shown in Figure 12-90(b).

12.5.3.4   "Turbo" Mode

Performing circuit simulations of PLLs and DLLs is particularly troublesome because the simulations usually run for durations of many times $1/\omega_1$ but at the same time require accuracy on a time scale that is small compared with the input clock period $1/\omega_{In} \le 10 \cdot 1/\omega_1$. To speed up simulations and to reduce lock-up time in the final running hardware, charge pumps and similar circuitry are often augmented with a "turbo" mode. A typical modification to a differential charge pump is shown in Figure 12-91. When the *Turbo* bit is asserted (for example, from a boundary-scan system), the pump currents are supplied from large devices, sized $K \cdot S_N$, causing the loop filter to converge toward lock much faster than

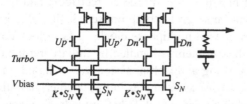

FIGURE 12-91   Differential Charge Pump with "Turbo" Mode

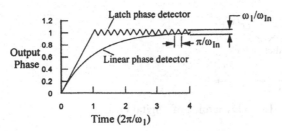

FIGURE 12-92 Loop Dynamics with High-Gain Latch Phase Detector

in normal operation. When *Turbo* is deasserted, devices S_N, sized to control the loop dynamics correctly, supply the pump current.

12.5.3.5 "Bang-Bang" Controllers

For very high-gain phase detectors, such as the latch (Figure 12-68), the continuous-time approximation we have been using to analyze loop filters is no longer valid, and the loop dynamics exhibits somewhat different behavior. Figure 12-92 shows the step response for a loop that uses an edge-triggered flip-flop with a very narrow aperture as its phase detector; the step response of a loop with the same loop-filter constants but with a linear (or "proportional") phase detector, is shown for comparison.

The step response is a linear ramp with slope $\omega_1/2\pi$. When the loop approaches lock, the loop response, coupled with the one-cycle delay in the phase detector, causes the loop to oscillate with a period twice that of the input frequency and with an amplitude ω_1/ω_{In}, as the input phase falls alternately on either side of the latch's narrow aperture. Because of its behavior at lock, this type of loop is sometimes called a "bang-bang" controller. In some applications, the small excursions around the lock point are not objectionable, and it is worth making the trade-off to gain the comparatively rapid lock time and circuit simplicity of this type of controller.

12.5.3.6 Digital Loop Controllers

For some applications the precision attainable using an analog control loop is not worth the cost in area and power, and a simpler digitally controlled loop is sufficient. An elementary example is shown in Figure 12-93.

The delay line is composed of delay elements that present small, fixed delays; inverters are shown by way of example, but any delay element could be used. The overall delay is set by a multiplexer that selects one of the delay outputs into *Out*.

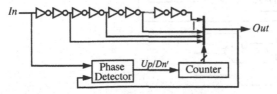

FIGURE 12-93 Digitally Controlled DLL

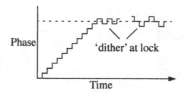

FIGURE 12-94   Loop Dynamics of Digital DLL

The loop is closed around a phase detector that drives a counter up or down, and the counter's output selects the multiplexer input. A loop of this sort operates in discrete time and discrete delay; its response to a step input in phase is shown in Figure 12-94.

Because phase is quantized into a set of discrete values, the loop cannot lock with zero error. In general the output phase will "dither" between two adjacent values (or three, if one of them is within the aperture of the phase detector).

In general, the loop-control elements (phase detector and counter) must be operated at a lower frequency than the input and output clocks. The phase detector must make a binary decision whether to drive the counter up or down on each cycle of operation. Assuming the phase detector is a latch, the loop is servoing the phase relationship between *In* and *Out* in such as way as to enhance the probability of metastability in the latch. If a metastable value were presented to the *Up/Dn′* input to the counter, the loop would loose lock in a catastrophic fashion, because the next value output by the counter would be undetermined. Time gain, in the form of additional regenerative latches between phase detector and counter, is required to reduce the probability of a metastable state at the output of the phase detector to acceptable levels. To accommodate this extra time and stabilize the loop, the loop sampling frequency must be lower than the input–output clock frequency.

In some applications dither is eliminated at the expense of increased phase error, by purposely inserting a dead band in the digital controller (e.g., [HataMochi97, EfenAfek94]). This idea is sketched in Figure 12-95.

Two phase detectors are used in this scheme, one of which gets the input clock delayed by an amount that is greater than the unit delay in the delay line (T_C must actually be larger than the sum of T_D and the aperture time of the phase detector).

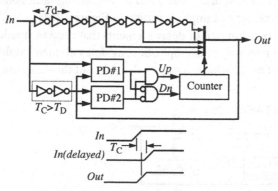

FIGURE 12-95   Inserting Dead Band in a Digital DLL

When the output clock falls within this window, the logic between the phase detectors and the counter causes the counter to hold its current value. The dead band injects a phase error between input and output that is, in general, greater than one unit delay.

12.6 CLOCK ALIGNERS

To conclude this chapter, we take up the problem of clock alignment, both a self-contained topic in timing circuits and a set of applications of the circuit techniques described in the preceding sections of this chapter.

In most digital ICs, the internal clock is buffered to drive a large load distributed across the chip. Clock buffer and distribution delays depend on process variations and environmental factors, and thus the input–output circuitry in pairs of chips that communicate synchronously receive clocks that have a perhaps bounded but unknown phase difference. A clock aligner's task is to phase-align a chip's internal clock with an external reference clock, effectively removing the variable buffer delay and reducing the uncertainty in clock phase between communicating chips. Clock aligners can be used on-chip, as well, to reduce clock skew among multiple clock buffers; this is the basis of the zero-delay driver (ZDD) of Figure 9-52.

12.6.1 PLL Versus DLL Implementations

Clock aligners can be built using either PLLs or DLLs, as shown in Figure 12-96.

In a PLL implementation (Figure 12-96(a)), the chip has its own clock oscillator (the VCO) that is phase-locked to an external reference clock. The phase shift introduced by the buffer delay, T_B, is assumed to be changing (for example, with temperature and supply voltage) slowly enough that any variation is within the control-loop bandwidth.

This phase shift simply adds a constant phase difference on a cycle by cycle basis and therefore does not change the control loop analysis. The buffer's delay is eliminated by inclusion in the control loop.

In the simple DLL implementation (Figure 12-96(b)) a variable delay line is inserted between the sreference clock and the internal clock. Its delay is servoed

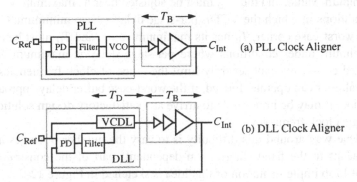

FIGURE 12-96 Clock Aligner Implementations

so that $T_D + T_B = N \cdot T_{Clk}$ (usually $N = 1$). As in the PLL implementation, the buffer delay is placed within a control loop and eliminated.

Phase-locked loop and DLL implementations have complementary advantages and disadvantages. For comparison purposes, assume the VCO is a ring oscillator built from the same delay elements as the VCDL. In the PLL, any jitter introduced during a cycle of operation is fed back through the ring oscillator on the next cycle. [KimweiGr94] shows that delay-element jitter in a PLL is amplified by an "accumulation factor" inversely proportional to the control loop bandwidth. As the bandwidth is increased, the loop is able to cancel the low-frequency part of its self-induced jitter but at the expense of admitting higher frequency components of jitter on the reference clock. The DLL does not recirculate its self-induced jitter, and therefore it has no accumulation factor. If the reference clock itself is noisy, the PLL reduces the incoming jitter by virtue of its low-pass behavior; the self-contained oscillator acts much like a flywheel in a mechanical system. The DLL, of course, passes whatever noise is present on the reference clock directly to the internal clock.

In summary, a PLL clock aligner will be superior in applications where noise on the reference clock dominates, and self-induced jitter within the VCO is negligible (PLLs were developed historically to recover data and timing from noisy communication channels). A DLL will provide superior jitter performance when a clean reference clock is available, and this is often the situation for multichip digital systems with a well-designed system clock distribution network. The simpler loop dynamics of the DLL is also an advantage insofar as it simplifies the design of the control-loop filter. However, as we will see, high-performance DLL-based clock aligners are not necessarily simpler circuits than PLL-based ones.

For the remainder of this section we will discuss various ways to implement DLL-based clock aligners. Phase-locked loop aligners are described in several of the references.

12.6.2 Simple DLL-Based Aligners

The simplest DLL-based clock aligner is shown in Figure 12-96(b). Not surprisingly, this naive implementation presents a problem that may be severe for some applications. At the best-case corner of operation, the buffer delay, T_B, has its minimum value, and thus T_D must be adjusted near its maximum value but under conditions in which the VCDL per-stage delay is also minimum. Conversely, at the worst-case corner, T_B has its maximum value, and T_D must be adjusted near minimum under conditions where per-stage delay is maximum. This double-ended constraint may severely limit the range of clock frequencies over which the aligner can operate. Indeed, if the worst-case buffer delay approaches a clock period, it may be impossible to arrive at a satisfactory design solution even for a single clock frequency.

One way around this difficulty is to vary the number of stages in the VCDL to adapt to the fixed (fabrication-dependent) part of the constraint. A hybrid, dual-loop implementation of this idea is sketched in Figure 12-97.

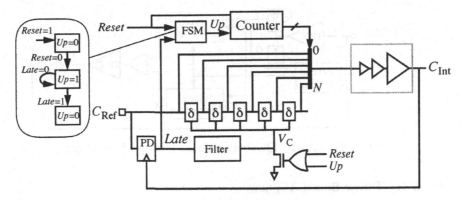

FIGURE 12-97 Dual-Loop DLL Clock Aligner

When (system-generated) *Reset* is asserted, the counter is preset to 0 (minimum number of delay stages, here one), the delay-element control voltage V_C is forced to its minimum-delay value, and the FSM is initialized. When *Reset* is deasserted, the FSM asserts *Up*, which increments the counter on each cycle of operation until the FSM detects *Late* asserted by the PD, indicating that the delay through the currently selected number of VCDL stages and the buffer is slightly longer than required. A this point the FSM halts and deasserts *Up*, enabling the analog portion of the delay control, which implements a conventional DLL with the number of delay elements preset and now fixed.

The digital loop in this aligner is very similar to the digital loop controller presented in Section 12.5.3.6, and the cautions regarding phase-detector metastability apply. The digital loop is allowed to operate only until it achieves a "coarse" lock; then the analog loop is enabled to acquire and maintain a "fine" lock.

This idea can be made to work reasonably well in practice but has some drawbacks. The number of stages, and thus the amount of self-induced jitter, varies, depending on fabrication parameters and on clock period. Further, control range is more restricted at the worst-case corner than at best case. Suppose that at the worst-case fabrication corner and highest clock frequency, the coarse delay adjustment procedure selects just one delay element. Then the range over which the fine delay loop can operate is only the adjustment range of one element. In some cases, this range may not be enough to accommodate subsequent changes in temperature and voltage.

Finally, jitter is increased in a DLL proportional to the number of stages of delay, because jitter, injected at each stage, accumulates along the delay line. On the other hand, a short delay line requires large delay per stage, and delay elements tuned for long delay have increased sensitivity to noise on the control input and thus more jitter. Because these two effects do not scale in the same way, an optimal number of stages exist for generating a given delay using a particular circuit approach. The variable-length delay line, unfortunately, guarantees that one will have to operate away from this optimum point at the extremes of fabrication, voltage, and temperature.

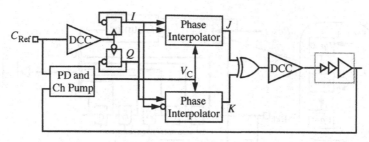

FIGURE 12-98   Quadrature Phase-Mixing Clock Aligner

12.6.3   Phase-Based Aligners

In the simple DLL-based clock aligner, a variable delay is inserted between the reference clock and the chip's internal clock buffer; its purpose is actually to shift the phase of the reference clock to cancel the phase shift in the buffer. The problems with delay-based aligners arise because of two-sided constraints on the delay that must be generated.

These problems could be avoided entirely by constructing an aligner that uses *phase* directly as the controlled quantity. [LeeDonn94] presents a clock aligner that works in this way and uses no controlled delay elements at all. A simplified sketch of the architecture of this aligner is shown in Figure 12-98 (signal paths are differential pairs).

A duty-cycle corrected (DCCs are outlined in Section 12.2.4.3) version of the input reference clock drives two toggle cells that generate I and Q, which are therefore half-frequency quadrature (90° phase difference) clocks. The Phase Interpolator blocks are similar in operation to the interpolators described in Section 12.2.4.2 but somewhat different in circuit details; they produce outputs that are interpolated smoothly between their inputs, depending on the control voltage, V_C. Interpolator outputs I, J are therefore also a half-frequency quadrature clock pair; they are mixed together in an XOR to generate a full-frequency clock. As shown in Figure 12-99, the arrangement so far described can introduce a phase shift between reference and internal clock that can be varied over a 180° range.

The remaining 180° of adjustment range can be achieved with some additional circuitry not shown in the simplified schematic of Figure 12-99. Suppose that, as V_C increases, the upper interpolator's output is weighted more heavily toward the Q input. At the upper limit of V_C, output J is entirely determined by input

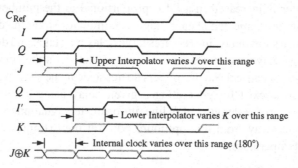

FIGURE 12-99   Waveforms in Quadrature Phase-Mixing Clock Aligner

Q, and input I is ignored. If, at this point, input I is inverted, then, if V_C heads back toward the lower limit, the phase *advances* farther, moving toward I'. In the implementation described in the reference, a monitor circuit detects when the control voltage is at one of the limits. When a limit is reached, a state machine that keeps track of the current phase shift takes two actions; it inverts the appropriate input to each interpolator and reverses the sense of the charge pump that drives V_C. This mechanism allows a full 360° phase adjustment range over which the internal clock can be varied.

This clock aligner implementation has the potential advantage over conventional DLL implementations that it can accommodate a wide range of input frequencies and essentially any value of clock buffer delay. It has a fairly serious problem, however; two successive like edges of the internal clock are generated by opposite polarities of one of the J, K signals. Therefore, if either J or K does not have exactly 50% duty factor, the internal clock will be subject to a systematic form of jitter that cannot be removed by the output duty-cycle corrector. The quadrature mixing clock aligner of [LeeDonn94] was used in the first Rambus memory devices but evidently replaced in later production devices, perhaps because of this flaw. Nevertheless, [LeeDonn94] contains descriptions of several clever and interesting circuits useful in other contexts, and the underlying idea of aligning two clocks by adjusting phase (rather than frequency or delay) is still attractive.

12.6.4 A Hybrid Phase/Delay-Based Clock Aligner

It is possible to obtain the benefits of stable, low-jitter delay that can be generated in a well-designed DLL while performing clock alignment with phase adjustment. The underlying idea for this approach is to generate a group of equiphase clocks from the reference clock using a DLL and then phase lock the internal and reference clocks by picking the two DLL outputs that bracket the desired output phase and interpolating between them. An architecture that implements this idea is shown in Figure 12-100; it is essentially a greatly improved adaptation of the dual-loop DLL of Figure 12-97.

The arrangement in Figure 12-100 has two independent control loops, a DLL that generates the set of equiphase clocks and a PLL that selects and interpolates between these phases. The digital PLL consists of a phase detector driving an

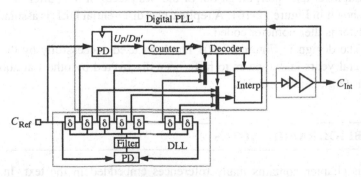

FIGURE 12-100 Hybrid Dual-Loop Clock Aligner

TABLE 12-1   **Example Decoder for Dual-Loop Aligner**

Counter Value	Even Multiplexer	Odd Multiplexer	Int (Even)	Int (Odd)
0	0	1	1	0
1	0	1	3/4	1/4
2	0	1	1/2	1/2
3	0	1	1/4	3/4
4	2	1	0	1
5	2	1	1/4	3/4
6	2	1	1/2	1/2
7	2	1	3/4	1/4
8	2	3	1	0
9	2	3	3/4	1/4

up/down counter. The counter's output is decoded to drive "even" and "odd" multiplexers that select neighboring phases from the DLL and the interpolator that outputs a phase between the two phases selected.

The interpolator and multiplexers are coordinated in a way suggested in [LeeDonn94]. When the interpolator is set so that only one input affects the output, the other input can be switched without introducing any disturbances on the interpolator output. Table 12-1 shows an example of how the decoder might work with a four-level interpolator for a short segment of the counter's range.

Some optimizations of this circuit are fairly obvious. First, the number of delay stages can be cut in half by constructing the DLL as a 180° loop (as in Figure 12-90), with the reminder that a modified sequential phase detector will be required to avoid initialization problems. This optimization reduces size and power by a factor of 2 but also reduces jitter by eliminating unneeded stages. The multiplexers and interpolator must be modified to insert an overall inversion when interpolating between the end values of the delay line. For example, in an N-stage delay line, when the phase advances to the point at which the interpolator is weighting stage $N - 1$ at unity, the next step in phase interpolates stage $N - 1$ with the *inverse* of stage 0.

The design of the multiplexer and interpolator requires some care to avoid power supply sensitivity and its resultant jitter. One possibility is to build the multiplexer and interpolator out of the two pieces of the buffer of Figure 12-48, as shown in Figure 12-101. A replica-bias differential DLL is assumed; the interpolator is thermometer coded.

The design in Figure 12-101 has been used successfully by the authors for several years and appears to have been discovered by others at about the same time (e.g., [SidiHoro97]).

12.7   BIBLIOGRAPHIC NOTES

This chapter contains many references embedded in the text. In addition to these, various textbooks, such as [WestEshr93] and [GuShaElm96], provide good

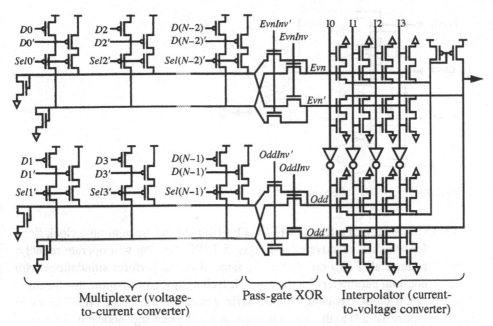

FIGURE 12-101 A Supply-Insensitive Implementation for Multiplexer–Interpolator

surveys of CMOS circuit techniques not described in detail in this book, including Domino logic, Zipper CMOS, NORA, and others that combine logic and latching functions. The survey [Razavi96] contains several papers on the problem of clock generation, synchronization, and distribution, along with an excellent introductory tutorial by the editor. Some additional papers not referenced in the text include [Bazes85], which describes a differential version of the capacitor-loaded delay line and a clever phase detection scheme; [KimKim96] describes a novel, SCR-like controlled delay element; [HeinScot88] provides an introduction to the use of the z-transform to analyze digital PLLs; [JohnHuds88] is a classic paper on the use of DLLs for clock alignment; [LeeLand97] describes an interesting PLL built from a digitally controlled first-order oscillator; [YounGrea92] describes a replica-biased PLL design, somewhat different in detail from those outlined in this chapter; and [YuanSven97] describes the latest results in Yuan and Svensson's continuing investigation of high-performance dynamic latches. As mentioned previously, [Maneat96] provides the essential introduction to self-biasing techniques. There are several excellent texts on the design and analysis of phase-locked loops, including [Gardner79], [Best84], and [Stensby97].

12.8 PROBLEMS

12-1 Master/Slave Latches: A schematic of the venerable TTL 7474 edge-trigger flip-flop is shown in Figure 12-102. Explain its operation in detail, showing the decomposition into master and slave latches.

12-2 Asynchronous Reset Flip-Flop: Design a static pass-gate positive edge-triggered flip-flop with an asynchronous reset input.

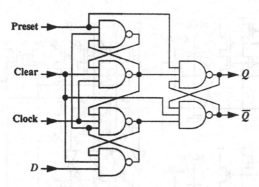

FIGURE 12-102   Schematic of TTL 7474 Flip-Flop

12-3 Clock Slope Failures in TSPC Flip-Flops: Find the minimum clock slope for which a negative-edge-triggered TSPC flip-flop will operate reliably; assume all FETs are drawn the same size and perform simulations with nominal parameters for the example technology. Now assume that the maximum clock frequency is 200 MHz; resize the precharge NFET ($mn1$ in Figure 12-23) to the minimum size that will precharge node b under *worst*-case conditions. Resimulate under *best*-case conditions to find the minimum clock slope for the improved flip-flop.

12-4 Sequential Phase Detectors: Decompose the cross-coupled NAND gates in the MC4044 sequential phase detector (Figure 12-71(a)) to show how they form edge-triggered, resettable flip-flops. Perform the same analysis for Figure 12-71(b).

12-5 Self-Biased DLLs: Show that in the self-biased DLL loop filter, the loop bandwidth is related to the input reference frequency by

$$\frac{\omega_1}{\omega_{\text{Ref}}} \propto \frac{C_{\text{L}}}{C}$$

where C_{L} is the load seen by each differential output in the delay line and C is the loop filter capacitor. Show also that for the self-biased PLL loop filter of Figure 12-87, the loop bandwidth and damping factors are

$$\frac{\omega_1}{\omega_{\text{Ref}}} \propto \sqrt{\frac{C_{\text{L}}}{C}}$$

$$\zeta \propto \sqrt{\frac{C}{C_{\text{L}}}}$$

REFERENCES

[AbidRofo97] Abidi, A., Rofougaran, A., Chang, G., Rael, J., Chang, J., Rofougaran, M., and Change, P., "The Future of CMOS Wireless Transceivers," *1997 IEEE International Solid State Circuits Conference Digest of Technical Papers*, pp. 118–119.

[AfghSven90] Afghahi, M., and Svensson, C., "A Unified Single-Phase Clocking Scheme for VLSI Systems," *IEEE Journal of Solid State Circuits*, Vol. 25, No. 1, February 1990, pp. 225–233.

[AfghYuan91] Afghahi, M., and Yuan, J., "Double Edge-Triggered D-Flip-Flops for High-Speed CMOS Circuits," *IEEE Journal of Solid State Circuits*, Vol. 26, No. 8, August 1991, pp. 1168–1170.

[AllsBlac83] Allstot, D., and Black, W., "Technological Design Considerations for Monolithic MOS Switched-Capacitor Filtering Systems," *Proceedings of the IEEE*, Vol. 71, No. 8, August 1983, pp. 967–986.

[AnamYosh83] Anami, K., Yoshimotot, M., Shinohara, H., Hirata, Y., and Nakano, T., "Design Considerations of a Static Memory Cell," *IEEE Journal of Solid State Circuits*, Vol. 18, No. 4, August 1983, pp. 414–417.

[AntoMass88] Antognetti, P., and Massobrio, G., *Semiconductor Device Modeling with SPICE*, McGraw–Hill, New York, 1988.

[BabaTeme84] Babanezhad, J., and Temes, G., "A Linear NMOS Depletion Resistor and Its Application in an Integrated Amplifier," *IEEE Journal of Solid State Circuits*, Vol. 19, No. 6, December 1994, pp. 932–938.

[Bakoglu90] Bakoglu, H. B., *Circuits, Interconnections, and Packaging for VLSI*, Addison–Wesley, Reading, Massachusetts, 1990.

[BassGlass86] Bassett, P., Glasser, L., and Rettberg, R., "Dynamic Delay Adjustment: A Technique for High-Speed Asynchronous Communication," *Proceedings of the Fourth MIT Conference on Advanced Research in VLSI*, MIT Press, 1986, pp. 219–232.

[Bazes85] Bazes, M., "A Novel Precision MOS Synchronous Delay Line," *IEEE Journal of Solid State Circuits*, Vol. 20, No. 6, December 1985, pp. 1265–1271.

[Bazes91] Bazes, M., "Two Novel Fully Complementary Self-Biased CMOS Differential Amplifiers," *IEEE Journal of Solid State Circuits*, Vol. 26, No. 2, February 1991, pp. 165–168.

[Berlekam84] Berlekamp, E. R., *Algebraic Coding Theory*, Agean Park Press, Laguna Hills, CA, 1984.

[Best84] Best, R., *Phase-Locked Loops Theory, Design, and Applications*, McGraw–Hill, New York, 1984.

[Blahut83] Blahut, R. E., *Theory and Practice of Error Control Codes*, Addison–Wesley, Reading, Massachusetts, 1983.

[BreuFrie76] Breuer, M., and Friedman, A., *Diagnosis and Reliable Design of Digital Systems*, Computer Science Press, Potomac, MD., 1976.

[BuehBlae89] Buehler, M., Blaes, B., Sayah, H., and Lieneweg, U., "Parameter Distributions for Complex VLSI Circuits," *Proceedings of the 1989 Decennial Caltech Conference on Advanced Research in VLSI*, MIT Press, Cambridge, Massachusetts, 1989.

[BurnMart88] Burns, S., and Martain, A., "Syntax-Directed Translation of Concurrent Programs into Self-Timed Circuits," *Proceedings of the Fifth MIT Conference on Advanced Research in VLSI*, MIT Press, Cambridge, Massachusetts, 1988, pp. 35–65.

[BurnMart91] Burns, S., and Martain, A., "Performance Analysis and Optimization of Asynchronous Circuits," *Proceedings of the 1991 University of California Santa Cruz Conference on Advanced Research in VLSI*, MIT Press, Cambridge, Massachusetts, 1991, pp. 71–86.

[Chaney83] Chaney, T., "Measured Flip-Flop Responses to Marginal Triggering," *IEEE Transactions on Computers*, Vol. C-32, No. 12, December 1983, pp. 1207–1209.

[ChanMoln73] Chaney, T., and Molnar, C., "Anomalous Behavior of Synchronizer and Arbiter Circuits," *IEEE Transactions on Computers*, Vol. C-22, No. 4, April 1973, pp. 421–422.

[Chap88] Chappell, B., Chappell, T., Schuster, S., Segmuller, H., Allen, J., Franch, R., and Restle, P., "Fast CMOS ECL Receivers With 100-mV Worst-Case Sensitivity," *IEEE Journal of Solid State Circuits*, Vol. 23, No. 1, February 1988, pp. 59–67.

[ChenYuan93] Cheng, C., and Yuan, L., "Electrical Design of A 1GByte/Sec High Performance Backplane Using Low Voltage Swing CMOS (GTL)," *Proceedings of the 1993 Symposium on Research on Integrated Systems*, MIT Press, Cambridge, Massachusetts, 1993, pp. 291–299.

[Chi94] Chi., V., "Salphasic Distribution of Clock Signals for Synchronous Systems," *IEEE Transactions on Computers*, Vol. 43, No. 5, May 1994, pp. 597–602.

[ChoeRigb97] Choe, S., Rigby, G., and Hellestrand, G., "Half-Rail Differential Logic," *1997 IEEE International Solid State Circuits Conference Digest of Technical Papers*, IEEE, New York, 1997, pp. 420–421.

[ClarMoln74] Clark, W., and Molnar, C., "Macromodular Computer Systems," in *Computers in Biomedical Research*, Vol. IV, B. Waxman and R. Stacey, eds., Academic Press, New York, 1985.

[CranStey95] Craninckx, J., and Steyaert, M., "A CMOS 1.8GHz Low-Phase-Noise Voltage-Controlled Oscillator with Prescaler," *1995 IEEE International Solid State Circuits Conference Digest of Technical Papers*, IEEE, New York, 1995, pp. 266–267.

[DallPoul96] Dally, W., and Poulton, J., "Transmitter Equalization for 4Gb/s Signalling," *Proceedings of Hot Interconnects IV*, Stanford University, Stanford, California, August 15–17, 1996, pp. 29–39.

[DeaWilDil91] Dean, M., Williams, T., and Dill, D., "Efficient Self-Timing with Level-Encoded 2-Phase Dual Rail (LEDR)," *Proceedings of the 1991 University of California Santa Cruz Conference on Advanced Research in VLSI*, MIT Press, Cambridge, Massachusetts, 1991, pp. 55–70.

[DeHoKnig93] DeHon, A., and Knight, T., "Automatic Impedance Control," *1993 IEEE International Solid State Circuits Conference Digest of Technical Papers*, IEEE, New York, 1993, pp. 164–165.

[DenDalXan95] Dennison, L., Dally, W., and Xanthopoulos, D., "Low-Latency Plesiochronous Data Retiming," *Proceedings of the 16th Conference on Advanced Research in VLSI*, Chapel Hill, North Carolina, March 27–29, 1995, Computer Society Press, Washington, DC, pp. 304–315.

[DenLeDal93] Dennison, L., Lee, W., and Dally, W., "High-Performance Bidirectional Signalling in VLSI Systems," *Proceedings of the 1993 Symposium on Research on Integrated Systems*, MIT Press, Cambridge, Massachusetts, 1993, pp. 300–319.

[DjorHarr89] Djordjevic, A., Harrington, R., Sarkar, T., and Bazdar, M., *Matrix Parameters for Multiconductor Transmission Lines: Software and User's Manual*, (User's Manual for LINPAR), Artech House, Boston, 1989.

[DobbWite92] Dobberpuhl, D., Witek, R., et al., "A 200-MHz 64-b Dual-Issue CMOS Microprocessor," *IEEE Journal of Solid State Circuits*, Vol. 27, No. 11, November 1992, pp. 1555–1565.

[Dworsky88] Dworsky, L., *Modern Transmission Line Theory and Applications*, Robert E. Krieger Publishing Company, Malabar, Florida, 1988.

[EfenAfek94] Efendovich, A., Afek, Y., Sell, C., and Bikowsky, Z., "Multifrequency Zero-Jitter Delay-Locked Loop," *IEEE Journal of Solid State Circuits*, Vol. 29, No. 1, January 1994, pp. 67–70.

[FiedMact97] Fiedler, A., Mactaggart, R., Welch, J., and Krishnan, S., "A 1.0625Gbps Transceiver with 2x-Oversampling and Transmit Signal Pre-Emphasis," *1997 IEEE International Solid State Circuits Conference Digest of Technical Papers*, IEEE, New York, 1997, pp. 238–239.

[FuruOsha89] Furuyama, T., Ohsawa, T., Nagahama, Y., Tanaka, H., Watanabe, Y., Kimura, T., Muraoka, K., and Natori, K., "An Experimental 2-bit/Cell Storage DRAM for Macrocell or Memory-on-Logic Application," *IEEE Journal of Solid State Circuits*, Vol. 24, No. 2, April 1989, pp. 388–393.

[GabaKnau92] Gabara, T., and Knauer, S., "Digitally Adjustable Resistors in CMOS for High-Performance Applications," *IEEE Journal of Solid State Circuits*, Vol. 27, No. 8, August 1992, pp. 1176–1185.

[GabaThom88] Gabara, T., and Thompson, D., "Ground Bounce Control in CMOS Integrated Circuitry," *1988 IEEE International Solid State Circuits Conference Disgest of Technical Papers*, IEEE, New York, 1988, pp. 88–89.

[GabaThom88a] Gabara, T., and Thompson, D., "High Speed, Low Power CMOS Transmitter-Receiver System," *Proceedings of the 1988 IEEE International Conference on Computer Design*, IEEE, New York, October 1988, pp. 344–347.

[Gardner79] Gardner, F., *Phaselock Techniques*, 2nd ed., John Wiley & Sons, New York, 1979.

[Gardner80] Gardner, F., "Charge-Pump Phase-Lock Loops," *IEEE Transactions on Communications*, Vol. 28, No. 11, November 1980, pp. 1849–1858.

[GersGray92] Gersho, A., and Gray, R., *Vector Quantization and Signal Processing*, Kluwer Academic Publishers, Norwell, Massachusetts, 1992.

[GlassDobb85] Glasser, L., and Dobberpuhl, D., *The Design and Analysis of VLSI Circuits*, Addison–Wesley, Reading, Massachusetts, 1985.

[Gray90] Gray, R., *Source Coding Theory*, Kluwer Academic Publishers, Norwell, Massachusetts, 1990.

[GrayLiu94] Gray, C., Liu., W., and Cavin, R., *Wave Pipelining: Theory and CMOS Implementation*, Kluwer Academic Publishers, Norwell, Massachusetts, 1994.

[GrayMeye84] Gray, P., and Meyer, R., *Analysis and Design of Analog Integrated Circuits*, 2nd ed., John Wiley & Sons, New York, 1984.

[GregTeme86] Gregorian, R., and Temes, G., *Analog MOS Integrated Circuits for Signal Processing*, John Wiley & Sons, New York, 1986.

[GuShaElm96] Gu, R., Sharaf, K., and Elmasry, M., *High-Performance Digital VLSI Circuit Design*, Kluwer Academic Publishers, Norwell, Massachusetts, 1996.

[GunnYuan92] Gunning, B., Yuan, L., Nguyen, T., and Wong, T., "A CMOS Low-Voltage-Swing Transmission-Line Transceiver," *1992 IEEE International Solid State Circuits Conference Digest of Technical Papers*, IEEE, New York, 1992, pp. 58–59.

[HanaDenn92] Hanafi, H., Dennard, R., Chen, C.-L., Weiss, R., and Zicherman, D., "Design and Characterization of a CMOS Off-Chip Driver/Receiver with Reduced Power-Supply Disturbance," *IEEE Journal of Solid State Circuits*, Vol. 27, No. 5, May 1992, pp. 783–791.

[Harper92] Harper, C., *Handbook of Plastics, Elastomers, and Composites*, 2nd ed., McGraw–Hill, New York, 1992.

[HataMochi97] Hatakeyama, A., Mochizuki, H., et al., "A 256Mb SDRAM Using a Register-Controlled Digital DLL," *1997 IEEE International Solid State Circuits Conference Digest of Technical Papers*, IEEE, New York, 1997, pp. 72–73.

[HeinScot88] Hein, J., and Scott, J., "z-Domain Model for Discrete-Time PLL's," *IEEE Transactions on Circuits and Systems*, Vol. 35, No. 11, November 1988, pp. 1393–1400.

[HellGriff84] Heller, L., Griffin, W., Davis, J., and Thoma, N., "Cascode Voltage Switch Logic: A Differential CMOS Logic Family," *1984 IEEE International Solid State Circuits Conference Digest of Technical Papers*, IEEE, New York, 1984, pp. 16–17.

[HennJoup91] Hennessy, J., and Jouppi, N., "Computer Technology and Architecture: An Evolving Interaction," *IEEE Computer*, Vol. 24, No. 9, September 1991, pp. 18–29.

[HillPete93] Hill, F. J., and Peterson, G. R., *Computer-Aided Logical Design with Emphasis on VLSI*, John Wiley & Sons, New York, 1993.

[HodgJack83] Hodges, D., and Jackson, H., *Analysis and Design of Digital Integrated Circuits*, McGraw–Hill, New York, 1983.

[HoroHill86] Horowitz, P., and Hill, W., *The Art of Electronics*, Cambridge University Press, New York, 1986 (reprinted in 1990 and 1991).

[Hu82] Hu, C., "Alpha-Particle Induced Field and Enhanced Collection of Carriers," *IEEE Electron Device Letters*, Vol. 3, No. 2, February 1982, pp. 31–34.

[HuijPlass96] Huijsing, J., van de Plassche, R., and Sansen, W. (eds.), *Analog Circuit Design*, Kluwer Academic Publishers, Norwell, Massachusetts, 1996.

[IEEE1596] *IEEE Standard for Low-Voltage Differential Signals (LVDS) for Scalable Coherent Interface (SCI)*, IEEE Std 1596.3-1996.

[IngeStey97] Ingels, M., and Steyaert, M., "Design Strategies and Decoupling Techniques for Reducing the Effects of Electrical Interference in Mixed-Mode IC's," *IEEE Journal of Solid State Circuits*, Vol. 32, No. 7, July 1997, pp. 1136–1141.

[IPA31093] *IPA310 Interconnect Parameter Analyzer Instruction Manual*, Tektronix, Inc., Publication 070-8764-00, 1993.

[IPCD91] *Design Standards for Rigid Printed Boards and Rigid Printed Board Assemblies*, Institute for Interconnecting and Packaging Electronic Circuits, Northbrook, Illinois Publication IPC-D-275, 1991.

[IPCD95] *Design Guidelines for Electronic Packaging Utilizing High-Speed Techniques*, Institute for Interconnecting and Packaging Electronic Circuits, Northbrook, Illinois Publication IPC-D-317A, 1995.

[IPCSM96] *Surface Mount Design and Land Pattern Standard*, Institute for Interconnecting and Packaging Electronic Circuits, Northbrook, Illinois Publication IPC-SM-782, 1996.

[ISMVL97] *27th IEEE International Symposium on Multiple Valued Logic*, St. Francis Xavier College, Anitgonish, Nova Scotia, Canada, May 28–30, 1977.

[JohnEssi97] Johns, D., and Essig, D., "Integrated Circuits for Data Transmission Over Twisted-Pair Channels," *IEEE Journal of Solid State Circuits*, Vol. 32, No. 3, March 1997, pp. 398–406.

[JohnGrah93] Johnson, H. W., and Graham, M., *High-Speed Digital Design, A Handbook of Black Magic*, Prentice–Hall, Englewood Cliffs, New Jersey, 1993.

[JohnHuds88] Johnson, M., and Hudson, E., "A Variable Delay Line PLL for CPU-Coprocessor Synchronization," *IEEE Journal of Solid State Circuits*, Vol. 23, No. 5, October 1988, pp. 1218–1223.

[JuhnKlar95] Juhnke, T., and Klar, H., "Calculation of the Soft-Error Rate of Submicron CMOS Logic Circuits," *IEEE Journal of Solid State Circuits*, Vol. 30, No. 7, July 1995, pp. 830–834.

[KimKim96] Kim, G., Kim, M.-K., Chang, B.-S., and Kim, W., "A Low-Voltage, Low-Power CMOS Delay Element," *IEEE Journal of Solid State Circuits*, Vol. 31, No. 7, July 1996, pp. 966–971.

[KimWeiGr94] Kim, B., Weigandt, T., and Gray, P., "PLL/DLL System Noise Analysis for Low Jitter Clock Synthesizer Design," *Proceedings of the 1994 International Symposium on Circuits and Systems*, Vol. 4, 1994, pp. 31–38 (also appears in [Razavi96]).

[KnigKrym88] Knight, T., and Krymm, A., "A Self-Terminating Low-Voltage Swing CMOS Output Driver," *IEEE Journal of Solid State Circuits*, Vol. 23, No. 2, April 1988, pp. 457–464.

[KrauBost80] Krauss, H., Bostian, C., and Raab, F., *Solid State Radio Engineering*, John Wiley & Sons, New York, 1980.

[LaksHada86] Lakshmikurmar, K., Hadaway, R., and Copeland, M., "Characterization and Modeling of Mismatch in MOS Transistors for Precision Analog Design," *IEEE Journal of Solid State Circuits*, Vol. 21, No. 6, December 1986, pp. 1057–1066.

[LamDenDa90] Lam, K., Dennison, L., and Dally, W., "Simultaneous Bidirectional Signalling for IC Systems," *Proceedings of the 1990 Conference on Computer Design (ICCD)*, Cambridge, Massachusetts, September 1990, pp. 430–433.

[LandRuss71] Landman, B., and Russo, R. L., "On a Pin vs. Block Relationship for Partitioning of Logic Graphs," *IEEE Transactions on Computers*, Vol. C-20, No. 12, December 1971, pp. 1469–1479.

[LarsSven94] Larsson, P., and Svensson, C., "Impact of Clock Slope on True Single Phase Clocked (TSPC) CMOS Circuits," *IEEE Journal of Solid State Circuits*, Vol. 29, No. 6, June 1994, pp. 723–726.

[LaudLeno97] Laudon, J., and Lenoski, D., "The SGI Origin, A ccNUMA Highly Scalable Server," *Proceedings of the 24th Annual International Symposium on Computer Architecture (ISCA-24)*, ACM, Denver, Colorado, June 1997, pp. 241–251.

[LavaSang93] Lavagno, L., and Sangiovanni-Vincentelli, A., *Algorithms for Synthesis and Testing of Asynchronous Circuits*, Kluwer Academic Publishers, Norwell, Massachusetts, 1993.

[LeeDonn94] Lee, T., Donnelly, K., Ho, J., Zerbe, J., Johnson, M., and Ishikawa, T., "A 2.5V CMOS Delay-Locked Loop for an 18MBit, 500 Megabytes/s DRAM," *IEEE Journal of Solid State Circuits*, Vol. 29, No. 12, December 1994, pp. 1491–1496.

[LeeKim95] Lee, K., Kim, S., Ahn, G., and Jeong, D.-K., "A CMOS Serial Link for Fully Duplexed Data Communication," *IEEE Journal of Solid State Circuits*, Vol. 30, No. 4, April 1995, pp. 353–364.

[LeeLand97] Lee, W., Landman, P., et al., "A 1V DSP for Wireless Communications," *1997 IEEE International Solid State Circuits Conference Digest of Technical Papers*, IEEE, New York, 1997, pp. 92–93.

[LeeMess94] Lee, E., and Messerschmitt, D., *Digital Communication*, 2nd ed., Kluwer Academic Publishers, Norwell, Massachusetts, 1994.

[LINPAR89] Djordjevic, A., Harrington, R., Sarkar, T., and Bazdar, M., *Matrix Parameters for Multiconductor Transmission Lines: Software and User's Manual*, Artech House, Boston, 1989.

[Maneat96] Maneatis, J., "Low-Jitter Process-Independent DLL and PLL Based on Self-Biased Techniques," *IEEE Journal of Solid State Circuits*, Vol. 31, No. 11, November 1996, pp. 1723–1732.

[ManeHoro93] Maneatis, J., and Horowitz, M., "Precise Delay Generation Using Coupled Oscillators," *IEEE Journal of Solid State Circuits*, Vol. 28, No. 12, December 1993, pp. 1273–1282.

[MarbCofl93] Marbot, R., Cofler, A., Lebihan, J.-C., and Nezamzadeh, R., "Integration of Multiple Bidirectional Point-to-Point Serial Links in the Gigabits per Second Range," *Proceedings of Hot Interconnects*, Stanford University, Standford, California,1993.

[Martain90] Martain, A., "Synthesis of Asynchronous VLSI Circuits," in *Formal Methods for VLSI Design*, J. Staunstrup, ed., North-Holland, Amsterdam, 1990.

[MartLine97] Martain, A., Lines, A., Manohar, R., Nystrom, M., Penzes, P., Southworth, R., Cummings, U., and Lee, T., "The Design on an Asynchronous MIPS R3000 Microprocessor," *Proceedings of the 17th Conference on Advanced Research in VLSI*, September 15–16, 1997, Ann Arbor, Michigan, Computer Society Press, pp. 164–181.

[Matick95] Matick, R., *Transmission Lines for Digital and Communication Networks*, IEEE, New York, 1995.

[MayWood79] May, T., and Woods, M., "Alpha-Particle-Induced Soft Errors in Dynamic Memories," *IEEE Transactions on Electron Devices*, Vol. ED-26, No. 1, January 1979, pp. 2–9.

[McPartla81] McPartland, R., "Circuit Simulation of Alpha-Particle-Induced Soft Errors in MOS Dynamic RAMs," *IEEE Journal of Solid State Circuits*, Vol. 16, No. 1, January 1981, pp. 31–34.

[MeadConw80] Mead, C., and Conway, L., *Introduction to VLSI Systems*, Addison–Wesley, Reading, Massachusetts, 1980.

[MECL88] Blood, W., *MECL System Design Handbook*, 4th ed., Motorola Semiconductor Products, Inc., Publication HB205, 1988.

[MijuBaye94] Mijuskovic, D., Bayer, M., Chomicz, T., Garg, N., James, F., McEntarfer, P., and Porter, J., "Cell-Based Fully Integrated CMOS Frequency Synthesizers," *IEEE Journal of Solid State Circuits*, Vol. 29, No. 3, March 1994, pp. 271–279.

[MolnFang85] Molnar, C., Fang, T.-P., and Rosenburger, F., "Synthesis of Delay-Insensitive Modules," *Proceedings of the 1985 Chapel Hill Conference on Very Large Scale Integration*, Computer Science Press, Washington, DC, 1985, pp. 67–86.

[MontWite96] Montaro, J., Witek, R., et al., "A 160-MHz, 32-b, 0.5-W CMOS RISC Microprocessor," *IEEE Journal of Solid State Circuits*, Vol. 31, No. 11, November 1996, pp. 1703–1714.

[MoonDike95] Mooney, R., Dike, C., and Borkar, S., "A 900 Mb/s Bidirectional Signaling Scheme," *IEEE Journal of Solid State Circuits*, Vol. 30, No. 12, December 1995, pp. 2015–2023.

[MoonZagh90] Moon, G., Zaghloul, M., and Newcomb, N., "An Enhancement-Mode MOS Voltage-Controlled Linear Resistor with Large Dynamic Range," *IEEE Transactions on Circuits and Systems*, Vol. 37, No. 10, October 1990, pp. 1284–1288.

[Moore79] Moore, G., "VLSI: Some Fundamental Challenges," *IEEE Spectrum*, Vol. 16, 1979, p. 30.

[MuroNari97] Murotani., T., Naritake, I., et al., "A 4-Level Storage 4Gb DRAM," *1997 IEEE International Solid State Circuits Conference Digest of Technical Papers*, IEEE, New York, 1997, pp. 74–75.

[NovoAust95] Novof, I., Austin, J., Chmela, R., Frank, T., Kelkar, R., Short, K., Strayer, D., Styduhar, M., and Wyatt, S., "Fully-Integrated CMOS Phase-Locked Loop with 15 to 240MHz Locking Range and ±50ps Jitter," *1995 IEEE International Solid State Circuits Conference Digest of Technical Papers*, IEEE, New York, 1995, pp. 112–113.

[PartBurd96] Partovi, H., Burd, R., Salim, U., Weber, F., DiGregorio, L., and Draper, D., "Flow-Through Latch and Edge-Triggered Flip-Flop Hybrid Elements," *1996 IEEE International Solid State Circuits Conference Digest of Technical Papers*, IEEE, New York, 1996, pp. 138–139.

[PelgDuin89] Pelgrom, M., Duinmaijer, A., and Welbers, A., "Matching Properties of MOS Transistors," *IEEE Journal of Solid State Circuits*, Vol. 24, No. 5, October 1989, pp. 1433–1440.

[PeteWeld72] Peterson, W. W., and Weldon, E. J., *Error Correcting Codes*, 2nd ed., MIT Press, Cambridge, Massachusetts, 1972.

[PoulDall97] Poulton, J., Dally, W., and Tell, S., "A Tracking Clock Recovery Receiver for 4Gb/s Signaling," *Proceedings of Hot Interconnects V*, Stanford University, Stanford, California, August 21–23, 1997, pp. 157–169.

[PratNguy95] Pratt, G., and Nguyen, J., "Distributed Synchronous Clocking," *IEEE Transactions on Parallel and Distributed Systems*, Vol. 6, No. 3, March 1995, pp. 316–329.

[Rabaey96] Rabaey, J., *Digital Integrated Circuits: A Design Perspective*, Prentice–Hall, Englewood Cliffs, New Jersey, 1996.

[RabaPedr96] Rabaey, J., and Pedram, M., *Low Power Design Methodologies*, Kluwer Academic Publishers, Norwell, Massachusetts, 1996.

[Rajsuma95] Rajsuman, R., *Iddq Testing for CMOS VLSI*, Artech House, Boston, 1995.

[Raver87] Raver, N., "Open-Loop Gain Limitations for Push-Pull Off-Chip Drivers," *IEEE Journal of Solid State Circuits*, Vol. 22, No. 2, April 1987, pp. 145–150.

[Razavi96] Razavi, B. (ed.), *Monolithic Phase-Locked Loops and Clock Recovery Circuits – Theory and Design*, IEEE, New York, 1996.

[Razavi97] Razavi, B., "A 1.8GHz CMOS Voltage-Controlled Oscillator," *1997 IEEE International Solid State Circuits Conference Digest of Technical Papers*, IEEE, New York, 1997, pp. 388–389.

[RefDat93] *Reference Data for Engineers – Radio, Electronics, Computer & Communications*, SAMS, Prentice–Hall Computer Publishing, Englewood Cliffs, New Jersey, 1993.

[RenshLau90] Renshaw, D., and Lau, C. H., "Race-Free Clocking of CMOS Pipelines Using a Single Global Clock," *IEEE Journal of Solid State Circuits*, Vol. 251, No. 3, June 1990, pp. 766–769.

[RoddCool81] Roddy, D., and Coolen, J., *Electronic Communications*, 2nd ed., Reston Publishing Company, Reston, VA, 1981.

[RofoRael96] Rofougaran, A., Rael, J., Rofougaran, M., and Abidi, A., "A 900MHz CMOS LC-Oscillator with Quadrature Outputs," *1996 IEEE International Solid State Circuits Conference Digest of Technical Papers*, IEEE, New York, 1996, pp. 392–393.

[SakuTama83] Sakurai, T., and Tamaru, K., "Simple Formulas for Two- and Three-Dimensional Capacitances," *IEEE Transactions on Electron Devices*, Vol. 30, No. 2, February 1983, pp. 183–185.

[Scott96] Scott, S., "Synchronization and Communication in the T3E Multiprocessor," *Proceedings of the 7th Symposium on Architectural Support for Programming Languages and Operating Systems (ASPLOS-VII)*, ACM, Cambridge, Massachusetts, October 1996, pp. 26–36.

[Seitz80] Seitz, C., "System Timing," Chapter 7 in [MeadConw80], pp. 218–262.

[SentPrin93] Senthinathan, R., and Prince, J., "Application Specific CMOS Output Driver Circuit Design Techniques to Reduce Simultaneous Switching Noise," *IEEE Journal of Solid State Circuits*, Vol. 28, No. 12, December 1993, pp. 1373–1383.

[ShicHodg68] Shichman, H., and Hodges, D., "Modeling and Simulation of Insulated-Gate Field-Effect Transistors," *IEEE Journal of Solid State Circuits*, Vol. SC-3, No. 5, September 1968, pp. 285–289.

[SIA94] *The National Technology Roadmap for Semiconductors*, Semiconductor Industry Association, 1994.

[SidiHoro97] Sidiropoulos, S., and Horowitz, M., "A Semi-Digital DLL with Unlimited Phase Shift Capability and 0.08–400MHz Operating Range," *1997 IEEE International Solid State Circuits Conference Digest of Technical Papers*, IEEE, New York, 1997, pp. 332–333.

[SidiHoro97a] Sidiropoulos, S., and Horowitz, M., "A 700-Mb/s/pin CMOS Signaling Interface Using Current Integrating Receivers," *IEEE Journal of Solid State Circuits*, Vol. 32, No. 5, May 1997, pp. 681–690.

[Smith81] Smith, K., "The Prospects for Multivalued Logic: A Technology and Application View," *IEEE Transactions on Computers*, Vol. 30, September 1981, pp. 619–634.

[StanRute96] Stanisic, B., Rutenbar, R., and Carley, L., *Synthesis of Power Distribution to Manage Signal Integrity in Mixed-Signal ICs*, Kluwer Academic Publishers, Norwell, Massachusetts, 1996.

[Stensby97] Stensby, J., *Phase-Locked Loops – Theory and Applications*, CRC Press, Boca Raton, Florida, 1997.

[Sutherl89] Sutherland, I., "Micropipelines," *Communications of the ACM*, Vol. 32, No. 6, July 1989, pp. 720–738.

[SuthSpro91] Sutherland, I., and Sproull, R., "Logical Effort: Designing for Speed on the Back of an Envelope," *Proceedings of the 1991 Conference on Advanced Research in VLSI*, MIT Press, Cambridge, Massachusetts, 1991, pp. 1–16.

[TakaUchi95] Takahashi, T., Uchida, M., Takahashi, T., Yoshino, R., Yamamoto, M., and Kitamura, N., "A CMOS Gate Array with 600 Mb/s Simultaneous Bidirectional I/O Circuits," *IEEE Journal of Solid State Circuits*, Vol. 30, No. 12, December 1995, pp. 1544–1546.

[Tewksbur94] Tewksbury, S. (ed.), *Microelectronic System Interconnections – Performance and Modeling*, IEEE, New York, 1994.

[ThamKwas97] Thamsirianunt, M., and Kwasniewski, T., "CMOS VCO's for PLL Frequency Synthesis in GHz Digital Mobile Radio Communications," *IEEE Journal of Solid State Circuits*, Vol. 32, No. 10, October 1997, pp. 1511–1524.

[Thomas97] Thomas, K., *LC User's Guide*, available from Cray Research, Inc. (available at http://www.cray.com/lc/doc), 1997.

[Tsividis87] Tsividis, Y., *Operation and Modeling of the MOS Transistor*, McGraw–Hill, New York, 1987.

[TsivAnto85] Tsividis, Y., and Antognetti, P. (eds.), *Design of MOS VLSI Circuits for Telecommunications*, Prentice–Hall, Englewood Cliffs, New Jersey, 1985.

[UngerTan86] Unger, S., and Tan, C.-J., "Clock Schemes for High-Speed Digital Systems," *IEEE Transactions on Computers*, Vol. C-35, No. 10, October 1986, pp. 880–895.

[Uyemura92] Uyemura, J., *Circuit Design for CMOS VLSI*, Kluwer Academic Publishers, Norwell, Massachusetts, 1992.

[VergSchm95] Verghese, N., Schmerbeck, R., and Allstot, D., *Simulation Techniques and Solutions for Mixed-Signal Coupling in Integrated Circuits*, Kluwer Academic Publishers, Norwell, Massachusetts, 1995.

[Vittoz85] Vittoz, E., "Micropower Techniques," Chapter 4 in [TsivAnto85], pp. 104–144.

[vonKaen96] von Kaenel, V., Aebischer, D., Piguet, C., and Dijkstra, E., "A 320 MHz, 1.5mW @ 1.35 V CMOS PLL for Microprocessor Clock Generation," *IEEE Journal of Solid State Circuits*, Vol. 31, No. 11, November 1996, pp. 1715–1722.

[von KaVit 96] von Kaenel, V., Vittoz, E., and Aebischer, D., "Crystal Oscillators," in [HuijPlass96], pp. 369–382.

[WardHals90] Ward, S. A., and Halstead, R. H., *Computation Structures*, MIT Press, Cambridge, Massachusetts, 1990.

[WestEshr93] West, N., and Eshraghian, K., *Principles of CMOS VLSI Design, A Systems Perspective*, 2nd ed., Addison–Wesley, Reading, Massachusetts, 1993.

[WidmFran83] Widmer, A., and Franaszek, P., "A DC-Balanced, Partitioned-Block 8B/10B Transmission Code," *IBM Journal of Research and Development*, Vol. 27, No. 5, September 1983, pp. 440–451.

[WillHoro87] Williams, T., Horowitz, M., Alverson, R., and Yang, T., "A Self-Timed Chip for Division," *Proceedings of the 1987 Stanford Conference on Advanced Research in VLSI*, MIT Press, Cambridge, Massachusetts, 1987, pp. 75–95.

[Wilson97] Wilson, J., *Optoelectronics: An Introduction*, Prentice–Hall, Upper Saddle River, New Jersey, 1997.

[YangHoro96] Yang, K. C.-K., and Horowitz, M., "A 0.8μm CMOS 2.5 Gb/s Oversampling Receiver and Transmitter for Serial Links," *IEEE Journal of Solid State Circuits*, Vol. 31, No. 12, December 1996, pp. 2015–2023.

[YounGrea92] Young, I., Greason, J., and Wong, K., "A PLL Clock Generator with 5 to 110 MHz of Lock Range for Microprocessors," *IEEE Journal of Solid State Circuits*, Vol. 27, No. 11, November 1992, pp. 1599–1607.

[YuanSven89] Yuan, J., and Svensson, C., "High-Speed CMOS Circuit Technique," *IEEE Journal of Solid State Circuits*, Vol. 24, No. 1, January 1989, pp. 62–70.

[YuanSven97] Yuan, J., and Svensson, C., "New Single-Clock CMOS Latches and Flipflops with Improved Speed and Power Savings," *IEEE Journal of Solid State Circuits*, Vol. 32, No. 1, January 1992, pp. 62–69.

[YuanTric82] Yuan, C., and Trick, T., "A Simple Formula for the Estimation of the Capacitance of Two-Dimensional Interconnects in VLSI Circuits," *IEEE Electron Device Letters*, Vol. 13, No. 12, December 1982, pp. 391–393.

INDEX